Louis Kenoyer (*baχawádas*), date and location unknown. The picture appears unattributed in *Smithsonian Miscellaneous Collections*, 1916, in a report by Leo J. Frachtenberg on linguistic fieldwork he conducted with Kenoyer and other informants in 1915. It bears the legend: "Louis Kenoyer, the last of the Atfalati." Kenoyer was the last known speaker of Tualatin (or Atfalati, Tfalati, Tuality) Northern Kalapuya, which to Frachtenberg and his fellow scholars made him, ipso facto, the "last" of his tribe.

My Life, by Louis Kenoyer

REMINISCENCES OF A GRAND RONDE RESERVATION CHILDHOOD

A Text in Tualatin Northern Kalapuya

Dictated to Melville Jacobs, Jaime de Angulo, and L. S. Freeland

Introduction and commentaries by Henry Zenk

Translation by Jedd Schrock and Henry Zenk

Foreword by Stephen Dow Beckham

Oregon State University Press, Corvallis
Published in cooperation with the Confederated Tribes of Grand Ronde

Library of Congress Cataloging-in-Publication Data

Names: Kenoyer, Louis, 1868–1937, author.
Title: My life / by Louis Kenoyer ; reminiscences of a Grand Ronde Reservation childhood ; a
    text in Tualatin Northern Kalapuya ; text transcript by Melville Jacobs ; introduction and
    commentaries by Henry Zenk ; translation by Jedd Schrock and Henry Zenk ; foreword by
    Stephen Dow Beckham.
Other titles: Reminiscences of a Grand Ronde Reservation childhood
Description: Corvallis, OR : Oregon State University Press, [2017] | "Published in cooperation with
    The Confederated Tribes of Grand Ronde, Oregon." | Includes bibliographical references and
    index. | Text in the English and in Tualatin Northern Kalapuya languages.
Identifiers: LCCN 2017006114 | ISBN 9780870718830 (original trade pbk. : alk.paper)
Subjects: LCSH: Kenoyer, Louis, 1868–1937—Childhood and youth. | Kalapuya Indians—Oregon—
    Biography. | Grand Ronde Indian Reservation (Or.) | Kalapuya Indians—Oregon—Social life and
    customs. | Kalapuya Indians—Oregon—History. | Kalapuya language—Texts.
Classification: LCC E99.K16 K46 2017 | DDC 979.5/004970092 [B] —dc23
LC record available at https://lccn.loc.gov/2017006114

♾This paper meets the requirements of ANSI/NISO Z39.48-1992
(Permanence of Paper).

First published in 2017 by Oregon State University Press
Printed in the United States of America

Oregon State University Press
121 The Valley Library
Corvallis OR 97331-4501
541-737-3166 • fax 541-737-3170
www.osupress.oregonstate.edu

Contents

Foreword

The autobiography of Louis Kenoyer is in a class of its own. It is one of the rare first-person narratives by a Native American discussing life on an Oregon reservation. While a few native informants dictated short autobiographical narratives to linguists and ethnographers in the early twentieth century, nothing compares with the length and depth of content shared by Kenoyer. This volume rescues from obscurity the story of his life, conditions on the Grand Ronde Reservation, and, for the first time, completes the translation of his narrative from the Tualatin dialect of Northern Kalapuya into English.

Autobiographies come in several genres, including tales of migration, rags-to-riches narratives, or self-justifying accounts where the author sets the world straight about what really happened. One of the most notable western Indian autobiographies is Sarah Winnemucca's *Life Among the Paiutes* (1883). The book is an amalgam of reminiscences, speeches, primary documents, letters of endorsement, and Winnemucca's plea for better treatment of the Paiutes. Heralded as an autobiography, the book may, however, be more of an "as-told-to" narrative edited and crafted into a publication by the Peabody sisters of Boston, who became ardent defenders and promoters of Winnemucca and Indian rights.

Native Americans of the twentieth century have produced more traditional autobiographies, including James Sewid's *Guests Never Leave Hungry: The Autobiography of James Sewid, a Kwakiutl Indian* (1969) written with James Spradley; Florence Edenshaw Davidson's *During My Time: Florence Edenshaw Davidson, A Haida Woman* (1982), dictated in fifty hours of tapes to anthropologist Margaret B. Blackman; and Peter S. Webster's *As Far As I Know: Reminiscences of an Ahousat Elder* (1983). These life histories recount the experiences of twentieth-century adults in coastal British Columbia. Horace Axtell's *A Little Bit of Wisdom: Conversations with a Nez Perce Elder* (2010) is another "as-told-to" autobiography orchestrated into print by Margo Aragon. As Blackman points out in Davidson's autobiography, the lives of these people spanned periods of "critical and rapid cultural change" and thus offer a personal, longitudinal view of the impact of events.

Louis Kenoyer's autobiography was dictated from the heart and head to tell the story of his childhood on the Grand Ronde Reservation. The narrative reveals no prompting from an interrogating anthropologist. It is Kenoyer's story recounted in the traditional narrative style of the Tualatin speakers of the northern Willamette Valley. The account covers the 1870s to the 1880s and provides a heretofore unavailable record of the forced acculturation and transformation of Oregon Indians from their traditional fishing, hunting, and gathering cultures into sedentary agrarians speaking English and worshipping the deity of their conquerors.

From the nurturing of his hardworking parents, Kenoyer learned a work ethic. His parents, however, insisted he attend the reservation Catholic school and church of St. Michael the Archangel. He was a student of the Catholic sisters and an altar boy for Father Adrien Croquet, a Belgian missionary priest at Grand Ronde. Kenoyer's upbringing was shaped by precepts that linked cleanliness and godliness. Both were drilled into him, and his account repeatedly refers to washing, bathing, and living an ordered life. His teachers used strict discipline with schedules for rising, instruction, play, and going to bed—all governed by voice orders and bell ringing. They employed rote learning, memorization, and recitation. Consequently, Kenoyer was a literate man who liked to read, and he felt at home with the scholars who interviewed him. In the case of Jaime de Angulo and his wife Lucy S. Freeland, Kenoyer became a member of their household in Berkeley, California, for a number of months. He was a man who could move in different worlds.

Kenoyer's autobiography documents the persistence of aboriginal lifeways in spite of the "civilization" programs at Grand Ronde. Most especially his account speaks to the unceasing labor demanded of nineteenth-century Indians in order to survive. Tilling, harvesting, fencing, hunting, picking berries and hops, gathering, washing clothes, and cutting immense amounts of cordwood and fence-rails were among the tasks he and his parents faced on a regular basis. Kenoyer was not judgmental about his life of hard labor. He reported it and also provided fascinating vignettes of happy times: games, horse races, wrestling, hunting, camping, and other events that were part of his social world. Kenoyer's narrative fills part of the void in understanding the impact of federal Indian policy and the toll it inflicted on the native peoples compelled to reside on reservations.

The translator/editors have successfully wrestled a long-forgotten manuscript from obscurity into this narrative. A deft team, they have used their linguistic skills to translate a language not spoken by anyone since Louis Kenoyer's death in 1937. Their account is buttressed by observations on Tualatin narrative structure and phrasing. They have also provided extensive notes on people, places, and events to put Kenoyer's autobiography in historical and ethnographic context.

Stephen Dow Beckham
Pamplin Professor of History, Emeritus, Lewis & Clark College

Acknowledgments

This book could not have come to fruition without the collaboration and support of the Grand Ronde community. Transcripts and notes from two of the Grand Ronde elders Zenk interviewed during the early 1980s, Wilson Bobb Sr. and Clara Riggs (a step-niece of Kenoyer), proved invaluable for fleshing out Kenoyer's rather spare descriptions of life on the old reservation. These two elders had also known Kenoyer well, and although Zenk unfortunately did not think to ask them about the man at the time, such information as they gave in passing has contributed significant detail to our picture of Kenoyer's life and times. For filling in many of the inevitable remaining gaps in this man's story, we are indebted to June Olson, Grand Ronde's foremost genealogist, who drew upon her own extensive archival research to compile a biographical fact sheet on Kenoyer. We are also indebted to Fr. Martinus Cawley of Our Lady of Guadalupe Trappist Abbey, Lafayette, Oregon, to Sr. Alberta Dieker of the Benedictine Sisters of Mount Angel, Oregon, and to Fr. Augustine DeNoble of Mount Angel Abbey, Oregon, for their help with Catholic missionary sources; to Gary Lundell of the University of Washington Libraries, Special Collections, for his help in accessing and navigating the Melville Jacobs Papers; to Howard Berman for making available his extensive unpublished research on Kalapuyan languages; to Stephen Dow Beckham for his valuable corrections and comments to our original manuscript; to Gui Mayo for sharing her memories of her parents, Jaime de Angulo and Nancy Freeland; and to the following tribal members, tribal employees, and members of the greater Grand Ronde community for their technical and logistical support: David Lewis, Jan Reibach, David Harrelson, Briece Edwards, Jessica Curteman, Jordan Mercier, Bobby Mercier, Darrell Mercier, Greg Archuleta, Lisa Archuleta, Veronica Montano, and Dennis Werth.

Introduction

THE STORY OF *MY LIFE,* BY *LOUIS KENOYER*

My Life, by Louis Kenoyer is an extended autobiographical narrative, dictated in the Tualatin (ˈtwä lə tən; also *tfálat'i, twálat'i,* Tuality, Atfalati)[1] dialect of Northern Kalapuya to three linguist transcribers. The narrator, Louis Kenoyer, belonged to the first cohort of northwest Oregon tribal people born at Grand Ronde Reservation, to which most of the surviving indigenous population of interior western Oregon was removed in 1856. His narrative consists of his reminiscences of growing up in that reservation community. His exact birthdate is unrecorded. Thanks to the vital statistics meticulously kept by Grand Ronde's Catholic missionary priest, Fr. Adrien-Joseph Croquet (locally, "Father Crockett"), one of the individuals featured in the narrative, we at least know that a "Louis (Louison)," said to have been born ten days earlier to "Marc Peter Gonoya [Peter Kenoyer] Twalaty [*sic*] Indian and Nancy, of this mission" (St. Michael the Archangel Parish, Grand Ronde), was baptized on September 3, 1868 (Munnick and Beckham 1987, Register I P. 55).

The Kenoyer family name appears variously spelled: Kennoyer, Kenayer, Conoyer, Cornoyer, Conoya, Konoi, Kenoi, and Kinai. The spelling "Kinai" reflects his father's usually given Tualatin-language name, *k'inái,* converted into a Euro-American style family surname. While northwest Oregon personal names could pass from father to son, strict tribal tradition would dictate that the father then adopt a new name—lest the son find himself in the tabooed situation of having to use the name of someone recently deceased. More often, formal family names were taken from long-deceased ancestors. Nicknames and multiple names, both formal and informal, were also common, adding to the woes of historians trying to track northwest Oregon tribal people through historical sources, a task made difficult enough already by the incommensurability of indigenous sound systems with English, a source of considerable confusion in the transliteration of indigenous names into English.[2] Consequently, few formal family names of northwest Oregon tribal individuals were reliably recorded. Louis Kenoyer is noteworthy for having borne one such name, *baxawádas* (spelled вaxawa'ᴅas in the older Americanist alphabet in which the Tualatin text of Kenoyer's narrative appears; anglicized as Bahawadas), inherited from a paternal great-grandfather (his father's mother's father) remembered as village chief at *čabánaxdin,* an aboriginal Tualatin-speaking group located in the vicinity of modern Mountaindale and North Plains, Washington County, Oregon.

Peter Kenoyer came to the reservation as an adult from a part of the old Tualatin homeland that centered on Wapato Lake, a large shallow lake and associated wetlands that, before being drained for agriculture in the late nineteenth century, occupied the mountain valley extending to the southeast of modern Gaston, Oregon. He usually spoke Tualatin Northern Kalapuya at home, but he also spoke English and the reservation community's original common language, Chinuk Wawa (Jargon, in local English; historically encountered as Chinook or as Chinook Jargon). Louis Kenoyer's mother, Nancy Kenoyer (*túnišni, k'úpan*; she appears also under the subsequent married names Nancy Apperson, Nancy Tipton, and Nancy Pratt, having long outlived Peter Kenoyer), was natively a speaker of the Ahantchuyuk (*hánč'iyuk*) or French Prairie dialect of Central Kalapuya, originally spoken in the Willamette Valley to the southeast of Northern Kalapuya.

Louis Kenoyer's language biography is touched on by the first two linguists to transcribe his narrative, Jaime de Angulo and his wife L. S. (Nancy) Freeland, who hosted him at their home in Berkeley, California, during the winter of 1928–1929. Franz Boas, known as the founder of modern American anthropology, had assigned them the task of documenting Northern Kalapuya, by then presumed to be spoken only by Kenoyer (the story of Angulo and Freeland's association with Kenoyer is told in Leeds-Hurwitz 2004:140–145 and G. de Angulo 2004:289–293).

> Our informant avers that when he was born his people were already civilized and had left off the old customs, except the language. At home he spoke Tfalati [Tualatin]. At school he and his comrades (from various tribes) spoke the "Chinook Jargon" [Chinuk Wawa], the lingua franca of all the people along the lower course of the Columbia River.
>
> He could not remember any tales or myths. For texts he dictated to us reminiscences from his own childhood. He proved to be an excellent informant for dictation, speaking slowly, enunciating carefully, and never losing the trend of his sentence. It must be added that he is an educated man, reading and writing English fluently. Indeed, he is an omnivorous reader, spending a great deal of his time while with us in the Public Library.
>
> We have given all these details about our informant in order to provide the reader with as many data as possible by which he may exercise his own judgment in appraising the factors that render the present study somewhat unreliable: a single informant; who has not used his language for twenty years [more likely, for over forty years—see below]; who has used the Chinook Jargon from infancy; the crowding into small reservations, in the first part of the last century, of the remnants of scattered tribes which spoke diverse tongues—all of them factors that make for the disintegration of grammatical forms and leveling to a common analytical structure. (Angulo and Freeland 1929:2–3)

These linguists clearly acknowledge Kenoyer's background as a reservation Indian, citing the reservation experience among factors rendering their study "somewhat unreliable." Of course, their research goal was to secure enough data on the language to support a full linguistic description of it. It is a fair point that the Tualatin heard from its last known speaker may not be fully representative of the language heard when it still sustained daily life in an independent Tualatin-speaking polity.

Angulo and Freeland accorded their informant's personal history due attention, devoting considerable time and effort to transcribing his story of his reservation childhood. At the same time, they failed to place that story in a broader regional and historical context. They even have the place of Kenoyer's birth and baptism wrong—giving it as Salem, Oregon, some thirty miles from Grand Ronde. They have it from Kenoyer himself that the last person he had spoken Tualatin with was his father—who died in 1886 (Munnick and Beckham 1987, Register II P 21), not "twenty years ago," as they write. The school referred to is never identified, although it figures prominently in the narrative. Without a doubt it was the original source of Kenoyer's adult literacy, Grand Ronde's old on-reservation boarding school, known in the community as the "Sisters' School." It was established under government auspices and staffed and run by Fr. Croquet and two Catholic orders: the Sisters of the Holy Names of Jesus and Mary (from 1874 to 1881) and the Benedictine Sisters (represented by several mother-houses, the two most important being the Benedictine Sisters in St. Cloud, Minnesota, from 1881 to 1882 and the Benedictine Sisters in Gervais, Oregon, later in Mount Angel, Oregon, from 1882 to 1900) (Anonymous 1960, Cawley 1996:59–62, Sr. Alberta Dieker personal communication 2015). Phrases like "lingua franca of all the people along the lower course of the Columbia River" and "crowding into small reservations" probably reflect impressions gathered from Kenoyer himself, as there is no evidence that the linguists independently researched the history of the reservation system in western Oregon.

Nor could they have gleaned much social and historical background from Kenoyer's very spare storytelling style. As in other recorded examples of the lower Columbia narrative art, the focus of Kenoyer's narrative is on overt action, details of external set and setting being acknowledged only as they help move the action along. Very frequent in the narrative are turns of quoted speech attributed to its dramatis personae, which Kenoyer seldom identifies by name in the narrative itself. For example, the aforementioned Fr. Croquet, who makes multiple appearances in the narrative, is consistently referred to in Tualatin by a euphemism—in literal translation, "the good man." In this case, we have not only the evidence of historical time and place (Fr. Croquet was the sole Catholic priest at Grand Ronde throughout the period of Kenoyer's childhood; see Cawley 1996 for a biography), but a positive identification as well, consisting of a note in the field translation to one of the passages dictated to the third linguist transcriber, Melville Jacobs.[3] Lacking external evidence, as in this example, it often proves problematic indeed to reference Kenoyer's narrative to documentable places and persons.

Such lack of historical perspective is a factor to be reckoned with for all three transcribers of Kenoyer's narrative, including Melville Jacobs, the linguist to whom Angulo turned over his Tualatin manuscripts, and to whom we owe the final form of the narrative as presented here. Upon joining the Department of Anthropology at the University of Washington in 1928, Jacobs began assuming primary responsibility for documenting the endangered indigenous languages of western Oregon (Seaburg and Amoss 2000:3–36). It was he who had first alerted Franz Boas that a last speaker of Northern Kalapuya was alive at Yakama Reservation, Washington, Kenoyer's usual place of residence since about 1914. And it was Boas who had enlisted Angulo and Freeland to work with Kenoyer, Jacobs at the time having been preoccupied with other linguistic fieldwork (Leeds-Hurwitz 2004:140–141).

In the summer of 1936, Jacobs finally found the time to work with Kenoyer. He painstakingly re-elicited all of Angulo and Freeland's previous transcriptions, aligning them to his own perceptions of Kalapuyan phonetics. Then, as Jacobs himself writes, "When I asked Kenoyer, at Wapato, Wash[ington] in July 1936, if he would like to continue with his autobiography, starting from the place where he had left off before, he acquiesced" (Jacobs ca. 1936a, <¶12(14)>, note). In raw field-transcribed form (Jacobs 1936a), this extension of the original autobiography takes up some 221 pages in Jacobs's field notebooks. Jacobs also copied out the greater part of the narrative, organizing it using the same system of paragraph and paragraph-segment numbers that he used to divide his various published collections of texts in Northwest indigenous languages. We dub this version the Printer's Manuscript, since it was obviously intended for publication. It consists of a free-hand, phonetic transcript and close translation of the Tualatin (Jacobs ca. 1936a), with a typed, free English translation (Jacobs ca. 1936b) bearing the title *My Life, by Louis Kenoyer*.

Why did this significant work by Jacobs, in which he incorporated earlier important work by colleagues, never appear in print? Quite possibly, the answer lies in the last quarter, roughly, of Kenoyer's narrative, which is missing from the Printer's Manuscript. It exists only as an untranslated phonetic transcript in the field notebooks. In Jacobs's own words: "The translation, up to and including paragraph 54 [10<54> in our prepared transcript: 10 is our chapter number, <54> Jacobs's paragraph number], is by Kenoyer, given by him upon me reading his text dictation back to him. The text material in <55> to the end [absent from the

Printer's Manuscript; 10<55> to the end in this book's narrative] was not translated by Kenoyer because of his untimely death" (Jacobs ca. 1936a, <¶12(14)>, note).

Jacobs had a remarkable grasp of the phonetic nuances of Northwest indigenous languages, enabling him to produce accurate phonetic transcripts of languages in which he never gained much, if any, practical competency. No doubt, he was fully expecting to return to Kenoyer to finish the autobiography when he learned of Kenoyer's unexpected demise during the following winter (1937). It is unclear whether Jacobs had ever envisaged some way of eventually securing a complete translation. In the end, the passing of the language's last known fluent speaker rendered this large chunk of the narrative, for all practical purposes, unusable to him.

We have taken it upon ourselves to repair this damage—by learning to read Tualatin (or well enough, we trust, for the purpose at hand). Schrock entered the entire Tualatin narrative, including its untranslated portions, into an SIL Fieldworks database. Working from Kenoyer's field translations in Angulo and Freeland's and Jacobs's manuscripts, he has been able to gloss approximately 99 percent of the lexical items appearing in the complete narrative. Using the concordancing tool provided by Fieldworks, which automates searches of items already entered and glossed in the database, he was able to assign glosses to almost every word-stem appearing in the untranslated one-quarter of the narrative. Zenk adopted a more traditional dictionary-based approach, glossing with reference to a word-stem list compiled from Howard Berman's (1988b) Tualatin slip-files.[4] It should be noted that Schrock's database and Zenk's stem-list were compiled from the same original sources. While there are other sources documenting Northern Kalapuya, those remain to be analyzed and compiled; the translations appearing here are therefore based primarily on English glosses originating from one multilingual Tualatin-English speaker—Louis Kenoyer (see Text Presentation and Translation: The Tualatin Text for further detail on the Tualatin transcript).

While Jacobs had a keen appreciation of the stylistic nuances of regional narrative genres, he never evinced much interest in his narrators' contemporary lives and communities. His main interest lay in the worldviews and values intrinsic to their intact indigenous cultures, which he presumed could be approached, if not grasped in full, through texts dictated in the original languages. Yet, he did transcribe nearly three full field notebooks worth of Kenoyer's story of his reservation childhood, notwithstanding the obviously attenuated state of aboriginal Tualatin culture revealed there. Moreover, these field texts are largely free of the kinds of distortions and errors noted in our discussion of Jacobs's predecessors' work with Kenoyer. Issues of interpretation arise, rather, in Jacobs's Printer's Manuscript free translation. It is important to understand that Jacobs's prepared translations were based on his informants' English field translations, modified somewhat by his own interpretations. After his early Sahaptin work (see Jacobs 1931:282-291), he seldom, if ever, incorporated results of formal linguistic analysis into his translations. Rather, he reproduced his field-notebook translations in edited form, adding parenthetical comments that in some cases supply background cultural knowledge presumed to be obvious to a hypothetical tribal auditor; in others, clarify possibly ambiguous wording; and in yet others, supply textual interpretations original to Jacobs (Seaburg and Amoss 2000:23). Since the latter category in particular is not identified as Jacobs's own original contribution, a reader could be forgiven for taking all of Jacobs's parenthetical interpolations as explications of his narrators' intended meanings. This issue is illustrated by the following excerpt from 7<38(3)> (our narrative chapter 7; Jacobs's paragraph-segment ¶38(3)). The original field translation (Jacobs 1936a, 123:11, 13) reads:

> Now everybody entered the church when they heard the bell. Now the priest said prayers to God. Now fin[ished] his talk he spoke/preached to the people. He said all-good-words to those people who were in church.

The Printer's Manuscript shows the following translation of the same passage, as edited and interpreted by Jacobs (ca. 1936b, <¶38(3)>).

> Now everyone entered the good house (the church) when they heard the bell. And the good man (the priest) said words (he prayed) to the headman above (to God). Then when he finished his talking (his praying), he spoke (he preached) to the people. He said all (sorts of) good words (good thoughts) to the bunch (to his Tualatin people) who were in the house (in church).

Guided by his understanding of the Tualatin original, Jacobs has provided literal glosses ('the good house', 'the good man', 'the headman above') where Kenoyer himself evidently used familiar English translation equivalents ('church', 'priest', 'God'). While this raises some thorny issues of translation, it does not affect the historical veracity of the dictation, unlike the last sentence of the passage, which flies in the face of historical reality. The field translation shows the gloss 'people' for two different Tualatin terms: the first-occurring (*di-mé·nmi*) usually refers specifically to Indians and shows the third-person-singular possessive *di-*, implying that these are the priest's Indian people; the second (*gáwakil*) also translates as 'tribesfolk' and is the term that Jacobs renders as "bunch." In context, *gáwakil* can indeed refer to the Tualatin "bunch," but it also appears in Kenoyer's narrative with reference to other tribes (for example, to Luckiamute Kalapuyans in 6<33(2)>), as well as to the people of the Grand Ronde Reservation generally (as in 6<33(1)>). In 5<27>, it refers to a hundred-person Grand Ronde hop-picking party organized by Kenoyer's father, at a time when there were less than half that number of Tualatins alive on the reservation—rendering Jacobs's parenthetical comments identifying the party as Tualatin patently absurd.

Instead, historical reality identifies *gáwakil* with the priest's (multi-tribal and multi-ethnic) Grand Ronde "flock." Here and elsewhere in the narrative, Jacobs appears to take it for granted that a narrative told in Tualatin must somehow concern an intact Tualatin cultural group—a Tualatin "bunch." However, Kenoyer's Catholic church (St. Michael the Archangel Church, Grand Ronde) existed in a reservation community that was tribally and ethnically thoroughly mixed from its very inception. On any given Sunday, Fr. Croquet would have been preaching to speakers of up to a dozen different tribal languages, joined by a fair number of speakers of Canadian Métis French. Jacobs's field annotations from Kenoyer, as well as accounts left by some of the Catholic sisters assigned to the Grand Ronde school, establish that he conducted his services using a combination of Latin, Chinuk Wawa, and English.[5]

In this book, we have assembled available historical and ethnographic documentation to fill in the background missing from the manuscript versions of Kenoyer's narrative, in order to recover a sense of its real historical place and moment. Jacobs's phonetic workmanship and skill at transcribing rapid dictation remain unexcelled; however, he occasionally interpolated his own textual interpretations—almost exclusively into the Printer's Manuscript free translation. Therefore, we refer to the Printer's Manuscript mainly to register Jacobs's division of the narrative into paragraphs and paragraph-segments and use Jacobs's Tualatin field texts and (insofar as possible) translations as our models. Also, while we retain the Printer's Manuscript system of paragraph numbers to provide orientation for referring to the transcript, we feel under no obligation to reproduce Jacobs's organization of the text into paragraphs. Rather, using Jacobs's field punctuation as a guide, we have laid out the narrative in lines, guided by Kenoyer's patterned use of certain Tualatin syntactic constructions and related sentence-initial grammatical elements—see Text Presentation and Tranlsation: Parsing Kenoyer's Narrative.

THE GRAND RONDE TRIBES

Grand Ronde Reservation was established to consolidate the indigenous peoples of interior western Oregon—the Willamette, Umpqua, and Rogue River Valleys—under the authority of a single Indian agency. Political organization in aboriginal western Oregon was, to begin with, highly atomistic and village centered. Precipitous declines in the region's indigenous populations following contact gave rise to the wholesale consolidation of many originally autonomous aboriginal local groups into a relatively small number of treaty "bands" and "tribes," each represented by leaders whose status as "chief" was a function not only of their prominence within their own groups, but also of the US government's demand to negotiate with authoritative leaders of named indigenous constituencies.

It is impossible to say with certainty just how many autonomous local groups originally occupied the lands covered by the treaties and executive orders leading up to the establishment of Grand Ronde Reservation. Sixteen named groups represented by signing "chiefs and headmen" are listed in the treaty concluded at Dayton, Oregon, in 1855 (Kappler 1904:665-669). They were joined by eight more groups from the Umpqua, Cow Creek, and Rogue River Valleys, listed in several additional treaties signed between 1853 and 1855 (Kappler 1904: 603–607, 654–660). These twenty-four named groups were the treaty "tribes" removed to Grand Ronde, with some complications affecting the "hostile" Rogue River Valley and Cow Creek groups, whose populations ended up being divided between Grand Ronde and the neighboring Siletz Reservation. The reservation site (named from *grande ronde*, a French Canadian voyageur term for a valley ringed by mountains) was selected for its available agricultural land and its location in Oregon's northern Coast Range, relatively isolated from the Willamette Valley's rapidly expanding Euro-American settlements.[6]

Kenoyer's Tualatin treaty "band" consisted of the remnants of at least sixteen originally autonomous village groups indigenous to the Tualatin, Chehalem, and North Yamhill drainages of the northern Willamette Valley, all speaking a dialect of Northern Kalapuya, the northernmost of three languages constituting the Kalapuyan family (Zenk 1994). Government records show a total of just seventy-five Tualatin survivors arriving at Grand Ronde. Other northern Willamette Valley groups removed to Grand Ronde at the same time included the Yamhills (population 26 on arrival), speakers of another dialect of Northern Kalapuya; the Clackamas (85) along with Chief John's Oregon City or Tumwater band (26); plus a few Portland-Vancouver region survivors, often referred to as the Multnomahs, or, with reference to their last intact village, the Wakanasisi (see narrative chapter 1), all speaking Upper Chinook dialects; and the Molalas (103), speakers of Molala, an isolated language. (These enumerations, as well as those given below, partially recapitulate a Grand Ronde Agency census dated November 25, 1856 [Grand Ronde 1856], with added details on identification and geography gleaned from Belden 1855; refer to map 1). These several groups occupied adjoining enclaves in the northeastern corner of the original reservation, reflecting ties of intertribal marriage and cultural affinity far predating the reservation.

Across the South Yamhill River, which bifurcated the original reservation into northern and southern halves, lay the southern Oregon peoples relocated to Grand Ronde: Umpquas (228 on arrival), speakers of an Athapaskan language (named Upper Umpqua to distinguish it from Lower Umpqua, an unrelated language spoken along lower Umpqua River and the adjacent ocean coast); and the various Rogue River and Cow Creek region groups, nearly one thousand on arrival, but subsequently divided between Siletz and Grand Ronde. According to a later government enumeration (Grand Ronde ca. 1872), by about 1872 that number was reduced at Grand Ronde to eighty-three Rogue River region tribespeople (belonging to two main "tribes," Rogue River and Shasta) and twenty-three Cow Creeks. Rogue Rivers and Cow Creeks were predominantly speakers of Takelma (today classified as an isolated language, formerly as a distant relative of Kalapuyan), while Shastas spoke a Shastan language.

Located in between these northern and southern clusters were the majority of Kalapuyan-speaking groups, most speaking dialects of Central Kalapuya: the Santiams (81), "Calapooias" (Kalapuyas of French Prairie and Pudding River, 22), "Calapooias" of Calapooia River (16), Marysvilles or Marys Rivers (22), Luckiamutes (22), Muddy Creeks (22), Long Toms (16), and "Calapooias" both of Mohawk River (20) and of the Coast Fork of Willamette River (23). The original locations of two Umpqua Valley groups on the reservation is not entirely clear: "Calapooias" (Yoncalla Kalapuyas, speakers of Southern Kalapuya, 30) and "Molallas" (Southern Molalas, speakers of Molala, 36).

The reservation's original tribal clusters were still remembered by one of the Grand Ronde elders interviewed by Zenk in the early 1980s (map 2); they are also evident from the tribal affiliations noted for family heads receiving agricultural allotments, made official in 1891 (see narrative chapter 3, note 1).

Extant records of the nineteenth-century reservation's representative assembly, known as the Grand Ronde Indian Legislature (Grand Ronde 1876–1882), show that until 1876 participants represented tribes (thereafter, they represented not tribes but precincts). The lists of tribes appearing in the proceedings of the earlier assemblies are unique in that they originated not with the record-keeping of government employees but with the community's conduct of its own internal business. The 1873 proceedings name eleven Grand Ronde "tribes," the 1876 proceedings twelve: common to the two lists are Clackamas, Oregon City, Wapato Lake (synonym of Tualatin; given simply as "Wapatos" in the 1873 proceedings), Yamhill, Molala (spelled "Molels" in the 1873 proceedings), Luckiamute, Santiam, Marys River, Umpqua, and Rogue River; the 1876 list adds Cow Creek and Shasta (combined), while the 1873 list includes "Calapooias" (who, judging from the representatives named, appear to be Yoncalla Kalapuyas).[7]

Members of other ethnic groups speaking other languages also found their way to Grand Ronde, typically to join relatives by marriage already living there. Reflecting the reservation's makeup—minority ethnicities lacking an ethnic majority tongue—Chinuk Wawa (autonym of the language usually referred to in English as Chinook Jargon), the first lingua franca of the greater Pacific Northwest, was

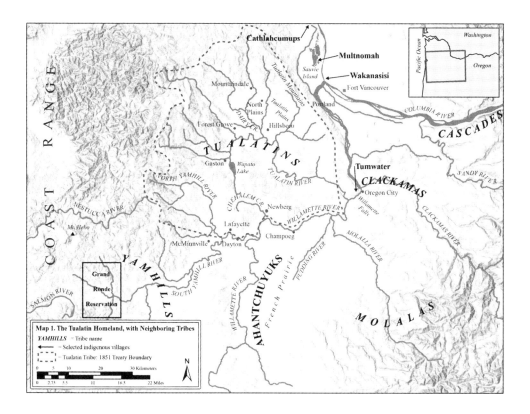

Map 1. The Tualatin Homeland, with Neighboring Tribes

YAMHILLS = Tribe name
= Selected indigenous villages
= Tualatin Tribe: 1851 Treaty Boundary

adopted as the community's first common language. All Grand Ronde Indians of Kenoyer's generation grew up speaking it along with their natal tribal languages and local English (Zenk 1988, Chinuk Wawa Dictionary Project 2012:12–18, 369–382; also see narrative chapter 10, note 1).

The abrupt consolidation of these disparate populations on one small Indian reservation brought many tribes that had had little or no previous experience of one another into close, daily proximity. Some tribes, indeed, found themselves near-neighbors of hereditary enemies. Notwithstanding the potential for social disharmony inherent in such a situation, there are few reports of disturbances arising from intertribal conflict on the reservation. Kenoyer's narrative provides some insight into how residents of the nineteenth-century reservation were able to remain fully cognizant of their different tribal identities while finding common cause as co-participants in one reservation community. Of particular interest are Kenoyer's extended descriptions of games and gambling on the reservation— favorite topics of his. Such activities provided occasions for friendly (or friendly enough) competition, permitting a safe release of community tensions. In 13<73> and chapter 6 we see that when sides were drawn up for competition, or when money was pooled to assemble bets, tribesmen naturally lined up first with fellow tribesmen, then with tribesmen from other tribes within their same reservation

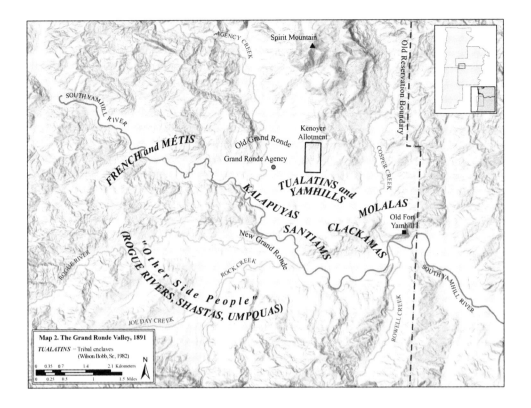

Map 2. The Grand Ronde Valley, 1891
TUALATINS — Tribal enclaves
(Wilson Bobb, Sr., 1982)

tribal cluster. In 6<33>, for example, the Tualatin leading man Shilikwa, here racing his horse against a Luckiamute-owned horse, assembles a stake from fellow Molalas, Clackamas, and Yamhills, as well as from fellow Tualatins; the Luckiamutes, in turn, are backed by Umpquas, Rogue Rivers, and Shastas, all tribes residing on the south side of South Yamhill River (map 2). The historical bifurcation of the reservation into two principal halves is also suggested by Kenoyer's account in 13<68> of an assembly of Grand Ronde leading men: he remembers the names of the Tualatin, Santiam, Ahantchuyuk, Yamhill, and Clackamas leading men but evidently misre-members the name of the Umpqua leader, while forgetting entirely the names of the Rogue River and Shasta leaders.

Each reservation tribe consisted of a rather small circle of people who typically considered themselves closely related, irrespective of demonstrable biological kin-ship. The tendency to impute close blood kinship to everyone within extended circles of perceived kin, combined with a strong cultural taboo on marriage within any degree of recognized blood relationship, meant that very few intra-tribal marriages took place on the reservation. It also means that Grand Ronde family histories often present dauntingly complex webs of interconnection. Although he grossly mischaracterized the community's positive valuation of extended kinship, one Grand Ronde agent's observations were in some respects prescient.

A shinny game. Kenoyer mentions shinny a number of times in his narrative. Narrative chapter 2<11> describes a gathering of many tribes, all playing shinny for high stakes. According to information accompanying this photo, Grand Ronde and Siletz Indians are playing at the C. W. Young place in Eugene on September 15, 1884. Lane County Historical Museum, photo WR131.

One of the greatest causes of trouble in the future is the fact that they do not seem to attach any value to their relationship [*sic*] and names. In many cases there are several classes of persons living in the same house, yet belonging to different families. They are in no way related: but they all go under the same name. It is not the name of perhaps half of them and in a few years no one will be able to tell what their real names are: of how they are related—if related at all. . . . In many cases parents die and their children are absorbed in families and have taken the names of the family that raises them. (Brentano 1894:259)

The agent appears to be concerned primarily about issues of individual property rights and inheritance. However, even a cursory glance at Fr. Croquet's register of Grand Ronde births, marriages, and deaths makes it obvious that the drastic decline of the region's indigenous population did not cease with removal to the reservation. Mortality remained high there, especially among the youngest members of the community. In this light, the widespread extension of mutual obligations implied by close blood kinship functioned to preserve a degree of group integrity in the face of continuing collective trauma.

The soil of the Grand Ronde Valley turned out to be less than ideally suited to productive agriculture, although Grand Ronde Indians were expected to (and many, including Kenoyer's father, tried hard to) transform themselves into Euro-American style small farmers.[8] Additionally, many benefits promised in treaty failed to materialize, a fault that the community laid squarely at the door of the era's notoriously corrupt federal Indian service. The Upper Umpqua–speaking elder John Warren, a contemporary of Kenoyer, encapsulated the history of the reservation system at Grand Ronde in a 1934 interview:

The first Indians were satisfied with this reservation. The agents showed them the hills with lots of deer and elk, the rivers, Salmon River, Little Nestucca and Big Nestucca, full of fish, and they thought that was fine. They expected to live like they had before by hunting, fishing, and gathering wild food. They knew nothing

INTRODUCTION

of farming. But game was soon gone, and the rivers taken away, and the land not very good for farming. Indians never had much land, and not enough tools. Agents sold lots of it that had been allotted to Indians. Sinnott, and Kershaw and Lamson [three of the nineteenth-century agents] especially, cheated Indians out of the best land, and out of much money. McLane [John B. McClane, agent from 1886 to 1889] was the best agent. He got wagons and stock, and helped the Indians. But honest men never lasted long, only crooked ones stayed a long time. (Berreman 1935:46-47)

LIFE ON THE NINETEENTH-CENTURY RESERVATION

While hunting and fishing supplied an important supplement to the local diet (and continue to do so for many in the contemporary community), the Grand Ronde tribes' traditional hunting and gathering economies yielded abruptly on the reservation to subsistence farming on the Euro-American model. Euro-American families of the Willamette Valley also came to depend on the reservation community as a source of farm and domestic labor. With this shift of economy there came a wholesale adoption of Euro-American rural dress, housing, technology, and work habits. Kenoyer's narrative is an important addition to the record of this transformation, as exemplified by 2<7-13>, which features daily farm work on the reservation and an off-reservation trip to work for local Euro-Americans and harvest wild crops. An extended narrative of a hunting and berrying trip into the Coast Range to the northwest of Grand Ronde makes up narrative chapter 4.

General O. O. Howard, stationed at Fort Vancouver shortly before leading the US Army on its famed pursuit of Chief Joseph's Nez Perce band, recorded his impressions of an 1876 tour of Grand Ronde Reservation. Proceeding into the northeastern

Contemporary view from the top of Mt. Hebo. The country hunted by Yamhill Joe in narrative chapter 4, and by generations of Grand Ronde people since.

The steeple of St. Michael's church and the picket fence surrounding the church are seen behind the riders in this view to the east. The picture is undated and the identities of the riders a subject of some controversy. The second rider from the right has been conjectured to be either Judge Joseph Shangretta (Iroquois-Kalapuyan, judge of the Court of Indian Offences at Grand Ronde) or Frank Quenel (French-Chinook, one of the agency policemen). The rider on the far left may be Dan Robinson (Rogue River Takelma, another agency policeman), whose third wife was Kenoyer's younger sister, Caroline Kenoyer. Andrew H. Kershaw Collection, Oregon Historical Society, photo 661Z011.

(Tualatin-Yamhill-Clackamas-Molala) sector of the Grand Ronde Valley from the former site of Fort Yamhill, where US Army soldiers had overseen the reservation during its first ten years of existence, the general was greeted with a seemingly idyllic vista.

> When we reached the top of the hill, the former site of the fort, and looked west and south, what an evening prospect was before us! A beautiful panoramic view of a cultivated valley apparently surrounded by a short line of hills—it is like an extended lake with swelling waves—but the waves are only the rising and falling of a rolling prairie. It is the "Grandronde [sic] Reservation."
>
> What houses are those all along the sides of this valley as far as the eye can reach, many of them evidently new? Mr. [James] Brown says they all belong to the Indians! Their farms have been allotted them, and they are improving rapidly.

It filled my heart with joy to see these evidences of civilization, even here where I had learned the poor people had been so often plundered of means that the government had appropriated to their benefit: even here where their women had been corrupted, and where all their education had been withholden! It was two miles and a half to the agency buildings. . . . The agency doctor conducted us through the lanes, fields, swamps and road to the agent's house.

Mr. P[erry] B. Sinnott, the agent, is an Irishman. He gave us a warm-hearted welcome to his house. . . . Looking north from the porch of Mr. Sinnott's house, you notice a fine new building a hundred yards distant. It is the new school-house, with accommodations for a hundred scholars. Just beyond I saw a larger old building, with a small belfry and cross upon it; this was the Catholic church. To my left, and no more than fifty yards off, was "the home," where "the Sisters," four in number, took care of the Indian girls who were scholars.

. . . We accompanied the agent to several Indian houses; these had generally two main rooms and a kitchen—the bed-rooms, with one well-made bed in each, were neat. I noticed in one there was a baby, [in?] a curious little basket-cradle, as broad as it was long, but having in it a clean sheet. The clothing in the house was tidy; the walls of the sitting-room papered with pictures taken from pictorial papers. Nearly every head of a family had a wagon, plow, and horses. Before ten a. m. we returned to visit the school. . . .

Father Croquet, a Belgian priest, was there. He has a happy, Christian face, and all love him. I do not think he draws the broad line we do between the converted and the unconverted. I tried to learn from him if any of the elder Indians had really found the Saviour [sic]. He answered that many of them were careful in their conduct and sincere. From the school-room we went to the agency office near the "children's home." Here the Indians wished me to talk to them. I did so, expressing my gratification at the school, the farms, the evident progress of the people of the several tribes here gathered. One after another the Indians made answer. The younger Indians could speak plain English, but for fear the old ones would not understand them, they all talked the Chinook, or "Jargon," as they call the language, and had it interpreted to me.

Polygamy has almost ceased among them. Nothing seems to offend them so much as the wicked attempts of certain white men to get their wives away from them. They thanked me over and over again for my visit and for my words to them. Some white men near by had said that they were not better than wild Indians. "You can see," they said, "we dress like you, we have a school and a church, we have houses and lands, teams and plows; we are no longer *wild Indians*."

(O. O. Howard, quoted in Van der Heyden 1906:87–89)

These very interesting observations touch on aspects of life on the nineteenth-century reservation also visible in Kenoyer's narrative. Along with accounts of day-to-day economic activity, Kenoyer provides a student's perspective on life in the on-reservation schools, especially the boarding school known in the community as "the Sisters' School," an inevitable rite of passage for almost all Indians born

Grand Ronde boarding school boys and girls posing with school staff in front of the blockhouse at Grand Ronde Agency. This blockhouse had originally been part of Fort Yamhill several miles to the east, where a military garrison oversaw the reservation during its early years. In 1911 it was moved again, to Dayton, Oregon, where it remains today as the only surviving vestige of the old agency. Andrew H. Kershaw Collection, Oregon Historical Society, photo 661Z025.

on the nineteenth-century reservation (see narrative chapter 2<4-5> and chapters 8 and 9). Fr. Croquet, who was instrumental in founding and organizing the school, appears in these chapters and chapter-segments, as well as in Kenoyer's recollections of serving as one of his altar boys—as told in chapter 9, for which we are fortunate to have been able to secure annotations from Fr. Martinus Cawley of Our Lady of Guadalupe Trappist Abbey, Lafayette, Oregon, an authority on Fr. Croquet's life and career (see Cawley 1996).

But the school and the mission were not the whole story of the reservation's cultural life, as Fr. Croquet's perhaps coy response to General Howard's query about whether "any of the elder Indians had really found the Saviour [sic]" hinted. General Howard, a devout evangelical Christian, doubtless knew that Fr. Croquet was faulted by some for accepting an outward show of devotion to Catholic ritual rather than demanding his charges' genuine conversion to Christianity. In fact, the old indigenous religion, centered on healing ceremonialism and the animistic ideology underlying it, flourished on the nineteenth-century reservation. Leading this indigenous religious life was a multi-tribal assortment of traditional healers patronized in common by all the reservation tribes. These practitioners are usually referred to by anthropologists as shamans; in the local English of the reservation, they were usually known as Indian doctors, or Tamanawas doctors, from Chinuk Wawa *t'amánawas*, referring to the spirit-beings to whom these doctors' powers

Group of sisters and girls posing on the steps of the main government boarding school build-ing, where the girls' dormitory was located. One of the plank walkways that criss-crossed the agency is in the foreground. Note the toddler, lower right, perhaps an orphaned child. Two of the elders interviewed by Zenk in the early 1980s lost their mothers as small children, and were subsequently taken in by sisters at the school. Andrew H. Kershaw Collection, Oregon Historical Society, photo 661Z008.

to heal (and, not infrequently, to harm) were attributed, as well as to the power conferred by such spirits—not only upon doctors, although doctors were thought to possess the strongest Tamanawas power. By all accounts, Fr. Croquet did not actively oppose the Tamanawas doctors. Rather, he placed his own hope for the community's Christian future in the school and its Catholic sisters.

Much detail on the community's indigenous religious ceremonialism appears in the texts that Jacobs transcribed from two other members of the first cohort of tribal people born at Grand Ronde: John B. Hudson, a speaker of Santiam Central Kalapuya (Jacobs 1945:1–142), and Victoria (Wishikin) Wacheno Howard, a speaker of Clackamas Upper Chinook (Jacobs 1958-59). Jacobs's field notebooks from both Hudson and Howard also contain a good deal of supplemental information in English on personalities and cultural practices animating daily life on the nineteenth-century reservation. Many of Howard's contributions in this regard, if far fewer of Hudson's, were published by Jacobs—see especially the endnotes accompany-ing Howard's Clackamas text dictations (Jacobs 1958–59:629–663), which sup-ply biographical detail important for situating her Clackamas-language cultural descriptions in their reservation context.

Kenoyer's narrative adds a third perspective on daily life at nineteenth-century

Grand Ronde Reservation, one much more attuned to the meeting and inter-penetration of old indigenous practices and beliefs with newly introduced Euro-American influences. Such comingling can be seen especially in 2<6>, Kenoyer's account of a death in the family, featuring appearances both by Fr. Croquet and the Tualatin Tamanawas doctor Shumkhi (šúmxi, šúmxən); and in chapter 11, Kenoyer's account of his own illness, featuring the agency doctor's ineffective attempt to cure, followed by success at the hands of an old Tamanawas doctoress.

If the indigenous cultures often seem to shine through in far purer form in the Hudson and Howard dictations, this is only natural, considering that Jacobs invited these speakers to use their indigenous languages and narrative conventions to frame ethnographic descriptions that they were equally, if not more, capable of delivering in English (Jacobs 1945:5–6). Aside from several short texts recorded by Angulo and Freeland (including their text reproduced as narrative chapter 1), none of the linguists who worked with Kenoyer attempted to elicit ethnographic texts from him. That Kenoyer possessed traditional knowledge comparable in many respects to Hudson's is shown by a manuscript identified as *Jacobs Kalapuya Element List . . . Santiam Kalapuya / Tualatin Kalapuya,* submitted by Jacobs to A. L. Kroeber of the University of California. This exists in two versions, one a draft (Jacobs ca. 1937a, evidently the field manuscript) archived at the University of California, Berkeley, under the title *Northwest Coast Culture Element list: Kalapuya, Santiam and Tualatin* (which is misleading, because it erroneously implies that there are lists for three coordinate groups, not two). The other is a copy (Jacobs ca. 1937b) archived in Jacobs's papers at the University of Washington. We have so far been unable to locate any background information on this list, not even the names of informants. However, the draft version contains internal evidence pointing to Hudson as the Santiam informant and Kenoyer as the Tualatin informant.[9]

One striking feature of these lists is their paucity of detail on material aspects of culture. This deficit could reflect Jacobs's lack of familiarity with many details of material culture (his own interests lay in narrative genres and the intersection of culture and individual psychology), his reservation-raised informants' hazy recollections in this regard, or both. It is interesting to compare the assessment of one of Kroeber's students, Philip Drucker, regarding the reliability of ethno-graphic data he himself had recorded from three tribal-language-speaking Grand Ronde contemporaries of Hudson and Kenoyer (John Warren, a speaker of Upper Umpqua Athapaskan; John Wacheno, a Clackamas Upper Chinook speaker; and William Simmons, a Takelma speaker). The last page of his Grand Ronde field notes (Drucker 1934) shows the following (later) appended note:

> This all is a lovely example of what you're liable to get among these shattered cultures—This info is a mixture of true abor[iginal] customs, reservation mixed

practices, and damn lies—I'll stake my soul—but how the hell are you going to know which is which? PD. (1935)

The two anthropologists' field methodologies present a stark contrast. Jacobs followed in his teacher Boas's footsteps, focusing on the encoding of culture in language; Drucker was limited to local English—his transcriptions of key terms from the languages are none too reliable—but he excelled at describing material aspects of indigenous cultures. The two were united by a common goal of uncovering the region's "true aboriginal customs." Quite possibly, the utter obscurity to which Kroeber and/or his school consigned Jacobs's Kalapuya culture element list reflects an assessment of its limited value as a record of "true" aboriginal culture.

Nevertheless, allowing for the influence of "reservation mixed practices" (unavoidable for the generation of Hudson and Kenoyer), the sections in the draft element list treating indigenous religious and healing ceremonialism show not only a high percentage of responses from both informants, but a good number of expansions on that list in the form of additional traits inserted in Jacobs's own hand. Based on the numbers and kinds of responses from each informant, it appears that Kenoyer and Hudson were about equally knowledgeable on the subject, demonstrating that the indigenous religious life of the reservation was very much a part of Hudson's and Kenoyer's experience, as well as of Victoria Howard's.

It is of note that none of the texts dictated by these three indigenous-language speakers reveal whether they themselves had acquired Tamanawas power. The usual traditional means to this end was a solitary preadolescent quest at an isolated spot in the wilderness, followed by dreamed encounters with spirits in human form, followed by the learning of songs unique to these spirits, culminating in participation in winter Tamanawas dances, considered necessary for raising and controlling the powers conferred by Tamanawas spirits. Less typically, power could be acquired through direct encounter at a Tamanawas dance or in the course of being cured by a Tamanawas doctor. Jacobs understood that this dimension of the tradition was considered deeply personal by Northwest tribal people—indeed, revealing one's power was thought to risk weakening it—and he scrupulously avoided asking direct questions about such matters.

One of Jacobs's Clackamas texts from Victoria Howard, *I was ill and dúšdaq doctored me* (Jacobs 1958–59:653–654), is very reminiscent of Kenoyer's own account in chapter 11 of being treated by a Tamanawas doctor. The former has the advantage, though, of detailed textual annotations, secured by Jacobs on reading back the field texts to Howard for translation. Much of the content of these annotations was published, divided between parenthesized additions to the English translation and appended endnotes. Kenoyer's very spare telling, coming as it does in the untranslated portion of his narrative, lacks such supplementary detail. But taken together, the two accounts invite some general observations on the rather long and drawn-out waxing, followed by the rather brief final waning, of the community's indigenous religious ceremonialism.

Dushdak (*dúšdaq*), also known as Doctor (or Doc) Smith (appearing as "Dr. Smith" in Jacobs 1929-30, 58:118, the field version of the text, but misconstrued in publication as "Mr. Smith"), is usually identified (as in Howard's account) as a Tualatin, although another account has him as Clackamas, yet another as Yamhill. Such confusion of tribal identities was not unusual on the nineteenth-century reservation. For the tribal cluster occupying the northeast corner of the reservation in particular, it often reflected ties of intertribal marriage (Dushdak was married to a Clackamas woman) and extended kinship (Yamhills and Tualatins were ethnically closely akin and sometimes lumped together).[10]

In Victoria Howard's account of her illness, her mother has called in a number of Tamanawas doctors with no success—leading her finally to summon "Dushdak himself," by implication the most powerful doctor available. Dushdak extracts and kills the infecting disease-causing "worm" (*wímqt* in Clackamas, *lá·l* in Tualatin: we translate as 'lahl-worm'). While lahl-worms lurk in the environment and can be encountered by accident, they can also be sent with hostile intent by persons with malevolent Tamanawas power. It is not clear from Howard's account how she became infected. In Kenoyer's account of his illness, the treating Tamanawas doctoress (unnamed) explicitly attributes Kenoyer's lahl-worm infection to the hostile intent of another Tamanawas doctor.

Complete recovery from illness following a Tamanawas doctor's treatment was thought to be contingent on the complete restoration of the patient's vitality. Dushdak's prescription for Howard's recovery was the usual one for ensuring that result: her mother must host a Tamanawas dance (in local English, doctor's dance) for her daughter. Such dances were always held in winter and customarily lasted until around midnight for four consecutive nights, then all the way through to dawn on the fifth night. Usually, doctors led the dances, dancing and singing their Tamanawas songs first, followed by other participants dancing and singing their own Tamanawas songs. Each singer's songs were taken up by the other participants, who kept time by jumping up and down in place and pounding canes on the wooden floor of the house hosting the dance.[11] Dushdak led the dance for restoring Howard.

Kenoyer's account of his own cure mentions dancing, the singing of Tamanawas songs, the beating of time using sticks, and a five-day recovery period—all indicative of a Tamanawas dance, although explicit identification is lacking. Kenoyer is, however, quite explicit that the hostile doctor, spiritually weakened by the treating doctoress's destruction of his lahl-worm, did host a five-night Tamanawas dance in an attempt to renew *his* vitality—without success, since he fell sick afterward, dying some undetermined time later. In a similar vein, Howard tells of an Umpqua doctoress who came to her dance, evidently with the intent of stealing some of Dushdak's power—an outcome anticipated by Dushdak, or rather, by some one or another of his many Tamanawas spirits, who were keeping watch over the proceedings for him. Omitted from the published annotations of Howard's text is the additional detail (Jacobs 1929–30, 58:130, 132) that either Dushdak himself, or "his *q'ašxínašxina* or some other of his many powers," stole the Umpqua doctoress's power, causing her to die within the year.

Two features of the Tamanawas dance are key to understanding its persistence on the reservation, even in the face of sporadic official persecution. First, while it could indeed be held as a highly orchestrated formal occasion, with a sponsoring family or individual (usually, but not necessarily, a Tamanawas doctor) and many participants, it could also occur as an informally organized sequel to the curing ritual proper, as in the case of Dushdak's prescription (and probably of Kenoyer's cure) above. Second, many older community members, especially those of the northwest Oregon tribal cluster where these dances represented deeply rooted tradition, believed that a productive life, even survival itself, presupposed relationship with one or more Tamanawas spirits, and that these spirits required, indeed themselves compelled, periodic expression in the dances.

In Kenoyer's account, he had fallen ill while boarded at the Sisters' School. Although the school was located at Grand Ronde Agency (by his own account only a mile from the Kenoyer family home), children were required to spend the entire school year boarded there, visiting home only for three days each month. Illness was not uncommon among the children, and it was a serious concern for many Indian parents, whose reluctance to give up their children to the school created some difficulty for the authorities, especially during the school's founding period (see 2<3-8>, in which the agent is quoted as threatening parents with arrest for not surrendering their children to the school; also see Cawley 1996:27, 55–58). In cases of more serious illness, however, the authorities could be persuaded to set aside their adamant opposition to the Tamanawas doctors, letting a child go back home to be treated in the traditional manner.[12] This is apparently what happened in Kenoyer's case, and in a case mentioned in an anonymously written (Catholic) *History of Grand Ronde,* quoted from the *Chronicles of the Holy Names* (a record of the first Catholic order to serve at the school):

> Although the savages of the Reservation are considered to be fully civilized they still preserve the old habits of their nation, such as calling the witch doctors close to the sick. These perform the Tamonoise [Tamanawas], or superstitious dance. Just recently we heard these songs and dances around one of our neighboring

houses which was sheltering a dying child. The poor little one was our pupil and desired nothing of the savage doctors, but his old parents, urged by the Indians, permitted the Tamonoise. Their cries and groans could be heard at a great distance. (Anonymous 1960:17)

While these "superstitious" Tamanawas dances were subject to official repression on the reservation, it is unclear how effective this ever was. They are not to be confused with the so-called Earthlodge cult (known at Siletz and Grand Ronde as the Warm House Dance), a nativistic revival movement characterized by large organized dances and associated festivities, which spread to the reservation from the south in the early 1870s and took hold especially among the southern Oregon tribes at Grand Ronde (Youst and Seaburg 2002:89-107, Du Bois 1939:26–32). According to the Clackamas-speaking elder John Wacheno, another contemporary of Kenoyer interviewed by Joel Berreman in 1934, this movement was effectively suppressed during the tenure of agent Perry B. Sinnott (1872–1885). Another elder of the same generation, John Warren (quoted previously on the founding of the reservation), added that the authorities enlisted the support of tribal chiefs to stop these dances (Berreman 1935:45, 107–108). This points to a crucial difference between the Warm House Dance and the indigenous healing traditions, which were so firmly embedded in the tribal cultures as to rate regulation under the bylaws of the reservation's self-governing assembly, the Grand Ronde Indian Legislature. The laws for the legislature's seventh annual session, held in 1878, include the following provision (spelling as in original):

> Any Doctor who doctors any Person and think[s] he cant cure the person he must tell the person he cant cure him. So that he dont rob him of all his property. he is to receive $2.50 for his cervices, but if the Doctor Keeps on doctoring and dont cure. after he is to be fined $10.00 and Cost of Court if proven. (Grand Ronde 1876–82)

Not that the agents did not also attempt to suppress the Tamanawas dances. Jacobs (1929–30, 58:98) has it from Victoria Howard that "the last time such power [Tamanawas] dances were held at Gr[and] Ronde were about 1885–1890; the agent and police finally stopped it." The dates given point to the tenure of agent John B. McClane (1886–1889), one of the more proactive government agents assigned to Grand Ronde. Notwithstanding McClane's evident disapproval of indigenous ways, the elders interviewed by Berreman in 1934 were in unanimous agreement that he was the best agent they ever had, proactive in trying to "civilize" his charges away from their ancient beliefs, yes, but proactive also in helping community members develop practical occupational skills, while seeing to it that government benefits intended for them by Congress actually reached them.[13] According to John Wacheno, Victoria Howard's brother-in-law during the years of her first marriage at Grand Ronde, McClane's campaign against the Tamanawas dances was in point of fact not exactly decisive:

> McLane [sic] tried to stop the Indian spirit or doctor's dance, and to stop Indian doctors from practicing. Wacheno and others talked to him and persuaded him to let it go, as people believed in it, etc. Wacheno challenged him to go to one and prove he could hold the magic cane that Doc Smith used in his dances, but he would not go. (John Wacheno interview; Berreman 1935:108)

The following passage from one of McClane's annual agent's reports provides an instructive counterpoint to Wacheno's account. Evidently frustrated by the influence of the doctors on the reservation, McClane was moved to issue a challenge of his own.

> When I came here there were very few of the Indians or half-breeds but what believed in the power of Indian doctors. Some of them even went so far as to believe they had the power of merely going through a little incantation of words and, blowing their breath towards you, even if you were twenty feet away, kill you instantly; or make you stand against a tree so you couldn't get away, and say to them, do you want to die now or to-morrow, and if they say to-morrow their life would be prolonged until that time. There is many believe this, and it is not confined to the Indians; the half-breeds are just as bad; they believe that they can kill a horse in the same way by tieing [sic] him up to a fence; or standing him anywhere in close proximity. There was a number in my office one day, and among them some of those would-be doctors. One, a part Spanish [Mexican] and part Indian, a quite intelligent man, with considerable property, stated that his wife had the power of doing that thing. I told him I would give him $100 if he would bring her and all the rest of the doctors that possessed that power to practice on me, and if they succeeded in killing me they should have the $100 and not be prosecuted for the killing. "Oh, no,["] says he, ["]we can't do that; we can't kill a white man, but can kill an Indian or a horse." (McClane 1886:211)

It is unclear what effect McClane's campaign had on the conduct of the dances, whether they ceased for a time or were reduced in scale to their more informal variety, or whether, as Wacheno had it, McClane finally just "let it go." In any case, the dances were back in full swing by 1895, judging by the then-agent's report.

> The "medicine men" still have a great hold on the Indians of this reservation. Whenever any one of them is sick they will call in one of these frauds and night after night one can hear the monotonous "music" of their "medicine dance." These "medicine men" lose no opportunity to cause the Indians to lose confidence in the agency physician who is a most competent and reliable officer. (Brentano 1895:267–268)

While departing from the usual local English terminology of the reservation, the agent's word choices—"night after night," "monotonous 'music,'" "medicine

Spirit Mountain, Grand Ronde Indian Reserve

Grand Ronde vertical board and batten farmhouse, with Spirit Mountain in the background, dated 1904. Spirit Mountain was an important ceremonial site during the early years of the reservation. Lee Moorhouse, 1904, Oregon Historical Society, photo 338P097.

dance"—all point to ongoing Tamanawas dances. Regarding the competition between the agency doctor and his Tamanawas doctor counterparts, note that Kenoyer's account of his successful cure by one of the latter follows his account of an unsuccessful treatment at the hands of the agency doctor. The agency physician in 1895 was Dr. Andrew Kershaw, who became the last resident superintendent of Grand Ronde Reservation. Interviewed by Berreman in 1934, Kershaw (then retired and living in Willamina, Oregon, neighboring Grand Ronde) confirmed the late persistence of the doctor's dances on the reservation, as well as the government's (that is, his own, as representative of the government's authority) at best sporadic attempts to stop them.

> He states that he used to forbid native doctors practicing, and elsewhere he had put them in jail for it. Here for the most part he overlooked it. One had to just ignore lots of such things in dealing with Indians. But sometimes he went and broke up the doctor's dances. Frequently threatened, once with a knife, but bluffed it through and was never hurt. (Berreman 1935:140)

The Tamanawas dances ceased, finally, when there were no more active Tamanawas doctors left to lead them. According to John Warren (Berreman

1935:44), the community's last active Tamanawas doctor was the Yoncalla-Molala practitioner Polk Scott (featured in Victoria Howard's Clackamas-language text, *The shaman at my mother's last illness*; Jacobs 1958–59, 2:512–514), who died about 1908. The elders interviewed by Berreman in 1934 were in agreement that no new doctors were "made" on the reservation. While many youngsters of Kenoyer's generation were sent on preadolescent quests to encounter Tamanawas spirits (Kenoyer himself was able to contribute significant detail on the subject for Jacobs's culture element list), apparently no one completed the subsequent long and arduous training period required to become a practicing Tamanawas doctor. The best known questing place on the reservation was Spirit Mountain, overlooking the Grand Ronde Valley from the north. Children sent there on quests were required to retrieve an object or bundle left at the questing site.[14] It is probably Spirit Mountain that Wacheno refers to in his following explanation of the final demise of the reservation's ancient indigenous religion.

> He says nobody became doctors here, they didn't get out and go after the power. When he was small he was called at three in the morning to go to the mountain to find the magic bundle the doctor had hid, but he never became a doctor. The boys and girls here never did that much, all went to school, and neglected such things. (John Wacheno interview; Berreman 1935:108)

Of all the indigenous-language texts and field notes recorded by Jacobs and his fellow linguists and anthropologists, Kenoyer's autobiographical narrative stands as perhaps the most well-rounded reflection of real life on a late nineteenth-century Northwest reservation. The older generations' traditional beliefs and practices—grist for the scholars' academic mills—are there, but so too is the reality, inescapable for most tribal people of Kenoyer's generation, that "all went to school."

LOUIS KENOYER IN LATER LIFE

Louis Kenoyer's own life during and following the period of his childhood narrative well exemplifies the community population dynamics of the nineteenth-century reservation. Out of perhaps ten children of Peter and Nancy Kenoyer, only he and a much younger sister survived to later adulthood. He was away from Grand Ronde in 1886, boarded at Chemawa Indian School in Salem, Oregon, when his father died. By his own account, his father was the last person with whom he spoke Tualatin. In 1891 he received an allotment at Grand Ronde (the location of which is consistent with that given in the narrative for the old Kenoyer family farm: map 2), where he became, by turns, the head of two Grand Ronde families, with two boys of his own and two stepchildren—all of whom died young. In 1899–1900, according to a ledger of *Employees at Grand Ronde, 1884-1907,* he and Joseph Dowd (brother of Rosa Dowd, later to be Kenoyer's second wife) were employed as Indian school teachers for the agency, working under the supervision of two government teachers, Luther Parker and Cora B. Egler. Otherwise, his occupations were various: farmer, laborer, yard-man for a Salem logging company. Sometime before 1914 he left Grand Ronde, sub-sequently being reported in various locations, but mostly at Yakama Reservation in Washington State (the foregoing sketch was extracted from a fact-sheet compiled by June Olson 2013).

We have no record of Kenoyer's tenure at the agency school (the same on-reservation boarding school providing the setting for much of his childhood nar-rative), nor of the circumstances under which it ended. Perhaps he departed the school along with the Catholic sisters so prominent in his narrative. Their era, which had begun with the arrival in 1874 of a contingent of Sisters of the Holy Names of Jesus and Mary, ended with the secularization of government Indian schools in 1900. Last to leave were two Benedictine Sisters, who had to return to their mother-house at Mount Angel, Oregon.[15] That Benedictine community, which was represented by up to five sisters during the heyday of the school, had taught and largely run the school since 1882. It may be appropriate to point out that the work of the sisters and of Fr. Croquet was not without lasting effect in the commu-nity. Most Grand Ronde Indians of the previous generations were at least nomi-nally Catholic; and more than a few of them were devoutly Catholic.[16]

While we have no specific information on what induced Kenoyer to relocate to Yakama Reservation, we do know that his second wife and last surviving step-child died in 1904, and that his mother died not long after that (Olson 2013). Quite possibly, he was led to Yakama Reservation through extended networks of kinship and community from his earlier years at Grand Ronde. Through his mother's first remarriage following the death of Peter Kenoyer—to Joseph Apperson, a son of Chief John of the Oregon City tribe—he was related to Homer Hoffer, a brother of Joseph Apperson who had been living at Yakama Reservation for some time. Grand Ronde Reservation was home to hardly over three hundred people by the end of the nine-teenth century, and it is very likely that both Hoffer and Kenoyer would have known Ed Wheeler, a southern Willamette Valley Kalapuyan from Grand Ronde who had also relocated to Yakama (in fact, we have family information that a granddaughter of Homer Hoffer married a son of Ed Wheeler; Greg Archuleta personal communica-tion 2014). Ed Wheeler was involved in the sheep business (Duane Wheeler personal communication 2014), and a note from Jacobs (n.d.), evidently dating to a period when Jacobs was trying to locate Kenoyer on the Yakama Reservation, reads, "lives usually at Ed. [sic] Wheeler, White Swan [Yakama Reservation]." As of 1928, accord-ing to a letter from Jacobs to Boas (Leeds-Hurwitz 2004:140), Kenoyer was working as a sheepherder in the Yakama Reservation region.

A first communion at St. Michael the Archangel Catholic Church, date unrecorded. This, the second St. Michael's church, was dedicated in 1883 and was replaced by the present-day St. Michael's church in 1938. Grand Ronde elder Darrel Mercier remembers the church being well attended during his boyhood in the mid-1930s, 75–80 percent of the congregation at that time being Indian. Donated to the Cultural Archive of the Confederated Tribes of Grand Ronde by Peachie Hamm.

Kenoyer's first experience as a linguistic consultant came in 1915, when Leo J. Frachtenberg, a Boas student belonging to the generation preceding Jacobs's, tracked him to Yakama Reservation.[17] On locating Kenoyer, Frachtenberg brought with him the original field notes of the first scholar to have recorded extensively at Grand Ronde, the Bureau of American Ethnology linguist Albert S. Gatschet, who in 1877 had transcribed 402 pages of Tualatin "texts, sentences, and vocables" from Kenoyer's father, Peter Kenoyer, as well as from Dave Yachkawa (*yáčgawa*), father of Daniel Yachkawa, Kenoyer's fellow altar boy in narrative chapter 9 (Gatschet 1877, Jacobs 1945:155). Frachtenberg confined himself to checking and correcting Gatschet's earlier transcriptions, made at a time when the phonetics of Northwest indigenous languages were not well understood. He methodically re-elicited Gatschet's transcriptions of selected words, writing his corrections in red ink directly into the pages of Gatschet's original notebooks.[18]

Jaime de Angulo's colorful recollection of his own trip to Yakama Reservation in search of Kenoyer appears in a 1950 letter to the imprisoned poet Ezra Pound, excerpted below. The reference to "Kroeber's girl" in this account is to Alfred L. Kroeber, head of the Anthropology Department at the University of California, Berkeley, and to Angulo's wife, Lucy S. (Nancy) Freeland. Kroeber had considered Freeland a particularly promising student, and he was not at all pleased when she left the university's anthropology program to marry Angulo (Leeds-Hurwitz 1982, Gui Mayo personal communication 2013). Spelling and punctuation as in the original.

> Boas who was a darling and a great man but he took no interest in the petty political quarrels of the anthropological world in America, discovered that my stuff was being published in Europe, in Vienna, in Paris "Who is this fellow Angulo?... Living in California? Why isnt he publishing here?" "Oh he had a fight with Kroeber—he married Kroeber's girl . . . he is a dissolute drunkard he is crazy" Boas didnt give a damn about my private morals as long as my phonetics were right So he took me up It was a joy to work for the Old Man! ... He had a golden heart but he was brusque One day I get a telegram "I need the Kalapooya [*sic*] language of the lower Columbia to settle a question of comparative linguistics. According to information there is only one man left who speaks that language Lives somewhere in the Yakima Reservation and is drinking himself to death Will you undertake it? I can get only $500 from Committee When can you go?" I answered from Portland "I am on the way" (I thot it rather amusing to send one drunkard looking for another drunkard "somewhere on the Yakima Reservation (in Washington State)" But i was used to Indian ways and it took me only a week to locate him and I drove him back to Berkeley We arrived in the middle of the afternoon nobody at home when the gang returned they found a drunken anthropologist and a drunken Indian (last of his race) snoring in each other's arms. (G. de Angulo 2004:424–425)

Gui Mayo (Gui de Angulo), in whose lively telling of her father's life this letter appears, attributes the account of Kenoyer's drunkenness to her father's penchant for dramatic exaggeration. Her mother, Nancy Freeland, became quite fond of Kenoyer during his winter-long stay with them at their home in Berkeley, and was firmly convinced that he was a non-drinker. She especially appreciated his help in caring for the couple's two small children (one of whom was Gui Mayo, too young however to remember Kenoyer—Gui Mayo personal communication 2013). Jaime de Angulo made rather short work of Tualatin, considering it unchallenging linguistically, but that was not the end of Kenoyer's stay in Berkeley, as Nancy Freeland remembered.

> In ten days or so, Jaime closed his notebooks and said he had it in the bag. There was no special reason for Konoi [Kenoyer] to stay on, but he did—almost all winter. We liked him very much, and for his part, he seemed to enjoy being in a metropolis. He was an educated man and spent a lot of time poring through our anthropological library. Sitting of a morning, with his glasses on, reading the Chronicle,

in his dark suit and vest, he looked a bit like a member of the Berkeley Chamber of Commerce. (Freeland in G. de Angulo 2004:291) [19]

With respect to Kenoyer as a teetotaler, however, two notices of arrests for public drunkenness—of "Lewis Cornoyer, an Indian from the Grand Ronde reservation" (*Morning Oregonian,* March 16, 1901) and of "Chemawa Graduate . . . Lewis Kenoyer" (*Oregon City Courier,* September 4, 1904)—lend historical credence to Jaime de Angulo's memory on this point (thanks to David Lewis for locating these items). It should be pointed out that the first notice comes around the time that Kenoyer's two small boys, Frederick and Joseph, died, and the second comes some months after the death of his second wife, Rosa (Dowd) Taylor Kenoyer (Olson 2013). He does seem to have been capable of abstaining when he put his mind to it, as he evidently did manage to do while caring for the two small children of his freethinking Berkeley hosts.

Zenk missed an opportunity to learn more about Kenoyer the man. Two of the Grand Ronde elders he interviewed at length between 1978 and 1983 had close family and personal ties to him: Wilson Bobb Sr., whose Tualatin mother, Lucinda (Metzger) Apperson Bobb Wacheno, had been married to a brother of Joseph Apperson, one of Kenoyer's stepfathers (even lacking that special connection, she was close kin simply by virtue of being Tualatin); and Clara (Robinson) Riggs, a stepdaughter of Kenoyer's late-surviving sister, Caroline (Kenoyer) Robinson Larson. Among the few mentions of Kenoyer in Zenk's field notes is the following from Wilson Bobb (Zenk 1978–93, 5:51).

> Where we lived at G[rand] R[onde] / The Tualatin, Yamhill, Kalapuyas / They'd practically claim each other as relatives . . . I knew Louis Kenoyer well—we lived next to him for years (at G[rand] R[onde]) / He used to get me drunk as a little kid—By the spoonful / mixed alcohol-water
>
> HZ [Zenk asking]: Do you think you talked Jargon w[ith] him? /
>
> [WB answering:] Oh yeah
>
> He got to be a real boozehound / He belonged to the same outfit as we were / a Tuality
>
> . . .
>
> lówi kənóyər
>
> Incident that WB rem[ember]s so well / They were drinking at a Frenchman's place (they had to get booze from Frenchmen—Ind[ian]s couldn't legally drink) / He (the Frenchman) told L[ouis] K[enoyer] to throw me out / As I was g[oing] out door—[I] swung at him / Hit the door & him at same time / I'll never forget the face he made

Just as there was a flourishing indigenous religious culture on the reservation, notwithstanding official disapproval, so too was there a flourishing drinking culture, notwithstanding the authorities' earnest efforts to keep alcohol away from Indians. Incidents of high drama punctuating the humdrum of daily reservation life were often attributable to one or the other of these underground cultures. The alcohol-related kind all too often came with tragic consequences, as in the case of the family of Kenoyer's childhood friend, Daniel Yachkawa. Daniel's father, the Tualatin Tamanawas doctor "Wapato Dave" Yachkawa, began going blind after drinking bad bootleg whiskey. According to Victoria Howard (Jacobs 1929–30, 58:12), he danced in an attempt to restore his vision, but must have started too late, since the condition kept worsening. He also turned informant against the bootleggers, a move that cost both him and his wife their lives. The two were brutally murdered in their home by an axe-wielding assailant, identified as the Molala community member (and bootlegger) Tom Gilbert (*giugíuš*) (Jacobs has accounts from both Hudson and Howard, and a fragment of the murder story turned up in Zenk's field notes from Wilson Bobb). Daniel Yachkawa was seriously wounded in the attack, barely escaping with his life; his parents were nearly decapitated (*Daily Astorian*, December 5, 1882). Gilbert was tried for the crime and duly sentenced to hang, but the Oregon Supreme Court later reversed the conviction on a technicality (Olson 2011:153–154). He was apparently living as a free man in Portland in 1890, where Franz Boas (1890) happened by and transcribed Molala vocabulary and sentences from him.

The deaths of Kenoyer's two young sons appear to have made an indelible impression on Clara Riggs; the subject comes up unsolicited several times in Zenk's tape-recorded interviews with her. In the following two excerpts, she is addressing a fellow Grand Ronde elder, Eula (Hudson) Petite, one of John B. Hudson's daughters. Clara elsewhere correctly remembers both boys' names (Frederick and Joseph), but here confuses Rosa (Dowd) Taylor Kenoyer (Kenoyer's second wife and the mother of his two stepchildren) with her sister Annie Dowd. Evidently, she had forgotten his first wife, Nellie Frank (also known as Nellie Silas), mother of Frederick and Joseph—she and Kenoyer separated in 1898, when Clara Riggs would have been five or six years old (Olson 2013).

> Caroline [kʰɛrəláyn] and Louis [lówi]. See Louis married one of the Dowd girls, remember? And he had two boys. . . . Then the boys got typhoid fever, and they both died in one week's time they're buried up over here, in the cemetery, I remember them well (Zenk 1978–93, sound file 28.23:15).

> That was Caroline's brother, Louis Kenoyer. Then his father was, look-like named Peter, Kenoyer. . . . Her [Caroline's] father died then her mother married a man

named, John Pratt look-like Pratt. . . . He [Louis] had two boys he had married Annie Dowd [*sic*]. Well he blamed some of the Indian doctors throw the spirit. You see both of the boys died in one week, Frederick and I don't know what the other boy's name, he had two boys. But he blamed some Indian doctor 'cause throwed the spirit and killed those two boys 'cause they died about a week apart I remember so well. (Zenk 1978–93, sound file 35.25:29)

The two causes of death cited—by typhoid fever and by evil Tamanawas power—are not mutually exclusive. As John Wacheno observed to Drucker (1934:n.p. [typed copy p. 25]), "nearly everyone" among the Clackamas (the same applies to older generations of northwest Oregon tribal people generally) had some kind of Tamanawas power; anyone lacking such power would very likely die in the "first epidemic that came along." Tamanawas spirits were traditionally not deliberately sought until the onset of adolescence, leaving younger children especially vulnerable. Herein may be the key to what must strike us as a contradiction: a traditional belief system focused on vitality and healing, stubbornly persisting even as so many in the community—and most especially, its youngest members—succumbed to infectious diseases.

As we have seen, Louis Kenoyer and Victoria Howard were among the more fortunate children of the reservation, both having survived evidently life-threatening childhood illnesses. Their accounts crediting the charismatic powers of the two Tamanawas doctors who treated them are echoed in Berreman's 1934 interviews of about fifteen Grand Ronde elders. It is remarkable, indeed, how closely aligned these elders' views were when it came to certain aspects of the nineteenth-century reservation experience: all of them acknowledged John B. McClane as their best agent, while evincing considerable bitterness toward selected other agents, and almost all professed belief in the powers of the old-time Tamanawas doctors, many offering testimonials based on their own experience.

Also belonging to the collective experience of this entire generation was the Sisters' School, which constituted an inescapable rite of passage for almost all children born on the nineteenth-century reservation.[20] We lack any definite information connecting Victoria Howard to the school, but then, were we to go only by Jacobs's field notes, we would have no basis either for connecting John B. Hudson to it; we know that Hudson put in two full years there, because his daughters happened to mention it to Zenk. In fact, Jacobs had not the slightest interest in his consultants' experiences with the nineteenth-century Indian education system. But he could hardly have avoided the subject during his sessions with Kenoyer. Kenoyer, much more than Hudson or Howard, was a product of that school system. We cannot help but feel that the result was ultimately ruinous for him personally: here was a man nurtured, encouraged, and groomed by the Indian education system of the time, only to make his way in a world that had virtually no use or place for an educated Indian. The disjunct between the quiet, dignified "educated man" that so captivated Nancy Freeland and the "real boozehound" remembered by a younger member of his own family and tribal circle, Wilson Bobb, leaves us with a very disjointed picture indeed of the man. Without a doubt, his memory is best served by his childhood narrative. We are aware of no other account that brings the nineteenth-century Northwest reservation experience quite so intimately and palpably to life.

Louis Kenoyer died on January 16, 1937, at Town of Harrah, Yakama Reservation, Washington. In a handwritten addition to his Printer's Manuscript, Jacobs (ca. 1936a, Preface) observes that he died "probably of exposure due to poverty." The official cause of death was influenza (Olson 2013).

NOTES AND COMMENTARY

1   See Text Presentation and Translation (The Tualatin Text: Spelling) for an explanation of the conventions used to display names and terms from Tualatin and other local indigenous languages. The usual form of the tribe name in Tualatin is *tfálat'i*, which with the addition of the Tualatin nominal prefix becomes *atfálat'i* (hence, the non-technical spellings Tfalati, Atfalati). In neighboring languages and in Chinuk Wawa (Chinook Jargon), the name was usually heard as *twálat'i* (hence, the historical synonym Tuality, variously spelled).

2   An example is the individual identified as "Tualatin Peter" in the Rev. R. W. Summers's narrative of an 1876 visit to Grand Ronde Reservation (Cawley 1994:33–34). This was not Peter Kenoyer, but, judging from the Summers party's struggle to pronounce and spell the name given them, the man known usually by the name *čéxyan* (also *číxyan*) in the community, and as Peter Chekete (variously spelled and misspelled) in English. His home village was Chehalem (*čahé·ʔlim*), located in the Chehalem Valley near the modern town of Newberg, Oregon. Like many northwest Oregon individuals, he bore multiple names; others on record are *šápnana, sébina* (though these may be variant forms of the same name: Jacobs ca. 1930:49; 1928–36, 36:192). In testimony to a government commission convened in 1901 (Applegate 1905), his name appears as (English:) Peter Cheekee and ("Indian":) "Chafean." The latter spelling has led some scholars to identify him erroneously with another Kalapuyan resident at Grand Ronde, known as "Shoefan" or "Chufan" (variously spelled).

3   Jacobs (1936b, 122:143), in a passage featuring "the good man," with Jacobs's accompanying field identification: "(a Belgian, Father Crockett)—he spoke in Jargon [Chinuk Wawa] and English both during services."

4   We also drew upon previous work on the Central Kalapuya language, consulting stem-lists by Takeuchi (1969) and Berman (1988c, 1988d), as well as a dictionary compiled by McCartney (2014). These permitted identifications of a number of items left unglossed in our Fieldworks database.

5   In the *Chronicles of the Holy Names*, quoted in Anonymous (1960:16), there is this from an account of a Grand Ronde Mass attended by sisters of that Order in 1874: "On Sunday

we had Mass in Church. . . . The singing at Mass is part Latin and part Chinook, and the voices are sweet and harmonious. The sermon is in English and Chinook."

Other sources indicate that it was Fr. Croquet's normal practice to accompany sermons delivered in English, whether by himself or by visiting priests, with Chinuk Wawa translations, provided for the express benefit of older Indians: see narrative chapter 9, note 1.

6   Excluded from consideration here are some Tillamook (Salishan-speaking) groups occupying the ocean coast to the immediate west of the Grand Ronde Valley. While these people were historically under the authority of Grand Ronde Agency, for the most part they remained in their indigenous coastal homeland.

7   We lack proceedings for 1874 and 1875. The 1876 manuscript original is accompanied by a typed copy in which the order of tribes and tribal representatives is scrambled. The manuscript is, however, legible enough to make out the following list of named tribal groups and representatives (spellings as in original, allowing for our own misreadings): Umpqua—Solomon Riggs, Winchester Jo; Wappato Lake—Peter Cheteke (misconstrual of Chekete), John Pratt; Oregon City—Jo Apperson; Shasta & Cow Creeks—Jim Bruce, Jack Lony; Clackamas—Tom Foster, Wachena Foster; Santiams—French Prairie Mack, Tom Hudson; Molallaz—Joel Hubbard, S. Savage; Yamhills—Peter Selkeah; Marys River—Joseph Sangaretta; Cow Creek—Cow Creek Jake, Bob Spores; Rogue Rivers—Bob Riley; Luckiamutes—[unintell.]. The 1873 list shows Luckiamutes—James Durban, Jacob Wheeler; Yamhills—Peter Selkirk (misconstrual of Selkeah, above); Calapooias—Polk Scott, Wm Williamson; Santiams—Jno [John] Hutchins, Frank Machell, Peter Carey; Umpquas—Peter McKay, Solomon Riggs, Jas. Rose; Rogue River—Robt Riley, [unintell.], Jno [John] Edmonchoey; Clackamas—Foster Wachano, Jas Winslow; Oregon City—Jo Apperson, Chas. Petite; Molels—[?]Kilkie; Marys River—Jo Sangaretta, Wm Barlow; Wapato (should be Wapato Lake)—Jim Shiloquy, Geo Sutton, Wm Wichigan, P. Kennoyer.

Note that Louis Kenoyer's father, Peter Kenoyer, was a Tualatin (Wapato Lake) representative in 1873. William Wishikin ("Wichigan"), also representing the Tualatins in 1873, was the father of Jacobs's Clackamas-speaking consultant, Victoria Howard, while John Hutchins, representing the Santiams in 1873, was the father of Jacobs's Santiam-speaking consultant, John B. Hudson (see Life on the Nineteenth-Century Reservation).

8   Stephen Dow Beckham (personal communication 2015) comments: "Superintendent Joel Palmer envisioned Grand Ronde becoming the granary producing the cereal crops to feed the Indians of the Coast Reservation. That vision was checked by the clay soil and cold breezes sweeping in over the low summit of the Coast Range to the west. There is a contrary article (Leavelle 1998) insisting that the agrarian programs at Grand Ronde were a resounding success. In my opinion the author failed to confront the demographic calamity that continued at Grand Ronde, the annual exodus of residents seeking subsistence and employment off-reservation in order to survive, and the reality that by the mid-twentieth century there was virtually no farming at Grand Ronde, a situation that continues to the present."

9   Jacobs depended almost exclusively on information from trusted informants, rarely acknowledging historical sources, the ethnographic work of predecessors, or informants that he felt were less trustworthy. See, for example, his historical map of The Kalapuya Communities in Jacobs (1945:154), which literally reproduces Hudson's recollections, disregarding all other sources including his own information from another Santiam-speaking informant. Specific to this case, a number of phonetic spellings of

Kalapuyan terms in his own hand appearing in the draft element list are identifiable elsewhere with his transcriptions from Hudson and Kenoyer (one of these is discussed in narrative chapter 11, note 9). What is not at all clear from the copy version is that its list of traits was not original to Jacobs. The copy version only reproduces traits for which informant responses were recorded: presence, absence, informant uncertainty. In the draft version, the informant responses appear in Jacobs's handwriting, while the traits themselves appear in a typed list which is quite unlike any of Jacobs's own ethnographic contributions. Very likely, the list originated with the work of Kroeber's associates, among whom Harold Driver, Philip Drucker, and Homer Barnett published culture element lists covering most of the greater Northwest Coast. While Jacobs's draft list is not identical to any of the foregoing authors' lists, it shows various similarities of trait identification and wording to Barnett (1939). The draft version, but not the copy version, shows page upon page, literally, of traits accompanied by few or no responses. This is especially apparent for many aspects of material culture.

10 The name Doctor (or Doc) Smith appears on Grand Ronde Reservation census schedules, including those for 1885, 1887 (where his Indian name is given as "Toos-ta"), 1888 (where his tribe is given as Wapato Lake, a synonym for Tualatin), and 1889. His name also appears in the 1900 Census of the United States, where his birth year is given as ca. 1810. He apparently died shortly following that census. We fail to find the name Dushdak (however spelled) in the Tualatin corpus, which includes Louis Kenoyer's texts and supporting data. In all probability, he went by a different name or names within his own Tualatin tribal community. Zenk strongly suspects that he was the same Tualatin "second chief" who signed the Willamette Valley Treaty of 1855 as "Le Medicin or Doctor" (cf. Chinuk Wawa *lamacín* 'medicine', recorded in fur-trade era sources also with the meaning 'doctor'). In Peter Kenoyer's Tualatin telling of events surrounding the treaty (Gatschet 1877:125–135, 312; Jacobs 1945:167–170), this second chief is identified as Kualítchadax̣ (Jacobs: ç̌ali'ɖjaɖax̣), the other two chiefs being Peter Kenoyer's uncle, Kayakach, and Dave Yachkawa, another Gatschet informant. Louis Kenoyer was the source of Jacobs's re-elicitation of the name, and of the following note appearing in Jacobs's (ca. 1937a, 000302) Tualatin culture-element list:

cɢwı'ɖıt [šgwídit], a kind of dead people's stick—representing dead people's power. Jake Wheeler—a Luckiamute had it / also ɢalı'ɖjaɖak.

That Gatschet's "second chief" was also a practicing Tamanawas doctor on the reservation during Gatschet's visit in 1877 is suggested by the following additional note in that source. The quotation marks surrounding the word "doctor" there are anomalous and may hint that the word is to be taken as the man's English name:

One "doctor" on the reserve, Kwalítchadax̣, can swallow fire and bring it back mixed with blood. (Gatschet 1877:401).

Doctor Smith was remembered by some of the elders of 1934 interviewed by Berreman. An interview with Mrs. Josephine Shirley is of particular interest as a testament to the reverence and awe with which many community elders of 1934 still regarded the traditional healers.

She remembers an Indian doctor named Doc Smith, a Yamhill, about whom she tells marvelous tales. She thinks he was about two hundred years old. She says he must have been a real devil. He could cure when he chose, and kill by a wave of his cane. She has seen him tie a handkerchief around his cane and change it to a rattle snake [*sic*] (the kerchief), so it would be a snake wrapped around the cane. Then he took the cane, held it over the sick man, and lifted him up with it, and he got well and lived a long time. He got his power supernaturally, then went off to the wilds and lived alone five years. Then he came back a powerful doctor. (Berreman 1935:100–101)

The individual identified as "Captain John Smith" by Rev. R. W. Summers (Cawley 1994:26–28) appears to be in reality a conflation of Doctor Smith with a Shasta-identified man named John Smith. John Smith played a prominent role in the introduction of the Earthlodge cult (locally, the Warm House Dance) to Grand Ronde and Siletz Reservations (Stephen Dow Beckham personal communication 2015). The religious beliefs and practices that Summers attributes to his Captain Smith reveal elements both of the Warm House Dance and of Tamanawas ceremonialism: his "Great Yearly Festival" suggests the former, while his allusions to "the sacred Spirit Mountain fastings and mysteries" point to the latter (Spirit Mountain, just north of the old agency, was the community's best known Tamanawas-questing place). The same passage in Summers' narrative confuses the locations and names of a number of different reservation tribes, grouping "Rogue Rivers" (which could be taken broadly to include John Smith's Shasta tribe) and "Tualatins" together in "the quarter of some of the less civilized tribes" while assigning the "Wapato Lake" tribe (the name is a synonym for Tualatin) to the reservation's "other tribes."

11 This description of late nineteenth-century Tamanawas ceremonialism at Grand Ronde Reservation is a digest of information from Gatschet (1877), Jacobs (1929–30, ca. 1937a), Drucker (1934), and Zenk (1978–93). Zenk's main source on the subject was Wilson Bobb Sr. (1891–1985), a stepson of John Wacheno, Victoria Howard's brother-in-law during the years of her first marriage at Grand Ronde. Bobb demonstrated the "jumping" dance-step (Chinuk Wawa *súpna-supna*) during a 1983 interview: the heels are held together, the toes angled outward, the trunk held erect; all the "action" comes from the alternate bending and flexing of the knees. Mr. Bobb's step was remarkably "springy" and sprightly, his singing voice remarkably strong and clear, considering that at the time he was ninety-two years of age. He retained vivid childhood memories of his mother in dance-induced ecstatic transport, pounding a cane against the floor while jumping in place.

That children were present at Tamanawas dances, but required some protection from the full effect of Tamanawas power, was explained by Victoria Howard:

One did not go with babies to a winter tamanwis [Tamanawas] dance lest the baby, when the dancers are "warm" with their power, be caught in their power. When 4–8 to 14–15 your child may be taken there, but it is kept way back in the corner or far from the dancers. One can get closer when larger. A person with no power, but adult, however does not hesitate to get closer. Elders are not all so afraid, some are, some are not. Further, when drunken, hence full of poison, power cannot hurt one; drunkards mingle then, in a winter dance, without qualms. (Jacobs 1929–30, 53:72)

12 For older Indians holding to a traditional belief system, a special concern was the failure of the school authorities to provide protection against—or even to acknowledge the reality of—harmful Tamanawas power. According to Victoria Howard (Jacobs 1929–30, 53:72), "a bad mean [Tamanawas] doctor may kill a person by looking at them, at their food, when eating or drinking." An example was the Klickitat-identified member of the reservaton community known as x̣ímštani or Susan Hollingsworth:

Joe Hollinsworth's [sic] Klikitat [sic] wife Susan (a powerful mean medicine woman) killed lots of children at the Grand Ronde government boarding school by coming in just at luncheon and go [*sic*] around watching them closely at eating. Child after child died, the Indians complained but the govt. authorities at first refused to prohibit Susan from coming in at mealtime.

x̣ímštani is also mentioned by Kenoyer in his narrative: see narrative chapter 4, note 1. The name, since mutated under English influence to *hám-štini*, was still remembered by the generation of elders interviewed by Zenk in the early 1980s. The Hudson sisters (surviving daughters of John B. Hudson), recalling their mother's firm belief in *hámští-ni*'s fearsome reputation, said that when *hám-štini* came by where people were eating, the people would invite her to partake with them: her acceptance meant she bore no ill will and all could continue; her refusal would cause everyone to immediately stop eating. On the other hand, another of Zenk's consultants, Esther LaBonte, had actually lived as a young girl in the same household as *hámštini* and remembered her there as but a harmless, useless old woman: "All she'd do is just sit there all day. She wouldn't help with dishes or nothing, just sit there." (Zenk 1978–93, sound file 93.02:03 [7/29/1983])

13 McClane's first annual report upon assuming his duties at Grand Ronde offers some insight into why the elders of 1934 held him in such high regard, despite his evidently gruff manner and hostility to indigenous ways (see narrative chapter 10, note 1). As this passage shows, he was forthright in recognizing actual conditions on the reservation, where other agents often painted rosy pictures highlighting the Indians' supposed progress under their tenures.

> When I arrived at the agency I found the Indians very poor, some of them nearly in a starving condition. Come to inquire into the causes of their poverty, I found that where they had been accustomed to bring three or four thousand dollars from hop-picking in the fall of the year, they only brought three or four hundred dollars. They had raised but a small crop of grain and very few potatoes in the fall of 1885, and had sold the most of that off to get something to live upon. I was under the necessity to call upon the Indian department for rations of beef and flour to keep them from starving, and they granted it. Not being acquainted with the situation or necessities of the Indians at that early date, I thought I would have but thirty or forty to feed, but soon found the number increased very fast, but managed to get along with it until spring. (McClane 1886:210)

14 Jacobs's re-elicitations of Angulo and Freeland (1929: n.p.) include an added snatch of Tualatin text from Kenoyer, introduced and translated as follows: "[English:] what a father tells his son to help him get power: [Tualatin, source translation:] 'you go to that m[oun]t[ain] / you stay till dawn / you get that stick which I left there.'"

15 Anonymous (1960) identifies the two sisters as Sr. Mary Xavier and Sr. Mary Walburge, but excerpts from the *Annals* of the Benedictine Sisters of Mount Angel compiled in Anonymous (ca. 1949) identify them as Sr. M. Agnes and Sr. M. Margaret. Sr. Walburg[e]'s name is mentioned in these excerpts as the (then) last surviving sister to have worked at Grand Ronde.

16 Darrel Mercier, who as a boy in the 1930s attended the second St. Michael's church (dedicated in 1883 during Fr. Croquet's tenure), remarks (personal communication 2013) that the church was well attended then, and that over three-quarters of the congregation were Indian. The organist was Suzette Simmons, one of the last surviving speakers of a Kalapuyan language.

17 Frachtenberg seems to have had some difficulty in locating Kenoyer. Notices requesting the public to forward information on Kenoyer's whereabouts to Frachtenberg appear in

the *Oregon Daily Journal*, October 23, 1914, and in the *Morning Oregonian*, October 25, 1914.

18 See Zenk and Schrock (2013b) for a discussion of linguistic aspects of Frachtenberg's project and Jacobs's subsequent role in it. See also the notes to narrative chapter 1, which contain observations on some textual issues posed by Jacobs's published presentation of one of the Frachtenberg-Gatschet texts.

19 At least at the outset, making Kenoyer feel at home seems to have been something of a project for the couple—part of the job. In a letter to Jacobs dated December 8, 1928 (in Angulo and Freeland 1929), Angulo recalled:

> At first I was terribly worried lest he [Kenoyer] should get lonesome and peter out on me. He is so terribly taciturn. So we took great care not to hurry him. All danger is now past. He is perfectly at home and having a good time. I have got him safe for all winter, I think.

20 Zenk's tape-recorded interviews with Kenoyer's step-niece, Clara Riggs (born 1892), include the following reminiscence of her experience at Chemawa Indian School, Salem, Oregon, in the early 1900s. This is the same school that Kenoyer earlier attended, after leaving the Sisters' School of his narrative. Besides providing a vivid portrayal of conditions encountered by young people sent to the school from the reservation, this excerpt also provides a good sampling of Mrs. Riggs's local rural English.

> When you went to Chemawa well they uh, takin' you away from the old Indian custom making you more of a White custom you know more, more which they, what they, probably be more civilized, see? More White custom ways of doing. You know they taking you away from the old Indian life you know, the Indian custom the Indian belief and all that, you know. So I didn't talk none of it [my Indian language, Chinuk Wawa] there you see, all I did is go to school you see.
>
> Then they learnt you to, to respect everybody. They learnt you how to you know, to greet people and they learnt you all good manners and you know all that. You know, they learnt you all that, to respect yourself you know. To always take your showers when you need. You know they had, they [had] nothing but showers they didn't have no bathtubs you know, I never seen a bathtub all they had [was] showers. Always have your hair done up they didn't have your hair stringing all over your face you know. They had your hair, you had to have your hair all done up nice you know. And you couldn't holler or laugh or anything in the McBride [residence] Hall. You have to be respectable and, and uh you always had to have your room nice and clean and for inspection you know.
>
> An' but uh they learnt you an awful lot of good manners you know. They learnt you a lot of different things to do, they learnt you. I learnt everything there. I like crocheting, my knitting and everything that I did, learnt in the line of handwork, I learnt it there. You always sat down every evening in the room, had a big room where you sat down where they [*unfin.*]. Half an hour of study for the next day, half an hour of some kind of line, or line of fancy work.
>
> And that you know then when you went to bed you had to go very quietly. There's two stairways they had in the McBride Hall, one they call the Golden Stairs, that's where the matron rode up, we was not allowed to go up that stairway we went the other stairway, you know. And when you went to bed you always had to kneel down and pray then you had to go to bed and go to sleep you wasn't allowed to talk or anything like that. (Zenk 1978–93, sound-file 47.15:49 [10/24/1982]; transcribed by Abigail Pecore)

Grand Ronde Agency, appearing here in an undated panoramic photograph, made probably around 1900. The view is from the northeast (very likely, from near, if not actually on, Louis Kenoyer's allotment: map 2) looking toward the timbered banks of the South Yamhill River. Clearly identifiable are the main boarding school building—larger building with steeple; the second St. Michael's church, dedicated in 1883—smaller building with steeple; the boys' dormitory—two-story building half-visible at the left margin of this cropped view; the government blacksmith shop—the long, low building sitting third to the left of the right margin; and the old Fort Yamhill blockhouse—the small square building fourth from the right margin (thanks to Dennis Werth for determining the exact orientation of the camera in this photograph). The contemporary landscape shows no obvious traces of the old agency, and not all of its features can be identified with confidence now. Some details are revealed by the following collection of photographs from the archive of the Benedictine Sisters of Mount Angel, Oregon, the Catholic community that administered and taught the boarding school through most of its existence. St. Paul Mission Historical Society, photograph 2008.1.0014.

The following photographs, most appearing in print for the first time here, provide firsthand glimpses of Grand Ronde Reservation life shortly after the period of Kenoyer's narrative. We are indebted to Sr. Alberta Dieker, OSB, of the Benedictine Sisters of Mount Angel for granting us access to her community's archives, as well as for permission to reproduce these pictures. (Grand Ronde photographs in the archives of the Benedictine Sisters of Mount Angel, Oregon.)

Unidentified man and girl. The picture is labeled "Grand Ronde."

An elderly woman identified as "Charlotte" standing next to the plank walkway leading toward St. Michael's Catholic Church.

Two intimate views of the old reservation. The photo on the top is labeled simply "old couple." The same couple is visible in the background of the photo below, which is labeled "Indian huts."

At the "mess kitchen" during a Fourth of July celebration. Sr. Clara with a group of Grand Ronde elders, among whom "Mr. Barlow" (presumably, Billy Barlow or *yé•mantguʔ*, a Marys River Kalapuyan) is identified sitting on the left.

Three of the Benedictine sisters who taught and managed the Grand Ronde boarding school during the 1890s. Left to right: Sr. Clara, Sr. Margaret, and Sr. Walburg(e).

Grand Ronde Agency, northern section. A view from the southeast toward the blockhouse (left), the government blacksmith shop (center long building), and the doctor's residence (two-story building nearest the shop).

While unfortunately poorly preserved, this photograph of the school complex from the southwest is of special value for the key accompanying the numbers visible on the picture—1: "school—girls' home"; 2: "barn"; 3: "boys home." Building 1, the combined main school building and sisters' living quarters, was originally also the girls' dormitory; the two-story building semi-visible here to the immediate right (but fully visible just to the left of the main school building in the panoramic vista beginning this section) is a later addition, function unknown to us. The "boys' home" was a separate dormitory building for the older boys boarded at the school.

Frank Quenel, who served the reservation for many years as one of its Indian policemen, poses here in front of the blockhouse. The blockhouse had been built originally as part of Fort Yamhill, which once oversaw the reservation from a vantage point several miles to the east. After being moved to the agency, it served for many years as the community jail.

View of the agency from the west. Agency Creek is in the foreground.

Picket fences surrounded the church and main agency buildings, and plank walkways linked buildings.

Main Grand Ronde boarding school building: view from the east.

The "good man" of Kenoyer's narrative, Fr. Adrien-Joseph Croquet ("Father Crockett"), Grand Ronde's resident missionary priest from 1860 to 1898. "To judge from his appearance, his shabby clothes, & his poor English, . . . one would be tempted to think that he hardly knew the most necessary Latin to be a priest—& yet . . . he was one of the best scholars, & one of the most profound & learned Theologians among the Catholic Clergy" (Fr. Adelhelm Odermatt, founder of the Mount Angel Benedictine Priory; see narrative chapter 9, note 1).

Group picture of students and staff, Grand Ronde boarding school. Fr. Croquet is in the back row, sixth from right.

Two of the government employees assigned to the Grand Ronde boarding school: Eugenie M. Edwards, girls' matron; and Cora B. Egler (or Egeler), principal teacher. The picture is dated 1900, the year that government Indian schools were secularized.

These three photographs appear to show Grand Ronde boarding school children on recreational outings. The large log on which they are seated (top) may be a log bridge.

Text Presentation and Translation

All of the texts reproduced and translated here originated as oral dictations performed with deference to an accompanying linguist's ability to manually transcribe what was said as it was being said. We take it as obvious that a line-by-line layout provides a more natural representation of oral dictation than the more customary English literary model of sentences and paragraphs. Had we an audio record of Kenoyer's dictations, we might have gone further, lining out the texts to match Kenoyer's actual breath groups as he dictated to the linguists. Lacking such a record, we have posited lines consisting of grammatical main clauses plus (where present) accompanying subordinate clauses.

Besides providing at least a rough approximation to Kenoyer's original order and style of dictation—"slowly, word by word" (Angulo)—a line-by-line layout also proves more helpful than a conventional sentence-and-paragraph arrangement for observing how Kenoyer constructed his narratives in the course of dictating them. To a considerable extent, Kenoyer's narratives, in common with lower Columbia indigenous narratives generally, are organized around turns of quoted speech attributed to their dramatis personae. The demarcation of passages of quoted speech is not always clear in Angulo and Freeland's and Jacobs's manuscripts. Laying out the text in lines often clarifies where quoted speech begins and ends; it also clarifies the narrative context, permitting recognition of quoted speech in the (not unusual) instances in which its identification is unsupported by clear marking in the field translations.

The fundamental point that oral narratives are built of lines owes much to the work of Dell Hymes, who devoted his final productive years to exploring the inner architectures of oral narratives told in a variety of indigenous languages (see Hymes 1981). Pointing especially to selected lower Columbia region narratives (most transcribed by linguists from direct dictation in an era before modern audio technology), he proposed a hierarchy of structural levels unified by a shared fundamental underlying design. On the lower Columbia, that design is apparent in segmentation usually into three or five narrative units at each level of structure. Threefold segmentation as a feature of narrative design is of course familiar enough to any survivor of an English composition course (a proper story must have a beginning, middle, and end; Hymes uses the terms *onset*, *ongoing*, and *outcome*). Indeed, this structure is very frequently seen in Kenoyer's narratives. Also seen there, and according to Hymes especially characteristic of the lower Columbia region where five happens to be the cultural pattern number, are sequences in which the end point of one set of three is the starting point of a subsequent set of three, yielding a fivefold set of onset-ongoing-outcome|onset-ongoing-outcome, as in this set from narrative chapter 4<21(5–6)>:

> Then [=*pé·ʔma*] that man shot that deer.
>> She leaped up.
>> She ran.
>> She ran maybe two hundred paces.
>> There she fell.

In this set of five lines, the third line can be seen as climax or outcome of a three-fold set of onset (gets shot)—ongoing (leaps up)—outcome (runs). The same third line in turn initiates a new threefold sequence of onset (runs)—ongoing (runs some distance)—outcome (falls). Also, as Hymes observes, all lower Columbia languages have initial particles that typically, if not invariably, introduce narrative units: in Kenoyer's Tualatin, this is *pé·ʔma* ('then, and then; now, and now,' which for clarity we usually translate as 'then'). In Hymes's terminology, the foregoing set of five lines would compose a *verse*. Verses in turn combine to form *stanzas*; stanzas combine to form *scenes*; and scenes combine to form *acts*, the maximal level of structure below the narrative as a whole.

What complicates the application of Hymes's model to Kenoyer's narrative is that Hymes's higher-level units (scenes and acts) are meaning-based and can only be determined based on a grasp of the narrative action as a whole. Strictly linguistic clues (like initial particles) are of limited relevance at this level of analysis. Kenoyer's narrative presents an extended series of episodes that often segue seamlessly into one another. This is in marked contrast to the self-contained narratives (myths, speeches, anecdotes, mostly from printed text collections) analyzed by Hymes. We are not confident in our ability to identify Hymes's higher levels of segmentation within Kenoyer's smoothly flowing narrative stream, and we would not want to impose arbitrary divisions simply for the sake of exhibiting an assumed underlying pattern. Accordingly, we have opted for a much more straightforward text layout, highlighting the special function of *pé·ʔma* as a marker of line-sets—as in the above example. This layout was developed by Schrock, whose explanation follows as Parsing Kenoyer's Narrative.

Chapters

We have split up the Louis Kenoyer story into thirteen chapters. Each chapter has commentary material to give the reader further knowledge of the thematic content of that chapter. It is our hope that the commentary provided will help the reader better understand the context in which the narrative takes place. These chapters are our delineation—Jacobs made no indication of chapters in his Printer's Manuscript.

Paragraphs

Jacobs marked "¶1," "¶2," "¶3" (we transliterate here as <1>, <2>, <3>) and so on in his Printer's Manuscript. These points of division feel more like starting and stopping points of anecdotes rather than what we conventionally think of as "paragraph" boundaries in English. In paragraphs <55> to <74>—the material Jacobs never translated in the field—we added paragraph headings to divide up that part of the narrative to match Jacobs.

The task of matching Jacobs, however, was not without its complications. In the part of the narrative appearing in Jacobs's Printer's Manuscript, <46> clearly is a complete memory, while <19> to <25> are more like episodes of a larger single anecdote. In the untranslated part of the narrative, <55> to <59> and <65> to <74> are each coherent units, similar to <19> to <25>. Were we to leave these longer anecdotes undivided, they would be very long and in that respect unlike the paragraph divisions that Jacob himself outlined.

Lines

We have attempted to devise a lining system for Kenoyer's narrative that is simple, transparent, and empirically reproducible. Our goal is to use a system that is guided by structures found in the language itself—to delineate Tualatin sentences based on lexical and grammatical signs that are empirically observable rather than based on our own interpretations of the content.

Quoted Speech

Quoted speech is in quotation marks, indented, and italicized. Any introductory words such as "he said," or "my father said," receive no indentation unless they follow the quote. Sometimes there is an implied shift in speaker that is not indicated with a "she said," or "my father said." We note this with a bracketed triple-hyphen [---], and if further clarification is needed the speaker is named: for example, [---] (Kammach speaks:).

Punctuation and Transcription

The punctuation and the orthography of the presented Tualatin are as they appear in Jacobs's own field notebooks and in his re-elicitations as written into the pages of Angulo and Freeland (1929). We have painstakingly tried to reproduce all the variation and inconsistency in the field transcriptions because this data represents the rawest version with least interference from transcriber interpretation. On the Tualatin side we have reproduced only the punctuation that Jacobs marked. Our lining system indicates our interpreted sentence boundaries, so punctuation is less necessary. Likewise, our lining system indicates quoted speech, so on the Tualatin side we have not added any omitted quotation marks, question marks, or exclamation points.

We have not standardized Tualatin orthography in the narrative because we feel it is premature to do so. Citations in the commentaries and notes are respelled for consistency, using the Americanist phonemic alphabet of the *Handbook of North American Indians*. Much further comparative Kalapuyan research is needed, especially comparison with Louis Kenoyer's father's Tualatin, which is recorded in Gatschet (1877). There are four different orthographies employed by the five different linguists who have conducted significant studies of Northern Kalapuya: Gatschet (1877), Frachtenberg (1913–14, 1915, ca. 1915), Angulo and Freeland (1929), and Jacobs (1936a). We have no recorded Tualatin audio to analyze ourselves. The goal of this project has been primarily to make the content of Louis Kenoyer's life story accessible to a wider audience. A thorough study of comparative Kalapuyan morphology and phonology must wait. Hence the raw Jacobs field transcript is what is presented in this book.

We have punctuated the English side of the narrative as conventionally as we can. With few exceptions, each line starts with a capital letter and ends with a period. A clause introducing quoted speech ends with a comma, and the quoted speech on the following line is treated like another sentence. We have freely added punctuation to the English side—question marks, quotation marks, etc. We have also added exclamation points to sentences marked in the Tualatin for imperative mood (giving a command).

pé·ʔma Clusters

One thing that might jump out at the reader from the Tualatin text is the oft-repeated pɛ·ʼma (*pé·ʔma*) 'then' that starts so many sentences. Linguists have called this kind of word a *discourse marker*—a word that does not carry much meaning other than to mark continuation of a narrative or a place in conversation. We are using *pé·ʔma* as an explicit clue to the beginning of an implied cluster of sentences that clarify each other or complete a thought. This clustering is our interpretation and our way to display Louis Kenoyer's spoken narrative.

Most speakers of English have been taught to write in paragraphs. When one analyzes oral narratives it quickly becomes apparent that the paragraph is not a very useful concept for that purpose. Louis Kenoyer did not speak in paragraphs, so why display his narrative in paragraphs? Our segmentation into *pé·ʔma* clusters is our attempt to present his narrative in a form more reflective of his oral style, as opposed to the artificial confines of English-style paragraphs.

Louis Kenoyer's most common narrative device is to make a statement and then clarify the idea further with supporting sentences; hence a cluster of sentences takes shape. In our system the supporting sentences are indented on lines following the initial *pé·ʔma* sentence or clause. Together, these sentences outline a full idea or description with supporting information. The appearance of the next *pé·ʔma* signals that a new cluster is starting.

(1) *pé·ʔma* cluster— *pé·ʔma* sentence followed by supporting sentences (chapter 2):

pɛ·''ma ɢʋdɪdɪ'tɢwɪn a-wa'm·ʋ ha'ŋklu·p
  ɢʋdɪtʙʋ'n alʋ''lʋ.
  ha'l·ʋ alʋ''lʋ ɢʋdɪtʙʋ'n.
pɛ''ma q̓ʋ'pfan asi''wei ɢɪ'n·ʋk ɢɪnɪdɛ'cdap la'ɢ·ai nau q̓ʋ'pfan hɛ'caʙɛ·d.<3(2)>

Then we went and got white clay.
  We made balls.
  Lots of balls we made.
Then half of the children stood far off and half nearby.   <3(2)>

Adverbial phrases signaling a change of time can also begin a cluster—we classify such instances as a kind of *pé·ʔma* cluster.

(2) Temporal adverbial phrase beginning a *pé·ʔma* cluster (chapter 2):

me'ɪdj-ɢʋt-hɛ'l'wan tcɪ''ɪ ɢʋdɪdɪ'twʋ dɪkɪ'udɑn   <10(4)>
  tcɪ''ɪ nau dɛna·'na ɢɛ·'m dɪʙʋ'k·wʋk du·'l sʋ'du ɢʋdɪti·'d u·'dnɪ'ɢwan a-dza·'ɢʋʙlʋ.
  ɢʋdɪdɪ'tku ha'l·u· t̓ɪ'w·ɑt,
pɛ''ma‿ɢʋd·ɛ'cdɛc ha'l·u· a-dza·'ɢʋplʋ ɢa'ya''an.

Early morning I went to get the horses.   <10(4)>
  I and my mother's two brothers' wives, we went to look for strawberries.
  We took many buckets.
Then we found lots of strawberries.

The term *pé·ʔma* can be repeated rapid-fire in a chain of occurrences (chapter 2):

(3) Rapid-fire *pé·ʔma* clusters—chain of occurrences:

pɛˈ'ma q̣uˈpfan ɑsiˈ'wei ɢɪˈn·ʋk ɢɪnɪdɛˈcdɑp laˈɢ·ai nau q̣uˈpfan hɛˈcaʙɛ·d.   <3(2)>
pɛˈ'ma ɢʋdɪtwaˈqnaif tcɛ-ɢʋˈsa waˈm·ʋ haˈŋklu·p.
pɛˈ'ma ɢʋdɪt_lʋˈ'ʋn ɢʋsa haˈŋklu·p tcɛ-t̓wɛ·lɪt ɢʋsa-waˈd·ɪk.
pɛˈ'ma ɢʋdɪt-ɪˈd·ʋp ʙʋˈɢʋlfan haˈl·ʋ.

Then half of the children stood far off and half nearby.   <3(2)>
Then we battled with those white clays.
Then we placed the clays on the ends of those switches (as catapults).
Then we jumped all over.

Bare *pé·ʔma* and temporal adverbial phrases are the empirical elements we have used to determine the beginnings/ends of *pé·ʔma* clusters in non-quoted speech. Quoted speech does not show the pattern of the *pé·ʔma* cluster as much as basic narration does, though sometimes it does. Louis Kenoyer's quoted speech often has a structure that is more conversational than narrative.

(4) *pé·ʔma* cluster not always meaningful in quoted speech (chapter 2):

ɢʋsa-yuˈhʋ'yʋ paˈ'-u-mɪ'ut   <12(7)>
  tɛˈn·a, maˈha sk̓wɪˈt̓kwat ɑ-hʋˈ'lʋ tcɪd·aˈmdjʋ.
  waˈŋq dam-nɪˈs·ɪn iˈ'ya daˈ'iwa'an a-mɛˈ'nmɪ.
  waˈŋq tcɪˈ'ɪ ɢɪd·aˈmdjʋ ɢɪˈn·ʋk dʋmdɪt-laˈtswu·t dɛɢaˈy·aˈan
  ɪˈ'y·a tcɪˈ'ɪ ɢʋˈmdɪdɛˈcdɛc ɢʋt-laˈtswu·t dɛɢaˈy·aˈan tcɪˈ'ɪ ɢʋdɪˈtɢwin dɛsaˈɢ·walala
  pɛˈ'ma tcɪˈ'ɪ ɢʋt̓waˈ'n.

The old man said,   <12(7)>
  "Alright! you pick as much as you may want!
  Do not tell any other Indians!
  I do not want them to get to stealing my berries.
  If I catch someone stealing my berries, I will take my gun.
  Then I'll shoot!"

Translation

Our approach to translation is relatively simple. Our goal is to make the English reader's experience of reading this narrative similar to a Tualatin listener's experience of hearing it in Tualatin. Just as spoken English has a natural flow, Louis Kenoyer's Tualatin has its own flow—what feels natural in Tualatin should feel natural in English ("natural" of course is *our* natural). As a result of strictly adhering to a parallel lining scheme, the length and complexity of our English sentences is artificially short, but within those short, simple sentences we are trying to present an English that sounds natural.

Angulo and Freeland and Jacobs translated much of this narrative directly with Louis Kenoyer in the field. We have used these field translations as the basis of our translations for <A1> to <54>. We do not follow Jacobs's Printer's Manuscript edited translations, because we find them often quite wordy and awkward. Here, an example of Jacobs's Printer's Manuscript translation is followed first by Jacobs's field translation, and then by our own translation:

(5) Jacobs's (ca. 1936b, <36(1-2)>) Printer's Manuscript ("he"= Louis Kenoyer's father):

> And then on the above headman's day (i.e. on the Lord's day—Sunday) he did not work. We went to the above headman's house (to God's house—the Catholic Church). (2) Everybody came to that house (to Church). And then the good man (the priest) made (rang) the bell, and everybody of those who were standing outside entered the good house (entered church).

Jacobs's (1936a, 122:143) field notebook translation of the same passage:

> Now on the above-chief's-day/Sunday he didn't work. We went to Church/ (Catholic). Everybody came to the (church) house. Now that good man/priest rang the (church) bell. Now everyone of those who were standing outside entered church.

Our translation of this passage (chapter 7):

> Then on the day of the Lord Above he didn't work.
>   We were to go to the house of the Lord Above.
>   Everybody came to that (church-)house.   <36(2)>
> Then the priest rang the bell.
> Then all of those who were standing outside entered the church.

We believe Jacobs's proposed display is partially a product of technical constraints. Jacobs used the same method of display in all of his ethnolinguistic publications, and it is a clever device. A translator must make choices as to how literally to translate. Literal meaning is often lost when one chooses a translation that reads well. Jacobs's method of parenthetical fleshing-out appears to be his attempt at keeping both a literal translation and a more standard English within the same display.

Current technology allows us easily to create interlinear representations like (6) below. Academic literature is filled with this sort of display, and for good reason—great insight into the language of study is gained by creating such displays. While it was typographically possible to create such displays in Jacobs's era, it appears Jacobs was trying to devise a simpler system that accomplished a similar goal.

(6) Chapter 7<36(1-2)>: interlinear representation (our glossing).

pɛ·"ma-	ɢʊ'ca	ha'lʙam	ᴅJa'mʙak	ᴅɪ'a"mpyan	wa'ŋq	ɢʊᴅ.lu"nafʊn.
then-	that	high	headman	his-the-day	not	he.did-work

'Then on the day of the Lord Above he didn't work.'

su'ᴅ·u	ᴅɪ'ᴅ	ᴅJɛɢʊ'sa	aha'lʙam-	ᴅJa'mʙak-	ᴅu'm·aɪ.	<36(2)>
we	we.will-go	to-that	the-high	headman	his-house	

'We were to go to the house of the Lord Above.'

ʙʊ'ɢʊlfani'y·a	ɢʊcma"a	ᴅJɛɢʊ'ca-	ha'm·i.
every-who	s/he.did-come	to-that	the-house

'Everybody came to that (church-)house.'

pɛ·"ma-	ɢʊ'ca-	tɛ'n·a-	aᴅJa'ŋku	ɢʊᴅʙʊ'n-	aᴅɪ'nᴅɪn.
then	that	good	the-man	he.did-do	the-bell

'Then the priest rang the bell.'

pɛ·"ma	ʙʊ'ɢʊlfani'y·a	ɢʊ'cawʊnᴅa·'ʙɪt	hɛ·"lʊm	ɢʊᴅɪnɪla'm·ʊ
then	every-who	that-who-they-stand	outside	did-they-enter

-	tcaɢʊ'ca-	tɛ'n·a	ha'm·i.
	to-that	good	the-house

'Then all of those who were standing outside entered the church.'

In summary, we have chosen to translate using simple English lined in a system that is meant to reflect Kenoyer's oral style. Our primary goal is to present Louis Kenoyer's story in the clearest way possible, in a natural English that will be maximally accessible to a general audience.

THE TUALATIN TEXT

Spelling
In the English text of the narrative, as well as in the introduction and in our commentarial notes, we usually cite names and terms from Tualatin and other indigenous languages in anglicized form. Technical spellings employing the Americanist

phonemic alphabet of the *Handbook of North American Indians* (for example, volume 7: The Northwest, 1990, x–xi) are mostly reserved for first appearances of key terms and names: such spellings are italicized (for example, *tfálat'i, twálat'i*, for the name Tualatin). Anglicized spellings reproduce conventional English spellings, where established in local usage (for example, Tualatin, Tuality, Atfalati for the name Tualatin); otherwise, most follow the *Handbook*'s table of Nontechnical Equivalents (see above reference).

Our Tualatin transcript preserves Jacobs's field spellings throughout, including those found in the sections originally transcribed by Angulo and Freeland and later re-elicited by Jacobs. Jacobs's phonetic alphabet is explained in Jacobs (1945:13–15, 151–153). The approximations in the accompanying key may serve as a rough guide to pronunciations of symbols lacking obvious roman-letter equivalents in English.

KEY TO JACOBS'S PHONETIC ALPHABET

a, e, i, u	as in English f*a*ther, m*a*te, b*ea*t, b*oo*t
ɪ, ʊ, ɛ, α, ꞷ	as in English p*i*t, p*u*t, p*e*t, p*u*tt, New York
ə	an unaccented vowel of obscure quality, as in English logic*a*l
в, ᴅ, ɢ	as in English s*p*in, s*t*eam, s*k*ip
q, ɢ̣	like English *k*eep, s*k*ip, but articulated deeper in the throat
c, tc, ᴅJ	as in English *sh*ip, *ch*ip, mis*ch*ief
˙	_ (=a consonant or vowel) pronounced long (drawn out)
ˀ	the catch in the voice heard in English "uh-oh"
k̓, q̓, p̓, t̓, t̓c, t̓s	glottalized consonants, usually heard in Kalapuyan languages as a slight "catch" in the voice (as opposed to the sharp "crack" heard in other local languages)
ł	a voiceless "l" made with a slight hissing sound (the sound of *ll* in Welsh *Llewellyn*)
x̣	as in German Ba*ch*, but articulated deeper in the throat

While Angulo and Freeland's transcription of consonants is less differentiated than that of Jacobs, it shows finer degrees of discrimination within some vowel continua. For example, where Jacobs writes only <a, ɛ> they write <a, ɛ, a, á)>, the latter two symbols being about equivalent to IPA [a] (in technical terminology, a lower low front unrounded vowel, as in French *patte*). In some instances, such finer discriminations may have implications for analyzing the morphology. By way of illustration, we note variances between Angulo and Freeland's and Jacobs's transcriptions of grammatical morphemes in the Tualatin text of narrative chapter 1:

brackets there (as in: ᴅᴇɢᴇ'f [ta..], [hʊ-]nɑ'ɢ·ɪt) restore Angulo and Freeland's original transcriptions, while curly brackets (as in {ᴅʊmnɪ}ᴅɑ'mᴅʒu) show morphemes (usually prefixes) absent from Angulo and Freeland's original phonetic transcript, but added by Kenoyer during Jacobs's re-elicitation of that transcript. Linguists interested in analyzing Kenoyer's Tualatin morphology may benefit from examining Angulo and Freeland's original transcriptions in greater detail.

Inflectional Morphology

We cannot claim to have definitively parsed Kenoyer's more complex, inflected word-forms. While Central Kalapuya morphology has received some attention from linguists (Takeuchi 1969, Hajda 1978, Rude 1986, Berman 1988a, Lewis 2003, Banks 2007), the results are difficult to assess, owing to the different analytic approaches used. While Angulo (Angulo and Freeland 1929) and Jacobs (1936b) did devote some effort to exploring Tualatin morphology while working with Kenoyer, their results are sketchy and incomplete. We have drawn upon all the foregoing sources to develop our own individual sets of working hypotheses for resolving Kenoyer's inflected word-forms into constituent lexical and grammatical elements. Zenk's working hypotheses draw on the analyses presented in Zenk and Schrock (2013a, 2013b), while Schrock's are more informed by Banks's (2007) description of Santiam verbal morphology. Comparison of these linguists' divergent analytic frameworks would make for a very interesting study in its own right—one that might offer insights into the nature of linguistic description itself.

While also difficult to evaluate, records of Northern Kalapuya obtained from an older generation of speakers (Gatschet 1877, Frachtenberg 1913–14) suggest that, by comparision, Kenoyer's version of the language operates with a smaller—"unusually poor" (Angulo)—lexicon; is more-or-less idiosyncratic with respect to the most productive part of Kalapuyan grammar, its system of verbal prefixation (Zenk and Schrock 2013b); and employs a limited set of verbal suffixes (Howard Berman personal communication to Zenk 1988). It is likely relevant that Kenoyer was the last speaker of a language that by his own account he had not used since his youth. Angulo raised the possibility that such features may, to some extent, be related to Kenoyer's lifelong use of Chinuk Wawa, a pidgin-creole language featuring a limited lexicon and virtually zero inflectional morphology. It is interesting that in the Kalapuyan recorded from other speakers, borrowings from Chinuk Wawa are for the most part restricted to newly introduced items and articles, while Kenoyer shows such borrowings even where inherited Kalapuyan forms would be expected: q'áiʔwut 'be bent' (from Chinuk Wawa q'áiʔwa 'crooked'), ɬúkɬa·t 'to break' (reduplication of Chinuk Wawa ɬuk 'break'), q'ʷáɬq'ʷa·d 'to hit, pound' (reduplication of

Chinuk Wawa *q'ʷəɬ* 'hit, knock'), *k'ʷítk'ʷa·t* 'to pick, pluck' (reduplication of Chinuk Wawa *k'ʷit* 'pick, break off'), and (identically Chinuk Wawa:) *t'ú·ʔwan* 'have, keep,' *lú·ʔlu* 'round,' *líkre·m* 'yellow.' Kenoyer's Tualatin also shows instances of Chinuk-Wawa-like semantic generalization (for example, *lakʷ* 'hand' also translates 'arm,' where Gatschet's record of Tualatin shows two different words), even where there is no phonetically resemblant corresponding Chinuk Wawa lexeme (Chinuk Wawa for 'hand, arm, branch' is *líma*) (Zenk and Schrock 2015).

In linguists' terminology, the Tualatin texts and data recorded from Kenoyer are best seen as expressions of an *obsolescent* Tualatin. Their definitive evaluation must await a fuller description of Northern Kalapuya, factoring in the record from older fluent speakers. Preliminary indications are that Kenoyer spoke a kind of household hybrid Tualatin, incorporating elements of his mother's Central Kalapuya dialect (compare Berman 1990:39–40) as well as influences traceable to his lifelong use of Chinuk Wawa.

Until we are able to give a fuller account of the many and various morphological inconsistencies presented by the Kenoyer corpus, we feel it advisable not to let our own imperfect understanding of the morphology override the speaker's interpretations, as preserved in the field translations. This does not mean that we feel bound to reproduce the field translations word-for-word. We have permitted ourselves latitude to fine-tune our translations, reflecting our sense of Kenoyer's style in Tualatin, including his deployment of the language's inflectional morphology. Our intensive experience with the corpus has enabled us to assign approximate English glosses to all of Kenoyer's more frequently used inflectional elements. That we are at least on the right track in this regard is indicated by our independent translations of the untranslated one-fourth of the narrative, which has come out looking very similar in almost all cases.[1]

Circumlocutions

Another aspect of Kenoyer's Tualatin grammar with implications for the translator is his frequent resort to circumlocution to express his meanings (another Chinuk-Wawa-like feature). In Kenoyer's Tualatin, Fr. Croquet is invariably "the good man" (one wonders why he didn't use the Chinuk Wawa word for 'priest,' *liprét*, considering how freely he resorts to Chinuk Wawa elsewhere); church is "the good house" (but why not Chinuk Wawa *lamés*?); school is "the language house"; the teachers are "language women"; and so on. In the field translations, such circumlocutions are usually rendered by corresponding English common nouns: "priest," "church," "school," "teacher." Our policy is to introduce the first occurrence of such a circumlocution with a parenthetical explanation: hence, "the priest (lit., the good man)."

Thereafter, we usually use the English common noun.

Another kind of circumlocution is posed by Kenoyer's repeated use of certain complex phrasal constructions, for example: "go upstairs to where you all sleep" (referring to the dormitory in the Sisters' School); "the place where you fix yourselves up" (for a washroom); "stand where it is you stand" (for stand in line); and so on. While the English meanings of such phrases would be more naturally conveyed by adding the appropriate simplifying English terms, the field translations for the most part preserve Kenoyer's literal Tualatin phrasings. Here again, we elect to keep closely to field translation, on the assumption that it provides the most faithful reflection of Kenoyer's style in Tualatin.

NOTES AND COMMENTARY

1   The question still arises as to how, or to what extent, or whether it is even advisable to attempt to make our English translations sensitive to (putative) indicators of language obsolescence in the Tualatin text. Compare our interlinear literal translations of the following examples with their original field translations—by Angulo and Freeland in (7), (8), (9) and by Jacobs in (10) and (11) (free translation line 1)—and with Jacobs's Printer's Manuscript free translations (free translation line 2):

(7) Chapter 2<5(11)>

ɢɪnɪ-tʊ'ɢɪ	kwe'ɪnafʊn	pɛ''ma	ɢʊnɪ-ɒɪ'tya	tcɛ-la'kwɪt·	ha'm·ɪ
did-they-finish	food	then	did-they-go	into-play	the-room

1) 'Finished eating they all go back to the play-house.'
2) 'When they finished eating, then they went to the play house.'

(8) Chapter 2<6(2)>

ɢʊɒɪtʊ'ɢɪ	kwe'ɪnafʊn	pɛ''ma	ɢʊnɪ-sɪ'y·ʊ	ɢʊ'sa-	tcɛ-ha'm·ɪ
s/he.did-finish	food	then	did-they-sit	that	in-the-house

1) 'Finished eating then they sit down in the house.'
2) 'When through with eating, then they sat in the house.'

(9) Chapter 2<6(7)

ɢɪn·ɪtʊ'ɢɪ	ɒɪk̓we'ɪnafʊn	ʙʊ'ɢʊlfan	a-kwɪ'ɒ·an	ɢʊɒɪnɪk̓u''wɪł
did-they-finish	his/her-food	all	the-dishes	did-they-wash

1) 'Finished eating they washed all the dishes.'
2) 'When they had finished eating, they washed all the dishes.'

(10) Chapter 3<14(13)>

tʊ'ɢɪ-	ɒɪnɪk̓we'ɪnafʊn	ɢʊɒ·ɪnɪsɪ'y·ʊ	pʊ't'cnaq
finish	their-food	did-they-sit	a.little

1) 'When done eating they sat a little while.'
2) 'Finished their meal, they sat a little while.'

(11) Chapter 3<16(4)>

ɢʊᴅɪɴɪt̓·ʊ́ɢɪ	ᴅɪɴɪkweʼɪnafʊn	ɢɪɴɪᴅɪ́ʼt	hɛ·ʼlʊm
did-they-finish	their-food	did-they-go	outside

1) 'Fin. [*sic*] eating they went outside.'
2) 'Finished their eating, they went outside.'

The foregoing pattern, in which a clause with -*t'ug·i* (-*t̓ʊ́ɢɪ*) 'stop, finish, be finished with' precedes a succeeding focal action, is frequently seen in the narrative.
Field translation uniformly glosses such -*t'ug·i* –clauses as subordinate, regardless of
how or whether the verb -*t'ug·i* appears prefixed. Note also that the noun -*k'ʷéinafun*
(-*kweʼɪnafʊn*) 'food, meal' lacks a prefix in (7) and (8); while showing the third-person
singular possessive *di*- in (9) and the third-person plural possessive *dini*- (more usually
seen as a Central Kalapuya form) in (10) and (11). The third-person plural verbal subject (or depending on context, object) prefix *ni*- appears on -*t'ug·i* in (7), (9), (11), but
not in (8) and (10). All of the prefixed verbs show the element *gu*-/*gi*-, corresponding to
a Central Kalapuya prefix variously analyzed as a marker of habitual aspect (Takeuchi),
past tense (Hajda), aorist tense (Berman), past realis (Banks). In Kenoyer's narrative,
gu-/*gi*- appears more often than not where context points to past time, but not always;
it also appears in clauses where expected or customary action is implied (Takeuchi's
habitual, as in the account of a typical day in the Sisters' School making up 2<5>, for
which Angulo and Freeland's original translation shows the English present indefinite throughout—all changed to past tense in Jacobs's Printer's Manuscript translation); while in quoted speech especially, it frequently has a predictive force (as in the
agent's mandate in 2<4>, and in the sister's instructions to the schoolchildren making
up 8<42(8-14)>). The text sample cited as example (6) (Parsing Kenoyer's Narrative:
Translation) shows an example of another TMA (tense-mode-aspect) prefix: future/
potential *di*- (in ᴅɪ́ᴅ, contracted for *di-í·d* 'we will-go'). Also frequent in the narrative:
present/progressive *u(m)*-. These account for most of the TMA prefixes appearing in
main clauses (as opposed to subordinate clauses, which come with their own set of
complications), except that the first-person singular shows the special form *čum*-/ *čim*-
(present/progressive), and the second-person plural the special forms *čidup*- (pres-
ent/progressive) and *dup*- (future/potential). Many of Kenoyer's prefixes have variant
forms; some show many variant forms.

Following the TMA prefixes, we often encounter the third-person plural form
dini- (ɢʊᴅɪɴɪlaʼmʊ [6], ɢʊᴅɪɴɪkuʼʼwɪɫ [9], ɢʊᴅ·ɪɴɪsɪʼyʊ [10], ɢʊᴅɪɴɪt̓·ʊ́ɢɪ [11]), identical
to Kenoyer's usual form for the third-person plural possessive. He also uses *ni*- alone
(as in ɢɪɴɪ-t̓ʊ́ɢɪ, ɢʊɴɪ-ᴅɪʼtyα in [7]), the verbal and nominal form usually recorded
from older speakers of Northern Kalapuya. Just what *di*- is doing in second position
in Kenoyer's verb-prefix complex is not at all clear from the translations. There is a
temporal/subordinate prefix *di·*- in Central Kalapuya, and as in (8) and (11), Kenoyer
often prefixes *di*- to second position in a verb appearing in a subordinate clause. But
as (7), (9), (10) also illustrate, *di*- does not always appear where field translations and/
or context point to such a meaning in such a clause. Also, as (9) and (10) illustrate,
Kenoyer often prefixes *di*- to second position in a verb appearing in a main clause,
with no discernable temporal meaning (although, note that Berman observes the same
restriction in Santiam).

A clearer analogy with the Central Kalapuya prefix complex is shown by the forms
ɢʊᴅ.luʼnafʊn (6) (*gu-d-lúʔnafún*), ɢʊᴅBʊ́ʼn (6) (*gu-d-bún*), ɢʊᴅɪɴɪt̓·ʊ́ɢɪ (11) (*gu-di(-)*

ni-t-t'úg·i), which all appear to show a *d-/t-* prefix immediately preceding the verb stem, evidently corresponding to a Central Kalapuya directive prefix (Banks: translocative; Takeuchi: completive). Also frequently appearing directly before verb stems in Kenoyer's Tualatin: the element *dit-*, as in ɢʊnɪ-ᴅɪ'tya (7) (*gu-ni-dít-ya*); and the imperative prefixes *š-* (singular) and *b(š)-* (plural) (both with variants). The function of *dit-* is uncertain: Angulo suggested that it may contribute an inceptive meaning; Frachtenberg analyzed it as a "discriminative" case-marker (presumably, something like the elements he so labelled in Hanis Coos and Lower Umpqua; Frachtenberg 1922a:324-25, 1922b:462–63, 575–77). Imperative-marked forms are straightforward imperatives when preceded by no other prefixes; however, there are many instances in which the imperative prefixes are preceded by the TMA prefixes, in which cases an imperative meaning is usually not obvious from field translation: as in (6), where the verb-form ɢʊcmɑ"ɑ (*gu-š-máʔa*) appears with the field translation '(everybody [every-who]) came.'

It was apparent irregularities such as those illustrated above that led Jaime de Angulo to conclude that Tualatin has hardly any productive morphology at all, and that the many permutations of recurring elements preceding verb roots in Kenoyer's Tualatin are to be taken as the mere fossilized detritus of a no longer productive morphology. We are inclined to consider that evaluation highly premature. Much yet remains to be learned about the morphosyntax of Northern Kalapuya and the other Kalapuyan languages, and future analysis may well reveal more sense to Kenoyer's Tualatin inflectional morphology than met Angulo's eye.

The Narrative

CHAPTER ONE
Three Chiefs of the Bygone Era[1]

<A1> My Grandfather and His Brother

My grandfather and his brother. ||d1:1||

My grandfather's name was Kammach.
His brother's name was Kayakach.
These two young men were important chiefs.
Whenever they wanted to say anything they gathered all the people.   <A1(1)>
  The people wanted all sorts of things.
  The people wanted various kinds of games.[2]
One man stands up, he speaks like this,
  "All the young men want to play shinny."   <A1(2)>
[---]
  "Very good!"
Kayakach stands up, he says to one old man,
  "What do you want to play?" ||d1:2||
This old man says,   <A1(3)>
  "I want to play the handgame."
One man says,
  "I want to race horses."
Kayakach stands up,   <A1(4)>
  "Alright, which young men want to go deliver this message?"
Five young men speak,
  "I want to go."
[---]
  "Alright,"   <A1(5)>
says Kayakach,
  "You five boys, don't do anything (untoward) to foreign people.
  You will go early in the morning.
  I will give you the message.   <A1(6)>
  Tell these people they are to come in one month! ||d1:3||
    We will gather in our country.
  I give you ten days to return."
Those young men say,   <A1(7)>
  "Okay."

CHAPTER ONE
Three Chiefs of the Bygone Era

<A1> My Grandfather and His Brother

tcɪ"ɪ ᴅɛɢɛ'f [ta..] na' [nau] ᴅɪkʊ'nɪ.   ‖d1:1‖

tcɪ"ɪ ᴅɛɢɛ'f [ta..] ᴅu'ŋkwɪt [ta'm..] q̇ɛ'm·ats.

ɢɔ'k ᴅɪʙɪ'ɢ·wak ᴅʊ'ŋkwɪt [ta'n..] q̇aya'kats.

ɢʊsa ɢɛ'm sɪ'nfaf ɢɪ'n·ʊk ɢʊnɪʙa'l [kwɪn-pa'l] ᴅja'mʙɑk·.

a'ɢ·a ɢɪ'n·ʊk {ᴅʊmnɪ}ᴅa'mᴅju ᴅʊm{nɪ}-na'ɢ·ɪt ᴅɪn{ɪ}ɢɛ'uweɪ ʙʊ'ɢʊlfan a'm·ɪm.   <A1(1)>

    ɢɪ'n·ʊk a'm·ɪm ʙʊ'ɢʊlfan a'ɢ·a {ᴅʊmnɪ}ᴅa'mᴅju

    a'w·ɛu la'ɢɪt ɢɪn·ʊk a'm·ɪm ᴅa'mᴅju.

wa"an ᴅja'ŋku ᴅɛ'sᴅap pa'-{u-}mɪ'ut

    ʙʊ'ɢʊlfan sɪ'nfaf ᴅa'mᴅju ᴅʊmla'ɢ·ɪt {a}skɑ'lkɑl.   <A1(2)>

[---]

    ʙʊ'f·an tɛ'n·ɑ!

q̇aya'kats ᴅɛ'sᴅap [hʊ-]na'ɢ·ɪt tcɛ-wa"ɑn [tcɑ_..] yu'hu'yu,

    a'ɢ·a ma'ha tcuᴅa'mᴅju [tcɪ-..] ᴅʊmla'ɢ·ʊt [tʊn_..].   ‖d1:2‖

hɛ'sa [hasa] yu'hu'yu na'ɢ·ɪt,   <A1(3)>

    tcɪ"ɪ ᴅa'mᴅju ᴅʊmla'ɢ·ɪt ma'lha.

wa"an tca'ŋku na'ɢ·ɪt,

    tcɪ"ɪ ᴅa'mᴅju ma'nfu kɪ'uᴅən.

q̇aya'kats ᴅɛ'cᴅap,   <A1(4)>

    ɢu'c-wɪ, ɪ'y·a sɪ'nfaf ᴅa'mᴅju ᴅʊmɢu'ʊm ᴅɪ'tɢu hɛ'sa-ha'mha [hasa_..].

hu"wan sɪ'nfaf na'ɢ·ɪt,

    tcɪ"ɪ ᴅa'mᴅjyu ᴅʊmɢʊ"ʊm.

[---]

    ɢʊ'c-wɪ,   <A1(5)>

q̇a'yakats na'ɢ·ɪt,

    mɪ'ᴅɪ ɢʊ'c·a hu"wan sɪ'nfaf wa'ŋq a'ɢ·a ᴅʊm-hɪ'u'nan tcɛ [tca] ᴅa'ɪ'wan a'm·ɪm.

    me'ɪᴅj ha'l'wan mɪ'ᴅɪ ᴅɪ{ᴅʊp}ɢʊ'ʊm [tɪ-..].

    tcɪ"ɪ ᴅɪᴅɪ'ᴅ·ʊp ha'mha.   <A1(6)>

    nɪ's·ɪn hɛ'sa [hasa] a'm·ɪm ɢɪ'n·ʊ'k cma"a wa"an ᴅꞷ'ʙ.   ‖d1:3‖

      tcɪᴅɪ{t}ɢɛ'wʊfan sa'ᴅ·ʊ tcɛᴅʊt-a'n·ʊ [tca t- ʊnno].

    tcɪ"ɪ ᴅɪᴅɪ'ᴅ·ɑp [tcɪ-tɛ'tt-ɔp] ᴅɪ'nfyuf a'mpyan mɪ'ᴅɪ ᴅʊm{ᴅʊp}me'yʊ.

ɢʊ'sa sɪ'nfaf na'ɢ·ɪt   <A1(7)>

    hɛ·"a.

That same day Kayakach spoke a great deal to his people.

   "You boys and girls, don't do anything (untoward) to the (visiting) foreign people.
   This is all I have to say."

<A2> Kammach

Long ago the people traded. ||d2:1||

   From a certain chief they obtained slaves.

   This chief, Kammach, was a very brave young man.[3]

   He took along his tribesmen, his people.

   They went far off to another tribe.

   They would go off maybe nine, maybe ten days. ||d2:2|| <A2(2)>

   They would arrive at that tribe.

   There they obtained poor people.

      These poor people, they had no family.

   He bought those people there.   <A2(3)>

      He gave some few things.

Thereupon he left.

   Those slaves of his were just the lot he bought.[4]

   Half of his tribesmen watched over (them) there. ||d2:3||

[---] (Kammach speaks:)

   "Here you will camp.   <A2(4)>

   Tomorrow my (remaining) tribesmen and I will go on to another tribe far off.

   There I will buy slaves.

   Then we will come back here to all of you. ||d2:4||

   Then all of us will return home.

      We'll take back these slaves.   <A2(5)>

      We'll trade them to another chief, named Kiesno.

      That chief lives far away across the Big River.[5]

      He has all kinds of edibles. ||d2:5||

      He has Indian potatoes, pulverized salmon.

      He has all kinds of beads, Indian money.   <A2(6)>

      I will give these slaves to him. ||d2:6||

      Only ten slaves do I wish to take back to our country, when[6] we get back to my
         brother's[7] place."

Then he took those slaves.

ɢʊ́sa-weɪ-ɪ′pyan q̇aya′kats nɪ′san ʙʊ′ɢʊlfan a′weɪ ha′mha ɢω̇k tcɛ-ᴅɪ-a′m·ɪm [tca t-..].

mɪ′ᴅɪ ɢʊsa sɪ′nfaf na ʙɪna·′tst wa′ŋɢ a′ɢ·a ᴅʊm{nɪ}hɪ′u′nan tcɛ [tca]-ᴅa′ɪ′wan a′m·ɪm.

pɛ′ca hω·″lʊ tcɪ″ɪ {tcɪ}ᴅa′mᴅjyʊ ᴅʊm-na′ɢ·ɪt.

<A2> Kammach

lώk a′m·ɪm ɢɪ′n·ʊ′k ɢʊnɪ-hu′ɪfaf [kɪn-..]. ||d2:1||

  tcɛ-wa″an [tcȧ ..] tca′m·ʙɑk ɢʊnɪᴅɪ′tɢwɪn a-wa′(′)k.

  ɢʊ́sa tca′m·ʙɑk k̇ɛ′m·atc ɢω̇k mɛ·′nfan u{m}tω·′qᴅɛlʊq ɑsɪ′nfaf.

  ɢω̇k ɢʊ-ᴅɪ′tku ᴅɪku′nɪyaʙ ᴅa′m·ɪm

  ɢʊᴅnɪ″ɪ la′ɢ·a′aɪ tcɛ-ᴅa′ɪ′wan [tcȧ ..] ɢa′wakɪl.

  ᴅɪnɪᴅɪ′f eɪkɪn k̇wi′st e′ɪkɪn ᴅɪ′nfyaf a′mpyan. ||d2:2|| <A2(2)>

  {ᴅɪn}ᴅɪnɪ-wa′l tcɛ-ɢʊ′sa [tcȧ ..] ɢa′wakɪl.

  ɢʊ́saʙɛ·ᴅ ɢω̇k ɢʊ{ᴅɪ}ᴅɪ′tɢwɪn hɛ′ɪʙantcyʊ a′m·ɪm.

    ɢɪ′n·ʊ′k ɢʊ́sa hɛ′ɪʙantcyʊ a′m·ɪm ɢɪ′n·ʊ′k wa′ha ᴅɪnɪ_ᴅω′m·ɪm.

  ɢω̇k ɢʊsa ɢʊtya′nᴅ ɢʊ́sa a′m·ɪm.   <A2(3)>

    ɢʊᴅɪᴅɪ′ᴅ [kʊt-ti′t] ʙʊ′ᴅzɑk a′kfan.

ɢʊ′saʙɛ·ᴅ ɢʊtha′ɢ·u·t.

  ɢʊ́sa ᴅu-wa′k ha′l·ʊ [ha·lo′] ɢʊ{ᴅɪ}ᴅya′nᴅ.

  k̇ʊ′ʙfan ᴅɪk̇ʊ′n·ɪyaʙ ɢɪ′n·ʊ′k yu′ᴅnɪɢwan ɢʊ′ṣaʙɛ·ᴅ. ||d2:3||

[---] (Kammach speaks:)

  hɛ′saʙɛ·ᴅ [ha·sa ..] mɪ′ᴅɪ ᴅʊpᴅɪᴅa′fᴅjʊ [tɪp-ta′ftso].   <A2(4)>

  meɪᴅj tcɪ″ɪ na ᴅɛk̇ʊ′n·ɪyaʙ [tȧ-..] ᴅɪᴅɪᴅu′haq tcɛ-ᴅa′ɪ′wan [tcȧ ..] hɛɢa′ukɪl [ha-ka′wakɪl]

    la′ɢ·aɪ.

  ɢu′caʙɛ·ᴅ tcɪ″ɪ ᴅɪtya′nᴅ wa′k.

  pɛ″ama ᴅɪᴅɪtme·′yɪ hɛ′sa [ha·sa] tcɛ-mɪ′ᴅɪ [tcȧ ..]. ||d2:4||

  pɛ″ama sʊ′ᴅ·ʊ ʙʊ′ɢʊlfan ᴅɪᴅɪᴅu′yɪ [tɪt-tɔ′yi].

    ᴅɪᴅɪᴅɪ′tk̇u [tɪt-tɪ′tko·] hɛ′sa [ha·sa] a-wa′k̇   <A2(5)>

    ᴅɪ{ᴅɪ}tyu′hat tcɛ-ᴅa′ɪ′wan [tcȧ ..] atca′m·ʙɑk ᴅa′ŋɢʊt q̇ɪyɛ′snu.

    ɢʊ́sa tca′m·ʙɑk ʊmʙi·′nᴅ [ɪm-..] la′ɢ·aɪ ᴅjʊ′hu· tcɛ-ʙa′l [tcȧ ..] ama′mpɢa.

  ɢω̇k umṗi·′n ʙʊ′ɢʊlfan ha′wɛu k̇wɛ′ɪnafʊn′yak. ||d2:5||

  ɢω̇k ʊmṗi·′hɪn mɛ·′nmɪyak ma′mpᴅʊ, αṗu′ɪṗyu·n ka′wan.

  ʊmṗi·′hɪn ʙʊ′ɢʊlfan a′wɛu ɢa′uᴅzan mɛ·′nmɪyak sq̇ɪ′nwa′ɪmax.   <A2(6)>

  tcɪ″ɪ ᴅɪᴅɪ′st [tɪt-tɛ′st] ɢʊ́sa wa′ɢ tcɛ-ɢω̇k [tcȧ ..]. ||d2:6||

  yɛ′lfan ᴅɪ′nfyʊf a′-waɢ tcɪ″ɪ tcɪᴅa′mᴅjʊ ᴅʊmᴅɪ′tku [tam ..] sʊ′ᴅ·ʊ tcɛᴅʊ′n·ʊ [tcȧ ..],

    ᴅɪᴅɪtwa′l [tam tɪt-..] tcɛha′m·ɪ [tcȧ ..] tcɛtcɪ″ɪ [tcȧ ..] ᴅɛʙɪ′kwɑkyʊp [tȧ-pɪ′kkwak]

    ᴅʊ′m·ɪ.

pɛ′ama ɢω̇k ɢʊᴅɪ′tɢwɪn ɢʊ′s·a wa′k.

He gave two to his uncle, three to his grandfather, two to his aunt.

Three he kept.

<A3> His Brother, Kayakach, Speaks[8]
Kayakach says,

> *"Tomorrow we will get two young men,*
> > *I will put forth a message to my tribes-people.* ‖d2:7‖
> > *I want all to come to my place.*
> > *Here we will play all sorts of games.*
> *When it gets dark we will stand to our dance.*
> *When it gets daybreak two lads will make a sweathouse for the people here.*

<A3(2)>

> > *The women will prepare food.*
> *When the sun is up all of the people will eat.* ‖d2:8‖
> *When they finish their meal, the lads will play their shinny.*

> *When it is afternoon the old men will play the hand-game.*

<A3(3)>

> *Next day I will send five hunter-boys out.*
> > *They will hunt deer.*
> *When it is nearly evening I will send two lads, five slaves.* ‖d2:9‖
> > *They will bring back the meat of the deer.*
> > *Women will cut up the meat of the deer.*   <A3(4)>
> > *Some they will boil.*
> > *Some they will roast.*
> *Again in the evening you will stand to your dance.*
> *When it is morning the women will play the thing called women's shinny."*

ɢ⍵·k ɢᴜdı'ct ɢɛ·'m tcɛ'ᴅısı'm'wı [tcȧ ..], hᴜ'psın tcɛᴅıkɛ·'f [tcȧ ..], ɢɛ·'m tcɛᴅıɢa'ɢa
   [tcȧ ..],

hᴜ'psın ɢ⍵·k ɢᴜtp̣i'n.

<A3> His Brother, Kayakach, Speaks

q̇aya'ɢats u-nɑ'ɢ·ıt,

   me'ıᴅj ᴅıᴅıᴅı'tɢwın [tıt-tı'tkwın] ɢɛ·'m sı'nfaf
      ᴅıtk̇u ha'mha tcɛᴅɛɢa'wakıl [tcȧ tȧ-ka'okıl],   ‖d2:7‖
      tcı''ı ṫa'mᴅjᴜ· ʙᴜ'ɢᴜlfan ᴅᴜmnısma'k [tam smak] tcı'i tcɛᴅᴜ'm·aı [tcȧ-..].
      hɛ'saʙɛ·ᴅ [ha'sa ..] ᴅıᴅ·ıtlɑ'kwɑk [tıt-lɑ'kwat] ʙᴜ'ɢᴜlfan a'wɛu lɑ'ɢat.
   ɢı'mᴅıthu'wı [kam tıt-..] ᴅı{ᴅı}tya'twan ᴅı-yɛ'l'wa.
   ɢamᴅıme'ıᴅıtcın [kam ıtmɛ'ytcıtın] a'mpyan ɢɛ·'m ası'nfaf ɢᴜᴅınıtʙᴜ'n [kᴜtın-pᴜ'n]
      aɢᴜ'ᴅ·ıp tcɛhɛ'sa [tcȧ ha'sa] a'm·ım.   <A3(2)>
      ɢı'n·ᴜ'k aʙᴜ'm·ık ᴅınʙᴜ'n·ı akwi·'nafᴜ [tın-p ᴜ'n (a)kwi'naf].
   ɢa'm{nı} [kam ı-]ha'lʙam a'mpyan ʙᴜ'ɢᴜlfan a'm·ım ɢᴜ'ᴅ·ınıkwi·'nafᴜn. ‖d2:8‖
   ɢᴜᴅ·ınıṫᴜ'ɢ·ı [kunnıt-tᴜ'ki] ᴅın{ı̣}kwi·'nafᴜn ɢı'n·ᴜ'k ṣı'nfaf ɢᴜᴅ·ınılɑ'ɢᴜt [kᴜnnı-..] ᴅı{nı}
      sɢɑ'lkɑl.
   ɢᴜmıᴅıtya'hampyan [kam (ıt)..] ɢı'n·ᴜ'k yu·tcɛᴅyu ɢᴜ'ᴅ·ınılɑ'ɢıt [tınnı-..] cma'l·a.
                                                                        <A3(3)>
   me'ıᴅj tcı''ı ᴅıt-ᴜ'mhat hu''wan ayᴜ'wa'lɑq sı'nfaf,
      ɢı'n·ᴜk ɢᴜᴅ·ını-yu''wan [tınıt-..] ᴅa'l·ım.
   yɛ'tc ɢam{n}ıthu'ı tcı''ı ᴅıtɢısɢat ɢɛ·'m sı'nfaf hu''wan a'-waq   ‖d2:9‖
      ɢı'n·ᴜk ɢınıcwı''ıl ɢᴜsa-ᴅa'l·ım ᴅımu·'kʷ.
      ɢı'n·ᴜ'k ʙına·'ᴅsıt ɢın·ı-sɢᴜ'ʙ·an [kınnı-skᴜ'pka] ɢᴜsa-ᴅa'l·ım ᴅımu·'kʷ.   <A3(4)>
      q̇ᴜ'ʙfan ɢᴜ's·a-mu·'kʷ ᴅını-ʙᴜ'tʙa·t,
      q̇ᴜ'ʙfan ɢᴜᴅ·ınıt'cᴜ'xyat.
   ɢwɛ'l·ᴜ ɢamᴅıthu'wı· [kam-(ıt)..] ᴅᴜpya'twan [tıp-..] {ᴅı-}yɛ'l'wa.
   ɢamıtme'ıᴅj [kam-(ıt)..] ɢı'n·ᴜk ınʙı'n·ats [(a)pınna·ts] ɢın·ıt_lɑ'ɢᴜt [tınnık-..] a'ɢ·a
      ɢᴜsa ta'ŋkwıt sɢwı'mxan [a-..].

CHAPTER TWO
Kenoyer's Reminiscences, as told in 1928[1]

<1> Family

My father was Tualatin.[2] ||d1:1||

  His name was Kinay.

My mother was half Tualatin, half Ahantchuyuk.[3]

Then their children were nine.

  Seven of my brothers died.   <1(2)>

  Just myself, named Bahawadas, and one older sister,[4] just we two were living in
    this land.

<2> The Grand Ronde Day School

When I was eight years old my father says to me, ||d1:2||

  "You will go to the White people.

  They will teach the White people's language."

  We were three, one was my older brother, the other my older sister.

[---]

  "Every day you will all go to that school (lit., language house)."   <2(2)>

  Many different children went to that school. ||d1:3||

One day in the early morning it clouded up.   <2(3)>

I spoke like this to my father,

  "I don't want to go to school today.

  I am afraid of that rain.

  I am afraid of thunder."

My father said, ||d1:4||

  "You will go.

  It makes no difference about that rain.

  It makes no difference about that thunder."

  I got myself ready.   <2(4)>

Then we went.

  We hadn't gone far.

Then the thunder roared.

  I cried.

My brother speaks like this,

  "Come on! come on! don't cry!"

[---]

CHAPTER TWO
Kenoyer's Reminiscences, as told in 1928

<1> Family

tcɪ″ɪ ᴅɛma′ma atfa′latɪn.   ‖d1:1‖

  ɢω′k uᴅa′ŋk̦wɪt k̦ɪna′y.

ᴅɛna′na k̦o′pfan tfa′latɪn k̦o′pfan ha′nt′cyok.

pɛ″ma ɢɪ′n·ok ᴅɪnɪ-wa′p̦ɪ k̦wi·′st [deA: ʋ-kwa′its (cf. Ch. Wawa *k'ʷáic* '9')].

  pcɪ′n′wɪ ᴅɛʙo′kwokyap ɢoᴅɪnɪfʋ″ʋ.   <1(2)>

  yɛ′lfan tcɪ″ɪ ᴅɛᴅa′ŋk̦wɪt ʙax̦awa′ᴅɑs nɑu wa″an ᴅɛʙu·′tsat yɛ′lfan ɢɛ·′m sʋ′ᴅʋ

    tcɪᴅɪᴅa′fʋts tcɛhɛ′c·a a′n·ʋ.

<2> The Grand Ronde Day School

tcɪ″ɪ ɢoᴅɪtɢɛ′m′wa ᴅɛmi·′t′s ᴅɛma·′ma pa′-ʋᴅnɪ′tsfan,   ‖d1:2‖

  ma′ha ᴅɪtɢʋ″ʋm tcɛ-wa′m·ʋ a′m·ɪm.

  ɢɪ′n·ok ɢɪn·ɪ-ᴅɛ″adɑk wa′m·ʋ a′m·ɪm ᴅɪnɪha′mha.

  sʋ′ᴅʋ ɢoᴅɪthʋ′psɪn wa″an ᴅɛʙɪ′k·wak wa″an ᴅɛʙu·′tsat.

[---]

  ʙʋ′ɢʋlfan a′mpyan mɪ′ᴅ·ɪ ᴅʋp-i·′ᴅɪt tcɛɢʋ′sa ha′mha ᴅʋ′m·ai.   <2(2)>

  ha′l·ʋ waᴅɪ′ᴅ·ai si″wei ɢɪn·ok ɢʋnɪt-ɪ·′ᴅ tcɛ ɢʋ′sa ha·mha ha′me·. ‖d1:3‖

wa″an waha′l′wan a′mpyan ɢʋtlʋ′pɢʋyʋ.   <2(3)>

tcɪ″ɪ pa″a ɢʋtnɪ′cɪn ᴅɛma·′ma,

  wa′ŋk ța′mᴅjyu ᴅʋmᴅɪᴅi·′t tcɛha′mha ha′m·ɪ hɛ′s·a-wi· ɪ′pyan.

  tcɪ″ɪ tcɪ-nɪ′ʋhɪn ɢʋsa ɢwi·′ᴅɪt

  tcɪ-nɪ′ʋhɪn a′mpkʷ.

ᴅɛma·′ma ɢʋtna′ɢ·ɪt,   ‖d1:4‖

  ma′ha ᴅɛt-i·′t

  wa′ŋɢ a′ɢ·a ɢʋsa ɢwi·′ᴅɪt

  wa′ŋk a′ɢ·a ɢʋ′sa a′mpkʷ.

  tcɪ″ɪ ɢʋtɛ′n·antcwʋ″ʋn   <2(4)>

pɛ″ma sʋ′ᴅʋ ɢoᴅʋt-i·′ᴅ,

  wa′ŋk̦ la′ɢai ɢoᴅɪt-ɪ′ᴅ

pɛ″ma ɢʋsa a′mpkʷ ɢʋt_lʋ″lʋwai.

  tcɪ″ɪ ɢoᴅ·ɛ′s·ᴅak̦

ᴅɛʙɪ′k·wak pa′-u′mi′ut,

  sma′k sma′k wa′ŋk ᴅʋmta′x̦ᴅɪt.

[---]

"I am afraid of that thunder."   <2(5)>
Then it really roared.
Then hail began to fall. ||d1:5||
    It struck my face and my ears.
Then I ran to the house.
When I got home I told my father,   <2(6)>
    "That hail whipped me!"
That day I stayed at home.
    One day I didn't go to that school.

<3> Playing Hooky and the Consequences
Many of us different children were going to play on the road. ||d1:6||
    We went and got little, long switches.
Then we went and got white clay.
    We made balls.
    Lots of balls we made.
Then half of the children stood far off and half nearby.   <3(2)>
Then we battled with those white clays. ||d1:7||
Then we placed the clays on the ends of those switches (as catapults).
Then we jumped all over.[5]
Thereupon, when they had battled all their clay away, one boy said,

                                                                <3(3)>

    "Let's race!
    Who wants to run?" ||d1:8||
One boy says,
    "I'm running one hundred paces!"
[---]
    "Alright,"   <3(4)>
    says that one boy.
Then one boy wants to jump.
Then another says,
    "I'm jumping with you!"
Having finished their playing, then they returned to their homes.
Come (next) day, then we went to school.   <3(5)>
That teacher (lit., language man) said,
    "For what reason did you not all come yesterday?
    Don't you lie!

tcɪ″ɪ tcɪ-nɪˊʊhɪn ɢʊsa αˊmpkʷ.   <2(5)>
pɛ″ma ʙʊˊfαn ɢʊt_lʊ″lʊwai
pɛ″ma ɒαˊ″yʊ ɢʊɒɪt-ɒJɛˊɪkfɪt.
    ɢʊɒɪtˑwaˊ″yαˑt ɒɛkwaˊlˑαk naˊu ɒɛɒαˊnqɒα .
pɛ″ma tcɪ″ɪ ɢʊɒɪtmɪˊnɒJɪt tcɛhaˊmˑɪ. ||d1:5||
tcɪ″ɪ ɢʊɒɪɒɪˊtwʊk ɢʊt_nɪˊsˑɪn ɒɛmaˊma,   <2(6)>
    ɢʊˊsˑα ɒαˊ″yʊ ɒαˊnˑaɪf.
ɢʊˊsa-wi-ɪˊpyan tcɪ″ɪ ɢʊɒɪtʙɪˊn tcɛhaˊmˑɪ.
    waˊ″an αˊmpyan waˊŋq ɢʊɒɪɒʊ″ʊ tcɛɢʊˊsa haˊmha haˊmˑɪ.

<3>Playing Hooky and the Consequences
haˊlˑʊ ɒɪˊɒˑaɪ siˊ″wei ɒɪɒɪt-laˊɢʊt tcɛɢuˊn. ||d1:6||
    ɢʊɒɪɒɪˊtɢwɪn wa-ɒɪˊnt'cat ɢʊˊmʙuˑs α-waˊɒˑɪk.
pɛ″ma ɢʊɒɪɒɪˊtɢwɪn α-waˊmˑʊ haˊŋkluˑp
    ɢʊɒɪtʙʊˊn αlʊ″lʊ.
    haˊlˑʊ αlʊ″lʊ ɢʊɒɪtʙʊˊn.
pɛ″ma ɋʊˊpfan αsiˊ″wei ɢɪˊnˑʊk ɢɪnɪɒɛˊcɒαp laˊɢˑai nau ɋʊˊpfan hɛˊcαʙɛˑɒ.   <3(2)>
pɛ″ma ɢʊɒɪtwaˊqnaɪf tcɛ-ɢʊˊsa waˊmˑʊ haˊŋkluˑp. ||d1:7||
pɛ″ma ɢʊɒɪt_lʊ″ʊn ɢʊsa haˊŋkluˑp tcɛ-ṫwɛˑlɪt ɢʊsa-waˊɒˑɪk.
pɛ″ma ɢʊɒɪt-ɪˊɒˑʊp ʙʊˊɢʊlfan haˊlˑʊ.
ɢʊˊsaʙɛˑɒ ɢʊɒɪɒɪnwaˊqnaɪf ʙʊˊɢʊlfan ɒɪnɪhaˊŋkluˑp ɢʊɒɪtwɛ″yʊ, waˊ″an αɒ'uˊɪɒɪn
    ɢʊɒnαˊɢˑɪt,   <3(3)>
    tcɪˊɒˑa tcɪɒmaˊnfʊṫwɪ.
    iˊ″ya ʊmṫaˊmɒJu ɒʊmtmaˊnfɪt? ||d1:8||
waˊ″an αṫuˊɪtɪn naˊɢˑɪt,
    tcɪ″ɪ tcɪɒmaˊnfɪt waˊ″an αɒʊˊmṗɪ ɒϖˊf.
[---]
    ɢʊˊswɪ   <3(4)>
    nαˊɢˑɪt ɢʊˊsa waˊ″an.
pɛ″ma waˊ″an αṫuˊɪtɪn ṫaˊmɒJʊ ɒʊmɪɒɪt-ɪˊɒˑαp.
pɛ″ma waˊ″an ɢʊtnαˊɢˑɪt,
    tcɪ″ɪ tcɪt-ɪˊɒˑαp tcɛ-maˊha.
ɢɪˊnˑɪtʊˊɢˑɪ ɒɪnˑɪ-laˊkwαk pɛ″ma ɢʊɒɪnɪɒɪˊtyɪ tcɛˊɒɪnɪhaˊmˑɪ.
ɢʊɒɪtmeˊɪɒJ pɛ″ma sʊˊɒˑʊ ɢʊɒɪt-ɪˊɒ tcɛ-haˊmha ɒɪhaˊmˑɪ.   <3(5)>
ɢʊsa haˊmha α-muˊi ɢʊɒnαˊɢɪt
    tcɛˊ αˊɢˑαʙɛˑɒ mɪˊɒˑɪ waˊŋq ɢʊɒmaˊ″a kuˊwɪ?
    waˊŋq ɒʊpt'cɪˊnˑαl!

I know what you children did yesterday."
One boy said,   <3(6)>
   "We played on the road."
Then the teacher spoke like this to those children,
   "Don't you do like that.
   I will whip you when you do like that."

<4> A Mandate
Maybe two years, and we quit that day-school.
   There was built a big (school-)house.
   One building there was the girls' building. ||d1:9||
   The other building was the boys' building.
Then two men drove to that White boss, the Indians' boss (the agent).

                                                                        <4(2)>

This is what he told the two men,
   "All the Indians are to come to my 'talking-house' (office).[6]
   I want to tell these Indians they are to bring their children to this big school-building.

[As the agent talks, his implied audience shifts to an assembly of Indians]
   Everything is kept in this building.   <4(3)>
   There the children will sleep.
   There they will eat.
   There they will learn (lit., acquire language).
   Here the teacher women (lit., language women) are those the White people call 'sisters'.
   You Indians need not worry yourselves.   <4(4)>
   These sister women are good people.
   They are people of the Lord Above.
   They will take care of you Indians' children.   <4(5)>
   They will give them nice things.
   On the seventh day they will bathe the children's bodies. ||d1:10||
   Then they will give them nice clothes to put on.
   Then in one month, you Indians, I will give you back your children to return to your homes.

   Three days later, then you will bring your children back to the school.

                                                                        <4(6)>

   Whenever one of your children becomes ill, there is a White doctor there.
   He will doctor the child.

tcɪʹʹɪ tcɪ-yʊʹɢɪn aʹɢ·a mɪʹdɪ siʹʹweɪ ɢʊdʊʙʊʹnhɪn kʊʹwɪ.

waʹʹan aťuʹɪtin ɢʊdɪdnaʹɢ·ɪt,   <3(6)>

    sʊʹdʊ ɢʊdɪd_laʹkwɪt tcɛɢʊʹn.

pɛʹʹma ɢʊsa haʹmha a-muʹɪ paʹʹa ɢʊdnɪʹcɪn ɢʊʹsa siʹʹweɪ,

    waʹŋq paʹca dɪmphɪʹuʹnan,

    tcɪʹʹɪ dɪdɪdaʹn·aɪf mɪʹdɪ paʹca ɢʊdɪdhɪʹuʹnan.

<4> A Mandate

eɪkɪn ɢɛʹm amɪʹt'cʊ ɢʊsa ɪʹpyan dɪhaʹmha haʹm·ɪ ɢʊdɪtpaʹslu·.

    ɢʊdʙʊʹn aʙaʹl haʹm·ɪ.

    waʹʹan haʹm·ɪ ɢʊʹsaʙɛ·d aʙɪn·aʹdjɪt ɢɪʹn·ʊk dɪn·ɪ-haʹm·ɪ. ||d1:9||

    [Angulo: waan haʹmme·] ɢʊsa ťuʹɪtin dɪnɪhaʹm·ɪ.

pɛʹʹma ɢɛʹm a-muʹɪ ɢɪʹn·ʊk ɢɪnɪɢɪʹcɢat ɢʊsa waʹm·ʊ adja'mʙak mɛʹnmaʹyʊq

    dɪnɪdjaʹmʙak,   <4(2)>

paʹʹa ɢʊdnɪʹcɪn ɢʊsa ɢɛʹm adjaʹŋǩʊ.

    ʙʊʹɢʊlfan mɛʹnmɪ ɢɪnɪsmaʹk tcɪʹʹɪ tcɛ dɛhaʹmha-haʹm·ɪ.

    tcɪʹʹɪ tcɪťaʹmdjʊ dʊmnɪʹs·ɪn hɛʹsa-mɛʹnmɪ ɢɪʹn·ʊk dʊmsmʊʹǩʊ dɪnɪ-waʹpɪ tcɛhɛʹsa aʙaʹl

        haʹmha dʊʹm·aɪ.

    tcɛ·ɢʊʹsa haʹm·ɪ ʙʊʹɢʊlfan aꞇfan maɢaʹɢdɪn.   <4(3)>

    ɢʊʹsaʙɛ·d siʹʹweɪ ɢʊdɪnɪweʹif.

    ɢʊʹsaʙɛ·d ɢʊdɪnɪkweʹɪnafʊn.

    ɢʊʹsaʙɛ·d ɢʊdɪnɪdɪʹtɢwɪn haʹmha.

    hɛʹsa haʹmha ʙʊʹm·ɪk ɢɪʹn·ʊk waʹm·ʊ aʹm·ɪm ɢɪnɪ·daʹŋgwɪt ʙʊʹdjat

    mɪʹdɪ mɛʹnmɪ waʹŋq dʊm-yaʹkladɪn dʊmuʹpɪn.   <4(4)>

    ɢʊʹsa ʙʊʹdjat a-waʹɪst ɢɪʹn·ʊk tɛʹn·a aʹm·ɪm.

    ɢɪʹn·ʊk ɢɪnɪ·haʹlʙam atcaʹmʙak dɪnɪ-aʹm·ɪm.

    ɢɪnɪ-yuʹdnɪgwan mɪʹdɪ mɛʹnmɪ dɪsiʹʹweɪ.   <4(5)>

    ɢɪʹn·ʊk ɢɪnɪdɛʹct atɛʹn·a aʹkfan.

    ɢʊnɪ·-pcɪʹn·ʹwɪ aʹmpyan ɢɪʹn·ʊʹk ɢɪnɪkuʹwal ɢʊʹsa asiʹʹweɪ dɪnɪɢaʹpyɑ. ||d1:10||

pɛʹʹma ɢɪnɪdɪʹct tɛʹn·a aʹqfan ɢʊmɪnɪʙʊʹn

pɛʹʹma waʹʹan adꞷʹp mɪʹdɪ mɛʹnmɪ tcɪʹʹɪ tcɪdɪʹdʊp dɪsiʹʹweɪ dʊmdɪdɪ·tǩʊ tcɛ-mɪʹdɪ

        dʊʹm·aɪ.

    hʊʹpsɪn aʹmpyan pɛʹʹma mɪʹdɪ ɢʊdʙɪswɪʹyɛl dɪsɪʹʹweɪ hɛʹsa tcɛhaʹmha haʹm·ɪ.

                                                                  <4(6)>

    ɪʹya mɪʹdɪ dɪsɪʹʹweɪ ɢʊdɪd-ɪʹlfʊt hɛʹsa waʹm·ʊ apaʹlɪq maʙɪʹnd.

    ɢꞷʹk ɢʊtyɪʹꞇlat ɢʊsa asiʹʹweɪ.

He will give something that will drive away that illness.
If there should be something not good in that school, you all come to me.   <4(7)>
   I will fix it.
In one day you will bring your children here to the school.
Should anyone not bring their child I will send two men.
   I will take ahold of (arrest) you.
   I will put you in jail (lit., the 'bad house').   ‖d1:11‖   <4(8)>
(If) you say,
   'Alright, come and get our children!'
Then I will let you out.
Then you will return to your home.
That is all I have to say to you Indians."
Then the Indians brought their boys and girls here to the school-house.

<5> Life in the Sisters' School[7]
Then it is they, those five sisters, taking care of all those children.[8]
   The smaller children sleep apart.
   That's where one of those sisters takes care of the little children.
   The bigger children sleep apart.   <5(2)>
When it is early morning, maybe 6 o'clock, one of those sisters wakes up the big
   children.
   They wash their faces.
Then they go into the school-room.   ‖d1:12‖
   The sisters and a man are there.[9]
   The man prays the words of the Lord Above.   <5(3)>
   Right there a little house (Angulo: a chapel) stands.
   The little house has a little door.
   In the little house is kept a little bowl.
Then that man takes out that little bowl.
   There in that bowl he pours some wine (lit., berry-water).
   He goes and drinks that wine.   <5(4)>
Then one boy—that boy helps that man.
   He takes two bottles.
   From one bottle he pours the wine, from the other, water.
Then he gives that man the wine.
Then he drinks the wine.   <5(5)>
Then when he finishes, he prays the words of the Lord Above.

ɢʊdɪ'ct a'ɢ·a ɢʊ'ṣa ɢʊdɢɪ'cɢɑ·t ɢʊ'ṣa wa'yfʊn.

a'ɢ·a wa'ŋq dɑmtɛ'n·a tcɛɢʊ'sa ha'mha dʊ'm·ai, mɪ'dɪ dɪdjɪpsmɑ'k tcɛtcɪ'ɪ.   <4(7)>

   tcɪ''ɪ dɪtɛ'n·a''an.

ɢʊmdɪtwa''an ɑha'mpyan mɪ'dɪ dɪdɪt_smʊ'ɢ·ʊ dɪsi·''wei tcɛhɛ'sa-ha'm·ɪ.

ɪ'ya wa'ŋq dʊmsmʊ'ɢ·ʊ dɪsi·''wei tcɪ'ɪ dɪdɪtɢɪ'cɢɑ·t ɢɛ'm α-mu'i

   ɢʊdɪdɪ'tɢwin tcɛma'ha.

    tcɪ''ɪ ɢʊt_lu''ʊn ma'ha tcɛqɑ'sq ha'm·ɪ. ||d1:11|| <4(8)>

ma'ha ɢʊtna'ɢ·ɪt,

     ɢʊ'c·wi·, tcɑ'k cɪ'ɢ·wɪn dɪsi·''wei,

pɛ''ma tcɪ''ɪ ɢʊtɢʊ' hɛ''lʊm tcɛma'ha.

pɛ''ma ma'ha dɪ'tyɪ tcɛpʊ'm·ɪ·.

pe'ca hɷ''lʊ tcɪ''ɪ tcɪ-nɑ'ɢ·ɪt tcɛ-mɪ'dɪ mɛ'nmɪ.

pɛ''ma ɢɪ'n·ʊ'k mɛ'nmɪ ɢɪnɪ-smʊ'k̓ʊ dɪnɪ-t̓u'ɪtɪn dɪnɪbɪ'n·a'ts tcɛhɛ'sa ha'mha ha'm·ɪ.

<5> Life in the Sisters' School

pɛ''ma ɢɪ'n·ʊk ɢʊsa hu'wan bʊ'djat ɢɪ'n·ʊ'k ɢɪnɪ-yu'dnɪɢwan bʊ'ɢʊlfan ɢʊsa asi·''wei.

   dɪ'n·tcɪt dɪsi·''wei ɢɪ'n·ʊ'k dɑ'ɪ'wan ɢɪnɪnɪtweif.

ɢʊ'sabɛ·d wa''an ɢʊsa bʊ'djat ɢʊtyu'dnɪɢwan ɢʊ'ca dɪ'n·tcɪt si·''wei.

ɢʊ'sa wadɷ'f asi·''wei dɑ'ɪ'wan ɢɪ'n·ʊk ɢʊdɪnɪwe'ɪf.   <5(2)>

ha'ɪ'wan ɢɑmɪtme'ɪdj e'ɪkɪn dɑ'f αdɪ'ndɪn wa''an ɢʊ'sa bʊ'djat ɢʊnɪṣbʊ'kli ɢʊ'ṣ·a αBa'l

   si·''wei.

ɢʊnɪku'wał dɪn·ɪkwa'l·ɑk.

pɛ''ma ɢɪ'n·ʊk ɢʊdɪnɪwa'l·ʊ tcɛha'm·ɪ. ||d1:12||

   ɢʊ'cabɛ·d ɢʊsa bʊ'djat nau wa''an α-mu'i

   ɢʊsa α-mu'i ɢʊtnɑ'ɢ·ɪt ha'lBam ɑtcɑ'mBɑk dɪha'mha.   <5(3)>

   ɢʊ'sabɛ·d tcɛɢʊ'sa dɪ'dzɑq ɑha'm·ɪ mɑ-yɑ't.

   ɢʊ'ca dɪ'dzɑq ɑha'm·ɪ ɢɑ'ɢdɪn αdɪ'dzɑq αɢu'djʊm.

   ɢʊ'ca tcɛdɪ'dzɑq ɑha'm·i mɑɢɑ'ɢdɪn dɪ'dzɑq ɑk̓wɑ't.

pɛ''ma ɢʊ'sa α-mu'ɪ ɢʊdmɪ'n·ɪ ɢʊsa dɪ'dzɑq ɑk̓wɑ't

   ɢʊ'cabɛ·d tcɛɢʊ'sa k̓wɑt ɢʊt-mu'wɪ a'ɢ·a ɢɑ'yan dʊ'mpq.

   ɢʊca ɢɑ'yan dʊ'mpq ɢɷ'k ɢʊdɪ'tkwɪt.   <5(4)>

pɛ''ma wa''an αt̓u'ɪtɪn, ɢʊsa αt̓u'ɪtɪn ɢʊdyu'dnɪɢwɑn ɢʊ'ca α-mu'ɪ.

   ɢʊdɪ'tɢwɪn kɛ·m α-nɑ'd·ʊ.

   wa''an α-nɑ'd·ʊ ɢʊtmu'wɪt ɢʊ'sa ɢɑ'yan dʊ'mpq, wa''an α-nɑ'd·ʊ ɑmɑ'mpɢɑ.

pɛ''ma ɢʊd·ɛ'ct ɢʊca a-mu'ɪ ɢʊca ɢɑ'yan dʊ'mpq.

pɛ''ma ɢɷ'k dɪ'tkwɪt ɢʊca ɢɑ'yan dʊ'mpq.   <5(5)>

pɛ''ma ɢʊdɪdʊ'ɢɪ ɢʊdyʊ''wan ha'lBam ɑtcɑ'mBɑk dʊ'mha.

Then the sisters and the children all pray the words of the Lord Above.

||d1:13||

Then when they finish their praying, all the children go into their playroom.

<5(6)>

Then the little children get up.

Then they wash their faces.

When they all finish, then all the children go into the dining room.

  All stand at the dining table.

Then the sisters pray the words of the Lord Above.   <5(7)>

When they finish their prayers,

  "You children all sit down! Eat!"

Then when they finish the meal, they go into the (play-)room.

  There they all stand.

Then those sisters say,

  "You five boys go cut wood!

    Each boy cut ten sticks.

  You (other) five boys, you all help the one Sister and those girls (in) the wash-house.

||d1:14|| <5(8)>

  You boys will work at the big tub that has an arm."

  Into that tub are put clothes and warm water.

Then the girls take the clothes out of the tub.

  They put the clothes into another tub.

  There the girls wash the clothes in clean water.   <5(9)>

Then they wring them out.

  They bring them outside.

  They hang those clothes on a line.

Then having finished their work, they go to their playroom.

  There they await the midday meal.   <5(10)>

Those children in the lesson-listening room, once they have finished their lessons

  to the point of learning everything, they come on out.

  They get ready to eat.

Then they sound the bell.

  All the children run into that room. ||d1:15||

  They all stand in one line (lit., one trail).

Then the sister speaks like so,

  "Let's go into the dining room!"   <5(11)>

  They all stand up then.

pɛ″ma ɢʊca bu′ᴅjat nau si″wei ʙʊ′ɢʊlfan ɢɪ′n′ʊ′k ɢɪnɪ-yʊ″wan ha′ʙam ɑtca′mʙɑk
    ᴅʊ″mha. ||d1:13||

pɛ″ma ɢuᴅɪnɪᴅʊ′ɢ·ɪn ᴅɪyʊ″wan ʙʊ′ɢʊlfan si″wei ᴅɪnɪ-ᴅɪ′tmɪn tcɛɢɪ′n′ʊk ᴅɪnɪ-la′ɢwɪt
    ha′m·ɪ.   <5(6)>

pɛ″ma ɢʊsa ᴅɪ·nt′cɪt ɑsi″wei ɢɪ′n′ʊ′k ɢɪnɪʙʊ′ḳlai.

pɛ″ma ᴅɪnɪku′wł ᴅɪnɪkwa′l·ɑk.

ʙʊ′ɢʊlfan ᴅɪnɪᴅʊ′ɢ·ɪ pɛ″ma ʙʊ′ɢʊlfan ɑsi″wei ɢuᴅɪnɪᴅɪ′t tcɛkwe′ɪnafʊn ha′m·ɪ.
    ʙʊ′ɢʊlfan ɢɪnɪᴅe′cᴅap tcɛ ɢʊ′ca k̇we′ɪnafʊn la′ᴅɑm.

pɛ″ma ɢʊca ɑʙu′ᴅjat ɢuᴅɪnɪyu″wan ɑ-ha′ʙam ɑtca′mʙɑk ᴅʊ″mha.   <5(7)>

ɢuᴅɪnɪᴅʊ′ɢ·ɪ ᴅʊ″mha,
    mɪ′ᴅ·ɪ si″wei ʙɪsɪ·′yʊ, ʙɪck̇we′ɪnafʊn.

pɛ″ma ɢɪᴅɪnɪᴅʊ′ɢ·ɪ k̇we′ɪnafʊn ɢuᴅɪnɪᴅɪ′t tcɛha′m·ɪ.
    ɢʊ′saʙe·ᴅ ʙʊ′ɢʊlfan ɢunɪᴅe′cᴅap.

pɛ″ma ɢʊsaʙu′ᴅjat ɢuᴅɪnɪ-na′ɢɪt,
    hu″wan ɑ̇tu′ɪᴅɪn mɪ′ᴅ·ɪ sk̇ʊ′pɢɑt ɑ-wa′ᴅ·ɪk,
      wa″an ɑ̇tu′ɪᴅɪn ku′pɢɑt ᴅɪ′nfyaf a-wa′ᴅ·ɪk.
    hu″wan ɑ̇tu′iᴅɪn mɪ′ᴅ·ɪ ɢa′m′yat tcɛwa″an aʙu′ᴅjat nau ɢʊsa-aʙɪ′n·a·ts ɢu′sa k̇u′luł
    ha′m·ɪ. ||d1:14|| <5(8)>

mɪ′ᴅ·ɪ ṫu′iᴅɪn ᴅuplu″nʊf tcɛɢʊ′sa-a-ʙa′l a-ṫe′mʊltc waɢa′ɢᴅɪn ᴅɪla′q͙ʷ.
    tcɛɢʊ′sa ṫe′mʊltc mu′wɪᴅ a′ɢfan nau wa′m·ai ma′mpɢa.

pɛ″ma ɢɪ′n′ʊ′k aʙɪ′n·a·ts ɢuᴅɪnɪt-mɪ′n·ɪ ɢʊsa a′ɢfan tcɛ ṫe′mʊltc.
    ɢɪ′n′ʊk ɢɪnɪlu″wan ɢʊ′sa a′ɢfan tcɛ ᴅa′ɪwa″n aṫe′mʊltc.
    ɢʊ′saʙe·ᴅ ɢɪ′n′ʊk a-ʙɪ′n·a·ts k̇u′wał ɢʊ′sa a′ɢfan tcɛ-ṫe′n·a ama′mpɢa.   <5(9)>

pɛ″ma ɢɪnɪt′sa′m·a·t,
    ɢɪnɪᴅɪ′ṫku hɛ″lʊm
    ɢʊnɪtqa′l·ał ɢʊ′sa a′ɢfan tcɛ-a′mt′cal.

pɛ″ma ṫʊ′ɢ·ɪ ᴅɪnɪ-lu″nafan ɢɪnɪti′ᴅ tcɛ-ᴅɪnɪ-la′k̇wɪt ha′m·i.
    ɢʊ′saʙe·ᴅ ɢɪ′n′uk ɢɪnɪ-yu·′wat tcɛ-wɪ′lf a′mpyan k̇we·ɪnʊf.   <5(10)>

ɢʊ′sa si″wei ɢɪ′n′ʊk tcɛ-ɢɑ′pᴅɪn ha′mha ha′m·ɪ ɢɪ′n′ʊk ṫʊ′ɢ·ɪ ᴅɪnɪha′mha ᴅʊmɪnɪ-yʊ′ɢ·ɪn
    ʙʊ′ɢʊlfan ɢɪnɪ-ma″a hɛ″lʊm
    ɢɪnɪ-sʊ″atcɪn ᴅʊmnɪkwe′ɪnafɪn.

pɛ″ma ɢɪnɪ-yu·″wʊn ɢʊ′sa ᴅɪ′nᴅɪn
    ʙʊ′ɢʊlfan si″wei ɢʊnɪ-mɪ′nᴅjɪs tcɛ-ɢʊ′sa-ha′m·ɪ. ||d1:15||
    ʙʊ′ɢʊlfan ɢʊnɪ-ᴅe′cᴅap tcɛ-wa″an a·ɢʊ′n.

pɛ″ma ɢʊ′saʙu′ᴅjat pa′-mi′ut,
    tcɪ′ᴅ·a smak tcɛ-ᴅɪ′k̇we′ɪnafʊn-ha′m·ɪ.   <5(11)>
    ʙʊ′ɢʊlfan ɢʊnɪ-ᴅe′cᴅap ɢʊ′saʙe·ᴅ

Then the sister prays the words of the Lord Above.
Then having finished her prayer, she tells those children,
  "Sit down! Eat!"
When they finish eating, then they go into the playroom.
Then all the children play.
  Big children play outside.
  The sister takes a ball.
    I don't know what that ball is called in Indian.
    White people call that ball "rubber-ball." [unfinished?]

<6> A Death in the Family
That winter my brother got sick.
For maybe two months he lay sick.
Then in the spring he died.[10]
For two days he remained in the house.   ‖d1:16‖
  Many people, our people (relatives), brought many things.   <6(2)>
Then the women folks made lots of food.
Early in the afternoon they fed these different people.[11]
Finished eating, they sat down there in the house.
  One of my aunts[12] brought many things.   <6(3)>
  She put them in the middle of the room.
Then she took one thing.
  She gave it to a man.
  She took a necklace.
    She gave it to a woman.
  She did likewise to all the different people.   <6(4)>
  All those things that our relatives brought, she gave away all.
When the sun was up next day, then we were to take this dead person's body to
  the graveyard.
  All the visiting people left for home.   <6(5)>
Then those relatives of ours, the grown-ups and Tamanawas doctors, they took
  care of that dead person's body all night long.   ‖d1:17‖
  We children went to my aunt's house.
  There we slept, and those Tamanawas doctors sang all night.

                                         <6(6)>

  They sang wanting to drive away the sickness that killed my brother.
Near the day's dawning, then our relatives arrived where the dead person lay.

pɛ″ma ɢʊsa-ʙʊ′ᴅjat ɢʊt-yu″wan ha′lʙam a-tca′mʙak ᴅɪha′mha.

pɛ″ma ɢʊtʊ′ɢɪ ᴅɪha′mha ɢʊᴅ-nɪ′sɪn ɢʊ′sa-asi·″wei,

   ʙɪsɪ′yʊ ʙɪskwe′ɪnafʊ.

ɢɪnɪ-tʊ′ɢɪ kwe′ɪnafʊn pɛ″ma ɢʊnɪ-ᴅɪ′tya tcɛ-la′kwɪt· ha′mɪ,

pɛ″ma ʙʊ′ɢʊlfan si·″wei ɢʊnɪ-la′kwɪt.

   ʙa′l a-si·″wei ɢɪ′n·ʊk ɢʊnɪ-la′kwɪt he′ɪ′lum.

   ɢʊsa-ʙʊ′ᴅjat ɢʊᴅɪ′tɢwɪn wa″n a-lu·″lu.

      wa′ŋq tcɪ″ɪ ɢʊᴅɪtyʊ′ɢʊn a′ɢ·a ɢʊsa-alu·″lu ta′ŋkwɪt tcɛ-mɛ′ɪnma′yak

      wa′m·u· a′m·im ɢʊnɪ-ku′wan ɢʊ′sa lu·″lu rubberball.

<6> A Death in the Family

ɢʊ′sa-wi·-ya′m̓pyʊs, tcɪ″ɪ ᴅeʙɪ′kwak ɢʊᴅɪt-ɪ′lfɪt.

e′ɪkɪn ɢɛ′m aᴅɷ·′p ɢʊᴅɪt-we′ɪᴅɪt

pɛ″ma ɢʊᴅɪt-mɛ·′kʷ ɢʊtfʊ′ʊ.

ɢɛ′m a′mpyan ɢʊᴅɪtp̓i′n tcɛ-ha′m·i. ||d1:16||

   ha′l·ʊ a′m·ɪm sʊ′ᴅ·ʊ ᴅʊ′m·ɪm ɢɪ′n·ʊk ɢɪnɪ-smʊ′k̓u ha′l·ʊ a′ɢfan.   <6(2)>

pɛ″ma ɢɪ′n·ʊk ʙʊ′m·ɪk a′m·ɪm ɢɪ′n·ʊk ɢʊnɪ-ʙʊ′n ha′l·ʊ akwe′ɪnaf yak.

ᴅɪ′s ɢamɪt-ya′hampyan ɢɪ′n·ʊk ɢʊnɪ-ʊ′k hɛ′ca waᴅɪ′ᴅ·aɪ a′m·ɪm.

ɢʊᴅɪtʊ′ɢɪ kwe′ɪnafʊn pɛ″ma ɢʊnɪ-sɪ′yʊ ɢʊ′sa-tcɛ-ha′m·ɪ.

   wa″n ᴅeɢa′ɢa ɢʊt_smʊ′k̓u ʙʊ′ɢʊlfan a′ɢfan.   <6(3)>

   ɢʊᴅɪtɢʊ′ wɪ′lf tcɛ-ha′m·ɪ.

pɛ″ma ɢʊᴅɪ′tɢwɪn wa″an a′ɢfan

   ɢʊᴅɪ′ct wa″an a-ᴅja′ŋku.

   ɢʊᴅɪ′tɢwɪn wa″an aɢa′ʊᴅzan

      ɢʊᴅ′ɪst wa″an a-ʙʊ′m·ɪk.

   pɛ′ca ɢʊᴅ-mɪ′u′nan tcɛ-ʙʊ′ɢʊlfan ɢʊ′sa ᴅeᴅɪ′ᴅ·aɪ [Angulo: tɪ′ttaɪ] a′m·ɪm. <6(4)>

   ɢʊ′sa ʙʊ′ɢʊlfan a′ɢ·a sʊ′ᴅ·ʊ ᴅʊ′m·ɪm ɢɪnɪ-smʊ′k̓u ke′ᴅ·ak ɢʊtɢʊ′ ʙʊ′ɢʊlfan.

ɢamɪt-me′ɪᴅj ha′lʙam a′mpyan ɢʊtya′ᴅ pɛ″ma sʊ′ᴅ·ʊ ᴅɪᴅɪt_sᴅɪ′tku hɛ′sa a″wus

   ᴅɪka′pya tcɛ-kwɪ′l̓yu·.

   ɢɪ′n·ʊk ɢʊsa waᴅɪ′ᴅ·aɪ a′m·ɪm ɢɪnɪᴅɪ′tyɪ.   <6(5)>

pɛ″ma ɢʊ′sa sʊ′ᴅ·ʊ ᴅʊ′m·ɪm waʙa′l a′m·ɪm pa′laq a′m·ɪm ɢɪ′n·ʊk ɢʊᴅɪnɪ-yu′ᴅnɪɢwan

   ɢʊ′sa a″wus ᴅɪka′pya ʙʊ′ɢʊlfan wɪ′fyu. ||d1:17||

   sʊ′ᴅ·u waᴅɪ′nt′cɪt a′m·ɪm ɢʊᴅɪti·′ᴅ tcɛ-ᴅeɢa′ɢa ᴅʊ′m·aɪ.

   ɢʊ′saʙe·ᴅ sʊ′ᴅ·ʊ ɢʊᴅɪtwe′ɪᴅ nau ɢɪ′n·ʊk ɢu′sa pa′laq a′m·ɪm ɢʊᴅɪnɪtq̓u·′ᴅɪt

      ʙʊ′ɢʊlfan-wɪ′fyʊ.   <6(6)>

   ɢʊᴅɪnɪt-q̓u·′ᴅɪt t̓a′m·ᴅju ᴅʊmɢɪ′sɢa·t ɢʊ′sa ʙʊ′ɢʊlfan ɢʊsa wa′yfʊn ɢʊᴅ·a′haɪ ᴅeku′nɪ.

yɛ′ts ɢamɪtme′ɪᴅj pɛ″ma sʊ′ᴅ·ʊ ᴅʊ′m·ɪm ɢɪnɪswa′l tcɛ-ɢʊ′sa ha′l·a a″wʊs ɢʊᴅɪtp̓ɪ′ᴅ

The old women cried. <6(7)>
Half the women made breakfast.
When they finished the meal, they washed all the dishes.
   Many people arrived.
Then my aunt took all those dishes. <6(8)>
Then she gave things (dishes, etc.) to those people.
   She got rid of everything in the house.
Then two men brought the coffin (lit., dead person's box). ||d1:18||
Then they put all kinds of nice things into the coffin.
Then they covered the coffin. <6(9)>
   They took hold of it and carried it outside.
   They put in on the wagon.
Then they carried that dead person on ahead.
Then my father my mother and us, we came along behind in another wagon.
   All the people came along behind us.
   They took the dead person's body to the house of the Lord Above. <6(10)>
Then they took the dead person's coffin into that church (lit., good house).
   There that man of the Lord prayed prayers (lit., good words).
   He sang the chants (on which) they took it to the graveyard.
Then when he finished his chants, he cast the good (holy) water of the Lord
   Above. <6(11)>
Then four men took the coffin.
   They took it outside.
   They took it to the graveyard. ||d1:19||
At the grave four men dug a hole in the ground.
Then the man of the Lord arrived. <6(12)>
   There he chanted.
   He cast the holy water into that hole in the ground.
Then they put the coffin in the ground.
Then those four men covered it with earth.
Then we went back home. <6(13)>
   Many people followed us to the house.
At home five young men killed two big cows.
   They cut up all the meat of those cows.
Then my father gave everybody a little meat.
   He gave away all the meat.

ɢɪ′n·ʊk ɢʊsa wayu′fatyu ʙʊ′m·ɪk ɢɪn·ɪ-ta′xɒɪt.   <6(7)>

  k̇ʊpfan aʙʊ′m·ɪk ɢɪ′n·ʊk ɢɪn·ɪ-ʙʊ′n hɛ′l′wan ɒɪkwe′ɪnafʊnaq.

ɢɪn·ɪṫʊ′ɢɪ ɒɪkwe′ɪnafʊn ʙʊ′ɢʊlfan a-kwɪ′ɒ-an ɢʊɒɪnɪku′′wɪɫ.

  ha′l·ʊ a′m·ɪm ɢɪɒɪnɪwa′l.

pɛ′′ma ɒɛɢa′′ɢa ɒɪ′tɢwɪn ʙʊ′ɢʊlfan ɢʊ′sa akwɪ′ɒ,   <6(8)>

pɛ′′ma ɢʊɒɪɒɪ′ct tcɛ-a′m·ɪm

  ʙʊ′ɢʊlfan ɢʊsa a′′ɢfan tcɛ-ha′m·ɪ ɢʊtɢʊ′.

pɛ′′ma ɢɛ′′m a-mu′ɪ ɢɪn·ɪ-smʊ′k̇ʊ ɢʊsa a′′wʊs ɒɛkwɪ′ɒ.   ‖d1:18‖

pɛ′′ma ɢʊɒɪnɪɢu′ tcɛ-ɢʊ′sa-kwɪ′ɒ ʙʊ′ɢʊlfan a′ɢ·a watɛ′n·a.

pɛ′′ma ɢʊɒɪnɪ-lʊ′k·wat ɢʊsa-a-kwɪ′ɒ   <6(9)>

  ɢʊɒɪnɪɒɪ′tɢwɪn ɒɪ′tɢu· hɛ′ɪ′lʊm

  ɢʊɒɪnɪlu′′ʊn tcɛ-tcɪ′ktcɪk.

pɛ′′ma ɢʊɒɪnɪɒɪ′tɢu· ɢʊ′sa a′′ws tcɪ′m·ei.

pɛ′′ma ɒɛma′′ma ɒɛna′′na nau sʊ′ɒ·u ɢʊɒɪt-i′′f ha′nt′c tcɛ-ɒa′ɪ′wan a-tcɪ′ktcɪk.

  ʙʊ′ɢʊlfan a′m·ɪm ɢʊɒman-i′′f ha′nt′c tcɛ-sʊ′ɒ·ʊ.

  ɢʊɒɪnɪɒɪtk̇ʊ ɢʊ′sa a′′ws ɒɪka′′pya tcɛ ha′lʙam atca′mʙak ɒʊ′m·aɪ.   <6(10)>

pɛ′′ma ɢʊɒɪnɪ-la′m·ɪ ɢʊsa a′′ws ɒɪkwɪ′t tcɛ-ɢʊ′sa-watɛ′n·a ha′m·ɪ.

  ɢʊ′sʙɛ·ɒ ɢʊsa ha′lʙam a-tca′mʙak ɒɪ-mu′ɪ ɢʊt-yu′′wan a-tɛ′n·a ha′mha.

  ɢʊɒɪtq̇u′ɒ ɢʊ′sa q̇u′ɒ ɢɪnɪɒɪ′tk̇u tcɛ-kwɪ′ɫyʊ

pɛ′′ma ɢʊɒɪṫʊ′ɢɪ ɒɪq̇u′ɒ ɢʊtɢu′ a-tɛ′n·a ha′lʙam atca′mʙak ɒɪma′mpɢa.

                                                          <6(11)>

pɛ′′ma ta′ʙ a-mu′ɪ ɢʊɒɪnɪɒɪ′tɢwɪn ɢʊ′sa akwɪ′t

  ɢʊɒɪnɪɒɪ′tɢwɪn hɛ′ɪ′lʊm

  ɢʊɒɪnɪɒɪ′tk̇u tcɛ-kwɪ′ɫyu.   ‖d1:19‖

ɢʊ′sa tcɛ-kwɪ′ɫyu ta′ʙ a-mu′ɪ ɢʊɒɪnɪ-lʊ′lkɫat wa′ɒzɪt ha′ŋk̇lu·p.

pɛ′′ma ɢʊt-mu′ɢ ɢʊsa-ha′lʙam a-ɒja′mʙak a-mu′ɪ,   <6(12)>

  ɢʊ′saʙɛ·ɒ ɢʊtq̇u′ɒɪt,

  ɢʊt-ɢu′ ɢʊ′sa-tɛ′n·a ama′mpɢa tcɛ-ɢʊ′sa wa·′ɒzɪt ha′ŋk̇lu·p.

pɛ′′ma ɢʊɒɪnɪ-ɢu′ ɢʊsa a-kwɪ′t tcɛ-ha′ŋk̇lu·p.

pɛ′′ma ɢʊsa ta′ʙ a-mu′ɪ ɢʊnɪt-lʊ′pɢat tcɛ-ha′ŋk̇lu·p.

pɛ′′ma sʊ′ɒ·ʊ ɢwɪɒɪɒɪ′tyɪ tcɛ-ha′m·ɪ.   <6(13)>

  ha′l·ʊ a′m·ɪm ɢʊɒɪtyu′′wafʊm tcɛ-ha′m·ɪ.

tcɛ-ha′m·ɪ hu′′wan a-sɪ′nfaf ɢʊɒɪnɪɒa′′haɪ ɢɛ′′m wa-ʙa′l a-mu′smʊs.

  ʙʊ′ɢʊlfan ɢʊsa-a-mʊ′smʊs ɒɪka′′pya ɢʊn·ɪtk̇ʊ′pka·t.

pɛ′′ma tcɪ′′ɪ ɒɛma′′ma ɢʊɒɪɒɪ′ct ʙʊ′ɢʊlfan a′m·ɪm ɒɪ′nt′cɪt a-mu·′kʷ.

  ʙʊ′ɢʊlfan ɢʊ′sa-a-mu·′kʷ ɢʊtɢu′.

We couldn't prepare any more food. <6(14)>
We had nothing to prepare food (with).
Then these people shook hands with my father and mother.
All the people went back home.
Our relatives went back to their homes. ||d1:20||
They went to get things, every kind of thing, bedclothes, cooking utensils (to resupply us). <6(15)>
Then women cooked food.
Then they ate.
All of them having finished their meal, they washed all the dishes.
Then they sat in the house.
One man, a half-woman named Shumkhi, a great Tamanawas doctor, her power was dead-people (Tamanawas).[13] <6(16)>
Then she "threw" her song.
She took five bundles of pitch sticks.
She took one pitch bundle.
Then she lit it.
Then she shook it everywhere in the house.
She drove away the dead person's spirit-breath.
Having finished one, she took a second, she did the same thing again. <6(17)>
(With) these five bundles of pitch sticks he[14] stood to his dance all night long.
At first dawn, she finished those sticks.
Then two young men prepared a sweat-bath. <6(18)>
Then they hollered,
"Come on and have a sweat!"
The old men went in to their sweat.

<7> At Home on the Farm
That spring I did not go to school. ||d1:21||
I stayed at home.
My father plowed the earth.
He sowed wheat in the ground.
I helped my father. <7(2)>
He took three horses.
He sowed the wheat in the ground.
I drove three horses behind him.
I harrowed maybe thirty of what are called "acres."

wa'ŋq la'fʊ ɢʊᴅɪtʙʊ'n k̓we'ɪnafʊnaq.   <6(14)>

   wa'ha a'ɢ·a ᴅʊmʙʊ'm [Angulo: -pun] ak̓we'ɪnafʊnaq.

pɛ''ma ɢʊ'sa, a'm·ɪm ɢɪn·ɪᴅɪ'tɢwɪn ᴅɛma''ma ᴅɛna''na ᴅɪn·ɪ-la'kʷ.

   ʙʊ'ɢʊlfan a'm·ɪm ɢʊᴅɪnɪᴅɪ'tyɪ.

    sʊ'ᴅ·ʊ ᴅʊ'm·ɪm ɢʊn·ɪᴅɪ'tyɪ ||d1:20||

    ɢʊn·ɪᴅɪ'twʊ a'ɢfan, ʙʊ'ɢʊlfan a'ɢfan, a-we'ɪ'naq a'ɢfan, k̓we'ɪnafʊnaq a'ɢfan.
                                                        <6(15)>

pɛ''ma ʙʊ'm·ɪk, ɢɪ'n·ʊk ɢɪnɪʙʊ'n a-k̓we'ɪnafʊnaq.

pɛ''ma ɢɪn·ɪ-k̓we'ɪnafʊn.

ʙʊ'ɢʊlfan ɢʊᴅɪn·ɪtʊ'ɢ·ɪ ᴅɪnɪk̓we'ɪnafʊnaq, ɢʊnɪku'wał ʙʊ'ɢʊlfan a-kwɪ't,

pɛ''ma ɢɪn·ɪsɪ'y·u tcɛ-ha'm·ɪ.

   wa''an a-mu'ɪ k̓ʊ'pfan aʙʊ'm·ɪk cʊ'mxɪ ᴅɪᴅa'ŋkwɪt, a-ʙa'l apa''laq, ç̓e'ᴅ·ak ᴅɪ'yu'łmɪ

    a''ws.   <6(16)>

pɛ''ma ɢʊᴅɪtɢu'ᴅɪq̓u'ᴅ.

   ɢʊᴅɪ'tɢwɪn hu''wan ɢʊᴅɪ-ta'x̣t a-ma'ŋk̓l

   ɢʊᴅɪ'tɢwɪn wa''an ma'ŋk̓l,

pɛ''ma ɢʊt-ya'lɪt,

pɛ''ma ɢʊt-wɪ'fyat ʙʊ'ɢʊlfan ha'l·a tcɛ-ɢʊ'sa-ha'm·ɪ.

   ɢʊt-ɢɪ'sɢat ɢʊsa-a''ws ᴅuwe'ɪʙ

ɢʊt·ʊ'ɢ·ɪ wa''an ɢʊᴅɪ'tɢwɪn ɢɛ'm, pɛ'sɛ-yu ɢut-hɪ'u'nan.   <6(17)>

   ɢʊ'sa hu''wan ɢʊᴅɪta'x̣t a-ma'ŋk̓l ʙʊ'ɢʊlfan a-wɪ'fyu ɢɷ'k ɢʊᴅɪtya'twan ᴅɪ-yɛ'l'wɛl.

yɛ'ts ɢʊᴅɪt-me'ɪᴅj ɢʊᴅɪt·ʊ'ɢ·ɪ ɢʊ'sa a-ma'ŋk̓l.

pɛ''ma ɢɛ'm a-sɪ'nfaf ɢʊᴅɪnɪʙʊ'n a-ɢu'ᴅɪp.   <6(18)>

pɛ''ma ɢʊᴅɪnɪsla'l'wɪ

   sma'ksᴅa ʙɪɢu'ᴅɪp.

   ɢɪ'n·ʊk yu'tcatyu' a-mu'ɪ ɢʊnɪt-i·'ᴅ ᴅɪnɪɢu'ᴅɪp.

<7> At Home on the Farm

ɢʊ'sa a-me'kʷ wa'ŋq tcɪ''ɪ ᴅɪti'·ᴅ tcɛ-ᴅa'mha ha'm·ɪ. ||d1:21||

   tcɪ''ɪ ɢʊt-ʙɪ'nᴅ tcɛ-ha'm·ɪ,

   ᴅɛma'·ma ɢʊtk̓ʊ'plu·t ha'ŋk̓lu·p.

   ɢʊtɢu' a-sa'p·lɪl tcɛha'ŋk̓lu·p.

    tcɪ''ɪ ɢʊt-ɢɛ'm'yat ᴅɛma'·ma   <7(2)>

   ɢʊᴅɪᴅɪ'tk̓ʊ hu'psɪn a-kɪ'uᴅɪn.

   ɢɷ'k ɢʊtɢu' a-sa'p_lɪl tcɛ-ha'ŋk̓lu·p.

    tcɪ''ɪ ɢʊt-ɢɪ'sɢa·t hu'psɪn a-kɪ'uᴅɪn ha'nt'c tcɛ-ɢɷ'k.

    tcɪ''ɪ ɢʊt-k̓ʊ'm·a·t ha'ŋk̓lu·p e'ɪkɪn hʊ'psɪn ᴅɪ'nfyʊf a'ɢ·a ɢʊ'sa ta'ŋkwɪt acres.

Having finished it all, then I fixed fences.   <7(3)>

Having finished fixing fences, then we turned all the horses and cattle loose in
    the mountains.

<8> Getting Papers

Then my father went to the White boss (agent).

This is what he said,

    "I want to go away from our place.

    I want you to give me a two months' paper (pass).

    I want to go across the Willamette River.   <8(2)>

    There I mean to work." ||d1:22||

Then the White agent gave him the paper,

    "In two months you are to return to this place."

<9> Going Off-Reservation

It was then July, and then one morning my mother got everything ready.

Two days later my father got up early.

    My mother got up, she prepared food outside.

My mother called me, she spoke like this,   <9(2)>

    "Bahawadas, get up! Let's go! Let's eat!"

    I got up and washed my face.

Then I called to my father,

    "Come on! Come on! Let's eat!"

[---]

    "Alright, my boy."

Then we ate.   <9(3)>

Then my father and I went to get two horses, one dun and the other a bay horse.

Then we loaded the wagon.

    We brought it close to the house.

    Then we loaded the wagon.

When we finished all that, then we locked the house. ||d1:23|| <9(4)>

Then we went onto the road.

    My father took a rope (actually, a chain).

    He locked the gate to the fence.

Then we went on.

ʙʊ'ɢʊlfan ɢʊtʊ'ɢɪ, pɛ''ma ɢʊtɛ''n·a'an k̓a'l·aχ   <7(3)>
ɢʊtʊ'ɢɪ ɒʊmʙɪtɛ'n·a'n ka'l·aχ, pɛ''ma ɢʊtɢʊ' ʙʊ'ɢʊlfan kɪʊ'ɒɪn na'm·ʊ'smʊs tcɛ-mɛ'fʊ.

<8> Getting Papers

pɛ''ma ɒɛma'ma ɢʊti'ɒ tcɛ-ɢʊ's·a wa'm·ʊ tca'mʙak.

pa'-ɢʊt-nɪ's·ɪn,

   tcɪ''ɪ tcɪta'mɒjʊ ɒʊmɢʊ''ʊm he'ɪ'lʊm sʊ'ɒʊ ɒʊ'n·ʊ.

   tcɪ''ɪ tcɪta'mɒjʊ ma'ha ɢʊmɒɪ'ɒa·t ɢɛ'm a-ɒ⍵'p ʙɪ'ʙa'

   tcɪ''ɪ tcɪta'mɒjʊ ɒʊmɢʊ''ʊm ɒjʊ'hu tcɛ-Willamette ma'mpɢa.   <8(2)>

   ɢʊ'saʙɛ·ɒ tcɪ''ɪ ɒʊ'mɒɪtlu''nafʊn. ||d1:22||

pɛ''ma ɢʊ'sa wa'm·ʊ tca'mʙak ɢʊɒɪɒɪ'ct a-ʙɪ'ʙa'

   ɢɛ'm a-ɒ⍵'ʙ, ma'ha ɒʊmɪsme·'yɪ tcɛ-he'sa a'n·u.

<9> Going Off-Reservation

ɢʊ'saʙɛ·ɒ ɢʊma-ʙa'l-a-ɒ⍵'ʙ, pɛ''ma ɢʊt-me'ɪɒj ɒɛna'na ɢʊɒɪt_sʊ''natswu·n ʙʊ'ɢʊlfan
   a'ɢfan

ɢɛ'm ɢʊt-me'ɪɒj ɒɛma'ma ɢʊɒɪt-ʙʊ'klaɪ ha'l'wan.

   ɒɛna'na ɢʊɒɪtʙʊ'klaɪ ɢʊt-ʙʊ'n a-k̓we'ɪnafʊn he'ɪ'lʊm.

ɒɛna'na ɢʊt-la'l'wanfɪ, pa''a-ɢʊt-mɪ'ut,   <9(2)>

   paχawa'tɪs cʙʊ'klaɪ! tcɪ'ɒ·a cʙʊ'klaɪ tcɪ'ɒ·a c̓kwe'ɪnafʊn.

   tcɪ''ɪ ɢʊɒ-ʙʊ'klaɪ k̓u'wɪł ɒɛkwa'l·ak,

pɛ''ma tcɪ''ɪ ɢʊt-lɛ'l'wan ɒɛma'ma.

   sma'k! smak! cɒɛck̓we'ɪnafʊn!

[---]

   u'-u' ɒɛ'-ʊp.

pɛ''ma sʊ'ɒ·u ɢʊɒɪtk̓we'ɪnafʊn,   <9(3)>

pɛ''ma tcɪ''ɪ na'u ɒɛma'ma ɢʊɒ·ɪ'twʊ ɢɛ'm a-kɪ'utɪn wa''an a-lɪ'krɛ·m wa''an a-t'sa'l
   a-kɪ'utɪn.

pɛ''ma ɢʊ'ɒ·ɪtla'f·ʊt tcɛ-tcɪ'ktcɪk,

   ɢwɒɪt-smʊ'k̓ʊ yɛ'tc tcɛ-ha'm·ɪ,

   pɛ''ma ɢʊɒɪt-la'f·ʊt ɢʊ'sa-tcɪ'ktcɪk.

ʙʊ'ɢʊlfan ɢʊɒɪtʊ'ɢɪ, pɛ''ma ɢʊɒɪt-la'kla·t ha'm·ɪ, ||d1:23|| <9(4)>

pɛ''ma ɢʊɒɪti'ɒ tcɛ-ɢʊ'n.

   ɒɛma'ma ɢʊɒɪ'tɢwɪn a'mt'sal

   ɢʊt-la'klat ɢʊsa-ka'l·aχ ɒɪɢu'tcɪm.

pɛ''ma sʊ'ɒ·ʊ ɢʊɒɪti'ɒ

On that day we made a great distance.

Then at midday we arrived at a small stream. <9(5)>

    There we rested.

    We unhitched the horses from the wagon.

    I took the horses.

    I gave them water.

    My mother prepared food.

    We finished the horses' feeding.

When we finished our meal, then we went on.

    We reached the Willamette River around six o'clock. <9(6)>

    In those days the White people had a big boat (ferry) there.

Then my father drove our wagon onto that boat.

    Those horses were scared.

    They reared up on that boat.

Then two White men led the horses.

    Three Whites' wagons went across. ||d1:24|| <9(7)>

    Four wagons in all went across.

    The Indian name of the place across there is Chemeketa (*čamígidi*, Salem).

    He gave half a dollar to the boat man.

<10> Sojourn at Chemeketa (Salem)

    Across there at Chemeketa, there my mother's brothers were camped.

    We got there to the place where they had their tent.

    Two of my mother's brothers had a big job.

    My father helped them cut a big oak tree and also small brush. <10(2)>

    The White man paid three dollars a cord.

Then my father worked there.

    My mother worked in White people's houses. <10(3)>

    She washed clothes.

    About three days she washed clothes.

Then one day we went off to get strawberries. ||d1:24||

Early morning I went to get the horses. <10(4)>

    I and my mother's two brothers' wives, we went to look for strawberries.

    We took many buckets.[15]

Then we found lots of strawberries.

    We filled all the buckets.

ɢʊ'sawi· ɪ'pyan la'ɢ·a'aɪ ɢʊdɪtwu·'ɢ.

pɛ''ma ɢʊt-wɪ'lfʊ a'mpyan ɢʊdɪtwa'l tcɛ-wa''an a-dɪ·'dzɑq ma'mpɢa   <9(5)>

  ɢʊ'saʙɛ·d ɢʊtyu'w·ʊf

  ɢʊdɪt_sɢwɪ'l a-kɪ'utɪn tcɛ-tcɪ'ktcɪk.

  tcɪ''ɪ ɢʊdɪ'tku kɪ'utɪn

  ɢʊdɪ't ma'mpɢa.

  ᴅɛna'na ɢʊt-ʙʊ'n a-kwe'ɪnafʊn.

  ɢʊdɪtʊ'ɢɪ a-kɪ'uᴅan ᴅɪnɪkwe'ɪnafʊn.

ɢʊdɪtʊ'ɢɪ ᴅɪk̇we'ɪnafʊn pɛ''ma ɢʊdɪtɪ'ᴅ

  ɢʊdɪt-wa'l tcɛ-Willamette ma'mpɢa e'ɪkɪn ᴅa'f a-ᴅɪ'nᴅɪn   <9(6)>

  ɢʊ'sawi· ɪ'pyan wa'm·u· a'm·ɪm ɢɪ'n·ʊk ɢɪn·a̦p̣ɪ'n ɢʊsa-a-ʙa'l a-kwʊ''ʊn

pɛ''ma ᴅɛma'ma ɢʊt-ɢɪ'sɢat ᴅɪtcɪ'ktcik tcɛ-ɢʊ'sa a-kwʊ''ʊn.

  ɢʊ'sa a-kɪ'uᴅan ɢʊnɪ-nɪ'uhan

  ɢʊdɪnɪᴅe'cᴅap tcɛ-ɢʊ'sa a-kwʊ''ʊn.

pɛ''ma ɢɛ'm wa'm·u· a'm·ɪm ɢʊnɪ-wʊ'twʊt ɢʊsa-a-kɪ'uᴅɪn.

  hʊ'psɪn a-wa'm·u· tcɪktcɪk ɢʊdɪnɪ-ᴅɪ·'f ᴅjʊ'hʊ. ||d1:24|| <9(7)>

  ta'ʙ a-tcɪ'ktcɪk tcɛ-ʙʊ'ɢʊlfan ɢʊdɪnɪ-ᴅɪ·'f ᴅjʊ'hʊ.

  tcɛ-ɢʊ'sa a'n·ʊ ᴅjʊ'hʊ ᴅɪnɪ-me'ɪnmɪ-yak ᴅa'ŋkwɪt tcɛmɪ'ɢɪᴅɪ

  k̇ʊ'pfan a-k̇ɪ'nmaɪwʊx̣ [?] ɢʊdɪ'ct tcɛ-ɢʊ'ca kwu·'ᴅ ᴅɪᴅja'ŋkʊ.

<10> Sojourn at Chemeketa

  ɢʊ'saʙɛ·d ᴅjʊ'hʊ tcɛmɪ'ɢɪᴅɪ ɢʊ'saʙɛ·d ᴅɛna'na ᴅɪʙɪ'ɢ·wakyaʙs [?] ɢɪ'n·ʊk ɢʊ'saʙɛ·d

    ɢɪn·ɪᴅa'fʊts.

  ɢʊ'saʙɛ·d sʊ'ᴅ·ʊ ɢʊt-wa'l tcɛ-ɢɪ'n·ʊk ha'l·a-ɢʊ'sa ɢɪnɪsɪ'lhaus [ɢwɪᴅ·ɪnɪsɪ'lhaus]

  ᴅɛna'na ɢɛ'm ᴅɪʙɪ'k·wʊkyap ɢɪ'n·ʊk ɢɪnɪtʊ''wan a-ʙa'l lu''nafyap.

  ᴅɛma'ma ɢʊnɪ-ɢa'mpyat ɢʊnɪ-k̇ʊ'pɢa·t ʙa'l amɛ'f nau ᴅɪ'nt'cɪt a-wa'ᴅ·ɪk.   <10(2)>

ɢʊsa-wa'm·u· a-mu'ɪ ɢʊnɪ-ᴅa'pyat hʊ'psɪn k̇ɪ'nwaimax̣ wa''an a-cord

pɛ''ma ᴅɛma'ma ɢʊtlu''lʊfan ɢʊ'saʙɛ·d.

  ᴅɛna'na ɢɛ'ᴅ·ak ɢʊt-lu''nafʊn tcɛ-wa'm·u· a'm·ɪm ᴅɪnɪ-ha'm·ɪ.   <10(3)>

  ɢɛ'ᴅ·ak ɢʊt-k̇u'w·ał a'ɢfan.

  e'ɪkɪn hʊ'psɪn a'mpyan ɢʊt-k̇u'w·ał a'ɢfan.

ɢʊ'saʙɛ·d-wi-ɪ'pyan ɢʊdɪt-hʊ'l·ʊ a-dza'ɢʊplʊ. ||d1:24||

me'ɪᴅj-ɢʊt-he'l'wan tcɪ''ɪ ɢʊdɪᴅɪ'twʊ ᴅɪkɪ'uᴅan   <10(4)>

  tcɪ''ɪ nau ᴅɛna'na ɢɛ'm ᴅɪʙʊ'k·wʊk ᴅu·'l sʊ'ᴅu ɢʊdɪtɪ·'ᴅ u'ᴅnɪ'ɢwan a-ᴅza'ɢʊʙlʊ.

  ɢʊdɪᴅɪ'tku ha'l·u· ṫɪ'w·at.

pɛ''ma ɢʊᴅ·ɛ'cᴅɛc ha'l·u· a-dza'ɢʊplʊ ɢa'ya''an.

  ɢʊdɪt-lʊ'fʊt ʙʊ'ɢʊlfan ɢʊsa-ṫɪ'w·at

Then we took the berries.
  We sold them to White women.
  We sold them at a half-dollar a small bucket, called a "gallon."

<10(5)>

  We took those berries everywhere.
When we had sold them all then we went back to our camp.   <10(6)>
The next day we went to that berry patch.
For three days we picked those strawberries.
  We sold them to White people each day.

<11>The Lord's Day
Then on that day that they call the Lord's Day, no one worked.

  Everyone rested that day. ||d1:26||
On that day all kinds of Indians gathered at one open place.
  The names of those Indians were Siletz,[16] Luckiamute, Santiam, the Ahantchuyuk
    people.
  They gathered there.
Then they played shinny.   <11(2)>
  They bet everything.
  Such and so much did one man bet—silver dollars, nice clothes, their shirts, their
    coats.
  So many men on that side, so many on this other side.
  About fifteen men (each).
Then they took up their shinny ball.   <11(3)>
Then they played all day long.
When the sun was almost down, then they quit.
  All the Indians went back to their camps.
  They had work (at) all different places.[17]

<12>Huckleberry-Picking
On the next day our people went to work.
  My mother went to the place where she washed clothes.
  I stayed in camp to watch things. ||d1:27||
Near midday my mother came back to prepare food.   <12(2)>
  My father returned, he ate.
Having finished his meal, he went back to his work.

pɛ″ma ɢʊdɪdɪ′tku ɢʊ′sa-ɢa′ya″an

   ɢʊt-lʊ″wʊt tcɛ-hʊ′m·u· a-ʙʊ′m·ık

   ɢʊdɪtɢu′ tcɛ-kʊ′ʙfan ı-kı′nwaimax̣ wa″an dı·′t′caq a-tı′w·at ᴅa′mkwɪt gallon

                                                                                           <10(5)>

   ʙʊ′ɢʊlfan hɛ′l·a ɢʊdɪdɪ′tku ɢusa-ɢa′y·a″an

ɢʊdɪnɪt-lʊ″wat ʙʊ′ɢʊlfan, pɛ″ma sʊ′ᴅ·ʊ ɢʊdɪdɪ′tyı tcɛ-dɪt-sı′lhaus.   <10(6)>

ɢwɪdɪt-me′ɪᴅj sʊ′ᴅ·ʊ ɢwɪdɪti·′ᴅ tcɛ-ɢʊ′sa ɢa′y·a·an a′n·ʊ.

hʊ′psɪn a′mpyan ɢwɪdɪt-kwı′tkwa·t ɢʊsa-ᴅza′ɢʊʙlʊ ɢa′y·a·an

   ɢʊdɪt-lʊ″wat tcɛ-wa′m·u· a′m·ım ʙʊ′ɢʊlfan a′mpyan.

<11> The Lord's Day

pɛ″ma ɢʊ′sa a′ɢ·a ᴅɪnɪ-kwu·′n a-ha′lʙam a-tca′mʙak dı′a′mpyan wa′ŋq ı′ya

   ɢʊdɪt-lu′nafʊn.

   ʙʊ′ɢʊlfan ı′y·a ɢʊdɪnɪt-yu′wʊf ɢʊ′sa-wı-ı′pyan. ||d1:26||

ɢʊ′sa-weɪ-a′mpyan ʙʊ′ɢʊlfan a′wɛʊ mɛ′nmı ɢʊdɪnɪt-ɢɛ′w·ʊ tcɛ-wa″an a-hɛ′l′yʊ.

   ɢʊ′sa mɛ′nmı ᴅɪnɪᴅa′ŋkwɪt qu″ʊs, la′q̓mayut, sɛ′nᴅɪyɛ·m ɢʊsa-ha′nt′cɪyʊk a′m·ım.

   ɢʊ′saʙɛ·ᴅ ɢʊdɪnɪ-ɢɛ′w·ʊ

pɛ″ma ɢʊdɪnɪ-la′ɢʊt sɢa′lkɑl,   <11(2)>

   ʙʊ′ɢʊlfan a′ɢfan ɢʊdɪnɪt-ɢu′,

   pahɷ″lu· wa′an a-mu′ı ɢʊtɢu′ wa′m·u· sk̓ı′nwaimax̣, tɛ′n·a a′ɢfan, ᴅɪnɪca′t

      ᴅɪnɪɢa′ʙ·u·

   pa′sa hɑ′l·u· a-mu′ı ᴅjʊ′hʊ, pa′sa hɑ′l·u· hɛ′sa-wı-yʊ′fan.

   e′ıkın ᴅı′nfyaf-nau-hu″wan mu′ı.

pɛ″ma ɢʊdɪnɪdɪ′tɢwɪn ᴅɪn·ılʊ″lʊ.   <11(3)>

pɛ″ma ɢɪnᴅɪnɪ-la′kwɪt ʙʊɢʊlfan-wı-ı′pyan

yɛ′ts a′mpyan ɢʊdɪdjɛɢ·u, pɛ″ma ɢʊdɪnɪt-pa′clʊ.

   ʙʊ′ɢʊlfan mɛ′nmı ɢʊdɪnɪdɪ′tyı tcɛ-ᴅɪnɪsı′lhaus.

   ʙʊ′ɢʊlfan hɛ′l·a ɢɪ′n·ʊk ɢɪnɪtu″wan lu″nafʊn.

<12> Huckleberry-Picking

ɢʊdɪt-me′ɪᴅj sʊ′ᴅ·ʊ ᴅʊ′m·ım ɢɪ′n·ʊk ɢɪnᴅɪt-lʊ″nafʊn.

   ᴅɛna′·na ɢɛ′ᴅ·ɑk ɢʊt·ı·′ᴅ tcɛ-ɢʊ′sa hɛ′l·a ɢɛ′ᴅak ɢʊdɪtku′lafʊn a′ɢfan.

   tcı″ı ɢʊt-ʙı′nᴅ tcɛ-sı′lhaus yu″ᴅnɪɢwan a′ɢfan. ||d1:27||

yɛ′ts ɢut-wı′lfyʊ a′mpyan ᴅɛna′·na ɢʊt-mu·′ɢ ʙʊ′n k̓we′ınafʊn.   <12(2)>

   ᴅɛma′·ma ɢʊt-mu·′ɢ ɢʊt-k̓we′ınafʊn.

ɢʊt·ʊ′ɢı ᴅɪk̓we′ınafʊn ɢʊdı·′t ᴅɪᴅ·ılu″nafʊn.

My mother went to the White peoples' house.

She worked every day.

Pretty near sundown she came back. <12(3)>

Every day she went to work.

Maybe three days, maybe four days she did not work.

Then she said to me,

"Tomorrow when it is early, you will get the horses.

We will go look for berries.

Maybe the berries are nearly all gone.

If there are no more of those strawberries, we will go to a certain White man's place.

<12(4)>

On his place there are those small berries called 'huckleberries' (há?mui).[18]

I will speak to that old White man.

That old man knows about us.

He was keeping (?) one of my aunts.[19] ||d1:28|| <12(5)>

That aunt of mine has died."

Then we reached the house of that old man.

Then he spoke like this,[20]

"Hello, hello, grandchildren, where do you come from?

How long have you been here in Chemeketa?"

[---]

"Oh, maybe twenty-one days." <12(6)>

[---]

"When do you go back to Indian country (the reservation)?"

[---]

"In about a month."

My mother spoke like so,

"I want to pick huckleberries."

The old man says, <12(7)>

"Alright! You pick as much as you may want!

Do not tell any other Indians.

I do not want them to get to stealing my berries.

If I catch someone stealing my berries, I will take my gun.

Then I'll shoot!"

My mother says, ||d1:29|| <12(8)>

"I will not say anything to anyone."

ᴅɛna′na ɢʊᴅ·ɪ′t tcɛ-wa′m·ʊ· a′m·ɪm ᴅʊ′m·aɪ
ɢʊt-lʊ′′nafʊn ʙʊ′ɢʊlfanɪ-a′mpyan.

yɛ′ts ɢʊᴅJɛ′ɢ·ʊ a′mpyan kɛ′ᴅ·ak ɢʊt-mu·′ɢ.   <12(3)>

ʙʊ′ɢʊlfan a′mpyan kɛ′ᴅ·ak ɢʊti·′ᴅ lʊ′′nafʊn.

e′ɪkɪn hʊ′psɪn a′mpyan e′ɪkɪn ta′ʙ a′mpyan wa′ŋq kɛ′ᴅ·ak ɢʊdɪt-lʊ′′nafʊn.

pɛ′′ma pa′-ɢʊt-nɪ′sfan,

me′ɪᴅJ ɢamɪt-hɛ′l′wan ma′ha ᴅɪᴅɪ′twʊ kɪ′uᴅan

ᴅɪᴅɪt-i·′ᴅ u′ᴅnɪgwan ɢa′y·a′an,

e′ɪkɪn yɛ′ts wa·′′yʊ ɢa′y·a′′an.

ɢʊmɪt-wa·′′yu ɢʊsa-ᴅza′ɢʊʙlʊ ɢa′ya′′an tcɪᴅɪᴅu·′′ʊ tcɛ-wa·′′an wa′m·ʊ· a-mu·′ɪ ᴅʊn·ʊ.

                    <12(4)>

ɢ⊙·k tcɛ-ᴅʊ′n·ʊ ɢʊsa-ᴅɪ′nt·cɪt ɢa′y·a′′an ᴅa′ŋkwɪt ha′′muɪ

ᴅɪ′s tcɪ′′ɪ ɢʊᴅɪt-nɪ′s·ɪn ɢʊ′sa yu′hu′yu wa′m·ʊ ᴅJa′ŋkʊ

ɢʊ′sa yu′hu′yu a-mu·′ɪ yʊ′k·ʊn tcɛ-sʊ′ᴅ·ʊ.

ɢ⊙·′k upɪ′n wa·′′an tcɪ′′ɪ ᴅɛɢa·′ɢa ||d1:28|| <12(5)>

ɢʊ′sa ᴅɛɢa·′ɢa kɛ′ᴅ·ak ufu·′′ʊ.

pɛ′′ma sʊ′ᴅ·ʊ ɢʊᴅɪt-wa′l ɢʊsa-yu′hu′yu mu·′ɪ ᴅʊ′m·aɪ.

pɛ′′ma pɛ′sa ɢu-mɪ′ut,

ka·′ʙaɪ ka·′ʙaɪ wa′snaɢɪwaɪ hɛ′l·a tcəm·atcu′y·amp

hɛ′saʙɛ·ᴅ tcɛ-tcɛmɪ′ɢɪᴅɪ la′fʊ mɪ′ᴅ·ɪ ɢʊp-wa′l ɢʊ′saʙɛ·ᴅ.

[---]

u·′ e′ɪkɪn ɢɛ·′m ᴅɪ′nfyaf nau wa·′′an a′mpyan   <12(6)>

[---]

la′fʊ ᴅʊpᴅɪ′tyɪ tcɛ-me′ɪnmɪ′yak a′n·ʊ

[---]

e′ɪkɪn wa·′′an a-ᴅ⊙·′p.

ᴅɛna·′na pa′-ɢʊt-nɪ′s·ɪn,

tcɪ′′ɪ tcɪ-t́a′mᴅJʊ ᴅʊmk̓wɪ′t́kwa·t ɢʊ′sa-ha′′muɪ ɢa′y·a′an.

ɢʊsa-yu′hʊ′yʊ pa′-u-mɪ′ut,   <12(7)>

tɛ′n·a, ma′ha sk̓wɪ′t́kwat α-hʊ′′lʊ tcɪᴅa′mᴅJʊ.

wa′ŋq ᴅam-nɪ′s·ɪn i·′ya ᴅa′ɪwa·′′an a-me′nmɪ.

wa′ŋq tcɪ′′ɪ ɢɪᴅ·a′mᴅJʊ ɢɪ′n·ʊk ᴅʊmᴅɪt-la′tswu·t ᴅɛɢa′y·a·′an

i·′y·a tcɪ′′ɪ ɢʊ′mᴅɪᴅɛ′cᴅɛc ɢʊt-la′tswu·t ᴅɛɢa′y·a·′an tcɪ′′ɪ ɢʊᴅɪ′tɢwin ᴅɛsa′ɢ·walala

pɛ′′ma tcɪ′′ɪ ɢʊt́wa·′′n.

ᴅɛna·′na pa′u-mɪ′ut, ||d1:29|| <12(8)>

wa′ŋq tcɪ′′ɪ ɢʊt-nɪ′s·ɪn tcɛ-ɪ′y·a

[---]

    "Alright, go pick berries!"

[---]

    "Bahawadas, get your bucket!
      Pick these berries!
    All so good to eat—the kind of thing you will like."

    Those berries were hard to pick.

All day we were at that berrying ground.   <12(9)>

Pretty near sundown, then we went back to the tent.

Then my mother prepared food.

    My father returned when the sun was already down.

Then we ate.

My father said,   <12(10)>

    "Where did you go today?"

[---]

    "We went to the old White man named Delaney.
    We picked these huckleberries there."

My father said,

    "I did not know there was that kind of berry in this country."

[---]

    "The old man planted these berries in the ground. ||d1:30|| <12(11)>
    He just covered them up when he planted the berry roots.
    Then one year later these berries came out of the ground.
    That's when he found out for himself that these berries grow well in this place.
    That's how he found out about these berries.
    The berries are very good."   <12(12)>

[---]

    "What are you going to do with these berries?"

[---]

    "I will sell them to White women.
    They like this kind of berry very much.
    I may sell them for a dollar and a half a gallon."   <12(13)>

    My mother and I went to the White people's house.

    We got rid of all those berries we had picked.

    We did not have to go far.

    She, my mother, went to she who was her boss.   <12(14)>

[---]
ᴄᴜ'swɪ. tca'k s̓kwɪ'tkwaᐧt ça'yᐧaᐧ'n.

[---]
paxawaᐧ'tɪs sɪ'ᴄwɪn ʙɪtɪ'wᐧat,
  s̓kwɪ'tkwaᐧt hɛ'sa ça'yᐧaᐧ'n.
ma'ha ᴅɪ's ᴅɪt̓a'mᴅᴊᴜ ʙᴜ'ᴄᴜlfan a'ᴄfan tɛ'nᐧa k̓we'ɪnafᴜnək
ᴄᴜsa-ça'yᐧaᐧ'n tca'ŋᴄᴜt ᴅᴜmk̓wɪ'tkwaᐧt.
ʙᴜ'ᴄᴜlfan a'mpyan sᴜ'ᴅᴜ ᴄᴜt-ʙɪ'nᴅ tcɛ-ᴄᴜ'sa ça'yᐧaᐧ'n a'nᐧᴜ.   <12(9)>
yɛ'ts ᴄᴜᴅᴊe'ᴄᴜ a'mpyan, pɛ''ma sᴜ'ᴅᴜ ᴅɪ'tyɪ tcɛ-sɪ'lhaus.
pɛ''ma ᴅena'na ᴄᴜt-ʙᴜ'n a-k̓we'ɪnafᴜn.
  ᴅema'ma ᴄᴜt-muᐧ'ᴄ ᴄwaᴅɪᴅᴊe'ᴄᴜ a'mpyan.
pɛ''ma sᴜ'ᴅᴜ ᴄᴜᴅɪt-k̓we'ɪnafᴜn.
ᴅema'ma ᴄᴜt-naᐧ'ᴄɪt   <12(10)>
  hɛ'lᐧa mɪ'ᴅɪ ᴄᴜᴅɪt-ɪ'f hɛ'sa-weɪ-ɪ'pyan?

[---]
  sᴜ'ᴅᴜ ᴄᴜᴅɪᴅ-ɪ'ᴅ tcɛ-ᴄᴜ'sa yuᐧ'hu'yu waᐧ'mᐧuᐧ a-mu'ɪ ᴅa'ŋkwɪt Delaney.
  ᴄᴜ'saʙɛᐧᴅ sᴜ'ᴅᴜ ᴄᴜt-k̓wɪ'tkwaᐧt hɛ'sa ha''muɪ.
ᴅema'ma ᴄᴜt-naᐧ'ᴄɪt,
  waᐧ'nq tcɪ''ɪ ᴄɪt-yᴜ'ᴄᐧɪn ᴄᴜt-p̓ɪ'n pɛ'ca aᐧ'-wɛᴜ aça'yᐧaᐧ'n tcɛ-hɛ'sa-aᐧ'nᐧᴜ.

[---]
  ᴄᴜ'sa yuᐧ'hu'yu a-mu'ɪ ᴄᴜtᴄu' hɛ'sa ça'yᐧaᐧ'n tcɛ-ha'ŋkluᐧp.   ‖d1:30‖   <12(11)>
  k̓ᴜ'nfᴜ'ᴜ ᴄᴜt-laᐧ'ᴄᴜt ᴄᴜᴅɪtᴄu' hɛ'sa ça'yᐧaᐧ'n ᴅu''mal.
  pɛ''ma waᐧ''an a-mɪ't'cu hɛ'sa-ça'yᐧaᐧ'n ᴄᴜt-mɪ'nᴜ tcɛ-ha'ŋkluᐧp.
  pɛ''ma ᴄᴡ̓'k ᴄᴜᴅɪᴅe'cᴅeᴄ tcɛ'-ᴅɪmu'ʙɪn hɛ'sa-ça'yᐧaᐧ'n ᴄᴜt-ʙa'l'yᴜ tcɛ-hɛ'sa a'nᐧᴜ.
  hɛ'sa aᐧ'-wɛᴜ ᴄᴡ̓'k ᴄᴜᴅᐧe'cᴅeᴄ hɛ'sa-ça'yᐧaᐧ'n.
  ʙᴜ'ᴄᴜlfan tɛ'nᐧa ᴄᴜsa-ça'yᐧaᐧ'n   <12(12)>

[---]
  a'ᴄᐧa ma'ha ᴅɪᴅɪt-mɪ'u'nan tcɛ-hɛ'cᐧa-ça'yᐧaᐧ'n?

[---]
  ᴅɪ's ᴅɪᴅ-lᴜ''wat tcɛ-waᐧ'mᐧuᐧ wa'ɪᴅᴊᴜf.
  ᴄɪ'nᴜk p̓ᴜ'fan nɪᴅɪta'mᴅᴊᴜ hɛ'sa paᐧ'ca-awɛ'ᴜ a-ça'yᐧaᐧ'n.
  e'ɪkɪn ᴅɪt-lᴜ''wat tcɛ waᐧ''an nau ᴅɪtk̓ᴜ'pfan kɪ'nweɪmax waᐧ''an a-gallon.   <12(13)>
  tcɪ''ɪ nau ᴅena'na ᴄᴜᴅɪtɪ'ᴅ tcɛ-waᐧ'mᐧuᐧ a'mɪm ᴅᴜ'mᐧaɪ.
  ᴄᴜᴅɪtᴄu' ʙᴜ'ᴄᴜlfan ᴄᴜsa ça'yᐧaᐧ'n sᴜ'ᴅᴜ ᴄᴜᴅɪt-k̓wɪ'tkwaᐧt.
  waᐧ'ŋq sᴜ'ᴅᴜ ᴄᴜᴅɪt-ɪ'ᴅ laᐧ'ᴄᐧaɪ.
  k̓ɛ'ᴅ·ak ᴅena'na ᴄᴜᴅɪt-i'ᴅ tcɛ-ᴄᴜ'sa çɛ'ᴅ·ak ᴄᴜᴅᐧɪᴅᴊa'mʙak.   <12(14)>

There we disposed of all the berries.
Then we went to the store.
    She bought all kinds of foods.
Then we went back to the camp.

<13> Conclusion of Off-Reservation Trip[21]
In the morning father said to my mother, ||122:11||
    "What will you do today?"
My mother said:
    "I will go to the White boss.
        I will wash clothes.
    I do not know what my boy will be doing today."
Then my father said,
    "I know what my boy will do today.
    I want him to cut wood.   <13(2)>
    I want him to cut five cords.
    I will buy a good small axe.
    Only one more month will we stay here.
    Twenty-five cords, and I will finish my work.
    My boy will cut five cords. ||122:13|| <13(3)>
    Then I will have finished all my work.
    When I've finished my work then I will get my pay from that man.
    Then we will go back to our country."
My mother spoke in this way,
    "Alright, I will work for that White woman."
When my father finished his work he went to that man.   <13(4)>
Then they settled everything up there.
    My father got it from him.
[---]
    "Tomorrow my boy and I will go get our horses.
    You get everything ready!
    We will go back on that day."
Then early the next morning my father (says), ||122:15|| <13(5)>
    "Get up Bahawadas!
    Let's go after our horses!"
    We got our horses.
    We came back to our camp.

ɢʊ'saʙɛ·ᴅ ɢʊᴅɪtɢʊ' ʙʊ'ɢʊlfan ɢʊsa ça'y·a'n.
pɛ''ma ɢʊᴅɪt-i'ᴅ tcɛ kwe'ɪnafyak ha'm·ɪ,
    ɢʊt-ya'nᴅ ʙʊ'ɢʊlfan a'wɛʊ kwe'ɪnafʊnək.
pɛ''ma sʊ'ᴅ·ʊ ᴅɪ'tyɪ tcɛ-sɪ'lhaus.

<13> Conclusion of Off-Reservation Trip

ɢʊᴅɪt-me'ɪᴅj ama'ma ɢʊᴅɪtna'ɢat tcaᴅɛna'na, ||122:11||
    a'ɢ·a mɪ'ᴅɪ mɪ'u'nan hɛ'ca-wɛɪ-ɪ'pyan.
ᴅɛna'na na'ɢat,
    tcɪ''ɪ ᴅɪti'ᴅ tcɛᴅawa'm·ʊ ᴅja'mʙak
        ᴅɪtku''uł a'ɢfan.
    ᴅanᴅa''ʊp wa'ŋq tcɪ'ɢɪ'yʊ'ɢʊn a'ɢ·a ɢ⍵'k ɢʊmɪtmɪ'u'nan ha'cɪ-wɪ-ɪ'pyan
pɛ''ma ᴅama'ma na'ɢat,
    tcɪ''ɪ tcɪ'yʊ'ɢʊn a'ɢ·a ᴅa''ʊp ɢʊtmɪ'u'nan hɛ'ca-wɪ-ɪ'pyan.
    tcɪ''ɪ tcɪta'mᴅjʊ ɢ⍵'k ᴅʊmɪtkʊ'pɢa·t a'wa'ᴅ·ɪk.   <13(2)>
    tcɪ''ɪ tcɪta'mᴅjʊ ɢ⍵'k ɢʊmtkʊ'ʙ·ʊn hu'wan acord.
    tcɪ''ɪ ᴅɪtya'nᴅ watɛ'n·a aᴅɪ'ᴅzaq aq̇ɛ'sᴅɪn.
    ye'lfan. wa''an-aᴅ⍵'p sʊ'ᴅ·ʊ ɢʊᴅɪtʙɪ'n hɛ'saʙe·d.
    ɢɛ'mᴅɪ'nfyan nauhu'wan acord tcɪ''ɪ ɢʊtwe'l·ɪ ᴅɛlu''nafʊn
    ᴅa''ʊp ɢʊtkʊ'ʙ·an hu'wan a'cord. ||122:13|| <13(3)>
        pɛ''ma ᴅɪᴅɪtʊ'ɢ·ɪ ʙʊ'ɢʊlfan tcɪ''ɪ ᴅɛlu''nafʊn.
        ɢwɪᴅɪtʊ'ɢ·ɪ ᴅɛlu''nafan nautcɪ''ɪ ɢʊᴅɪ'tɢwɪn ᴅaka'ɪwanmax̣ tcɛɢʊ's·a ha'm·uɪ.
        pɛ''ma sʊ'ᴅ·ʊ ɢʊᴅ·u'y·ɪ tcɛᴅʊ'n·ʊ.
ᴅɛna'na pa-mɪ'ut,
    ɢʊ'cwɪ. tcɪ''ɪ ᴅɪt_lʊ''nafʊn tcɛɢʊ's·a hu'm·u ʙʊ'm·ɪk.
ᴅɛma'ma ɢwɪᴅɪtʊ'ɢ·ɪn ᴅɪlu''nafʊn ɢʊᴅɪ't tcɛɢʊ's·a a'mu'ɪ.   <13(4)>
pɛ''ma ɢɪ'n·ʊk ɢanɪtɛ'n·an ʙʊ'ɢʊlfan a'ɢ·a ɢʊ's·a.
    ᴅɛma'ma ɢʊᴅɪ'tɢwɪn tcɛɢ⍵·'k.

[---]

    ɢa'mɪt_me'ɪᴅj tcɪ''ɪ nauᴅ⍵''ʊp ɢʊᴅɪ'twʊ sʊ'ᴅ·ʊ ᴅɪkɪ'uᴅɪn.
    ma'ha st·ɛ'n·an ʙʊ'ɢʊlfan a'ɢ·a.
    ᴅɪ'sᴅɪᴅu'y·ɪ ɢʊ'c-wɪ'pyan.
pɛ''ma hɛ'l'wan ᴅɛma'ma ||122:15|| <13(5)>
    cʙʊ'klaɪsᴅa ʙax̣awa'ᴅas!
    tcɪ'ᴅ·ɛ·ᴅɪsᴅu'w·u ᴅɪkɪ'uᴅɪn.
    sʊ'ᴅ·ʊ ɢʊᴅ·ɪ'tɢwɪn ᴅɪkɪ'uᴅɪn,
    ɢʊt_sme'y·ɪ tcɛ'-ᴅusɪ'lhaus.

I threw the harness over the horse.
Then I hitched it to the wagon.
My mother put everything in the wagon.   <13(6)>
Then we went on.
We got to the Big River (the Willamette).
Then my father drove the horses onto the (ferry-)boat.
Then he got across.
He gave that man half a dollar.
Then we went along the road all day long.
We got to our place as the sun was going down.

ɢʊtɢu′ ᴅıtɢu′ [?] ᴅıharness tcɛᴅukı′uᴅın

pɛ″ma ɢʊtɢɛ′m·at tcɛtcı′ktcık.

ᴅɛna′na ɢʊtṗı′n ʙʊ′ɢʊlfan a′ɢfan tcɛtcı′ktcık. <13(6)>

pɛ″ma sʊ′ᴅ·ʊ ɢwıᴅıt·ı′ᴅ,

ɢʊᴅwa′l ɢʊ′s·a tcaʙa′l ama′mpɢa.

pɛ″ma ᴅɛma′ma ɢʊtɢı′sɢat ᴅıkı′uᴅın tcaɢʊ′sa-akwu′ᴅ.

pɛ″ma ɢʊᴅwa′l ᴅju′hu,

ɢʊᴅ·ı′t ɢusa-a′mu′ı k̇ʊ′ʙfan sk̇ı′nwaımax̣.

pɛ″ma ɢwıᴅıt·ı′ᴅ tcɛɢu′n ʙʊ′ɢʊlfan a′mpyan.

ɢuᴅıᴅwa′l sʊ′ᴅ·ʊ tcɛᴅ·ʊ′m·aı ɢʊᴅıᴅjˑɛ′ɢ·ʊ a′mpyan.

Daily Life on the Farm[1]

<14> Back Home on the Farm

Then everything was fine at our place. ||122:17||

  My mother made food.

  We ate.

Then she washed all the dishes.

  She fixed my bed where I was to sleep.

The next day my father went to the Indian agent. <14(2)>

Then that man says,

  "So you have come back!"

[---]

  "Yes,"

  my father replies.

Then my father said to the agent,

  "I want a hay mower."

[---]

  "Very well, you may take it whenever you want it."

My father returned home when it was midday. <14(3)>

  My mother finished the midday meal. ||122:19||

  We ate.

Then we took two horses.

  "Now we'll go hunt for our horses and our cattle."[2]

  We found our horses and two cows.

    They had calves. <14(4)>

Then we drove the two cows and four horses along.

  We got back home.

  We put those two cows in a small corral.

  We put the four horses in a large corral.

Then my mother said,

  "You all come eat!"

Then when it got dark, we went to sleep.

Early the next day my mother made food. <14(5)>

  My father got up. ||122:21||

  He went to the small corral.

  He milked those two cows.

Daily Life on the Farm

<14> Back Home on the Farm

pɛˈʼma bʊˈɢʊlfan aˈɢꞏa ɢʊtɛˈnꞏa sʊˈdꞏʊ tcetʊˈnꞏu.   ‖122:17‖

   dɛnaˈna ɢʊtbʊˈn k̓weˈɪnafʊn,

   ɢʊtk̓weˈɪnafʊ.

pɛˈʼma qɛˈdꞷꞏk ɢʊtk̓uˈʼʊ̵ bʊˈɢʊlfan akwɪˈd.

   ɢʊtɛˈnꞏan dɛweˈɪnafyak haˈlꞏaꞏɢʊˈsꞏa ɢʊdɪd-sduˈwꞏɪ.

ɢʊdɪtmeˈɪdj· dɛmaˈma ɢʊdꞏɪˈt djɛɢʊˈsꞏa umɛˈnmɪyak adjaˈm_bak.   <14(2)>

pɛˈʼma ɢʊsꞏaˈmuˈɪ uˈnaˈɢɪt,

   maˈha tcumuˈɢ

[---]

   hɛˈʼnʼaⁿ

   dɛmaˈma paˈ-umɪˈut.

pɛˈʼma dɛmaˈma ɢʊdnɪˈsꞏɪn ɢʊsa-adjaˈmbak aˈmuˈɪ,

   tcɪˈʼɪ tcɪt̓aˈmdjʊ k̓ʊˈʙyanꞏaq alʊˈq̓ʊ.

[---]

   ɢʊˈc-wɪ maˈha ɢʊdꞏɪˈtɢwɪn laˈfʊ maˈha tcɪt̓aˈmdjʊ.

dɛmaˈma ɢʊdmeˈyꞏɪ djɛhaˈmꞏɪ ɢwdɪtwɪˈlfyʊ aˈmpyan.   <14(3)>

   dɛnaˈna ɢʊt̓ʊˈɢꞏɪ wɪˈlfyuq-aˈmpyan dɪk̓weˈɪnafʊn.   ‖122:19‖

   sʊˈdꞏʊ ɢwɪdk̓weˈɪnafʊ.

pɛˈʼma ɢwɪdꞏɪˈtɢwɪn ɢɛˈm akɪˈʊdɪn.

   pɛˈʼma tcɪdʊˈʼʊ tcɪdɪt_lʊˈpɢwan sʊˈdꞏʊ dɪkɪˈʊdɪn naˈu-dɪmʊˈsmʊs.

ɢʊdꞏɛˈsdɛs sʊˈdꞏʊ dɪkɪˈʊdɪn naˈu-ɢɛˈm-amuˈsmʊs.

   ɢʊnɪp̓iˈʼn dɪˈntˈcɪt dʊˈʼwaɪ.   <14(4)>

pɛˈʼma ɢwdɪdɢɪˈcɢaꞏt ɢɛˈm-amuˈsmʊs taˈʙ-akɪˈʊdɪn.

   ɢwɪdwaˈl tcɛdɪdʊˈmꞏaɪ.

   ɢwɪdɢuˈ ɢʊsa-ɢɛˈm-amuˈsmʊs tcɛdɪˈʼdzaq aq̓aˈlax̣.

   ɢwɪtɢuˈ ɢʊˈc-ataˈʙ-akɪˈʊdɪn tcɛʙaˈl aq̓aˈlax̣.

pɛˈʼma dɛnaˈna naˈɢɪt,

   mɪˈdꞏɪ smaˈk s̓k̓weˈɪnafʊ.

pɛˈʼma ɢʊdɪthuˈwɪ ɢʊd_sduˈʼwɛɪ.

haˈlˈwan ɢʊdɪtmeˈɪdj dɛnaˈna ɢʊdbʊˈn-akweˈɪnafʊn   <14(5)>

   dɛmaˈma ɢʊdbʊˈklaɪ   ‖122:21‖

   ɢʊd_ɪˈt djɛɢʊˈsa dɪˈdzaq aq̓aˈlax̣.

   ɢʊdmɪˈlɢwaꞏt ɢʊˈsa-ɢɛˈm-amʊˈsmʊs.

Then he returned home.

My mother (said),

   "Eat now!"

Then when they finished eating, he went to get two horses.

   He placed the harness over their bodies.   <14(6)>

Then my father went to the agent.

   He went to get that hay mower.

   He came back.

   He brought that hay mower.

   He brought it to our place.

Then he cut that hay.

When it was midday, he unhitched the horses from the mower.

   He went back home.

   He fed his horses.

Then he went inside the house. ||122:23||

   He washed his face and his hands.

Then we ate.   <14(7)>

At one o'clock he went outside and got his horses.

   He went to work.

   He worked all afternoon.

When the sun was nearly down, he unhitched his horses, and he went back to the
   house.

   He loosened his harness.

   He hung it on a tree.

Then he went to the small corral.   <14(8)>

   He milked those two cows.

   He left them there, in the small corral all night.

Then he got back to the house.

   He gave the milk to my mother.

Then,

   "Now you all wash your faces and your hands! ||122:25||
   You all eat!"

Through eating, she washed all the dishes,   <14(9)>

   and I went to sleep.

   My father went outside.

      He looked after his horses.

pɛ·''ma ɢʊtme'-yɪ tcɛha'm·ɪ.

ᴅɛna'na,

　ṡkwe'ɪnafʊcᴅa.

pɛ·''ma ɢwntʊ'ɢɪ c̓kwe'ɪnafʊn ɢʊᴅɪ'twʊ ɢɛ'm akɪ'uᴅɪn

　ɢwɪtɢʊ' ᴅɛharness tcɛᴅɪᴅɪnk̓a'pya.　　　　　　　　　　　<14(6)>

pɛ·''ma ᴅɛma·'ma ɢʊᴅɪ't tcɛɢʊ's·a ᴅja'mʙɛk

　ɢʊᴅɪ'twʊ ɢʊ's·a k̓ʊ'pfanɪk lʊ'q̓u.

　ɢʊm·e'y·ɪ,

　ɢʊtk̓wɛ·'n ɢʊ'sa k̓ʊ'pfanɪk lʊ'q̓u.

　ɢʊᴅ_la'm·ɪ tcɛᴅɪᴅʊ'n·ʊ.

pɛ·''ma ɢʊtk̓ʊ'ʙ·ʊn ɢʊ's·a-alʊ'q̓ʊ.

ɢwᴅɪtwɪ'lfyʊ-a'mpyan ɢʊᴅ_ṡkwɪ''ɪl ᴅɪkɪ'uᴅɪn tcɛɢʊ'sa k̓ʊ'pfanɪk-lʊ'q̓ʊ.

　ɢʊᴅɪ'tyɪ tcɛha'm·ɪ.

　ɢʊt-ʊ'k ᴅɪkɪ'uᴅɪn

pɛ·''ma ɢʊ·'k ɢʊᴅ_sla'm·ʊ tcɛha'm·ɪ,　　　　　　　　　||122:23||

　ɢʊtk̓u''uɬ ᴅɛkwa'l·ak na'u-ᴅɪlaqʷ.

pɛ·''ma sʊ'ᴅ·ʊ ɢʊtk̓we'ɪnafʊ.　　　　　　　　　　　　14(7)

wa''an-aᴅɪ'nᴅɪn ɢʊᴅɪ't hɛ·''lʊm, ᴅɪ'tɢwɪn-ᴅɪkɪ'uᴅɪn,

　ɢʊᴅɪ't ᴅɪlu''nafʊn.

　ɢʊᴅ_lʊ''nʊf ʙʊ'ɢʊlfan aya'hampyan,

yɛ'tc-ɢwᴅɪᴅjɛ'ɢ·ʊ-a'mpyan ɢʊᴅ_ṡkwɪ'lṡkwa·t ᴅɪkɪ'uᴅɪn na'u ɢʊᴅɪ'tyɪ tcɛha'm·ɪ.

　ɢʊᴅ_ṡkwɪ'lṡkwa·t ᴅɪharness

　ɢʊᴅ_qa'l·aɬ tcɛ'wa'ᴅ·ik.

pɛ·''ma ɢʊᴅɪ't tcɛɢʊ's·a-ᴅɪ·'ᴅzaq q̓a'l·ax.　　　　　　14(8)

　ɢʊt_smɪ'lq̓ma·t ɢʊ's·a-ɢɛ'm-amʊ'smʊs.

　ɢʊ'saʙɛ·ᴅ ɢʊᴅp̓i'n ᴅjɛɢʊ's·a ᴅi·'ᴅzaq-aq̓a'l·ax ʙʊ'ɢʊlfan-awɪ'fyʊ.

pɛ·''ma ɢʊᴅwu'ɢ ᴅjɛha'm·ɪ,

　ɢʊᴅɪ'st ɢʊca-aᴅʊᴅu''c ᴅjɛᴅana'na.

pɛ·''ma

　mɪ'ᴅɪ ṡku''uɬ ᴅɪkwa'l·ak ᴅɪ'la'qʷ.　　　　　　　　||122:25||

　mɪ'ᴅɪ ʙʊck̓we'ɪnafu.

ɢʊt·ʊɢɪ ᴅɪck̓we'ɪnafʊ qɛ'ᴅ·ak ɢʊtk̓u''ʊɬ ʙʊ'ɢʊlfan ɢʊca-akwɪ'ᴅ.　　<14(9)>

　nau tcɪ''ɪ ɢʊᴅɪ'twei.

　ᴅɛma·'ma ɢʊᴅɪ't hɛ·''lʊm

　　ɢʊᴅ_lu'ᴅnikwaɪ ᴅɪkɪ'uᴅɪn

Then he came back.

    He went to lie down.

When it was early morning my father arose.

    He went outside.

    He fed his horses.

    He went to the little corral.

    He milked the cows.

Then he came back to the house.   <14(10)>

    He washed his face and his hands.

Then my mother said,

    "Bahawadas, get up!

    Don't sleep all day!"

[---]

    "Oh," ||122:27||

my father said,

    "Never mind! Let him sleep!

    Whenever he wants to get up, he can get up."

    I rolled over (and) I went back to sleep.   <14(11)>

The sun was high in the sky.

    I got up.

    I washed my face and my hands.

    I ate.

I said to my mother,

    "Where is my father?"

[---]

    "Your father is working.

    Your [Tualatin shows "my"] *father isn't here."*

Then,

    "Maybe he took the hay mower back to where he got it."

    My father came back.   <14(12)>

      He brought something that he might pile up hay (with).

Then two of my mother's brothers arrived at the house.

    My mother prepared food. ||122:29||

Then my father got back to the house.

    He put away his horses.

    He fed them water and he fed them hay.

pɛ·''ma ɢʊtme·'y·ɪ
  ɢɶ·'k ɢʊdɪ'twɪ
me'ɪdj ɢʊtha'l'wan dɛma·'ma ɢʊtbʊ'klaɪ,
  ɢʊdɪ't hɛ·''lʊm,
  ɢʊd'ʊ'k dɪkɪ'ʊdɪn,
  ɢʊdɪ't dje-dɪ·'dzaq aq̇a'laẋ,
  ɢʊd_smɪ'lk̇wa·t ɢʊ'ca-amʊ'smʊs.
pɛ·''ma ɢʊdma·''a djɛha'm·ɪ.   \<14(10)>
  ɢʊtk̇u''ʊł dɛkwa'l·ak dɛl·a'qʷ.
pɛ·''ma dɛna·'na ɢʊdna'ɢɪt,
  ʙaẋawa'das cʙʊ'klaɪsdʌ
  wa'ŋq dɛtwe'ɪdɪt ʙʊ'ɢʊlfan a'mpyan.
[---]
  u' ||122:27||
dɛma·'ma na'ɢɪt,
  pɛ'caksɪ'ut ɢʊtwe'ɪdɪt.
  lʊ'fʊ ɢɶ·'k ɢʊmṫa'mdju dʊmbʊ'klaɪ, ɢɶ·'k ɢʊdbʊ'klaɪ.
  tcɪ''ɪ ɢʊdbɪ'lk̇wɪ· ɢʊtɢʊ'mweɪ.   \<14(11)>
ha'lʙam a'mpyan ɢʊd·a·'ʙɪt.
  tcɪ''ɪ ɢʊdbʊ'klaɪ
  ɢʊtk̇u''ʊł dɛkwa'l·ak dɪ'la'qʷ.
  ɢʊtk̇we'ɪnafʊ.
tcɪ''ɪ ɢʊdnɪ'c·ɪn dɛna·'na,
  ha'l·a dama·'ma
[---]
  ʙʊma·'ma ʊmlu·''nafʊn
  wa'ha dama·'ma ɢʊ'caʙɛ'd.
pɛ·''ma
  e'ɪkɪn ɢʊdɪ'tk̇u ɢʊ'c·a k̇ʊ'pfyana'q lʊ'q̇u tcɛha'l·a ɢʊdɪdɪ'tɢwɪn.
  dama·'ma ɢʊd_sme'y·ɪ,   \<14(12)>
    ɢʊd_sk̇wɛ'n a'ɢ·a ɢʊ'c·a ɢʊd_la'l·ɪnfʊ lʊ'q̇u.
pɛ·''ma ɢɛ·'m dɛna·'na dɪʙɪ'kwakyap ɢʊnɪwa'l djɛha'm·ɪ
  dɛna·'na ɢʊdbʊ'n-akwe'ɪnafʊn. ||122:29||
pɛ·''ma tcɪ''ɪ dama·'ma ɢʊtmu'ɢ djɛha'm·ɪ.
  ɢʊt_lʊ''ʊn dɪkɪ'ʊdɪn
  ɢʊt'ʊ'k ma'mpɢa na'u-ɢʊt'ʊ'k lʊ'q̇u.

He entered the house.   <14(13)>
He shook hands with his brothers-in-law.[3]
Then they all washed their faces and their hands.
Then they ate.
Finished with their meal, they sat a little while.
   They talked about all sorts of things.
Then when they finished their talking, they went outside.
   My father took his horses.   <14(14)>
   He went to work.
One of those uncles of mine speaks to me like this,
   "Where are those pitchforks?"
[---]
   "Huu, I don't think I know." ||122:31||
[---]
   "Oh, you do too know!
   Go get them!"
Then I went.
   I found those pitchforks.
   I took three, two for my uncles.
      I took one.   <14(15)>
Then we piled up that hay.
   We did not finish piling up the hay that afternoon.
When the sun was nearly down, we all went to the house.
Then my mother said,
   "Wash your faces and your hands!
   Come and eat!"
   They finished (that).
Then when they finished their meal, those uncles of mine went back to their
   home.   <14(16)>
   "Come tomorrow we will return," ||122:33||
   he told my father.
My father said,
   "Alright."
Then my father went out.
   He milked the cows.
Then he gave water to the horses.

ɢʊt_la′m·ʊ ᴅjɛha′m·ɪ   <14(13)>
   ɢʊᴅ·ɪ′st ᴅɪ′la′qʷ tcɛᴅɪʙɪ′kwaɢyap.
pɛ·″ma ʙʊ′ɢʊlfan ɢʊᴅɪnɪku″ʊɬ ᴅɪnɪkwa′l·ak ᴅɪn·ɪ′la′qʷ.
pɛ·″ma ɢwɪᴅɪnɪkwe′ɪnafʊ.
tʊ′ɢ·ɪ-ᴅɪnɪkwe′ɪnafʊn ɢʊᴅ·ɪnɪsɪ′y·ʊ pʊ′t'cnaq.
   ɢɪ′n·ʊk ɢʊᴅɪnɪfa·′l ʙʊ′ɢʊlfan a′ɢ·a.
pɛ·″ma ɢʊᴅɪnɪtʊ′ɢ·ɪ ᴅɪn·ɪfa·′l ɢʊnɪ·ᴅɪ′t hɛ·″lʊm.
   ᴅɛma′ma ɢʊᴅ·ɪ′tku ᴅɪkɪ′ʊᴅɪn   <14(14)>
   ɢʊᴅ_lu″nafʊ.
wa″an ɢʊ′ca-ᴅɛsɪ·″muɪ pa″u′na′ɢɪt tcɛtcɪ·″ɪ,
   ha′l·a ɢʊ′sa fa′lqfya·t.
[---]
   hu′ e′ɪkɪn wa′ŋq tcɪ·″ɪ-ɢɪ′yʊ′ɢ·ʊn.   ‖122:31‖
[--]
   u′ ma′ha-tcɪ′yʊ′ɢ·ʊn
   ᴅja′k-cᴅjɪ′w·u.
pɛ·″ma tcɪ·″ɪ-ɢʊᴅ·ɪ′t
   ɢʊᴅ·ɛ′sᴅɛs ɢʊ′s·a fa′lqfʊnfaɪ.
   hu′psɪn ɢʊᴅ_ɪ′tku ɢɛ·′m tcɛᴅɪcɪ·″muɪ,
      tcɪ·″ɪ-ɢʊᴅ·ɪ′tku wa″an.   <14(15)>
pɛ·″ma sʊ′ᴅ·ʊ ɢʊtɢe′ɪ′wʊt ɢʊ′s·a alʊ′q̣ʊ
   wa′ŋq ɢʊᴅ·ɪtʊ′ɢ·ɪ ɢʊmɢe′ɪ′wʊt. ɢʊ′s·a-alʊ′q̣ʊ ɢʊ′sa-weɪ_ya′hampyan
yɛ′ts-ɢʊᴅɪᴅje′ɢ·ʊ a′mpyan ʙʊ′ɢʊlfan sʊ′ᴅ·ʊ ɢwɪᴅɪᴅɪ′t tcɛha′m·ɪ.
pɛ·″ma ᴅɛna′na na′ɢɪt
   cku″ʊɬ mɪ′ᴅ·ɪ ᴅɪkwa′l·ak ᴅɪ′la′qʷ.
   tcɪ′ᴅ·a ᴅɪskwe′ɪnafʊ.
   ɢwɪnɪtʊ′ɢ·ɪ,
pɛ·″ma ɢʊnɪtʊ′ɢ·ɪ ᴅɪnɪkwe′ɪnafʊn ɢʊ′c·a ᴅɛcɪ·″muɪ ɢʊnɪᴅɪ′tyɪ ᴅjɛnɪᴅʊ′m·aɪ
                                                              <14(16)>
   ɢʊmame′ɪᴅj sʊ′ᴅ·ʊ ᴅɪtma″a   ‖122:33‖
   ɢω′k-nɪ′c·ɪn ᴅɛma′ma.
ᴅɛma′ma ɢʊᴅna′ɢɪt
   ɢʊ′c-wɪ.
pɛ·″ma ᴅɛma′ma ɢʊᴅ·ɪ′t
   ɢʊᴅ_smɪ′lqwa·t ɢʊ′ca-amu′smus.
pɛ·″ma ɢʊᴅ_ɪ′st ma′mpɢa tcɛᴅɪkɪ′ʊᴅɪn

He fed them hay.
　I went to sleep.
My mother said,   <14(17)>
　　"*I am going to wash everything up now.*"
　My father came back.
He entered the house,
　"*Where's my boy?*"
[---]
　"*Oh, he went to sleep!*"
[---]
　"*Alright, I want to go to sleep too.*"
　My mother finished all of her work.
　　　She, too, went to sleep.

<15> Bahawadas Rides the Calf
Early the next day she arose.
　She prepared food.
My father went to look after his horses.
　He milked the cows.
Then we ate. ||122:35||
When we had finished our meal, my father speaks like this to me,
　"*You go put the cow outside the small corral.*"
　I went and put the big cow outside.   <15(2)>
　I found a rope in that small corral.
　　I took that rope.
　　I lassoed one of the calves.
Then I tied the rope and that calf to a tree.
Then I climbed on top of that calf.
Then that calf leaped up.
Then I fell off.   <15(3)>
Then I rode him a second time. ||122:37||
　That calf leaped.
　Five times it leaped.
Then it bawled.
Then the big cow came on a run towards the small corral.
Then my mother came up over the hill,   <15(4)>
　"*Bahawadas, what are you doing to that calf?*

ɢʊt'ʊ'k a'lʊ'q̇u
tcɪ''ɪ ɢʊDɪʹtweɪ.
Dena'na ɢʊDna'ɢɪt,   <14(17)>
  Bʊ'ɢʊlfan-a'ɢ·a tcɪ''ɪ Dɪ's-Detku''uł.
  Dema'ma ɢʊDme'y·ɪ
ɢʊDla'm·ʊ DJɛha'm·ɪ,
  ha'l·a-Da''ʊp!
[---]
  u' ɢʊDɪʹtweɪ!
[---]
  ɢʊ'c-wɪ· tcɪ''ɪ-yu· tcɛta'mDJɪ-Dʊmɢʊʹmweɪ.
  Dena'na ɢʊt'ʊ'ɢɪ Bʊ'ɢʊlfan Dɪ'lu''nafʊn
    ɢ̇ɛ'D·ak yu·' ɢɪDɪʹtweɪ.

<15> _baẋawádas_ Rides the Calf
hɛ'l'wan ɢʊDɪtme'ɪDJ ɢ̇ɛ'D·ak ɢʊDBʊ'klaɪ
  ɢʊDBʊ'n ak̇we'ɪnafʊn.
Dema'ma ɢʊDɪ't lu'DnɪɢwaɪDɪkɪ'uDɪn.
  ɢʊD_smɪ'lqwa·t amʊ'smʊs.
pɛ·''ma sʊ'D·ʊ ɢwiDɪtk̇we'ɪnafʊ. ||122:35||
ɢʊDɪt'ʊ'ɢɪ Dɪk̇we'ɪnafʊ Dema'ma pa''-una'ɢɪt tcɛtcɪ''ɪ
  ma'ha Detɢu·' hɛ·''lʊm ɢʊ'ca-amu'smus ɢʊ'caweɪ-Dɪʹtsaq aq̇a'l·aẋ.
  tcɪ''ɪ ɢʊDɪ't ɢu'-hɛ·''lʊm ɢʊ'ca-waBa'l-amu'smus.   <15(2)>
  tcɪ''ɪ ɢʊDɛ'cDɛc a'mt'sal tcɛɢʊ's·a-Dɪʹt'saq aq̇a'l·aẋ.
    tcɪ''ɪ ɢʊDɪ'tɢwɪn ɢʊca-a'mt'sal
    ɢʊtyʊ'Gla·t wa''an ɢʊ'caweɪ-Dɪʹt'saq amu'smus.
pɛ·''ma tcɪ''ɪ ɢut·a'ẋDa·t ɢʊ'sa-a'mt'sal na'u ɢʊ'sawɪ-Dɪʹt'saq amu'smus tcɛ'wa'D·ɪk.
pɛ·''ma tcɪ''ɪ ɢʊD_sa'mfnakwɪt ɢʊ'sa waDɪ't'saq amu'smus.
pɛ·''ma ɢʊ's·a-Dɪʹt'saq amu'smʊs ɢʊt·ɪ'D·ʊp
pɛ·''ma tcɪ''ɪ ɢʊDJɛ'ɢ·ʊ.   <15(3)>
pɛ·''ma ɢʊD_sa'mfnakwɪt ɢɛ'f·ʊ. ||122:37||
  ɢʊ'sa-aDɪ·'t'saq-amu'smus ɢʊD·ɪ'D·ʊp
  wa'nf·ʊ ɢʊD·ɪ'D·ʊp
pɛ·''ma ɢut·a·'ẋDɪt
pɛ·''ma ɢʊ'ca-aBa'l amʊ'cmʊc ɢʊmamɪ'nDJɪc tcɛɢʊ'ca aDɪ·'t'saq aq̇a'l·aẋ.
pɛ·''ma Dena'na ɢʊm·ɛ'B·af.   <15(4)>
  Baẋawa'Das a'ɢ·a-ma'ha tcɪmɪ'u'nan tcɛɢʊ's·a Dɪ·'t'saq-am'ʊcmʊc!

Untie that rope!"
I untied the rope.
    I threw it down on the ground.
[---]
  "Come back to the house!"
I was afraid of my mother,
  "Don't whip me, mother!   <15(5)>
  I was just playing with that calf."
[---]
  "Then you go to where those uncles of yours are working." ||122:39||
  I went there.
    I worked.
Then when it was nearly midday, we finished our work.
Then we went back to the house.
  We washed our faces and our hands.   <15(6)>
[---]
  "Now you all eat!"
When we finished our meal, my uncles went back to their home.
My father said as follows,
  "On the sixth day (Saturday?) *then we'll haul the hay to the barn."*
[---]
  "Alright,"
  said the uncles.
[---]
  "You bring your horse and your wagon!"   <15(7)>
During those five days we did nothing.
  Me alone, I took the five horses to water[4] twice each day.
  That was my kind of work each day of those five days. ||122:41||

<16> A Sunday Afternoon
Then when it dawned on the Lord's Day (Sunday), we got ourselves ready.
  We went to the House of the Lord (St. Michael's Catholic church, Grand Ronde).[5]
  There many people came.
  The priest rang his bell.
Then all the people entered the church.
  There they said prayers.   <16(2)>
Then at nearly midday they finished their prayers.

sɪˈkwɪlt ɢʊˈs·a-aˈmtˈsal.

tcɪˈˈɪ ɢʊᴅ_sɪˈkwɪlt ɢʊˈs·a-aˈm·tˈcal.

ɢʊtɢʊˈ tcɛhaˈŋkluˈp.

[---]

cmeˈyɪ ᴅjɛhaˈm·ɪ!

tcɪˈˈɪ ɢʊᴅnɪˈuhɪn ᴅɛnaˈˈna.

waˈŋq maˈha ᴅamᴅaˈn·aɪf! naˈˈna!　　　　　　　　　　<15(5)>

k̓ʊˈnfu· [q̓ʊnfu·] tcɪˈˈɪ ɢʊᴅ_laˈɢ·ɪt tcɛɢʊˈs·a-ᴅɪˈtˈsaq amʊˈcmʊc.

[---]

pɛˈˈma maˈha ctcaˈk tcɛhaˈl·a ɢʊˈc·a ᴅɛsɪˈˈmuɪ ᴅɪˈluˈˈnafʊn.　　||122:39||

tcɪˈˈɪ ɢʊᴅ·ɪˈt ɢʊˈsaᴅɛ·ᴅ.

ɢʊt_luˈˈnʊf.

pɛˈˈma yɛˈts ɢwɪᴅɪtwɪˈlfu-aˈmpyan ɢuᴅɪt·ʊˈɢ·ɪ ᴅɪluˈnafʊn,

pɛˈˈma sʊˈᴅ·ʊ ɢʊᴅ·ɪˈtyɪ tcɛhaˈm·ɪ,

ɢʊᴅɪtkʊˈˈʊɬ ᴅɛkwaˈl·ak-ᴅɪlaˈqw.　　　　　　　　　<15(6)>

[---]

tcɪˈᴅ·ɛ-mɪˈᴅ·ɪ ʙʊc̓kweˈɪnafun.

ɢʊᴅɪt·ʊˈɢ·ɪ ᴅɪkweˈɪnafʊn ᴅɪsɪˈˈmuɪ ɢʊᴅɪnɪᴅɪˈtyɪ tcɛɢɪˈn·ʊk nɪᴅʊˈm·aɪ

ᴅɛmaˈˈma paˈˈ-ɢʊᴅnɪˈc·ɪn,

ɢʊmɪᴅaˈf-aˈmpyan pɛˈˈma ɢʊᴅɪᴅwaˈt ɢʊˈc·aluˈq̓u tcaˈlʊˈq̓w-ᴅʊˈm·aɪ.

[---]

ɢʊˈcwɪ

ɢʊmˈnaˈɢɪt si·ˈˈmuɪ.

[---]

mɪˈᴅ·ɪ ᴅɪsmʊˈkʊ ʙɪkɪˈuᴅan naˈu-ʙɪtcɪˈktcɪk.　　　　　<15(7)>

ɢʊˈs·a-wɪ huˈwan-aˈmpyan waˈŋq aˈɢ·a sʊˈᴅ·ʊ ɢʊᴅɪᴅʙʊˈnhɪn.

yɛˈlfan tcɪˈˈɪ ɢʊᴅɪˈtku ᴅɪhuˈw·an ᴅɪkɪˈuᴅɪn tcɛmaˈmpɢa ɢɛˈf·ʊ waˈˈan-aˈmpyan.

pɛˈc·a·ˈwɛˈw tcɪˈˈɪ ᴅɛluˈˈnafʊn ʙʊˈɢʊlfan aˈmpyan ɢʊˈc·a huˈwan aˈmpyan. ||122:41||

<16> A Sunday Afternoon

pɛˈˈma ɢʊᴅɪtmeˈɪᴅj ɢʊˈc·a ahaˈlʙam ᴅjaˈmʙak ᴅɪˈaˈmpyan, sʊˈᴅ·ʊ ɢʊᴅ_suˈˈyɛtcwuˈn

ɢʊᴅ·ɪᴅɪˈt tcɛhɛˈs·a haˈlʙam ᴅjaˈmʙak ᴅʊˈm·aɪ.

ɢʊˈs·aʙ·ɛ·ᴅ haˈl·u· aˈm·ɪm ɢʊn·ɪwaˈl.

ɢʊˈs·a-atɛˈn·a aˈmuˈɪ ɢʊtʙʊˈn ᴅɪᴅɪˈnᴅɪn.

pɛˈˈma ʙʊˈɢʊlfan aˈm·ɪm ɢʊᴅɪnɪlaˈm·ʊ tcɛɢʊˈc·a-atɛˈn·a haˈm·ɪ.

ɢʊˈs·aʙɛˈ·ᴅ ɢʊᴅɪnɪnɪˈc·ɪn tɛˈn·a-haˈmha.　　　　　<16(2)>

pɛˈˈma yɛˈtc wɪˈlfu-aˈmpyan ɢʊᴅ·ɪnɪtʊˈɢ·ɪ ᴅɪnɪtɛˈn·a-haˈmha.

Then we went back, back to the house. ||122:43||

I went outside,

"Oh! Mother! Lots of people are on the way coming this way."

Then my mother replies like so, <16(3)>

"Never mind.

Those are our relatives who are coming."

Then my mother made all sorts of food.

Part of those people brought camas roots[6], cat-ear lily roots, blackberries, tarweed seeds.[7]

They gave them to my mother.

Then my mother finished with all the food.

She speaks like so to those people, <16(4)>

"All of you come in! Eat!"

Then all those people entered.

They sat down.

They ate.

When they finished their meal, they went outside, ||122:45||

and I and my mother ate.

When we finished eating, four girls came into the house.

They cleared up all the dishes.

Then they washed them.

When they finished, we were all going to go where they were going to play shinny. <16(5)>

At that place were many, of all kinds[8] of Indians.

They played games.

One tribe played the hand game.

Another tribe played the nahf (guessing) game.

Another tribe played shinny.

There they played that afternoon. <16(6)>

Then everyone went back to their own homes when it was nearly sundown. ||122:47||

We went back to our home.

Then when it is nearly dark,

"Take the horses to water!"

I got all five of the horses.

I took them to the water.

When I came back my father fixed hay for the horses.

pɛ''ma sʊ'ᴅ·ʊ ɢʊᴅɪᴅɪ'tyɪ ᴅɪ'twʊk tcɛha'm·ɪ. ||122:43||

tcɪ''ɪ ɢʊᴅɪ't hɛ''lʊm.

    hu·' na'na! ha'l·u a'm·ɪm ɢu''ʊm nɪtc'i''f.

pɛ''ma ᴅɛna'na pɛ'c-um·ɪ'ut   <16(3)>

    wa'ŋq a'ɢ·a.

ɢʊ'c·a sʊ'ᴅ·ʊ tʊ'm·ɪm ɢʊca-nɪtc'i''f.

pɛ''ma ᴅɛna'na ɢʊtbʊ'n ʙʊ'ɢʊlfan ha'w·ɛw akwe'ɪnafu'nak.

    kʊ'ʙfan ɢʊ's·a-a'm·ɪm ɢɪnɪsma'kwa am·a'm·ɪc, aᴅza·'ts, a'a'ntkwɪl, ac·a''wal,

    ɢʊnɪᴅɪ'st tcɛᴅana'na.

pɛ''ma ᴅana'na ɢʊtʊ'ɢ·ɪ ʙʊ'ɢʊlfan akwe'ɪnafun'yak

pa'-uknɪ'c·ɪn tcɛɢʊ's·a a'm·ɪm,   <16(4)>

    mɪ'ᴅ·ɪ psla'm·ʊ ʙɪskwe'ɪnafʊ.

pɛ''ma ʙʊ'ɢʊlfan ɢʊ'sa-a'm·ɪm ɢɪnɪsla'm·ʊ

    ɢɪnɪsɪ'y·ʊ

    ɢɪnɪkwe'ɪnafʊn.

ɢʊᴅɪnɪtʊ'ɢ·ɪ ᴅɪnɪkwe'ɪnafʊn ɢɪnɪᴅɪ't hɛ''lʊm. ||122:45||

    nautcɪ''ɪ nauᴅɛna'na ɢʊᴅkwe'ɪnafʊ.

ɢʊtʊ'ɢ·ɪ ᴅɪkwe'ɪnafʊn ta'ʙaʙɪna'tst ɢʊn·ɪt_sla'm·ʊ tcɛha'm·ɪ,

    ɢʊn·ɪt_skwɪlskwa·t ʙʊ'ɢʊlfan ɢʊca-ama'l·ax̣

pɛ''ma ɢɪ'n·ʊk ɢʊᴅɪnɪku''uł

ɢʊᴅɪnɪtʊ'ɢ·ɪ ʙʊ'ɢʊlfan sʊ'ᴅ·ʊ tcɪᴅɪt_sᴅʊ''ʊ tcɛɢʊ's·aʙɛ·ᴅ ha'l·a. ᴅɪnɪla'k·wɪt ᴅɪska'lɢal.

                                             <16(5)>

    ɢʊ'c·aʙɛ·ᴅ hu'l·u· ʙʊ'ɢʊlfan a''wɛw amɛ·'nmɪ.

        ɢʊn·ɪla'kwɪt.

    wa''an aɢɛw'wakɪl ɢʊn·ɪla'kwɪt asma'l·a,

    wa''an aɢɛ'wʊkɪl ɢʊn·ɪla'ɢ·ʊt ana·'f

    wa''an aɢɛ'wʊkɪl ɢʊnɪla'k·wɪt aska'lkal.

    ɢʊ'saʙɛ·ᴅ ɢʊn·ɪla'k·wɪt ɢʊ's·a-wɪ·-ya'mpyan.   <16(6)>

pɛ''ma ʙʊ'ɢʊlfan-ɪ'y·a ɢʊᴅɪnɪᴅɪ'tyɪ tcɛ'ᴅɪnɪᴅʊ'm·aɪ yɛ'tc-ɢʊᴅjɛ'ɢ·ʊ-a'mpyan. ||122:47||

    sa'ᴅ·ʊ ɢwɪᴅ·ɪ'tyɪ tcɛᴅɪᴅʊ'm·aɪ.

pɛ''ma yɛ'tc-ʊmhu·'wɪ,

    sᴅɪ'ᴅku ɢʊca-akɪ'uᴅɪn tcɛma'mpɢa.

    tcɪ''ɪ ɢʊᴅɪ'tɢwɪn ʙʊ'ɢʊlfan hu'w·an ɢʊ'ca-akɪ'uᴅɪn,

        ɢʊᴅɪ'tkʊ ɢʊca-ama'mpɢa.

tcɪ''ɪ ɢʊᴅɪtme'y·ɪ ᴅɛma'ma ɢʊᴅ_su''wu·n al·u'q̣u ᴅjɛhɛ'sa-akɪ'uᴅɪn.

He finished milking the cows.

He cut up a lot of (fire-)wood. <16(7)>

Then my mother says,

"*You come eat!*

We are going to eat!"

When finished eating, my mother said,

"*I want to go to bed.*

Go to sleep if you want to. ||122:49||

We will be asleep pretty soon, for sure."

<17> Uncles Help with Hay

Early next day they arose.

My mother prepared food early.

My uncles came early.

They fed their horses hay.

My mother called out,

"*You come to the house!*

Get ready so you can eat soon!" <17(2)>

My uncles washed their faces and their hands.

My father washed his face and his hands.

My mother said,

"*You sit down and eat!*"

When they finished their meal, they went and got their horses.

They went to haul hay with two wagons. ||122:51||

They loaded up one of the wagons. <17(3)>

When they finished loading that wagon, then they loaded my uncle's wagon.

They took it to the hay barn.

They unloaded one wagon.

When they finished that wagon, they took the uncle's wagon.

Then they went out to the hay field.

Then they loaded the second wagon.

At nearly midday my mother says this to me, <17(4)>

"*Go tell your father it is almost midday!*"

My father said,

"*Very well, my son.*

We will unhitch the horses from this wagon." ||122:53||

Then they took their horses.

ɢⱳ′ɢʊtʊ′ɢɪ amɪ′lɋwaˑn tcɛɢʊ′ca-amʊ′smʊs.
ɢʊtkʊ′ʙɢaˑt haˈlˑ·ɪu a′wa′ɒɪk.   <16(7)>
pɛˑ′′ma ɒɛna′na uˑ′na′ɢɪt
    mɪ′ɒɪ smaˑ′k ɒɪk̇we′ɪnafʊn.
    sʊ′ɒˑʊ ɢʊtk̇we′ɪnafʊ.
ɒɪtʊ′ɢɪ ɒɪk̇we′ɪnafʊn ɢʊɒnɪ′sˑɪn ɒɛna′na,
    tcɪˑ′ɪ tˑcɪṫa′mɒju ɒʊmɢʊ′mwaɪ
    ɒja′k-cɪ′′weɪ ma′ha-ɒʊmṫa′mɒju. ||122:49||
    pa′c-nuˑc sʊ′ɒˑʊ ɒɪɒ_cɪ′w·eɪ.

<17> Uncles Help with Hay

me′ɪɒj-ɢʊmha′l′wan ɢʊɒɪnɪɒʙʊ′klaɪ.
    ɒɛna′na ɢʊɒʙʊ′n ak̇we′ɪnafʊn hɛ′l′wan.
    ɒasɪˑ′′muɪ ɢʊɒnɪwa′l hɛ′l′wan.
        ɢʊɒɪnɪṫʊ′ɢ lʊ′ɋu ɒɪnkɪ′uɒɪn
ɒɛna′na ɢʊɒ_la′l′waɪ,
    mɪ′ɒɪ sma′hak ɒjɛha′m·ɪ.
    su′′yatswuˑn tcɪ′ɒˑa pa′c-nuˑc ɢɪɒɪpk̇we′ɪnafʊ.   <17(2)>
    ɒɛsɪˑ′′muɪ ɢʊɒɪnɪku′′uɬ ɒɪnɪkwa′l·ak na′u-ɒɪnɪla′qʷ.
    ɒɛma′′ma ɢʊɒku′′uɬ ɒɪkwa′l·ak na′u-ɒɪ′la′qʷ.
ɒɛna′na ɢʊɒna′ɢɪt,
    mɪ′ɒɪ sɪ′y·u k̇we′ɪnafʊ.
ɢɪnɪṫʊ′ɢɪ ɒɪnk̇we′ɪnafʊ ɢʊnɪɒɪ′tɢwɪn ɒɪnkɪ′uɒɪn,
    ɢʊnɪɒɪ′ɒ ɒʊmwʊ′twaˑt a′lʊ′ɋu. tcɛɢɛˑ′m-atcɪ′ktcɪk. ||122:51||
    ɢʊnɪlʊ′fʊt wa′′an-atcɪ′ktcɪk.   <17(3)>
ɢɪnɪṫʊ′ɢɪ ɒʊmlʊ′fuˑt ɢʊ′ca-atcɪ′ktcɪk. pɛˑ′′ma ɢʊnɪlʊ′fuˑt ɢʊ′ca-ɒasɪˑ′′muɪ ɒɪtcɪ′ktcɪk.
    ɢʊnɪɒɪ′tk̇u tcɛ-lʊ′ɋu ɒʊ′m·aɪ.
    ɢʊnɪtɢuˑ′′wal [ɢʊmtɢuˑ′′wal] wa′′an-atcɪ′ktcɪk.
ɢʊnɪṫʊ′ɢɪ ɢʊ′ca-atcɪ′ktcɪk ɢʊnɪɒɪ′tk̇u asɪˑ′′muɪ ɒɪtcɪ′ktcɪk.
pɛˑ′′ma ɢʊɒɪnɪtiˑ′ɒ ɢusa-tcɛlʊ′ɋu amɛ′w·a.
pɛˑ′′ma ɢʊnɪlʊ′fʊt ɢʊ′ca-aɢɛˑ′m-atcɪ′ktcɪk.
yɛ′tc-wɪ′lfʊ-a′mpyan ɒɛna′na pa′-uˑnɪ′tsfan   <17(4)>
    ɒja′kcnɪ′cˑɪn ʙʊma′′ma yɛ′tc umwɪ′lfʊ-a′mpyan.
ɒama′′ma umna′ɢɪt
    ɢʊ′cwɪ ɒaˑ′′ʊp
    tcɪɒɪck̇wɪ′lakwaˑt kɪ′uɒɪn tcɛ-hɛ′ca-atcɪ′ktcɪk. ||122:53||
pɛˑ′′ma ɢɪ′n·ʊk ɢɪnɪɒɪ′tk̇u ɒɪnkɪ′uɒɪn

They gave them water and hay. <17(5)>
Then when they went inside the house, they washed themselves.
Then they ate.
At one o'clock they went to their work.
   They worked all afternoon.
At nearly sundown they quit their work.
   They unhitched their horses.
   They put them into the barn.
   They fed their horses. <17(6)>
Then they went into the house.
   They washed up.
Finished with their washing up, my mother says,
   "You all go ahead and eat!" ||122:55||
When they finished their meal, my uncle says,
   "We are going to go back home."
[---]
   "Why would that be?"
[---]
   "Oh,"
one of my uncles says,
   "Our horses are staked out on the prairie." <17(7)>
My mother says,
   "Alright."
Then we went to sleep.
Early the next morning my mother got up.
   She prepared food.
In the early morning my uncles got there.
   My father had already fed their horses and his own horse. <17(8)>
Then they washed up.
When they finished their washing, then they ate.
When finished with their meal, they went outside to their horses.
   They threw the harnesses on their horses' bodies.
Then they went to work hauling hay.
   They worked all that forenoon. ||122:57|| <17(9)>
When it was nearly midday, they finished all that hay.
   They unharnessed their horses.

ɢʊnɪdɪ't ma'mpɢa na'u-lʊ'qu. <17(5)>

pɛ·''ma ɢɪ'nu'k ɢʊdɪnɪla'mʊ tcɛha'mɪ ɢʊn·ɪku'lɪtswu·n.

pɛ·''ma ɢudɪnɪkwe'ɪnafʊ.

ɢʊtwa''na-dɪ'ndɪn ɢɪ'n·ʊ'k ɢɪnɪdɪ't dɪnɪlu'nafʊn.

  ɢɪnɪlu'nafʊn ʙʊ'ɢʊlfan-aya''hampyan

yɛ'tc ɢʊdjɛ'ɢ·u-a'mpyan ɢɪ'n·ʊ'k ɢʊnɪpa'clu· dɪnɪlu'nafʊn

  ɢʊnɪckwɪ'lckwa·t dɪnɪkɪ'udɪn

  ɢʊnɪt_lu''un tcɛlʊ'qu-ha'm·ɪ.

  ɢʊdɪnɪ'ʊ'k dɪnɪkɪ'udɪn. <17(6)>

pɛ·''ma ɢʊdɪnɪt_la'mʊ tcɛha'mɪ,

  ɢʊdɪnɪtku''uł.

tʊ'ɢ·ɪ-dɪnɪku''uł dɛna''na na'ɢɪt

  tcɪ'd·a mɪ'dɪ pckwe'ɪnafʊ. ||122:55||

ɢɪdɪnɪtʊ'ɢ·ɪ dɪnɪkwe'ɪnafʊn dɛsi·''muɪ na'ɢɪt,

  sʊ'd·ʊ tcɪd·ʊ'ɪhɪ.

[---]

  tcɛ-a'ɢ·a-nʊ'f·an.

[---]

  u·'

wa''an dɛsi·''mui u'na'ɢɪt,

  sʊ'd·ʊ dɪkɪ'udɪn ɛ'mɪtcɪ djɛhɛ'l'yu. <17(7)>

dɛna''na pa''-umɪ'ut

  ɢʊ'cwɪ.

pɛ·''ma sʊ'd·ʊ ɢʊd·ɪ'twɪ·.

mɛ'ɪdj ɢamɪtha'l'wan dɛna''na ɢʊtʙʊ'klaɪ

  ɢʊʙʊ'n-akwe'ɪnafʊn

ha'l'wa·n dɛsi·''muɪ ɢʊnwa'l.

  dɛma''ma dɪ'l·aq ɢʊd·ʊ'k·ɪn ɢɪ'n·ʊk dɪnɪkɪ'udɪn na'u-ɢⱷ'k dɪkɪ'udɪn. <17(8)>

pɛ·''ma ɢɪ'n·ʊk ɢɪnɪku''uł,

ɢɪnɪtʊ'ɢ·ɪ dɪnɪku''uł, pɛ·''ma ɢɪnɪtkwe'ɪnafʊn.

tʊ'ɢ·ɪ-dɪnɪkwe'ɪnafʊn ɢʊnɪdɪ't-hɛ·''lʊm tcɛ·-dɪnɪkɪ'udɪn.

  ɢu·'-harness tcɛn·ɪkɪ'udɪn dɪnɪka'pya.

pɛ·''ma ɢɪ'n·ʊk ɢɪn·ɪdɪ't dɪlu'nafʊn wʊ'twat dɪlʊ'qu.

  ɢɪnlu'nafʊn ʙʊ'ɢʊlfan ɢʊ'ca-weɪ-hɛ'l'wan ||122:57|| <17(9)>

yɛ'ts ɢʊ'dɪtwɪ'lfʊ-a'mpyan ɢʊnɪtʊ'ɢ·ɪ ʙʊ'ɢʊlfan ɢʊ'sa-alʊ'qu.

  ɢʊnɪskwɪ'lskwa·t dɪkɪ'udɪn,

They fed their horses.

Then they made themselves ready to eat.

    They ate.

When finished with their meal, they went back home.

<18> Father Reaps Wheat

Then my father went to get a wheat reaper.

Then he got that reaper.

    He brought it to our place.

Then he got four young men.

    One young man drove that wheat reaper.

    Four went behind.

      They bound the wheat.

    The four young men stood at each corner.[9]

Then they followed that wheat reaper. ||122:59|| <18(2)>

    Maybe thirty acres they worked.

In four days then they finished.

Then they piled (shocked) the wheat.

When they were all done, then my father paid them.

ɢʊnɪtʊ′ç ᴅɪnɪkɪ′uᴅɪn.

pɛ·″ma ɢɪnɪtɛ′n·ɪtcwu·n ᴅʊmɪnɪsk̇we′ɪnafʊ.

  ɢɪ′n·ʊ′k ɢʊᴅɪnɪkwe′ɪnafʊ,

tʊ′ɢɪ ᴅɪnɪkwe′ɪnafʊn ɢʊᴅɪnɪᴅɪ′tyɪ tcɛ′ᴅɪnɪᴅʊ′m·aɪ.

<18> Father Reaps Wheat

pɛ·″ma tcɪ″ɪ ᴅɛma′ma ɢʊᴅɪ′twʊ ak̇ʊ′ʙnɪyɪk asa′ʙlɪl.

pɛ·″ma ɢʊᴅ·ɪtɢwɪn ɢʊca-ak̇ʊ′ʙnɪyɪk

  ɢʊᴅɪt_sma′ku sʊ′ᴅ·u tcɛᴅu′n·u.

pɛ·″ma ɢʊᴅ·ɪ′tɢwɪn ta′ʙ sɪ′nfaf

  wa″an-asɪ′nfaf ɢʊᴅɢɪ′cɢa·t ɢʊ′ca-k̇ʊ′ʙnɪyɪk sa′ʙlɪl.

  ta′ʙ ɢʊnɪtɪ′f ha′nt′c

    ɢʊnɪ′ɛ′m·at ɢʊ′sa sa′ʙlɪl.

  ɢʊ·sa-ta′ʙ sɪ′n′faf ɢʊnɪᴅa′ʙat tcɛᴅɪtwɛ·′l.

pɛ·″ma ɢɪ′n·ʊk ɢʊᴅɪnɪtyu′wɪ ɢʊ·sa-kʊ′ʙnɪyak sa′ʙlɪl.　　　　　||122:59||　　　　<18(2)>

  e′ɪkɪn hʊ′psɪn-ᴅɪ·′nfya acres ɢʊnɪt_lu″nafʊn

ta′ʙ-a′mpyan pɛ·″ma ɢʊn·ɪtʊ′ɢɪ.

pɛ·″ma ɢɪ′n·ʊk ɢʊᴅɪnɪt_lu′pla·ᴅ ɢʊ′sa-sa′ʙlɪl.

ɢʊᴅɪnɪtʊ′ɢɪ ʙʊ′ɢʊlfan pɛ·″ma ᴅɛma′ma ɢʊᴅ·a′pna·t.

CHAPTER FOUR
Hunting Mt. Hebo with Yamhill Joe[1]

<19> Mounting a Hunting and Berrying Trip

Then my mother said to my father, ||122:59||

   "I want to go to the mountains.

   I will go after all sorts of berries."

My father replies like so,

   "Who all is going with you?"

[---]

   "Four women, one man, and me and Bahawadas.

   We are getting all of our food ready this very day.

   I want four horses.   <19(2)>

      Two horses to take our food and our blankets.

   Tomorrow early we will go.

   They will await us at their house."

Then we all went to the mountains.

When we got to those people, then we all went. ||122:61||

   That man (Yamhill Joe) went ahead,   <19(3)>

      and I went behind that man.

   We went all day.

When it was nearly mid-afternoon, that man says,

   "Here we will sleep tonight.

   You women go look for berries!

   And I will look for deer.

   Bahawadas will remain.

      He will look after our horses."

When the sun set, they all came back.   <19(4)>

   That man came back.

In this way he speaks,

   "I didn't see a deer."

His wife tells it like this,

   "There are no berries in this place."

[---]

   "Tomorrow early we will go on yonder to the Big Mountain (Mt. Hebo)."

When it was early morning they all arose.

Hunting Mt. Hebo with Yamhill Joe

<19> Mounting a Hunting and Berrying Trip
pɛ·''ma ᴅana·'na ɢʊᴅnɪ's·ɪn ᴅɛma·'ma ||122:59||
   tcɪ''ɪ tcɪ́ta'mᴅjʊ ᴅʊmɢʊ''ʊm tcɛmɛ'fʊ.
   ɢwɪᴅ·ɪ'twʊ [~ɢʊᴅ..] ʙʊ'ɢʊlfan a'wɛʊ ɢa'y·a'an
ᴅɛma·ma pa'-ʊtmi'ut
   e'y·a· mɪ'ᴅ·ɪ ʙʊ'ɢʊlfan ɢʊᴅɪt'i·'f
[---]
   ta'ʙ ʊʙu'm·ɪk wa''an-aᴅja'n̓ku nau-tcɪ''ɪ nau-ʙa'x̣awa'ᴅas.
   tcɪᴅ.sʊ'nɪtswu·n hɛ'sa-weɪ-i'pyan ʙʊ'ɢʊlfan ᴅɪkwe'ɪnafʊn.
   tcɪ''ɪ tcɪ́ta'mᴅjʊ ta'ʙ-aki'uᴅɪn.   <19(2)>
      ɢɛ·'m ɢʊᴅɪnk̓we·'n ᴅɪkwe'ɪnafunak, na'u sʊ'ᴅ·ʊ ᴅɪʙa'cicɢwa.
   me'ɪᴅj ɢʊmha'l'wan ᴅɪᴅɪt.sᴅʊ''ʊ.
   ɢʊ'saʙɛ·ᴅ ɢɪ'n·ʊk ɢɪnɪ'yu''watsfu·n tcɛ'ᴅ·ɪntha'm·ɪ.
pɛ·''ma ʙʊ'ɢʊlfan sʊ'ᴅ·ʊ ɢʊᴅ'i·'ᴅ tcɛ·mɛ'fʊ.
ɢʊᴅitwʊ'ɢu·ᴅ ɢʊ'sa-a'm·ɪm pɛ·''ma ʙʊ'ɢʊlfan sʊ'ᴅ·ʊ ɢʊᴅɪt'i·'ᴅ. ||122:61||
   ɢʊ'sa-aᴅja'ŋ̓ku ɢʊᴅɪt'i·'ᴅ tcɪ'm·ɪ,   <19(3)>
      nɪtcɪ''ɪ ɢʊᴅɪt'ɪ·'ᴅ ha'nt'c tcɛɢʊ'sa a'mu'ɪ.
   ɢʊᴅɪt'i·'ᴅ ʙʊ'ɢʊlfan a'mpyan,
yɛ'ts ɢʊᴅɪtya'hampyan ɢʊ'ca-a'mu'ɪ na'ɢɪt,
   hɛ'sa sʊ'ᴅ·ʊ ᴅɪᴅɪt.sɪ''weɪ hɛca-wɪ·-wɪ'fyu.
   mɪ'ᴅ·ɪ wa'ɪ'wa·tst pcɪ'ʊ'ᴅnɪɢwan aɢa'ya'n̥.
   nau-tcɪ''ɪ ᴅɪᴅ'ʊ'tnɪɢwan [~ᴅɪᴅ'ʊ'ᴅ..] aᴅa'l·ɪm.
   pa'x̣awa'ᴅas [ʙ..] ɢʊᴅ.sʙɪ'nt
      ɢʊtlʊ'ᴅnɪɢwan sʊ'ᴅ·ʊ ᴅɪki'uᴅɪn.
ɢʊᴅɪᴅjɛ'ɢ·ʊ-a'mpyan ʙʊ'ɢʊlfan ɢɪ'n·ʊk ɢʊᴅɪnɪtwa'l.   <19(4)>
   ɢʊ'ca-a'mu'ɪ ɢʊtmu·'ɢ,
pa'-una'ɢɪt,
   wa'ŋq tcɪ''ɪ ɢʊᴅhɷ·'ᴅ aᴅa'l·ɪm.
ɢɷ'k-ᴅʊ'l pa'-uᴅnɪ'c·ɪn,
   wa'ha ɢa'y·a''an tcɛhɛ'ca a'n·ʊ.
[---]
   me'ɪᴅj-ɢamha'l'wan ᴅɪᴅɪᴅ.sᴅu'hak la'ɢ·ai tcɛɢʊ'sa-ʙa'l-amɛ'fʊ.
ɢʊᴅɪtha'l'wan ʙʊ'ɢʊlfan ɢɪ'n·ʊk ɢʊᴅɪnɪtʙʊ'klaɪ

They prepared food.

Then we ate.

Having finished their food, they got everything ready. ||122:63||

    We threw it all on the horses' backs.

    We went on.

    That man went in front, his wife behind him, along with my mother and the two women.

    I went behind.

<20> Hunting Mt. Hebo

    We came up high on top of that mountain.

Then I looked out across.

    I saw a deer.

    They were going on ahead.

        They were laughing and talking about everything.

I hollered,

    "All of you stand still!

    Over there stands a deer!"

That man says,

    "Where? where?"

[---]

    "He's standing there.   <20(2)>

       He's standing across there!"

Then he saw it.

    He ran behind a big fir tree.

Then he shot that deer.

    The deer fell. ||122:65||

Then his dog ran to that deer.

    He bit at its throat.

That man ran over there.   <20(3)>

    He cut that deer's throat.

Then he skinned it completely.

    He cut off four limbs and its legs.

Then each of those women got one of its legs.

    I got the deer's hooves.

    That man got its back.

    We took it all to our horses.

ɢʊᴅɪɴɪtʙʊ'n-ak̓we'ɪnafʊn
pɛ·''ma-sʊ'ᴅʊ ɢʊᴅɪtk̓we'ɪnafʊ.
tʊ'ɢɪ-ᴅɪɴɪk̓we'ɪnafʊn ɢʊᴅɪɴɪtɛ'n·an ʙʊ'ɢʊlfan a'ɢfan ||122:63||
  ɢʊᴅɪɴɪtɢʊ' tcɛkɪ'ʊᴅan ᴅɪɴɪʙi·'l.
  sʊ'ᴅʊ ɢʊᴅ.sᴅʊ'hak.
  ɢʊ'sa-a'mu'ɪ ɢʊti·'ᴅ ᴅjɪ'm·ei, ᴅɪᴅu·'l ha'nt'c tcɛɢⱷ·'k nau-tcɪ''ɪ-ᴅɛna·'na nau·ɢʊ'ca-
    ɢɛ·'m aʙʊ'm·ɪk,
  tcɪ''ɪ-ɢʊt'i·'ᴅ ha'nt'c.

<20> Hunting Mt. Hebo
  ɢʊᴅmɛ'ʙ·af ha'ʙam tcɛ-ɢʊ'sa-mɛ'fʊ
pɛ·''ma tcɪ''ɪ ɢʊᴅtc'ɪʙlu·t yɛ'lɕfan [~..qfan]
  tcɪ''ɪ-ɢʊthⱷ·'ᴅ wa''an aᴅa'l·ɪm.
  ɢɪ'nʊk-ɢʊɴɪᴅ'i·'f ᴅjɪ'm·ei
    ɢʊᴅɪɴɪt.li·'lɪf yu''wɪn ʙʊ'ɢʊlfan a'ɢ·a.
tcɪ'ɪ-ɢʊt.la'l̓wɪ,
  mɪ'ᴅ·ɪ ʙcᴅɛ'cᴅap!
  ɢʊ·''aʙɛ·ᴅ wa''an aᴅa'l·ɪm maᴅa'ʙɪt!
ɢʊ'sa-a'mu'i na'ɢ·ɪt,
  ha'l·a? ha'l·a?
[---]
  ɢʊ'sa -waᴅa'ʙɪt   <20(2)>
    ɢʊ'sa-waᴅa'ʙɪt ᴅjʊ'hʊ!
pɛ·''ma-ɢʊthⱷ·'ᴅ.
  ɢʊtmɪ'nᴅjɪs hɛ'nt'c tcɛʙa'l ha'n̓twał.
pɛ·''ma-ɢʊt̓wa''an ɢʊ'sa-aᴅa'l·ɪm.
  ɢʊ'sa-aᴅa'l·ɪm ɢʊᴅjɛ'ɢ·ʊ. ||122:65||
pɛ·''ma ᴅʊ'n̓tal ɢʊtmɪ'nᴅjɪs ɢʊ'sa-tcɛ-ᴅa'l·ɪm.
  ɢʊᴅyɪ'kla·t tcɛᴅʊʙu'mɪq.
ɢʊ'sa-a'mu'ɪ ɢʊtmɪ'nᴅjɪs ɢʊ'saʙɛ·ᴅ   <20(3)>
  ɢʊt̓kʊ'ʙ·ʊn ɢʊ'sa-ᴅa'l·ɪm ᴅʊʙu'mɪq.
pɛ·''ma ɢʊtyɪ'fla·t ʙʊ'ɢʊlfan
  k̓ʊ'ʙɢa·t ta'ʙ-ᴅɪ'la'qʷ nau-ᴅɪlu''un.
pɛ·''ma ʙʊ'ɢʊlfan ɢʊ'ca wa'ɪtcwaf ɢʊn·ɪᴅɪ'tɢwɪn wa''an-ᴅɪlʊ''ʊn
  tcɪ''ɪ-ɢʊᴅɪ'tɢwɪn ɢʊ'sa ᴅa'l·ɪm ᴅⱷ·'f.
  ɢʊ'sa-a'mu'ɪ ɢʊᴅɪ·'tɢwɪn ᴅʊʙi·'l.
  ɢʊᴅɪt.smʊ'k̓ʊ tcɛ-ᴅɪki'ʊᴅɪn.

<21>Bahawadas Helps Yamhill Joe Hunt

Then we moved along to where there were lots of berries.

    We got there when it was mid-afternoon.

Then we set up our tents.

Then they prepared food.

    We ate.

When our meal was finished, one woman gave my mother a basket of berries. <21(2)>

    Many people were staying there.

    They were picking berries.

That woman (that) had given my mother berries, she says, ||122:67||

    "There aren't many berries, and not many deer.

    My husband went hunting every morning.   <21(3)>

        He never saw a deer."

Then that man who had killed a deer, his wife gave food to that hunter's wife.

Then that man said to me,

    he said,

    "Tomorrow early morning we will go.

    We will hunt.

    I want you to go with me.

    Your eyes are good.   <21(4)>

        You see far off.

        I can't see far off at all."

Then we took our horses.

Early morning we went on our hunt.

When we hadn't gone very far, then I saw a female deer.

In this way I spoke,

    "There stands a female deer!"

    He jumped to the ground. ||122:69|| <21(5)>

Then he ran.

    He hid behind a big fir tree.

    The deer looked towards me and my horse.

Then that man shot that deer.

    She leaped up.

    She ran.

    She ran maybe two hundred paces.   <21(6)>

<21> *baxawádas* Helps Yamhill Joe Hunt

pɛ·''ma sʊ'ᴅ·ʊ ɢʊᴅ·u'hak ᴅjɛha'l·a ɢʊ'ca-uha'l·u ça'y·a''an.
  ɢʊtwa'l ɢʊ'caʙɛ·ᴅ ɢʊᴅɪtya'hampyan.
pɛ·''ma ɢʊᴅɪtɛ'n·an ᴅɪsɪ'lhaus
pɛ·''ma ɢʊnɪʙʊ'n-akwe'ɪnafʊn.
  sʊ'ᴅ·ʊ-ɢʊtkwe'ɪnafʊ.
tʊ'ɢɪ-ᴅɪkwe'ɪnafʊn, wa''an-aʙʊ'm·ɪk ɢʊᴅɪ'st-ᴅɛna'na wa''an aťa'n·ana aça'y·a''n̥. <21(2)>
  ha''lu [~ha'l·ω] a'm·ɪm ɢʊn·ɪʙɪ'nᴅ tcɛɢʊ'caʙɛ·ᴅ.
  ɢɪnɪḱwɪ'tkwa·t aça'y·a'n̥.
ɢʊ'sa-aʙʊ'm·ɪk ɢʊᴅɪ'st ᴅɛna'na aça'y·a'n̥ qɛ'ᴅ·ak ɢʊᴅna'ɢɪt ||122:67||
  wa'ŋq ha'l·ʊ aça'y·a'n̥, nau-wa'ŋq ha'l·u aᴅa'l·ɪm.
  tcɪ''ɪ ᴅɛ'mu'ɪ ɢʊtyu''wuɬ ʙʊ'ɢʊlfan-ha'l'wan.   <21(3)>
    wa'ŋq-la'f ɢʊmɪthω'ᴅ aᴅa'l·im.
pɛ·''ma ɢʊ'ca-a'mu'ɪ ɢwaᴅ·a'haɪ wa''an aᴅa'l·im. ᴅɪᴅu'l ɢʊt'ʊ'k ɢʊ'sa a'yu''alaq ᴅɪᴅu'l.
pɛ·''ma ɢʊ'sa-a'mu'ɪ ɢʊᴅnɪ'tcfan,
  ɢʊᴅna'ɢɪt
  me'ɪᴅj-ha'l'wan ᴅɪᴅʊ''ʊ
  ᴅɪtyu''wal.
  tcɪ''ɪ-tcɪťa'mᴅju ma'ha ᴅʊmᴅɪt'ɪ''ᴅ tcɛ-tcɪ''ɪ.
  ma'ha-ʙʊkwa'l·ak ʊmtɛ'n·a   <21(4)>
    ɢʊthω'ᴅ la'ç·ai,
    tcɪ''ɪ wa'ŋq-la'f ɢamɪᴅithω·'ᴅ la'ç·ai.
pɛ·''ma sʊ'ᴅ·ʊ ɢʊᴅɪ'tɢwin ᴅɪkɪ'uᴅɪn,
hɛ'l'wan ɢwɪᴅɪᴅɪ't ᴅɪyʊ''wal.
wa'ŋq-ṗʊ'fan la'ç·ai ɢʊᴅɪt'ɪ''f [~..ťɪ'f], pɛ·''ma tcɪ''i ɢwthω·'ᴅ [~ɢʊt..] wa''an ʙʊ'm·ik
  ᴅa'l·ɪm.
pa''a-ɢʊᴅnɪ'cɪn,
  ɢʊ'ca-waᴅa'ʙɪt wa''an ʙʊ'm·ik aᴅa'l·ɪm!
  ɢʊtɪ'ᴅ·ʊp tcɛha'ŋklʊp, ||122:69|| <21(5)>
pɛ·''ma ɢʊtmɪ'nᴅjɪs
  ɢʊᴅɪ'plʊ ha'nt'c [hɛ'nt'c] tcɛwa''an ʙa'l ha'nťwa'ɬ.
  ɢʊ'sa-aᴅa'l·ɪm ɢʊᴅjɪ'ʙ·ɪl tcɛtcɪ''ɪ nau-tcɛᴅiki'uᴅɪn.
pɛ·''ma-ɢʊ'ca-a'mʊ'ɪ ɢʊťwa''an ɢʊ'ca-aᴅa'l·ɪm.
  ɢʊt'ɪ'ᴅ·ɪp,
  ɢʊᴅmɪ'nᴅjɪs.
  ɢʊᴅmɪ'nᴅjɪs e'ɪkɪn ɢɛ'm ᴅʊ'mṗɪ ᴅω·'f   <21(6)>

There she fell.
That man said,
   "Which way did that deer run?"
[---]
   "Oh not very far.
   She fell over there."
[---]
   "You saw her when she fell?"
[---]
   "Yes."
Then we went to the place where that deer fell.   <21(7)>
   I went ahead.
   I found that deer.
In this way I spoke,
   "Here it lies."
Then he cut its throat (to bleed it).
   He skinned it.
   He threw it on his horse.
Then we went on back to our camp. ||122:71||
The sun was not yet high in the sky when we got back to camp.   <21(8)>
   He threw that deer to the ground.
He said to his wife,
   "You go cut up this meat!
   Give food to everyone!"[2]
Then we, I and that man, washed up.
Then we ate.
When our meal was finished, we changed our horses.
Then we went looking everywhere for berries.   <21(9)>
   He carried his rifle.[3]
Oh, then we went everywhere.[4]
   Way far off we found a lot of berries.
Then we returned to camp.
In this way he spoke,
   "Wife! yonder far away we found lots of berries.
   Tomorrow you all are to go on horseback.
   Bahawadas and I will go to the other side of the Big Mountain."

ɢʊ'cɑʙɛ·ᴅ ɢʊᴅ·ᴊe'ɪɢ·ʊ.

ɢʊ'sɑ-ɑ'mu'ɪ nɑ'ɢɪt,

  hɑ'l·ɑi'-yʊ'fɑn ɢʊ'sɑ-ɑᴅɑ'l·ɪm ɢʊᴅmi'nᴅᴊɪs?

[---]

  u wɑ'ŋq-p̓ʊ'fɑn-lɑ'ɢ·ɑɪ

  ɢʊ'cɑʙɛ·ᴅ ɢʊᴅ·ᴊe'ɪɢ·ʊ.

[---]

  mɑ'hɑ-ɢʊᴅhɷ·'ᴅ ɢʊᴅɪᴅᴊe'ɢ·ʊ?

[---]

  hɛ·''ɑⁿ.

pɛ·''mɑ sʊ'ᴅ·ʊ ɢʊᴅɷ·''ɷ ɢʊ'sɑʙɛ·ᴅ tcɛhɑ'l·ɑ ɢʊ'sɑ ᴅɑ'l·ɪm ɢʊᴅᴊe'ɢ·ʊ [ɛ~ei~e·].   <21(7)>

  tcɪ·''ɪ-ɢʊᴅ'i·'ᴅ ᴅᴊɪ'm·ei,

  ɢʊᴅe'sᴅɛs ɢʊ'sɑ-ɑᴅɑ'l·ɪm.

pɑ·''ɑ-ɢʊᴅnɑ'ɢɪt

  hɛ'cɑ-mɑwe'ɪᴅ.

pɛ·''mɑ ɢɷ·'k ɢʊtk̓ʊ'ʙ·ɑn ᴅɛʙɷ·'mʊq,

  ɢʊᴅyɪ'flɑ·t

  ɢʊᴅɢu·' hɑ'lʙɑm tcɛᴅiki'uᴅɪn.

pɛ·''mɑ sʊ'ᴅ·ʊ ɢʊᴅ·u'y·ɪ tcɛ'ᴅu·sɪ'lhɑus. ||122:71||

wɑ'ŋq-me·'fɑn hɑ'lʙɑm ɑ'mpyɑn ɢʊᴅɪᴅwɑ'l tcɛᴅu·sɪ'lhɑus.   <21(8)>

  ɢʊtɢu·' ɢʊcɑ-ɑᴅɑ'l·ɪm tcɛhɑ'ŋk̓lu·p.

ɢʊᴅnɑ'ɢɪt tcɛᴅu·'l,

  mɑ'hɑ sk̓ʊ'pɢɑ·t hɛ'sɑ-ɑmu·'kʷ.

  s'u'k ʙʊ'ɢʊlfɑn e'yɑ.

pɛ·''mɑ sʊ'ᴅ·ʊ tcɪ·''ɪ-nɑu-ɢʊ'cɑ-ɑ'mu'i ɢʊtk̓u·''ʊł

pɛ·''mɑ ɢʊᴅɪtk̓we'inɑfʊ.

ᴅɪt̓ʊ'ɢɪ-ᴅɪkwe'ɪnɑfʊn ɢʊᴅyu·'hɪ ᴅɪkɪ'uᴅɪn.

pɛ·''mɑ sʊ'ᴅ·ʊ ɢʊᴅɪt'ʊ'ᴅnɪgwɑn ɑɢɑ'y·ɑ'ṇ ʙʊ'ɢʊlfɑn-hɑ'l·ɑ [~hɛ'l·ɑ].   <21(9)>

  ɢɷ·'k ɢʊᴅk̓we·'n ᴅɪsɑ'ɢwɑlɑl [~ᴅɪpɑ'ɢwɑlɑl].

u·' pɛ·''mɑ ɢʊᴅ'i·'f ʙʊ'ɢʊlfɑn-hɑ'l·ɑ,

  lɑ'ɢ·ɑ'ɑi sʊ'ᴅ·ʊ ɢʊᴅ·ɛ'sᴅɛs hɑ'l·u· ɑɢɑ'y·ɑ'ṇ.

pɛ·''mɑ sʊ'ᴅ·ʊ ɢʊᴅɪ'tyi tcɛᴅusɪ'lhɑus.

pɑ·''ɑ-ɢʊᴅnɪ'sɪn

  ᴅu·'l ɢu·'-ɑlɑ'ɢ·ɑɪ ɢʊᴅe'cᴅɛc hɑ'l·u· ɑɢɑ'yɑ'ṇ.

  ɢʊmɪme'ɪᴅᴊ mɪ'ᴅ·ɪ ᴅʊmɪt̓i·'f tcɛkɪ'uᴅɪn.

  tcɪ·''ɪ nɑu-ʙɑ'x̣ɑwɑ'ᴅɑs ᴅɪᴅɷ·''ɷ ye'lqfɑn tcɛɢʊ'sɑ-ʙɑ'l-ɑmɛ'fʊ.

<22>Two More Kills

My mother got me up early. ||122:73||

That man arose.

He went after our horses.

He brought them back to camp.

Then I got myself ready.

I got my horse ready.

Then we went to the Big Mountain.

That man knew all the trails of this country. <22(2)>

Then when we arrived at that mountain.

"Dismount, Bahawadas!

Tie up your horse!

We're going on the ground (by foot).

Down below right here there are always big buck deer.

They play around there. <22(3)>

Look out there down below!"

I looked down there.

I saw two buck deer jump.

In this way I speak,

"Two are jumping over there."

In this way he speaks to me,

"You stay here! ||122:75||

Watch those deer!

I will crawl like this. <22(4)>

I will hide by that big rock.

There I will shoot."

Then he shot one of those deer.

It fell there.

That other deer was confused.

He just looked around.

Then that man shot that deer. <22(5)>

Then he came to me,

"This other way here, we'll go down to where those deer will be lying."

Then he cut their throats.

Then he took his jacket.

He covered those deer with his jacket.[5]

<22> Two More Kills

    ᴅᴇna'na ɢʊᴅʙʊ'klɪnfaɪ ha'l'wan. ||122:73||

    ɢⱷ·'k ɢʊ'sa-a'mu'ɪ ɢʊᴅʙʊ'klai.

    ᴅɪ'twʊ sʊ'ᴅ·ʊ ᴅɪkɪ'uᴅɪn.

    ɢʊᴅ.smʊ'k̊ʊ tcɛᴅu·sɪ'lhaus.

pɛ·''ma tcɪ''ɪ-ɢʊtɛ'n·ɪtcwu·n

    ɢʊtɛ'n·an ᴅɪkɪ'uᴅɪn.

pɛ·''ma ɢʊᴅɪᴅɪ't tcɛɢʊ'sa-ʙa'l ʊmɛ'fʊ.

    ɢʊ'sa-amu'ɪ ɢʊᴅyʊ'kʊn ʙʊ'ɢʊlfan ɢʊ'sa-ha'n·ʊ ᴅʊɢu·'n.   <22(2)>

pɛ·''ma ɢʊᴅɪtwa'l tcɛ-ɢʊ'sa-amɛ'fʊ.

    shʊ'l·aɪsᴅa ʙax̄awa'ᴅas.

    s'ɛ'm·a·t ʙɪkɪ'uᴅɪn.

    tcɪᴅɪti·'f tcɛha'ŋ̊klu·p.

    hɛ'ca-wɪ·ɪ'w·a mu'ɪnu mɪnɪʙi·'nᴅ ʙal ʊᴅja'ŋ̊ku ᴅa'l·ɪm.

    ɢʊ'caʙɛ·ᴅ ɢɪ'n·ʊk nɪl·a'kwɪt.   <22(3)>

    ṣyu'ᴅnɪkwan ɢʊ'sa-amu'.

    tcɪ''ɪ-ɢʊt·cɪ'plu·t ɢʊ'sa-amu'

        ɢʊthⱷ'ᴅ ɢɛ·'m ᴅja'ŋ̊ku aᴅa'l·ɪm ɢʊnɪ·ɪ'tfʊt.

pa''uᴅnɪ'cɪn,

    ɢɛ·'m ɢʊ'caʙɛ·ᴅ ni'ɪ'tfɪt.

pa''una'ɢɪt tcɛtcɪ''ɪ,

    ma'ha hɛ'caʙɛ·ᴅ sᴅa'ʙit. ||122:75||

    cyu'ᴅnɪgwan ɢʊ'sa-ᴅa'l·ɪm.

    tcɪ''ɪ hɛ'ca-wɛ'u ᴅɪtʙa'ŋkʙʊk,   <22(4)>

    ᴅɪt'ɪ'plu tcɛɢʊ'sa waʙa'l a'nᴅ.

    ɢʊ'saʙɛ·ᴅ tcɪ''ɪ ᴅɪtwa''an.

pɛ·''ma ɢʊt·wa''an wa''an ɢʊ'sa-aᴅa'l·ɪm

    ɢʊᴅ·je'ɢ·u ɢʊ'saʙɛ·ᴅ.

    ɢʊ'sa-awa''an ʊᴅa'l·ɪm ɢʊᴅwa''yʊ ᴅɪmu'p̊ɪn.

    k̊u'nfʊ [~k̊wa'nfʊ] ɢʊtɢwɛ'ltcɢwɛltc.

pɛ·''ma ɢʊ'ca-a'mʊ'ɪ ɢʊt·wa''an ɢʊ'ca aᴅa'l·ɪm.   <22(5)>

pɛ·''ma ɢʊtma''a tcɛtcɪ''ɪ,

    hɛ'ca-wɛɪ-yʊ'fan tcɪᴅɪthʊ'l·aɪ ᴅjɛha'l·a ɢʊ'sa-aᴅa'l·ɪm ᴅɪᴅɪnɪtwe'ɪf.

pɛ·''ma ɢʊᴅk'ʊ'pɢa·t ᴅɪnɪʙⱷ'mʊq.

pɛ·''ma ɢʊᴅ·ɪ'tɢwin ᴅɪɢa'ʙʊ·

    ɢʊᴅlʊ'pɢa·t ɢʊ'sa-aᴅa'l·ɪm tcɪᴅɪɢa'ʙʊ·.

Then we came back to the horses.   <22(6)>
   We returned to our camp.
   We went for two horses.
   We got those two deer. ||122:77||
When we returned to our camp, all of the women had gone off to where there
   were lots of berries.[6]
Then we ate.
Finished with our meal, we go after two horses.
Then they went to where the killed deer were.
[Rather,] then we went.   <22(7)>
   It was very rough country.[7]
When we got back to those deer, we threw one on each horse.
   One horse carried one.
   That other horse carried one.
Then we went back to our camp.
   We cut up all that meat.
Then we covered it with brush.[8]   <22(8)>
Then we fixed up the place[9] where we dried that meat.
When we finished, then we went after a lot of firewood. ||122:79||
Then when it was early afternoon his wife got back.
   Lots of berries they brought back.
   They prepared food.
Finished with their meal, then those women cut those two deer into small strips.
                                                                    <22(9)>

Then they dried it.[10]
Then my mother says to me,
   "You go gather fir bark!
   With it I will then dry the berries.[11]
   Early tomorrow morning we will fix it up where the berries are to be dried."

<23> Drying Venison and Berries
All day they stayed there.
   They worked on their berries.[12]
   I and that man prepared lots of firewood that day.
Having finished everything where they dry berries, then they put their berries on
   the fir-bark. ||122:81||
Then they put down firewood near those berries.

pɛ·"ma sʊ'ᴅʊ ɢʊtwu'ɢ tcɪᴅukɪ'utɪn,   <22(6)>
   ɢʊᴅɪ'tyi tcɛᴅusɪ'lhaus.
   ɢʊᴅɪ'twʊ ɢɛ·'m akɪ'uᴅɪn.
   ɢʊmnɪtkwɛ·'n ɢʊ'ca-ɢɛ·'m ʊᴅa'lɪm. ||122:77||
ɢʊᴅwa'l tcɛᴅɪsɪ'lhaus. ʙʊ'ɢʊlfan ɢʊ's·a ʙʊ'm·ɪk ɢʊᴅɪnɪtɪ'ᴅ tcɛɢʊ'sa ha'l·a waha'l·u·
   aça'y·a·'an.
pɛ·"ma sʊ'ᴅʊ ɢʊᴅk̓we'ɪnafʊ.
tʊ'ɢɪ ᴅɪkwe'ɪnafʊn ᴅɪ'twʊ ɢɛ·'m-akɪ'uᴅɪn.
pɛ·"ma ɢwɪnɪtɪ'ᴅ ᴅjɛha'l·a ɢʊ'ca uᴅ·a'haɪ ᴅa'l·ɪm.
pɛ·"ma ɢʊᴅɪtɪ'f   <22(7)>
   p̓ʊ'fan qa'sqayu a'n·u.
ɢʊtwa'l tcɛɢʊ'sa ᴅa'l·ɪm ɢʊtɢu·' wa·''an tcɛwa·''an-akɪ'uᴅɪn,
   wa·''an-akɪ'uᴅɪn ɢʊtk̓wɛ·'n wa·''an,
   ɢʊ'ca-wa·''an-akɪ'uᴅɪn ɢʊtk̓wɛ·'n wa·''an.
pɛ·"ma sʊ'ᴅʊ ɢʊᴅ_sᴅu'yɪ tcɛᴅusɪ'lhaus.
   ɢʊtk̓ʊ'pɢa·t ʙʊ'ɢʊlfan ɢʊ'c·a-amu·'kʷ.
pɛ·"ma ɢʊᴅ.lʊ'pɢa·t tcɛᴅɪ'nt'cɪt-awa'ᴅɪk.   <22(8)>
pɛ·"ma ɢʊtɛ'n·an ha'l·a ɢʊ'ca ɢʊᴅɪᴅja'kliwa'an [~..ɢliwa'an] ɢʊ'ca-amu·'kʷ.
ɢʊᴅɪtʊ'ɢɪ pɛ·"ma ɢʊᴅɪᴅɪ'twʊ ha'l·u·-a'wa'ᴅɪk. ||122:79||
pɛ·"ma pʊ'tsnaŋq ɢʊᴅɪtya'hampyan ᴅɪᴅu'l ɢʊᴅɪnɪtwʊ·'ç.
   ha'l·u aça'y·a·'an ɢʊᴅɪnɪmwɪ·''ɪl.
   ɢʊᴅɪnɪtʙʊ'n-ak̓we'ɪnafʊn,
tʊ'ɢɪ-ᴅɪnɪkwe'ɪnafʊn pɛ·"ma ɢɪ'n·ʊk ɢʊ'ca-ʙʊ'm·ɪk ɢʊᴅɪnɪwa'łwa·t ɢʊ'ca ɢɛ·'m aᴅa'l·ɪm.
                                                <22(9)>
pɛ·"ma ɢʊᴅɪnɪᴅja'kliwa·n.
pɛ·"ma ᴅɛna'na u'na'ɢɪt tcɛtcɪ''ɪ
   ma'ha ᴅja'k-cᴅjɪ''wʊ aha'nt̓_wał ᴅɪᴅa'ɢɪł.
   tcɛɢʊ'sa ᴅɪ's ᴅɪtca'klɪwan aça'ya'n̥.
   ɢamɪtme'ɪᴅj ɢamɪᴅɪtha'l'wan sʊ'ᴅʊ ᴅɪᴅɪta'n·an ha'l·a ɢʊ'sa ɢʊᴅɪtca'klɪwa·n aça'ya'n.

<23> Drying Venison and Berries

ʙʊ'ɢʊlfan-a'mpyan ɢʊᴅɪnɪʙi'ᴎᴅ
   ɢʊᴅɪnɪlu''nafʊn tcɛ'ᴅɪnɪça'y·a·n.
   tcɪ''ɪ-nau-ɢʊ'ca-a'mu·'ɪ ɢʊᴅɪtʙʊ'n ha'l·u· a'wa'ᴅɪk ɢʊ'ca-we-ɪ'pyan·.
ɢʊnɪtʊ'ɢɪ ʙʊ'ɢʊlfan ɢʊ's·a-ha'l·a ɢʊᴅɪnɪᴅja'ɢalwa·n-aça'ya·n, pɛ·"ma ɢʊᴅɪnɪɢu·'
   ᴅɪnɪça'y·a·n tcɛɢʊ'sa aᴅa'ɢɪł. ||122:81||
pɛ·"ma ɢʊᴅɪnɪlu''ʊn a'wa'ᴅɪk yɛ'ts tcɛɢʊ'sa-aça'ya'n,

They set fire to that wood.

They watched over those berries half the night.   <23(2)>

I and that man went to sleep.

Then when it was the next day, the women went back picking berries.[13]

I and that man remain in camp.

He tended the drying meat and his wife's berries.   <23(3)>

I tended my mother's berries and those two women's berries.[14]

When it was nearly sundown they returned.

Then those women prepared food.

We all ate.   <23(4)>

Finished with our meal, then those women replaced their berries.[15] ||122:83||

I prepared lots of firewood.

They went to work.[16]

Half the night they dried their berries.

<24> Back to the Hunt

Then when it was the next day, that man and I went to hunt.

We travelled half the day.

We saw nothing.

He got tired at heart, he says to me,

"We will never find a deer today.

Let's look for berries."

Then we found one place with lots of berries.   <24(2)>

The women were in camp.

They were working at their berries.

Then when the next day came I stayed in camp.

That man took those women to where those quantities of berries were.

Then he hunted. ||122:85|| <24(3)>

He found one two-horned male deer.[17]

He shot that deer.

He threw its entire body on his horse.

Then he returned.

He got to our camp.

He threw down that deer.

Then he skinned it.

He hung it on a tree.[18]

ɢʋꝺɪnɪme·'yat ɢʋ'ca-a'wa'ꝺ·ɪk.

ɢʋꝺɪnɪlʋ·'ꝺnɪgwan ɢʋ'ca-aɢa'ya'n k'ʋ'ʙfan awɪ'fyu.　　　　　　　　<23(2)>

tcɪ''ɪ-na'u-ɢʋca-a'mu'ɪ ɢʋꝺɪ'twi.

pɛ·''ma ɢʋꝺɪtme'ɪꝺj ɢɪ'n·ʋk aʙʋ'm·ɪk ɢʋꝺɪnɪꝺɪ't ꝺɪꝺkwʋ'tkwa·t aɢa'y·a'n.

tcɪ''ɪ-nau-ɢʋ'ca-a'mʋ'ɪ aꝺa'fʋts tcɛsɪ'lhaus.

ɢꙍ'k ɢʋꝺyu'ꝺnɪgwan ꝺja'ɢlɪwan-amu·'kʷ na·u-ꝺɪꝺu·'l ꝺɪɢa'y·a'n.　　　　<23(3)>

tcɪ''ɪ-ɢʋꝺyu'ꝺnɪgwan ꝺɛna·'na ꝺɪɢa'y·a'n na·u-ɢʋ'ca-aɢɛ·'m aʙʋ'm·'ɪk ꝺɪnɪɢa'y·a'n.

yɛ'ts-ɢʋꝺɪꝺ·jɛ'ɢ·u-a'mpyan ɢʋꝺɪnɪtwa'l.

pɛ·''ma ɢʋ'sa ʙʋ'm·ɪk ɢʋꝺɪnɪtʙʋ'n akwe'ɪnafʋn.

ʙʋ'ɢʋlfan-su'ꝺ·ʋ ɢʋꝺɪtkwe'ɪnafʋ.　　　　　　　　　　　　　　　<23(4)>

tʋ'ɢ·ɪ ꝺɪkwe'ɪnafʋn pɛ·''ma ɢɪ'n·uk ɢʋ'sa ʙʋ'm·ɪk ɢɪnɪ'yu'ha·t ꝺɪnɪɢa'ya'n. ||122:83||

tcɪ''ɪ-ɢʋtʙʋ'n ha'l·u· a'wa'ꝺ·ɪk.

ɢɪ'n·ʋ'k ɢɪnɪ·la'ftwɪ

k'ʋ'ʙfan-awɪ'fyʋ ɢʋnɪꝺja'klɪwa·n ꝺɪnɪɢa'ya'n.

<24> Back to the Hunt

pɛ·''ma ɢʋꝺɪꝺme'ɪꝺj ɢʋ'ca-a'mu'ɪ nautcɪ''ɪ ɢʋꝺɪ'ꝺ·ɪyu''wal.

sʋ'ꝺ·ʋ ɢʋꝺɪt'i·'f k'ʋ'pfan-a'mpyan,

wa'ŋq a'ɢ·a ɢʋꝺɪthꙍ·'ꝺ.

ɢʋꝺ·u'ɢyu [ꝺ~t] ꝺʋmu·'p̓ɪn, pa'-unɪ'tsfan,

wa'ŋq-lʋ'f sʋ'ꝺ·ʋ ɢʋꝺɪꝺ·ɛ'ʂꝺɛʂ a'ꝺa'l·ɪm hɛ'ca-wɪ-ɪ'pyan.

tcɪꝺɪtyʋ'ꬶnu'f aɢa'y·a''an.

pɛ·''ma sʋ'ꝺ·ʋ ɢʋꝺɪꝺ·ɛ'ꝺɛc wa''an a'n·ʋ ha'l·u·-aɢa'ya''an.　　　　　<24(2)>

ɢɪ'n·ʋɢ·ɪnɪʙʋ'm·ɪk ɢʋnɪʙi·'nꝺ tcɛsɪ'lhaus.

ɢʋn·ɪlʋ''nafan tcɛꝺɪnɪɢa'ya''n.

pɛ·''ma ɢʋꝺɪtme'ɪꝺj tcɪ''ɪ-ɢʋtʙi·'nꝺ tcɛsɪ'lhaus.

ɢʋ'ca-amu'ɪ ɢʋnɪꝺɪ'tku ɢʋ'ca-aʙʋ'm·ɪk tcɛ-ha'l·a ɢʋ'ca-ʋha'l·u·-aɢa'ya''an.

pɛ·''ma ɢꙍ'k-ɢʋtyu''wuɬ　　　　　　　　||122:85||　　<24(3)>

ɢʋꝺ·ɛ'cꝺɛc wa''an ɢɛ·'m-ꝺuwa'i waꝺja'ŋ̓ku aꝺa'l·ɪm.

ɢʋtwa''an ɢʋ'sa-aꝺa'lɪm

ɢʋtɢu·' ʙʋ'ɢʋlfan-ꝺɪk'aʙya tcɛꝺɪkɪ'uꝺɪn.

pɛ·''ma ɢʋm·e'y·ɪ.

ɢʋm·u·'ɢ tcɛꝺɪsɪ'lhaus,

ɢʋtɢu·' ɢʋ'sa-aꝺa'l·ɪm.

pɛ·''ma ɢʋtyɪ'fla·t

ɢʋtqa'l·ɪɬ tcɛ'wa'ꝺ·ɪk.

<25> Finishing Up on Mt. Hebo

Then he prepared lots of firewood.

   I too prepared lots of firewood.

When it was early afternoon, those women returned.

   All of their berry-baskets they had filled.

Then they prepared food.

Then when they finished their meal, they went to work on their berries.   <25(2)>

   They replaced those dried berries.

Then they placed those fresh berries on that fir-bark.

Then they set the wood afire to dry their berries.   ‖122:87‖

They worked half of that night.

When it was morning [said my mother],   <25(3)>

   "Soon we will finish picking berries.

   In two days we will return to our homes."

Then they fixed up all of their berries.

   And that man gave my mother dried meat, and those two women.

When it was early morning, I and that man went after all of our horses.   <25(4)>

Then they loaded up their meat and their berries.

Then they put them on the horses' backs.

   What little bit of food was left they gave to everyone camped there.

   We travelled all day (before) we got back to our houses.   ‖122:89‖   <25(5)>

<25> Finishing Up on Mt. Hebo

pɛ·''ma ɢɷ·'k ɢʊDBʊ'n ha'lʊ· a'wa'Dɪk,

tcɪ''ɪ-yu ɢʊDBʊ'n ha'lɪ'yu a'wa'Dɪk.

pu'tsnaq ɢʊDɪtya'hampyan ɢɪ'n·ʊk-ɢʊ'ca-aBʊ'm·ɪk ɢʊDɪnɪtswa'l.

Bʊ'ɢʊlfan DɪnɪtȧʼnʼanaɢʊDɪnɪtBʊ'yɪ.

pɛ·''ma ɢɪ'n·ʊk ɢʊDɪnɪtBʊ'n-akwe'ɪnafʊn.

pɛ·''ma ɢʊnɪṫʊ'ɢɪ Dɪnɪkwe'ɪnafʊn ɢʊDɪnɪt.lu''nʊf tcɛDɪnɪɢa'ya''n̩,   <25(2)>

ɢʊnɪtyʊ'ha·D ɢʊ'sa-wɪ-tca'klɪwɛɪ-aɢa'ya'n.

pɛ·''ma ɢʊDɪnɪtɢʊ' ɢʊ'ca waBa''al aɢa'ya'an tcɛɢʊ'sa-aDa'ɢɪɫ.

pɛ·''ma ɢɪnɪme'y·at a'wa'Dɪk DʊmɪnɪDja'klɪwan Dɪnɪɢa'ya'n. ||122:87||

ɢɪ'n·ʊ'k ɢʊDɪnɪlʊ''nʊf k'ʊ'Bfan ɢʊ'ca-wɪ-wɪ'fyʊ.

ɢʊmɪnɪDme'ɪDj   <25(3)>

sʊ'D·ʊ Dɪ's-DɪDɪt.stʊ'ɢɪ Dʊmɪnɪtkwɪ'tkwa·t aɢa'ya'an.

ɢɛ'mDɪtme'ɪDj sʊ'D·ʊ DɪD.sDʊ'yɪ tcɛDɪt.sDʊ'm·ai.

pɛ·''ma ɢʊDɪnɪsʊ''yʊtswu·n Bʊ'ɢʊlfan Dɪnɪɢa'ya'n.

nau-ɢʊ'ca-a'mu'ɪ ɢʊDɪ'ct Dɛna'na waDja'ɢlɪwɛɪ-amu·'kʷ, nau-ɢʊ'ca-aɢɛ·'m aBʊ'm·ik.

ɢʊDɪtha'l'wan tcɪ''ɪ-nau-ɢʊ'ca-a'mu'ɪ ɢʊDɪ'twʊ Bʊ'ɢʊlfan sʊ'D·ʊ DɪɢɪʼuDan.   <25(4)>

pɛ·''ma Bʊ'ɢʊlfan ɢʊnɪD.lʊ'fu·t Dɪnɪmu·'kʷ Dɪnɪɢa'ya''n.

pɛ·''ma ɢʊ·Dɪnɪtɢʊʼ tcɛkɪ'uDɪn DɪnɪBi·'l.

a'ɢ·a-ɢʊ'ca pu'nʊk akwe'ɪnafʊn ɢʊn·ɪDɪ't Bʊ'ɢʊlfan e'y·a ɢʊ'caBɛ·D ɢʊnɪBɪ'nD.

sʊ'Dʊ-ɢʊDɪD'i·'f Bʊ'ɢʊlfan-a'mpyan ɢʊDɪtwa·'l tcɛsʊ'D·ʊ Dʊ'm·ai. ||122:89|| <25(5)>

More Daily Life on the Farm; a Hop-Picking Excursion[1]

<26> Young Men Help Thresh Wheat
Then my mother got ready.
   She fixed lots of food.
Two mornings later the wheat thresher arrived.
   Many young men came.
Then they got the thresher ready.
When they finished all of that, then they threshed the wheat.
   Four young men stood on top there keeping the wheat in a pile.   <26(2)>
   One young man stood on the platform.
      He cut the bound wheat.
   One man fed the wheat thresher. ||122:91||
They worked all day long.
Then at midday all those young men went to the house.
   They washed up.
Then my mother made all sorts of food.   <26(3)>
   Many girls assisted my mother.
Then all the young men ate.
When they finished all the food, then they went outside.
   They sat down under a grove of trees.
Then at one o'clock my father said,
   "Everybody go to your work."
   All those young men stood up.   <26(4)>
      They went to work.
Then my mother, all the girls, the old men, and the old women ate.

When they finished their meal, then the girls fixed everything up.
   They washed the plates.
Then all the girls made lots of food.
At sundown my father said to those young worker men, ||122:93|| <26(5)>
   "Let's quit!
   All of you go on to the house.
   Get yourselves ready for mealtime."
When all the young men finished the meal, then they went back to their homes.

More Daily Life on the Farm; a Hop-Picking Excursion

<26> Young Men Help Thresh Wheat

pɛ·''ma ᴅɛna'na ɢʊt·ɛ'natcwu·n,
   ɢʊᴅвʊ'n ha'l·u· aḱwe'ınafʊn.
ɢʊᴅɪᴅɢɛ'm ᴅɪme'ıᴅj ɢʊ's·a k̓lʊ'ɢᴅıfʊn sa'вlıl ɢʊtmu·'ɢ.
   ha'l·u ası'nfaf ɢʊ'nᴅınımu·'ɢ.
pɛ·''ma ɢʊᴅɪntɛ'n·a·n ɢʊca-ḱlʊ'ɢᴅıfun [fan] sa'вlıl.
вʊ'ɢʊlfan ɢʊᴅɪnɪtʊ'ɢ·ı. pɛ·''ma ɢʊᴅɪnɪḱlʊ'ɢᴅa·t ɢʊ'ca-asa'вlıl.
   ta'в-acı'nfaf ɢʊᴅɪnᴅa'вɪᴅ tcɛɢʊ'ca ha'lвam ɢʊᴅɪlʊ''lınfʊı asa'вlıl.   <26(2)>
   wa·''an-ası'nfaf ɢʊᴅ·a'вaᴅ tcɛɢʊ'ca laᴅa'm.
      ɢω·'k ɢʊᴅḱʊ'вɢa·t ɢʊ's·a ᴅω'qᴅınıfʊ'q sa'вlıl.
   wa·''an-amu·'ı ɢʊtʊ'ɢ ɢʊ's·a k̓lʊ'ɢᴅınfʊı sa'вlıl. ||122:91||
вʊ'ɢʊlfan a'mpyan ɢʊᴅɪnılu·''nuf.
pɛ·''ma ɢʊᴅɪnɪtwı'lfu-a'mpyan вʊ'ɢʊlfan ɢʊ'ca-sı'nfaf ɢʊᴅɪnɪt̓_ı'ᴅ tcɛha'm·ı.
   ɢʊᴅɪnɪtḱu·'ł.
pɛ·''ma-tcı·'ı-ᴅɛna'na ɢʊᴅṕı'n вʊ'ɢʊlfan a·''wɛʊ k̓we'ınafʊn.   <26(3)>
   ha'l·u·-aвı'na·tst ɢʊn·ıɢɛ'm'ya·t ᴅɛna'na.
pɛ·''ma вʊ'ɢʊlfan ɢʊ's·a-ası'nfaf ɢʊᴅɪntḱwe'ınafʊ.
ɢınıtʊ'ɢ·ı-вʊ'ɢʊlfan ᴅıḱwe'ınafan pɛ·''ma ɢʊnıᴅı't hɛ·''lʊm,
   ɢʊᴅɪnsı''wɛı ha'l·u tcɛ'wa'ᴅ·ık.
pɛ·''ma ɢʊᴅwa·''an-aᴅı'nᴅın ᴅɛma·'ma ɢʊᴅna'ɢıt
   вʊ'ɢʊlfan-ı'y·a ᴅı't ᴅılu·''nafʊn.
   вʊ'ɢʊlfan-ɢʊ'ca-ası'nfaf ɢʊnıᴅɛ'cᴅap   <26(4)>
      ɢʊnıᴅı't ᴅılu·''nafʊn.
pɛ·''ma ᴅɛna'na, вʊ'ɢʊlfan вına·'tst, yu'hu'yu a'mu·'ı, yu'hu'yu aвʊ'm·ık
   ɢʊᴅɪnɪtḱwe'ınafʊ.
ɢı'n·ʊk-ɢıᴅınıtʊ'ɢ·ı ᴅınḱwe'ınafʊn pɛ·''ma ɢʊca-вı'na·tst ɢʊᴅɪntɛ'n·a'n вʊ'ɢʊlfan-a'ɢ·a
   ɢʊᴅɪnḱu''uł kwa'ᴅ·ın.
pɛ·''ma вʊ'ɢʊlfan-ɢʊ'ca-вına·'tst ɢʊᴅɪnвʊ'n ha'l·u k̓we'ınafʊn.
ɢʊᴅɪᴅjɛ'ɢ·ʊ-a'mpyan ᴅɛma·'ma ɢʊᴅna'ɢıt tcɛɢʊ's·a lu·''nafyaq sı'nfaf ||122:93|| <26(5)>
   pa'cl·u· tcı'ᴅa.
   вʊ'ɢʊlfan mı'ᴅı tcıᴅıt'ı·'ᴅ tcɛha'm·eı,
   mı'ᴅı tɛ'n·etcwu·n k̓we'ınafʊn.
вʊ'ɢʊlfan-ɢʊsa-ası'nfaf ɢʊᴅɪnɪtʊ'ɢ·ı ᴅıḱwe'ınafʊn pɛ·''ma ɢʊᴅɪnıᴅı'tyı ɢı'n·ʊk
   tcɛᴅınıᴅʊ'm·aı.

[---]
   "Tomorrow morning all of you come back here and eat!"
My mother and the girls[2] worked nearly half that night.   <26(6)>
Then they all lay down.
At three o'clock in the morning, my mother woke up those girls.
Then they prepared food.
At five o'clock all those young men arrived.
Then they washed up.
Then they ate.
Finished with their meal, they went outside to their work.   <26(7)>
When they had worked that half day, they had finished the threshing of the wheat.
Then they went to the house. ||122:95||
Once they fixed themselves up washing all their faces, then they ate.
When they were through with their meal, my father told those young men,
   "You go stay outside.
   As soon as I finish eating, then I'll pay all of you young men."

                                                              <26(8)>

My father said,
   "Give me money!"
   My mother took the money.
      She gave it to my father.
   All the young men assembled outside,
      and my father paid all those young men.

<27> Picking Hops in Salem
Then my father said,
   "In maybe ten days we'll go to the hop-yard.
   I want one-hundred people to pick the hops at that White man's place."

Then the young men, all the people who were standing there, said,
   "Okay. We'll get ready on that day." ||122:97||
Then they took the thresher to another man.   <27(2)>
Then my father and two of my mother's older brothers helping my father go and
   haul the wheat to the little house (granary).
When they finished all of it, then they went home.
Then the next day my father went to hunt up the people he wanted to take to the
   hop-yard.

[---]

me'ɪdj-ɢʊmha'l'wan mɪ'ᴅɪ pcma''ak hɛ'saʙɛ''ᴅ pɪckwe'ɪnafʊn.

ᴅɛna'na nau-ɢʊ'sa-aʙɪ'na·tst ɢʊnɪlu'nafʊn yɛ'ᴅj tcɛkʊ'fyu· ɢʊ'ca wuhu'wɪ.   <26(6)>

pɛ·''ma ʙʊ'ɢʊlfan ɢɪ'n·ʊk ɢʊᴅɪnɪsɪ'w·eɪ

hu'psɪn-aᴅɪ'nᴅɪn ɢwaᴅɛtha'l'wan ᴅɛ'na'na ɢʊᴅʙʊ'klɪ ɢʊ'sa-ʙɪna'tst.

pɛ·''ma ɢɪ'n·ʊ'k ɢʊᴅɪnɪtʙʊ'n-akwe'ɪnafʊn.

ɢwaᴅɪthu'wan-aᴅɪ'nᴅɪn ʙʊ'ɢʊlfan ɢʊ'sa-asɪ'nfaf ɢʊᴅɪnɪmu'ɢ.

pɛ·''ma ɢʊᴅɪnɪtku'ɬ

pɛ·''ma ɢʊᴅɪnɪtkwe'ɪnafʊn.

tʊ'ɢɪ-ᴅɪnɪkwe'ɪnafʊn ɢɪnɪᴅɪ't-hɛ·''lʊm ᴅɪnɪlu'nafʊn.   <26(7)>

ɢʊᴅɪnɪtlu·''nuf ɢʊ'sa kʊ'ʙfan a'mpyan ɢʊᴅɪnɪtʊ'ɢɪ ɢʊ'sa kʊɢtya·t asa'ʙlɪl.

pɛ·''ma ɢʊᴅɪnɪᴅɪ't-tcɛha'm·ɪ   ‖122:95‖

ɢʊᴅɪnɪtɛ'n·ɛtcwu·n ku·'ɬ-ʙʊ'ɢʊlfan ᴅɪn·ɪkwa'l·ak pɛ·''ma ɢʊᴅɪnɪtkwe'ɪnafʊn.

ɢʊᴅɪnɪtʊ'ɢɪ-ᴅɪnkwe'ɪnafʊn ᴅɛ'ma'ma ɢʊᴅnɪ's·ɪn ɢʊ'sa-asɪ'nfaf

   mɪ'ᴅɪ ᴅʊʙi·'nᴅ hɛ·''lʊm.

   ᴅɪ's-tcɪ''ɪ-ᴅɪtʊ'ɢɪ-ᴅɪkwe'ɪnafʊn pɛ·''ma tcɪ''ɪ ᴅɪᴅa'ʙna·t ʙʊ'ɢʊlfan mɪ'ᴅɪ sɪ'nfaf.

                              <26(8)>

ᴅɛma'ma ɢʊᴅnɪ'cɪn

   sᴅɪ'ᴅ·at skɪ'nweɪmaẋ.

   ᴅɛna'na ɢʊᴅɪ'tɢwɪn ɢʊ'ca-askɪ'nweɪmaẋ

      ɢʊᴅɪ'st ᴅɛma'ma.

   ʙʊ'ɢʊlfan-sɪ'nfaf ɢʊn·ɪɢɛ'w·u hɛ·''lʊm.

      na'u-ᴅɪma·'ma ɢʊᴅ·a'ʙna·t ʙʊ'ɢʊlfan ɢʊ'sa-asɪ'nfaf.

<27> Picking Hops in Salem

pɛ·''ma ᴅɛma·'ma ɢʊᴅna'ɢɪt

   e'ɪkɪn ɢʊmɪᴅɪ'nfyaf a'mpyan ᴅɪ's-ᴅɪᴅω''ω tcɛɢʊ'sa aha'ps a'a'n·ʊ.

   tcɪ''ɪ-tcɪta'mᴅju wa·''an ᴅʊ'mp̣ɪ a'm·ɪm. ᴅʊmkwʊ'ᴅɢwa·t ɢʊ'ca-aha'pc tcɛɢʊ'ca

      wa'm·u-amu'ɪ.

pɛ·''ma ɢʊ'ca-acɪ'nfaf ʙʊ'ɢʊlfan-a'm·ɪm ɢʊ'saʙɛ·ᴅ ɢʊᴅɪnɪᴅa'ʙɪt ɢʊᴅɪnɪᴅna'ɢɪt

   ɢʊ'cwɪ. sʊ'ᴅʊ ᴅɪtɛ'n·ɛtcwu·n tcɛɢʊ'ca a'mpyan.   ‖122:97‖

pɛ·''ma ɢʊᴅɪnᴅɪ'tku ɢʊ'sa aklʊ'ɢᴅɪfʊn tcɛᴅa'ɪwan a·''muɪ.   <27(2) >

pɛ·''ma ᴅɛma·'ma nau-ɢɛ'm ᴅɛna'na ᴅɪnɪku'n·ɪyaʙ ɢʊn·ɪɢɛ'm'yat ᴅɛma'ma

   ᴅɪnɪtwʊ'ᴅwa·t ɢʊ'ca-asa'ʙlɪl tcɛᴅɪ·'t'saq-aha'm·ɪ.

ʙʊ'ɢʊlfan ɢɪnɪtʊ'ɢɪ pɛ·''ma ɢɪ'n·ʊ'k ɢʊᴅɪnɪᴅɪ'tyɪ.

pɛ·''ma-ɢʊᴅɪtme'ɪᴅj ᴅɛma'ma ɢʊᴅ·ʊ'ᴅnɪɢwan a'm·ɪm ɢʊᴅɪta'mᴅju. ᴅʊmᴅɪ'tku tcɛɢʊ'ca

   ha'ps a'n·u.

He told his group,   <27(3) >
   "In ten days we'll go to the hop-yard."
Then on that day all of those hundred people went to the hopyard.

   They travelled one day, when they got to the hop-yard.[3]
   Everyone set up their tents.
Then my father said to the White man,   <27(4)>
   "Where can we turn loose all these people's horses?" ||122:99||
The White man says this,
   "There are one hundred acres of good grass over there.
   Your people will take their horses over there."
   One young White man took them there where they released their horses.<27(5)>
Then my father [unfin.], and that White man said this to my father,
   "Here are ten acres of potatoes.
   I'll just give them to your people."[4]
My father said,
   "Okay, good."
Then next day all his people went to pick the hops.

                                                   <27(6)>

Then my father watched over all his people.
He told his people,
   "You do a good job for this White man!
   He has given you ten acres of potatoes. ||122:101|| <27(7)>
   You will eat (will have food)."
   My father worked for five dollars a day.
   There they picked hops for twenty-five days.
Then they finished all the hops.
Then that man went to Chemeketa (Salem).   <27(8)>
   He went to get money at the money-house (bank).
Next day he paid all the people.
Then they went to get the horses.
   They got ready.
Then they went off all different ways.

<28> Grinding Wheat at the Gristmill
My father and my mother (and I) went back home.
When he got to the house, my father fixed up everything at our place.

ɢʊᴅnɪ'sɪn ᴅɪɢɑ'wakɪl   <27(3) >
   ɢʊmaᴅi'nfyaf-a'mpyan tcɪᴅɪᴅɯ''ɷ tcaɢʊ'ca-ha'ps-wɪ-a'n·u.
pɛ·''ma ɢʊ'cawi-a'mpyan ʙʊ'ɢʊlfan ɢʊ'ca wa''an ᴅʊ'mp̣ɪ am·ɪ'm ɢʊᴅɪnɪᴅɪ't tcɛɢʊ'ca
   ha'ps a'n·u.
   ɢʊᴅɪntiˑ'f wa''an-a'mpyan ɢʊᴅɪnɪtwa'l tcɛɢʊ'sa ha'ps a'n·u.
   ʙʊ'ɢʊlfan-ɪ'y·a ɢʊᴅɪnɪtɛ'n·an ᴅɪnɪsɪ'l·haus
pɛ·''ma ᴅɛma''ma ɢʊᴅna'ɢɪt tcɛɢʊ'sa wa'm·u am'ʊɪ.   <27(4) >
   haˑl·a tcɪᴅɪtɢʊ' ʙʊ'ɢʊlfan hɛ'sa a'm·im ᴅɪnɪkɪ'ʊᴅɪn. ||122:99||
ɢʊ'sa-wa'm·uˑ amu'ɪ pa'-utmɪ'ut,
   wa''an ᴅʊ'mp̣ɪ ᴅɪ-a'cre tɛ'n·a lʊ'q̇ʊ ɢʊ'caʙɛ·ᴅ.
   ɢʊ'saʙɛ·ᴅ ma'ha ʙɪɢa'wakɪl ɢʊnɪᴅɪ'tk̇u ᴅɪnɪkɪ'ʊᴅɪn.
   wa''an huˑm·uˑ sɪ'nfaf ɢʊᴅɪnɪᴅɪ'tk̇u tcɛɢʊ'sa hɛ·l·a ɢʊᴅɪnɪtɢʊ' ᴅɪnɪkɪ'ʊᴅɪn. <27(5)>
pɛ·''ma ᴅɛma''ma nauɢʊ'sa-awa'm·uˑ-amu'ɪ pa'-umɪ'ut tcɛᴅɛma''ma
   hɛ'saʙɛ·ᴅ ᴅɪˑ'nfyaf acre ama'mpᴅu.
   k̇ʊ'nfʊ tcɪ''ɪ tcɪᴅɪᴅɪ'st tcɛma'ha ʙʊɢa'wakɪl.
ᴅɛma''ma
   ɢʊ'cwɪ tɛ'n·a
pɛ·''ma ɢʊᴅɪᴅme'ɪᴅj ʙʊ'ɢʊlfan ᴅɪɢa'wakɪl ɢʊᴅɪnɪᴅɪ't ᴅʊmɪnɪkwʊ'tk̇waˑt ɢʊ'sa-ha'ps.
                                                                             <27(6)>
pɛ·''ma ᴅɛma''ma ɢʊᴅyu'ᴅnɪɢwan ʙʊ'ɢʊlfan ᴅɪɢa'wakɪl.
ɢʊᴅnɪ'sˑɪn ᴅɪɢa'wakɪl.
   mɪ'ᴅɪ sʙʊ'n tɛ'n·a alu''nafʊn tcɛhɛ'sa wa'm·uˑ-a'mu'ɪ.
   ɢɯ'k ɢʊᴅɪ'ᴅ·ʊp ᴅɪˑ'nfyaf an'acre ama'mpᴅʊ. ||122:101|| <27(7)>
   mɪ'ᴅɪ ɢʊᴅʊpk̇we'ɪnafʊ.
   tcɪ''ɪ-ᴅɛma''ma ɢʊᴅ_luˑ''nʊf tcɛhu'w·an sq̇ɪ'nweɪmax̣ wa''an-a'mpyan.
   ɢʊ'saʙɛ·ᴅ ɢʊnɪᴅkwʊ'tk̇waˑᴅ ɢʊ'sa-ha'ps ɢɛ'm-ᴅɪ'nfyʊf nauhu'w·an a'mpyan.
pɛ·''ma ɢʊnˑɪṫʊ'ɢɪ-ʙʊ'ɢʊlfan ɢʊ'sa-aha'ps.
pɛ·''ma ɢʊca-a'mu'ɪ ɢʊᴅɪ't tcɛtcemɪ'ɢɪᴅɪ   <27(8)>
   ɢʊᴅɪ'twʊ cq̇ɪ'nweɪmax̣ tcɛɢʊ'ca acq̇ɪ'nweɪmax̣ ᴅʊ'm·aɪ.
ɢʊᴅɪtme'ɪᴅj ɢʊᴅ·a'ʙna·t ʙʊ'ɢʊlfan ɢʊ'sa a'm·ɪm.
pɛ·''ma ɢʊᴅɪnɪᴅɪ'twʊ ᴅɪkɪ'ʊᴅɪn,
   ɢʊnɪtɛ'natswuˑn,
pɛ·''ma ɢʊᴅɪnɪṫiˑ'f ʙʊ'ɢʊlfan ha''lʊ [or halʊ].

<28> Grinding Wheat at the Gristmill
ᴅɛma''ma nau-ᴅɛna''na su'ᴅ·ʊ ɢʊᴅɪ'tyɪ tcɛᴅʊᴅʊ'n·ʊ.
ɢʊᴅɪtwa'l tcɛha'm·ɪ ᴅɛma''ma ɢʊtˑɛ'n·aˑn ʙʊ'ɢʊlfan a'ɢfan tcɛᴅʊᴅʊ'n·ʊ.

Then next day he got ten sacks of wheat.

He took them to where they ground the wheat.[5] ||122:103||

Then near nightfall he came back.

He brought back five hundred pounds of the ground flour. <28(2)>

Then the old men, the old women, he gave a little to all those old people.

Then they went back home.

pɛ·"ma-ɢʊᴅɪᴅme'ɪᴅj ɢʊᴅʌ'tɢwɪn ᴅɪ'nfyaf lʊ'm·ʊɪfʊɪ ɢʊ'ca-asa'ʙlɪl.

    ɢʊᴅʌ'tku. tcɛha'l·a ɢʊ'ca ɢʊᴅɪnɪtᵽu'ɪᵽya·t asa'ʙlɪl. ||122:103||

pɛ·"ma yɛ'ᴅj-ɢʊmɪthu'wɪ ɢʊᴅme'y·ɪ.

    ɢʊmwɪ"ɪl hu'w·an ᴅʊ'mᵽi ɢʊ'sa ᵽu'ɪᵽyɪm sa'ʙlil.   <28(2)>

pɛ·"ma ɢɪ'n·ʊk ayu·'tcatyu a'mu'ɪ ayu·'tcatyu aʙu'm·ɪk ɢʊᴅʌ'st pʊ't'snaq tcɛʙʊ'ɢʊlfan

    ɢʊ'ca yu·'fatyu a'm·ɪm.

pɛ·"ma-ɢɪ'n·ʊk ɢʊᴅɪnɪᴅɪ'tyɪ.

CHAPTER SIX
Horse-Racing[1]

<29> Shilikwa Races a White Man

Then the next day my father and I went to fetch two race-horses.

   One of those horses, my horse, my father gave me that horse.

He said to me,

   "This is your race-horse.

   Take good care of it.

     Give it good food.

   You are to wash the entire body of that horse!"

He gave me a blanket,   <29(2)>

   "You are to cover your horse with this."

   (As for) his own horse, it was a fine one. ||122:105||

   All the people took their horses, all kinds of horses.

     They trained common saddle-horses.

Then on the sixth day (Saturday?) everyone went to that race-track.[2]

In the afternoon many White people came to the race-track.

                                            <29(3)>

   They brought their race-horses.

One Indian (Shilikwa[3]) led out a very fine race-horse.

   "Who wants to race against my horse?"

One White man said,   <29(4)>

   "I'll race against you.

   I want to race six hundred paces against you."

That Indian said,

   "Okay. How much money do you want to race?"

That White man said, ||122:107||

   "One hundred and fifty dollars."

Then that Indian said,   <29(5)>

   "Okay."

   All the Indians collected their money.[4]

Then they gave it to one good man (to hold the stake).

Then that Indian says this,

   "I'll take two Indian men,

     One there where they start,

     One here at the end."

Horse-Racing

<29> šílikʷa Races a White Man

pɛ·''ma ɢʊdɪdmɛ'ɪdj tcɪ''ɪ-na'u-dɛma'ma ɢʊd·ɷ''ɷ ɢʊd_ɪ'twʊ ɢɛ·'m ma'nfyak akɪ'ʊdɪn.

  wa''an-ɢu'sa-akɪ'ʊdɪn tcɪ''ɪ-dɛkɪ'ʊdɪn dɛma'ma ɢʊdɪ'd·at ɢʊ'ca-akɪ'ʊdɪn.

ɢʊdna'ɢɪt tcɛtcɪ''ɪ,

  hɛ's·a ma'ha ʙɪm·a'nfyak akɪ'ʊdɪn.

  ma'ha cyu·'dnɪɢwan tɛ'n·a·n,

    dɪ'st watɛ'n·a k̓wɛ'ɪnafʊn.

  ma'ha sk̓u'uł ʙʊ'ɢʊlfan dɪk̓a'pya tcɛɢʊ'sa-akɪ'ʊdɪn.

ɢʊdɪ'dat wa''an aṗa'cɪcɢwa.   <29(2)>

  ha'sa ma'ha dɛlʊ'm·ʊt dɪkɪ'ʊdɪn.

  ɢɷ'k utɛ'n·an ɢɷ'k dɪkɪ'ʊdɪn. ||122:105||

  ʙʊ'ɢʊlfan mɛ·'nmɪ ɢʊnɪdɪ'tɢwɪn dɪnɪkɪ'ʊdan ʙʊ'ɢʊlfan ha'w·ɛu kɪ'ʊdɪn.

    k̓ʊ'nfʊ akɪ'ʊdɪn ɢʊnɪtɛ'n·a'n.

pɛ·''ma ɢʊdɪda'f-a'mpyan ʙʊ'ɢʊlfan-ɪ'y·a ɢʊdɪnɪdɪ't tcɛɢʊ'sa ma'nfyak aɢu'n.

ɢʊdɪtya'hampyan ha'l·u· wa'm·u· a'mɪm ɢʊdɪnɪdma''a tcɛɢʊ'sa ma'nfyak dɪɢu'n

                                                 <29(3)>

  ɢʊdɪnɪtk̓wɛ·'n ɢɪ'n·ʊk dɪnɪma'nfyak akɪ'ʊdɪn.

wa''an-amɛ·'nmɪ ɢʊtwʊ'twa·t ṗʊ'f·an tɛ'n·a ama'nfyak dɪkɪ'ʊdɪn.

  ɪ'y·a ṫa'mdju dʊm·a'ntfʊ tcɛtcɪ''ɪ dɪkɪ'ʊdɪn

wa''an-wʊ'm·u· amu'ɪ ɢʊdna'ɢɪt,   <29(4)>

  tcɪ''ɪ-tcɪdma'nfʊ tcɛ'ma'ha.

  tcɪ''ɪ tcɪṫa'mdju dʊma'nfʊ tcɛma'ha da'f-ʊdu'm̓ṗɪ dɷ'f.

ɢʊ'ca-amɛ·'nmɪ ɢʊdna'ɢɪt

  ɢʊ'cwɪ. a'hu·''lʊ [ha·''lʊ] sɋ̣ɪ'nwɛɪmaẋ ma'ha tcɪṫa'mdju dʊma'nfʊ.

ɢʊ'sa-wa'mu·-amu'ɪ ɢʊdna'ɢɪt ||122:107||

  wa''an dʊ'm̓ṗɪ nau-hu'w·an-dɪ'nfyaf nɪsɋ̣ɪ'nwɛɪmaẋ.

pɛ·''ma ɢʊca-amɛ·'nmɪ ɢʊdna'ɢɪt   <29(5)>

  ɢʊ'cwɪ.

  ʙʊ'ɢʊlfan mɛ·'nmɪ ɢʊn·ɪɢɛ'w·a·t dɪnɪsɋ̣ɪ'nwaɪmaẋ

pɛ·''ma ɢʊnɪdɪ'st wa''an tɛ'n·a adja'ŋk̓u.

pɛ·''ma ɢʊ'ca-amɛ·'nmɪ pa'-ʊdna'ɢɪt,

  tcɪ''ɪ dɪdɪ'tɢwɪn ɢɛ·'m amɛ·'nmɪ.

    wa''an ɢʊ'sa ha'l·a ɢʊdɪnɪd·ɪ'd·ʊp.

    wa''an hɛ'caʙɛ·d tc'ɪm·ɪ.

That White man took two White men (as *his* judges). <29(6)>
Then that jockey (lit., race-boy) rode the Indians' horse.
    A White man rode the Whites' horse.
Then they went to where they started.
Then there when they turned (to start), the White boy wanted to get a head-start
    ahead. ||122:109||
    The Indians' horse knew that sort of turn-around. <29(7)>
       That horse was unexcitable (literally, cool-hearted).
Then they started.
    The second (other) horse was a very good race horse.
When nearly at the end of the race track, the Indians' horse won by two paces.
Then all the Indians jumped up. <29(8)>
    They hollered.
    They threw their hats up.
    They were glad.
    They had beaten the White persons' horse.
    They took their money.
    They paid all the people who had given their money (to stake) that man's race-
    horse. <29(9)>
Then all kinds of horses raced. ||122:111||
    Common saddle-horses raced all that afternoon.
At sunset everybody went home.

<30> Frank Bond Jockeys a Win Against the Whites

The next day they gathered at that race-track.
    White people came.
    They brought lots of race-horses.
In the afternoon they all gathered at the race-track.
One White man brought his race-horse,
    "I want to race this horse four hundred and twenty paces for two hundred and fifty
      dollars." <30(2)>
    Those Indians got one good race horse.
      They led him out.
      They showed it to the White man. ||122:113||
The White man said,
    "Okay! We'll race."
Then the Indians collected two hundred and fifty dollars.

ɢʊ'ca-awa'm·u· u'mu'ɪ ɢʊɒɪ'tɢwɪn ɢɛ'm wa'm·u· ɒja'ŋ̊ku.   <29(6)>

pɛ·''ma ɢʊ'ca-ama'nfyak åtu'ɪɒɪn ɢʊɒyu'wufɢwu·t (~..ɢwa·t) ɢʊ'ca mɛ·'nmɪ ɒɪnɪkɪ'ʊɒɪn.

   wa'm·u· aɒja'ŋ̊ku ɢʊɒyu'wufɢwu·t (~..ɢwa·t) ɢʊ'ca wa'm·u· ɒɪnɪkɪ'ʊɒɪn.

pɛ·''ma ɢʊɒɪnɪɒɪ't ha'l·a ɢʊ'ca ɢʊɒɪnɪɒ'ɪ'ɒ·ʊp.

pɛ·''ma ɢʊ'caʙɛ·ᴅ ɢʊɒɪnɪɒckɪ'lck̊ʊl ɢʊ'sa-awa'm·u· åtu'ɪɒɪn tå'mɒju ᴅʊmɒɪt'ɪ'ɒ·ʊp mɛ·'n.
                                                              ||122:109||

   ɢʊ'sa mɛ·'nmɪyak [~..q] akɪ'ʊɒɪn ɢʊɒyʊ'k·ʊn pɛ·'cawɛu ɪck̊u'lck̊ul.   <29(7)>

      ɢʊ'sa-akɪ'ʊɒɪn ɢʊmtʊ'k̊yu·t ᴅɪmu·'p̊ɪn.

pɛ·''ma. ɢʊɒɪnɪɒ'ɪ'ɒ·ʊp.

   ɢʊ'ca-aɢɛ·'m-akɪ'ʊɒɪn p̊ʊ'fan ɢʊnɪ-tɛ·'n·a ma'nfyak akɪ'ʊɒɪn.

yɛ·'ɒj ɢʊɒɪtwɛ·'l·ʊ ɢʊ'ca-ma'nfyak aɢu'n ɢʊ'sa-amɛ·'nmɪyak akɪ'ʊɒɪn ɢʊɒʊ'l·u ɢɛ·'m-ɒʊ·'f.

pɛ·''ma ʙʊ'ɢʊlfan ɢʊca-amɛ·'nmɪ ɢʊɒɪnɪɒ'ɪ'ɒ·up   <29(8)>

   ɢʊɒɪnɪɒ_la'lwɛɪ

   ɢʊɒɪnɪtɢu·' ᴅɪnɪmu'yus ha'lʙam.

   ɢɪ'n·ʊk ɢʊɒɪnɪɒ'ɛ·'l·ʊ.

   ɢʊɒɪnɪɒʊ'l·ʊ tcɛɢʊ'sa-wa'm·u· a'm·ɪm ᴅɪnɪkɪ'ʊɒɪn.

   ɢʊɒɪnɪɒɪ'tɢwɪn ᴅɪnɪsq̊ɪ'nwaɪmaẋ

   ɢʊɒɪnɪɒa'pna·t ʙʊ'ɢʊlfan ɢʊca-amɛ·'nmɪ ɢʊɒɪnɪɒ'ɪ'ct ᴅɪnɪcq̊ɪ'nwaɪmaẋ ɢʊ'ca-amu'ɪ
      ᴅʊma'nfyak akɪ'ʊɒɪn.   <29(9)>

pɛ·''ma ʙʊ'ɢʊlfan a'w·ɛu akɪ'ʊɒɪn ɢʊɒɪnɪma'nfya·t. ||122:111||

   k̊ʊ'nfʊ-akɪ'ʊɒɪn ɢʊɒɪnɪma'nfʊ ʙʊ'ɢʊlfan ɢʊ'ca-aya'hampyan.

ɢuᴅɪᴅjɛ·'ɢ·u-a'mpyan ʙʊ'ɢʊlfan-ɪ'y·a ɢʊɒɪnɪɒɪ'tyɪ.

<30> Frank Bond Jockeys a Win Against the Whites

ɢʊɒɪnɪɒmɛ·'ɪɒj ɢʊn·ɪɢɛ·'w·u tcɛɢʊ'ca ma'nfyak ᴅɪɢu·'n

   ɢɪ'n·ʊk wa'm·u·-a'm·ɪm ɢʊɒɪnɪɒ_cma·''a,

   ɢʊɒɪnɪɒ_cmʊ'k̊u ha'l·u· ma'nfyak ᴅɪkɪ'ʊɒɪn.

ɢʊɒɪnɪɒya'hamp_yan ʙʊ'ɢʊlfan ɢʊn·ɪɢɛ·'w·u tcɛɢʊ'ca ma'nfyak-ᴅɪɢu·'n.

wa''an-aha'm·u· a'mu'ɪ ɢʊɒ_smʊ'k̊u ᴅɪma'nfyak-akɪ'ʊɒɪn

   tcɪ''ɪ-tcɪta'mɒju ᴅɪma'nfu hɛ·'ca-akɪ'ʊɒɪn ta'ʙ-ᴅʊ'mp̊ɪ nau-ɢɛ·'m-ᴅɪ·'nfyʊf ᴅʊ·'f.

      tcɛɢɛ·'m-ᴅʊ'mp̊ɪ nau-hu'w·an-ᴅɪ·'nfyaf asq̊ɪ'nwɛɪmaẋ.   <30(2)>

   ɢɪ'n·ʊɢʊ'ca-amɛ·'nmɪ ɢʊnɪɒɪ'tɢwɪn wa''an tɛ·'n·a ma'nfyʊk-akɪ'ʊɒɪn.

      ɢʊnɪtwʊ'ᴅwa·t,

      ɢʊnɪthʊ·'ᴅnɪɢwan tcɛɢʊ'sa-awa'm·u·-amu'ɪ. ||122:113||

ɢʊ'sa-wa'm·u·-amu'ɪ ɢʊɒna'ɢɪt,

   ɢʊ'swi·! tcɪɒma'nfu.

pɛ·''ma ɢɪ'n·ʊk a'mɛ·'nmɪ ɢʊnɪɢɛ·'w·a·t ɢɛ·'m-ᴅʊ'mp̊ɪ nau-hu'w·an-ᴅɪ·'nfyaf asq̊ɪ'nwɛɪmaẋ.

<30(3)>

Then that Indian boy (Frank Bond[5]) rode the Indians' race horse.

   One White boy rode the White man's horse.

The White man said,

   "I don't want to get four men (as judges)."

Those boys spoke, one spoke.   <30(4)>

Then one did speak,

   "Yes.

   Oh, there at the starting place, the White boys want to steal the start."[6]

   The Indians' boy did not yield the start.[7] ||122:115||

Then the White man's horse got sweaty.   <30(5)>

Then that White man called to that (White) boy,

   "You better start now!

   That horse of ours is getting into a big sweat."

Then they started.

   The two boys whipped them "killing" their horses.[8]

When they were almost to the end, the Indians' horse went ahead.   <30(6)>

   It won by maybe six paces.

Then the Indians were glad.

   They threw their hats up.

   They hollered.

Then they took their money.

Then they raced all sorts of other horses.

At sunset everybody went back home.

<31> A Near Tie Between Two Fine Horses

For the next six days everyone came to this race track.

                                        ||122:117||

Now on this particular day many White people came.

   They brought all sorts of horses.

   One man brought a very fine horse.

   Those Indians were afraid of that horse.

They said,   <31(2)>

   "We lack a good horse to race against that horse of yours."

Another White man said,

   "I have a race horse I will race against you."

<30(3)>

pɛ·''ma ɢʊ'ca-amɛ·'nmɪ aᴛu'ɪᴅɪn ɢʊᴅyu'wʊfɢu·t ɢʊ'sa-amɛ·'nmɪyak ma'nfyak akɪ'uᴅɪn.

 wa·''an-awa'm·u· aᴛu'ɪᴅɪn ɢʊᴅyu'wʊfɢu·t ɢʊ'sa-wa'm·u·-a'mu'ɪ ᴅɪnɪkɪ'uᴅɪn.

ɢʊ'sa-wa'm·u·-a'mu'ɪ.

 wa'ŋq tcɪ''ɪ-ɢʊᴛa'mᴅju ᴅʊmᴅɪ'tɢwɪn ta'ʙ-a'mu'ɪ.

ɢɪ'n·u'k ɢʊ'sa-aᴛu'ɪᴅfaf ɢɪnɪᴅna'ɢɪᴅ, wa·''an ɢʊᴅna'ɢɪᴅ,   <30(4)>

pɛ·''ma wa·''an ɢʊᴅna'ɢɪᴅ

 hɛ·'ⁿ'a.

 u·', ɢʊ'caʙɛᴅ tcɛha'l·a ɢʊᴅɪnɪᴅ'ɪ'ᴅʊf ᴅɪnɪkɪ'uᴅɪn ɢʊ'sa-wa'm·u· aᴛu'ɪᴅfaf ɢʊᴛa'mᴅju

  ᴅʊmᴅɪᴅ_l_a'tswu·t aᴅ'ɪ'ᴅʊp.

 ɢʊ'sa-amɛ·'nmɪ ᴅɪᴛu'ɪᴅɪn wa'ŋq ɢʊmɪᴅɪ''st ɢʊ'sa-aᴅ'ɪ'ᴅʊp [aᴛɪ'ᴅʊp]. ||122:115||

pɛ·''ma ɢʊ'sa wa'm·u· amu'wɪ [amu'ɪ] ᴅɪnɪkɪ'uᴅɪn ɢʊᴅma·''yʊ.   <30(5)>

pɛ·''ma ɢʊ'sa-wa'm·u·-amu'ɪ ɢʊᴅ_la'l'wɪ tcɛɢʊ'sa aᴛu'ɪᴅɪn,

 mɪ'ᴅɪ ʙɪcma·'k.

 ɢʊ'sa sʊ'ᴅu ᴅɪkɪ'uᴅɪn p̓ʊ'f·an um·a·''yu.

pɛ·''ma ɢʊᴅɪnɪᴅ'ɪ'ᴅʊp.

 ᴅɪnɪɢɛ·'m ɢʊ'sa aᴛu'ɪᴅ·ɪn ɢʊᴅɪnɪᴅa'haɪ ᴅɪnɪkɪ'uᴅɪn ɢʊnɪk̓lu'ɢla·t.

yɛ'ᴅj ɢʊᴅɪnɪᴅma'l·a ɢʊ'ca a'mɛ·'nmɪyak akɪ'uᴅɪn ɢʊᴅ·ɪ't tc'ɪm·eⁱ,   <30(6)>

 ɢʊᴅ·u'l·u e'ɪkɪn ᴅa'f ᴅɷ·'f.

pɛ·''ma ɢɪ'n·ʊk a'mɛ·'nmɪ ɢʊᴅɪnɪt'ɪ'l·u

 ɢʊᴅɪnɪᴅɢu·'ᴅ ᴅɪnɪmu'y·us ha'lʙam

 ɢʊᴅɪnɪᴅ_la'l'wɛɪ.

pɛ·''ma ɢʊᴅɪnɪᴅɪ'tɢwɪn ᴅɪnɪsq̓ɪ'nwɛɪmaχ.

pɛ·''ma ɢʊᴅɪnɪᴅma'ntfa·f ʙʊ'ɢʊlfan ha'w·ɛu kɪ'uᴅɪn.

ɢʊᴅɪnᴅjɛ'ɢ·u-a'mpyan ʙʊ'ɢʊlfan-ɪ'y·a ɢʊᴅɪnɪᴅɪ'tyɪ.

<31>A Near Tie Between Two Fine Horses

ɢʊmɪᴅa'f-a'mpyan ʙʊ'ɢʊlfan-ɪ'y·a ɢʊnɪcma·''a tcɛha'sa ma'nfyak-aɢu·'n.

||122:117||

pɛ·''ma hɛ'sɪ-wɪ·-ɪ'pyan hʊ'l·u· wa'm·u· a'm·ɪm ɢʊᴅɪnɪtwa'l,

 ʙʊ'ɢʊlfan a'wɛu akɪ'uᴅɪn ɢʊᴅɪnɪtkwɛ·'n.

 wa·''an-a'mu'ɪ ɢʊᴅɪtk̓ɛ·'n p̓ʊ'f·an wa-tɛ'n·a akɪ'uᴅɪn.

ɢɪ'n·ʊ'k ɢʊ'sa mɛ·'nmɪ ɢʊᴅɪnɪᴅnɪ'uhɪn ɢʊ'ca-akɪ'uᴅɪn.

ɢʊᴅɪnɪᴅna'ɢɪt,   <31(2)>

 wa'ha sʊ'ᴅʊ wa-tɛ'n·a akɪ'uᴅɪn ᴅʊmᴅɪᴅma'nfɪt tcɛɢʊ'ca ma'ha ʙɪɢɪ'uᴅɪn.

wa·''an uwa'm·u· a·''muɪ ɢʊᴅna'ɢɪt,

 tcɪ''ɪ p̓ɪ'n wa·''an ama'nfyak akɪ'uᴅɪn tcɪ''ɪ-ᴅɪtma'nfʊ tcɛma'ha

That other man says,
  "Where is your horse?
    I want to see it."
  The other White man went to get his race horse.   <31(3)>
Then the man saw that horse. ||122:119||
Then he said,
  "Okay. Let's race.
  How much do you want to bet?"
[---]
  "It's up to you.⁹
  How much do you want to bet?"
[---]
  "I am betting three hundred dollars."
The other man said,   <31(4)>
  "Okay. I want it to run five hundred paces."
[---]
  "Okay."
Then they went and got those who rode (jockeyed) their horses.
Then they went to where they started.
After they had gotten to where they started, they bolted back around twice.   <31(5)>
Then they started.¹⁰
Then they ran.
  They were very fine horses.
  One of those horses won by one pace.
Then (to) those who were betting on that one ahead, one of those other men¹¹ said,
  "No one won." ||122:121||
That other man said,   <31(6)>
  "We won by one pace."
Then all the people were arguing.
  That man on the other side had bet his money on that other horse.
This is what he said,
  "No one won."
Then the other man said,
  "That horse of his won by one pace.
  Then let's run it once more."
[---]

ɢʊ'ca-wa''an-a'mu'ɪ ʊᴅna'ɢɪt,
  ha'l·a ma'ha ʙɪɢɪ'uᴅɪn.
    tcɪ''ɪ t̓a'mᴅju ᴅʊmthɷ'ᴅ.
  ɢʊ'sa-wa''an-wa'm·u-amu'ɪ ɢʊᴅɪ'twʊ ᴅɪma'nfyak akɪ'uᴅɪn.   <31(3)>
pɛ·''ma ɢʊ'sa-amu'ɪ ɢʊthɷ'ᴅ ɢʊ'sa akɪ'uᴅɪn.   ‖122:119‖
pɛ·''ma ɢʊᴅna'ɢɪt,
  ɢʊ'cwɪ tcɪᴅma'nfɪᴅʊ.
  a'hʊ'l·u ma'ha tcɪt̓a'mᴅju ᴅʊmlu''ut.
[---]
  ma'ha-ʙʊmhu·'ṗɪn
  a'hu'lu ma'ha tcɪt̓a'mᴅju ᴅʊmlu''ut.
[---]
  tcɪ''ɪ-tcɪlu''ut hu'psɪn ᴅʊ'mṗɪ q̓ɪ'nweɪmax.
ɢʊ'sa-wa''an-amu'ɪ ɢʊᴅna'ɢɪt   <31(4)>
  ɢʊ'cwɪ. tcɪ''ɪ tcɪt̓a'mᴅju amɪ'tcnafɢwɪ·n hu'w·an aᴅʊ'mṗɪ ᴅɷ'f.
[---]
  ɢʊ'cwɪ.
pɛ·''ma ɢʊᴅɪnɪᴅnɪ'ɢwɪn ɢɪ'n·ʊk ɢʊ'ca ɢʊᴅyu'wʊfɢu·t ᴅɪnɪkɪ'uᴅɪn.
pɛ·''ma ɢʊᴅɪnɪᴅɪ't tcɛɢʊ'sa ha'l·a ɢʊᴅɪnɪᴅ'ɪ'ᴅ·ʊp.
ɢʊᴅɪnɪtwa'l tcɛha'l·a ɢʊ'saʙɛ·ᴅ ɢʊᴅɪnɪᴅ'ɪ'ᴅ·ʊp ɢɛ'm'wa ɢʊᴅɪnɪᴅ_sk̓ɪ'lskul   <31(5)>
pɛ·''ma ɢʊᴅɪnɪᴅ'ɪ'ᴅ·ʊp.
pɛ·''ma ɢʊᴅɪnɪᴅmɪ'nᴅjɪc
  ṗʊ'f·an ɢʊnɪtɛ'n·a-kɪ'uᴅɪn.
  wa''an ɢʊ'sa kɪ'uᴅɪn ɢʊᴅʊ'l·ʊ wa''an ᴅɷ'f.
pɛ·''ma ɢɪ'n·ʊk ɢuca ɢʊᴅɪnɪᴅ_lʊ'ᴅɢwɪfu·n ɢʊ'sa ᴅjɪm·eɪ wa''an ɢʊca-a'mu'ɪ ɢʊᴅna'ɢɪt
  wa'ŋq-ɪ'y·a ɢʊᴅu'l·u.   ‖122:121‖
ɢusa-wa''an-a'mu'ɪ ɢʊᴅna'ɢɪt   <31(6)>
  su'ᴅ·ʊ ɢʊᴅ_cᴅʊ'l·ʊ wa''an-aᴅɷ'f.
pɛ·''ma ʙʊ'ɢʊlfan a'm·ɪm ɢʊᴅɪnɪᴅyu''wɪn.
  ɢʊ'ca-a'mu'ɪ ᴅjʊ'hu ɢɷ'k ɢʊᴅ_lʊ'ʙfu·n ᴅɪcq̓ɪ'nwaɪmax tcɛɢʊ'sa-akɪ'uᴅɪn.
pɛ'ca ɢɷ'k ɢʊᴅna'ɢɪt,
  wa'ŋq-ɪ'y·a ɢʊᴅʊ'l·u.
pɛ·''ma ɢʊ'ca-wa''an a'mu'ɪ ɢʊᴅna'ɢɪt
  ɢu'ca ɢɷ'k ᴅɪkɪ'uᴅɪn ɢʊᴅ·u'l·u wa''an-aᴅɷ'f
  pɛ·''ma tcɪᴅma'nfʊ wa''an mɪ'ᴅ·a.
[---]

"Okay, let's run it once more." <31(7)>

Then they went to where they started.

Then they started, and that one horse won by five paces.

    That horse won twice.

<32> Siletz People Come to Race

Then in the late morning all the people brought their horses. ||122:123||

    An Indian (Pinky Logan) came from Siletz country.

    They brought one fast horse to our country.[12]

    They brought one good horse.

Then they raced with the Siletz Indians' horse.

    Those Siletz Indians[13] collected a lot of money. <32(2)>

    They collected two hundred dollars.

Then our Indians made up this same amount, two hundred dollars.

    Those Siletz Indians wanted to run their horse three hundred paces.

Our people said,

    "Okay."

Then they got their lads to ride their horses. <32(3)>

Then our people got one good lad. ||122:125||

Then he rode our people's race-horse.

    They took four men,

        two to here where they started the horses,

        two to here where the end of the race-track was.

Then they brought the race-horses to where they started. <32(4)>

    The two men watched the race-horses (so that) one would not steal the start.

They said,

    "Now you start!"

Then they started the horses.

Then they "killed" their horses.

    Those two young men rode those race-horses.

    Near the end of the course our Indians' horse left the Siletz people's horse

        behind. <32(5)>

    He won by maybe four paces. ||122:127||

Then they took their money.

    They paid off all those who had put money on that horse.

ɢʊ′cwɪ tcɪɒma′nfɪt wa′'an-mɪ′ɒ·a.   <31(7)>

pɛɛ·″ma ɢɪ′nʊ̇k ɢʊɒnɪ′'ɪ tcɛha′l·a-ɢʊ′ca ɢʊɒɪnɪɒ′'ɪ′ɒʊp.

pɛɛ·″ma ɢʊɒɪnɪɒ′'ɪ′ɒʊp nau-ɢʊ′ca-wa′'an akɪ′uɒɪn ɢʊɒ·ʊ′l·ʊ hu′w·an ɒɷ·′f.

ɢʊ′ca akɪ′uɒɪn ɢʊɒ·ʊ′l·ʊ ɢɛ′fʊ.

<32> Siletz People Come to Race

pɛɛ·″ma ɢʊ′ca-wɪ-ya′hampyan ʙʊ′ɢʊlfan a′m·ɪm ɢɪnɪkwɛ′'n ɒɪnɪkɪ′uɒɪn. ||122:123||

wa′'an-amɛ′'nmɪ ɢʊɒ_cme′y·amp tcaqu″ʊc wɪ-a′n·ʊ.

ɢɪ′nʊ̇k ɢʊɒɪnɪɒkwɛ′'n wa′'an ɢʊ′mcu·k akɪ′uɒɪn tcɛsʊ′ɒ·ʊ-ɒʊ′n·ʊ,

ɢɪnɪɒkwɛ′'n wa′'an tɛ′n·a akɪ′uɒɪn.

pɛɛ·″ma ɢʊɒɪnɪɒma′nfɪt tcɛɢʊ′ca-qu″ʊs mɛ′'nmɪ ɒɪnɪkɪ′uɒɪn.

ɢʊɒɪnɪɢɛ′w·ʊ ha′l·u· ɪsɋɪ′nwaɪmax ɢʊ′sa aqu″us mɛ′'nmɪ.   <32(2)>

ɢɛ′m-ɒʊ′mᵽya asɋɪ′nweɪmax ɢɪ′nʊ̇k ɢʊɒɪnɪɒnɪ′ɢ·ʊn.

pɛɛ·″ma sʊ′ɒ·ʊ ɒʊmɛ′'nmɪ ɢɪnɪʙʊ′'n pa′ca′yu-hɷ·″lʊ ɢɛ′mɒʊ′mᵽɪ asɋɪ′nweɪmax.

ɢɪ′nʊ̇′k ɢʊ′ca-qu″us amɛ′'nmɪ ɢʊnɪta′mɒjʊ ɒʊmɪmɪ′tcɢwanfɪn ɒɪnɪkɪ′uɒɪn hu′psɪn

[hu′pcɪn] ɒʊ′mᵽɪ ɒɪɒɷ·′f.

sʊ′ɒ·ʊ ɒɪ′a′m·ɪm ɢʊnɪ′na′ɢɪt

ɢʊ′cwɪ.

pɛɛ·″ma ɢʊnɪɒɪ′tɢwɪn ɒɪnɪ′u′ɪfaf ɢʊɒyu′wafɢwʊt ɢɪ′nʊ̇k ɒɪnɪkɪ′uɒan.   <32(3)>

pɛɛ·″ma sʊ′ɒ·ʊ ɒɪ′a′m·ɪm ɢʊnɪɒɪ′tɢwɪn wa′'an wa·-tɛ′n·a atu′ɪɒɪn. ||122:125||

pɛɛ·″ma ɢʊtyu′wafɢwʊt ɢʊ′c·a-sʊ′ɒ·ʊ ɒʊ′m·ɪm ɒɪnɪma′nfyak akɪ′uɒɪn.

ɢʊɒɪnɪnɪ′kwɪn ta′ʙ a′mu′ɪ

ɢɛ′m-tcɛhɛ′′ca ɢʊɒɪnɪɒ′'ɪ′ɒʊp. akɪ′uɒɪn,

ɢɛ′m tcɛhɛ′′c·a ɒɪtwɛ′l·ʊt ma′nfyak-aɢʊ′n.

pɛɛ·″ma ɢʊɒɪɒnɪ′ku ɢʊ′ca-ma′nfyak-akɪ′uɒɪn tcɛhɛ′l·a ɢʊ′ca ɢʊɒɪnɪɒ′'ɪ′ɒʊp.   <32(4)>

ɢʊ′ca ɢɛ′m-am′u′ɪ ɢʊɒɪnɪɒ_lʊ′ɒnɪɢwan ɢʊ′ca-ma′nfyak akɪ′uɒɪn wa′ŋq-wa′'an

ɢʊ′mɒɪɒɪɒ_la′tswu·t ɒɪ′'ɪ′ɒʊp.

ɢɪ′nʊ̇k-ɢʊɒɪɒna′ɢɪt

pɛɛ·″ma mɪ′ɒɪ pc′'ɪ′ɒʊp.

pɛɛ·″ma ɢʊɒɪnɪɒ′'ɪ′ɒʊp akɪ′uɒɪn

pɛɛ·″ma ɢʊɒɪnɪɒa′haɪ ɒɪnɪkɪ′uɒɪn

ɢʊca-ɢɛ′m-asɪ′nfaf ɢʊɒɪnɪyu′wafɢwɪt ɢʊca-ma′nfyak akɪ′uɒɪn.

yɛ′tc tcɪɒɪtwɛ′lɒɪɢu·ɒ sʊ′ɒ·ʊ ɒɪmɛ′'nmɪ ɒɪnɪkɪ′uɒɪn ɢʊɒha′ɢ·u·ɒ ɢʊca-qu″ʊc a′m·ɪm

ɒɪnɪkɪ′uɒɪn.   <32(5)>

e′ɪkɪn ta′ʙ-ɒɷ·′f ɢʊɒ·ʊ′l·ʊ. ||122:127||

pɛɛ·″ma ɢʊɒɪnɪɒnɪ′kwɪn ɒɪnɪsɋɪ′nwaɪmax

ɢʊɒɪnɪɒa′ʙ·a·t ʙʊ′ɢʊlfan e′y·a ɢʊ′ca-ɢʊtɢʊ′ tcɛɢʊ′ca-akɪ′uɒɪn.

<33> Silvertail Wins $500 for the Tualatins and Their Clackamas and Molala Friends
Then our own (Grand Ronde) Indian community[14] raced.

    One tribe, called the Luckiamutes, lead out one of their race horses.

They said,
    "We want to race you Tualatin people!"
Then the Tualatin people said,
    "Okay."
    They knew their own horses.   <33(2)>
    "How much money do you want to get together?"
Then the Luckiamute people, the Umpquas, Rogue Rivers, Shastas, all of those
    people put their money together on the Luckiamute people's horse.
Then one Tualatin man said this, ||122:129|| <33(3)>
    "How much money do you have?"
The Luckiamute people said,
    "Five hundred."
Our man said,
    "We will get together that much money."
Then they got together their money.
    Tualatins, Yamhills, Clackamas, and Molala people got together that five hun-
        dred dollars.
    They tied it up in a handkerchief.   <33(4)>
    They tied up those two handkerchiefs in another.
Then they got their horses.
    They went to the race-track.
    They ran six hundred paces.
Then they started the race-horses.
    Those two race horses were extremely good ones.   <33(5)>
    They ran the six hundred yards.[15]
Then, at perhaps five hundred (yards), the Luckiamute people's horse got winded.
                               ||122:131||

Then our horse (Silvertail) left their horse behind.
    Our people were glad.   <33(6)>
    They threw their hats up.
Then they hollered.
    They laughed when our horse won.

<33> Silvertail Wins $500 for the Tualatins and Their Clackamas and Molala Friends

pɛˑ″ma sʊ′ᴅ·ʊ ᴅɪmɛ′nmɪyak ɢa′wakɪl ɢɪ′nʊk ɢʊᴅɪnɪtma′nfyak.

   wa″an aɢa′wakɪl ᴅɪnɪᴅa′ŋkwɪt la′q̇mayʊt ɢɪ′nʊk nɪwʊ′ᴅwaˑt wa″an ᴅɪnɪma′n-

      fyak nɪkɪ′ʊᴅɪn.

ɢɪ′nʊk-ɢɪnɪᴅna′ɢɪt

   sʊ′ᴅ·ʊ tcɪᴅɪṫa′mᴅjʊ ᴅʊmɪnɪᴅma′nfɪyʊ tcɛ-mɪ′ᴅɪ ɢʊ′ca tfa′laṫɪ-a′mˑɪm.

pɛˑ″ma ɢʊ′ca-atfa′laṫɪ-a′mˑɪm ɢʊᴅna′ɢɪt

   ɢʊ′cwɪ.

   ɢɪ′nʊk ɢɪnɪ′yʊ′ɢɪn ᴅɪnɪkɪ′ʊᴅɪn.   <33(2)>

   aha″lu· isq̇ɪ′nwɛɪmaẋ mɪ′ᴅɪ tcɪṫa′mᴅjʊ sɢɛ′wˑat

pɛˑ″ma ɢɪ′nʊk ɢʊ′sa la′q̇mayʊt a′mˑɪm a′mᴘɢwa Rogue Rivers ɢʊᴅjɛ′sᴅɪ ʙʊ′ɢʊlfan-ɢɪ′nʊk

   ɢʊ′sa-a′mˑɪm ɢʊᴅɪnɪɢɛ′wˑʊ ᴅɪnɪsq̇ɪ′nwaɪmaẋ tcɛɢʊ′sa la′q̇mayʊt a′mˑɪm ᴅɪnɪkɪ′ʊᴅɪn.

pɛˑ″ma wa″an tfa′laṫɪ-a′muˑɪ pa″-ɢʊᴅna′ɢɪt ||122:129|| <33(3)>

   a′hɷ″lʊ mɪ′ᴅɪ ᴅɪpsq̇ɪ′nwaɪmaẋ.

ɢɪ′nʊk la′q̇mayʊt a′muˑɪ ɢʊᴅna′ɢɪt,

   huˑ′wˑan-ᴅʊ′mᴘi.

sʊ′ᴅ·ʊ-ᴅumuˑɪ ɢʊᴅna′ɢɪt,

   sʊ′ᴅ·ʊ ɢɪᴅɪᴅɪ′tɢwɪn pa′c-ahuˑ″lu asq̇ɪ′nwaɪmaẋ

pɛˑ″ma ɢɪ′nʊk ɢʊnɪɢɛ′wˑʊ ᴅɪnɪsq̇ɪ′nwaɪmaẋ

   tfa′laṫɪ ya′mhala ɫa′kamas na′u amʊ′lɛˑlɪs a′mˑɪm ɢɪnɪᴅɪ′tɢwɪn ɢʊ′ca-huˑ′wˑan

      ᴅʊ′mᴘi sq̇ɪ′nwaɪmaẋ.

   ɢʊᴅɪnɪᴅ′_ɛ′mˑaᴅ tcɛhɪ′ktcʊm   <33(4)>

   ɢʊᴅɪnɪᴅ′ɛ′mˑaᴅ ɢʊ′ca-ɢɛ′m ahɪ′ktcʊm tcɛwa″an.

pɛˑ″ma ɢʊᴅɪnɪᴅɪ′tɢwɪn ᴅɪnɪkɪ′ʊᴅɪn

   ɢʊᴅɪnɪᴅni·′ tcɛ-ɢʊ′ca-ma′nfyak aɢuˑ′n.

   ɢʊᴅɪnɪᴅmɪ′nᴅjɪs ᴅa′f ᴅʊ′mᴘi ᴅɷ′f.

pɛˑ″ma ɢʊᴅɪnɪᴅ′ɪ′ᴅ·ʊp ɢʊ′ca-amɪ′nfyak akɪ′ʊᴅɪn.

   ᴅɪɢɛ′m ɢʊ′ca amɪ′nfyak akɪ′ʊᴅɪn ᴘu′fan ɢʊᴅɪnɪtɛ′nˑa.   <33(5)>

   ɢʊᴅɪnɪᴅmɪ′nᴅjɪs ɢʊ′ca-ᴅa′f ᴅʊ′mᴘi. ᴅʊlʊ″ʊn.

pɛˑ″ma e′ɪkɪn hʊ′wˑan-aᴅʊ′mᴘi ɢɪ′nʊk ɢʊ′sa-la′q̇mayʊt a′mˑɪm ᴅɪnɪkɪ′ʊᴅɪn ɢʊtwa″yʊ

   ᴅʊ′maˈkaˑn. ||122:131||

pɛˑ″ma sʊ′ᴅ·ʊ ᴅɪkɪ′ʊᴅɪn ɢʊtha′ɢ̇uˑt ɢʊ′ca-ɢɪ′nʊk ᴅɪnɪkɪ′ʊᴅɪn.

   sʊ′ᴅ·ʊ-ᴅʊ′mˑɪm ɢʊᴅɪnɪᴅ′ɛ′lˑʊ   <33(6)>

   ɢʊᴅɪnɪᴅɢuˑ′ ᴅɪnɪmu′yuc tcɛ′a′myaŋk (ha′lʙam)

pɛˑ″ma ɢɪ′nʊk ᴅɛlɛˈl′waɪ

   ɢʊnɪᴅ_lɪ′lʊfʊᴅ sʊ′ᴅ·ʊ kɪ′ʊᴅɪn ɢʊᴅɪᴅʊ′lˑʊ.

They took their money.
Then our man gave to everyone that had contributed money.[16]

<34> John Wacheno Organizes a Win Against the Umpquas
Then they led out plain, common saddle-horses.
    They ran for little money.
Then at sunset that Luckiamute man said,
    "We want to play the nahf game."[17]
Our people said,
    "Okay."
Then on that night there were all sorts of games.   <34(2)>
    They went back to their houses, they ate. ||122:133||
Then they went to where they gathered.
    There all the Indians played all night.
The next morning they went home.
Then on the sixth day (Saturday?) they gathered at that race-track.   <34(3)>
Then it rained.
    My father worked.
    He plowed the ground all day.
    He gave his race horse to his "brother-in-law" (John Wacheno).[18]
        He was a fine race-horse.[19]
On the sixth day all the people came to that race-track in the early afternoon.

Then my father's brother-in-law (Wacheno) led out our horse.   <34(4)>
He said to one man,
    "I want to race against your race-horse." ||122:135||
    Those people were Umpquas.[20]
Then they got together their money.
    They got one-hundred-fifty (dollars).
    Our people got together that much also.   <34(5)>
They said,
    "We want to race our horse four hundred paces."
[---]
    "Our people want to race six hundred paces."
The Umpquas said,
    "It is too far for our horse."
Then our people said,   <34(6)>

ɢʊnɪdɪ'tɢwɪn dɪnɪsɋɪ'nwaɪmax̣
pɛˑ''ma sʊ'dʊ dʊmuˑ'ɪ ɢʊdˑɪ'st ʙʊ'ɢʊlfan e'yˑa ɢʊ'ca ɢʊdɢʊ' asɋɪ'nwaɪmax̣.

<34> John Wacheno Organizes a Win Against the Umpquas

pɛˑ''ma ɢʊnɪwʊ'dwaˑt k̓ʊ'nfʊ ha'wɛw akɪ'ʊdɪn.
  ɢʊdɪnɪdmɪ'ndjɪs apuˑ't'saq asɋɪ'nwaɪmax̣.
pɛˑ''ma ɢʊdjɛ'ɢʊ-a'mpyan ɢʊ'sa la'ɋmayʊt a'muˑ'ɪ ɢʊdna'ɢɪt
  sʊ'dʊ tcɪdɪta'mdjʊ dʊmɪnɪd_la'ɢʊt anaˑ'f.
sʊ'dʊ dʊ'mˑɪm ɢʊdna'ɢɪt
  ɢʊ'cwɪ.
pɛˑ''ma ɢʊ'cwɪ-huˑ'wɪ ʙʊ'ɢʊlfan a'wˑɛu a'la'ɢʊt.   <34(2)>
  ɢʊdɪnɪdɪ'tyɪ tcɛdɪnɪdʊ'mˑaɪ dɪdɪnɪdkwe'ɪnafʊ ||122:133||
pɛˑ''ma ɢʊdɪnɪdɪ't tcɛha'lˑa ɢʊ'ca ɢʊdɪnɪdɢɛ'wˑʊ.
  ɢʊ'caʙɛˑd ɢɪ'nˑʊk ʙʊ'ɢʊlfan-amɛˑ'nmɪ ɢʊdɪnɪd_la'kwak ʙʊ'ɢʊlfan-awɪ'fyu.
ɢʊdɪdmɛ'ɪdj ɢʊdɪnɪdɪ'tyɪ tcɛˑ'dˑɪnɪdʊ'mˑaɪ.
pɛˑ''ma ɢʊmdɪda'f-a'mpyan dɪdɢɛ'wˑu tcɛɢʊ'sa-ma'nfyak-aɢuˑ'n.   <34(3)>
pɛˑ''ma ɢʊdɢwiˑ'dɪt.
  dɛmaˑ'ma ɢⱷˑk ɢʊd_lu''nafʊn
  ɢʊdpla'ɋpluˑt aha'ŋk̓luˑp ʙʊ'ɢʊlfan-a'mpyan.
  ɢʊdˑɪ'ct ɢⱷˑk dʊma'nfyak akɪ'ʊdɪn tcɛdɪʙa'nˑak.
    ɢⱷˑk ɢʊtˑɛˑnˑaˑ'n̥ ɢʊca-ma'nfyak-akɪ'ʊdɪn.
ɢʊdɪdˑaˑ'f-hampyan ʙʊ'ɢʊlfan-a'mˑɪm ɢʊdɪnɪdmaˑ'a tcɛ-ɢʊ'ca ma'nfɪyak aɢuˑ'n
  ɢwadɪdya'hampyan.
pɛˑ''ma ɢʊ'ca dɛmaˑ'ma dɪʙa'nˑak ɢʊtwʊ'twuˑt sʊ'dʊ dɪkɪ'ʊdɪn   <34(4)>
ɢʊdna'ɢɪt tcɛwaˑ''an amu'ɪ,
  tcɪˑ'ɪ-tcɪta'mdjʊ dʊma'nfɪt tcɛ'mɪ'dɪ dɪma'nfɪyak akɪ'ʊdɪn. ||122:135||
  hɛˑ'cˑa-a'mˑɪm ɢʊnɪ-a'mpɢwa.
pɛˑ''ma ɢɪ'nˑʊk ɢɪnɪɢɛ'wˑu dɪnɪsɋɪ'nwaɪmax̣
  ɢɪnɪdɪ'tɢwɪn waˑ''an-dʊ'mp̣ɪ nau-hu'wˑan-dɪˑ'nfyaf.
  sʊ'dʊ-dʊ'mˑɪm ɢʊnɪɢɛ'wˑʊt pa'cyu-huˑ''lu.   <34(5)>
ɢɪ'nˑʊk-ɢʊnɪdna'ɢɪt,
  sʊ'dʊ-tcɪdɪta'mdjʊ ma'nfɪd sʊ'dʊ dɪkɪ'ʊdɪn taˑʙ dʊ'mp̣ɪ dⱷ'f.
[---]
  sʊ'dʊ dʊ'mˑɪm ɢʊnɪta'mdjʊ dʊmnɪma'nfɪd daˑ'f dʊ'mp̣ɪ dⱷˑ'f.
ɢɪ'nˑʊk-ɢʊca-a'mpɢwa ɢʊnɪ'na'ɢɪt
  p̣ʊ'fan laˑ'ɢˑaɪ tcɛsʊ'dʊ dɪkɪ'ʊdɪn.
pɛˑ''ma sʊ'dʊ dʊ'mˑɪm ɢʊdna'ɢɪt   <34(6)>

"Let's run five hundred paces."
They said,
  "No."
My father said,
  "Never mind. You race the way they want."
Then they got ready. ||122:137||
  They got them, they were boys, (who) would ride their horses.
  We did the same.   <34(7)>
  They got four men to watch the race-horses.
Then they went to where they started.
My father said to that boy,[21]
  "You watch this horse
  It will be very hard to hold back.
  Do not give a single pace away to the other horse."   <34(8)>
[---]
  "Okay,"
  said that boy.[22]
Then they started.
  That boy of ours stole maybe two paces.
Then they ran.
  They got to the finish.
  Our horse couldn't get away with any more than those two paces that he had
    stolen. ||122:139||
  He won by just that much.
Our people were glad.   <34(9)>
  They hollered.
  They jumped and threw their hats up.
Then when they were done hollering, my father went to get the money.
  He untied the handkerchiefs.
  He took the money.
He said to my people,   <34(10)>
  "How much did you contribute?"
One said,
  "I put in ten dollars."
  All those people had put in a little each.
  My father won fifty dollars.

tcɪɒma'nfɪt hu'w·an. hu'w·an-aɒʊ'mɓɪ-aɒɷ'f.
ɢɪ'n·ʊk ɢʊɒɪnɪɒna'ɢɪt,
  wa'ŋq.
ɒɛma·'ma ɢʊɒna'ɢɪt,
  paca'kcɪ'ut. ɒɪpma'nfɪt ɢʊ'ca a'wɛu ɢɪ'n·ʊk ɢɪnɪʈa'mɒju.
pɛ·''ma ɢʊn·ɪtɛ''n·atcwu·n ||122:137||
  ɢʊɒɪnɪɒnɪ'kwɪn ɢɪ'n·ʊk ɢʊnɪtu'ɪfaf ɢʊɒyu·'wʊfɢwu·t ɒɪnɪkɪ'uɒɪn.
  sʊ'ɒ·ʊ-yu· pa'c·a'wɛu.   <34(7)>
  ɢʊɒɪnɪɒɪ'tɢwɪn ta'ʙ-amu'ɪ ɢʊɒɪnɪɒ_lʊ'ɒkunu·n ɢʊ'ca-ma'nfɪyak akɪ'uɒɪn.
pɛ·''ma ɢʊɒɪnɪɒɪ't tcɛha'l·a ɢʊ'ca ɒɪɒɪnɪɒ'ɪ'ɒʊp [ɒɪɒnɪɒ'i'ɒʊp].
ɒɛma·'ma ɢʊɒnɪ'cɪn ɢʊ'ca aʈu'ɪɒfa·f,
  ma'ha cyu'ɒnɪɢwan hɛ'ca ɒɪkɪ'uɒɪn.
  ṗʊ'f·an ɒa'lqɒʊɢʊ ɒuwa'ɒʊfun.
  wa'ŋq ɒʊmɪɒɪ'c ɢʊca-wa''an akɪ'uɒɪn wa''an-ɒɷ'f.   <34(8)>
[---]
  ɢʊ'cwɪ
  ɢʊɒna'ɢɪt ɢʊ'ca-aʈu'ɪɒɪn.
pɛ·''ma ɢʊɒɪnɪɒ'ɪ'ɒʊp
  ɢʊ'ca-sʊ'ɒ·ʊ ɒɪtu'ɪɒɪn ɢʊɒ_la'tswu·t e'ɪkɪn ɢɛ'm-aɒɷ'f.
pɛ·''ma ɢʊɒnɪɒmɪ'nɒjɪs.
  ɢʊɒnɪtwɛ'l·u
  sʊ'ɒ·ʊ-ɒɪkɪ'uɒɪn wa'nq-lʊ·f ɢʊmɪtha'ɢu·t ɢʊsa-ɢɛ·'m-aɒɷ'f ɢʊɒɪt_la'tswu·t
                                           ||122:139||
  pa'sa-hɷ·''lʊ ɢʊɒɪɒʊ'l·ʊ.
sʊ'ɒ·ʊ-ɒʊ'm·ɪm ɢʊɒɪɒ'ɛ'l·ʊ   <34(9)>
  ɢʊɒnɪɒ_la'l'wɛɪ
  ɢʊɒnɪɒ'ɪ'ɒʊp ɢu·'-ɒɪnɪmu'yuc ha'lʙam
pɛ·''ma ɢɪnɪtu'ɢɪ ɒʊmnɪɒ_lɛ'l'wɛɪ tcɪ''ɪ-ɒɛma·'ma ɢʊɒɪ'twu· ɢʊ'ca-sɋ̇ɪ'nwaɪmax̣.
  ɢʊɒ_skwɪ'lskwa·t ɢʊsa-hɪ'ktcʊm
  ɢwaɒɪ'tɢwɪn [ɢʊaɒɪ't] ɢʊca-sɋ̇ɪ'nwɛɪmax̣.
ɢʊɒna'ɢɪt tcɛɒa'm·ɪm,   <34(10)>
  a'hɷ·'''lu ma'ha ɢʊɒɢu' ?
wa''an-ɢʊɒna'ɢɪt,
  tcɪ''ɪ-ɢʊtɢu' ɒɪ·'nfyaf-asɋ̇ɪ'nwaɪmax̣.
  ʙʊ'ɢʊlfan ɢɪ'n·ʊk ɢʊ'ca-a'm·ɪm ɢɪnɪɒɢu' ṗʊ't'snaq.
  tcɪ''ɪ-ɒɛma·'ma ɢʊɒ·ʊ'l·ʊ hu''wan-ɒɪ·'nfyaf sɋ̇ɪ'nwaɪmax̣.

Then all those people of ours got their money.

<35> Racing Free-for-All
Then all different kinds of people raced one another.
  (From) White people and Indians they took horses, anybody's horses.

||122:141||

  A White person got an Indian's horse.
  Another White man borrowed another Indian's horse.
  They made up a race.   <35(2)>
[---]
  "However much you collect will be alright!
    We will collect just that much too."
Then they raced.
  They merely went to the track.
    They did not race by (measured) paces.[23]
  They went part-way along on the race-track.   <35(3)>
    There they started.
Then they raced.
  One of the horses won by a long ways.
Then they did like that all that afternoon.
Then all the people went back to their homes.

pɛ·''ma ʙʊ'ɢʊlfan ɢu'ca-ᴅʊ'm·ɪm ɢʊnɪᴅnɪ'kwɪn ɢɪ'n·ʊk ᴅɪnɪsq̓ɪ'nwaɪmax̣.

<35>Racing Free-for-All

pɛ·''ma ʙʊ'ɢʊlfan a'wɛu a'm·ɪm ɢʊᴅnɪᴅma'nfɪᴅaɪ.

    wa'm·u-a'm·ɪm nau-amɛ·'nmɪ ɢɪ'n·ʊk ɢʊᴅnɪᴅnɪ'kwɪn akɪ'uᴅɪn ʙʊ'ɢʊlfan e'y·a
        ᴅɪnɪkɪ'uᴅɪn. ||122:141||

    wa''an wa'm·u-amu'ɪ ɢʊᴅɪ'ᴅɢwɪn wa''an-amɛ·'nmɪ ᴅɪkɪ'uᴅɪn.

    wa''an-yu· a'wa'm·u-amu'ɪ ɢʊᴅyʊ'f·ut wa''an-amɛ·'nmɪ ᴅɪkɪ'uᴅɪn.

    ɢɪ'n·ʊk-ɢɪnɪʙʊ'n ᴅɪma'nfɪyak,   <35(2)>

[---]

    a'hu''lʊ ma'ha ᴅʊmnɪcɢɛ'w·ɪ pɛ'cakcɪ'ut,
        sʊ'ᴅ·ʊ-ᴅɪᴅɪsɢɛ'w·u pɛ'ca-hω''lʊ [hʊ''lʊ].

pɛ·''ma ɢʊᴅnɪᴅma'nfɪyak
    k̓ʊ'nfʊ ɢʊᴅnɪᴅ'i·'f tcɛɢʊ'ca-ɢu'n.
        wa'ŋq ɢʊᴅnɪᴅma'nfʊ tcɛhu'f.

    ɢʊᴅɪnɪᴅɪ't k̓ʊ'ʙfan tcɛɢʊ'ca ma'nfɪyak-aɢu·'n   <35(3)>
        ɢʊ'caʙe·ᴅ ɢʊᴅɪnɪᴅ'ɪ'ᴅ·ʊp [-ʊf].

pɛ·''ma ɢʊᴅɪnɪᴅma'nfɪ.

    wa''an ɢʊ'c·a-akɪ'uᴅɪn ɢʊᴅʊ'l·ʊ la'ɢ·aɪ.

pɛ·''ma pɛ'ca-ɢʊnɪmɪ'uf ʙʊ'ɢʊlfan ɢʊ'ca-aya'hampyan.

pɛ·''ma ʙu'ɢʊlfan a'm·ɪm ɢʊᴅɪnɪ'yɪ tcɛᴅʊnɪᴅum·aɪ.

CHAPTER SEVEN
Working and Going to Church[1]

<36> Sunday Comes

Then the next day my father plowed the ground. ||122:143||
    He worked all of those six days.
Then on the day of the Lord Above he didn't work.
    We were to go to the house of the Lord Above.
    Everybody came to that (church-)house.   <36(2)>
Then the priest rang the bell.
Then all of those who were standing outside entered the church.
Then the priest prayed the words of the Lord Above.
When he finished his praying, then he spoke good words (preached) to all of those
    Indians.   <36(3)>
When he finished his preaching, then he prayed to the Lord Above. ||123:9||

Then all the people went outside.
When they got outside, they shook hands with everyone.
Then everyone went back to their homes.
    We went back to our own home.

<37> No Time to Gamble—Too Much Work!
    My mother made food.
Then we ate.
When we were through eating, my father said,
    "Let's go to the race-track.
    Lots of people will be at the race-track.
    Lots of White people are coming here."
Then they got all sorts of horses to race.   <37(2)>
Then that's what they did that afternoon.
At sunset they all went back home.
Then Shilikwa and his tribes-people (and) those Luckiamute Indians played the
    hand-game that night.
    My father did not go to where they played.
He said to Shilikwa,   <37(3) >
    "I won't go. ||123:11||
        Tomorrow I work."

Working and Going to Church

\<36\> Sunday Comes

pɛˑ''ma ɢʊDɪDɪDmeˈɪDJ Dɛmaˑ'ma ɢʊDplaˈqʊn (~..g̣ʊn) haˈŋkluˑp. ‖122:143‖

   Bʊ'ɢʊlfan ɢʊˈcˑa Dʌ'f-a'mpyan ɢʊD_luˑ''nafʊn.

pɛˑ''ma-ɢʊˈcˑa haˈlʙam DJaˈmʙak Dɪˈaˈmpyan waˈŋq ɢʊD_luˑ''nafʊn.

   suˈDˑu Dɪ'D DJɛɢʊ'sa ahaˈlʙam-DJaˈmʙak-Duˈmˑaɪ.

   Bʊ'ɢʊlfanɪ'yˑa ɢʊcmaˑ'a DJɛɢʊ'cˑa-haˈmˑɪ.   \<36(2)\>

pɛˑ''ma-ɢʊˈcˑa-tɛ'nˑa-ʌDJaˈŋku̇ ɢʊDʙʊ'n-ʌDɪˈnDɪn.

pɛˑ''ma Bʊ'ɢʊlfanɪ'yˑa ɢʊˈcawʊnDaˑ'ʙɪt hɛˑ''lʊm ɢʊDɪnɪlaˈmˑʊ tcaɢʊ'cˑa-tɛ'nˑa haˈmˑɪ.

pɛˑ''ma ɢʊˈcawɪ-tɛ'nˑa-DJaˈŋku̇ ɢʊtɢu' atɛ'nˑa haˈmha DJɛɢʊ'cˑa haˈlʙam DJaˈmʙak.

ɢʊṫʊˈɢɪ-Dɪhaˈmha pɛˑ''ma ɢʊDnaˈɢɪt DJɛBʊ'ɢʊlfan ɢʊ'cˑa amɛ'nmɪ watɛ'nˑa haˈmha.   \<36(3)\>

ɢʊṫʊˈɢɪ-Dɪyuˈwɪn pɛˑ''ma ɢʊtɢu' tɛ'nˑa haˈmha tcɛɢʊ'cˑa haˈlʙam DJaˈmʙak.

                  ‖123:9‖

pɛˑ''ma Bʊ'ɢʊlfan-a'mˑim ɢʊDɪnɪ'yɪ hɛˑ''lʊm.

ɢʊDɪnwa'l-hɛˑ''lʊm pɛˑ''ma ɢʊnɪDɪ't Dɪnɪ'laˈqʷ tcɛʙʊ'ɢʊlfanɪ'yˑa.

pɛˑ''ma Bʊ'ɢʊlfanɪ'yˑa ɢʊnɪDɪ'tyɪ tcɛDɪnɪDʊˈmˑaɪ.

   sʊ'Dˑʊ-ɢʊDɪ'tyɪ tcɛDuDuˈmˑaɪ,

\<37\> No Time to Gamble—Too Much Work!

   Dɛnaˈ'na ɢʊDʙʊ'n aˈkweˈɪnafʊn,

pɛˑ''ma sʊ'Dˑu-ɢʊDɪDkweˈɪnafu.

ɢʊDɪṫʊˈɢɪ-Dɪkweˈɪnafʊn Dɛmaˑ'ma naˈɢɪt,

   tciˈDˑa tcɪDɪsDʊˈ''ʊ tcɛɢʊ'sa maˈnfɪyak aɢu'n.

   ha''lu a'mˑɪm ɢʊnɪʙɪ'nD DJɛɢʊ'cˑa maˈnfɪyak aɢu'n.

   haˈlˑuˑ wa'mˑuˑ a'mˑɪm ɢʊDɪnɪDJiˑ'f.

pɛˑ''ma ɢʊDɪnɪ'tɢwɪn Bʊ'ɢʊlfan a'wɛw akɪ'uDɪn DʊmnɪDmaˈnfu.   \<37(2)\>

pɛˑ''ma pa'cˑ-ɢanɪmhɪ'uf ɢʊ'cˑa wayaˈhampyan.

ɢwDɪDJɛˈɢˑʊ-a'mpyan Bʊ'ɢʊlfan ɪ'yˑa ɢʊDɪnɪDɪ'tyɪ.

pɛˑ''ma ɢɪ'nˑʊk cɪ'lɪkwa naˈu-DɪɢAˈwakɪl ɢʊ'cˑa laˈq̇mayut mɛ'nmɪ ɢɪ'nˑʊk ɢʊDɪnɪlaˈkwɪt.

   smaˈlˑa ɢʊ'cawɛɪ-wɪ'fyu.

   Dɛmaˑ'ma waˈŋq ɢʊDˑɪ't tcɛɢʊ'cˑa-haˈlˑa ɢɪnɪlaˈkwɪt.

ɢʊnɪ'cˑɪn tcɛcɪ'lɪkwa,   \<37(3)\>

   waˈŋq-laˈf tcɪ''ɪ DʊmɪDɪ't.   ‖123:11‖

     ɢamɪmeˈɪDJ tcɪ''ɪ ɢɪ'laˈfʊtwaɪ.

Shilikwa said,

"*Okay. We will play against those Luckiamute Indians by ourselves.*"

Then they went back to their homes to eat.

We, too, went back home.

<38> Going to Church

My father got up early, he fed his horses.

My mother made food.

Then my father went to work.

He worked all those six days.

Then it rained.

It rained really hard.

We stayed at home on that Sunday.   <38(2)>

My father and my mother said prayers to the Lord Above.

On the next day the ground was very muddy.

My father didn't work at all on that one day.

On the next Sunday they went to church.

Then everyone went into the church when they heard the bell.   <38(3)>

Then the priest said prayers to the Lord Above.

||123:13||

Then when he finished his prayer-talk, he spoke to the Indians.

He said inspirational things ("all-good-words") to the community[2] who were in
the (church-)house.

He said,   <38(4)>

"*You Indians, do nothing bad to anyone.*

Do not steal anything.

You must have a good heart towards everyone!

When you see an old man or old woman, you must help them!

Then the Lord Above will watch over you.   <38(5)>

He will give you all manner of food.

Then when you die, then He will say to come to the Lord Above."[3]

Then everybody went out.

They shook hands with everyone.   <38(6)>

They went back to their homes.

We went back home.

My mother prepared food.

cɪ'lɪk̓wa na'ɢɪt

    ɢʊ'cwɪ. γɛ'lfan sʊ'ᴅʊ ᴅɪᴅ_la'kwɪt ᴅJɛɢʊ'sa la'q̓mayut mɛ'nmɪ.

pɛ'"ma ɢʊnɪᴅɪ'tyɪ tcɛnɪᴅʊ'm·aɪ ᴅʊkwe'ɪnafʊn.

    sʊ'ᴅʊ-yu' ɢʊᴅɪ'tyɪ tcɛᴅɪᴅʊ'm·aɪ.

<38> Going to church

ᴅɛma'·ma ɢʊᴅʙu'klaɪ ha'lw'an hu'k·ᴅɪkɪ'ʊᴅɪn,

    ᴅɛna'·na ɢʊtʙʊ'n k̓we'ɪnafʊn.

pɛ'"ma-ᴅɛma'·ma ɢʊᴅɪ't ᴅɪlu'"nafʊn.

    ɢʊᴅ_lu'"nʊf ʙʊ'ɢʊlfan ɢʊ'ca-wɪ-ᴅa'f-a'mpyan.

pɛ'"ma ɢʊᴅɢwi'ᴅɪt,

    p̓ʊ'f·an ɢʊᴅɢwi'ᴅit.

    sʊ'ᴅʊ-ɢʊᴅɪᴅʙi'·nᴅ ᴅJɛɢʊ'sa tɛ'n·a-a'mpyan.   <38(2)>

ᴅɛma'·ma na'ʊ-ᴅɛna'·na ɢɪ'n·ʊk ɢʊᴅɪnɪyu'w·ɪn [yu'"wɪn] tɛ'n·a-ha'mha ᴅJɛha'lʙam

    aᴅJa'mʙak.

ɢwᴅɪᴅme'ɪᴅJ [ɢʊᴅɪᴅ-] p̓ʊ'f·an ha'ŋk̓lu·p ɢʊᴅɪᴅ_ła'ʙł'yu.

    ᴅɛma'·ma wa'ŋq-lʊ'f ɢʊmlu'"nafʊn ᴅJɛɢʊ'ca wa'nfʊ a'mpyan.

ᴅJɛɢʊ'ca atɛ'n·a a'mpyan ɢɪnɪᴅɪ't ᴅJɛɢʊ'ca atɛ'n·a ha'm·ɪ.

pɛ'"ma ʙʊ'ɢʊlfan-ɪ'y·a ɢʊᴅ_la'm·ʊ ᴅJɛɢʊ'ca tɛ'n·a ha'm·ɪ ɢʊᴅɪnɪɢa'pᴅɪn ɢʊ'ca-ᴅɪ'nᴅɪn. <38(3)>

pɛ'"ma ɢʊ'ca watɛ'n·a aᴅJa'ŋk̓u ɢʊᴅyu'"wɪn ᴅʊ'mha ᴅJɛɢʊ'ca ha'lʙam aᴅJa'mʙak.

                                   ||123:13||

pɛ'"ma ɢʊt̓ʊ'ɢɪ ᴅɪyu'"wɪn ɢʊᴅyu'"wɪn ᴅJɛᴅɪme'·nmɪ.

    ɢʊᴅna'ɢɪt ʙʊ'ɢʊlfan atɛ'n·a ha'mha tcɛɢʊ'ca ɢa'wakɪl ɢʊᴅɪnɪʙi'·nᴅ ᴅJɛha'm·ɪ.

ɢʊᴅnɪ'c·ɪn,   <38(4)>

    mɪ'ᴅɪ mɛ'·nmɪ wa'ŋq a'ɢ·a ᴅʊmnɪᴅʙʊ'n qa'sq ᴅJa'ɪ'y·a

    wa'ŋq-ᴅʊmnɪ'la'tswʊt a'ɢ·a.

    mɪ'ᴅɪ sʙɪtɛ'n·a ᴅʊmhu'p̓ɪn ᴅJɛʙʊ'ɢʊlfan-e'y·a.

    mɪ'ᴅɪ ɢwᴅɪᴅhɷ'ᴅ yu'huyu am'u'ɪ yu'huyu a'wa'ɪtst mɪ'ᴅɪ ʙɪsɢɛ'm'yat.

pɛ'"ma ɢʊ'sa ha'lʙam-aᴅJa'mʙak ɢʊᴅyu'ᴅnɪfnɪ'ɢwan ᴅJɛmɪ'ᴅɪ.   <38(5)>

    ɢʊᴅ·ɛ'ᴅ·ap ʙʊ'ɢʊlfan a'w·ɛu yukwe'ɪnafʊnik.

pɛ'"ma ɢʊt̓ʊ'ɢɪ ma'"a pɛ'"ma ɢʊᴅna'ɢɪt ᴅʊm·a'·a ᴅJaɢʊ'ca-ha'lʙam-aᴅJa'mʙak.

pɛ'"ma ʙʊ'ɢʊlfan-e'y·a ɢʊᴅɪ'twɪn.

    ɢʊᴅɪnɪᴅɪ't ᴅɛn'la'q^u (~ᴅɪn-) ᴅJɛʙʊ'ɢʊlfan-e'y·a.   <38(6)>

    ɢʊᴅɪnɪᴅɪ'tyɪ ᴅJɛnɪᴅʊ'm·aɪ.

    sʊ'ᴅʊ-ɢɪᴅɪ'tyɪ ᴅJɛᴅuᴅʊ'm·aɪ.

ᴅɛna'·na ɢʊᴅʙʊ'n ak̓we'ɪnafʊn.

Finished preparing food, then she said, ||123:15||
    "Come! eat!"
Finished eating, we stayed in all that afternoon. <38(7)>
When it became dark my father took his horses.
    He put them in the barn.
    He came back to the house.

<39> Sowing Wheat
Then he said to me,
    "My boy! Tomorrow, if it's a nice day, I'll sow wheat.
    I want you to drive that harrow with three horses."[4]
I said,
    "Okay! I'll do that."
Early next day my father arose. <39(2)>
    My mother also arose.
    She made food.
My father fed the horses.
My mother called to me,
    "Bahawadas! get up!
        You will help your father today!"
    I got up.
        I washed my face.
Then my father came in.
    He washed up. <39(3)>
Then we ate. ||123:15a||
Finished eating, my father and I went to the horse-barn.
    He put the harness on those three horses.
Then he took two horses, he goes and hitches them to the wagon.
    He went to the granary. <39(4)>
    He got ten sacks of grain.
    He took them to where he would sow grain.
He said,
    "I'll go ahead and sow the grain.
    Once I've gone a ways, then you come along behind!
    You watch! <39(5)>
        Do not skip any ground!

tʊ'ɢɪ-ᴅᴜmbʊ'n akwe'ɪnafʊn p̓ɛ·''ma ɢʊᴅna'ɢɪt,　　　　　　　　　||123:15||

　　sma·'ksᴅa pckwe'ɪnafu!

tʊ'ɢɪ ᴅukwe'ɪnafʊn, sʊ'ᴅʊ ɢʊᴅʙɪ'nᴅ ʙʊ'ɢʊlfan ɢʊ'ca ya'hampyan.　　　　<38(7)>

ɢwᴅɪᴅhu'wɪ ᴅɛma'·ma ɢʊᴅɪ'tɢwɪn ᴅɪkɪ'uᴅɪn,

　　ɢʊᴅ_lu''un ᴅjaha'm·ɪ.

　　ɢʊᴅme'y·ɪ ᴅjɛha'm·ɪ

<39> Sowing wheat

p̓ɛ·''ma ɢʊᴅna'ɢɪt tcɛtcɪ''ɪ,

　　ᴅa''ʊp! me'ɪᴅj ɢamɪtɛ'n·a a'mpyan tcɪ''ɪ ᴅɪtɢu' asa'ʙlɪl.

　　tcɪ''ɪ tcɪt̓a'mᴅju ma'ha ᴅʊmᴅɪtɢɪ'cɢa·t hu'pcɪn nɪkɪ'uᴅɪn ᴅjɛɢʊ'ca qu'm·ɪlɪt.

tcɪ''ɪ ɢʊᴅna'ɢɪt,

　　ɢʊ'cwɪ! ɢʊ'cwɪ pa'c·a ɢʊᴅmɪ'u'nan.

ɢʊᴅɪtme'ɪᴅj-hɛ'l'wan ᴅɛma'·ma ɢʊᴅʙʊ'klaɪ.　　　　　　　　　<39(2)>

　　ᴅɛna'·na-yu' ɢʊᴅʙʊ'klaɪ,

　　ʙʊ'n-kwe'ɪnafʊn,

ᴅɛma'·ma ɢʊᴅ'ʊ'k ᴅɪkɪ'uᴅɪn.

ᴅɛna'·na ɢʊᴅ_la'l'waɪ tcɛtcɪ''ɪ,

　　pax̱awa'ᴅas! cʙʊ'klaɪcᴅa!

　　　　ᴅɪ's-ᴅɛtɢɛ'm'ya·t ʙʊma'·ma hɛ'ca-wɪ-ɪ'pyan.

　　tcɪ''ɪ-ɢʊᴅʙʊ'klaɪ,

　　　　ɢʊᴅ̓ku''ułᴅ ᴅɛkwa'l·ak,

p̓ɛ·''ma ᴅɛma'·ma ɢʊm·ɪla'm·u.

　　ɢⱷ'k ɢʊᴅku''uł.　　　　　　　　　　　　　　　　　<39(3)>

p̓ɛ·''ma sʊ'ᴅu ɢʊᴅɪtkwe'ɪnafʊ.　　　　　　　　||123:15a||

tʊ'ɢɪ-ᴅɪkwe'ɪnafʊn ᴅɛma'·ma-nau-tcɪ''ɪ ɢwɪᴅɪ't ᴅjɛɢʊ'ca kɪ'uᴅɪn ᴅʊ'm·aɪ.

　　ɢⱷ'k ɢʊtɢu' ᴅɪharness ᴅjaɢʊ'ca hu'pcɪn-akɪ'uᴅɪn.

p̓ɛ·''ma ɢʊᴅɪ't̓ku ɢɛ'm-akɪ'uᴅɪn ᴅɪtɢu' tcɛtcɪ'ktcɪk.

　　ɢʊᴅɪ't ᴅjɛɢʊ'ca sa'ʙlɪl-ha'm·ɪ,　　　　　　　　　<39(4)>

　　ɢʊᴅɪ'tɢwɪn ᴅɪ'nfyaf lu'm·ʊf asa'ʙlɪl.

　　ɢʊᴅɪ't̓ku ᴅjɛha'l·a ɢʊ'ca ɢʊᴅɪtɢu' ɢʊ'ca-asa'ʙlɪl.

ɢʊᴅna'ɢɪt

　　tcɪ''ɪ-mɛ'n tcɪɢu' asa'ʙlɪl.

　　ᴅɪ's ᴅʊmɪtɪ·'ᴅ la'ɢ·aɪ, p̓ɛ·''ma ma'ha ᴅʊmɪ'ɪ'ᴅ ha'nt'c.

　　ma'ha ᴅɪtyu'ᴅnɪɢwan　　　　　　　　　　　<39(5)>

　　　　wa'ŋq ᴅʊmɪᴅjɪ'ʙ·ɪ ɢʊ'ca-ha'ŋ̓klu·p,

Having once come and gone over it, then on a second (pass) you will take half of (that is,
   you will lap) that harrow's row!"[5]
Then at midday we went back to the house.
   He took the horses.
   He gave them water.
Then he fed them oats and hay.
   I went into the house.   <39(6)>
   I washed my face.
   My father got back to the house. ||123:17||
   He got himself ready.
   He washed up.
Then we ate.
Three days we sowed wheat into the ground, 20 acres.

miˑˊs maɒɪtiˑˊɒ pɛˑˊ″ma ɒʊˊɢˑaf ɒɪɒˑɪˊtɢwɪn k̓ʊˊʙfan ɢʊsa kʊˊmˑ·ɪlˑaˑt ɒɪɢuˊn.

pɛˑˊ″ma ɢʊɒɪtwɪˊlfu aˊmpyan sʊˊɒˑʊ ɢʊɒ_sɒuˊyˑɪ ɒjɛhaˊmˑɪ.
  ɢ⍵ˑk-ɢʊɒɪˊtku ɒɪkɪˊuɒɪn
  ɢʊɒˑɪˊt-maˊmpɢa
pɛˑˊ″ma ɢʊɒɪnɪɒˊʊˊk alaˑˊ″wɛˊn naˊu-lʊˊq̓u.
  tcɪˊ″ɪ-ɢʊɒ_laˊmˑʊ ɒjahaˊmˑɪ,   <39(6)>
  ɢʊɒ̓kuˊ″uɫ ɒɛkwaˊlˑak.
  ɒɛmaˑˊma ɢʊɒmeˊyˑɪ ɒjahaˊmˑɪ ||123:17||
  ɢ⍵ˑˊk ɢʊtˑɛˊnˑɪtcwuˑn
  ɢʊtk̓uˊ″uɫ
pɛˑˊ″ma sʊˊɒˑu ɢʊɒɪtkweˊɪnafu.
huˊpcɪn aˊmpyan ɢwɒɪɒɢuˊ [ɢuɒɪɒ-] asaˊʙlil ɒjahaˊŋ̓kluˑp ɢɛˑm-ɒɪˊnfya ɒɪˊacre.

Daily Life in the Sisters' School[1]

<40> Bahawadas Goes to School

When he finished his work, then he said this to me,

"You will be going to that school all this coming year."

Then I said,

"I don't want to go to that school."

[---]

"That's no way to talk!

It is for your own benefit, when you become a grown man.

I won't be in this world forever.   <40(2)>

You will grow to be a man.

You will have to take care of your own self ('heart')."

Then I said nothing,

"Alright, my father.

I will go to that school tomorrow."

[---]

"Tomorrow I will take you there to the big boss (the agent).   <40(3)>

He will give you all manner of clothes, all sorts of food. ||123:19||

It won't be just you there.

Many of your 'brothers' (age-mates) will go to that school.

You will play all kinds of games."

Then when we got there,[2] he took me to the head sister.   <40(4)>

He said to the head sister,

"You take care of this son of mine."

Then the sister said,

"What is your son's name?"

My father said,   <40(5)>

"His Indian name is Bahawadas.

His White peoples' name is Louis Kinay."

My father said,

"Now I'll leave you.

You be a good boy!"

Then my father left.

Daily Life in the Sisters' School

<40> *baχawádas* Goes to School

ɢʊᴅ·ɪt·ʊʹɢɪ ᴅɪlu"nafʊn. pɛ·"ma paʹ-ɢʊmnaʹɢɪt ᴅ〕atcɪ"ɪ

  maʹha ᴅᴇᴅɪ't ᴅ〕ᴇɢʊʹca haʹmha haʹmˑɪ ʙʊʹɢʊlfan hɛʹca wiʹmiˑʹtʹcu.

pɛ·"ma tcɪ"ɪ-ɢʊᴅnaʹɢɪt,

  waʹŋq-tcɪ"ɪ-ɢʊtaʹmᴅ〕u ɢʊmᴅɪ't ᴅ〕ᴇɢʊʹca-haʹmha haʹmˑɪ.

[---]

  waʹŋq-paʹsa ᴅumnaʹɢɪt,

  maʹha ʙɪʙʊʹnt'caʹan, ᴅaʹm-ᴅɪᴅɪtʙaʹlʹyu amʹhuʹɪ.

  waʹŋq-laʹfa tcɪ"ɪ ᴅɪᴅɪtʙiʹnᴅ ᴅ〕ᴇhɛʹca aʹnˑu muʹinu.   <40(2)>

  maʹha ɢʊᴅʙaʹlʹyu aᴅ〕aʹŋku

  maʹha ɢʊᴅyuʹᴅnɪɢwan maʹha ʙʊmuʹp̓ɪn.

pɛ·"ma waʹŋq aʹɢˑa tcɪ"ɪ ɢʊᴅnaʹɢɪt.

  ɢʊʹcwɪ ᴅᴇmaʹma

  tcɪ"ɪ ᴅɪᴅɪ't ᴅ〕ᴇɢʊʹsa haʹmha haʹmˑɪ ɢamɪtmeʹɪᴅ〕.

[---]

  ɢamɪtmeʹɪᴅ〕 tcɪ"ɪ ᴅɪᴅɪ'tku maʹha tcɛɢʊʹsa-ʙᴇ·ᴅ ɢʊʹsa-ʙaʹl-aᴅ〕aʹmʙak   <40(3)>

  ɢɷ·k ɢɪnˑɪɢuʹ ʙʊʹɢʊlfan aʹwɛu aʹɢfan. ʙʊʹɢʊlfan aʹwɛu akwe'ɪnafʊnak. ||123:19||

  waʹŋq-yɛʹlfan-maʹha ɢʊᴅɪtʙiʹnᴅ ɢʊʹsaʙᴇ·ᴅ,

  haʹlˑuˑ ʙɪk̓ʊʹnˑayaʙ ɢɪᴅɪnɪᴅɪ't ᴅ〕ᴇɢʊʹca haʹmha haʹmˑɪ.

  maʹha ɢʊᴅ_laʹɢʊt ʙʊʹɢʊlfan aʹwɛu alˑaʹɢʊt.

pɛ·"ma ɢʊᴅɪtwaʹl-ɢʊʹsaʙᴇ·ᴅ ɢʊᴅɪ'tku tcɪ"ɪ tcɛɢʊʹca ʙʊʹᴅ〕at ᴅɪnɪᴅ〕aʹmʙak.   <40(4)>

ɢʊᴅnɪʹsɪn ᴅ〕ᴇɢʊʹca ʙʊʹᴅ〕at aᴅ〕aʹmʙak

  maʹha ᴅᴇtyuʹᴅnɪɢwan hɛʹca ᴅaʹ"ʊp.

pɛ·"ma ɢʊʹca-aʙʊʹᴅ〕at ɢʊᴅnaʹɢɪt,

  eʹyˑa-ᴅaʹŋkwɪt maʹha ʙʊᴅaʹ"ʊp.

ᴅᴇmaʹma ɢʊᴅnaʹɢɪt,   <40(5)>

  mɛ·ʹnmɪyɪk ᴅʊʹŋkwɪt ʙaʹχawaʹᴅɪs,

  waʹmˑuˑ aʹmˑɪm ᴅʊʹŋkwɪt Louis/Lewis k̓ɪnaʹɪ.

ᴅᴇmaʹma naʹɢɪt,

  pɛ·"a tcɪ"ɪ tcɪhaʹɢwɪtcuf.

  maʹha tɛʹnˑɑ at̓uʹɪᴅɪn.

pɛ·"ma ᴅᴇmaʹma ɢʊᴅɪ'tyɪ.

<41> Dividing into Grades

The sister says,

    "Go outside!

    Play with those children!

    Don't fight."

I said,

    "Okay."

    Lots of my "brothers" I knew. ||123:21||

They called to me,

    "Come on over here!

    We'll play!

    Don't go playing with those different (tribes-)children!"   <41(2)>

Then the sister rang her bell,

    "All you children go (outside) there to the washroom!

    Get ready!

    It's nearly mealtime."

Then, when she rang her bell (again), the sister said,

    "All you children stand here!"

    The big boys stood in front.   <41(3)>

    The small boys stood behind.

Then she, the sister, said,

    "Go on! Go inside!"

Then they went inside.

    They marched around the dining table.

    When they got to their plates (places), there they stood.

    All the children came in. ||123:23|| <41(4)>

Then the sister prayed prayers to the Lord Above.

When she finished her prayers, then she said,

    "Sit down!

    Go ahead and eat!"

    All the children finished their meal.

    She, the sister, had a little bell.   <41(5)>

        She rang it.

Then all the children stood up.

Then she prayed words of the Lord Above.

Having finished her words, then all the children went outside to their playing.

<41> Dividing into Grades

ɢʊ'sa-aʙʊ'ᴅzat u'na'ɢɪt,
  ᴅja'ks_ᴅa hɛ·''lʊm,
  cla'ɢʊt tcɛɢʊ'ca-ci·''wɛɪ.
  wa'ŋq ᴅʊmnɪtwa'qnɪfaɪ.
tcɪ''ɪ na'ɢɪt,
  ɢʊ'cwɪ.
  ha'l·u· tcɪ''ɪ ᴅʊkʊ'n·ɪyaʙ ɢʊᴅyʊ'ɢʊn. ||123:21||
ɢɪ'n·ʊk ɢɪnɪla'l'waɪ tcɛtcɪ''ɪ,
  sma'k hɛ'sɪ-yʊ'fan.
  sʊ'ᴅ·ʊ-ᴅɪᴅɪt_la'kwɪt.
  wa'ŋq ᴅamla'kwɪt tcɛɢʊ's·a waᴅɪ'ᴅ·aɪ asi·''waɪ.   <41(2)>
pɛ·''ma ɢʊ'sa-aʙʊ'ᴅzat ɢʊᴅɪ'nᴅa·t ᴅɪᴅɪ'nᴅɪn,
  ʙʊ'ɢʊlfan-mɪ'ᴅ·ɪ-sɪ''waɪ ʙɪsɪ''ɪ tcɛɢʊ'sa ha'l·a ku·'lfɪ'nak ha'm·i.
  tɛ'n·ɪtcwu·n
  yɛ'tc ʊmk̓we'ɪnafʊnak.
pɛ·''ma, ɢʊᴅɪnɪᴅɪ'nᴅɛ·t ᴅɪᴅɪ'nᴅɪn, ɢʊ'sa-aʙʊ'ᴅjat u'na'ɢɪt,
  ʙʊ'ɢʊlfan mɪ'ᴅ·ɪ ci·''wɛɪ hɛ'saʙɛ·ᴅ ʙɪsᴅɪ'sᴅap.
  waʙa'l-a t̓u'ɪᴅɪn ɢɪ'n·ʊk ɢɪnɪᴅa'ʙɪt ᴅjɪ'm·eɪ,   <41(3)>
  ɢʊ'c·a uᴅɪ·'t'saq ɢɪnɪᴅa'ʙɪt-ha'nt'c.
pɛ·''ma qɛ'ᴅ·ak ɢʊ'ca-ʙʊ'ᴅzat ɢʊᴅna'ɢɪt,
  ᴅja·'ksᴅa ʙɪsla'm·u.
pɛ·''ma ɢɪ'n·ʊk ɢʊᴅɪnɪsla'm·u,
  ɢʊᴅɪnɪwi·''ya·t tcɛɢʊ'sa-k̓we'ɪnafʊnak laᴅa'm.
  ɢʊᴅɪnɪtwa'l tcɛɢɪ'n·ʊk ᴅɪnɪɢwa't, ɢʊ'saʙɛ·ᴅ ɢɪnɪᴅɛ'sᴅap.
  ʙʊ'ɢʊlfan-si·''wɛɪ ɢʊᴅɪnɪt_la'm·u. ||123:23|| <41(4)>
pɛ·''ma ɢʊ'sa-aʙʊ'ᴅzat ɢʊᴅyu·''wɪn tɛ'n·a ha'mha ᴅjaha'lʙam-aᴅja'mʙak.
ɢʊt̓ʊ'ɢ·ɪ ᴅɪha'mha pɛ·''ma ɢʊᴅna'ɢɪt,
  pcɪ·''yu,
  tcɪ'ᴅ·a pck̓we'ɪnafu.
  ʙʊ'ɢʊlfan-aci·''wɛɪ ɢʊnɪt̓ʊ'ɢ·ɪ ᴅɪk̓we'ɪnafʊn,
  çɛ'ᴅ·ak ɢʊca-aʙʊ'ᴅzat ɢʊᴅp̓i'n wa·''an ᴅi·'t'saq aᴅɪ'nᴅɪn,   <41(5)>
    ɢʊᴅɪ'nᴅa·t.
pɛ·''ma ʙʊ'ɢʊlfan ci·''wɛɪ ɢʊnɪᴅɪ'cᴅap.
pɛ·''ma qɛ'ᴅ·ak ɢʊᴅyu'wun ha'lʙam-aᴅja'mʙak ᴅu'mha.
ɢʊt̓ʊ'ɢ·ɪ ᴅʊ'mha, pɛ·''ma ʙʊ'ɢʊlfan ci·''wɛɪ ɢʊnɪᴅɪ't hɛ·''lʊm ᴅɪnɪla'ɢwak.

When it got to be one o'clock, then she rang the bell.   <41(6)>
    All the children ran to be near the school-house.
    They all stood.
Then one of the sisters offered words (instructions) to the children.
She said,
    "You all come inside!"
    All the children went inside.
    They sat down at their desks.
Then the sister said to that big boy, ||123:25|| <41(7)>
    "Up to which reader (grade level) do you know?"
(That) one said that when he finished at the school (before),
    "I knew the fourth reader."
Then the sister said,
    "How many of you lads know the fourth reader?
        You all stand up!"
Then the sister took those lads,   <41(8)>
    She gave them different desks.³
[---]
    "How many of you know the third reader?
        You too stand up!"
    Just that many stood up.
Then she gave them different desks.
Then the sister said,
    "How many of you boys know up to the second reader?
        Stand up!"
    Those who knew the second reader, they stood up.   <41(9)>
Then she gave different desks to all.
Then the sister said,
    "How many of you lads know the first reader?" ||123:27||
    Those boys stood up.   <41(10)>
Then she gave them different desks.
    Those boys not knowing anything of any reader stayed where they were.

Then the sister gave (readers) to all the boys of the fourth reader.
    She gave them their fourth readers.
    They too, those knowing their third reader, in the same way she gave them their

ɢʊᴅɪtwa″an-aᴅɪ′ɴᴅɪn, pɛ·″ma ɢʊᴅɪᴅɪ′ɴᴅɑ·t aᴅɪ′ɴᴅɪn.   <41(6)>
   ʙʊ′ɢʊlfan ci·″wei ɢʊᴅɪnɪᴅmɪ′ɴᴅjɪs yɛ′tc ᴅjɛɢʊ′sa ha′mha ha′m·eɪ.
   ʙʊ′ɢʊlfan ɢʊᴅɪnɪᴅɛ′cᴅap.
pɛ·″ma wa·″an ɢʊ′sa-aʙʊ′ᴅzat ɢʊᴅɪᴅɪ′ct ha′mha tcɛsi·″wei,
ɢʊᴅna′ɢɪt,
   mɪ′ᴅ·ɪ pcla′m·ʊ.
   ʙʊ′ɢʊlfan asi·″wei ᴅɪnɪt_la′m·u·.
   ɢɪnɪsi·″yu tcɛɢɪ′n·ʊk ᴅɪnɪla′ᴅɑ·′m.
pɛ·″ma ɢʊ′ca-aʙʊ′ᴅzat ɢʊᴅna′ɢɪt tcɛɢʊ′sa ʙa′l aṭu′ɪᴅɪn, ||123:25|| <41(7)>
   a′hœ′lʊ aʙɪ′ʙa ma′ha tcɪyʊ′ɢʊn.
wa·″an-ɢʊᴅna′ɢɪt ɢwᴅɪṭʊ′ɢ·ɪ tcɛᴅɪha′mha-ha′m·ɪ,
   tcɪ″ɪ -ɢʊtyʊ′ɢʊn ta′ʙ ᴅuʙi·′ʙa.
pɛ·″ma ɢʊ′ca-ʙʊ′ᴅzat ɢʊᴅna′ɢɪt,
   a′hœ′lʊ mɪ′ᴅ·ɪ sɪ′nfaf tcɛᴅɪtyʊ′ɢʊn ta′ʙ-aʙɪ·′ʙa,
     mɪ′ᴅ·ɪ ʙɪsᴅɛ′sᴅap.
pɛ·″ma ɢʊ′sa-aʙʊ′ᴅzat ɢʊnɪᴅɪ′tku ɢʊ′sa sɪ′nfaf,   <41(8)>
   ɢʊnɪᴅɪ′st ᴅa′ɪ′wan ala′ᴅɑ·′m.
[---]
   a′hœ′lʊ mɪ′ᴅ·ɪ pcyʊ′ɢʊn hʊ′pcɪn-aʙɪ·′ʙa,
     mɪ′ᴅ·ɪ-yu· ʙcᴅɪ′cᴅap.
   pa′s-uhœ·″lʊ ɢʊnɪᴅɛ′cᴅap.
pɛ·″ma ɡɛ′ᴅ·ak ɢʊnɪᴅɪ′ct ᴅa′ɪ′wan ala′ᴅɑ·′m.
pɛ·″ma ɢʊ′ca-aʙʊ′ᴅjat ɢʊᴅna′ɢɪt,
   ahœ·″lʊ mɪ′ᴅ·ɪ -aṭu′ɪᴅɪn ɢʊᴅyʊ′ɢʊn ɡɛ′m-aʙɪ·′ʙa
     ʙɪsɪ′ᴅ·ap.
   ɢɪ′n·ʊk ɢʊ′sa ɢɪnɪ′yʊ′ɢʊn ɡɛ′m-aʙe′ɪʙa ɢʊᴅɪnɪᴅɛ′cᴅap.   <41(9)>
pɛ·″ma ɡɛ′ᴅ·ak ɢʊᴅɪnɪᴅɪ′ct ᴅa′ɪ′wan ala′ᴅɑ·′m ʙʊ′ɢʊlfan.
pɛ·″ma ɢʊ′sa-aʙʊ′ᴅjat ɢʊᴅna′ɢɪt,
   a′hœ′lʊ mɪ′ᴅ·ɪ aṭu′ɪᴅɪn tcɪᴅʊpyʊ′ɢʊn wa·″an-aʙe′ɪʙa. ||123:27||
   ɢɪ′n·ʊk ɢʊca-aṭu′ɪᴅɪn ɢʊᴅɪnɪᴅɛ′cᴅap.   <41(10)>
pɛ·″ma ɡɛ′ᴅ·ak ɢʊᴅɪnɪᴅɪ′ct ᴅa′ɪ′wan ala′ᴅɑ·′m.
   ɢɪ′n·ʊk ɢʊ′ca-aṭu′ɪᴅɪn wa′ŋq-a′ɢ·a nɪ′yʊ′ɢʊn tcɛʙi·′ʙa, ɢʊᴅɪnɪʙɪ′ɴᴅ ᴅjɛha′l·a ɢʊ′ca
     ɢʊᴅɪnɪʙɪ′ɴᴅ.
pɛ·″ma ɢʊ′ca-aʙʊ′ᴅjat ɢʊnɪᴅɪ′ct ʙʊ′ɢʊlfan ɢʊ′ca ᴅɪnɪṭu′ɪᴅɪn ᴅjɛᴅa′ʙ-aʙɪ·′ʙa,
   ɡɛ′ᴅ·ak ɢʊᴅɪnɪᴅɪ′ct ᴅɪnɪᴅa′ʙ ᴅɪʙi·′ʙa.
   ɢɪ′nuk-yu· ɢʊ′ca ɢɪnɪ′yʊ′ɢʊn hʊ′pcɪn ᴅɪnɪʙi·′ʙa, ɡɛ′ᴅ·ak-yu· ɢɪn·ɪᴅɪ′ct ᴅɪnɪhu′pcɪn

third readers. <41(11)>
Then to them who were up to the second reader, she did it the same way.
  She gave them all their second readers.
  That's the way likewise she did to those of the first reader.
    She gave them all their readers.
Then she took those who knew the fourth reader (and) those who knew the third reader. <41(12)>
  She took them to another room. ||123:29||
  The sister kept those who knew the second reader and those who knew the first reader and those who didn't know anything.
Then in a different room, one of the sisters did it the same way to the girls. <41(13)>

  The sister from that other room brought in the second-grade girls, and the first-grade girls, and those that knew nothing.

Then she said to the boys and to the girls, <41(14)>
  "You apply yourselves very diligently to these books.
  Whatever it is that you don't know, tell this to me.
  I'll teach you whatever you don't know." ||123:31||

<42> School Procedures
Come the next day, the sister said,
  "I'll give you readers."[4]
Then the sister had a small bell.
She rang the bell,
  "All of you stand!"
  All the children stood.
Then she said, <42(2)>
  "You all go outside to play for five minutes!"
Then she rang the bell.
  All the children came back in.
Then she took all those who knew nothing,
  "You come here!
  You stand here!"
  There was a large blackboard.
    She took a white "marker" (piece of chalk). <42(3)>
    On that blackboard she wrote what are called "ABCs."

DIBI'BA.   <41(11)>

pɛ·''ma ɢɪ'n·ʊk ɢʊ'ca tcɛɢɛ·'m-aвe'ıвa pɛ'ca-yʊ· ç̧ɛ'ᴅ·ak ɢʊtɪ'unan,
   ɢʊnıᴅɪ'st вʊ'ɢʊlfan ᴅɪnıɢɛ·'m-aвe'ıвa.
   pa'c·wi·yʊ· ɢʊt·ɪ'unan tcɛɢʊ'ca-wa''an-aвe'ıвa,
      ɢʊdɪnıᴅɪ'st вʊ'ɢʊlfan ᴅɪnıвe'ıвa.
pɛ·''ma ɢʊnıᴅɪ'tɢwın ɢɪ'n·ʊk ɢʊ'ca ɢʊn·ɪ'yʊ'ɢ·ʊn ᴅa'в-ᴅɪвe'ıвa, ɢʊ'ca ɢʊn·ɪ'yʊ'ɢ·ʊn hʊ'p-
   cın-ᴅɪвe'ıвa.   <41(12)>
   ɢʊnıᴅɪ'tku tcɛᴅa'ɪ'wa·n ha'm·ɪ. ||123:29||
   qɛ'ᴅ·ak ɢʊ'ca-aвʊ'ᴅjat ɢʊᴅp̧ɪ·'n ɢɪ'n·ʊk ɢʊ'ca ɢɪn·ɪ'yʊ'ɢ·ʊn ɢɛ·'m-ᴅɪвe'ıвa, nau-ɢɪ'n·ʊk
      ɢʊ'sa ɢɪn·ɪ'yʊ'ɢ·ʊn wa''an-ᴅɪвe'ıвa, nau-ɢɪ'n·ʊk ɢʊ'sa wa'ŋq-a'ɢ·a ɢɪn·ɪ'yʊ'ɢ·ʊn.
pɛ·''ma wa''an ɢʊ'sa-aвʊ'ᴅjat ᴅjaᴅa'ɪ'wan aha'm·ɪ, pa'sa-yʊ·' ɢʊtmɪ'u'nan tcɛɢʊ'sa
   waвına·'tst.   <41(13)>
   qɛ'ᴅ·ak, ɢʊ'sa-aвʊ'ᴅjat tcɛᴅa'ɪ'wan-ha'm·ɪ, ɢʊᴅ_cmʊ'kʊ ɢʊ'sa-ɢɛ·'m ᴅɪвe'ıвa
      aвına·'tst, ɢʊ'ca-wa''an-ᴅɪвe'ıвa вına·'tst, nau-ɢʊ'sa ɢɪ'n·ʊk wa'ŋq-a'ɢ·a
      nı'yu'ɢ·ʊn.
pɛ·''ma ɢʊᴅınıᴅnı's·ın tcɛɢʊ's·a a̓tu'ıᴅ·ın na'u-tcɛɢʊ'sa вına·'tst,   <41(14)>
   mɪ'ᴅ·ɪ p̧ʊ'fan ᴅʊmınıt̓ʊ'ɢnın ᴅɪmhu·'p̧in tcɛɢʊ'sa-aвɪ·'вa.
   a'ɢ·a mɪ'ᴅ·ɪ wa'ŋq ɢʊmınıᴅyʊ'ɢ·ʊn pa'sa, cna'ɢɪt tcɛtcɪ·''ɪ.
   tcɪ·''ɪ ᴅɪtyʊ'knıfʊp a'ɢ·a wa'ŋq ᴅam_ᴅɪt·yʊ'ɢ·ʊn. ||123:31||

<42> School Procedures

ɢamıtme'ıᴅj ɢʊ'ca-aвʊ'ᴅjat ɢʊᴅna'ɢɪt
   tcɪ·''ɪ ᴅɪt'ʊ'knıfaı tcɛ·'mɪ'ᴅ·ɪ tcɛɢʊ'sa-ᴅɪвɪ·'вa.
pɛ·''ma ɢɛ'ᴅ·ak ɢʊ'sa-aвʊ'ᴅjat ɢʊᴅp̧ɪ·'n uᴅɪ·'t'saq aᴅɪ'nᴅın,
ç̧ɛ'ᴅ·ak ɢʊᴅɪ'nᴅa·t ɢʊ'ca-aᴅɪ'nᴅın,
   вʊ'ɢʊlfan mɪ'ᴅ·ɪ sɛ'ᴅ·ap.
   вʊ'ɢʊlfan cı·''weı ɢınısɛ'ᴅ·ap.
pɛ·''ma ç̧ɛ'ᴅ·ak ɢʊᴅna'ɢɪt,   <42(2)>
   mɪ'ᴅ·ɪ ᴅja·'k hɛ·''lʊm вsla'ɢwɪt hu·''wan amɪ'nɪt.
pɛ·''ma ç̧ɛ'ᴅ·ak ɢʊᴅɪ'nᴅa·t aᴅɪ'nᴅın.
   вʊ'ɢʊlfan asɪ·''weı ɢʊᴅınıla'm·u.
pɛ·''ma ç̧ɛ'ᴅ·ak ɢʊᴅɪ'tɢwın вʊ'ɢʊlfan ɢʊ'ca wa'ŋq-a'ɢ·a ɢɪn·ɪ'yʊ'ɢ·ʊn,
   mɪ'ᴅ·ɪ sma·'k hɛ'caвɛᴅ,
   hɛ'saвɛᴅ mɪ'ᴅ·ɪ вcᴅɛ·'cᴅap.
   waвa'l amu·''yım la'вla·c
      ɢʊᴅɪ'tɢwın wa''an awa'm·u· yɛ·'mʊfʊn.   <42(3)>
         ɢʊᴅyɛ·'m·a·t tcɛɢʊ's·a amu'yım ala'вla·'c a'ɢ·a ɢʊ'sa ᴅʊ'ŋkwɪt ABC.

Then she "gave the words" (instructions) to the children. ||123:33||
She said,
   "This is named 'A.'
   All you children say this!"
Then she said,   <42(4)>
   "This is named 'B.'"
   All the children said it.
Then when they finished, they all sat down where they (usually) sat.
Then those second-graders and first-graders studied their readers hard.

Then when it was four o'clock she rang the bell.
   All the children stood.
She said to the children,   <42(5)>
   "You go outside to play!"
   That was all there was for that day.
Then at six o'clock all the children ran (outside) to where they got themselves ready.

   They washed.
Finished with their washing, they went there to where they (usually) stood.
                                    ||123:35||
The sister said,   <42(6)>
   "All you children stand at where your own place is!"
Then she said,
   "All of you are to take the places where you have been standing!"
The children said,
   "Yes."
She said,
   "Come inside to eat!"
   She did it the same way again.   <42(7)>
   She spoke words of the Lord Above.
She having finished, then they sat down to their meal.
Then all the children finished their meal.
   The sister told the children to stand.
Then she spoke words of the Lord Above.
When she finishes her prayer, she said to the children,   <42(8)>
   "You go outside! Play!

pɛ·"ma ɢʊDɪD·i'ct ɢʊ'ca Dʊ'mha tcɛɢʊ'ca-acɪ·"wɛɪ. ||123:33||

ɢɛ'D·ak ɢʊDna'ɢɪt

  ha'sa Dʊ'ŋkwɪt A.

  Bʊ'ɢʊlfan mɪ'D·ɪ si·"wɛɪ pa'c pɪsna'ɢɪt.

pɛ·"ma ɢʊDna'ɢɪt   <42(4)>

  ha'c·a Da'ŋkwɪt B.

  Bʊ'ɢʊlfan asi·"wɛɪ ɢʊDɪnɪtna'ɢɪt.

pɛ·"ma ɢʊDɪnɪtʊ'ɢ·ɪ Bʊ'ɢʊlfan ɢʊDɪnɪt_sɪ'y·u DJɛha'l·a ɢʊ'ca ɢʊDɪnɪsɪ'y·u.

pɛ·"ma ɢɪ'n·ʊk ɢʊ'ca ɢɛ·'m-DɪBɛ'ɪBa nau-wa·"an-DɪBɛ'ɪBa ɢɪ'n·ʊk p̓ʊ'fan ɢʊDɪnɪDJɪ'B·ɪ·lD

  DɪnɪBɪ'Ba.

pɛ·"ma ɢʊDɪta'B-aDɪ'nDɪn ɢʊDɪ'nDa·t

  Bʊ'ɢʊlfan-asi·"wɛɪ ɢʊnɪDɛ'sDap.

qɛ'D·ak ɢʊDna'ɢɪt tcɛDɪcɪ·"wɛɪ   <42(5)>

  mɪ'D·ɪ DJa'kcDa hɛ·"lʊm Dʊpla'kwak.

  pa'sa-hɷ·"lʊ tcɛɢʊ'ca-wɛɪ-ɪ'pyan.

pɛ·"ma ɢwDɪDa'f-aDɪ'nDɪn Bʊ'ɢʊlfan asi·'wɛɪ ɢʊDɪnɪDmɪ'nDJɪs tcɛɢʊ'sa ha'l·a

  ɢʊnɪtɛ'n·ɪtcwu·n

  ɢʊDɪnɪ·k̓u·"uɫ

tʊ̓'ɢ·ɪ-Dɪnɪ·k̓u·"uɫ ɢʊDɪnɪDɪ't DJɛha'l·a ɢʊ'caBɛ·D ɢʊDɪnɪDɛ'cDap.

                                   ||123:35||

ɢʊ'sa-aBʊ·'Dzat na'ɢɪt   <42(6)>

  Bʊ'ɢʊlfan mɪ'D·ɪ sɪ'w·ɛɪ BsDɛ'sDap DJɛha'laBɛ·D ɢʊ'sa-mɪ'D·ɪ ɢwDʊBDa'BɪD.

pɛ·"ma ɢɛ'D·ak ɢʊDna'ɢɪt

  Bʊ'ɢʊlfan mɪ'D·i ɢʊDɪ'tɢwɪn ha'laBɛ·D ɢʊ'ca ɢʊDʊpDa'f

ɢɪ'n·ʊk sɪ'w·ɛɪ ɢʊDna'ɢɪt,

  hɛⁿ·"a.

ɢɛ'D·ak ɢʊDna'ɢɪt

  Bɪcla'm·ucDa Dɪkwe'ɪnafʊn

  pɛ'ca-yu· ɢɛ'D·ak ɢʊDmɪ'u'nan,   <42(7)>

  ɢʊDna'ɢɪt ha'lBam aDJa'mBak Dɪha'mha.

ɢʊtʊ̓'ɢ·ɪ pɛ·"ma ɢʊDɪnɪt_sɪ'y·u Dɪnɪkwe'ɪnafʊn.

pɛ·"ma Bʊ'ɢʊlfan si·"wɛɪ ɢɪntʊ̓'ɢ·ɪn Dɪnɪkwe'ɪnafʊn

  ɢʊ'sa-aBʊ·'Dzat ɢʊDɪtnɪ's·ɪn Dɪsi·"wɛɪ DʊmnɪDɛ'cDap.

pɛ·"ma ɢɛ'D·ak ɢʊDna'ɢɪt ha'lBam-DJa'mBak Dʊ'mha.

DɪDɪtʊ̓'ɢ·ɪ Dʊ'mha ɢʊDnaɢɪt DJɛsi·"wɛɪ   <42(8)>

  mɪ'Dɪ BcDJa·'k hɛ·"lʊm pcla'k·wak.

When it begins getting dark, all of you are to come inside to the playroom!

||123:37||

Soon, when it is eight o'clock, I'll ring the bell.

All of you will go upstairs to the room where you all sleep.

A sister will be there.   <42(9)>

    She will give you a bed to sleep on.

Then you will go to sleep!

    No one talks.

    No one plays.

    Whoever plays or talks, tomorrow he will get the little whipping stick.[5]

    You mind what I am saying to you!

Tomorrow early in the morning that other sister will ring the bell for you to get up.

<42(10)>

    All of you get up!

You tidy up the blankets where you sleep!

Finishing that, all of you go downstairs.

    Go to the place where you fix yourselves up.

    All of you wash, comb your hair! ||123:39|| <42(11)>

Then you will go into the play-room.

    There you will stay.

Then the early bell for breakfast will ring.

    All of you will stand up where you are.

Then one of the sisters will be there.

Then she will tell you,

    'Go inside to eat!'

That is how you will do every day.   <42(12)>

I don't want to talk to you every day (like this, repeating myself).

You mind what I have said to all you children!

Whichever child does not want to mind, he'll get the whipping stick.[6]

That is all that I have to say to you children.

Finished with (your) breakfast, you will all go outside to play.   <42(13)>

Then when it is nine o'clock, they will ring the bell. ||124:3||

All of you will run to the cleaning-up room, (to) wash your faces, your hands, and (to)
   comb your hair.

Then when you have fixed yourselves up, you will go to the classroom.

When they ring the bell, all of you will stand in one row.

dɪˈs puˈnuk ᴅᴏmɪtcɪˈkmiˑ ʙᴏˈɢᴏlfan mɪˈᴅɪ ᴅᴏmɪpclaˈmˑuˑ tcɛɢᴏˈsa laˈɢᴏt haˈmˑɪ.

||123:37||

diˈs ɢamɪtɢɪˈmwei aᴅɪˈnᴅɪn ᴅɪᴅɪᴅɪˈᴅˑaˑt aᴅɪˈnᴅɪn.

ʙᴏˈɢᴏlfan mɪˈᴅɪ ɢᴏᴅɪpᴅɪˈt haˈlʙam ᴅjahaˈmˑɪ haˈlˑa ɢᴏˈca mɪˈᴅɪ ɢᴏᴅɪpcɪˈˈwei.

waˈˈan-aʙᴏˈᴅzat ɢᴏˈsaʙɛˑᴅ ɢᴏmaʙiˈnᴅ.   <42(9)>

   ɢɛˈᴅˑak ɢᴏᴅˈɛˑsᴅup waˈˈan yaweˈɪfyak abed.

pɛˈˈma mɪˈᴅɪ ᴅɪᴅᴏpcɪˈˈwei.

   waˈŋq eˈyˑa ɢᴏᴅɪpyuˈwˑᴏn

   waˈŋq-eˈyˑa ɢᴏᴅɪᴅˍlaˈɢᴏt.

   eˈyˑa ɢᴏᴅˍlaˈɢᴏt ɢᴏᴅyuˈˈun, meˈɪᴅj ɢᴡˈk ɢᴏᴅɪˈtɢwin aᴅiˈtˈsaq ᴅaˈˈnaˈyᴏk aˈwaˈᴅˑik.

   mɪˈᴅɪ pcyᴏˈɢˑᴏn aˈɢˑa tcɪˈˈɪ tcᴏˈnɪˈcˈɪn tcamɪˈᴅɪ.

meˈɪᴅj-ɢamhaˈlˈwan ɢu'sa-awaˈˈan-aʙᴏˈᴅzat ɢᴏᴅˈɪˈnᴅaˑt aᴅɪˈnᴅɪn

   mɪˈᴅɪ ᴅᴏmᴅɪᴅˍcʙᴏˈklaɪ.   <42(10)>

   ʙᴏˈɢᴏlfan-mɪˈᴅɪ cʙᴏˈklaɪ.

mɪˈᴅɪ ʙɪʙctɛˈnˑaˑn ɢᴏˈcˑa ᴅɪpaˈcɪcɢwa haˈlˑa ɢᴏᴅᴏpweˈɪf.

tᴏˈɢɪ-ɢᴏˈca ʙᴏˈɢᴏlfan mɪˈᴅɪ ɢᴏᴅˍshᴏˈlˑaɪ

   ɢᴏᴅɪˈt tcɛhaˈlˑa-ɢᴏˈcˑa-ʙɛˑˈᴅ mɪˈᴅɪ ɢᴏᴅtɛˈnˑatcwuˑn

   ʙᴏˈɢᴏlfan mɪˈᴅɪ ɢᴏᴅᴏpkuˈˈuł, ɢᴏᴅᴏpkuˈmˑaˑt ᴅɪᴅaˈmɪł. ||123:39|| <42(11)>

pɛˈˈma mɪˈᴅɪ ᴅɪᴅᴏpslaˈmˑᴏ tcɛɢᴏˈcˑa laˈɢᴏt-haˈmˑɪ

   ɢᴏˈsaʙɛˑᴅ ᴅɪᴅᴏʙˈɪˈnᴅ.

pɛˈˈma ɢᴏˈca haˈlˈwanyak aᴅɪˈnᴅɪn ᴅɪkweˈɪnafanak ɢᴏᴅɪˈnᴅɪn,

   ʙᴏˈɢᴏlfan-mɪˈᴅɪ ɢᴏᴅᴏpᴅɛˈcᴅap tcɛhaˈlˑa ɢᴏˈca mɪˈᴅɪ ɢᴏᴅᴏpᴅaˈʙɪt.

pɛˈˈma-waˈˈan-ɢᴏˈca-aʙᴏˈᴅzat ɢᴏmaᴅaˈʙɪt.

pɛˈˈma qɛˈᴅˑak ɢᴏᴅnaˈɢɪt tcɛˈmɪˈᴅɪ

   pclaˈmˑᴏcᴅa ᴅɪkweˈɪnafᴏn.

pɛˈca mɪˈᴅɪ ᴅᴏpsmɪˈuˈnan ʙᴏˈɢᴏlfan aˈmpyan.   <42(12)>

waˈŋq tcɪˈˈɪ ɢᴏᴅˈaˈmᴅju ᴅᴏmnɪtyuˈwan tcɛmɪˈᴅɪ ʙᴏˈɢᴏlfan aˈmpyan.

mɪˈᴅɪ ʙsɢaˈpᴅɪn aˈɢˑa tcɪˈˈɪ ɢᴏᴅnaˈɢɪt tcaʙᴏˈɢᴏlfan mɪˈᴅɪ ciˈˈwei.

eˈyˑa-cɪˈˈwei waˈŋq ɢᴏᴅˈaˈmᴅju ᴅᴏmɢaˈpᴅɪn ɢᴡˈk ɢᴏᴅɪˈtɢwin aᴅaˈnˈaˈyak waˈᴅˑik.

paˈsa-hᴡˈˈlᴏ tcɪˈˈɪ tcɪnaˈɢɪt tcaˈmɪˈᴅɪ-siˈˈwei.

tᴏˈɢɪ-ᴅɪkweˈɪnafᴏn mɪˈᴅɪ ᴅɪᴅhɛˈˈlᴏm ᴅɪᴅᴏplaˈɢwɪt   <42(13)>

pɛˈˈma ɢᴏᴅɪtˍkwiˈst aᴅɪˈnᴅɪn. ɢᴏnɪᴅɪˈnᴅaˑt aᴅɪˈnᴅɪn. ||124:3||

ʙᴏˈɢᴏlfan-mɪˈᴅɪ ɢᴏᴅɪpmɪˈnᴅjɪs tcɛɢᴏˈca tɛˈnˑaˈyak haˈmˑɪ, kuˈˈuł ᴅɪkwaˈlˑak ᴅɪˈlaˈqᵂ,

   kuˈmˑuˑt ᴅɪᴅaˈmɪł.

pɛˈˈma mɪˈᴅɪ ɢᴏᴅˍsuˈˈyatcwuˑn ɢᴏmᴅɪᴅɪˈt tcaɢᴏˈsa haˈmha haˈmˑɪ.

ɢᴏmnɪᴅɪˈnᴅaˑt-aᴅɪnᴅɪn ʙᴏˈɢᴏlfan-mɪˈᴅɪ ɢᴏᴅɪpᴅɛˈsᴅap ᴅjɛwaˈˈan-aɢᴏˈn.

Then the classroom sister will come to you there. <42(14)>
Then she will tell you,
  'Go inside to the classroom!'
You will sit down where your desks are.
Then she will give you your readers.
Then you will look at your readers.
 You all will apply yourselves very diligently to those readers."
[From here the aforementioned class-room sister takes center-stage:]
 Then the sister takes all the children (beginners) who know nothing.

<42(15)>

  She writes all the ABCs on the blackboard. ||124:5||
When she finishes her instructions to the small children, then she says,
 "You all go sit where it is you all sit!"
Then she tells the second-graders to stand.
 "All you girls and boys, you come up front!"   <42(16)>
Then she told them to recite from their readers.
When they got through reciting, (to) whoever did not know his lesson, she said,
 "You will stay.
 You will study your lesson.
 You will apply yourself very diligently to that lesson.
 You are to recite it when they come up front again.   <42(17)>
 I want you to know those reader lessons."
Then that's what she, the sister, did to those first-grade children.
 Whoever didn't know their lesson, they stayed in the classroom.
Then all the children went to play outside. ||124:7|| <42(18)>
 Those who didn't know their lesson, they stayed in the classroom.
Then the sister taught what those children didn't know.
Then she rang the bell.
 All the children ran and stood where it was they were to stand.
And then she said,   <42(19)>
 "You all go inside!"
 They sat down where it was they sat.
Then she said to the second-grade children,
 "You come up front!"
Then they looked at their readers.
 They said all that they knew.

pɛˑ"ma-ɢʊˈsa haˈmha ʙuˈⅮzat ɢʊˈsaʙɛˑⅮ ɢʊⅮmaˑ"a tcamıˈⅮˑɪ.   <42(14)>

pɛˑ"ma ɢ̧ɛˈⅮˑak ɢʊⅮnaˈɢıt mıˈⅮˑɪ
    pclaˈmˑʊcⅮa tcɛɢʊˈsa haˈmha haˈmˑɪ.

mıˈⅮˑɪ ɢʊⅮıpcıˈyˑu hɛˈlˑa ɢʊˈca mıˈⅮˑɪ ⅮıⅮʊplaⅮaˈm.

pɛˑ"ma ɢ̧ɛˈⅮˑak ɢʊⅮıⅮıˈⅮˑʊp mıˈⅮˑɪ Ⅾıʙiˈˑʙa.

pɛˑ"ma-mıˈⅮˑɪ tsıˈʙluˑt Ⅾıʙiˈˑʙa,
    p̧ʊˈfan mıˈⅮˑɪ ţʊˈɢnɪn Ⅾamhuˈˑp̧ın tcaɢʊˈsa-aʙiˈˑʙa.

pɛˑ"ma ɢ̧ɛˈⅮˑak ɢʊˈsa-aʙuˈˑⅮzat ɢʊⅮıˈtɢwın ʙuˈɢʊlfan ɢʊˈca asiˑ"weı waˈŋq-aˈɢˑa
    ɢʊnˑıyʊˈɢʊn.   <42(15)>

    ɢʊⅮyɛˈmˑaˑt tcaɢʊˈca-amuˈyˑım alaˑʙlaˈˑc. ʙuˈɢʊlfan-ɢʊˈca ⅮıABCs ||124:5||

    ɢ̧ɛˈⅮˑak ɢʊţʊˈɢˑɪ Ⅾıhaˈmha tcɛɢʊˈsa Ⅾıˈntˑcıt asıˈweı, pɛˑ"ma ɢʊⅮnıˈsın
        mıˈⅮˑɪ tcacıˈyˑu tcɛhaˈlˑa-ɢʊˈsa mıˈⅮˑɪ ʙıⅮıⅮ_sıˈyˑu.

pɛˑ"ma ɢ̧ɛˈⅮˑak naˈɢıt tcaɢʊˈsa ɢɛˈm-aʙiˈˑʙa ɢʊmnıⅮɛˈˑcⅮap,
    ʙuˈɢʊlfan ʙınaˈˑtst nau-aţuˈıⅮın, mıˈⅮˑɪ ʙıcmaˈˑk Ⅾȷıˈmˑɪ.   <42(16)>

pɛˑ"ma ɢ̧ɛˈⅮˑak ɢʊⅮnıˈsın tcɛɢıˈnˑʊk Ⅾʊmnıˈyuˈwˑan Ⅾınıʙiˈˑʙa.

ɢʊnıţʊˈɢˑɪ-Ⅾıyuˈwˑan eˈyˑa ɢʊˈsa waˈŋq ɢʊⅮıtyʊˈɢˑʊn Ⅾıʙeˈıʙa ɢ̧ɛˈⅮˑak-ɢʊⅮnıˈcın,
    maˈha ⅮɛⅮʙiˈˑnⅮ
    ⅮɛⅮȷıˈʙluˑt ʙʊʙiˈˑʙa.
    p̧ʊˈfan maˈha Ⅾɛţʊˈknın ʙʊmhuˈˑp̧ın tcaɢʊˈsa aʙiˈˑʙa,
    tcıⅮyaˈʙˑaf maˈha Ⅾʊmınısmaˑ"a.   <42(17)>
    tcı"ı-tcıţaˈmⅮȷu maˈha Ⅾʊmnıtyʊˈɢʊn ɢʊˈsa-aʙiˈˑʙa.

pɛˑ"ma ɢ̧ɛˈⅮˑak-ɢʊˈca-aʙuˈˑⅮzat pɛˈca ɢʊⅮmıˈuˈnan tcɛɢʊˈsa-waˈˑan aʙiˈˑʙa Ⅾınıcıˑ"weı.
    eˈyˑa ɢʊˈca waˈŋq ɢʊⅮyʊˈɢʊn Ⅾınıʙiˈˑʙa ɢıˈnˑʊk ɢınıʙiˈˑnⅮ Ⅾȷɛhaˈmˑɪ.

pɛˑ"ma ʙuˈɢʊlfan cıˑ"weı ɢʊnıⅮıˈt Ⅾınılaˈɢwaɢ hɛˑ"lʊm. ||124:7|| <42(18)>

    ɢıˈnˑʊk ɢʊˈca waˈŋq ɢʊⅮınıˈyuˈɢʊn Ⅾınıʙiˈˑʙa ɢıˈnˑʊk ɢʊnıʙiˈˑnⅮ Ⅾȷɛhaˈmˑɪ.

pɛˑ"ma ɢʊˈca-aʙuˈˑⅮzat ɢ̧ɛˈⅮˑak ɢʊⅮyʊˈklını aˈɢˑa ɢʊˈca cıˑ"weı waˈŋq ɢanıyʊˈɢʊn.

pɛˑ"ma ɢ̧ɛˈⅮˑak ɢʊⅮıˈnⅮaˑt-aⅮıˈnⅮın
    ʙuˈɢʊlfan cıˑ"weı ɢʊⅮnımıˈnⅮȷıs ɢʊⅮınıⅮɛˈcⅮap Ⅾȷahaˈlˑa-ɢʊˈca ɢʊⅮınıⅮaˈˑʙıt.

pɛˑ"ma ɢ̧ɛˈⅮˑak ɢʊⅮnaˈɢıt   <42(19)>
    mıˈⅮˑɪ pclaˈmˑʊcⅮa.
    ɢʊⅮınısıˈyˑu Ⅾȷahaˈlˑa-ɢʊˈca ɢıˈnˑʊk ɢʊnˑısıˈyˑu.

pɛˑ"ma ɢʊⅮnaˈɢıt Ⅾȷaɢʊˈca ɢɛˈm-aʙiˈˑʙa sıˑ"weı
    mıˈⅮˑɪ psmaˈˑk Ⅾȷıˈmˑɪ.

pɛˑ"ma ɢʊˈnˑʊk [?] ɢıˈnˑʊk ɢʊnˑıⅮȷıˈʙˑiˑl Ⅾınıʙiˈˑʙa
    ɢʊⅮınıˈnaˈɢıt ʙuˈɢʊlfan aˈɢˑa ɢʊⅮınıⅮyʊˈɢʊn.

Then (to) those who didn't know their lesson, this is what she said,   <42(20)>
    "Now you must recite your lesson!"
    They recited all they knew of their lesson. ||124:9||
Then having finished reciting their lessons, they went back to where they sat.
    That's the way likewise she did to the first-grade children.
All done with their reciting, then they quit.   <42(21)>
    They put away their readers.
Then all the children stood up.
    She, the sister, said prayers to the Lord Above.
Then she said to the children,
    "You all go outside! you play!"
Then every day, on those five (week) days, that's what they did.[7]

<43> Saturday Chores

On Saturday all the children cut five (four-foot blocks) of wood.
    Some of the children split the wood.
    The small children packed the split wood to where two sisters made food.
                                           ||124:11||
All that morning the children worked.   <43(2)>
At midday they went to where they washed their faces and hands.
All done with their washing, they awaited that bell to go eat.
Then a sister rang the bell.
    They all ran to where they were to stand.
        Every child knew where he was to stand.   <43(3)>
Then the sister said,
    "Go in and eat!"
    All the children sat down to eat.
When they finished their meal, the sister said,
    "All you children go upstairs to where you sleep!
    There you will find good (clean) clothes.   <43(4)>
    You go to where they wash clothes! ||124:13||
    Lots of tubs are there, lots of warm water."
    Ten big boys went in there.
    Ten of the small children went in there.
[---]
    "You ten big boys will wash the small children's bodies.   <43(5)>
    Having finished their washing, you will wipe their bodies (dry)!

pɛ·''ma ɢʊ'ca ɢɪ'n·ʊk wa'ŋq ɢɪnɪdyʊ'ɢ·un ɢɪnɪʙi·'ʙa pa''-ɢʊdna'ɢɪt.   <42(20)>

  hɛ'n·a ma'ha tcɪyu''wan ʙɪʙi·'ʙa.

  ɢɪ'n·ʊk ɢɪdɪnɪdyu'w·an ʙu'ɢulfan ɢanɪdyʊ'ɢ·un ɢʊ'ca-dɪnɪʙi·'ʙa. ||124:9||

pɛ·''ma ɢʊnɪtʊ'ɢɪ dɪnɪyu'w·an dɪnɪʙi·'ʙa ɢʊnɪdɪ'tyɪ djaha'l·a ɢʊ'ca ɢʊdɪnɪsɪ'y·u.

  pa'ca-yu-wɛ·'u ɢʊt·ɪ'unan tcaɢʊ'sa wa''an aʙɪ'ʙa dɪsɪ'w·eɪ.

ʙʊ'ɢʊlfan ɢʊnɪtʊ'ɢɪ dɪnɪyu'w·ɪn pɛ·''ma ɢʊnɪʙa'clu',   <42(21)>

  ɢʊnɪd_lu''un dɪnɪʙi·'ʙa

pɛ·''ma ʙʊ'ɢʊlfan ci·''weɪ ɢʊnɪdɛ'cɒap.

  ɡɛ'ɒ·ak ɢu'ca-aʙʊ'ɒzat ɢʊdna'ɢɪt watɛ'n·a ha'mha tcaha'lʙam-aɒja'mʙak.

pɛ·''ma ɢʊdna'ɢɪt tcɛɒɪcɪ'w·eɪ

  mɪ'ɒɪ ʙcɒja'ksɒa hɛ·''lʊm pcla'ɢwɪt.

pɛ·''ma ʙʊ'ɢʊlfan a'mpyan tcɛɢʊ'sa hu'w·an a'a'mpyan pɛ'ca-ɢʊnɪmɪ'u'nan.

<43> Saturday Chores

ɢwɒɪɒa'f-a'mpyan ʙʊ'ɢʊlfan sɪ·''waɪ ɢʊnɪku'ʙɢat hu'w·an· a'wa'ɒɪk.

  ku'pfan-asi·''weɪ ɢʊdɪnɪpla'kpla·t a'wa'ɒɪk.

  ɢɪ'n·ʊk waɒɪ'nt'cɪt-asi·''weɪ ɢʊnɪtɛ'k·u ɢʊ'sa-pla'kpla·t-awa'ɒɪk tcaha'l·a-ɢʊ'sa

    ɡɛ'm aʙʊ'ɒzat ɢʊnɪʙʊ'nhɪn akwe'ɪnafʊn. ||124:11||

ʙʊ'ɢʊlfan-ɢʊ'ca-wɪ-ha'l'wan ɢʊ'ca-aci·''weɪ ɢʊnɪlu·''nafʊn.   <43(2)>

wɪ'lfu-a'mpyan ɢʊdɪnɪdɪ't djɛha'l·a-ɢʊ'sa ku''uł dɪnɪkwa'l·ak dɪ'nɪ'la'qʷ.

ʙʊ'ɢʊlfan-ɢʊnɪtʊ'ɢɪ dɪnɪku''uł ɢʊdɪnɪyu'w·ut ɢʊ'sa-aɒɪ'nɒɪn ɒʊ'mɒɪnɪkwe'ɪnafʊ.

pɛ·''ma ɢʊ'ca-wa''an-aʙʊ'ɒza·t ɢʊdɪ'nɒa·t-aɒɪ'nɒɪn.

  ʙu'ɢʊlfan ɢʊdɪnɪmɪ'nɒjɪs djaha'l·a ɢʊ'ca ɢʊdɪnɪɒa·'ʙɪt.

  ʙu'ɢʊlfan-si·''weɪ ɢʊdɪnɪyʊ'ɢ·on ha'l·a ɢɪ'n·ʊk ɢʊnɪɒa·ʙɪt.   <43(3)>

pɛ·''ma ɢʊ'ca-aʙʊ'ɒzat ɢʊdna'ɢɪt,

  ʙɪcla'm·ʊcɒa dɪkwe'ɪnafʊn.

  ʙʊ'ɢʊlfan-ci·''weɪ ɢɪnɪsɪ'y·u dɪnɪkwe'ɪnafʊn.

ɢʊdɪnɪtʊ'ɢɪ dɪnɪkwe'ɪnafʊn ɢʊ'sa-aʙʊ'ɒzat ɢʊdna'ɢɪt,

  ʙʊ'ɢʊlfan mɪ'ɒɪ si·''weɪ dɪɒʊfɒɪ't ha'lʙam tcɛha'l·a ɢʊ'ca mɪ'ɒɪ ɢʊdʊpwe'ɪɒɪt.

  ɢʊ'saʙɛ·ɒ mɪ'ɒɪ ɒɛ·'cɒɛc utɛ'n·a a'ɢfan   <43(4)>

  dɪɒʊpɒɪ't djaha'l·a ɢʊ'ca ɢʊnɪku'luł a'ɢfan, ||124:13||

  ha'l·u· ata'multc ɢʊ'saʙɛ·ɒ, ha'l·u· wa'm·aɪ ma'mpɢa.

  dɪ·'nfyaf waʙa'l atu'ɪɒ·ɪn ɢʊdɪnɪcla'm·u ɢʊ'caʙɛ·ɒ,

  dɪ·'nfyaf hɛ'ca-waɒɪ'nt'cɪt ci'w·eɪ ɢʊnɪcla'm·ʊ ɢʊ'caʙɛ·ɒ.

[---]

  mɪ'ɒɪ dɪ·'nfyaf tu'ɪɒ·ɪn dɪɒʊpku''ul dɪnɪka'pya ɢʊ'sa-waɒɪ'nt'cɪt asi'w·eɪ.   <43(5)>

  ɢʊnɪtʊ'ɢɪ-dɪnɪku''uł mɪ'ɒɪ ɢʊnɪtya'fla·t dɪnɪka'pya

Put those clean clothes on all of them.

That is how you will do it for all these small children.

Having finished (with) them, then you big children go wash your bodies.

　　Put on clean clothes!

When all the children finish washing their bodies, then all of you go play.[8]

<43(6)>

You children are not to run away.

Whichever of you children runs away, they'll go after you.[9]　　||124:15||

Then when it's close to six o'clock, all you children go to where you wash.

　　Prepare for the meal!"

Then this sister rang the bell.

　All the children ran to where they stood.　　　　　　　　<43(7)>

Then the sister took one big boy.

　"You watch these children!

　You tell (them),

　　'Go into the dining room!'"

The sister stood in the middle of the room.

　Then she prayed words of the Lord Above.

Then she said,

　"Sit down! Eat!"　　　　　　　　　　　　　　<43(8)>

Their meal finished, she said,

　"All children stand!"

Then she prayed words of the Lord Above.

Then she said,　　　　　　　　　　　　　　||124:17||

　"All you children go outside to play!

　When it gets near dark, all you children go inside to the playroom.　　<43(9)>

　　There you will play.

　When eight o'clock approaches, then I will ring the bell.

　All of you children go upstairs to where you sleep.

　Tomorrow at seven o'clock I will ring the bell for you to get up."

ʙuˈɢulfan ɢɪnɪtʙʊˈn ɢʊˈsˑa tɛˈnˑa aˈɢfan

ʙɛˈsˑa mɪˈɒˑɪ ɒupmɪˈuˈnan tcɛʙuˈɢulfan hɛˈca-waɒɪˈntˈcɪt asiˈwˑeɪ.

ɢʊnˑɪʙtʊˈɢɪ ɢʊˈsa pɛˈˑˈma mɪˈɒˑɪ waʙaˈl siˈˈweɪ k̓uˈuɫ ɒɪk̓aˈʙya,

    ʙɪʙcʙʊˈn watɛˈnˑa-aˈɢfan.

ʙuˈɢulfan siˈˈweɪ ɢʊnɪtʊˈɢɪ ɒɪnɪk̓uˈuɫ ɒɪnika̓ˈʙya, pɛˈˑˈma mɪˈɒˑɪ ɢʊɒɪpɒɪˈt ɒɪlaˈɢwak.

                                                                                          <43(6)>

wa̓ˈŋq mɪˈɒˑɪ siˈˈweɪ ɒumnɪtmɪˈnʊɢwɪt.

eˈyˑa-mɪˈɒˑɪ-siˈˈweɪ ɢʊɒnɪɒmɪˈnaɢwɪt ɢʊɒnɪtwuˈwu tcɛmɪˈɒˑɪ. ||124:15||

pɛˈˑˈma yɛˈts-ɢamɒaˈf-aɒɪˈnɒɪn ʙuˈɢulfan-mɪˈɒˑɪ-siˈˈweɪ ɢuɒɪˈt tcɛhaˈlˑa-ɢʊˈsˑa

    ɢʊɒɪpk̓uˈuɫ

      tɛˈnˑatcwuˑn ɒɪk̓weˈɪnafʊn.

pɛˈˑˈma haˈsa-aʙuˈɒzat ɢʊɒɪˈnɒaˑt-aɒɪˈnɒɪn.

  ʙuˈɢʊlfan asiˈˈweɪ ɢʊɒɪnɪɒmɪˈnɒjɪs ɒjahaˈlˑa ɢʊˈsa ɢʊɒɪnɪɒaˈf.   <43(7)>

pɛˈˑˈma ɢʊˈsa-aʙuˈɒzat ɢʊɒɪˈtɢwɪn waˈˈan aʙaˈl at̓uˈɪɒˑɪn,

  maˈha ʙcluˈɒnɪɢwan haˈca ciˈˈweɪ.

  maˈha nɪˈcˑɪn

    pcɒ_laˈmˈʊcɒa ɒjɛhaˈmˑɪ ɒɪk̓weˈɪnafʊn.

ɢʊˈsa-aʙuˈɒjat ɢʊɒˑaˈʙɪt wɪˈlf ɒjɛhaˈmˑɪ.

  pɛˈˑˈma qɛˈɒˑak ɢʊɒyuˈwɪn haˈlʙam-ɒjaˈmʙak-ɒuˈmha.

pɛˈˑˈma qɛˈɒˑak naˈɢɪt

  pcɪˈyucɒa pck̓weˈɪnafʊn.   <43(8)>

t̓uˈɢɪ-ɒɪnɪk̓weˈɪnafʊn qɛˈɒˑak ɢʊɒnaˈɢɪt,

  ʙuˈɢulfan-ciˈˈweɪ cɒɛˈcɒap

pɛˈˑˈma qɛˈɒˑak ɢʊtyuˈwʊn ɢʊˈca haˈlʙam-ɒjaˈmʙak-ɒuˈmha.

pɛˈˑˈma ɢʊɒnaˈɢɪt ||124:17||

  ʙuˈɢulfan mɪˈɒˑɪ siˈˈweɪ cɒjaˑˈk hɛˈˈlum ɒuplaˈɢwt.

  yɛˈts-ɢamɪthuˈwɪ ʙuˈɢulfan mɪˈɒˑɪ siˈˈweɪ ɢʊɒuʙlaˈmˑu ɒjɛɢʊˈsa laˈɢʊt-haˈmˑɪ. <43(9)>

    ɢʊˈsaʙɛˑɒ mɪˈɒˑɪ ɢʊɒuplaˈɢut.

  dɪˈs yeˈɪɒj-ɢamɪɢɛˈmˈwa ɒɪˈnɒɪn, pɛˈˑˈma tcɪˈˈɪ ɒɪɒɪˈnɒaˑt ɒɪɒɪˈnɒɪn.

  ʙuˈɢulfan mɪˈɒˑɪ ciˈˈweɪ ɒɪˈt-haˈlʙam ɒjɛhaˈlˑa ɢʊˈsa mɪˈɒˑɪ ɢʊɒɪpweˈɪf.

  meˈɪɒj ɢamɪpcɪˈnˈwa aɒɪˈnɒɪn ɒjɪˈˈɪ ɒɪɒɪˈnɒaˑt ɒɪɒɪˈnɒɪn mɪˈɒˑɪ ɒɪmɒɪɒʙʊˈk̓laɪ.

Serving Mass for Fr. Croquet[1]

<44> Bahawadas Gets Picked as an Altar Boy

Then all the children got up.

   They went down and outside.

   They went to where it was they washed up.

Then they all washed up.

   They went into the playroom.

   There they awaited the bell to go to their meal.

||124:19|| <44(2)>

On that particular morning, then the big boy rang the bell.

   All the children went to where it was that they stood.

Then the big boy spoke like so,

   "Are all the children (boys) here?"[2]

Then the children (boys) said,

   "Yes." <44(3)>

[---]

   "Now all of you children turn around! Go on into the dining room!"

All of the children entered.

   They stood by their plates.

Then the sister stood in the middle at the end of the table.

Then she said,

   "I'll pray the words of the Lord Above. <44(4)>

   All of you children, too, you will pray the same as I say!"

Having finished her prayers, then she rang the little (hand-)bell, ||124:21||

   "All of you sit!

   Now all of you eat!"

She stayed there.

   She waited for the children to finish their meal. <44(5)>

Then she said to all the children,

   "When it is nine-o'clock, I will ring this bell.

   All you children will go to the place where you make ready (and) wash your faces, your hands.

   When you have all finished your washing, then all of you will go on into where your play-room is!" <44(6)>

Then this big boy rang the bell.

Serving Mass for Fr. Croquet

<44> *baxawádas* Gets Picked as an Altar Boy

pɛ·ʼma ʙʊʼɢulfan ci·ʼʼwei ɢʊᴅɪnɪᴅʙuʼklaɪ

ɢʊᴅɪnɪᴅhaʼl·u· hɛ·ʼʼlʊm

ɢɪᴅɪnɪᴅɪʼt tcɛhaʼlʼa-ɢʊʼsa ᴅɪn·ɪtǩuʼʼuł.

pɛ·ʼʼma ʙuʼɢulfan ɢʊᴅɪnɪtǩuʼʼuł.

ɢʊᴅ·ɪnɪlaʼm·ʊ tcɛ-ɢʊʼsa laʼɢʊʼthaʼm·ɪ,

ɢʊʼsaʙɛᴅ ɢʊᴅɪnɪyʊʼwʼʊᴅ ɢʊʼs·a-aᴅɪʼnᴅɪn ᴅʊmnɪᴅɪʼt tcɛᴅɪnɪǩweʼɪnafʊn.

||124:19|| <44(2)>

ɢʊʼsa-weɪ-halʼwan pɛ·ʼʼma ɢʊʼsa-ʊʙaʼl-aṭuʼɪᴅɪn ɢʊᴅɪʼnᴅaˑt aᴅɪʼnᴅɪn.

ʙʊʼɢulfan-ci·ʼʼweɪ ɢʊᴅɪᴅnɪʼʼɪ (~ɢʊᴅɪtnɪʼʼɪ) tcɛhaʼlʼa ɢʊʼca ɢʊnɪᴅaˑʼf.

pɛ·ʼʼma ɢʊʼsa-wɪ-ʙaʼl-aṭuʼɪᴅɪn paʼʼa-ɢʊᴅnaʼɢɪt,

ʙʊʼɢulfan ci·ʼʼweɪ hɛʼsaʙɛᴅ?

pɛ·ʼʼma ɢɪʼnˑʊk ci·ʼʼweɪ ɢʊᴅɪnˑaʼɢɪt,

hɛʼⁿʼʼa.   <44(3)>

[---]

pɛ·ʼʼma mɪʼᴅɪ ci·ʼʼwei pcǩɪʼlʼu tcaˑʼk ᴅɪʼlaʼm·ʊ tcɛǩweʼɪnafyak-haʼm·ɪ.

ʙʊʼɢulfan-ci·ʼʼweɪ ɢʊᴅɪnɪlaʼm·u

ɢʊᴅɪnɪᴅɛʼᴄᴅap tcɛɢɪʼnˑuk ᴅɪᴅɪnɪkwaʼᴅ.

pɛ·ʼʼma ɢʊca-aʙʊ·ʼᴅzat ç̧ɛʼᴅ·ak ɢʊᴅ·aʼʙɪt wɪʼlf tcɛɢʊʼc·a ťwɛ·ʼlt tcɛɢʊʼca-laᴅaʼm.

pɛ·ʼʼma ç̧ɛᴅˑak ɢʊᴅnaʼɢɪt,

tcɪʼʼɪ tcɪyuʼwʼan haʼlʙam-tcaʼmʙak-ᴅʊʼmha.   <44(4)>

mɪʼᴅɪ-yuʼ ʙʊʼɢulfan-ci·ʼʼweɪ ᴅɪᴅʊpyuʼʼwan pɛʼca-weɪ aʼɢ·a tcɪʼʼɪ tcɪʼnaʼɢɪt.

ɢʊťʊʼɢɪ-ᴅɪyʊʼʼwan pɛ·ʼʼma ɢʊᴅɪʼnᴅ·at ɢʊs-uᴅɪʼtʼsaq̇ aᴅɪʼnᴅɪn, ||124:21||

ʙʊʼɢulfan-mɪʼᴅɪ ʙɪsɪʼyʼu.

pɛ·ʼʼma ʙɪʙᴄǩweʼɪnafu.

ç̧ɛʼᴅˑak ɢʊᴅ·aʼʙɪt ɢʊʼsaʙɛᴅ

ɢʊᴅyuʼʼwuˑt ɢʊʼsa-asi·ʼʼweɪ ᴅʊmnɪtʊʼɢɪ ᴅɪnɪǩweʼɪnafʊn.   <44(5)>

pɛ·ʼʼma ç̧ɛʼᴅˑak-ɢʊᴅnaʼɢɪt tcɛʙʊʼɢulfan ɢʊs-asi·ʼʼweɪ,

ɢamɪǩwiʼst-aᴅɪʼnᴅɪn tcɪʼʼɪ-ᴅɪᴅɪʼnᴅˑat hɛʼsa-aᴅɪʼnᴅɪn.

ʙʊʼɢulfan-mɪʼᴅɪ-si·ʼʼweɪ ᴅɪᴅʊpᴅɪʼt tcɛ-ɢʊʼsa-haʼlʼa mɪʼᴅɪ ɢʊťɛʼnˑatcwuˑn. ǩuʼʼuł ᴅɪk-waʼlˑak ᴅɪʼlaʼqʷ,

ʙʊʼɢulfan-mɪʼᴅɪ ᴅʊmɪťʊʼɢɪ ᴅɪǩuʼʼuł, pɛ·ʼʼma ʙʊʼɢulfan-mɪʼᴅɪ ʙclaʼm·u tcɛɢuʼs·a-haʼlʼa

mɪʼᴅɪ ɢʊᴅɪplaʼɢwɪt-haʼm·ɪ.   <44(6)>

pɛ·ʼʼma hɛʼsa-aʙal-aṭuʼɪᴅɪn ɢʊʼᴅɪʼnᴅaˑt ɢʊca-aᴅɪʼnᴅɪn.

[---] (a sister speaks):

"All you children stand where you (always) stand!

Then you will go to where you sleep.

A sister is staying there. ||124:23|| <44(7)>

She will give you all good (clean) clothes, your pants, your coats, your shirts, and a
good hat.

Then all you children will put on those clean clothes.

Then you will go downstairs to where the playroom is.

There you will stay. <44(8)>

You will just stay there.

No one is to play!

When it is almost 10 o'clock, the priest at the house of the Lord Above will ring the big
(church-)bell.

Then the second time he rings the bell, you will all go outside to where it is you all stand!
<44(9)>

Then you will enter the house of the Lord Above.

You will go in front of all the people.

Then the girls, too, they will go into the church. ||124:25||

I want two boys to serve the priest. <44(10)>

Who wants to go serve the priest?"

None of the boys spoke.

Then the sister said,

"I know who to take."

Then she said,

"You, Louis Kenoyer and another boy, named Daniel (Yachkawa[3]), you both will go to the
priest's room.[4] <44(11)>

There you take off your coats and your hats, so I may give you a coat-dress, a white coat-
dress, and a red coat.[5]

Then you both will go with the priest.

He will go in front.

You will go behind (him).[6]

Then the priest will chant his songs,

You, Louis, will carry the good (holy) water." ||124:27||

[---] (a sister speaks):

ʙʊ′ɢʊlfan-mɪ′ᴅɪ-sɪ-′′wei ɢʊᴅʊpᴅɛ′cᴅap tcɛha′l·a-mɪ′ᴅ’i ɢʊᴅʊpᴅa′f.

pɛ-′′ma mɪ′ᴅɪ ɢʊᴅʊpᴅɪ′t ᴅjɛha′l·a mɪ′ᴅɪ ɢʊᴅʊpwe′ɪf.

   ɢu′saʙɛ·ᴅ wa-′′an-aʙu-′ᴅzat ɢamɪᴅa′ʙɪt. ||124:23|| <44(7)>

qɛ′ᴅ·ak ɢʊᴅ·ɛ′ᴅ·ʊp ʙʊ′ɢʊlfan watɛ′n·a a′ɢfan, ᴅɪla′mʊlu′n, ᴅɪɢa′ʙu·′, ᴅɪca′·t,
   nau-tɛ′n·a-amu′yuc.

pɛ-′′ma ʙʊ′ɢʊlfan-mɪ′ᴅɪ-ci-′′wei ɢʊᴅɪpcʙʊ′n ɢʊ′ca watɛ′n·a-a′ɢfan.

pɛ-′′ma mɪ′ᴅɪ ɢʊᴅʊpchʊ′l·aɪ tcɛha′l·a ɢʊ′ca-la′ɢwɪt-ha′m·ɪ.

ɢʊ′caʙɛ·ᴅ mɪ′ᴅɪ ɢʊᴅʊpcʙi′·nᴅ.   <44(8)>

   ǩʊ′nfu· mɪ′ᴅɪ ɢʊᴅʊpcʙi′·nᴅ ɢʊ′saʙɛ·′ᴅ.

   wa′ŋq-ᴅamnɪla′ɢwɪt.

ye′ts ɢamɪᴅɪ′nfyaf-aᴅɪ′nᴅɪn ɢʊ′s·a watɛ′n·a-aᴅja′ŋku tcɛha′lʙam-ᴅja′mʙak-ᴅʊ′m·aɪ
   ɢⱷ′k ɢʊᴅɪ′nᴅa·t ɢʊ′sa-waʙa′l-aᴅɪ′nᴅɪn.

pɛ-′′ma ᴅɪɢɛ′fʊ ɢⱷ′k-ɢʊᴅɪ′nᴅa·t ɢʊ′ca-aᴅɪ′nᴅɪn mɪ′ᴅɪ ɢʊᴅ_cᴅɪ′t-hɛ-′′lum tcɛha′l·a-
   ɢʊ′c·a-mɪ′ᴅɪ ɢʊᴅⱷ′f (~ɢʊᴅ·a′f).   <44(9)>

pɛ-′′ma-mɪ′ᴅɪ ɢʊᴅʊpcla′m·u tcɛɢʊ′c·a ha′lʙam-ᴅja′mʙak-ᴅʊ′m·aɪ.

   mɪ′ᴅɪ ɢʊᴅʊpᴅɪ′t ᴅjɪ′m·ei ᴅjɛʙʊ′ɢʊlfan-a′m·ɪm.

pɛ-′′ma ɢɪ′n·ʊk ɢʊnɪʙɪ′na·tst ɢɪ′n·ʊk-yu·-ɢɪnɪl·a′m·u tcɛɢʊ′sa tɛ′n·a-ha′m·ɪ. ||124:25||

tcɪ′ɪ-tcɪ′ta′mᴅju ɢɛ-′m aťu′ɪᴅfaf ᴅʊmnɪᴅyu′ᴅnɪɢwan tcɛɢʊ′ca tɛ′n·a-amu′ɪ. <44(10)>

e′y·a-ɢʊťa′mᴅju ᴅuɢu-′′um ɢʊᴅyu′ᴅnɪɢwan ɢʊ′ca-tɛ′n·a-amu′ɪ?

wa′ŋq-e′y·a sɪ′nfaf ɢʊᴅna′ɢɪt.

pɛ-′′ma ɢʊ′ca-aʙu′ᴅjat ɢʊᴅna′ɢɪt,

   tcɪ′′ɪ-tcɪ′yʊ′ɢʊn e′y·a ᴅʊmᴅɪ′tɢwɪn.

pɛ-′′ma ɢʊᴅna′ɢɪt,

   ma′ha Louis ǩɪnu′ɪ nau-wa-′′an-yu· aťu′ɪᴅfaf ᴅʊ′ŋkwɪt Daniel. mɪ′ᴅɪ pcᴅja′k tcɛ-ɢʊ′sa
   tɛ′n·a-amu′ɪ tcɛᴅɪᴅʊ′m·aɪ.   <44(11)>

   ɢʊ′saʙɛ·ᴅ-mɪ′ᴅɪ ʙckwɪ′lcǩwa·t ᴅɪɢa′ʙu· na′u-ᴅɪmu′yus nautcɪ′′ɪ ᴅʊmᴅɛ′sᴅup wa-′′an
   aku′t wa′m·u-aku′t nau-waᴅza′l aɢa′ʙu·.

   pɛ-′′ma-mɪ′ᴅɪ ɢʊᴅʊʙᴅɪ′t (~ɢʊᴅʊpᴅɪ′t) tcɛɢʊ′c·a tɛ′n·a-amu′ɪ.

      ɢⱷ′k-ɢʊᴅ’i′t ᴅjɪ′m·eɪ,

      mɪ′ᴅɪ ɢʊᴅɪʙ′i′ᴅ ha′nt′c.

   pɛ-′′ma ɢʊ′ca watɛ′n·a-amu′ɪ ɢʊᴅɢu′-ᴅiǫu′·ᴅ,

      ma′ha Louis ᴅɪtǩwɛ′n ɢʊ′sa watɛ′n·a-ama′mpɢa. ||124:27||

<45>Serving Mass for the "Good Man"[7]

The priest went in the middle (Jacobs: down the aisle) among all the people.

Then he cast the holy water onto the people (Jacobs: as he went).[8]

Then he went to where it is he stands (Jacobs: at the altar).

   There he spoke prayers.

   The sisters were above (in a gallery at the back end).[9]   <45(2)>

     There they sang.

Then having finished their singing, the priest offered good words (Jacobs: a sermon) to the people.

Then having finished his preaching, then the sisters sang.

When they were nearly done singing, then I and that other boy, we offered two
   small cups (jugs).[10]

   One cup (jug) was full of the wine (lit., berry water).   <45(3)>

   I offered the wine.

     I poured it. ||124:29||

     He took another cup (Jacobs: the chalice).

     I poured the wine into his cup (the chalice).

Then he drank of the wine.

Then that other boy poured the water.

   The priest washed his hands.[11]   <45(4)>

Then having finished all of that, the priest spoke prayers to the Lord Above.

Then everyone went out.

   I and that boy went to the next room to there where we took off our coat-dresses
     and our coats.

   All the children went out.   <45(5)>

     They went upstairs (at the school) to where they undressed up in the room
     they slept in.

Then they put on their ordinary ("bad") clothes.

Then all the children went downstairs and outside. ||124:31||

Then the big boy rang the bell for their midday meal.

               <45(6)>

   All the children ran to where they stood.

Then all of them entered the dining room.

   There too stood the sister.

Then she and all the children prayed to the Lord Above.

               <45(7)>

<45> Serving Mass for the "Good Man"

ɢʊ'sa-watɛ'nˑa-amu'ɪ ɢʊdɪdɪ't wɪ'lf tcɛɓʊ'ɢʊlfan ɢʊ'sa-a'mˑɪm.

pɛˑ''ma ɢɷ'k ɢʊtɢʊ' ɢʊ'sa-atɛ'nˑa-ama'mpɢa tcɛ'a'mˑɪm.

pɛˑ''ma ɢɷ'k-ɢʊdɪ'tyɪ tcɛha'lˑa-ɢʊsa ɢʊdɪda'ʙɪt.

  ɢʊ'sˑaˑʙɛˑd ɢɷ'k-ɢʊdnaˑ'ɢɪt watɛ'nˑa-ha'mha.

  ɢɪ'nˑʊk ɢʊ'sa ʙʊ'dzat ɢʊnɪdʙiˑ'nd haˑlʙam   <45(2)>

    ɢʊ'saʙɛˑd ɢɪ'nˑʊk ɢɪnɪtq̇u'dɪt.

pɛˑ''ma ɢɪnɪtʊ'ɢɪ-dɪnɪq̇u'd ɢʊ'sa-watɛ'nˑa-adɟa'ŋku ɢʊdɪnɪdɪ'ct atɛ'nˑa-ha'mha

  tcɛɢʊ'sa-a'mˑɪm.

pɛˑ''ma ɢʊtˑʊ'ɢɪ-dɪyu''wɪn, pɛˑ''ma ɢɪ'nˑʊk-ʙʊ'dzat ɢʊdɪnɪdq̇u'd.

yɛ'tc-ɢʊdɪnɪtˑʊ'ɢɪ-dɪq̇u'd, pɛˑ''ma tcɪ''i-nau-ɢʊ'ca-waˑ''an-aṫu'ɪdfaf sʊ'dˑʊ-ɢʊdɪ't ɢɛ'm

  waдɪ't'saq a'ʊ'sɢan.

  waˑ''an-a'ʊ'sɢan ɢʊd_lʊ'fˑaˑt tcɛɢʊ's·a aɕa'yˑaˑn-dɪma'mpɢa.   <45(3)>

  tcɪ''ɪ-ɢʊdɪ'st ɢʊsa-aɕa'y·a·n-dɪma'mpɢa

    ɢʊdk̇ʊ'mwalt. ||124:29||

    ɢɷ'k-ɢʊдk̇wɛˑ'n waдai''wan ʊ'sɢan,

    tcɪ''ɪ-ɢʊdɪ'twalt ɢʊca-aɕay·an-dɪma'mpɢa tcɛɢɷ'k-dɪ'ʊ'sɢan.

pɛˑ''ma ɢɷ'k ɢʊdɪ'tɢwɪt ɢʊca-aɕa'ya·n-dɪma'mpɢa.

pɛˑ''ma ɢʊsa-waˑ''an-aṫu'ɪdɪn ɢʊdɪ'twalt ɢʊsa-ama'mpɢa,

  ɢʊ'sa-tɛ'nˑa-adɟa'ŋku ɢʊtk̇u''uɬ dɪ'la'qʷ.   <45(4)>

pɛˑ''ma ʙʊ'ɢʊlfan-ɢʊtˑʊ'ɢɪ-ɢʊ'ca, ɢʊ'ca-atɛ'nˑa-adɟa'ŋku ɢʊdnaˑ'ɢɪt watɛ'nˑa-ha'mha

  tcaha'lʙam-dɟa'mʙak.

pɛˑ''ma-ʙʊ'ɢʊlfan e'yˑa (~i'yˑa) ɢʊdɪnɪdɪ'tmɪn.

  tcɪ''ɪ-nau-ɢʊca-aṫu'ɪdɪn sʊ'dˑʊ ɢʊdɪ't yɪ'm dɟɛha'lˑa-ɢʊ'ca hɛ'saʙɛˑd ɢʊd_ck̇wɪ'l-

    ck̇waˑt sʊ'dˑʊ-dɪku't nauдɪɢa'ʙʊ'.

  ʙʊ'ɢʊlfan-sɪ''wɛɪ ɢʊdɪnɪdɪ'tmɪn.   <45(5)>

    ɢʊnɪdɪ't ha'lʙam-dɟɛha'lˑa-ɢʊ'ca ɢʊnɪck̇wɪ'lck̇waˑt, ha'lʙam-tcɛha'mˑɪ ɢʊ'ca

    ɢʊdɪnɪdwe'ɪf.

pɛˑ''ma ɢʊnɪdʙʊ'n ɢʊ'sˑa waqa'sq dɪ'a'ɢfan.

pɛˑ''ma ʙʊ'ɢʊlfan-cɪ''wɛɪ ɢʊdɪnɪthʊ'lˑaɪ hɛˑ''lʊm. ||124:31||

pɛˑ''ma ɢʊ'ca-waʙaˑ'l-aṫu'ɪdɪn ɢʊdɪ'nдaˑt-adɪ'ndɪn ɢʊca-awɪ'lfʊ-a'mpyan

  dɪnɪk̇we'ɪnafʊn.   <45(6)>

  ʙʊ'ɢʊlfan-cɪ''wɛɪ ɢʊnɪdmɪ'ndɟɪs tcɛha'lˑa ɢʊ'sa ɢɪ'nˑʊk ɢʊdɪnɪdˑaˑ'f.

pɛˑ''ma ʙʊ'ɢʊlfan ɢʊdɪnɪd_la'mˑʊ tcɛk̇we'ɪnafʊnak-ha'mˑɪ.

  ɢʊ'saʙɛˑd-yu' ɢʊ'sa-aʙʊ'dɟat ɢʊdˑa'ʙɪt.

pɛˑ''ma ɕɛ'dˑak nau-ʙʊ'ɢʊˑlfan-acɪ''wɛɪ ɢʊdɪnɪdyu''wɪn watɛ'nˑa-ha'mha tcɛдɪha'lʙam-

  aдɟa'mʙak.   <45(7)>

All the children sat down.

Then they ate.

When they finished their meal, the sister rang the little (hand-)bell.

    All the children stood up.

    They said the words of the Lord Above.

Then all the children went outside.   <45(8)>

Then the children played outside. ||124:33||

The sister said to the big boy,

    "You watch over all the children!

        They are not to go far off!

    Soon, when it is 2 o'clock, we will go again to the church.   <45(9)>

    When you all hear the church bell, all of you will assemble where you all stand (Jacobs: in

        a row).

    Then you will take all of the children.

        All of you will go into the church.

        All of the girls will also go in.

        And all of us sisters will also go in.   <45(10)>

        There we will sing a little while and pray to our Lord Above.

    Then we will all come out.

    Then all of you children may play everywhere. ||124:35||

    Then when it is six o'clock, we'll ring the big bell.

        All of you children will come back.   <45(11)>

        You will get ready, washing your hands and your faces.

    Then you will await the bell.

    When the bell rings, you will all come back to where it is you stand.

    Then the big boy will say to you all,

        'Come on in for your meal!'"

Then the sister spoke the words of the Lord Above.

    "Now go and sit down to your meal!"   <45(12)>

Finished with their meal, then she said,

    "Stand up!"

Then she prayed the prayers to the Lord Above.

Then all the children went outside.

    There they all played. ||124:37||

ʙʊ'ɢʊlfan-aciˑ'ʼweɪ ɢʊdˑɪnsɪ'ʼyu,

pɛˑ'ʼma ɢʊdɪnɪk̓we'ɪnafu.

ɢʊdɪnɪtʊ'ɢɪ-dɪnɪk̓we'ɪnafɪn ɢʊ'sa-aʙʊ'dzat ɢʊdɪ'ndaˑt ɢʊsa-adɪ't'saq-adɪ'ndɪn,

    ʙʊ'ɢʊlfan-aciˑ'ʼweɪ ɢʊnɪdɛ'cdap,

      ɢʊdɪnɪɒna'ɢɪt ha'lʙam-ɒja'mʙak-dʊ'mha.

pɛˑ'ʼma ʙʊ'ɢʊlfan-cɪˑ'ʼweɪ ɢʊnˑɪdɪ't-hɛˑ'ʼlʊm.   <45(8)>

pɛˑ'ʼma siˑ'ʼweɪ ɢʊnˑɪla'ɢ_wak-hɛˑ'ʼlʊm.   ‖124:33‖

ɢʊ'sa-aʙʊ'dzat ɢʊdnɪ'cɪn ɢʊ'ca-aʙa'l-atʊ'ɪdɪn,

    ma'ha cyu'ɒnɪgwan ʙʊ'ɢʊlfan ciˑ'ʼweɪ.

      wa'ŋq ɢamnɪdˑɪ't-la'ɢaɪ.

    ɒiˑ'c ɢamɪɢɛˑ'm-adɪ'ndɪn ɢwɛˑ'lˑa'yu ɒɪdɪd_cdω''ω ɒjɛɢʊ'ca-watɛ'nˑa-ha'mˑɪ.   <45(9)>

    mɪ'ɒɪ ɒamnɪɒɢa'pɒɪn ɢʊca-tɛ'nˑa-ha'mˑɪ ɒɪdɪ'ndɪn ʙʊ'ɢʊlfan-mɪ'ɒɪ ɢʊdʊpcɢɛ'wʊ

      tcɛha'lˑa ɢʊ'ca mɪ'ɒɪ ɢʊdʊpɒa'f.

    pɛˑ'ʼma ma'ha ɒaɒɪ'tku ʙʊ'ɢʊlfan-ɢʊ'sa-aciˑ'ʼweɪ,

      ɒɛt_la'mˑɪ ɒjɛɢʊ'ca-watɛ'nˑa-ha'mˑɪ.

      ʙʊ'ɢʊlfan-yuˑ aʙɪ'nˑaˑtst ɢɪ'nʊk ɢɪnɪd_la'mˑu.

      nau-ʙʊ'ɢʊlfan-yuˑ suˑ'ɒʊ aʙʊ'dzat ɒɪdˑɪt_sla'mˑu.   <45(10)>

        ɢʊ'caʙɛˑd pu't'snaq ɒɪdɪtd̓qu'dɪd na'u-ɒɪtyu'ʼwɪn tɛ'nˑa-ha'mha

          tcɛdˑɪha'lʙam-aɒja'mʙak.

    pɛˑ'ʼma ʙʊ'ɢʊlfan sʊ'ɒʊ ɒɛɒɪɒma'mˑɪn,

    pɛˑ'ʼma ʙʊ'ɢʊlfan-mɪ'ɒɪ-siˑ'ʼweɪ ɢʊdʊpla'ɢʊt ʙʊ'ɢʊlfan-ha'lˑa.   ‖124:35‖

    pɛˑ'ʼma ɢamɪɒa'f-adɪ'ndɪn ɒɪdɪdɪ'ndˑat waʙa'l-adɪ'ndɪn.

      ʙʊ'ɢʊlfan-mɪ'ɒɪ-sɪ'ʼweɪ ɢʊdʊpcme'yɪ   <45(11)>

      ɢʊdɪptɛ'nˑatcwuˑn k̓u'ʼuɫ ɒɪ'la'qʷ ɒɪkwa'lˑak.

    pɛˑ'ʼma mɪ'ɒɪ yu'ɒnɪgwan ɢʊ'sa-adɪ'ndɪn.

    ɢʊdɪ'nɒa'ˑt-adɪ'ndɪn mɪ'ɒɪ ɢʊdɪpcma'k ɒjɛha'lˑa mɪ'ɒɪ-ɢʊdɪpɒa'ʙɪt.

    pɛˑ'ʼma ɢʊ'ca-aʙa'l-atʊ'ɪdɪn ɢʊdna'ɢɪt tcɛmɪ'ɒɪ,

      ɢʊd_cla'mˑʊcɒa-ɒɪk̓we'ɪnafʊn.

pɛˑ'ʼma ɢʊ'sa-aʙʊ'dzat ɢʊdna'ɢɪt ha'lʙam-ɒja'mʙak-dʊ'mha.

  tcɪ'ɒˑa ʙsɪ'ʼyusɒa ɒʊʙʊck̓we'ɪnafʊ.   <45(12)>

tʊ'ɢɪ-ɒɪnɪk̓we'ɪnafʊn pɛˑ'ʼma qɛˑ'ɒak-ɢʊdna'ɢɪt,

  psɒɪ'cɒapcɒa.

pɛˑ'ʼma-qɛˑ'ɒˑak ɢʊdyu'ʼwɪn ɢʊ'ca-atɛ'nˑa-ha'mha tcaha'lʙam-aɒja'mʙak.

pɛˑ'ʼma-ʙʊ'ɢʊlfan-ciˑ'ʼweɪ ɢʊnˑɪdɪ't-hɛˑ'ʼlʊm.

  ɢʊ'saʙɛˑd ʙʊ'ɢʊˑlfan-ɢʊnɪɒla'ɢˑwɪd .   ‖124:37‖

More Daily Life in the Sisters' School[1]

<46> Playing Black-Animal

Then the children played a different game.

One of them said, one of the big boys,

> *"I'll be the lone one ('it').*
>
> *I will be the 'black man.'"*[2]

Then those boys said,

> *"Alright!"*

[---]

> *"All you children stand fifty paces (away)."*

Then the "black lad" (said),   <46(2)>

> *"I will do like this,*
>
> *I will run after you."*

The other boys said,

> *"We will run!"*

[---] (one of the boys boasting:)

> *"This is how I will run!*
>
> *I'll do it here just like a deer.*
>
> *You can't ever catch us!"*

Then that one boy played the "black man."   <46(3)>

Then he ran after them.

> He chased all those boys.

Then he didn't catch a single one.

> He went to the other side to where all the other boys had started from. ||124:39||

Then he said,

> *"What will you do when I run after you?"*

Those boys said,   <46(4)>

> *"We will run just like deer."*

Then the "black man" ran after one of the boys.

> Then he caught one.

Then there were two "black persons."

> That's the way they played their game nearly to dusk.

Then two of those "black persons" chased all of those boys.   <46(5)>

> They caught two boys, and then there were four "black persons."

Again that "black person" said,

More Daily Life in the Sisters' School

<46> Playing Black-Animal

pɛˈˈma ɢɪˈnʊɢ·ʊsˈɪˈˈweɪ ɢʊɒɪnlaˈɢwak ɒaˈɪˈwan-alaˈɢʊt.

waˈˈan-ɢʊɒnaˈɢɪt, ɢʊs-awaˈˈan-aʙaˈl-asɪˈnfaf,

   tcɪˈˈɪ-tcɪmwaˈtafȧn

   tcɪˈˈɪ-tcɪmⱷˈˈyɪm aˈmuˈɪ

pɛˈˈma-ɢɪˈnʊ̇k ɢʊˈca-aṫuˈɪɒ·ɪn ɢʊˈnaˈɢɪt,

   ɢʊˈcwɪ!

[---]

   mɪˈɒ·ɪ-ʙʊˈɢʊlfan-siˈˈweɪ ɢʊɒɪnɪɒɛˈsɒap huˈwan-ɒɪˈnfya aɒⱷˈf.

pɛˈˈma-ɢʊˈca-aˈmⱷˈˈyɪm asɪˈnfaf,   <46(2)>

   paˈˈ-ɢɪmɪɒɪˈmɪˈuˈnan,

   tcɪˈˈɪ-ɒʊmɪnɪtyuˈwɪnfʊʙ

ɢɪˈnʊ̇ˈk ɒɪnɪṫuˈɪɒ·ɪn,

   sʊˈɒ·u ɢʊɒmɪˈnɒjɪs,

[---]

   paˈˈa tcɪˈˈɪ-ɒɪtmɪˈnɒjɪs

   paˈˈa-ɒɪtmɪˈut pɛˈsḱa hɛˈsa aɒaˈlˈɪm.

   waˈŋq-laˈf maˈha ɢʊmɒɪɒɪˈtɢwɪn tcɛsʊˈɒ·ʊ.

pɛˈˈma ɢʊsa-waˈˈan-aṫuˈɪɒfaf ɢⱷˈk-ɢʊɒaˈŋɢwt amⱷˈˈyɪm aˈm·ɪm.   <46(3)>

pɛˈˈma-ɢⱷˈk ɢʊtmɪˈnɒjɪs

   ɢʊtyuˈˈwan-ʙʊˈɢʊlfan ɢʊˈca-aṫuˈɪɒ·ɪn.

pɛˈˈma waˈŋq ɢʊɒ·ɪˈtɢwɪn waˈˈan.

   ɢʊɒ·ɪˈt-ɒ·juˈhu ɒjɛ-haˈl·a ɢʊˈca-haˈl·u·-sɪˈnfaf ɢʊɒɪnɪɒjuˈyamp. ‖124:39‖

pɛˈˈma ɢʊɒnaˈɢɪt,

   aˈɢ·a-mɪˈɒ·ɪ ɢʊɒpcɪˈuˈnan tcɪˈˈɪ-ɢʊɒɪtyuˈwɪnfʊʙ tcɛˈmɪˈɒ·ɪ.

ɢɪˈnʊ̇k-ɢʊca-aṫuˈɪɒ·ɪn ɢʊɒnaˈɢɪt,   <46(4)>

   sʊˈɒ·ʊ-ɢʊtmɪˈnɒjɪs paˈˈ-wɛˈu hɛˈsa-aɒaˈlˈɪm.

pɛˈˈma-ɢʊca-muˈˈyɪm-amuˈɪ ɢʊɒ-yuˈˈwan waˈˈan ɢʊˈsa-aṫuˈɪɒ·ɪn,

   pɛˈˈma ɢʊɒ·ɪˈtɢwɪn-waˈˈan.

pɛˈˈma ɢʊɒɢɛˈm muˈˈyɪm-aˈm·ɪm.

   paˈcḱa-naˈmɪˈut ɒɪnɪlaˈɢwak ɢʊˈsa-yɛˈtc-ɢʊthuˈwɪ.

pɛˈˈma ɢɛˈm-ɢʊca-muˈˈyɪm-aˈm·ɪm ɢʊɒɪnɪtyuˈwan ʙʊˈɢʊlfan ɢʊˈsa-aṫuˈɪɒ·ɪn.   <46(5)>

   ɢɪnɪɒɪˈtɢwɪn ɢɛˈm-aṫuˈɪɒ·ɪn. nau-pɛˈˈma ɢʊtˈa·ʙ ɢʊca-amuˈˈyɪm-aˈm·ɪm.

ɢwɪˈlˈyu ɢʊca-amuˈˈyɪm-aˈm·ɪm ɢʊɒnaˈɢɪt,

"What will you do when we chase you?"

[---]

    "We'll run like deer." ||124:41|| <46(6)>

Then there were eight "black lads."

Then when it was almost dark the big boy rang the bell.

Then all those children entered into their playroom.

    They stayed in the room there.

At eight o'clock they rang the bell.   <46(7)>

Then all the children went upstairs to where they slept.

Then they all took off their clothes.

Then they went to bed.

<47> A Typical Day at School

The next day one of the sisters rang the bell at five o'clock in the early morning,

"All you big boys get up![3]

Put on your clothes!

Go downstairs and outside!

Wash your faces!

Then come back into your sitting-room. ||124:43|| <47(2)>

Then, soon, a sister will ring the bell.

Then you will go to a particular 'little church' (upstairs chapel).[4]

There the priest will come.

Then all of us will pray prayers there to the Lord Above.[5]

We sisters want all of you children to know these prayers to pray to the Lord Above."

                                                  <47(3)>

Then, when they had finished those prayers, they went.

    They came down to the boys' playroom.

Then the big boy went upstairs to where the small children slept.   <47(4)>

  He woke up the small children at six o'clock. ||122:10||

Then all the small children put on their clothes.

Then they went down to where they washed their faces and their hands.

Then they all fixed themselves up.   <47(5)>

    They waited for the morning bell to eat.

When it was seven o'clock, then they rang the breakfast bell.

    All the children went outside to where it was that they stood.

a'ɢa-mι'ᴅι ɢʊᴩcmcι'u'nan su'ᴅʊ ɢʊᴅιᴅyu'wʊnfʊʙ?

[---]

su'ᴅʊ-ᴅιtmι'nᴅjιs pa''-uwɛ'u· hɛ'sa-aᴅa'lιm. ‖124:41‖ <46(6)>

pɛ·''ma ɢʊᴅιnιtɢɛ'm'wa ɢʊ'sa mⱷ''yιm sι'nfaf.

pɛ·''ma yɛ'tc-ɢʊthu'wι ɢʊ'sa-waʙa'l a̓tu'ιfaf ɢʊᴅι'nᴅa·t-ᴅιᴅι'nᴅιn.

pɛ·''ma-ʙu'ɢʊlfan ɢʊ'ca-asι''wει ɢʊᴅιnιt_la'm·u tcɛ'-ᴅιnιla'ɢwak-ha'm·ι.

  ɢʊ'caʙɛᴅ ɢι'n·ʊk ɢιnιʙι'nᴅ ᴅjɛha'm·ι.

ɢʊᴅιtɢι'm'wa-aᴅι'nᴅιn ɢʊnιᴅι'nᴅ·ɛt-aᴅι'nᴅιn, <46(7)>

pɛ·''ma-ʙu'ɢʊlfan cι''wει ɢʊᴅιnιᴅι't ha'lʙam tcaha'l·a ɢʊ'ca ᴅιᴅιnιsι'w·ει.

pɛ·''ma-ʙu'ɢʊlfan ɢʊᴅιnιckwι'lckwa·t ᴅιn'a'ɢfan.

pɛ·''ma ɢʊᴅιnsι''wει.

<47> A Typical Day at School

ɢʊᴅιtmе'ιᴅj ɢʊ'sa-wa''an-aʙu'ᴅzat ɢʊᴅι'nᴅa·t-aᴅι'nᴅιn tcɛ-hu'w'an-aᴅι'nᴅιn

  ɢwaᴅιtha'l'wan

  ʙu'ɢʊlfan-mι'ᴅι waʙa'l a̓tu'ιᴅ·ιn ʙιcʙu'ɢlaι.

  cʙu'n ʙι'a'ɢfan,

  ᴅja'kc-ha'l·u hɛ·''lʊm,

  c̓ku''uł mι'ᴅι-ᴅιkwa'l·ak

  pɛ·''ma ᴅʊᴅιpcla'm·u, tcɛ'mι'ᴅι ᴅιᴅιcι'yu ha'm·ι. ‖124:43‖ <47(2)>

  pɛ·''ma ᴅι·'s wa''an aʙu'ᴅzat ɢʊᴅι'nᴅa·t-aᴅι'nᴅιn

  pɛ·''ma cᴅιᴅιtι'ᴅ tcɛwa''an waᴅι'tʼsaq watɛ'n·a ha'm·ι.

  ɢʊ'caʙɛᴅ ɢʊ'c·a-watɛ'n·a-aᴅja'ŋk̓u ɢʊmcma''a ɢʊ'caʙɛᴅ.

  pɛ·''ma ɢʊ'saʙɛᴅ ʙu'ɢʊlfan-su'ᴅʊ ɢʊᴅyu''wʊn tɛ'n·a aha'mha ᴅjɛha'lʙam-aᴅja'mʙak.

  su'ᴅʊ ʙu'ᴅzat tcι-ᴅἰta'mᴅju ʙu'ɢʊlfan-mι'ᴅι-sι''wει ᴅʊmᴅιpyu'ɢʊn hɛ'ca tɛ'n·a-
    ha'mha ᴅʊpyu''wʊn tcɛha'lʙam-aᴅja'mʙak. <47(3)>

pɛ·''ma ɢʊᴅιnιtu'ɢιn ɢʊ'sa-atɛ'n·a-ᴅιnha'mha ɢʊᴅιnιᴅι't

  ɢʊᴅιnιmha'l·u· tcɛɢʊ'ca-a̓tu'ιᴅιn ᴅιᴅιnla'ɢwt-ha'm·ι.

pɛ·''ma ɢʊ'sa-waʙa'l-a̓tu'ιᴅιn ɢʊᴅι't-ha'lʙam tcɛha'l·a ɢʊ'sa ᴅι'ntʼcιt sι''wει ɢʊᴅιnιwειf
    <47(4)>

  ɢʊᴅιnιtʙu'klι ʙu'ɢʊlfan ɢʊ'ca ᴅι'nt'cιt-acι''wει ɢʊᴅιᴅ·a'f-aᴅι'nᴅιn. ‖122:10‖

pɛ·''ma ʙu'ɢʊlfan aᴅι'nt'cιt-acι''wει ɢʊᴅιnιʙu'n-ᴅιnι'a'ɢfan.

pɛ·''ma ɢʊᴅιnιha'l·u tcɛɢʊ'sa ha'l·a ᴅιnιk̓u''ul ᴅιnιkwa'l·ak nau-ᴅιnι''laqʷ.

pɛ·''ma ʙu'ɢʊlfan ɢι'n·ʊk ɢʊ'nιtɛ'nɛtcwu·n. <47(5)>

  ɢʊᴅιnιyu'w·u·t ɢʊ'sa ha'l'wanyak aᴅι'nᴅιn ᴅʊmιnιkwe'ιnafu.

ɢʊᴅιpcι'n'wι aᴅι'nᴅιn pɛ·''ma ɢʊnιᴅι'nᴅ·a·t ɢʊsa-akwe'ιnafyak-ᴅιᴅι'nᴅιn.

  ʙu'ɢʊlfan-sι''wει ɢιnιᴅι't-hɛ·''lʊm ᴅjɛha'l·a ɢʊ'sa ɢι'n·ʊk ɢʊᴅιnιᴅⱷ'f.

Then they went into the dining room. <47(6)>

   The sister was standing there.

   All the children stood.

Then the sister said the words of the Lord Above. ||122:12||

Then all the children said the words of the Lord Above.

Then they all sat down to their meal. <47(7)>

When they were through with their meal, then the sister prayed the words of the
   Lord Above.

   The children, too, prayed the words of the Lord Above.

Then she said,

   "Ten of you big boys cut wood, and ten of the older boys split the wood."

   The sisters cooking food had no more firewood. <47(8)>

Then ten of these smaller big boys, they took the wood to where those sisters
   prepared the food. ||122:14||

[---]

   "Now when you have finished your work, then you all go and play.

   Then, when nine o'clock comes, I'll ring the bell. <47(9)>

     All of you children will run to where it is you wash your faces and hands and comb
      your hair.

   Then you will come into the playroom.

   There you will await the bell.

   Then, when the bell rings, you all will come into the classroom." <47(10)>

   All the children entered and sat down at their desks.[6]

Then the classroom sister named (called the roll of) all the children who were in
   the classroom. ||122.16||

Then she called one boy's name.

That boy said, <47(11)>

   "Here I am."

She called all those second-graders' names.

   All were present.

Then she called all the first-grade boys.

   All of them were present, too.

Then they, the small children, she called their names.

   All the small children were present also.

Then the sister rang the bell, <47(12)>

pɛ·''ma ɢʊᴅɪnɪla'm·u tcɛɢʊ'sa-kwe'ɪnafyak-ha'm·ɪ.   <47(6)>

ʙʊ'saʙɛ·ᴅ ɢʊᴅɪᴅa'ʙɪt ɢʊ'sa-aʙʊ'ᴅzat.

ʙʊ'ɢʊlfan-si·''weɪ ɢʊᴅɪnɪᴅɪ'sᴅap,

pɛ·''ma ɢʊ'sa-aʙʊ'ᴅzat ɢʊᴅna'ɢɪt ha'lʙam-ᴅJa'mʙak-ᴅʊ'mha. ||122:12||

pɛ·''ma ʙʊ'ɢʊlfan ɢʊ'ca-asi·''weɪ ɢɪ'n·ʊk ɢʊnɪᴅna'ɢɪt ɢʊ'ca ha'lʙam-aᴅJa'mʙak-ᴅʊ'mha.

pɛ·''ma ʙʊ'ɢʊlfan ɢʊᴅɪnsi·'yu ᴅɪnɪkwe'ɪnafʊn.   <47(7)>

ɢʊᴅɪnɪtʊ'ɢɪ-ᴅɪnɪkwe'ɪnafʊn, pɛ·''ma ɢʊ'sa-aʙʊ'ᴅJat ɢʊᴅyu·''wʊn

ɢʊ'sa-ha'lʙam-ᴅJa'mʙak-ᴅʊ'mha,

ɢɪ'n·ʊk-yu' ɢʊca-asi·''weɪ ɢʊᴅɪnɪᴅyu·''wɪn ɢu'sa-ha'lʙam-ᴅJa'mʙak-ᴅʊ'mha.

pɛ·''ma qɛ'ᴅak ɢʊᴅna'ɢɪt

ᴅi·'nfyʊf mi'ᴅɪ ʙa'l-atʊ'ɪᴅ·ɪn ᴅɪᴅʊpkʊ'pka·t a'wa'ᴅɪk, nau-ᴅi·'nfyaf ɢʊ'sa sɪ'nfaf

ɢʊᴅɪnɪplʊ'q̩pla·t a'wa'ᴅɪk.

ɢʊ'sa-aʙʊ'ᴅzat ɢʊnɪʙʊ'nhɪn-akwe'ɪnafʊn ɢʊᴅwa·''yu· ᴅɪnɪ'wa'ᴅɪk.   <47(8)>

pɛ·''ma ᴅi·'nfyaf hɛ'ca ʙʊ't'saq waʙa'l-atʊ'ɪᴅɪn ɢɪ'n·ʊk ɢɪnɪᴅɪtku-a'wa'ᴅɪk ᴅJɛha'l·a

ɢʊ'sa-aʙʊ'ᴅzat ᴅɪnɪʙʊ'nhɪn akwe'ɪnafʊn. ||122:14||

[---]

pɛ·''ma mi'ᴅɪ ɢʊᴅʊʙtʊ'ɢɪ ᴅɪlu'nafʊn pɛ·''ma mi'ᴅɪ ɢʊᴅʊʙcɪ·'ɪ ᴅɪla'ɢwak.

pɛ·''ma ɢamᴅɪᴅkwi·'st-aᴅi'nᴅɪn tcɪ·'ɪ ᴅɪᴅɪ'nᴅa·t-aᴅi'nᴅɪn,   <47(9)>

ʙʊ'ɢʊlfan-mi'ᴅɪ-si'w·eɪ ɢʊᴅɪʙmi'nᴅJɪs ᴅJɛha'l·a ɢʊ'sa mi'ᴅɪ ᴅɛᴅʊpkʊ''uł ᴅɪkwal·ak

nau-ᴅɪ'la'qʷ, kʊ'm·u ᴅɪᴅa'mɪł

pɛ·''ma mi'ᴅɪ ɢʊᴅɪpcla'm·u tcɛᴅɪʙla'kwak-ha'm·ɪ.

ɢʊ'caʙɛ·ᴅ mi'ᴅɪ ɢʊᴅɪpyʊ''wu·t waᴅi'nᴅɪn.

pɛ·''ma ɢʊnɪᴅi'nᴅa·t-aᴅi'nᴅɪn mi'ᴅɪ ɢʊᴅɪpcla'm·u tcɛɢʊ'ca ha'mha-ha'm·ɪ.   <47(10)>

ʙʊ'ɢʊlfan-ci·''weɪ ɢʊᴅɪnɪᴅ_la'm·u ɢʊᴅɪnɪᴅsi'y·u· tcɛɢɪ'n·ʊk ᴅɪnɪ'la'ᴅam.

pɛ·''ma ɢʊ'sa-ha'mha-ʙʊ'ᴅJat ɢʊᴅɪnɪᴅkwu'hɪn ʙʊ'ɢʊlfan-ɢʊ'sa ci·''weɪ ɢʊᴅɪnɪᴅʙi'nᴅ

ᴅJɛɢʊ'ca-ha'mha-ha'm·ɪ ||122:16||

pɛ·''ma qɛ'ᴅak ɢʊtkwu''un wa''an-atʊ'ɪᴅ·ɪn ᴅʊ'ŋkwɪt.

ɢʊ'sa-atʊ'ɪᴅɪn ɢʊᴅna'ɢɪt   <47(11)>

hɛ'saʙɛ·ᴅ tcɪ·'ɪ tcɪʙi'nᴅ.

ɢʊtkwu''un ʙʊ'ɢʊlfan ɢɪ'n·ʊk ɢʊ'ca ɢɛ·'m-aʙɪ·'ʙa ᴅɪnɪᴅa'ŋkwɪt,

ʙʊ'ɢʊlfan ɢɪ'n·ʊk ɢʊᴅɪnɪᴅʙi'nᴅ.

pɛ·''ma ɢʊtkwu''un ʙʊ'ɢʊlfan ɢɪ'n·ʊk ɢʊca-awa''an-aʙɪ·'ʙa atʊ'ɪᴅɪn.

ʙʊ'ɢʊlfan-yu' ɢɪ'n·ʊk ɢɪnɪᴅʙi'nᴅ.

pɛ·''ma ɢɪ'n·ʊk ɢʊ'sa-waᴅi'nt'cɪᴅ-asi·''weɪ ɢʊnɪtkwu'hɪn ᴅɪnɪᴅa'ŋkwɪt

ʙʊ'ɢʊlfan-yu' ɢʊ'sa-aᴅi'nt'cɪt-asi·''weɪ ɢʊᴅɪnɪᴅʙi'nᴅ.

pɛ·''ma-ɢʊ'sa-aʙʊ'ᴅJat ɢʊᴅi'nᴅa·t aᴅi'nᴅɪn,   <47(12)>

"All of you stand up!
We will speak the words of the Lord Above." ||122:18||
Then she took all the second-grade readers.
  She gave them to the boys and girls.
  That's what she did also with the first-grade children.
    She gave all of them their readers.
Then she said,   <47(13)>
  "All of you study your readers diligently!"
Then she said to the small children,
  "You come here!"
Then she took the white marker.
  She wrote on the blackboard.
  She wrote,
    "1," "2," "3," "4," "5," "6," "7," "8," "9," "10."
Then she spoke to the children.   <47(14)>
Then she spoke that one called "one," ||122:20||
  "You children too, say it so after me."
Then she said all the (number-)names that she had written on the blackboard.

Then when they had finished their speaking of those words, then she wrote all of
  the ABC's.
Then she taught them their ABCs.   <47(15)>
When they finished, then she said,
  "All of you go sit down at your desks!"
Then she said,
  "Go outside to play five minutes!
  Then, shortly, I will ring the (hand-)bell."[7]
Then she goes and rings the bell. ||122:22|| <47(16)>
  All the children came back in.
    They sit down at their desks.
Then she said to the second-grade (boys and girls),
  "All of you come up front!"
Then she said to one of the boys,
  "First, you go look at your reader!
  Say what you know from your reader!"   <47(17)>
Then the second(-grade) boy, he, too, looked at his reader.

вʊ'гʊlfan-mı'dı вcdε'cdɑp.

sʊ'd·u dıdna'гıt гʊ'sa ha'lвam-adja'mвak-dʊ'mha. ||122:18||

pε·''ma гʊnıdı'tгwın вʊ'гʊlfan-гʊ'sa гε'm-aвı'вa dınıвı'вa,

  гε'd·ak гʊdı'ct tcεгʊ'c·a at·u'ıdın na'u-aвı'na·tst.

   pε'sı-yu-гʊt·ı'u'nan tcεгʊ'ca-wa''an dıвı'вa ası''weı,

     гʊdı'st вʊгʊlfan dınıвı'вa.

pε·''ma гʊdna'гıt,   <47(13)>

  mı'dı pʊ'fan dʊmıct'cı'вlu·t mı'dı-dıвı'вa.

pε·''ma qε'd·ak-гʊdna'гıt djεгʊ'ca wadı'nt'cıt-ası''weı,

  mı'dı psma·'k hε'saвε·d.

pε·''ma qε'd·ak гʊdı'tгwın гʊ'ca-awa'm·u· yε·'mafʊn,

  гʊtyε'm·at tcεгʊ'ca-amu'y·ım ala'вla·c.

  гʊtyε'm·at

    wa''an гε'm hu'pcın ta'в hu'w·an da'f pcı'n'wı гε'm'wı k̓wi·'st dı·nfyaf.

pε·''ma гʊdna'гıt djεгʊca-ci·''weı,   <47(14)>

pε·''ma qε'd·ak гʊdna'гıt ||122:20||

  гʊ'sa-ada'ŋгwt wa''an, mı'dı-yu· asi''weı pε'c-dumna'гıt ha'nt'c tcεtcı'·ı.

pε·''ma qε'd·ak гʊdna'гıt вʊ'гʊlfan гʊ'ca da'ŋkwıt гʊ'ca a'г·a гʊdyε'm·ut tcεгʊ'ca-

  mu'y·ım ala'вla·c.

pε·''ma гʊdınıt·ʊ'г·ı dı'na'гıt tcεгʊ'ca dʊ'mha, pε·''ma qε'd·ak гʊdyε'm·at гʊ'sa -dı'ABCs

  вʊ'гʊlfan.

pε·''ma гwdıdyʊ'kdnıfaı гʊ'ca -dını'ABCs.   <47(15)>

гʊd·ınıt·ʊ'г·ı pε·''ma гʊdna'гıt,

  mı'dı dja'kcda вcı'y·u tcεmı'dı dıla'dam.

pε·''ma qε'd·ak гʊdna'гıt,

  hu'w·an amı'nute mı'dı pcdja·'k hε·''lʊm dıdıpcla'гwak.

   pε·''ma dı's tcı'·ı dıdı'ndat-adı'ndın

pε·''ma qε'd·ak dıdı'ndat-adı'ndın ||122:22|| <47(16)>

  вʊ'гʊlfan si·''weı гʊdnmıla'm·u,

  dın·ısı'y·u tcεdı'nıla'da·m.

pε·''ma гʊdna'гıt tcεгʊ'sa гε'm-aвı'вa-ası''weı,

  mı'dı-вcma·'k djı'm·eı.

pε·''ma гʊdna'гıt tcεwa''an гʊ'ca at·u'ıdın,

  ma'ha mε'n ct'cı'вlu·t вıвı'вa

    ısna'гıt a'г·a ma'ha tcı'yʊ'г·ʊn tcεгʊ'c·a ma'ha aвı'вa.   <47(17)>

pε·''ma гʊ'sa гε'm dıtu'ıdın гɷ'k-yu· гʊt·'cı'вlu·d dıвı'вa

He said what he knew from his reader.

That's the way she did also with the girls.

Then, when they were all through, she said,   <47(18)>

"Sit down!"

Then she said to the first-grade boys and girls, ||122:24||

"You all come up front!"

They too said all they knew from their readers.   <47(19)>

All the first-grade children knew their lesson.

Then, at four o'clock, she said,

"That is all for today."

Then, when she rang her bell, all the children stand up.   <47(20)>

They said the words of the Lord Above.

Having finished, then all the children (only the boys?) went outside.

The girls went to their (separate) playroom.

<48> Playing Indian-Ball[8]

Then all the children played.

The big boys played what was called "Indian-ball."[9] ||122:26||

Then they took so and so many boys: nine on one, nine on the opposite side.

They marked the ground four times,

one trail here,

and one trail this other way,

and another trail this other way,

and another trail here to home (plate).   <48(2)>

Then the boys of the other side went out to where the trails were marked.

One stood in the middle.

One stood behind (the batter).

And one of them took a stick (bat) to hit the ball.   <48(3)>

The boy who was standing in the middle threw the ball. ||122:28||

Then that boy hit the ball.

Then those who were standing outside on the trails caught the ball.

Then they ran after the boy who hit the ball.   <48(4)>

Then they threw the ball hitting that boy's body.[10]

Then all the boys out there ran to home (plate).

Then the boy who had been hit on his body, he took the ball.

ɢʊᴅna′ɢɪt a′ɢ·a ɢʊca ɢɷ′k ɢʊᴅyʊ′ɢʊn tcɛᴅɪʙi′ʙa.

pa′cɪ-yu· ɢʊᴅmɪ′ut tcaɢɪ′n·ʊk ɢʊ′ca-aʙɪ′naᴅjit.

pɛ·″ma ʙʊ′ɢʊlfan ɢɪn·ɪt·ʊ′ɢɪ pɛ·″ma qɛ′ᴅ·ak ɢʊᴅna′ɢɪt,　　　　　　　<47(18)>

　pcɪ′yucda.

pɛ·″ma qɛ′ᴅ·ak ɢʊᴅna′ɢɪt tcɛɢʊ′ca-wa″an-aʙi′ʙa at·u′ɪᴅɪn nau-ʙɪ′na·tst ||122:24||

　mɪ′ᴅɪ pcma′k ᴅjɪ′m·ɛɪ.

ɢɪ′n·ʊk-yu· ɢʊᴅɪnɪᴅna′ɢɪt tcɛᴅɪnɪʙi′ʙa ʙʊ′ɢʊlfan ɢɪn·ɪᴅyʊ′ɢʊn.　　　　<47(19)>

　ʙʊ′ɢʊlfan ɢʊ′ca-wa″an-aʙi′ʙa asɪ·″wɛɪ ɢʊᴅɪnɪᴅyʊ′ɢʊn ᴅɪnɪʙi′ʙa′.

pɛ·″ma ɢʊᴅ·ita′ʙ-aᴅɪ′nᴅɪn qɛ′ᴅ·ak ɢʊᴅna′ɢɪt

　pɛ′sa-hɷ″lʊ tcɛhɛ′ca-wɪ-ɪ′pyan.

pɛ·″ma ɢʊᴅɪdɪ′nᴅa·t-ᴅɪᴅɪ′nᴅɪn ʙʊ′ɢʊlfan-cɪ·″wɛɪ nɪᴅɛ′cᴅap.　　　　　<47(20)>

　ɢʊᴅ·ɪnɪᴅna′ɢɪt ɢʊ′sa ha′lʙam-ᴅja′mʙak-ᴅʊ′mha.

ɢʊnɪt·ʊ′ɢɪ pɛ·″ma ʙʊ′ɢʊlfan ci·″wɛɪ ɢʊn·ɪᴅi′t-hɛ·″lʊm.

ɢɪ′n·ʊk-aʙɪ′na·ᴅzit ɢɪnɪᴅi′tyɪ tcɛɢɪ′n·ʊk ᴅɪnɪla′ɢwaɢ-ha′m·ɪ.

<48> Playing Indian-Ball

pɛ·″ma ʙʊ′ɢʊlfan-cɪ·″wɛɪ ɢʊnɪla′ɢwak.

　ʙa′l-at·u′ɪᴅɪn ɢɪ′n·ʊk ɢɪnɪla′ɢʊt a′ɢ·a ɢʊ′sa ᴅa′ŋkwɪt amɛ·′nmɪyɪk alɷ·″lʊ. ||122:26||

pɛ·″ma ɢʊᴅɪnɪᴅi′tɢwin pɛ′sa-hɷ″lʊ at·u′ɪᴅɪn: k̇wɪ·′st tcɛwa″an k̇wɪ·′st tcɛyɛ′lqfan.

　ɢʊn·ɪyɛ′m·ʊt ha′ŋk̇lʊp ta′ʙ

　　　wa″an ᴅɪɢu′n hɛ′caʙɛ·ᴅ,

　　　nau-wa″an ᴅɪɢu′n hɛ′cɪ-yʊ′f·an,

　　　nau-wa″an ᴅɪɢu′n hɛ′c·a-wɛɪ-yʊ′f·an,

　　　nau-wa″an ᴅɪɢu′n hɛ′sa tcaha′m·ɪ.　　　　　　　　　<48(2)>

pɛ·″ma ɢʊ′sa-yɛ′lqfan at·u′ɪᴅɪn ɢɪ′n·ʊk ɢɪn·ɪᴅi′t hɛ·″lʊm ᴅjɛha′l·a ɢʊ′ca-wɪ-yɛ′m·ɪᴅjɛɪ

　aɢu′n.

wa″an-ɢʊᴅ·ɛ′sᴅap wɪ′lf,

　wa″an ɢʊᴅ·ɛ′sᴅap ha′nt'c.

　nau-ɢɪ′n·ʊk ɢʊ′ca-wa″an ɢʊᴅɪᴅi′tɢwin a′wa′ᴅ·ɪk ɢʊmᴅ·ɪṫwa″an ɢʊ′ca-lu″lu. <48(3)>

　ɢu′-at·u′ɪᴅɪn ɢʊᴅ·a′ʙat tcɛwɪ′lf ɢɷ′k ɢʊtɢu′ ɢʊ′ca alu″lu　　||122:28||

pɛ·″ma ɢʊ′sa-at·u′ɪᴅɪn ɢʊṫwa″an ɢʊsa-alu″lu

pɛ·″ma ɢɪ′n·ʊk ɢʊ′ca-wa′n·ɪᴅa′ʙɪt hɛ·″lʊm tcɛɢʊ′ca-aɢu′n ɢʊn·ɪᴅi′tɢwin ɢʊ′ca-alu″lu.

pɛ·″ma ɢʊᴅɪnɪᴅyu″wan ɢʊ′ca-at·u′ɪᴅɪn ɢʊṫwa″an ɢʊca-alu″lu.　　　<48(4)>

pɛ·″ma ɢʊᴅɪnɪtɢu′ ɢʊca-alu″lu ṫwa″an tcɛɢʊ′ca-at·u′ɪᴅɪn ᴅɪka′ʙya

pɛ·″ma ʙʊ′ɢʊlfan ɢʊ′sa-at·u′ɪᴅɪn-hɛ·″lʊm ɢʊᴅ·ɪnɪtmɪ′nᴅjɪs tcɛɢʊ′ca tcaha′m·ɪ.

pɛ·″ma ɢʊ′ca-at·u′ɪᴅɪn ɢʊṫwa″yʊq tcɛᴅɪka′ʙya ɢɷ′k ɢʊᴅɪ′tɢwin ɢu′ca-alu″lu

He, too, wanted to hit the boys running to home (plate).

<48(5)>

He threw the ball.

He missed that other boy. ||122:30||

Then the ones that had (first) taken the bat, they went out to the marked
trails.[11]

And they, those other boys, they took the bat.

He (one of them) hit the ball far away.

Then he ran on the marked trails.

He ran around all of them.

He got back to home.   <48(6)>

Then one of the other boys took the bat.

He didn't hit the ball far.

The boys out there on the marked trails caught the ball.

Then they went after that boy.

They hit him on his body.

That boy, he jumped all over (trying to escape). ||122:32||

(Unless?) then another boy threw the ball to hit that boy's body.

(And) then he missed the boy's body.   <48(7)>

Then he ran along the marked trails.

He got back to home.

Then, when it was almost dark, they quit.

They went to where they fixed themselves up, to wash their faces and their hands.

Then the big boy rang the (hand-)bell for their meal.   <48(8)>

They all ran to where they stood.

They all stood.

They awaited the small children. ||122:34||

Then the big boy said,

"Turn around!

Go inside to the dining room!"

Then the sister spoke.

All the children prayed the words of the Lord Above.   <48(9)>

Then the sister said,

"You all sit down!

Eat!"

ɢɷˊk-yu· ɢuta̕ˊmɒjʊ ɒʊmṫwa''an ɢʊˊsa-aṫuˊɪɒ·ɪn ɢʊɒɪnɪmɪˊnɒjɪs tcɛɢʊˊca-haˊm·ɪ.

<48(5)>

ɢutɢuˊ ɢʊˊca-aluˊ'lu

ɢʊɒjɪˊʙ·ɪ (~t̕ˊcɪˊʙ·ɪ) ɢʊˊca ɒaˊɪˊwan aṫuˊɪɒɪn ||122:30||

pɛˊ''ma waˊ'an ɢɪˊn·ʊk ɢʊˊca-ɢɪnɪɒɪˊtɢwɪn aˊwaˊɒɪk ɢɪˊn·ʊk ɢʊɒɪnɪɒɪˊt heˊ''lum tcɛɢʊˊsa

   yɛˊmɪɒjɪ-aɢu·ˊn.

   nau-ɢɪˊn·ʊk ɢʊˊca yɛˊlqfan ṫuˊɪɒ·ɪn ɢɪnɪɒɪˊtɢwɪn aˊwaˊɒɪk

   ɢɷˊɢuṫwa''an ɢʊˊca-aluˊ'lu laˊɢ·aɪ.

pɛˊ''ma ɢɷˊɢʊtmɪˊnɒjɪs ɢʊˊca-ayɛˊmʊfʊn-ɢu·ˊn

   ɢuɒ·wɪˊ''yu ʙʊˊɢulfan

   ɢʊɒɪˊtwuk tcɛɢʊˊca-haˊm·ɪ.   <48(6)>

pɛˊ''ma waˊ'an aɒaˊɪˊwan aṫuˊɪɒ·ɪn ɢʊɒɪˊtɢwɪn ɒɪˊwaˊɒɪk,

   ɢɷˊk waˊŋɢuṫwa''an ɢʊˊsa-aluˊ'lu laˊɢ·aɪ.

   ɢɪˊn·ʊk ɢʊˊca-heˊ·''lum tcɛyɛˊmʊfʊn-aɢu·ˊn ɢɪnɪɒɪˊtɢwɪn ɢʊˊca-aluˊ·''lu

pɛˊ''ma ɢɪnɪtyuˊ''wan ɢʊˊsa-aṫuˊɪɒɪn.

   ɢʊɒɪnɪtwa''an tcɛɒɪkaˊʙya

   ɢɷˊk ɢʊˊsa-aṫ·uˊɪɒɪn ɢuɒˊɪˊɒ·ʊʙ ʙuˊɢulfan-haˊl·a. ||122:32||

pɛˊ''ma ɢʊˊca-waˊ'an-aṫuˊɪɒɪn ɢutɢuˊ ɢʊˊca-aluˊ'lu, ɒʊmɒɪˊtwa''an ɢuˊsa-aṫuˊɪɒɪn

   ɒɪkaˊʙya.

pɛˊ''ma ɢɷˊk ɢʊtˊcɪˊʙ·ɪn ɢʊˊsa-aṫuˊɪɒɪn ɒɪkaˊʙya.   <48(7)>

pɛˊ''ma ɢɷˊk ɢʊtmɪˊnɒjɪs tcɛyɛˊmɪɒjɪ-aɢu·ˊn

   ɢʊɒɪˊtwʊk tcɛhaˊm·ɪ.

pɛˊ''ma ɢʊn·ɪʙaˊclau yɛˊɒj-ɢʊɒɪɒhu·ˊwɪ.

   ɢʊɒɪnɪɒɪˊt tcɛhaˊl·a-ɢʊˊsa ɒɪnɪtɛˊnɪtcwu·n ɒʊmnɪku''uł ɒɪnɪkwaˊl·ak ɒɪnɪˊlaˊqᵂ.

pɛˊ''ma ɢʊˊca-waʙaˊl-aṫuˊɪɒɪn ɢʊɒɪˊnɒ·at-aɒɪˊnɒɪn ɒʊmnɪkweˊɪnafu.   <48(8)>

   ʙuˊɢulfan-ɢɪˊn·ʊk ɢʊnɪmɪˊnɒjɪs tcɛhaˊl·aʙɛˊɒ ɢʊˊca ɢʊɒɪnɪɒaˊˊf.

   ʙuˊɢulfan-ɢɪnɪɒaˊʙɪt,

   ɢʊnɪyuˊw·u·t ɢʊˊca-waɒɪˊnt̕ˊcɪt-asiˊ·''weɪ ||122:34||

pɛˊ''ma ɢuˊsa-waʙaˊl-aṫuˊɪɒɪn ɢʊɒnaˊɢɪt

   ʙskɪˊlyusɒa

   ɒjaˊˊk-pslaˊm·u tcɛ̇kweˊɪnafyak-haˊm·ɪ.

pɛˊ''ma ɢʊˊsa-aʙuˊɒzat ɢʊɒyuˊ''un,

   ʙuˊɢulfan siˊ·''weɪ ɢʊɒnɪtyuˊ''wn heˊca tɛˊn·a haˊlʙam-ɒjamʙak-ɒuˊmha. <48(9)>

pɛˊ''ma ɢʊˊca-aʙuˊɒjat ɢʊɒnaˊɢɪt,

   mɪˊɒ·ɪ pcɪˊy·u

   pċkweˊɪnafu.

All the children ate.

Having finished their meal, all the children stood.

They prayed the prayers to the Lord Above.

Then having finished, they went outside to their playroom.

Then they played there.

<49> Boisterous Boys Square-Dancing

One boy knew the White people's music known as "the fiddle."

||122:36||

Then another boy made himself leader,

"All you children sit down!

Now we'll dance (the) White people's dance.   <49(2)>

Anyone wanting to dance the White people's dance, stand up here in the center!

Anyone else wanting to dance, stand in the center!"

Another boy said,

"How many persons are you wanting to dance the White people's dance?"

The head boy said,

"I want eight boys." ||122:38| <49(3)>

Then they took eight boys.

Then the head boy,

"Make music!"

Then he tuned up his fiddle.

Then the head boy,

"Everyone join hands![12]

Circle to your right!"

They, the boys, went around.

Then he said,   <49(4)>

"Stop!

Jump (jig) every which way (solo fashion)!

Now take your partner's hand!

Swing around once and a half!

Now take that other boy's hand to the left!"

Then that's the way they went.

They kept going around.

Then they returned to their partners. ||122:40|| <49(5)>

Then he said,

"Everybody jump (jig) around every which way!"

ʙu'ɢʊlfan-ci·''wei ɢʊᴅɪnkwe'ɪnafu.

ɢʊn·i̇t·ʊ'ɢ·ɪ-ᴅɪnɪkwe'ɪnafɪn ʙu'ɢʊlfan-ci·''wei ɢʊᴅɪnɪᴅɛ'sᴅap.

ɢʊᴅɪnɪyu''wn ɢʊ'ca-atɛ'n·a-ha'mha tcɛha'lʙam-aᴅja'mʙak.

pɛ·''ma ɢʊn·i̇t·ʊ'ɢ·ɪ ɢʊᴅɪnɪᴅɪ't-hɛ·''lum tcɛᴅɪnɪla'ɢwak-ha'm·ɪ.

pɛ·''ma-ɢʊ'caʙɛ·ᴅ ɢʊᴅɪnɪᴅ_la'ɢwaɢ.

\<49\> Boisterous Boys Square-Dancing

wa''an-ȧtu'ɪᴅɪn ɢʊᴅyʊ'k·un ɢʊ'sa-awa'm·u· a'm·ɪ'm ᴅɪnɪᴅɪ'nᴅɪn ᴅa'ŋkwɪt afɪ'ᴅəl

||122:36||

pɛ·''ma wa''an-ȧtu'ɪᴅɪn ɢʊᴅʙʊ'ntca aᴅja'mʙak.

ʙʊ'ɢʊlfan-mɪ'ᴅ·ɪ -cɪ''wei pcɪ'y·u

ᴅi·'s ᴅɪᴅɪtya'twan wa'm·u·-a'm·ɪm ᴅɪnɪyɛ'l'wa.   \<49(2)\>

ɪ'y·a-ɢʊta'mᴅju ᴅʊmya'tʊn wa'm·u·-a'm·ɪm ᴅɪyɛ'l'w sɪ'ᴅ·aʙ hɛ'saʙɛ·ᴅ tcɛwɪ'lf.

ɪ'y·a-yu· wa''an ɢʊta'mᴅju ᴅɛmyɛ'l'w sɪ'ᴅ·aʙ tcɛwɪ'lf.

wa''an-ȧtu'ɪᴅɪn ɢʊᴅna'ɢɪt,

a'hω·'lu· a'm·ɪm ma'ha tcɪmta'mᴅju ᴅʊmɪnɪy·a'tʊn ɢʊ'sa-wa'm·u·-a'm·ɪm ᴅɪnɪyɛ'l'w?

ɢʊ'sa-aᴅja'mʙak-ȧtu'ɪᴅɪn ɢʊᴅna'ɢɪt

tcɪ''ɪ-tcɪta'mᴅju ɢɛ'm'wa ȧtu'ɪᴅɪn. ||122:38|| \<49(3)\>

pɛ·''ma ɢʊᴅɪnɪᴅɪ'tɢwɪn ɢɛ'm'wa ȧtu'ɪᴅɪn

pɛ·''ma ɢʊ'ca-aᴅjamʙak-ȧtu'ɪᴅɪn,

sʙʊ'nsᴅa ᴅɪᴅɪ'nᴅɪn.

pɛ·''ma ɢω'k ɢʊtyu''wʊn ᴅɪᴅɪ'nᴅɪn.

pɛ·''ma ɢʊ'ca-aᴅja'mʙak-ȧtu'ɪᴅɪn,

ʙʊ'ɢʊlfan-ɪ'ya ᴅɪ'tɢwɪn ᴅɪ'la'qʷ,

swɪ'y·u tcɛʙʊtɛ'n·aʙla'qʷ.

ɢɪ'n·ʊk ȧtu'ɪᴅɪn ɢɪᴅɪnɪᴅswɪ'y·u.

pɛ·''ma ɢʊᴅnɪ's·ɪn,   \<49(4)\>

sɪ'ᴅ·ap!

ʙɪs'ɪ'ᴅ·ʊp ʙʊ'ɢʊlfan-a'wɛw

pɛ·''ma ʙɪsᴅɪ'tɢwɪn ʙʊla'h·u ᴅɪ'la'qʷ.

ᴅɪskɪ'lskɪl'yʊ wa''an nau-ᴅɪkʊ'ʙfan.

pɛ·''ma sɪ'ɢwɪn ɢʊ'sa-waᴅa'ɪ'wan ȧtu'ɪᴅɪn waqa'sq-ᴅɪ'la'qʷ.

pɛ·''ma pɛ'ca-wɛ'w ɢʊᴅɪnɪᴅ'ɪ·'f

ɢʊᴅɪnɪᴅwɪ'yu.

pɛ·''ma ɢʊᴅɪnɪᴅmu'ɢ tcɛɢω·'k ᴅɪla'h·u, ||122:40|| \<49(5)\>

pɛ·''ma ɢʊᴅna'ɢɪt

ʙʊ'ɢʊlfan-ɪ'y·a ɢʊᴅ'ɪ'ᴅ·ʊp ʙʊ'ɢʊlfan-a'wɛw.

Then he said,

"Take your partner!

Turn once!

Now you all circle in the middle of the room!"

Then they finished.

Oh my, they laughed so hard.

They hollered.

They jumped around in the room.   <49(6)>

Then, when they were done, a sister came in there.

She said,

"You holler, you laugh so loudly.

People will hear you far away." ||122:42||

Then it was nearly eight o'clock.   <49(7)>

Then a big boy rang the bell.

All the children went outside to go pee (lit., make their water).

Then they came back into the building.

Then a big boy rang the bell.

All the children went upstairs to where they slept.   <49(8)>

Then he, the big boy, looked around to see if all the children were asleep.

Then he saw that all were in bed.

Then he, too, went to sleep.

<50> Morning Ritual

Then again, the next day, a sister rang the (hand-)bell at five A.M.

All the big boys got up. ||122:44||

The sister did likewise to the big girls.

The big girls got up.

The big boys went (out).   <50(2)>

They went downstairs to where they washed their faces and their hands.

Then when they finished their fixing up, they sat in their playroom.

They waited for the bell.

Then the sister rang the bell.

Then the head boy took all the big boys upstairs to an adjoined room (the chapel).

There the priest came. ||122:46|| <50(3)>

Then he spoke all manner of prayers of the book of the Lord Above (the Bible).

pɛˑˮma ɢʊᴅna'ɢɪt,
   sɪ'ɢˑwɪn ʙʊla'hˑu!
   skɪ'lskɪyu-wa''an!
   pɛˑˮma mɪ'ᴅɪ ʙɪswɪ'yˑat tcɛwɪ'lf tcɛha'mˑɪ.
pɛˑˮma ɢʊnˑɪtˑu'ɢɪ.
   uˑ' p̣u'fan haˑ'lˑuˑ ɢʊᴅɪnɪᴅ_lɪ'lufɪᴅ,
   ɢʊᴅɪnɪᴅ_la'l'waɪ.
   ɢʊᴅɪnɪᴅ'ɪ'ᴅˑʊp tcɛɢu'ca-tcɛha'mˑɪ.   <49(6)>
pɛˑˮma ɢʊᴅɪnɪtʊ'ɢɪ wa''an-aʙu'ᴅjat ɢʊmsla'mˑu ɢʊ'saʙɛˑᴅ.
qɛ'ᴅˑak ɢʊᴅna'ɢɪt,
   p̣ʊ'fan mɪ'ᴅɪ tcɪᴅuplɛ'l'wiˑfɪt tcɪᴅuplɪˑ'lfɪt
   a'mˑɪm ɢɪnɪɢa'ʙᴅɪn tcɛ'mɪ'ᴅɪ la'ɢaɪ ||122:42||
pɛˑˮma yɛ'ᴅj ɢʊᴅɢɛ'm'wa ᴅɪ'nᴅɪn.   <49(7)>
pɛˑˮma ɢʊ'ca-waʙa'l aṭu'ɪᴅɪn ɢʊᴅɪ'nᴅaˑt ᴅɪᴅɪ'nᴅɪn,
   ʙu'ɢʊlfan ciˑ''weɪ ɢʊᴅɪᴅnɪ''ɪ hɛˑ''lum, ᴅʊmnɪᴅɢuˑ'ᴅ nɪma'mpɢa.
pɛˑˮma ɢʊᴅɪnɪᴅ_la'mˑu tcɛha'mˑɪ.
pɛˑˮma ɢʊ'ca-waʙa'l-aṭu'ɪᴅɪn ɢʊᴅɪ'nᴅaˑt-aᴅɪ'nᴅɪn.
   ʙʊ'ɢʊlfan-aciˑ''weɪ ɢʊᴅɪnɪᴅɪ't ha'lʙam ᴅjɛha'l'a ɢʊ'sa ɢʊᴅɪnɪᴅɪ'tweɪ.   <49(8)>
pɛˑˮma-ɢω'k ɢʊ'sa-waʙa'l-aṭu'ɪᴅɪn ɢʊtˑcɪ'ʙluˑt ʙu'ɢʊlfan ɢʊ'sa-asiˑ''weɪ ɢʊmnɪᴅɪ'tweɪ.
pɛˑˮma ɢʊthω·'ᴅ ʙʊ'ɢʊlfan ɢʊᴅɪnɪᴅɪ'tweɪ
pɛˑˮma-yuˑ ɢω·'k ɢʊᴅɪ'tweɪ.

<50> Morning Ritual

pɛˑˮma ɢʊᴅɪᴅmeˑ'ɪᴅj ɢʊ'sa-yuˑ wa''an-aʙu'ᴅzat ɢʊᴅɪ'nᴅaˑt-aᴅɪ'nᴅɪn tcɛhu'wan-aᴅɪ'nᴅɪn.
   ʙʊ'ɢʊlfan-ɢʊ'sa waʙa'l-aṭu'ɪᴅɪn ɢʊᴅɪnɪsʙu'klaɪ ||122:44||
   pɛ'ca-yuˑ-wɛ'w ɢʊ'sa aʙu'ᴅzat tcɛʙa'l aʙɪna'tst.
      ɢɪ'nˑʊk-ɢʊsa-aʙa'l-aʙɪna'tst ɢɪ'nˑʊk-ɢɪnɪᴅʙu'klaɪ.
   waʙa'l-aṭu'ɪᴅˑɪn ɢʊnɪᴅɪ't   <50(2)>
      ɢʊntha'lˑuˑ tcɛɢu'sa-haˑ'l'a ɢʊᴅɪnɪᴅk̇u''uł ᴅɪnɪkwaˑ'l'ak ᴅɪnɪ'la'qʷ.
pɛˑˮma ɢʊᴅɪnɪtʊ̇'ɢɪ ᴅɪnɪtɛ'nˑɛtcwuˑn, ɢʊᴅɪnɪsɪ'yˑu ᴅjɛha'l'a-ɢʊ'sa ᴅɪnɪla'ɢˑut-ha'mˑɪ.
   ɢʊnɪyu'wˑuˑt ɢʊ'ca-aᴅɪ'nᴅɪn.
pɛˑˮma ɢʊ'sa-aʙu'ᴅzat ɢʊᴅɪ'nᴅaˑt-aᴅɪ'nᴅɪn
pɛˑˮma ɢʊ'sa-ᴅja'mʙak-aṭu'ɪᴅɪn ɢʊᴅɪ'tku ʙʊ'ɢʊlfan ɢʊ'sa-waʙa'l-waṭu'ɪᴅɪn ha'lʙam
   tcɛwa''an ayiˑ'm.
   ɢʊ'saʙɛˑᴅ ɢʊ'sa-tɛ'nˑa-aᴅja'ŋku ɢʊmuˑ'ɢ. ||122:46|| <50(3)>
pɛˑˮma ɢʊᴅɪnɪtyu''un ha'lʙam-ᴅja'mʙak-ᴅɪnɪbiˑ'ʙa ʙʊ'ɢʊlfan-a'wɛw watɛ'nˑa-ha'mha.

When they finished their praying of prayers, all of us boys came down to our
    playroom.
Then the big boy went upstairs.
    He woke up all the little children.
He woke them all up,
    "You all go!
    Go downstairs!
    Go outside to where they wash faces!   <50(4)>
    Then you fix yourselves up for the morning meal!"
Then the sister rang the bell.
Then they all went to where the lines (lit., trails) were where they stood.
Then he said,
    "Turn around! ||122:48||
    Go to the dining room!"
    The sister was in the dining room.
Then all the children stood.   <50(5)>
Then she spoke words of the Lord Above.
Then she said,
    "You all sit down! Eat!"
All the children, when they finished their meal, then they stood.
    She spoke those words of the Lord Above.

<51> A Storm
Then it was raining a little outside.
Then the sister said,
    "Don't play outside today.
    You all stay in your playroom!"
Then a wind came up.
    It rained hard.
    The wind was very strong. ||122:50||
        It was a south wind.   <51(2)>
    It rained two days and two nights.
        It rained hard.
    On the third day it was a fine day.
Then we (still) couldn't play outside (owing to the mud).
    (We) stayed in the (school-)house all day long for two days.

ɢʊɒɪnɪt̓ʊ′ɢɪ ɒɪnɪyu′w·un watɛ′n·a-ha′mha ʙʊ′ɢʊlfan-sʊ′ɒ·u at̓u′ɪɒɪn ɢʊɒcma′l·aɪ
    tcɛɒula′ɢwaɢ-ha′m·ɪ.

pɛ·′′ma ɢʊ′ca-aʙa′l-at̓u′ɪɒɪn ɢʊɒɪ′t-ha′lʙam,
    ɢʊɒʙʊ′kla·t ʙʊ′ɢʊlfan ɢʊca-waɒɪ′nt′cit-cɪ·′′wɛɪ.

ʙʊ′ɢʊlfan-ɢʊtʙʊ′klɪ,
    mɪ′ɒ·ɪ-ʙsɒɪ′t,
    ʙsha′l·u·
    ʙsɒɪ′t-hɛ·′′lʊm ɒjɛha′l·a ɢʊ′ca k̓u·′′uł-ɒɪnɪkwa′l·ak.   \<50(4)\>
    pɛ·′′ma mɪ′ɒɪ pctɛ′n·ɛtcwu·n ɒjɛha′l′wanyak k̓we′ɪnafʊn.

pɛ·′′ma ɢʊ′ca-aʙu·′ɒzat ɢʊɒɪ′nɒa·t-aɒɪ′nɒɪn

pɛ·′′ma ʙʊ′ɢʊlfan ɢʊɒɪnɪɒɪ′t ɒjɛha′l·a ɢʊ′sa-aɢu′n ɢʊɒɪnɪɒa′·ʙɪt.

pɛ·′′ma-ɢʊɒnɪ′s·ɪn,
    sk̓ɪ′lwɛɪcɒa! ||122:48||
    ʙsɒɪ′t tcɛɢʊ′sa-akwe′ɪnafʊnak-ha′m·ɪ.
    ɢʊ′sa-aʙu·′ɒzat ɢʊmaɒa′·ʙɪt wa′l tcɛɢʊ′sa k̓we′ɪnafʊnak-ha′m·ɪ.

pɛ·′′ma ʙʊ′ɢʊlfan-si·′′wɛɪ ɢʊɒɪnɪɒɛ′sɒap.   \<50(5)\>

pɛ·′′ma ɢʊɒna′ɢɪt ha′lʙam-aɒja′mʙak-ɒʊ′mha.

pɛ·′′ma qɛ′ɒ·ak ɢʊɒna′ɢɪt,
    mɪ′ɒɪ pcɪ′y·u, pck̓we′ɪnafu!

ʙʊ′ɢʊlfan-si·′′wɛɪ ɢʊɒɪnɪt̓ʊ′ɢɪ ɒɪnɪkwe′ɪnafʊn, pɛ·′′ma ɢʊɒɪnɪɒɛ′sɒap,
    ɢʊɒna′ɢɪt ɢʊ′sa-ha′lʙam-ɒja′mʙak-ɒʊ′mha.

\<51\> A Storm

pɛ·′′ma hɛ·′′lʊm ɢʊtɢwi′ɒɪt pu′t′snaq.

pɛ·′′ma ɢʊ′sa-aʙu·′ɒzat ɢʊɒna′ɢɪt,
    wa′ŋq mɪ′ɒɪ ɒɪn·ʊʙla′ɢwɪt hɛ·′′lʊm hɛ′sa-wɪ·ɪ′pyan.
    mɪ′ɒ·ɪ-ʙsʙi·′nɒ tcɛɒupla′ɢwɪt-ha′m·ɪ.

pɛ·′′ma a′we′ɪʙ ɢʊɒsma·′′a.
    p̓ʊ′f·an ɢʊɒɢwi·′ɒɪt.
    p̓ʊ′f·an ɒa′lqɒʊɢʊ a′we′ɪʙ ||122:50||
        waɒjʊ′ɢ·wam awe′ɪʙ   \<51(2)\>
    ɢʊtɢwɪ′ɒɪt ɢɛ′m-a′mpyan nau-ɢɛ′m-awɪ′fyu,
        p̓ʊ′f·an-ɢʊɒɢwi·′ɒɪt
    ɢʊɒɪthu′pcɪn-a′mpyan ɢʊt·ɛ′n·a′yu-a′mpyan.

pɛ·′′ma wa′ŋq-la′f sʊ′ɒ·ʊ ɢʊɒɪɒ_la′ɢwaɢ hɛ·′′lʊm,
    ʙɪ′nɒjaha′m·ɪ ʙʊ′ɢʊlfan-a′mpyan ɢʊ′ca-wɪ-ɢɛ′m-a′mpyan.

<52> Reading, Writing, Arithmetic

Then they rang the bell.

    All the children fixed themselves up to go to the classroom.

Then they rang the bell.

    All the children went into the classroom. <52(2)>

Then the sister called all the children by name.

They all said,

    "Here!"

Then she gave them their readers. ||122:52||

    She gave them another book: *Geography* (lit., 'here all lands their-book').

Then there were two of those books.

    The boys and girls had two books. <52(3)>

Then she said to the small children to come up front.

Then she wrote on the blackboard what it was she was teaching to those small children.

Then she wrote the (numeral) '1', and on to '10'. <52(4)>

Then she said,

    "You all say from this all the way to that!

      'One, two, three, four, five, six, seven, eight, nine, ten.'"

Then the small children said all of those names of what she had written on the blackboard. ||122:54||

Then she wrote all the ABCs.

Then she said to one of the children,

    "Now you will say your ABCs!"

    That one child said all of his ABCs.

Then she spoke to another of the small children. <52(5)>

    He, too, said all of those ABCs of his.

The sister said,

    "All you children say your ABCs!"

Then they, the children, all said their ABCs.

The sister said, ||122:56||

    "All you children know all your ABCs very well." <52(6)>

Then she said,

    "You all go sit down at your desks!"

Then she said to the second-grade boys and girls,

    "You all come up front!"

<52> Reading, Writing, Arithmetic

pɛ·″ma ɢʊdɪnɪdɪ′nda·t-adɪ′ndɪn.

  ʙʊ′ɢʊlfan-ci·″weɪ ɢunɪtɛ′n·ɛtcwu·n, dumnɪdɪ′t tcaha′mha-ha′m·ɪ.

pɛ·″ma ɢʊnɪdɪ′ndɛt-adɪ′ndɪn,

  ʙu′ɢulfan-acɪ·″weɪ ɢʊdɪnɪd_la′m·u tcɛɢʊ′ca-ha′mha-ha′m·ɪ.   <52(2)>

pɛ·″ma ɢu′sa-aʙu·″dzat ɢʊdkwu″ʊn ʙʊ′ɢʊlfan-cɪ·″weɪ dɪnɪda′ŋkwɪt.

ʙʊ′ɢʊlfan ɢʊdɪnɪdna′ɢɪt,

  hɛ′saʙɛ′d!

pɛ·″ma ɢʊn·ɪdɪ′st dɪn·ɪʙɪ·′ʙa. ||122:52||

  ɢʊnɪdɪ′st wada′ɪ′wan-aʙɪ·′ʙa ha′sa ʙʊ′ɢʊlfan a′n·u dɪnɪʙɪ′ʙa.

pɛ·″ma ɢɛ′m ɢʊ′sa-ɢɛ′m-aʙɪ·′ʙa,

  atu′ɪdɪn nau-ʙɪna·′tst ɢunɪp̓i′n ɢɛ·′m-aʙɪ·′ʙa.   <52(3)>

pɛ·″ma ɢʊdna′ɢɪt djɛɢʊ′ca-dɪ′nt′cɪt-asɪ′w·eɪ dumnɪsma′k djɪ′m·eɪ.

pɛ·″ma ɢʊtyɛ′m·at tcɛɢʊ′ca-amu′yɪm la′ʙla·c a′ɢ·a ɢʊ′ca ayu′knɪnfʊ tcɛɢʊ′ca-dɪ′nt′cɪt

  asɪ·″weɪ.

pɛ·″ma qɛ′d·ak ɢʊdyɛ′m·at ɢʊ′sa-wa″an na′u-dɪdi·′nfya   <52(4)>

pɛ·″ma qɛ′d·ak ɢʊdna′ɢɪt,

  mɪ′d·ɪ psna′ɢɪt djɛhɛ′ca ʙʊ′ɢʊlfan tcɛɢʊ′ca:

    wa″an ɢɛ·′m hu′psin ta′ʙ hu′w·an da′f pcɪ′n′wɪ ɢɛ′m′wɪ kwi·′st dɪ′nfya

pɛ·″ma ɢɪ′n·ʊk dɪ′nt′cɪt-asɪ·″weɪ ɢʊdna′ɢɪt tcɛʙu′ɢʊlfan ɢu′sa da′ŋɢwt tcɛ-a′ɢ·a qɛ′d·ak

  ɢʊd·ɪtyɛ′m·at tcɛɢʊ′ca amu′yɪm la′ʙla·c. ||122:54||

pɛ·″ma qɛ′d·ak ɢʊtyɛ·′m·a·t ʙʊ′ɢʊlfan ɢʊ′ca ABC's.

pɛ·″ma ɢʊdna′ɢɪt tcɛ′wa″an ɢʊ′sa-asɪ·″weɪ,

  hɪ′n·a ma′ha sna′ɢɪt ʙɪ′ABC.

  ɢʊ′ca-wa″an-acɪ·″weɪ ɢʊdna′ɢɪt ʙʊ′ɢʊlfan dɪ′ABC.

pɛ·″ma ɢʊdna′ɢɪt tcɛ′wa″an ɢʊ′sa wadɪ′nt′cɪt sɪ·″weɪ,   <52(5)>

  ɢω′k-yu· ɢʊdna′ɢɪt ʙʊ′ɢʊlfan ɢʊ′sa dɪ′ABC.

ɢʊ′sa-aʙu·″dzat ɢʊdna′ɢɪt,

  ʙʊ′ɢʊlfan mɪ′d·ɪ sɪ·″weɪ ʙɪsna′ɢɪt dɪ′ABC.

pɛ·″ma ɢɪ′n·ʊk nɪsɪ·″weɪ ʙʊ′ɢʊlfan ɢʊdɪdna′ɢɪt dɪn·ɪ′ABC.

ɢʊ′sa-aʙu·″dzat ɢʊdnaɢit ||122:56||

  p̓ʊ′fan tɛ′n·a mɪ′d·ɪ ci·″weɪ ɢʊtyu′ɢ·ʊn ʙʊ′ɢʊlfan dɪ′ABC.   <52(6)>

pɛ·″ma ɢʊdna′ɢɪt

  mɪ′d·ɪ tca′k sɪ′y·u tcɛdɪlada·′m.

pɛ·″ma ɢʊdna′ɢɪt tcɛɢʊ′sa ɢɛ·′m-aʙɪ·′ʙa t̓u′ɪdɪn na′u-dɪʙɪ′na·djɪt,

  mɪ′d·ɪ psma′k djɪ′m·eɪ.

Then she said to one standing up front,

    "You read from your book!

        You will say what you know.   \<52(7)\>

    If you miss one word, you will go to the rear.

    Then, whoever it is who knows all of your lesson, you will go up front."

    That is the way she did with all of them.

        Whoever missed two words went to the rear.   \<52(8)\>

Then, when they were all finished, then she said, ||122:58||

    "You all go sit down at your desks!"

Then, when she rang the bell, all the children stood.

The sister said,

    "You all go outside for five minutes!

    Then, soon, I will ring the bell."   \<52(9)\>

    All the children came in.

Then she said to the small children,

    "You all come up front!"

    She took one of the children.

        She gave him the chalk.

Then she said to that little child,

    "You write!:

        'One, two, three, four, five.'"   \<52(10)\>

    That child wrote all of that. ||122:60||

Then the sister rubbed off (erased) the blackboard.

Then she took another child.

She said,

    "Write that!

        'One, two, three, four, five.'"

Then she rubbed off all that writing.   \<52(11)\>

Then the sister said,

    "All you children stand next to that blackboard."

    She gave each of them a piece of chalk.

Then she said,

    "All you children write those,

        'One, two, three, four, five, six, seven, eight, nine, ten.'"   \<52(12)\>

Some of the children lost track while writing.

    Whoever it was that lost track of his writing—

pɛˑˊˊma ɢʊɒnaˊɢɪt ɢʊˊsa-awaˊˊan waɒaˊʙɪt ɒjɪˊmˑeɪ,

  maˊha stˊcɪˊʙlʊt ʙʊʙiˊˊʙɑ,

    ɒɛˊnaˊɢɪt aˊɢˑa maˊha tcɪˊyʊˊɢʊn.   <52(7)>

  ɒɛmnɪtˊcɪˊʙɪ waˊˊan haˊmha maˊha ɒɛɒɪˊt hɛˊntˊc.

  pɛˑˊˊma ɛˊya ɢʊˊsa ɢʊɒyʊˊɢʊn ʙʊˊɢʊlfan ʙʊʙiˊˊʙa ɢʊɒɪˊt ɒjɪˊmˑɪ.

  pɛˊsˑa-ɢʊtmɪˊuˊnan tcɛʙʊˊɢʊlfan ɢɪˊnˊʊk.

    eˊyˑa ɢʊtˊcɪˊʙɪ ɢɛˊm haˊmha ɢʊɒɪˊt hɛˊntˊc.   <52(8)>

pɛˑˊˊma ʙʊˊɢʊlfan ɢʊɒɪnɪtʊˊɢˑɪ, pɛˑˊˊma ɢʊɒnaˊɢɪt, ||122:58||

  mɪˊɒɪ ɒjaˊk pcɪˊyucɒa tcɛɒuplaɒaˊm.

pɛˑˊˊma ɢʊɒˑiˊnɒaˑt-aɒɪˊnɒɪn, ʙʊˊɢʊlfan ciˊˊweɪ ɢʊnɪɒɛˊcɒap.

ɢʊˊsa-aʙʊˊˊɒzat ɢʊtnaˊɢɪt,

  mɪˊɒɪ pcɪˊˊɪ hɛˑˊˊlʊm huˊwˑan-aminute.

  pɛˑˊˊma tcɪˊˊɪ ɒɪˊc-tcɪˊˊɪ-ɒɪɒɪˊnɒˑaˑt-aɒɪˊnɒɪn   <52(9)>

  ʙʊˊɢʊlfan siˊˊweɪ ɢʊɒɪnɪlaˊmˑu.

pɛˑˊˊma ɢʊɒɪnɪtnɪˊsˑɪn ɢʊˊsa-wɪ-ɒɪˊntˊcɪt-asɪˊˊweɪ,

  mɪˊɒɪ psmaˊk ɒjɪˊmeɪ.

  ɢʊɒɪˊtɢwɪn waˊˊan ɢʊsa-asɪˊˊweɪ

    ɢʊɒɪˊst ɢʊˊsa-awaˊmˑuˑ ayɛˊmˑafu

pɛˑˊˊma ɢʊɒnɪˊcɪn tcɛɢʊˊsa waɒiˊtˊsaq asɪˊˊweɪ,

  maˊha cyɛˊmˑaˑt

    waˊˊan ɢɛˊm huˊpsɪn taˊʙ huˊwˑan.   <52(10)>

  ɢʊˊsa asɪˊˊweɪ ɢʊtyɛˊmˑaˑt ʙʊˊɢʊlfan-ɢʊˊsa. ||122:60||

pɛˑˊˊma ɢʊˊsa-aʙʊˊˊɒzat ɢʊtyɪˊfyaˑt ɢʊˊsa-amuˊyˑɪm alaʙlaˊˊc.

pɛˑˊˊma ɢʊɒɪˊtɢwɪn waˊˊan-yuˑ-asɪˊˊweɪ

ɢʊɒnaˊɢɪt,

  maˊha cyɛˊmˑaˑt ɢʊˊsa,

    waˊˊan ɢɛˊm huˊpsɪn taˊʙ huˊwˑan.

pɛˑˊˊma qɛˊɒˑak ɢʊtyɪˊfyaˑt ʙʊˊɢʊlfan ɢʊˊsa yɛˊmafʊn.   <52(11)>

pɛˑˊˊma ɢʊˊsa-aʙʊˊˊɒjat ɢʊtnaˊɢɪt,

  ʙʊˊɢʊlfan mɪˊɒɪ ciˊˊweɪ pcɒɛˊcɒap yɛˊɒj tcɛɢʊˊsa muˊˊyɪm-laʙlaˊˊc.

  ɢʊnˑɪɒɪˊct ʙʊˊɢʊlfan ɢʊˊcˑa waˊmˑuˑ ɒiyɛˊmʊfʊn.

pɛˑˊˊma qɛˊɒˑak ɢʊɒnaˊɢɪt,

  ʙʊˊɢʊlfan mɪˊɒɪ siˊˊweɪ ɢʊɒyɛˊmˑaˑt ɢʊˊsa

    waˊˊan ɢɛˊm huˊpsɪn taˊʙ huˊwˑan ɒaˊf pcɪˊnˊwɪ ɢɛˊmˊwɪ ꞌkwiˊst ɒɪˊnfya.   <52(12)>

ꞌkuˊʙfan ɢɪnɪciˊˊweɪ ɢʊtˊsuˊlˑu tcɛɢʊˊcˑa yɛˊmʊfʊn.

  ɪˊyˑa ɢʊˊsa ɢʊtˊsʊˊlˊʊ ɒɪyɛˊmʊfʊn

[---]
   "You all stay there!" ||122:62||

Then (to) those who knew all of the writing, she said,
   "You all go sit down at your desks!"
Then she taught to them, those children who did not know all their writing.

                                                                  <52(13)>

She wrote on the blackboard,
   "You children will look at how I write it."
Then she rubbed out all of what she had written.
Then she said to those children,
   "You all write what I taught you!"
Then those children wrote it all.   <52(14)>
Having finished writing, the sister said this,
   "You all go sit down!"
   All the children sat down at their desks. ||122:64||
Then she said to them, the boys and girls,
   "You all come up front!
   Bring all the geography books!"   <52(15)>
Then she said,
   "You must learn the entire lesson!"
Then they said,
   "We don't know it."
Then the sister taught them from that geography book.
Then she said,
   "This coming afternoon you all study that lesson diligently!"   <52(16)>
Then she said,
   "You all go sit down!"
   They all sat down at their desks.
Then they worked on their lessons.
Then she rang the small bell.
   All the children stood. ||122:66||
   They spoke the Lord Above's words.
Then all the children went outside.
   They fixed themselves up, washing their faces and their hands.   <52(17)>
Then the big boy rang the bell for their midday meal.
Then all the children stood where it was that they stood.

[---]

mı'dɪ ɢʊ'caʙɛ·d dɪdɪpsda'ʙɪt!   ‖122:62‖

pɛ·''ma ɢɪ'n·ʊk ɢʊ'sa ɢʊdnɪyu'ɢ·ʊn ʙu'ɢʊlfan dɪ'yɛ·'mafʊn ɢʊdna'ɢɪt,
    mı'dɪ dja'k sı'y·u tcɛdɪlada'm.

pɛ·''ma qɛ'd·ak ɢʊdyu'kninfaɪ tcɛɢɪ'n·ʊk ɢʊ'sa-asi·''weɪ wa'nq ɢʊdnɪtyu'ɢ·ʊn ʙu'ɢʊlfan
    dɪnɪyɛ·'mafʊn.   <52(13)>

qɛ'd·ak ɢʊdyɛ·'m·a·t tcɛɢʊ'sa mu·''yɪm laʙla'c,
    mı'dɪ sı·''weɪ tcʊʙhꙍ·'d ha·''w·ɛw tcɪ'ɪ ɢʊdyɛ·'m·a·t.

pɛ·''ma qɛ'd·ak ɢʊtyɪ'fya·t ʙu'ɢʊlfan a'ɢ·a ɢʊ'ca qɛ'd·ak ɢʊdɪtyɛ·'m·a·t.

pɛ·''ma ɢʊdn'ɪcɪn tcɛɢʊ'ca-aci·''weɪ,
    mı'dɪ ʙcyɛ·'m·a·t ɢʊ'ca a'ɢ·a tcɪ'ɪ ɢʊdɪdyu'ɢnɪfʊʙ.

pɛ·''ma ɢʊ'ca asi·''weɪ ɢʊdnɪtyɛ·'m·a·t ʙu'ɢʊlfan.   <52(14)>

ɢʊdnɪtʊ'ɢ·ɪ dɪyɛ·'m·afʊn, ɢʊ'sa-aʙu·'dzat pa·''a-ɢʊdna'ɢɪt,
    mı'dɪ dja'k sı'y·usda.

    ʙu'ɢʊlfan-sı·''weɪ ɢʊdnɪsı'y·u tcɛɢɪ'n·ʊk dɪnɪlada'm.   ‖122:64‖

pɛ·''ma ɢʊdna'ɢɪt tcɛɢɪ'n·ʊk ɢʊ'sa-a̯tu'ɪd·ɪn nau-ʙɪ'n·atst,
    mı'dɪ pcma'k dɪ̯ɪ'm·eɪ.

    ʙɪcma'kwa ɢʊ'ca ʙu'ɢʊlfan a'n·u dɪʙi·'ʙa.   <52(15)>

pɛ·''ma qɛ'd·ak ɢʊdna'ɢɪt,
    mı'dɪ pcyʊ'k·ʊn ʙu'ɢʊlfan dɪʙi·'ʙa.

pɛ·''ma ɢɪ'n·ʊk ɢʊnɪdna'ɢɪt,
    wa'ŋq sʊ'd·ʊ ɢʊdɪdyʊ'ɢ·ʊn.

pɛ·''ma ɢʊ'sa-aʙu·'dzat ɢʊdɪnɪdyʊ'ɢ·ʊnfʊʙ tcɛɢʊ's·a a'n·u dɪnɪʙi·'ʙa.

pɛ·''ma ɢʊdna'ɢɪt,
    dɪ's-ɢamɪya·'hampyan mı'dɪ pct'cɪ'ʙlu·t p̓ʊ'fan tcɛɢʊ'sa-aʙɪ·'ʙa.   <52(16)>

pɛ·''ma ɢʊdna'ɢɪt,
    mı'dɪ dja'k sı'y·usda.

    ʙu'ɢʊlfan ɢʊdnɪsɛ'y·u tcɛ·'dɪnɪlada'm.

pɛ·''ma ɢʊdɪnɪd_lu·''un dɪnɪʙi·'ʙa.

pɛ·''ma ɢʊd·ɪ'nda·t ɢusa-waɖɪ't'saq-adɪ'ndɪn,
    ʙu'ɢʊlfan asi·''weɪ ɢʊnɪdɛ'sdap.   ‖122:66‖

    ɢʊdɪnɪdna'ɢɪt ɢʊ'ca ha'lʙam dja'mʙak dɪha·'mha.

pɛ·''ma ʙu'ɢʊlfan ci·''weɪ ɢʊdɪnɪdnɪ'ɪ hɛ·''lʊm.

    ɢʊdɪnɪtɛ'n·etcwu·n, ku·''uł dɪnɪ'la·'q^w dɪnɪkwa'l·ak.   <52(17)>

pɛ·''ma ɢʊ'sa-ʙa'l a̯tu'ɪdɪn ɢʊdɪ'nda·t-adɪ'ndɪn tcɛwɪ'lf-a·'mpyan dɪnɪkwɛ'ɪnafʊnak.

pɛ·''ma ʙu'ɢʊlfan-ci·''weɪ ɢʊdɪnɪdɛ'sdap tcɛha'l·a ɢʊ'ca ɢʊdɪnɪda'f.

Then he said,

"All children stand at their standing-places!"

All the children said,

"Okay."

[---]

"Now you all turn around!

Go to the dining room!"   <52(18)>

One of the sisters was there.

Then they stood at where their plates were.

Then all the children said the words of the Lord Above.   ‖122:68‖

Then all sat down to their meal.

Having finished eating, all the children stood.

They said those prayers of theirs to the Lord Above.   <52(19)>

Then the sister said,

"You are not to play outside.

It is very muddy.

You all go into your playroom!

There you will stay.

Then, at one o'clock, I'll ring the bell.

You all will go into the classroom."   <52(20)>

Then she rang the bell.

All the children went inside.

They sat down at their desks.   ‖122:70‖

Then the sister said to them, to the second-graders,

"You all come up front!"

All boys and girls went up front.   <52(21)>

Then she said to one of the boys,

"Do you know what the name of this entire land of all of you Indians is?"

Then that boy named that land's name.

Then she said,

"Who first found this land of yours?"

That boy named the man who found this land.

He named his name ("Columbus"!).[13]   <52(22)>

Then she said to all those children,

"You say all that you know of that geography book!"

Then she said to the children,   ‖122:72‖

pɛˑ''ma-ɢʊɒnaˈɢɪt,
  ʙʊ'ɢʊlfan ciˑ''weɪ ɒaˈʙɪt tcɛhaˈlˑa ɢʊ'ca ɒɪnˑɪɒaˈp.
ʙʊ'ɢʊlfan ciˑ''weɪ ɢʊɒnaˈɢɪt
      hɛⁿˑ''a.
[---]
  pɛˑ''ma mɪ'ɒɪ pckɪˈlweɪ!
  psɒɪ't tcɛɢʊ'ca kweˈɪnafʊnak-haˈmˑɪ.   <52(18)>
  ɢʊ'sa waˑ''an aʙʊ''ɒzat ɢʊɒˑaˈʙɪt.
pɛˑ''ma ɢʊnˑɪɒɛˈsɒap tcɛhaˈlˑa ɢʊ'sˑa ɢɪ'nˑʊk ɒɪnɪkwaˈt,
ʙɛˑ''ma ʙʊ'ɢʊlfan siˑ''weɪ ɢʊnˑɪɒnaˈɢɪt ɢʊ'cˑa haˈlʙam-ɒJaˈmʙak-ɒʊˈmha. ||122:68||
pɛˑ''ma ʙʊ'ɢʊlfan ɢʊɒɪnsi'y·u ɒɪnɪkweˈɪnafʊn.
ɢʊnˑɪtʊ'ɢˑi ɒɪnɪkweˈɪnafʊn ʙʊ'ɢʊlfan siˑ''weɪ ɢʊɒɪnɪɒɛˈsɒap,
  ɢʊɒɪnɪɒnaˈɢɪt ɢʊ'cˑa ɒɪnɪtɛˈnˑa-haˈmha tcɛhaˈlʙam-aɒJaˈmʙak.   <52(19)>
pɛˑ''ma ɢʊ'ca-aʙʊ''ɒJat ɢʊɒnaˈɢɪt,
  waˈŋq mɪ'ɒɪ ɒʊmnɪɒ_laˈɢʊt hɛˑ''lʊm.
      p̓ʊ'fan ʊmła'ʙłayu.
  mɪ'ɒɪ ʙclaˈmˑʊ tcɛɒʊplaˈɢwaɢ-haˈmˑɪ.
      ɢʊ'saʙɛ·ɒ mɪ'ɒɪ ɢʊɒʊpcʙɪ'nɒ.
  pɛˑ''ma ɢʊmwaˑ''an-aɒɪ'nɒɪn tcɪˑ''ɪ-ɒɪnɒɪ'nɒˑa·t-aɒɪ'nɒɪn.
      mɪ'ɒɪ ɢʊɒʊpclaˈmˑu tcɛɢʊ'sa haˈmha ɒʊ'mˑaɪ.   <52(20)>
pɛˑ''ma qɛ'ɒaˑk ɢʊɒɪ'nɒaˑt-aɒɪ'nɒɪn.
  ʙʊ'ɢʊlfan ciˑ''weɪ ɢʊɒɪnɪt_laˈmˑu,
  tcɛɒɪnɪlaɒaˈm ɢʊɒɪnɪsi'y·u. ||122:70||
pɛˑ''ma qɛ'ɒaˑk ɢʊ'sa-aʙʊ''ɒzat ɢʊɒnaˈɢɪt tcɛɢɪ'nˑuk tcɛɢʊ'ca-waɢɛˈm-aʙɪˈʙa ciˑ''weɪ.
  mɪ'ɒɪ ʙcmaˈk ɒJɪ'mˑeɪ.
  ʙʊ'ɢʊlfan t̓u'ɪɒfaf naˈu-ʙɪ'naˑtst ɢʊɒɪɒnɪˈ''ɪ ɒJɪ'mˑeɪ.   <52(21)>
pɛˑ''ma ɢʊɒnaˈɢɪt tcɛwaˑ''an ɢʊ'sa-at̓u'ɪɒɪn,
  maˈha-tcɪ'yʊ'ɢʊn aˈɢˑa ɒaˈŋkwɒ hɛ'sa mɪ'ɒɪ ʙʊ'ɢʊlfan mɛ'nmɪ ɢʊɒɪnɪɒʊ'nˑu?
pɛˑ''ma ɢʊ'sa-at̓u'ɪɒɪn ɢʊɒkwu'wˑut ɢʊ'ca-aˈnˑu ɒaˈŋkwt.
pɛˑ''ma ɢʊɒnaˈɢɪt,
  e'yˑa mɛ'n ɢʊɒˑɛ'sɒɛs hɛ'sa mɪ'ɒɪ ɒɪ'aˈnˑu?
  ɢʊ'sa-at̓u'ɪɒˑɪn ɢʊɒk̓wu'wˑut ɢʊ'ca-aˈmu'ɪ e'yˑa ɢʊ'sa-ɢʊɒɛ'sɒɛs hɛ'sa-wɪ-aˈnˑu,
  ɢʊɒk̓wu'wʊt ɒaˈŋkwɪt.   <52(22)>
pɛˑ''ma ɢʊɒnaˈɢɪt tcɛʙʊ'ɢʊlfan ɢʊ'sa-siˑ''weɪ,
  mɪ'ɒɪ psnaˈɢɪt ʙʊ'ɢʊlfan aˈɢˑa mɪ'ɒɪ tcɪyʊ'k̓un tcɛɢʊ'cˑa waʙaˈl aˈnˑu ɒɪʙɪˈʙa.
pɛˑ''ma ɢʊɒnaˈɢɪt tcɛɢʊ'ca-asiˑ''weɪ, ||122:72||

“*You all go sit down at your desks!*”

Then they went back to sit at their desks. <52(23)>

Then she said to the first-graders,

  “*You all come up front to this blackboard!*”

She said to them,

  “*You all write on this blackboard from one to one hundred.*”

Then they, those boys and girls, wrote from one to one hundred.

  All of them wrote that. <52(24)>

Then she, the sister, (said),

  “*Fine, you all know all of that very well.*”

Then she said,

  “*You all go sit down at your desks!*” ||122:74||

Then she rang the little bell.

  All the children stood.

  They said the prayers, the words to the Lord Above.

Then the sister said,

  “*You big boys will go to the woodshed.* <52(25)>

  All of you cut small sticks!

  Some of you will split the wood.

  Then the somewhat bigger children will take that split wood to the room where they
    prepare food.

  Then when you have finished that, then fix yourselves up, wash your hands and your
    faces. <52(26)>

  Then all of you go into your playroom. ||122:78||

    There you wait for the meal bell!

  Then you listen for that bell!

    All of you stand in that room!

  Then you will go into that dining room.”

<53> Wrestling

All the children entered their dining room.

Then the sister waited for the children to come in.

  All the children went in.

  They went around the table.

Then they stood where they (were to) sit.

mɪˈdɪ dja'k sɪ'y·u tcɛdɪlaɒa'm.

pɛˈ"ma ɢɪ'n·ʋk ɢʋdɪnɪdɪ'tyɪ ɒʋmɪnɪsɪ'y·u tcɛd·ɪnɪlaɒa'm.　　　　　<52(23)>

pɛˈ"ma ɢʋɒna'ɢɪt tcɛɢʋ'c·a wa"an-ɒɪbɪ·'ɓa asiˈ"wei,

　mɪˈdɪ psma·'k dJɪ'mei dJɛhɛˈsa mu'yɪm laˈɓla·c.

ɢʋɒna'ɢɪt tcɛɢɪ'n·ʋk,

　mɪˈdɪ ɒʋpyɛˈm·a·t tcɛhɛˈca-mu'yɪm laɓla·'c wa"an nautcuwa"an-ɒʋ'm̩pɪ.

pɛˈ"ma ɢɪ'n·ʋk ɢʋsa-aɛu'ɪdɪn na'u-ɓɪ'na·tst ɢɪ'n·ʋk ɢʋdɪnɪtyɛˈm·a·t tcɛwa"an

　na'utcɛɒuwa"an-ɒʋ'm̩pɪ.

　ɓʋ'ɢʋlfan ɢɪ'n·ʋk ɢʋdɪnɪtyɛˈm·a·t ɢʋ'ca.　　　　　<52(24)>

pɛˈ"ma qɛ'ɒak-ɢʋ'sa-aɓu'ɒzat,

　ɢʋ'cwɪ p̩ʋ'fan tɛ'n·a mɪˈdɪ tcɪɒʋpyʋ'ɢ·ʋn ɓʋ'ɢʋlfan ɢʋ's·a.

pɛˈ"ma ɢʋɒna'ɢɪt,

　mɪˈdɪ dj·a'k sɪ'y·u tcɛ'ɒ·ɪlaɒa'm.　　　　　||122:74||

pɛˈ"ma ɢʋd·ɪ'nɒa·t ɢʋsa-ɒɪ·'t'saq-aɒɪ'nɒɪn.

　ɓʋ'ɢʋlfan si"'wei ɢʋdɪnɪɒɛ'sɒap.

　ɢʋdɪnɪɒna'ɢɪt ɢʋ'sa watɛ'n·a ha'mha tcɛha'lɓam-aɒja'mɓak ɒɪha'mha.

pɛˈ"ma ɢʋ'ca-aɓu'ɒjat ɢʋɒna'ɢɪt,

　mɪˈdɪ ɢʋ'ca-waɓa'l ɛu'ɪdɪn tcɪɒʋpɒɪ't tcɛ-ɢʋ'ca-wa'ɒ·ik-ɒʋ'maɪ.　　　<52(25)>

　ɓʋ'ɢʋlfan mɪˈdɪ ɓɪɒskʋ'ɓ·ʋn ɓʋ't'saq a'wa'ɒik.

　k̩ʋ'ɓfan mɪˈdɪ ɢʋɒʋpsp̩la'kp̩la·t ɢʋ'sa-a'wa'ɒ·ik.

　pɛˈ"ma ɢɪ'n·ʋk ɢʋ'sa ɓʋ't'caq waɒɒʋ'f asiˈ"wei ɢʋnɪɒɪ'tku ɢʋ'sa wap̩la'kp̩lɪtcɪ wa'ɒik
　　tcɛɢʋ'sa ha'l·a ɒɪn·ɪɓʋ'n kwe'ɪnafʋnak ha'm·ɪ.

　　pɛˈ"ma mɪˈdɪ ɢʋɒʋpstʋ'ɢ·ɪ ɢʋ's·a, pɛˈ"ma mɪˈdɪ ɢʋdɪpstɛ'n·atcwu·n k̩u'uł ɒɪ'la'qʷ
　　na'u-ɒɪkwa'l·ak　　　　　<52(26)>

　　pɛˈ"ma mɪˈdɪ ɓɪsla'm·u tcɛɢʋ'sa mɪˈdɪ ɒɪl·a'ɢwt ha'm·ɪ.　　　||122:78||

　　ɢʋ'saɓɛ·ɒ mɪˈdɪ ɓɪcyu'w·ut ɢʋ'ca kwe'ɪnafʋnɪk-ɒɪ'nɒɪn.

　　pɛˈ"ma mɪˈdɪ ɓsg̩a'ɓɒɪn ɢʋ'sa-aɒɪ'nɒɪn,

　　　ɓʋ'ɢʋlfan mɪˈdɪ ɓcɒɛ'cɒap tcɛɢʋ's·a ha'm·ɪ.

　　pɛˈ"ma mɪˈdɪ ɢʋɒʋpɒɪ't tcɛɢʋ's·a k̩we'ɪnafʋnɪk-ha'm·ɪ.

<53> Wrestling

ɓʋ'ɢʋlfan-sɪ"'wei ɢʋdɪnɪɒ_la'm·u tcɛdɪnɪk̩we'ɪnafʋnɪk-ha'm·ɪ.

pɛˈ"ma qɛ'ɒak-ɢʋ'sa-aɓu'ɒzat ɢʋdɪdyu'w·ut ɢʋ'sa-asiˈ"wei ɒʋmɪnɪɒ_la'm·u.

　ɓʋ'ɢʋlfan-cɪ'w·ei ɢʋɒ_la'm·u,

　ɢʋnɪtwɪ'y·ɛt tcɛɢʋ'sa-laɒa'm.

pɛˈ"ma ɢʋdɪnɪɒɛ'sɒap djaha'l·a ɢɪ'n·ʋk ɢʋdɪnɪsɪ'y·u.

Then the sister said words of the Lord Above.

    All the children also said those words of the Lord Above. <53(2)>

Then all the children sat down to their meal. ||122:80||

Finished with their meal, then they all stood up.

    They said the prayers of words to the Lord Above.

Then the sister said,

    "All of you go into the playroom!

    You will play there." <53(3)>

Then the big boy said,

    "Who among you big boys wants to wrestle?"

One said,

    "I want to wrestle."

Then another said,

    "I'll wrestle with him."

Then they took off their coats and their vests. <53(4)>

Then the big boy said,

    "What kind of wrestling do you want?"

One of them said,

    "I want Indian wrestling."[14]

The other boy said,

    "Okay."

Then they wrestled. ||122:82||

    Those boys were very strong. <53(5)>

    They wrestled.

    Neither one ever fell.

Then the big boy said,

    "You guys quit!

        You are getting exhausted."

Then they quit.

Then the big boy said,

    "Who else wants to wrestle?" <53(6)>

One boy said,

    "I want to wrestle with anybody at all."

One boy said,

    "I'll wrestle with you."

[---]

pɛˑ″ma ɢʊ′sa-aʙʊ′djat ɢʊɒna′ɢɪt ha′lʙam ɒja′mʙak ɒʊ′mha.

   ʙʊ′ɢʊlfan-yuˑ′ asi″weɪ ɢʊɒɪnɪɒna′ɢɪt ɢʊ′sa-ha′lʙam-ɒja′mʙak-ɒʊ′mha.   <53(2)>

pɛˑ″ma ʙʊ′ɢʊlfan-si′weɪ ɢʊɒɪnɪsɪ′yˑu ɒɪnˑɪk̇we′ɪnafʊn. ||122:80||

tʊ′ɢɪ-ɒɪnɪk̇we′ɪnafʊn pɛˑ″ma ʙʊ′ɢʊlfan ɢʊɒɪnɪɒɛ′sɒap,

   ɢʊɒɪnɪɒna′ɢɪt ɢʊ′sa-watɛ′na ha′mha ɒjaha′lʙam-aɒja′mʙak-ɒɪha′mha,

pɛˑ″ma ɢʊ′sa-aʙʊ′dzat ɢʊɒna′ɢɪt,

   ʙʊ′ɢʊlfan mɪ′ɒɪ ʙɪsla′mˑu tcɛɢʊ′ca ɒɪ′la′ɢwak ɒʊ′mˑaɪ.

      ɢʊ′saʙɛ′ɒ mɪ′ɒɪ ɢʊɒʊpla′ɢˑwɢ.   <53(3)>

pɛˑ″ma ɢʊ′sa-waʙa′l atʊ′ɪɒˑɪn ɢʊɒna′ɢɪt,

   e′yˑa mɪ′ɒɪ ɢʊ′sa-waʙa′l-aṫu′ɪɒˑɪn ta′mɒju ɒuma′nfɪt.

wa″an ɢʊɒna′ɢɪt

   tcɪ″ɪ-tcɪṫa′mɒju ɒumˑa′nfʊt.

pɛˑ″ma wa″an-yuˑ ɢʊɒna′ɢɪt,

   tcɪ″ɪ ɒɪtma′nfɪt tcɛɢʊ″k.

pɛˑ″ma ɢʊɒɪnɪck̇wɪ′lck̇waˑt ɒɪnˑɪɢa′ʙuˑ ɒɪnˑɪla′ɒfan   <53(4)>

pɛˑ″ma ɢʊ′ca-aʙa′l-aṫu′ɪɒˑɪn ɢʊɒna′ɢɪt,

   a′wˑɛw ama′nfɪt ma′ha tcɪɒupṫa′mɒju.

wa″an ɢʊɒna′ɢɪt,

   tcɪ″ɪ tcɪṫa′mɒju a′mɛ′nmɪ′yɪk ma′nfʊp.

ɢʊ′sa-wa″an-aṫu′ɪɒɪn ɢʊɒna′ɢɪt,

   ɢʊ′cwɪ!

pɛˑ″ma ɢɪ′nˑʊk ɢʊɒɪnɪɒma′nfʊp. ||122:82||

   ṗʊ′fan ɢɪ′nˑʊk ɢʊ′ca aṫu′ɪɒɪn ɢʊnˑɪɒa′lqɒʊɢʊ.   <53(5)>

   ɢɪ′nˑʊk ɢɪnˑɪɒma′nfʊʙ,

      wa′ŋq-la′f e′yˑa ɢʊmɒɪɒjɛ′ɢˑuˑ.

pɛˑ″ma ɢʊ′ca-aʙa′l-aṫu′ɪɒɪn ɢʊɒna′ɢɪt,

   mɪ′ɒɪ cʙa′cluˑcɒa.

      mɪ′ɒɪ tcɪɒʊplʊ′k̇yu.

pɛˑ″ma ɢɪ′nˑʊk ɢʊɒɪnɪpa′cluˑ.

pɛˑ″ma ɢʊ′ca-aʙa′l-aṫu′ɪɒɪn ɢʊɒna′ɢɪt,

   e′yˑa-yuˑ ṫa′mɒju ɒuma′nfɪt?   <53(6)>

wa″an-aṫu′ɪɒɪn ɢʊɒna′ɢɪt,

   tcɪ″ɪ tcɪṫa′mɒju ɒuma′nfɪt tcɛʙu′ɢʊlfan-e′yˑa.

wa″an-aṫu′ɪɒɪn ɢʊɒna′ɢɪt,

   tcɪ″ɪ ɒɪɒma′nfʊp tcɛma′ha.

[---]

"Okay, what kind of wrestling do you want?"
The other boy said,
  "I want to wrestle White people's wrestling, the wrestling called 'sideholds."[15]

||122:84|| <53(7)>

  Then, if you should throw me down twice, then you will win."
Then the big boy said,
  "Go to it you guys, you go wrestle!
  All you children stand back!"
Then the two boys wrestled and wrestled.
Then one of those boys threw the other boy.   <53(8)>
Then they rested for five minutes.
Then the big boy said,
  "Go to it you guys, wrestle!"
They grabbed hands,
  then they wrestled and wrestled.
Then the other boy (that) fell first,
  then he threw that other boy.   <53(9)>
Then they rested five minutes.
Then the big boy said, ||122:86||
  "Go to it you guys, wrestle!"
Then they grasped hands.
Then they wrestled for a long time.
  Neither one fell.
Then they wrestled a long time.
Then that one boy threw the other.   <53(10)>
  He had thrown him twice.
Then they quit wrestling.
  That's how they played.
Then they rang the bell.
  All the children went outside.
  They fixed themselves up to go to bed.   <53(11)>
Then when they rang the bell again all the children went inside.
  They went upstairs to where they slept.
Then all the children took off their clothes. ||122:88||
Then they pulled open their blankets.[16]
Then they went to bed.

ɢʊ'cwɪ, a'w'ɛw ma'nfʊp ma'ha tcɪta'mɒju?

ɢʊ'ca-wa"an-aɫu'ɪdɪn ɢʊdna'ɢɪt,

   tcɪ"ɪ tcɪta'mɒju ɒum·a'nfɪt wa'm·u· a'm·ɪm ɒɪn·ɪma'nfɪt ɢʊ'sa-ma'nfɪt ɒa'ŋɢwt side-
      holds. ||122:84| <53(7)>

   pɛ·"ma ma'ha ɒatɢʊ'ɒjaf ɢɛ'fu, pɛ·"ma ma'ha ɒɛɒʊ'l·u.

pɛ·"ma ɢʊ'ca-aʙa'l-aɫu'ɪdɪn ɢʊdna'ɢɪt,

   tcɪ'ɒ·a mɪ'ɒ·ɪ ɒɪɒʊpcma'nfɪt.

   ʙʊ'ɢʊlfan-si·"wei ʙɪsɒa'ʙɪt la'ɢ·aɪ.

pɛ·"ma ɢʊ'ca-aɢɛ·'m-aɫu'ɪdɪn ɢʊdɪnɪɒma'nfɪt ɢʊdɪnɪɒma'nfɪɒ

pɛ·"ma wa"an ɢʊ'sa-aɫu'ɪd·ɪn ɢʊtɢu' ɢʊ'sa-wa"an-aɫu'ɪdɪn.   <53(8)>

pɛ·"ma ɢʊdɪnɪɒa'ʙɪt hu'w·an aminute.

pɛ·"ma-ɢʊ'ca-aʙa'l-aɫu'ɪdɪn ɢʊdna'ɢɪt,

   tcɪ'ɒ·a mɪ'ɒ·ɪ ʙɪcma'nfɪt.

ɢʊdɪnɪdɪ'tɢwɪn ɒɪn·ɪ'la'qʷ,

   pɛ·"ma ɢɪ'n·ʊk ɢʊdɪnɪɒma'nfɪt. ɢʊdɪnɪɒma'nfɪɒ

pɛ·"ma ɢʊ'sa wa"an aɫu'ɪd·ɪn ɢʊɒ·ɪɒje'ɢ·u me·'n

   pɛ·"ma ɢɶ·'k ɢʊtɢu' ɢʊ'sa ye'lqfa·n aɫu'ɪdɪn.   <53(9)>

pɛ·"ma ɢʊdɪnɪɒɛ'sɒap hu'w·an aminute.

pɛ·"ma ɢʊ'ca-aʙa'l-aɫu'ɪdɪn ɢʊdna'ɢɪt, ||122:86||

   tcɪ'ɒ·a mɪ'ɒ·ɪ ʙɪcma'nfɪt.

pɛ·"ma ɢʊdɪnɪdɪ'tɢwɪn ɒɪn·ɪ'la'qʷ,

pɛ·"ma ɢʊdɪnɪɒma'nfʊt hɛ'ɫ·af.

   wa'ŋq-la'f e'y·a ɢamɪɒɪɒje'ɢ·u.

pɛ·"ma ɢʊdɪnɪɒma'nfɪt hɛ'ɫ·af

pɛ·"ma ɢʊ'ca-wa"an aɫu'ɪdɪn ɢʊɒɪtɢu' ɢu'sa-awa"an,   <53(10)>

   ɢʊtɢu' ɢɛ'fu.

pɛ·"ma ɢʊn·ɪɫʊ'ɢ·ɪ ɒɪn·ɪma'nfɪt.

   pɛ'sa-wɛw ɢʊn·ɪla'ɢwɪt.

pɛ·"ma ɢʊ'sa-aɒɪ'nɒɪn ɢʊn·ɪɒɪ'nɒɛt.

   ʙʊ'ɢʊlfan ci·'wei ɢʊdɪnɪɒ·ɪ't hɛ·"lʊm.

   ɢʊdɪnɪtɛ'n·atcwu·n ɒʊmɒɪnɪɢʊ'mwaɪ.   <53(11)>

pɛ·"ma-yu· ɢʊn·ɪɒɪ'nɒɛt-aɒɪ'nɒɪn, ʙʊ'ɢʊlfan-ci·'wei ɢʊnɪɒ_cla'm·u,

   ɢʊn·ɪɒ·ɪ't ha'lʙam ɒjɛha'l·a ɢʊ'ca ɢɪ'n·ʊk ɒɪnɪwe·'ɪf.

pɛ·"ma ʙʊ'ɢʊlfan ci·'wei ɢʊnɪckwɪ'lkwa·t ɒɪnɪ'a'ɢfan ||122:88||

ʙɛ·"ma ɢʊnɪtwɪ'ɫ·wa·t ɒɪnɪpa'cɪcɢwa

pɛ·"ma ɢʊdɪnɪɒ_cɪ'w·eɪ.

The big boy blew out the candle.
Then he went to bed.

<54> Start of the Morning

At 5:00 o'clock in the morning one of the sisters rang the bell.

   All the big boys arose.

   They went downstairs to their playroom.

   They went outside to where they washed.

   All of them washed.

   They fixed their hair.

Then they went into the building.   <54(2)>

Then the sister sounded the bell.

   All the boys went upstairs to the little adjoined room (chapel). ||122:90||

   There they said the prayers.

   There also the priest said prayers to the Lord Above.

   All the girls and also the sisters came there.

Then all of them said all sorts of prayers to the Lord Above.

                                                                    <54(3)>

Then when they finished their prayers, all the boys went downstairs to their
   playroom.

Then the big boy went upstairs to where the little children slept.

   He rang the bell.

   He woke up all of the little children.

   Whosoever of those little children didn't get up, the big boy took their blanket.

                                              ||122:92|| <54(4)>

      He threw it aside.

Then he took hold of the little child.

   He made him stand up on the floor.

Then the little child woke up.

He spoke like this,

   "Put on your clothes!

   Follow the boys who have gone downstairs in the building!

   You go (out) to where they wash their faces!"

Then the sister rang the bell for them to go to their meal.   <54(5)>

   All the children went outside.

   They stood where it was that they stood.

ɢʊ'sa-waʙa'l-aᴛu'ɪᴅ·ɪn ɢʊᴅfu'w·ɪ ɢʊ'sa lɪ'caɴᴅɛ·'l.

pɛ·''ma-ɢω'k-ɢʊᴅɪ'twi·.

<54> Start of the Morning

ɢʊᴅɪthu'w·an-aᴅɪ'nᴅɪn ɢʊᴅɪᴅme'ɪᴅj ɢʊ'ca-wa''an-aʙu'ᴅjat ɢʊᴅɪ'nᴅa·t-aᴅɪ'nᴅɪn.

   ʙʊ'ɢʊlfan-ɢʊ'ca-waʙa'l-aᴛu'ɪᴅɪn ɢɪ'n·ʊk ɢɪnɪᴅʙʊ'klaɪ.

     ɢɪn·ɪhu'l·aɪ mu' ᴅjɛɢʊ'ca ᴅɪnɪla'ɢwaɢ-ha'm·eɪ

     ɢɪn·ɪᴅɪ't-hɛ·''lʊm ᴅjɛha'l·a ɢʊ'ca ɢʊᴅɪnɪtku'ɫ,

    ʙʊ'ɢʊlfan-ɢʊnɪtku'ɫ

    ɢʊnɪtɛ'n·a·n ᴅɪnɪᴅa'mɪɫ.

pɛ·''ma ɢʊn·ɪᴅ_la'm·u ᴅjɛha'm·eɪ.   <54(2)>

pɛ·''ma ɢʊ'sa-aʙu'ᴅjat ɢʊᴅɪ'nᴅa·t-aᴅɪ'nᴅɪn.

   ʙʊ'ɢʊlfan-ɢʊ'sa-aᴛu'ɪᴅ·ɪn ɢʊᴅɪnɪᴅnɪ''ɪ ha'lʙam ᴅjɛɢʊ'ca yɪ'm·eɪ. ||122:90||

   ɢʊ'saʙe·ᴅ ɢɪ'n·ʊk ɢɪn·ɪyu''wṅ ɢʊ'sa tɛ'n·a ha'mha.

   ɢʊ'saʙe·'ᴅ-yu' ɢʊ'sa-watɛ'n·a-aᴅja'ŋku ɢʊᴅɪᴅ_yu''un ᴅjaha'lʙam-aᴅja'mʙak-ᴅu'mha.

   ʙʊ'ɢʊlfan aʙɪna'tst nau-ɢɪ'n·uk-yu' ɢʊ'sa-aʙu'ᴅzat ɢʊ'saʙe·ᴅ ɢʊᴅnɪt_cma''a.

pɛ·''ma ʙʊ'ɢʊlfan ɢɪ'n·uk ɢʊᴅɪnɪtyu''un ʙʊ'ɢʊlfan a'w·ɛw watɛ'n·a ha'mha tcɛɢʊ's·a

   aha'lʙam-aᴅja'mʙak.   <54(3)>

pɛ·''ma ɢʊᴅɪnɪtʊ'ɢ·ɪ ᴅɪn·ɪha'mha ʙʊ'ɢʊlfan-aᴛu'ɪᴅɪn ɢʊᴅɪnɪtha'l·u tcɛɢɪ'n·ʊk

   ᴅɪnɪla'ɢwak-ha'm·ɪ.

pɛ·''ma ɢʊ'sa-waʙa'l-aᴛu'ɪᴅɪn ɢʊᴅɪ't-ha'lʙam ᴅjaha'l·a ɢʊ'ca ᴅɪ'nt'cɪt-asɪ''weɪ

   ɢʊᴅɪnɪwe'ɪf.

   ɢʊᴅɪ'nᴅ-aᴅɪ'nᴅɪn,

   ɢʊᴅɪnɪᴅʙu'klɪ ʙʊ'ɢʊlfan ɢʊ'ca-waᴅɪ'nt'cɪt asɪ''weɪ.

   e'y·a ɢʊ'sa-waᴅɪ'nt'cɪt asɪ''weɪ wa'ŋq-ɢʊᴅʙu'klaɪ ɢω'k ɢʊ'sa waʙa'l-aᴛu'ɪᴅɪn

     ɢʊᴅɪ'tɢwɪn ᴅɪnɪṗa'cɪcɢwa ||122:92|| <54(4)>

     ɢutɢʊ'.

pɛ·''ma ɢʊᴅɪ'tɢwɪn ɢʊ'ca-waᴅɪ't'saq-asɪ·''weɪ

   ɢʊᴅa·'pfq̇apnaɪ ᴅjɛlaʙla·'c.

pɛ·''ma ɢʊ'ca-waᴅɪ't'caq-asɪ·''weɪ ɢʊᴅʙu'klaɪ.

pa''a-ɢʊᴅnɪ'sɪn,

   sʙu'n ʙɪ'a'ɢfan

   cyu''wn ɢu'sa-sɪ·''weɪ ɢʊᴅ·ɪnɪᴅha'l·u mu' ᴅjɛha'm·ɪ.

   ma'ha cᴅja·'k ᴅjɛha'l·a ɢʊ's·a ɢɪ'n·ʊk ɢɪn·ɪku'ɫ ᴅɪnɪkwa'l·ak.

pɛ·''ma ɢʊ'sa-aʙu'ᴅzat ɢʊᴅɪ'nᴅɛ·t-aᴅɪ'nᴅɪn ᴅʊmnɪᴅɪ't tcɛ'ᴅ·ɪnɪkwe'ɪnafʊn.   <54(5)>

   ʙʊ'ɢʊlfan-cɪ·''weɪ ɢʊn·ɪᴅɪ't-hɛ·''lʊm

   ɢʊn·ɪᴅɛ'cᴅap ᴅjɛha'l·a ɢʊ'ca ɢɪ'n·ʊk ɢɪnɪᴅa·'f.

All the children stood.

Then the big boy said,

　"You all turn around!

　Go into the dining room!" ‖122:94‖ <54(6)>

　All the children entered.

　They went around the table.

Then they stood where they (were to) sit.

　The sister was there.

Then all the children and the sister said words of prayer to the Lord Above.

Then all the children sat down to their meal. <54(7)>

Finished with their meal, they all stood.

　They said the words of prayer to the Lord Above.

Then she said,

　"All you children will cut little sticks of wood.

　Everyone will work.

　When you have finished your work, then all of you go play." ‖122:96‖

<55> Back in the Classroom [beginning of untranslated field text][17]

Then, when it was nearly nine o'clock, the sister rang the bell.

　All the children ran to where they wash their hands and faces.

Then, finished with their washing, they came into the room where they played.

　There they waited for the bell.

Then the sister rang the bell. <55(2)>

　All the children stood up in their rows where it was that they stood.

Then the sister spoke,

　"All of you go in! Sit at your desks!"

Then she, the sister, rang the little bell.

　All the children stood up. <55(3)>

　She spoke the prayers. ‖122:98‖

Then she rang the little bell.

　All the children sat down.

Then the sister went and got the second graders' books.

　She gave the second graders their books.

Then she also got the first-grader books.

　She handed them out. <55(4)>

　Those books had the title *Spelling-book.*

ʙʊʹɢʊlfan ci·ʼʼweɪ ɢʊnɪɖaʹf.

pɛ·ʼʼma ɢʊʹca-waʙaʹl-atuʹɪɖɪn ɢʊɖnaʹɢɪt,
  mɪʹɖɪ ʙɪskɪʹlu!
  ʙɪslaʹm·u tcɛɢʊʹca kweʹɪnafʊnak-haʹmɪ.   ‖122:94‖   <54(6)>
  ʙʊʹɢʊlfan-ci·ʼʼweɪ ɢʊɖ·ɪnɪɖ_laʹmu·.
  ɢʊɖɪnɪɖwɪʹy·at ɢʊʹca-laɖaʹm.

pɛ·ʼʼma ɢʊn·ɪɖɛʹsɖap ɖjahaʹl·a ɢɪʹnʊk ɢʊɖ·ɪnɪsɪʹy·u.
  ɢuʹsa-aʙʊʹɖzat ɢʊʹca·ʙɛ·ɖ ɢʊmaɖaʹʙɪɖ.

pɛ·ʼʼma ʙʊʹɢʊlfan ci·ʼweɪ nau-ɢʊʹsa-aʙʊʹɖzat ɢʊɖɪɖnaʹɢɪt ɢʊʹca-watɛʹnʹ·a-haʹmha
  ɖjahaʹlʙam-aɖjaʹmʙak ɖʊʹmha.

pɛ·ʼʼma ʙʊʹɢʊlfan ci·ʼʼweɪ. ɢʊɖ·ɪnɪsɪʹy·u ɖɪnɪkweʹɪnafʊn.   <54(7)>
tʊʹɢɪ-ɖɪnɪkweʹɪnafʊn ʙʊʹɢʊlfan ɢʊn·ɪɖɛʹsɖap
  ɢʊɖɪnɪɖnaʹɢɪt heʹca-watɛʹnʹ·a-haʹmha ɖjahaʹlʙam-aɖjaʹmʙak ɖʊʹmha.

pɛ·ʼʼma ɢʊɖnaʹɢɪt
  ʙʊʹɢʊlfan-mɪʹɖɪ-si·ʼʼweɪ ɖupkuʹpɢa·t pʊʹtʼsnaq aʹwaʹɖɪk.
  ʙʊʹɢʊlfan eʹyʹa ɢʊɖ_luʹʼnuf!
  ɢʊɖʊptuʹɢɪ ɖɪʹluʹʼnafʊn pɛ·ʼʼma mɪʹɖɪ ɢʊɖʊpsɖɪʹɖ ɖɪlaʹɢʊt.   ‖122:96‖

<55> Back in the Classroom

pɛ·ʼʼma yɛʹtc ɢʊɖɪɖkwi·ʹst ɖɪɖɪʹnɖɪn ɢʊʹsa-aʙʊʹɖzat ɢʊɖɪʹnɖa·t-aɖɪʹnɖɪn.
  ʙʊʹɢʊlfan-ci·ʼʼweɪ ɢʊɖnɪmɪʹnɖjɪs ɖjɛhaʹl·a ɢʊʹsa nɪkuʹʼuɫ ɖɪnɪʹlaʹqʷ ɖɪnɪkwaʹl·ak.

pɛ·ʼʼma ɢʊnɪtʊʹɢɪ-ɖɪnɪkuʹʼuɫ ɢʊn·ɪlaʹmu tcɛɢʊʹsa haʹl·a ɢɪʹnʊk ɢɪnɪlaʹɢwaɢ ahaʹmɾ.
  ɢʊʹsaʙɛ·ɖ ɢʊɖɪnɪyuʹw·u·t ɢʊʹsa-aɖɪʹnɖɪn.

pɛ·ʼʼma ɢʊʹca-aʙʊʹɖjat ɢʊɖɪʹnɖa·t-aɖɪʹnɖɪn   <55(2)>
  ʙʊʹɢʊlfan-siʹwʼeɪ ɢʊɖɪnɪɖɛʹcɖap tcɛʹɖɪnɪɢuʹn haʹl·a ɢʊʹs·a ɢɪʹnʊk ɢʊɖɪnɪɖaʹf.

pɛ·ʼʼma ɢʊʹsa-aʙʊʹɖzat ɢʊɖnaʹɢɪt,
  mɪʹɖɪ pslaʹm·ucɖa sɪʹyʹu tcɛmɪʹɖɪ ɖɪɖuplaɖaʹm.

ʙɛ·ʼʼma qɛʹɖ·ak ɢʊʹsa-aʙʊʹɖjat ɢʊɖɪʹnɖa·t ɢʊʹsa-waɖɪʼtʼsaq-aɖɪʹnɖɪn.
  ʙʊʹɢʊlfan-siʹwʼeɪ ɢʊn·ɪɖɛʹsɖap.   <55(3)>
  qɛʹɖ·ak ɢʊɖnaʹɢɪt, ɢʊʹsa watɛʹnʹ·a haʹmha.   ‖122:98‖

pɛ·ʼʼma ɢʊɖɪʹnɖa·t ɢʊsa-waɖɪʼtʼsaq-aɖɪʹnɖɪn
  ʙʊʹɢʊlfan-siʹweɪ ɢʊɖɪnɪsɪʹy·u

pɛ·ʼʼma ɢʊʹsa-aʙʊʹɖzat ɢʊɖɪʹtɢwɪn ɢʊʹsa ɢɛʹm-asiʹweɪ ɖɪnɪʙɪʹʙa.
  ɢʊɖɪnɪɖɪʹst ɖɪnɪʙɪʹʙa ɢʊʹsa ɢɛʹm-ɖɪnɪʙɪʹʙa.

pɛ·ʼʼma ɢʊɖɪʹtɢwɪn waʹʼan-yu-aʙɪʹʙa
  ɢʊɖɪnɪɖɪʹst.   <55(4)>
  ɢʊʹsa-aʙɪʹʙa ɢʊɖ·aʹŋkwt aSpelling ʙɪʹʙa.

Then she spoke to the second-grade children.

    "You all will pay attention to these three books!

    You will give undivided attention ('heart') to these three books."

Then she spoke to these first-grade children.   \<55(5)\>

    She also gave the first graders books.

    Those books' title was *Arithmetic*.

[---]

    "You first graders, you study those two books that I have given you!

    You study those books this morning!

    You will put all your effort into those two books! ||122:100|| \<55(6)\>

    Shortly, this very morning, I will be wanting to know what you all will have learned from those books."

Then she finished her instruction to the first-graders.

Then she spoke to the little children,

    "All of you come up front here, to this blackboard!"   \<55(7)\>

Then she said,

    "I am writing on this blackboard.

    All of you pay attention to what I will be saying now."

Then that sister wrote: from "11" to "20."

    She wrote: \<55(8)\>

        "11," "12," "13," "14," "15," "16," "17," "18," "19," "20."

                                                             ||122:102||

Then she took the (pointer-)stick.

She spoke in this manner to these children,   \<55(9)\>

    "This one is named 'eleven.'

    All of you children repeat after me!"

She said the names of all of the numerals on the blackboard.

Then she said,   \<55(10)\>

    "All of you children go sit where it is you sit!"

Then she said,

    "All of you second graders will come up front.

    You first graders will go back."

Then she said to the one standing in front,   \<55(11)\>

    "You speak about that book of yours!

    I am wanting to know how much you have learned of your book."

pɛ·''ma-ɢʊɒna'ɢɪt tcaɢʊ'sa-ɢɛ·'m ɒɪʙi·'ʙa· asi·'wei

　mɪ'ɒɪ ʙɪst'ci'ʙlu·t hɛ·ca hʊ'pcɪn aʙi·'ʙa.

　p̀ʊ'fan mɪ'ɒɪ ɒɪʙtu'knɪ ɒɪmhʊ·'p̀ɪn tcɛhɛ'sa hu'psɪn aʙi·'ʙa.

pɛ·''ma ɢʊɒna'ɢɪt tcɛhɛ'sa-asi·'wei wa''an-ɒɪʙi·'ʙa　　　　　　　　　<55(5)>

　ɢʊnɪɒɪ'st wa''an-yu· aʙi·'ʙa.

　ɢʊ'sa ʙi·'ʙa ɒa'ŋkwt arithmetic .

[---]

　mɪ'ɒɪ wa''an-aʙi·'ʙa si·''wei ʙɪst'ci'ʙlu·t ɢʊ'sa ɢɛ·'m aʙi·'ʙa tcɪ''ɪ ɢuɒɪɒɪ'ɒ·up.

　hɛ'sa-wei-ha'l'wan mɪ'ɒɪ ʙɪst'ci'ʙlut ɢʊ'ca aʙi·'ʙa'

　　p̀ʊ'fan ʙɪctu'ɢnɪn tcɛɢʊ'ca ɢɛ·'m-aʙi·'ʙa.　　　　　||122:100||　　<55(6)>

　　ɒi·'s ɢamɪtya'hampyan tcɪ''ɪ tcɪta'mɒju ɒumyʊ'k·un a'ɢ·a mɪ'ɒɪ tcɪɒupyu'ɢ·ʊn tcɛɢʊ's·a
　　　aʙi·'ʙa.

pɛ·''ma ɢut·ʊ'ɢ·ɪn ɒʊmha'mha tcɛɢʊ'sa wa''an-aʙi·'ʙa-ci·''wei

pɛ·''ma ɢʊɒna'ɢɪt tcɛɢʊ'sa-ɒɪ'nt'cɪt-asi·''wei,

　mɪ'ɒɪ-ʙɪsma·'k tcɪ'm·ɪ ɒjaha'ca a'mu·''yɪm alaʙla·'c.　　　　　　　<55(7)>

pɛ·''ma ɢʊɒna'ɢɪt

　tcɪ''ɪ tcɪy·ɛ·'m·a·t hɛ·'sa tcɛmɯ·'yɪm-alaʙla·'c.

　mɪ'ɒɪ p̀ʊ'f·an tcɪpyu'ɒnɪɢwan a'ɢ·a tcɪ''ɪ ɒamɒɪɒnɪ'cnɪ.

pɛ·''ma ɢʊ'ca-aʙu·'ɒjat ɢʊtyɛ·'m·a·t, ɒi·'nfyaf-nau-wa''an tcɛɢɛ·'m-ɒi·'nfya.

　ɢʊɒyɛ·'m·a·t　　　　　　　　　　　　　　　　　　　　　　　　　<55(8)>

　　ɒi·'nfyaf-nau-wa''an　ɒi·'nfyaf-nau-ɢɛ·m　ɒi·'nfyaf-nau-hu'pcɪn　ɒi·'nfyaf-nau-
　　taʙ　ɒi·'nfyaf-nau-hu'wan　ɒi·'nfyaf-nau-ɒa'f　ɒi·'nfyaf-nau-pcɪn'wɪ　ɒi·'nfyaf-
　　nau-ɢɪ'm'wei ɒi·'nfyaf-nau-k̀wi·'st ɢɛ·'m-ɒi·nfya　　||122:102||

pɛ·''ma ɢʊɒɪ'tɢwɪn a'wa'ɒik

pa·''a-ɢʊɢnɪ'cɪn [?] tcɛha'ca-asi·''wei　　　　　　　　　　　　　<55(9)>

　ha's·a-ɒʊ'ŋkwɪt 'ɒi·'nfyaf-nau-wa''an

　ʙʊ'ɢʊlfan-mɪ'ɒɪ-ci·''wei pa's-ʙɪɒna'ɢɪt hu'ʙ·ʊn-tcɛtcɪ''ɪ.

ʙu'ɢʊlfan ɢʊɒnɪ'cɪn ɢʊ'ca ɒɪyɛ·'mafʊn tcɛɢʊ'ca-amɯ·'yɪm alaʙla·'c ɒʊ'ŋkwɪt.

pɛ·''ma-ɢʊɒna'ɢɪt　　　　　　　　　　　　　　　　　　　　　　<55(10)>

　mɪ'ɒɪ ci·'wei psɒɪ'tyɪ tcɛha'l·a ɢʊ'ca mɪ'ɒɪ ɢʊɒʊpcɪ'y·u.

pɛ·''ma ɢʊɒna'ɢɪt

　mɪ'ɒɪ ɢʊ's·a ɢɛ·'m-aʙi·'ʙa ɒɪpcma·'k tcɪ'm·ei.

　ɒɪpcmʊ'k̀u wa''an ɢʊ'ca ɒɪʙi·'ʙa'.

pɛ·''ma ɢʊɒna'ɢɪt tcɛɢʊ'ca ɒjɪ'm·ei ɢuɒa·'ʙit,　　　　　　　　　<55(11)>

　ma'ha sna'ɢɪt tcɛɢʊ'ca ma'ha-ʙɪʙi·'ʙa

　tcɪ''ɪ-tcɪta'mɒju ɒum'yu'k·ʊn a'hɯ·'lu ma'ha-tcɪ'yʊ'k·ʊn tcɛɢʊ'sa-ʙɪʙi·'ʙa.

Then that boy told everything he knew.

Then there was one of those girls, she told about everything she had learned from
    that book. ||122:104|| <55(12)>

    She knew the entire book.

Then one boy, he missed (failed at) his lesson.

    He told about his book.

    He got a lot wrong.

Then the sister said,   <55(13)>

    "You go to the rear behind everyone!"

Then the sister said to one girl,

    "You look over your book!

    How much do you know from this book?"

She went and looked at that book.   <55(14)>

    She knew it all.

    She didn't get anything wrong.

The sister did it the same way with all of the children.

    Whoever it was that got their lesson wrong, he or she went to the back.

Having finished with all the children, then the sister said,   <55(15)>

    "All of you go and sit at your desks!" ||122:106||

Then that sister said to the first-grade children,

    "All of you come forward here to the blackboard!"

    All the children stood up next to the blackboard.

    The sister got just that many white markers.   <55(16)>

        She gave each of those children a white marker.

Then the sister said,

    "You all write what I will be telling you!

    You all write '30'!

        And write '20' down underneath that '30'!   <55(17)>

    How much is '30' and '20'?

    Write how much (comes) from that!"

Then one boy wrote,

    "'50' altogether from that '30' and '20.'"

        ||122:108|| <55(18)>

    Not all of the children understood that lesson.

Then the sister saw who it was that understood the lesson.

Then she got the names of the children who didn't understand.

pɛ·''ma ɢʊ'sa-aɫu'ɪᴅɪn ɢʊᴅna'ɢɪt, ʙʊ'ɢʊlfan a'ɢ·a ɢʊ'ca ɢⱷ'k ɢʊtyu'ɢʊn.

pɛ·''ma wa''an ɢʊ'sa-aʙɪna·'tst qɛ'ᴅ·ak ɢʊᴅnɪ's·ɪn tcɛɢʊ'sa-aʙɪ'ʙa ʙʊ'ɢʊlfan-a'ɢ·a qɛ'ᴅ·ak
   ɢʊᴅɪᴅyu'ɢʊn. ||122:104|| <55(12)>

   qɛ'ᴅ·ak ɢʊᴅyu'ɢʊn ʙʊ'ɢʊlfan ᴅɪʙi·'ʙa'.

pɛ·''ma wa''an aɫu'ɪᴅ·in ɢⱷ·'k ɢʊt·'cɪ'ʙ·ɪ ᴅɪʙi·'ʙa'.

   ɢʊᴅna'ɢɪt ᴅjɛɢⱷ·'k ᴅɪʙi·'ʙa

   ɢⱷ·k ɢʊt·'cɪ'ʙ·ɪ ha'l·u·.

pɛ·''ma ɢʊ'ca-aʙu·'ᴅjat ɢʊᴅna'ɢɪt   <55(13)>

   ma'ha sᴅja·'k ha·'nt'c tcɛʙu'ɢʊlfan.

pɛ·''ma aʙu·'ᴅzat ɢʊᴅna'ɢɪt tcɛwa''an-aʙɪ'na·tst,

   ma'ha st'cɪ'plu·t ʙɪʙi'ʙa'

   a'hⱷ·lu ma'ha tcɪ'yʊ'ɢʊn tcɛɢʊ'ca-aʙɪ'ʙa.

qɛ'ᴅ·ak ɢʊt·'cɪ'ʙlu·t tcɛɢʊ'sa-aʙɪ'ʙa   <55(14)>

   ɢʊᴅyu''un ʙʊɢʊlfan

   wa'ŋq-a'ɢ·a ɢʊᴅɪt·'cɪ'ʙ·ɪ.

ɢʊ'sa-aʙu·'ᴅzat pa·'s-ɢʊtɪ'u'nan tcaʙʊ'ɢʊlfan-ɢʊ'sa-asi'wɛɪ.

   e'y·a-ɢʊ'sa ɢʊᴅ·ɪt·'cɪ'ʙ·ɪ ᴅɪha'mha ɢʊᴅ·ɪ't ha·'nt'c.

ɢʊt·ʊ'ɢ·ɪ ʙʊ'ɢʊlfan-acɪ''wɛɪ pɛ·''ma ɢʊ'sa-aʙu·'ᴅzat ɢʊtna'ɢɪt,   <55(15)>

   mɪ'ᴅ·ɪ ʙcᴅja·'k cɪ'y·u tcɛᴅuplaᴅa·'m ||122:106||

pɛ·''ma ɢʊ'ca-aʙu·'ᴅjat ɢʊᴅna'ɢɪt tcɛɢʊ'ca wa''an-aʙɪ'ʙa-acɪ''wɛɪ,

   mɪ'ᴅ·ɪ ʙɪcma·'k ᴅjɪ'm·eɪ ᴅjaha'sa-amⱷ·'yɪm-ala'ʙla·c.

   ʙu'ɢʊlfan-acɪ''wɛɪ ɢʊᴅɪnɪᴅɛ'sᴅap yɛ·'tc tcaɢʊ'ca-mⱷ·'yɪm-la'ʙla·c.

   ɢʊ'sa-aʙu·'ᴅzat ɢʊᴅ·ɪ'tɢwɪn pa'sa hⱷ·'lu ɢʊ'sa wa'm·u· ᴅɪyɛ·'mafʊn.   <55(16)>

     qɛ'ᴅ·ak ɢʊᴅ·ɪ'st tcɛʙu'ɢʊlfan ɢʊ·'sa-asi·''wɛɪ wa''an ɢʊ·'sa wa'm·u· ᴅɪyɛ·'mafʊn.

pɛ·''ma ɢʊ'sa-aʙu·'ᴅzat ɢʊᴅna'ɢɪt,

   mɪ'ᴅ·ɪ ʙɪcyɛ·'m·a·t a'ɢ·a tcɪ''·ɪ ᴅɪᴅɪᴅnɪ'cɪn.

   mɪ'ᴅ·ɪ ʙɪcyɛ·'m·a·t hu'pcɪn-ᴅɪ·'nfya

     na'u-ʙɪsyɛ·'m·a·t ɢɛ·'m-ᴅɪ'nfya ha'l·u· tcɛɢʊ'sa hu'psɪn-ᴅɪ·'nfya.   <55(17)>

   a'hⱷ·lʊ ɢʊ'ca hu'pcɪn-ᴅɪ·'nfya nau-ɢɛ·'m-ᴅɪ·'nfya.

   ʙɪcyɛ·'m·a·t ha'l·u· ᴅjɛɢʊ'ca.

pɛ·''ma wa''an aɫu'ɪᴅ·ɪn ɢʊᴅyɛ·'m·a·t.

   wa'nfʊf-ᴅɪ·'nfya ʙʊ'ɢʊlfan tcɛɢʊ'ca hu'pcɪn-ᴅɪ·'nfyaf nau ɢɛ·'m-ᴅɪnfyaf.
                                   ||122:108|| <55(18)>

   wa'ŋq-ʙu'ɢʊlfan ɢɪ'n·ʊk ɢu'sa-asi·'wɛɪ ɢun·ɪtyu'ɢʊn ɢʊ'ca ᴅɪyɛ·'mafʊn.

pɛ·''ma ɢʊ'sa-aʙu·'ᴅzat ɢʊthⱷ·'ᴅ e'y·a ɢʊ'sa ɢʊtyu'ɢʊn ᴅɪyɛ·'ɪmafʊn.

pɛ·''ma qɛ'ᴅ·ak ɢʊᴅ·ɪ'tɢwɪn ᴅɪn·ɪᴅa'ŋkwt ɢʊ'sa-asi·'wɛɪ wa'ŋq ɢʊᴅɪnɪyu'ɢʊn.

Then the sister said,

    "All of you go sit down!"   <55(19)>

Then she rang it, that little bell.

    All of the children stood up.

[---]

    "All of you go outside!

    You all play for five minutes!"

Then the sister went and rang her bell.   <55(20)>

    All the children came in.

Then she said,

    "You, those little children not getting your lesson, you all come forward!"

Then on the blackboard she wrote all of the 20s together with 30s.

                                                      ||122:110|| <55(21)>

She, the sister, wrote,

    "'20' and '1' and '3' and '4' and '5' and '6' and '7' and '8' and '9,' and '30.'"

Then she told those little children,   <55(22)>

    "All of you pay attention to what I am writing now."

Then she began teaching to those little children.

She said,

    "You all learn what I have written here!"

Then she erased what she had just written.   <55(23)>

Then she said to those little children,

    "All of you write what I have just taught you!"

Then they, the children, they wrote those 20s with 30s.

Then the sister,

    "Such excellent (work) from you children." ||122:112|| <55(24)>

Then she said,

    "All of you go sit at your desks!"

Then she said to the second-grade children,

    "All of you come up front here to the blackboard!

    You six children, stand near the blackboard."   <55(25)>

Then she gave out six white markers.

Then she said,

    "All of you write what I tell you on that blackboard.

        All of you write 'earth'!

pɛ·''ma ɢʊ'sa-aʙʊ'ᴅzat ɢʊᴅna'ɢɪt,

   mɪ'ᴅɪ ᴅja·'k sɪ'y·usᴅa.   <55(19)>

pɛ·''ma qɛ'ᴅak ɢʊᴅɪ'nᴅa·t ɢʊ'sa-wɪ-ᴅi·'t'saq-aᴅɪ'nᴅɪn

   ʙʊ'ɢʊlfan-ci·''weɪ ɢʊn·ɪᴅɛ'sᴅap

[---]

   mɪ'ᴅɪ ᴅja·'k hɛ·''lʊm

   ʙɪcla'ɢʊt hu'w·an aminute.

pɛ·''ma ɢʊ'ca-aʙʊ'ᴅjat ɢʊᴅɪ'nᴅa·t-ᴅɪᴅɪ'nᴅɪn.   <55(20)>

   ʙʊ'ɢʊlfan asi·''weɪ ɢʊᴅɪnɪt_la'm·u

pɛ·''ma ɢʊᴅna'ɢɪt,

   mɪ'ᴅɪ ɢʊ'ca-wɪ-ᴅɪ'nt'cɪt-acɪ·''weɪ, wa'ŋq-ɢʊᴅɪᴅyu'ɢʊn ᴅɪyɛ'ɪmafʊn ʙcma·'k ᴅjɪ'm·eɪ.

pɛ·''ma qɛ'ᴅak ɢʊᴅyɛ'm·a·t tcaɢʊ'ca-mɶ·''yɪm-alaʙla·'c. ʙʊ'ɢʊlfan ɢʊ'ca ɢɛ'm-ᴅi·'nfyaf

   nau-tcɛhʊ'psɪn-ᴅi·'nfyaf. ||122:110|| <55(21)>

qɛ'ᴅak ɢʊ'sa-aʙʊ'ᴅzat ɢʊᴅyɛ'm·a·t

   ɢɛ'm-ᴅi·'nfyaf nau-wa''an nau-hu'psɪn nau-ta'ʙ nau-hu'w·an nau-ᴅa'f nau-pcɪ'n'wɪ

      nau-ɢɪ'm-wɪ nau-k̓wi·'st nau-hu'pcɪn-ᴅi·'nfyaf.

pɛ·''ma ɢʊᴅna'ɢɪt ɢʊ'ca-aᴅɪ'nt'cit-acɪ·''weɪ   <55(22)>

   mɪ'ᴅɪ tcɪʙhɶ'ᴅʊn a'ɢ·a tcɪ·''ɪ ɢʊᴅɪᴅyɛ'm·a·t.

pɛ·''ma qɛ'ᴅak ɢʊᴅɪᴅyu'ɢnɪᴅnɪ tcɛɢʊ'ca-ᴅɪ'nt'cɪt-acɪ·''weɪ.

qɛ'ᴅ·ak-ɢʊᴅna'ɢɪt,

   mɪ'ᴅɪ ʙɪcyʊ'ɢʊn hɛ'ca a'ɢ·a tcɪ·''ɪ ɢʊᴅɪᴅyɛ'm·a·t.

pɛ·''ma qɛ'ᴅak ɢʊᴅyɪ'fya·t ɢʊ'ca a'ɢ·a qɛ'ᴅ·ak ɢʊᴅɪᴅyɛ'm·a·t.   <55(23)>

pɛ·''ma ɢʊᴅna'ɢɪt tcɛɢʊ'ca ᴅɪ'nt'cɪt asi·''weɪ.

   mɪ'ᴅɪ syɛ'm·a·t a'ɢ·a-tcɪ·''ɪ ɢʊᴅɪᴅyʊ'ɢnɪfʊʙ.

pɛ·''ma ɢɪ'n·ʊk asi·''weɪ ɢʊᴅnɪᴅyɛ'm·a·t ɢʊ'ca ɢɛ'm-ᴅi·'nfya na'u-tcɛ-hu'pcɪn-ᴅi·'nfya.

pɛ·''ma ɢʊ'sa-aʙʊ'ᴅjat

   p̓ʊ'fan-tɛ'n·a tcɛmɪ'ᴅɪ ci·''weɪ. ||122:112|| <55(24)>

pɛ·''ma qɛ'ᴅ·ak ɢʊᴅna'ɢɪt

   mɪ'ᴅɪ ᴅja·'k-ci'yucᴅa tcɛᴅɪplaᴅa'm.

pɛ·''ma ɢʊᴅna'ɢɪt tcɛɢʊ'ca ɢɛ'm-ᴅɪʙi·'ʙa-cɪ'weɪ,

   mɪ'ᴅɪ ʙɪcma·'k ᴅjɪ'meɪ ᴅjaha'sa mɶ·''yɪm-ala'ʙla·c.

   ᴅa'f-mɪ'ᴅɪ ci·''weɪ ᴅɛ'sᴅap yɛ·'tc tcɛɢʊ'ca mɶ·''yɪm la'ʙla·c.   <55(25)>

pɛ·''ma qɛ'ᴅak ɢʊᴅnɪᴅɪ'ct ᴅa'f ɢʊ'ca wa'm·u· ayɛ'mafʊn.

pɛ·''ma ɢʊᴅna'ɢɪt,

   a'ɢ·a tcɪ·''ɪ ɢʊᴅnɪ'cɪn mɪ'ᴅɪ ɢʊᴅɪpyɛ'm·a·t tcɛɢʊ'ca mɶ·''yɪm la'ʙla·c.

     mɪ'ᴅɪ pcyɛ'm·a·t ha'ŋklu·p.

All of you write 'water'!   <55(26)>
All of you write 'wood'!
All of you write 'morning'!"

Going on almost to evening, whoever it was that did not write everything she told
  them to, they went to the back.

  She got their names.   <55(27)>

Then she said,

  "All of you go sit at your desks!" ||122:114||

Then the sister said,

  "All of you seven boys and girls, all of you come here to the blackboard!"

                                                                         <55(28)>

The sister gave them all those white markers.

  "All of you will write what I name."

  The sister named "horse," "cow," "wagon," "trout," "deer," "black-bear," "rac-
    coon," and "person."   <55(29)>

Then the children, when they got what she had named wrong, she got their
  names.

Then she said,

  "All of you go sit at your desks!"

Then she said to all of the children,   <55(30)>

  "Tomorrow I will be wanting all of you children to know your lesson."

                                                              ||122:116||

Then she rang the little (hand-)bell.

  All the children stood up.

  She said, and the children said, prayers.   <55(31)>

When they finished,

  "All of you go outside, clean yourselves up at where you all wash your faces and your
    hands, for your midday meal-time.

  You are not to get to playing.   <55(32)>

  As soon as they ring the bell, all of you will go to where it is that you stand."

Then the sister rang the bell.

  All the children ran to where it is that they stand.

  The big lad stood there.   <55(33)>

  All the children got to where it was that they (were to) stand.

Then the big lad said,

pcyɛ'mɑ·t ama'mpɢa.   <55(26)>

pcyɛ'mɑ·t a'wa'ɒik.

pcyɛ'mɑ·t aha'l'wan.

yɛ'ɒj-ɢamɒhu'wɪ. e'y·a ɢʊ'ca wa'ŋq-ɢʊɒyɛ'mɑ·t ʙʊ'ɢʊlfan a'ɢ·a qɛ'ɒ·ak. ɢʊɒɪnɒnɪ'cɪn
ɢɪ'n'ʊk ɢɪnɪsma·'k ha'nt'c.

qɛ'ɒ·ak ɢʊɒɪ'tɢwɪn ɒɪnɪɒa'ŋkwɪt.   <55(27)>

pɛ·''ma ɢʊɒna'ɢɪt,

mɪ'ɒɪ cɒja'k sɪ'y·u tcɛɒɪplaɒa'm. ||122:114||

pɛ·''ma ɢʊ'ca-aʙʊ'ɒzat ɢʊɒna'ɢɪt

mɪ'ɒɪ ɢʊ'ca pcɪ'n'wɪ ańu'ɪɒɪn na'u-ɒɪʙɪ'na·tst ʙsma·'k hɛ'ca tca'mɷ·''yɪm-ala'ʙla·c.
                                                                       <55(28)>

ɢʊ'sa-aʙʊ'ɒzat ɢʊnɪɒɪ'st ʙʊ'ɢʊlfan ɢʊ'ca wa'mʊ-ayɛ·'mafʊn.

ʙʊ'ɢʊlfan-mɪ'ɒɪ ɒɪpyɛ'mɑ·t a'ɢ·a tcɪ''ɪ ɢʊtkwu'n.

ɢʊ'sa-aʙʊ'ɒjat ɢʊtkwu'n akɪ'ʊɒɪn, amu'cmuc, atcɪ'ktcik, aʙʊ'ɒ·u·f, aɒa'l·ɪm,
alu'tufan, ha'ŋ̇kwɪn, nau-a'm·ɪm.   <55(29)>

pɛ·''ma ɢʊ'ca-asɪ·''wɪ ɢʊɒɪnɪt·'cɪ'ʙ·in a'ɢ·a ɢʊ'ca qɛ'ɒ·ak ɢʊɒɪɒkwu'n ɢʊɒɪ'tɢwɪn
ɒɪnɪɒa'ŋkwɪt.

pɛ·''ma qɛ'ɒ·ak ɢʊɒna'ɢɪt

mɪ'ɒɪ ɒja·'k ci'yu tcɛɒɪlaɒa'm.

pɛ·''ma ɢʊɒna'ɢɪt tcaʙu'ɢʊlfan ɢʊ'ca acɪ·''wɪ,   <55(30)>

me'ɪɒj tcɪ''ɪ tcɪ́ta'mɒju ʙʊ'ɢʊlfan-mɪ'ɒɪ-cɪ·''wɪ ɢʊɒɪpyʊ'ɢʊn [unintel.] ɒɪnɪʙi'ʙa'.
                                                                       ||122:116||

pɛ·''ma ɢʊɒɪ'nɒa·t-ɢʊsa-waɒɪ·'t'saq-aɒɪ'nɒɪn.

ʙʊ'ɢʊlfan si·''wɪ ɢɪnɪɒe'cɒap.

qɛ'ɒ·ak ɢʊɒna'ɢɪt na'u-acɪ·''wɪ ɢɪ'n'ʊk ɢʊɒɪɒna'ɢɪt watɛ'n·a ha'mha.   <55(31)>

ɢʊɒɪnɪtʊ'ɢɪ,

mɪ'ɒɪ ɒja·'k hɛ·''lum tɛ'n·atcwu·n ɒjɛha'l·a ɢʊ'ca-mɪ'ɒɪ ɢʊɒɪpku·'ł ɒɪkwa'l·ak nau-
ɒɪ'la'qʷ. wɪ'lfu-a'mpyan ɒumpnɪkwe'ɪnafʊn.

wa'ŋq-mɪ'ɒɪ ɒɪɒɪpla'ɢwak.   <55(32)>

pa's-nu·s ɢʊnɪɒɪ'nɒa·t-aɒɪ'nɒɪn, ʙu'ɢʊlfan mɪ'ɒɪ ɢʊɒɪpɒɪ'ɒ tcaha'l·a ɢʊ'ca mɪ'ɒɪ
ɢʊɒɪpɒɷ·'f.

pɛ·''ma ɢʊ'ca-aʙʊ'ɒzat ɢʊɒɪ'nɒa·t aɒɪ'nɒɪn.

ʙu'ɢʊlfan acɪ·''wɪ ɢʊɒɪnɪɒmɪ'nɒjɪs ɒjaha'l·a ɢʊ'ca ɢɪ'n'ʊk ɢʊɒɪnɪɒa·'f
ɢʊ'sa-waʙa'l-ańu'ɪɒɪn ɢuɒa·'ʙɪt ɢʊ'saʙɛ·ɒ.   <55(33)>

ʙu'ɢʊlfan- si·''wɪ ɢʊɒɪnɪtwa'l ɒja·ha'l·a ɢʊ's·a ɢʊɒɪnɪɒa·'f.

pɛ·''ma ɢʊ'sa-waʙa'l-ańu'ɪɒɪn ɢʊɒna'ɢɪt

    "All of you turn around.

    Go! Go into the dining room!" ||122:118||

    All the children went in.   <55(34)>

    They went around by the tables.

    They stood at where they (were to) sit.

Then the sister stood (there).

    As always, she spoke the prayers.

Then all the children sat down.   <55(35)>

    They ate.

Then when they finished their meal, the sister said,

    "All of you stand up!"

    All the children stood up.

Then all the children, and that sister, they said the prayers.   <55(36)>

Then all the children went outside to their playing.

ʙʊʹɢʊlfan-eʹy·a ɢʊɒskɪʹlwi
ᴅjaʹk slaʹm·u ᴅjaɢʊʹca-k̓weʹɪnafʊnak ahaʹm·ɪ. ‖122:118‖
ʙʊʹɢʊlfan ci·ʹʹwei ɢʊᴅɪnɪᴅ_laʹm·u <55(34)>
ɢʊᴅɪnɪᴅwɪʹy·u ᴅjaɢʊʹca-alaᴅaʹm.
ɢʊᴅɪnɪᴅɛʹcᴅap ᴅjahaʹl·a ɢɪʹn·ʊk ɢʊᴅɪnɪᴅ_sɪʹy·u.
pɛ·ʹʹma ɢʊʹca-aʙʊʹᴅjat ɢuᴅ·aʹʙ·ɪt
muʹɪnu ɢʊᴅnaʹɢɪt ɢuʹsa-watɛʹn·a haʹmha.
pɛ·ʹʹma ʙʊʹɢulfan ci·ʹʹwei ɢʊᴅɪnɪsɪʹy·u <55(35)>
ɢʊᴅɪnɪk̓weʹɪnafʊ.
pɛ·ʹʹma ɢʊᴅɪnɪtʊʹɢɪ-ᴅɪnɪk̓weʹɪnafɪn ɢʊʹsa-aʙʊʹᴅzat ɢʊᴅnaʹɢɪt
ʙcᴅɛʹcᴅap,
ʙʊʹɢʊlfan-ci·ʹʹwei ɢun·ɪcᴅɛʹcᴅap.
pɛ·ʹʹma ʙʊʹɢʊlfan ci·ʹʹwei naɢʊʹsa-ʙʊʹᴅzat ɢʊn·ɪʹnaʹɢɪt ɢʊʹsa-watɛʹn·a-haʹmha. <55(36)>
pɛ·ʹʹma ʙʊʹɢʊlfan ci·ʹʹwei ɢʊᴅɪnɪʹʹɪ hɛ·ʹʹlʊm ᴅɪnɪlaʹɢwak.

A Tale of Two Doctoring Traditions[1]

[previously untranslated]

<56> Bahawadas Falls Ill; the White Doctor Is Called

I myself, Bahawadas, got to feeling unwell.

    I went a ways off, there I vomited everything I had eaten.

Then I went into the playroom. ||122:120||

    There I stayed.

At one o'clock the sister rang the bell.   <56(2)>

    All the children came into the place where they washed their hands and faces.

Then all the children came into the playroom.

Then they rang the bell.

    All the children came in.

    They sat down at their desks.

Then the sister rang the little (hand-)bell.   <56(3)>

    All the children stood up.

    They said the prayers.

When they finished, then all the children sat down.

Then I myself, Bahawadas, stood up.

I told that sister,   <56(4)>

    "My head is just about splitting open.

    I want to go upstairs to lie down."

    I was in bed all that afternoon. ||122:122||

In the evening I slept.

One of the sisters came to me,   <56(5)>

    "How are you?"

[---]

    "I am very sick."

She said,

    "I will go get the White doctor."   <56(6)>

Then that doctor came to where I was lying.

He said,

    "Of what sort is your illness?"

I said,

    "My head is just about splitting open."   <56(7)>

A Tale of Two Doctoring Traditions

<56> *baẋawádas* Falls Ill; the White Doctor Is Called

tcɪ"ɪ ʙaẋawa'ᴅɪs wa'ŋq ɢʊt·ɛ'n·a·yu ᴅɛmhu·'p̓ɪn

  tcɪ"ɪ ɢʊᴅ·ɪ't la'ɢaɪ ɢʊ'ca tcɪ"ɪ ɢʊtya·'ɢʊt. ʙʊ'ɢʊlfan ak̓we'ɪnafʊn.

pɛ·"ma tcɪ"ɪ ɢʊt_la'm·u tcɛɢʊ'ca la'ɢʊt ha'm·ɪ. ||122:120||

  ɢʊ'saʙɛ·ᴅ tcɪ"ɪ ɢʊᴅʙi·'nᴅ.

wa"an-aᴅɪ'nᴅɪn ɢʊ'sa-aʙʊ'ᴅzat ɢʊᴅ·ɪ'nᴅɛt-aᴅɪnᴅɪn.   <56(2)>

  ʙʊ'ɢʊlfan-si·"weɪ ɢʊᴅɪnɪᴅ_sma"a tcaha'l·a ɢʊ'sa ᴅɪnɪk̓u"ul ᴅɪnɪkwa'l·ak nau-ᴅɪ'la'qʷ.

pɛ·"ma ʙʊ'ɢʊlfan si·"weɪ ɢʊᴅɪnɪᴅ_la'm·u tcɛɢʊ'ca la'ɢʊt ha'm·ɪ.

pɛ·"ma ɢʊᴅɪnɪᴅɪ'nᴅɛt-aᴅɪ'nᴅɪn.

  ʙʊ'ɢʊlfan si·"weɪ ɢʊᴅɪnɪᴅ_la'm·u.

  ɢʊᴅɪnɪt_sɪ'y·u tcɛ'ᴅɪnɪlaᴅa'm.

pɛ·"ma ɢʊ'sa-aʙʊ'ᴅzat ɢʊᴅ·ɪ'nᴅɛt-ɢu'sa-aᴅi·'t'saq-aᴅɪ'nᴅɪn.   <56(3)>

  ʙʊ'ɢʊlfan-si·"weɪ ɢʊᴅɪnɪᴅɛ'ᴄᴅap.

  ɢʊᴅɪnɪᴅna'ɢɪt ɢʊ'sa watɛ'n·a ha'mha.

ɢʊᴅɪnɪtʊ'ɢɪ pɛ·"ma ʙʊ'ɢʊlfan ci·"weɪ ɢʊᴅɪnɪᴅ_sɪ'y·u.

pɛ·"ma tcɪ"ɪ ʙaẋawa'ᴅas ɢʊᴅ·ɛ'sᴅap

ɢʊᴅnɪ'sɪn ɢʊ'sa aʙʊ'ᴅzat   <56(4)>

  p̓ʊ'fan tcɪ"ɪ ᴅa'mɫ yɛ'ᴅj ʊmp̓la'qp̓laçu.

  tcɪ"ɪ t̓a'mᴅju ᴅʊmsᴅɪ't ha'lʙam tcaha'm·ɪ ᴅʊmsᴅɪ'twɪ·.

  tcɪ"ɪ ɢʊᴅ_sᴅɪ'twi· ʙʊ'ɢʊlfan ɢʊ'ca-waya'hampyan. ||122:122||

ɢʊᴅɪthu'wɪ tcɪ"ɪ ɢʊtwe'ɪᴅɪt.

wa"an-aʙʊ'ᴅzat ɢʊt_cma"a tcɛtcɪ"ɪ.   <56(5)>

  a'ha ma'tcʊmɪ'ut.

[---]

  p̓ʊ'fan tcɪ"ɪ tcum'ɪ'lfɪt.

qɛ'ᴅ·ak ɢʊᴅna'ɢɪt

  tcɪ"ɪ ᴅɪᴅɪ'tɢwɪn ɢʊ'sa-wa'm·u· apa'lɪq.   <56(6)>

pɛ·"ma ɢʊ'sa-apa'lɪq ɢumu'ɢ tcɛha'l·a tcɪ"ɪ ɢʊᴅɪᴅwe'ɪᴅɪt.

ɢʊᴅna'ɢɪt,

  a'wɛw ma'ha ʙɪ'ɪ'lfɪt?

tcɪ"ɪ ɢʊᴅn·a'ɢɪt

  ᴅa'm·ɫ yɛ'ᴅj ʊmp̓la'qwaɪ.   <56(7)>

Then the doctor gave me medicine.

   I drank that medicine.

Then I vomited it all up.

The doctor said to the sister,

   "In one hour, you will administer this medicine."   <56(8)>

Then they left.

   I slept.

   The sister brought in some fine food.

   I ate.

      I couldn't keep it down. ||122:124|| <56(9)>

      I vomited up all of that food.

Then all the children came upstairs to go to bed.

   All the children went to bed.

Then I couldn't get to sleep.

   I was suffering (?)[2] terribly.   <56(10)>

   That sister came back after one hour (and) gave me that medicine.

Then I drank that medicine.

   I threw it all up.

Then I said to that sister not to give me that medicine.   <56(11)>

   I was suffering (?) so terribly.

Early the next morning the sister rang the bell.

   All the big boys got up.

   They went downstairs.

Then the sister wanted to give me the medicine.   <56(12)>

I said,

   "I do not want that medicine." ||122:126||

   It was there, that medicine, in the cup.

      She wanted to give it to me.

      I sat there.   <56(13)>

Then I knocked the cup from her hand.

   The cup fell to the floor.

Then she, the sister, said,

   "You can't get better, not unless you drink this medicine."

I said,   <56(14)>

   "Not as long as it's anything of yours, I won't get better."

Then the big boy came upstairs.

pɛ·"ma ɢʊ'sa-aʙa·'laqya ɢʊdɪ'sdɛt ala'mɪtsi·'n.

  tcɪ"ɪ ɢʊdɪ'tɢwɪt ɢʊ'sa-la'mɪtci·'n

pɛ·"ma ʙʊ'ɢʊlfan tcɪ"ɪ ɢutya'ɢu·t.

ɢʊ'sa-aʙa·'laqya ɢʊdnɪ'cɪn tcaɢʊ'ca-aʙu'djat

  ɢʊmwa"an hour ma'ha ᴅɛdɪ'ct hɛ'ca la'mɪtsi·'n.   <56(8)>

pɛ·"ma ɢɪ'n·ʊk ɢʊdnɪᴅnɪ"ɪ

  tcɪ"ɪ ɢʊᴅwe'ɪᴅit.

  ɢu'sa-aʙu'djat ɢʊᴅ_cmu'ku tɛ'n·a kwe'ɪnafʊn.

  tcɪ"ɪ ɢʊᴅkwe'ɪnʊf

  wa'nq-la'f tcɪ"ɪ ɢʊᴅɪᴅp̓ɪ·'n. ||122:124|| <56(9)>

  ʙʊ'ɢʊlfan tcɪ"ɪ ɢutya'ɢu·t ɢʊ'ca-kwe'ɪnafʊn.

pɛ·"ma ʙʊ'ɢʊlfan si·"weɪ ɢʊdɪnɪᴅ_cma"a ha'lʙam ᴅumnɪᴅitwe'ɪf.

  ʙu'ɢʊlfan-ci·"weɪ ɢʊdɪnɪᴅɪ'tweɪ

pɛ·"ma tcɪ"ɪ wa'nq-la'f ɢʊdɪᴅɪ'tweɪ.

  p̓ʊ'fan tcɪ"ɪ ɢʊtya'tcfɪq.   <56(10)>

ɢu'ca-aʙu'djat ɢʊt_cma"a ɢʊ'ca wa"an hour ɢʊmᴅɛ'sᴅɛt ɢʊ'ca-lamtci·'n.

pɛ·"ma tcɪ"ɪ ɢʊdɪ'tɢwɪt ɢʊ'sa-lamtcɪ'n

  ʙʊ'ɢʊlfan ɢʊdya'ɢu·t.

pɛ·"ma tcɪ"ɪ ɢʊdna'ɢɪt tcɛɢʊ'sa-aʙu'djat, wa'nq ᴅumᴅɪ'sᴅat ɢʊ'ca-ala'mtci·'n.<56(11)>

  p̓ʊ'fan tcɪ"ɪ ɢʊᴅya'ᴅjfɪq.

ɢʊᴅ·aha'l'wan ɢʊ'ca-aʙu'djat ɢʊdɪ'nᴅat-aᴅɪ'nᴅɪn

  ʙu'ɢʊlfan ɢʊ'ca-waʙa'l atu'ɪᴅ·ɪn ɢɪ'n·ʊk ɢʊdɪnɪᴅʙu'klaɪ.

  ɢʊᴅɪnɪha'l·u· wa'l.

pɛ·"ma ɢʊ'sa-aʙu'dzat ɢut̓a'mᴅju ᴅumᴅɪ'sᴅat ɢu'sa-lamtci·'n   <56(12)>

tcɪ"ɪ ɢʊᴅna'ɢɪt

  wa'nq tcɪ"ɪ ɢut̓·a'mᴅju ɢʊ'ca-lamtci·'n ||122:126||

  ɢʊᴅp̓i·'n ɢʊ'sa-lamtcɪ·'n tca'u'cɢan.

    qɛ'ᴅ·ak ɢut̓a'mᴅju ᴅumᴅɪ'sᴅat

    tcɪ"ɪ ɢuᴅ.sɪ'y·u   <56(13)>

pɛ·"ma tcɪ"ɪ ɢuᴅ_la'pᴅa·t ɢʊ'sa ʊ'cɢan tcɛᴅɪ'la'qʷ.

  ɢʊ'ca-u'cɢan ɢuᴅje'ɢ·u ᴅjalaʙla·'c.

pɛ·"ma qɛ'ᴅ·ak ɢʊ'ca-aʙu'djat ɢʊᴅna'ɢɪt

  wa'nq-la'fa ma'ha ɢʊᴅitwe'l·u· wa'nq ᴅumɪᴅɪ'tɢwɪt hɛ'ca-ala'mᴅjɪ·n.

tcɪ"ɪ ɢʊᴅna'ɢɪt   <56(14)>

  wa'nq-a'ɢ·a ɢʊ'sa tcama'ha tcɪ"ɪ wa'nq ɢʊᴅitɛ'n·a'yu.

pɛ·"ma ɢu'sa-aʙa'l-atu'ɪᴅɪn ɢuᴅ_cma"a ha'lʙam

He rang the bell.

He woke up all the little children.

All the little children got up. <56(15)>

Then they went downstairs to where they got ready.

I laid in my bed.

There I tossed and turned.

Then the sister came to me. ||122:128||

She brought food. <56(16)>

She said,

"How are you doing this morning?"

[---]

"I am very sick.

All night long I tossed and turned. <56(17)>

I couldn't fall asleep."

Then the sister said,

"Do you want to eat?"

I told her,

"No, I want to go back to our home." <56(18)>

The sister said,

"You can't go home."

[---]

"I want to see my father today."

Then the head sister came to talk to me,

"How are you?" <56(19)>

[---]

"I am very sick.

I want to go home to my father and my mother."

[---]

"Alright, I will send word to your father. ||122:130||

He will come get you." <56(20)>

I laid in bed that morning.

Then my father arrived for me.

Then they took me downstairs in the (school-)building.

They took me to that buggy.

Then my father drove his horse. <56(21)>

We went back to our home.

ɢᴜᴅɪ'ɴᴅɛ·t ᴀᴅɪ'ɴᴅɪɴ
ɢᴜᴅʙᴜ'klɪ ʙᴜ'ɢʊlfan ᴀᴅɪ'nt'cɪt-si·''weɪ.
ʙᴜ'ɢʊlfan ᴅɪ'nt'cɪt-asi''weɪ ɢᴜᴅɪɴɪᴅʙᴜ'ɢlaɪ.   <56(15)>
pɛ·''ma ɢᴜᴅɪɴɪhᴜ'l·aɪ ᴅjɛha'l·a ɢᴜ'ca-ɢɪɴɪtɛ'n·ɛtcwu·n.
  tcɪ''ɪ ɢᴜᴅwe'ɪᴅɪt tcɛᴅaqwa''an
  ɢᴜ'saʙɛ·ᴅ tcɪ''ɪ ɢᴜᴅʙɪ'lᵏʙᴜᵏu.
pɛ·''ma ɢᴜ'sa-aʙᴜ'ᴅjat ɢᴜᴅ_cma''a tcɛtcɪ''ɪ ||122:128||
  ɢᴜᴅ_cmu'ᵏu aᵏwe'ɪnafᴜnak.   <56(16)>
qɛ'ᴅ·ak ɢᴜᴅna'ɢɪt
  a'ha ma'ha tcɪmɪ'ut hɛ'ca-wɪ-ha'l'wan.
[---]
  tcɪ''ɪ pᴜ'fan tcᴜm'ɪ'lfɪt.
  ʙᴜ'ɢʊlfan awɪ'fyu tcɪ''ɪ ɢᴜtʙɪ'lᵏʙᴜᵏu   <56(17)>
    wa'ŋq-la'f ɢamɪᴅɪ'tweɪ.
pɛ·''ma ɢᴜ'sa-aʙᴜ'ᴅjat ɢᴜᴅna'ɢɪt
  tcɪta'mᴅju ᴅᴜmᵏwe'ɪnafu.
tcɪ''ɪ ɢᴜᴅnɪ'cɪn,
  wa'ŋq. tcɪ''ɪ tcɪta'mᴅju ᴅᴜmɢᴜ'myɪ tcɛsᴜ'ᴅ·u ᴅu'm·aɪ.   <56(18)>
ɢᴜ'sa-aʙᴜ'ᴅzat ɢᴜᴅna'ɢɪt
  wa'ŋq-la'f ma'ha ɢᴜmᴅɪ'tyɪ.
[---]
  tcɪ''ɪ tcɪta'mᴅju ᴅᴜmhω''ωt ᴅama'·ma hɛ'ca-wɪ-ɪ'pyan.
pɛ·''ma ɢᴜ'sa-waᴅja'mʙak-aʙᴜ'ᴅjat ɢᴜᴅma''a tcɛtcɪ''ɪ.
  a'm·atcɪmɪ'ut.   <56(19)>
[---]
  pᴜ'fan tcɪ''ɪ tcᴜm'ɪ'lfɪt.
  tcɪ''ɪ tcɪta'mᴅju ᴅᴜmɢᴜ'myɪ tcaᴅama'·ma na'u-tcaᴅana'·na.
[---]
  ɢᴜ'cwɪ. tcɪ''ɪ ᴅɪᴅɢɪ'cɢa·t aha'm·a tcaʙuma'·ma ||122:130||
  ɢω'k ɢɪmɪwu'fᴜʙ.   <56(20)>
  tcɪ''ɪ-ɢᴜᴅwe'ɪᴅɪᴅ ɢᴜ'ca-wi-ha'l'wan.
pɛ·''ma ᴅama'·ma ɢᴜᴅmu'ɢ tcatcɪ''ɪ.
pɛ·''ma ɢᴜɴɪᴅɪ'tᵏu tcɪ''ɪ wa'l tcaha'm·ɪ.
  ɢᴜɴɪᴅɪ'tᵏu tcɪ''ɪ tcaɢᴜ'ca ᴅɪ't'saq atcɪ'ktcɪk.
pɛ·''ma ᴅɛma'·ma ɢᴜᴅɢɪ'cɢa·t ᴅɪkɪ'uᴅɪn   <56(21)>
  ɢᴜᴅ_sᴅu'yɪ su'ᴅ·ᴜ tcaᴅ·u'm·aɪ.

When we returned home, my mother fixed up the place where I was to sleep.
Then I lost consciousness (lit., then I didn't know anything).

<57> A Tamanawas Doctoress

For nine days I was unconscious.

On the tenth day I regained consciousness (lit., I awoke my heart).

   I looked around, one old woman was there.

   She rubbed my head, rubbed everywhere on my body.   <57(2)>

   I was lying near the fireplace. ||122:132||

Then that old doctor woman warmed her hands on the fire.

   Her hands were warmed for doctoring.[3]

Then she rubbed my head.

   She sang her (Tamanawas) song.   <57(3)>

Then the people who were there knocked sticks on the floor.

   All the people took up the doctor's song.[4]

   That doctor woman doctored me half the night.

Then they finished the doctoring.

Then my mother prepared food.   <57(4)>

   All of the people ate.

Finished with their meal, everyone went back to their homes.

Then the doctor said,

   "Tomorrow night I will doctor again."

All the people said,   <57(5)>

   "Okay, we'll come." ||122:134||

   I went to sleep.

   My whole body felt a little bit better.

In the morning my father got up.

   He went outside.   <57(6)>

   He fed his horses and his cows.

My mother made breakfast.

   They ate.

   I couldn't eat.

   My heart (state of being) was quite [_?_].[5]   <57(7)>

Then my mother killed a chicken.

   She boiled that chicken.[6]

Then she gave me that chicken broth.

   I drank a little of the broth.

ɢʊDɪ'twʊk tcaha'm·ɪ Dᴇna'na ɢʊD_su''un tcaha'l·a ɢʊ'ca tcɪ''ɪ ɢʊmDɪDwe'ɪDɪt.
pɛ·''ma tcɪ''ɪ wa'ŋq a'ɢ·a ɢʊDɪtyʊ'ɢ·un.

<57> A Tamanawas Doctoress

k̇wi·'st a'mpyan tcɪ''ɪ wa'ŋq a'ɢ·a ɢʊDɪtyʊ'ɢ·un.
tcᴇDɪ'nfyaf-a'mpyan tcɪ''ɪ ɢʊDbu'ɢlaɪ Damhu'p̣ɪn.
   ɢʊtɢwɛ'ltcɢwtc ha'saʙɛ·'D wa''an ayʊ'huyu aʙʊ'm·ik ɢʊmaʙi'nD.
   qɛ'D·ak uyɪ'fya·t DᴇDa'mɪł bʊ'ɢʊlfan ha'l·a tcᴇDᴇka'ʙya.   <57(2)>
   yɛ'Dj tcɛlɛ'camnɛ·' tcɪ''ɪ ɢʊDɪDwe'ɪDɪt. ||122:132||
pɛ·''ma ɢu'sa-ayʊ'huyu apa'laqya aʙʊ'm·ik qɛ'D·ak ɢʊD'u'q̇na·t Dɪ'la'qʷ tcᴇɢʊ'ca ha'm·ɪ.
   ɢʊDma·'yu Dɪ'la'qʷ.
pɛ·''ma ɢʊDyɪ'fya·t tcᴇDa'mɪł.
   qɛ'D·ak ɢʊtɢu' Dɪq̇u·'D.   <57(3)>
pɛ·''ma ɢʊ'ca a'm·ɪm ɢʊDɪnɪʙi·'nD ɢʊDɪnɪtu'xDa·D a'wa'Dik tcalaʙla·'c.
   ʙʊ'ɢʊlfan ɢɪ'n·ʊk ɢʊ'ca a'm·ɪm ɢɪnɪDɪ'tɢwɪn ɢʊ'ca pa'lak Dɪq̇u·'D.
   ɢu'sa-apa·'lak aʙʊ'm·ik ɢʊDyɪ'ɢlaDjaf ɢu'ca k̇ʊ'ʙfan awɪ'fyu.
pɛ·''ma ɢʊDɪnɪtʊ'ɢɪ Dɪyɛ'ɢlafʊn.
pɛ·''ma Dᴇna'na ɢut·ɛ'n·a·n ak̇we'ɪnafʊn.   <57(4)>
   ʙʊ'ɢʊlfan ɢʊ'ca a'm·ɪm ɢʊDɪnɪk̇we'ɪnafu.
ṫʊ'ɢ·ɪ-Dɪnɪk̇we'ɪnafɪn ʙʊ'ɢʊlfan ɢʊDɪnɪDɪ'tyɪ tcᴇDɪnɪDʊ'm·aɪ.
pɛ·''ma ɢʊ'sa-wapa·'lak aʙʊ'm·ik ɢʊDna'ɢɪt,
   me'ɪDj-yu·-ɢamɪhu'wɪ tcɪ''ɪ Dɪtyɛ'ɢla·t.
ʙʊ'ɢʊlfan-a'm·ɪm ɢʊnɪ'na'ɢɪt,   <57(5)>
   ɢʊ'cwɪ, sʊ'D·u DɪDɪDma''a. ||122:134||
   tcɪ''ɪ ɢʊDɪ'twi·.
   pu't'cnaq ɢut·ɛ'n·a'yu ʙʊ'ɢʊlfan Dᴇka'ʙya.
ɢʊDɪtha'l'wan Dᴇma'ma ɢʊDbu'k̇laɪ
   ɢʊDɪ't hɛ·''lʊm   <57(6)>
   ɢʊD'ʊ'k Dɪkɪ'uDɪn na'u-Dɪmu'smʊs.
Dᴇna'na ɢʊDbu'n ak̇we'ɪnafʊn.
   ɢɪ'n·ʊk ɢɪnɪk̇we'ɪnafʊ.
   tcɪ''ɪ wa'ŋq-la'f ɢʊD·ɪtk̇we'ɪnafʊ.
   ṗʊ'f·an tcɪ''ɪ Dᴇm·u'p̣ɪn ɢʊD·u'ṫyu.   <57(7)>
pɛ·''ma Dᴇna'na ɢʊDa'haɪ wa''an a'ntmat.
   ɢʊDpʊ'tpa·t ɢʊ'sa-a'ntmat.
pɛ·''ma qɛ'D·ak ɢʊDɪ'cDa·t ɢʊ'sa-a'ntmat Dɪkwɪ'tfʊn.
   tcɪ''ɪ ɢʊDɪ'tɢwɪt pu·'t'caq ɢʊ'ca-akwɪ'tfɪn.

Then when it got dark, the doctor woman arrived.   <57(8)>
   Everyone else, those who were to help the doctor, they arrived.
Then the doctor untied her shawl and her shoes.
Then she sat down close to the fire. ||122:136||
Then she warmed[7] her hands at the fire.
Then she took my head.   <57(9)>
  She did this also with my body.
  She warmed her hands.
  She rubbed her hands all over my head and my body.
Then she sang her songs.
  All the people took up her songs.   <57(10)>
  They beat their sticks.
  She sang the same song five times.
Then she sang a different song of hers.
  She sang the other song five times.
Then she went to work on my body and my head that half-night.   <57(11)>
Then, when she finished, all the people readied themselves.
  They went outside.
Then they washed their faces and their hands. ||122:138||
Then my mother fed all of those people.
  The doctor woman did not want to eat.   <57(12)>
Everyone having finished their food, then that doctor said to them, those people,

  "In two nights, then I will treat this sickness."
The people said,
  "Alright."   <57(13)>
Then my mother gave me the chicken broth.
  I took a half cup.
Then my father and mother went to sleep.
  I, too, slept that entire night.
Next day they got up.   <57(14)>
  My father went outside.
    He fed his horses and his cows.
  My mother made breakfast. ||122:140||
They having finished their meal, my father went outside.
  He did all of his work.   <57(15)>

pɛ·"ma ɢʊdıthu·'wı ɢu'ca-wapa·'laq-aʙʊ'm·ık ɢʊdʊomwa·'l. <57(8)>

ʙʊ'ɢʊlfan-yu· ɢʊ'ca-a'm·ım ɢʊdınıɢɛ'm'ya·t ɢʊsa-apa·'laq ɢıdınıwa·'l

pɛ·"ma ɢu'sa-apa·'laq ɢʊd_skwı'lskwa·t ɒılı'cœl na'u-ɒılʊ'm·ʊf.

pɛ·"ma ɢʊd_sı'y·u yɛ'ɒj ɒjaɢʊ'sa ha'm·ı. ||122:136||

pɛ·"ma ɢʊd·u'kna·t ɒı'la'qʷ ɒjɛɢʊ'sa-aha'm·ı.

ʙɛ·"ma ɢʊdı'tɢwın ɒa'mıł <57(9)>

pɛ'sa-ɢʊtmı'u'nan yu·' tcɛɒaka'ʙya.

ɢʊd·u'ɢ·na·t ɒı'la'qʷ

ɢʊty·ı'fya·t ɒı'la'qʷ tcɛʙʊ'ɢʊlfan ɒa'mıł na'u ɒɛka'ʙya.

pɛ·"ma qɛ'ɒ·ak ɢutɢu·'-ɒıɋu'ɒ.

ʙʊ'ɢʊlfan-a'm·ım ɢʊ·nıɒı'tɢwın-ɒıɋu'ɒ <57(10)>

ɢʊdınıɋwa·'łɋwa·ɒ ɒı'nı'wa'ɒık.

qɛ'ɒ·ak ɢutɢu·' ɢu'ca-wa·"an ɒıɋu'ɒ wa'nfu.

pɛ·"ma ɢutɢu·' aɒaı'wan ɒıɋu'ɒ.

ɢutɢu·' ɢu'sa ɒaı'wan ɒıɋu'ɒ wa'nfu.

pɛ·"ma qɛ'ɒ·ak ɢʊd·la'ftweı tcɛɒaka'ʙya tcɛɒa'mıł ɢʊ·'sa wakʊ'ʙfan awı'fyu. <57(11)>

pɛ·"ma ɢʊtʊ'ɢ·ı ʙʊ'ɢʊlfan a'm·ım ɢʊnıtɛ'n·atcwu·n

ɢʊdınıɒnı·"ı hɛ·"lʊm.

ʙɛ·"ma ɢʊdınıɒku·"uł ɒınıkwa'l·ak nau-ɒı'la'qʷ. ||122:138||

pɛ·"ma ɒɛna'na ɢʊdnıt·u'k ʙʊ'ɢʊlfan ɢʊ'sa-a'm·ım.

ɢʊ'sa-apa·'laq aʙʊ'm·ık ɢɛ'ɒ·ak wa'ŋq ɢutʾa'mɒju ɒʊmtkweı'nafʊ. <57(12)>

ʙʊ'ɢʊlfan-a'm·ım ɢʊnıtʊ'ɢ·ı ɒınıkweı'nafʊn. pɛ·"ma ɢʊ'ca wapa·'lak ɢʊdna'ɢıt tcɛɢı'n·ʊk ɢʊ'sa-a'm·ım,

ɢamıɢɛ'fʊ ɒıhu·'ı pɛ·"ma tcı·"ı ɒıtyɛ·'kla·t hɛ'ca-wa-ı'lfıt.

ɢı'n·ʊk-a'm·ım ɢʊn·ıɒna'ɢıt,

ɢʊ'cwı. <57(13)>

pɛ·"ma ɒɛna'na ɢʊdı'ɒ·at ɢʊ'ca chicken ɒʊ'mpça.

tcı·"ı ɢʊdı'tɢwıt kʊ'ʙfan a'u'cɢan.

pɛ·"ma ɢı'n·ʊk ɒɛma·'ma ɒɛna'na ɢʊdınıɒı'tweı.

tcı·"ı-yu· ɢʊdı'twı· ʙʊ'ɢʊlfan ɢʊ'sa-awıfyu.

ɢʊdıtme'ıɒj ɢı'n·ʊk ɢun·ıtʙu'klaı. <57(14)>

ɒɛma·'ma ɢʊdı't-hɛ·"lʊm

ɢʊd·ʊ'k ɒıkı'uɒın nau-ɒımu'smus.

ɒɛna'na ɢʊdʙʊ'n-akweı'nafʊn. ||122:140||

ɢʊnıtʊ'ɢ·ı-ɒınıkweı'nafʊn ɒɛma·'ma ɢʊdı't-hɛ·"lʊm

ɢʊd_lu·"nʊf ʙʊ'ɢʊlfan a'ɢ·a. <57(15)>

He turned out all his horses from the big corral, (also) all his cows.

My mother cleaned the house.

She washed the floors.

I laid in bed all day.

I could not sit (up). <57(16)>

I was in very poor health.

My body was not strong.

Then, when it got dark, my mother made supper.

My father put his horses in the stable.

He fed them hay. <57(17)>

When all the cows came back close to the barn, then my father fed all the cows.

Then my father came into the house.

He got ready to eat.

My mother, having finished all the food, she put it on the table. ||122:142||

Then they ate. <57(18)>

Finished with their meal, then my mother tidied up.

She washed all the dishes.

She put all the dishes into the cupboard.

Then my father and mother [_?_].[8]

When it was almost ten o'clock they got ready to go to bed.

Early the next day they got up early. <57(19)>

My mother made breakfast.

My father went outside.

He fed all his horses and his cows.

Then they ate. <57(20)>

Finished with their meal, then he put his horses outside.

He put a portion of those cows in the small corral.

<58> Diagnosis and Treatment

Then two of my mother's brothers arrived to help my father slaughter a one-year-old calf. ||123:2||

They killed that calf.

When they finished, then they hung the calf in the woodshed. <58(2)>

My father cut off one of its legs to carry into the house.

Then my mother made all kinds of good food to feed the people who were arriving that night.

ɢutɢu'ʹ ᴅɪkɪ'uᴅɪn hɛ·ʹʹlʊm tcɛʙa'l-aq̇a'l·aẋ ʙʊ'ɢʊlfan-ᴅɪmu'smus.

ᴅɛna'·na ɢʊt·ɛ'n·a·n tcɛha'm·ɪ·.

ɢʊtku'ʹuɫ ɢʊ'ca-ala'ʙla·c.

tcɪ'ʹ·ɪ ɢʊtwe'ɪᴅɪt ʙʊ'ɢʊlfan-a'ʹmpyan.

wa'ŋq-la'f ɢumᴅɪt_cɪ'y·u.   <57(16)>

ṗʊ'fan tcɪ'ʹ·ɪ ɢʊthe'ɪʙintcu.

ᴅɛk̇a'ʙyɑ wa'ŋq ɢʊᴅ·a'lqᴅjɢʊ.

pɛ·ʹʹma ɢʊᴅɪthu'ʹwɪ ᴅɛna'·na ɢʊᴅʙʊ'n-ak̇we'ɪnafʊn.

ᴅɛma'·ma ɢʊᴅlu'ʹun ᴅɪkɪ'uᴅɪn ᴅjɛha'm·ɪ;

ɢʊᴅ'ʊ'k a'lu'q̇ᵘ.   <57(17)>

ʙʊ'ɢʊlfan-amu'smus ɢamnɪtcme'y·ɪ yɛ'ᴅj ᴅjɛɢʊ'sa lʊ'q̇ᵘ-ᴅʊ'm·aɪ. pɛ·ʹʹma ᴅɛma'·ma

ɢʊᴅ'ʊ'k ʙʊ'ɢʊlfan amu'cmuc.

pɛ·ʹʹma ᴅɛma'·ma ɢʊᴅ_la'm·u tcɛha'm·ɪ

ɢʊt·ɛ'n·atcwu·n ᴅumnɪᴅk̇we'ɪnafʊ.

ᴅɛna'·na ɢʊt·ʊ'ɢ·ɪ ʙʊ'ɢʊlfan ᴅɪk̇we'ɪnafʊn ɢʊtṗɪ'n tcɛlaᴅa'm.   ‖122:142‖

pɛ·ʹʹma ɢɪ'n·ʊk ɢʊᴅɪnɪtk̇we'ɪnafʊ.   <57(18)>

ṫʊ'ɢ·ɪ-ᴅɪnɪk̇we'ɪnafʊn pɛ·ʹʹma ᴅɛna'·na ɢʊt·ɛ'n·a·n

ʙʊ'ɢʊlfan akwa'ᴅ ɢʊᴅk̇u'ʹuɫ.

ɢɛ'ᴅ·ak ɢʊṫu'w·an ʙʊ'ɢulfan akwa'ᴅ tcɛcupboard.

pɛ·ʹʹma ᴅɛma'·ma na'u-ᴅɛna'·na ɢɪ'n·ʊk ɢʊᴅɪnɪlɛ'ʙnɪtcfuɪ.

yɛ'ᴅj ɢumnɪᴅɪ'nfyaf-aᴅɪ'nᴅɪn pɛ·ʹʹma ɢɪ'n·ʊk ɢʊᴅɪnɪtɛ'n·atcwu·n ᴅumnɪcɢʊ'mwaɪ.

me'ɪᴅj ɢʊᴅɪtha'l'wan ɢʊᴅɪnɪcʙʊ'ɢlaɪ ha'l'wan.   <57(19)>

ᴅɛna'·na ɢʊᴅʙʊ'n-ak̇we'ɪnafʊn.

ᴅɛma'·ma ɢʊᴅ·ɪ't-hɛ·ʹʹlʊm

ɢʊᴅ'ʊ'k ʙʊ'ɢʊlfan ᴅɪkɪ'uᴅɪn nau-ᴅɪmu'cmuc.

pɛ·ʹʹma ɢʊᴅɪnɪtk̇we'ɪnafʊ.   <57(20)>

ṫʊ'ɢ·ɪ-ᴅɪnɪk̇we'ɪnafɪn, pɛ·ʹʹma ɢʊtɢu'ʹu hɛ·ʹʹlʊm ᴅɪɢɪ'uᴅɪn.

ɢʊᴅ_lu'ʹun k̇u'ʙfan ɢʊ'ca mu'cmuc tcɛᴅɪ'ʹt'saq aq̇a'l·aẋ

<58> Diagnosis and Treatment

pɛ·ʹʹma ɢɛ'm ɢʊ'ca ᴅɛna'·na ᴅɪʙɪ'ɢwak ɢʊᴅɪnɪmu·'ɢ ᴅamnɪɢɛ·'m'ya·t ᴅɛma'·ma.

ᴅʊmnɪᴅa'haɪ wa'ʹan ᴅɪ·'t'saq amu'cmuc. wa'ʹan ᴅɪmɪt'su.   ‖123:2‖

ɢʊᴅɪnɪᴅa'haɪ ɢʊ'sa-waᴅɪ·'t'saq-amu'cmuc

ɢʊᴅɪnɪṫʊ'ɢ·ɪ pɛ·ʹʹma ɢʊᴅɪnɪça'l·aɫ ɢʊ'ca-mu'cmuc tcɛ'a'waᴅ·ɪk ᴅʊ'm·aɪ.   <58(2)>

ᴅɛma'·ma ɢʊᴅk̇u'ʙ·ʊn wa'ʹan ᴅɪlu'ʹʊn aᴅɪ'tk̇u ᴅjaha'm·ɪ.

ʙɛ·ʹʹma ᴅɛna'·na ɢʊtʙu'n ʙu'ɢʊlfan a'w·ɛw waᴅɛ'n·a ak̇we'ɪnafʊnak ᴅamnɪ'ʊ'k ɢʊ'ca

a'm·ɪm ɢʊmnɪtwa'l ɢʊ'ca wahu'wɪ.

Then when it was nearly dark, my mother said to her brothers and my father,   <58(3)>
  "You all get ready for supper!"
Then she put all the food on the table.
Then she said,
  "Everybody eat!
  These people are almost here."   <58(4)>
Then, having finished their meal, they went outside. ||123:3a||
  They helped my father feed the horses and cows.
Then it got dark.
Then the doctor woman arrived.
  All the other people also arrived.   <58(5)>
Then that doctor made ready to doctor.
That night many people came.
  They filled that house of ours.
Then the doctor spoke to those people.
  She told them what sort of sickness I had.   <58(6)>
She said,
  "This child's sickness is very bad."
Then she sat down close to me and to the fire.
  She warmed her hands on the fire.
Then she rubbed my body and my head,   <58(7)>
  "There is a lahl-worm in this child's head.
  That lahl-worm is very strong. ||123:4a||
  Now I will try my heart.
  Soon I will take hold of that lahl-worm.
  Perhaps another Indian doctor sent this lahl-worm into the back of his head."
Then she sang her song.   <58(8)>
  Everyone took up her song.
  They knocked sticks.
  She sang her first song five times.
She finished that first song of hers, then she sang another one of her songs.   <58(9)>
  Five times she sang that song.
Then she sang a very strong song.
  That Tamanawas-power (*yúłmi*) of hers was very strong.
  They called her Tamanawas-power *agé·mšandi.*[9]
    That Tamanawas-power resides in five [lakes?[10]].   <58(10)>

ʙɛ·''ma yeꞌdj ɢuᴅɪᴅhuꞌwɪ ᴅɛnaꞌna ɢuᴅnɪ'cɪn tcɛᴅɪʙɪ'ɢwak na'u-tcɛᴅɛmaꞌma,   <58(3)>
  mɪꞌᴅɪ tɛ'n·atcwu·n tcɛᴅʊpkwe'ɪnafʊ.
pɛ·''ma qɛꞌᴅ·ak ɢuᴅp̓iꞌn ʙʊ'ɢʊlfan k̓we'ɪnafʊ tcɛlaᴅaꞌm
pɛ·''ma ɢuᴅnaꞌɢɪt
  mɪꞌᴅɪ pckwe'ɪnafʊ.
  yeꞌdj nɪwaꞌl ɢʊꞌsa-a·ꞌm·ɪm.   <58(4)>
pɛ·''ma t̓ʊꞌɢɪ-ᴅɪnɪkwe'ɪnafʊ ɢuᴅɪnɪᴅɪꞌt-hɛ·''lʊm ||123:3a||
  ɢuᴅɪnɪtɢaꞌm'yat ᴅɛmaꞌma ᴅʊmnɪꞌʊ'k ɢʊꞌca-kɪꞌuᴅɪn nau-muꞌcmuc.
pɛ·''ma ɢuᴅjɪꞌk̓yu·.
pɛ·''ma ɢʊꞌsa-apaꞌlaq-aʙʊꞌm·ɪk ɢuᴅmuꞌɢ.
  ʙʊ'ɢʊlfan-yu· aꞌm·ɪm ɢuᴅɪnɪmuꞌɢ.   <58(5)>
pɛ·''ma ɢu·sa-apaꞌlaq ɢʊt·ɛ'n·atcwu·n ᴅʊmᴅɪtyɛꞌɢlɪnfaɪ.
ɢuꞌca-wawɪꞌfyu, haꞌl·u· aꞌm·ɪm ɢuᴅɪnɪwaꞌl.
  ɢuᴅʙʊꞌyɛᴅju ɢʊꞌca sʊꞌᴅ·u ᴅɪᴅ·uꞌm·aɪ.
pɛ·''ma ɢu·sa-apaꞌlaq ɢutyuꞌ'un tcɛɢʊꞌsa-a·ꞌm·ɪm.
  ɢuᴅnɪꞌsɪn, aꞌw·ɛw tcɪꞌ'ɪ ᴅɪꞌɪꞌlfʊnyaq.   <58(6)>
ɢuᴅnaꞌɢɪt
  p̓ʊꞌf·an ʊmqaꞌsq hɛꞌca-awaꞌp̓ɪ ᴅɪꞌɪꞌlfan.
ʙɛ·''ma qɛꞌᴅ·ak ɢuᴅ_sɪꞌyu· yeꞌdj-djɛtcɪꞌ'ɪ na'u-tcɛɢʊꞌsa-ahaꞌm·ɪ.
  ɢuᴅ'ʊꞌq̓na·t ᴅɪꞌlaꞌqʷ djɛɢʊꞌsa-ahaꞌm·ɪ.
pɛ·''ma ɢʊtyɪꞌfya·t ᴅɛkaꞌbya na'u-ᴅɛᴅaꞌmɪł.   <58(7)>
  waꞌ'an ɢu·sa tcɛᴅɪᴅaꞌm·ɪł hɛꞌca-awaꞌp̓ɪ maʙɪꞌnᴅ waꞌ'an alaꞌl.
  ɢʊꞌca alaꞌl p̓ʊꞌf·an ʊmᴅaꞌlqᴅʊɢu. ||123:4a||
  ʙɛ·''ma tcɪꞌ'ɪ ᴅɪt·ʊꞌk̓nɪn ᴅʊmhuꞌp̓ɪn.
  ᴅɪꞌs ᴅɪᴅɪꞌtɢwɪn ɢu·sa alaꞌl.
  eꞌɪkɪn waꞌ'an amɛꞌnmɪyak apaꞌlaq ɢutɢuꞌ ɢʊꞌsa alaꞌl tcɛhɛꞌnt'c ɢⱳꞌk ᴅɪᴅaꞌmɪł.
pɛ·''ma qɛꞌᴅ·ak ɢutɢuꞌ-ᴅɪq̓uꞌᴅ.   <58(8)>
  ʙʊ'ɢʊlfan-aꞌm·ɪm ɢuᴅɪꞌtɢwɪn-ᴅɪq̓uꞌᴅ
  ɢunɪt̓ʊꞌx̣ᴅa·ᴅ-aꞌwaꞌᴅɪk.
  ɢutɢuꞌ waꞌ'an ᴅɪq̓uꞌᴅ waꞌnfu.
ɢut̓uꞌɢɪ ɢuꞌca-waꞌ'an-ᴅɪq̓uꞌᴅ pɛ·''ma ɢutɢuꞌ waꞌ'an aᴅaꞌɪ'wan ᴅɪq̓uꞌᴅ.   <58(9)>
  waꞌnfu ɢutɢuꞌ ɢuꞌca-aq̓uꞌᴅ.
ʙɛ·''ma ɢutɢuꞌ waꞌ'an waᴅaꞌlqᴅʊɢu ᴅʊq̓uꞌᴅ.
  ɢʊꞌca qɛꞌᴅ·ak waᴅaꞌlqᴅʊɢu ᴅɪyuꞌłmɪ.
  ɢuꞌca-ayuꞌłmɪ ɢuᴅnɪkwuꞌn aɢɛꞌmcanᴅɪ'.
    ɢuꞌsa ayuꞌłmɪ maʙɪꞌnᴅ huꞌw·an ᴅɪwaꞌmpɢɪ.   <58(10)>

No one ever saw that Tamanawas-power.
  It stayed in the mountains a long time.
She sang her Tamanawas-power song five times, ||123:6||
  "Soon now I will take hold of that lahl-worm."
Then two men grasped the doctor from behind.   <58(11)>
  They tied that doctor around the chest with a strong cloth strip.
Then the doctor told my mother,
  "Bring a pan and water!
  Soon I will throw that lahl-worm there."
Then she sang one more song.   <58(12)>
Then she sang the song four times.
When she had sung her song five times, then the doctor woman said to my mother,
  "Turn him like this.
    Down on his stomach!
  Then I will take hold of that lahl-worm."
Then my mother took my head.   <58(13)>
Then the two men took hold of the doctor by the back.
Then the doctor took hold of the lahl-worm in my head.
  She pulled out that lahl-worm. ||123:8||
Then those two men took hold of her from behind.
  She took hold of that lahl-worm   <58(14)>
Then she stood.
  Those two men fought with that doctor.
  One took her by her hands.
  They threw her on the floor.
  They put her hands in that water.   <58(15)>
Then the doctor sang her song.
Then she took the lahl-worm.
  She took it in her hand.
Then she blew[11] on the lahl-worm.
Then she showed it to the people.   <58(16)>
  That lahl-worm was red.
Then she bit that lahl-worm.
  She killed that lahl-worm.
Then she said to those people,
  "Whichever doctor placed this lahl-worm into this child, soon you will know.

wa'ŋq-la'f e'y·a ɢuthⱷ'ᴅ ɢʊ'ca-ayu'łmɪ.

mu'ɪnu maʙi·'nᴅ· ha'l·u· tcɛɢʊ'ca amɛ'fʊ.

wa'nfʊ qɛ'ᴅ·ak ɢutɢʊ' ɢʊ'ca ayu'łmɪ ᴅɪɋu'ᴅ.　　　　　　　　||123:6||

　　pɛ·''ma tcɪ'ɪ ᴅɪ·'s ᴅɪᴅɪ'tɢwɪn ɢu'sa ala'l.

pɛ·''ma ɢɛ·'m amu'ɪ ɢun·ɪᴅɪ'tɢwɪn tcɛɢu'sa pa'laq tcɛᴅɪ·ha'nt'c.　　　　　<58(11)>

　　ɢut'ɛ·'m·a·t ɢʊsa-apa'laq tcɛ'ᴅʊmhu·'ꝑɪn waᴅa'lqᴅuɕu ahɪ'ktcum.

pɛ·''ma ɢʊ'sa-apa'laq ɢʊᴅnɪ'cɪn ᴅɛna'na

　　cmʊ'k̓ʊ ama'lax na'u ama'mpɢa.

　　ɢʊ'ca·ʙɛ·ᴅ ᴅɪ'c ᴅɪᴅɢu' ɢʊ'ca-ala'l.

pɛ·''ma ɢutɢʊ' wa''an-yu' aᴅa'ɪfʊn ᴅɪɋu'ᴅ.　　　　　　　　　　　　<58(12)>

pɛ·''ma ɢutɋu'ᴅ ta'ʙ·af ɢʊ'ca-aɋu'ᴅ.

ᴅɪᴅɪwa'nfu-ᴅɪɋu'ᴅ pɛ·''ma qɛ'ᴅ·ak-ɢuca-apa'laq ɢʊᴅnɪ'cɪn ᴅɛna'na

　　ski̓'lfat hɛ'ca-awɛ''a

　　　tcɛᴅɪᴅʊmꝑu wa'l.

　　pɛ·''ma tcɪ'ɪ ᴅɪᴅɪ'tɢwɪn ɢʊ'sa-ala'l.

pɛ·''ma ᴅɛna'na ɢʊᴅɪ'tɢwɪn ᴅa'mł.　　　　　　　　　　　　　　<58(13)>

pɛ·''ma ɢʊ'ca-aɢɛ·'m-amu'ɪ ɢʊᴅɪnɪᴅɪ'tɢwɪn ha'nt'c tcɛɢʊ'sa-wapa'laq ᴅɪʙi'l.

pɛ·''ma ɢʊ'sa-apa'laq ɢʊᴅɪ'tɢwɪn hɛ'sa-ala'l tcɛᴅɪᴅa'mł.

　　ɢʊᴅmɪ'n·ɪ ɢʊ'sa-ala'l.　　　　　　　　　　　　　　　||123:8||

pɛ·''ma ɢu'sa-aɢɛ·'m-a'm'uɪ ɢʊᴅɪnɪᴅɪ'tɢwɪn tcɛᴅ·ɪha'nt'c.

　　ᴅɪᴅɪᴅɪ'tɢwɪn ɢʊ'sa-ala'l　　　　　　　　　　　　　　　<58(14)>

pɛ·''ma ɢʊᴅ·ɪ'sᴅap

　　ɢʊ'sa-aɢɛ·'m-amu'ɪ. ɢʊᴅɪnɪᴅwa'qnɪyaf tcɛɢʊ'sa-pa'laq

　　wa''an ɢʊᴅ·ɪ'tɢwɪn ᴅɪ'la'qʷ

　　ɢʊᴅɪnɪtɢʊ' ᴅjɛlaʙla·'c

　　ɢʊᴅɪnɪᴅɢʊ' ᴅɪ'la'qʷ tcɛɢʊ'ca-ama'mpɢa.　　　　　　　　　<58(15)>

pɛ·''ma ɢu'sa-apa'laq ɢutɢʊ'-ᴅɪɋu'ᴅ

pɛ·''ma ɢʊᴅ·ɪ'tɢwɪn ɢʊ'sa-ala'l.

　　ɢʊᴅ·ɪ'tɢwɪn tcɛᴅ·ɪ'la'qʷ

pɛ·''ma ɢʊᴅʙʊ'f·ɪ tcɛɢʊ'ca-ala'l

pɛ·''ma ɢutha'ᴅɪnɪ tcɛɢʊ'ca-a'm·ɪm.　　　　　　　　　　　　<58(16)>

　　ɢʊ'sa-ala'l ɢʊt_sa'l.

pɛ·''ma ɢʊᴅyɪ'kya·t ɢʊ'sa-ala'l.

　　ɢʊᴅ·a'haɪ ɢʊ'sa-ala'l.

pɛ·''ma ɢʊᴅnɪ'cɪn tcɛɢʊ'sa-a'm·ɪm,

　　e'ya ɢʊ'sa aʙa·'laq ɢʊᴅɪtɢʊ' hɛ'ca-ala'l tcɛhɛ'ca-u'wa'ꝑɪ ᴅɪ's mɪ'ᴅɪ ᴅɪᴅupyʊ'ɢʊn

Whichever doctor it was who did this to this child, that doctor will soon get sick."

Then she finished her doctoring. ||123:10|| <58(17)>
Then those people went outside.
   They washed their faces and hands to prepare for eating.   <58(18)>
Then my mother and two girls prepared the table.
   They laid out all kinds of food.
Then my mother said to the people,
   "Come in and eat!"
   A portion of the people ate.   <58(19)>
Finished with their meal, then they went outside.
   The two girls took all the dishes.
   They washed them.
Then they set out new dishes.
Then they laid out a lot of food.   <58(20)>
Then my mother spoke,
   "Whoever has not eaten, sit down to your meal!" ||123:12||
Then, all having finished their meal, the girls cleared the table.

   They washed everything.   <58(21)>
   They put it away.
Then my father said,
   "All you people come into the house!"
   Everyone entered.
   They sat down.   <58(22)>
Then my father spoke,
   "I will give this doctor woman one cow, one horse, and five blankets.

   I will pay this doctor woman."
Then everyone returned to their homes.   <58(23)>
Then my father and my mother got themselves ready.
   They went to bed.
   I slept very well.

<59> Recovery and Comeuppance
When it was morning, they got up.
   My father fed his horses and his cows.

ɢʊ'sa-wapa·'laq e'y·a ɢu'sa-apa·'laq pɛ'ca ɢʊtmɪ'u'nan tcɛhɛ'ca a'wa'pɪ. ɢʊ'sa-
  wapa·'laq ᴅɪ·'s ɢʊᴅ'ɪ'lfʊt.

pɛ·''ma qɛ'ᴅ·ak ɢʊt'ʊ'ɢɪ ᴅɪ'yɛ'klɪnfʊn. ||123:10|| <58(17)>

pɛ·''ma ɢɪ'n·ʊk ɢʊ'sa-a'm·ɪm ɢuᴅɪnɪᴅɪ't hɛ·''lʊm
  ɢʊᴅɪnɪtku''uł ᴅɪnɪkwa'l·ak ᴅɪnɪ'la'qʷ tɛ'n·atcwu·n ᴅamnɪkwe'ɪnafʊn.   <58(18)>

pɛ·''ma ᴅɛna·'na nau-ɢɛ·'m-aʙɪ'na·ᴅjt ɢuᴅɪnɪtɛ'n·an ala'ᴅ·a·'m
  ɢʊᴅɪnɪtp̓ɪ·'n ʙʊ'ɢʊlfan a·''wɛ·'w ak̓we'ɪnafʊnak.

pɛ·''ma ᴅɛna·'na ɢuᴅna'ɢɪt tcɛɢʊ'ca-a'm·im,
  mɪ'ᴅ·ɪ ʙcla'm·ʊ ʙck̓we'ɪnafʊ.
  k̓ʊ'pfan ɢʊ'sa-a'm·ɪm ɢuᴅnɪᴅk̓we'ɪnafʊ.   <58(19)>

ɢʊnɪtʊ'ɢɪ ᴅɪnɪk̓we'ɪnafʊn pɛ·''ma ɢʊᴅɪnɪᴅɪ't-hɛ·''lʊm.
  ɢɪ'n·ʊk-ɢʊ'sa-aʙɪ'na·tst ɢʊᴅɪnɪᴅɪ'tɢwin ʙʊ'ɢʊlfan ɢʊ'ca-akwɪ't
  ɢʊᴅɪnɪtku''uł.

ʙɛ·''ma ɢʊᴅɪntɛ'n·a·n waᴅa'ɪ'wan akwa't.

pɛ·''ma ɢʊᴅɪnɪtp̓ɪ·'n ha'l·u· akwe'ɪnafʊnak.   <58(20)>

pɛ·''ma ᴅɛna·'na ɢuᴅna'ɢɪt
  e'y·a wa'ŋq-ma·'ʙɪt ɢuᴅɪtk̓we'ɪnaf mɪ'ᴅ·ɪ psɪ'y·u ᴅɪk̓we'ɪnafun ||123:12||

pɛ·''ma ʙʊ'ɢʊlfan ɢʊn·ɪtu'ɢɪ-ᴅɪnɪk̓we'ɪnafʊn ɢʊ'sa-aʙɪ'na·tst ɢʊᴅɪnɪla'k̓la·t
  ɢʊ'sa-ala'ᴅ·a·'m
  ɢʊᴅɪnɪtk̓u''uł ʙʊ'ɢʊlfan a'ɢfan   <58(21)>
  ɢʊᴅɪnɪt_lu''un.

pɛ·''ma ᴅɛma·'ma ɢuᴅna'ɢɪt
  ʙʊ'ɢʊlfan mɪ'ᴅ·ɪ a'm·ɪm psla'm·ʊ ᴅjɛha'm·ɪ.
  ʙʊ'ɢʊlfan-a'm·ɪm ɢʊᴅɪnɪt_sla'm·ʊ
  ɢʊᴅɪnɪt_sɪ'y·u.   <58(22)>

pɛ·''ma ᴅɛma·'ma ɢutyu''wn
  tcɪ''ɪ ᴅɪᴅɪ'st hɛ'sa-pa·'laq aʙu'm·ɪk wa·''an amu'cmuc wa·''an-akɪ'uᴅɪn. nau hu'w·an
    aʙa'cɪcɢwa.
  qɛ'ᴅ·ak hɛ·'sa apa·'laq aʙu'm·ɪk tcɪ''ɪ ᴅɪᴅa'pna·t.

pɛ·''ma ʙʊ'ɢʊlfan a'm·ɪm ɢʊᴅɪnɪᴅɪ'tyɪ tcɛᴅɪnɪᴅu'm·aɪ.   <58(23)>

pɛ·''ma ᴅɛma·'ma nau-ᴅɛna·'na ɢuᴅɪnɪtɛ'n·atcwu·n
  ɢʊᴅɪnɪᴅɪ'twɪ·.
  tcɪ''ɪ ɢuᴅɪ'twi· p̓u'f·an tɛ'n·a.

<59> Recovery and Comeuppance

ɢuᴅɪᴅme'ɪᴅj ɢɪ'n·uk ɢun·ɪtʙʊ'ɢlaɪ.
  ᴅɛma·'ma ɢut'u'k ᴅɪkɪ'uᴅɪn nau-ᴅɪmu'cmuc

My mother made food.

Then they ate. ||123:14|| <59(2)>

I was sound asleep.

When it was the middle of the morning near ten o'clock, I felt like getting up.

Then my mother washed (her? my?) face and hands.

She gave me a little of the chicken broth and chicken meat.

I ate a little of the chicken meat. <59(3)>

Then I slept.

For five days I just sat.

On the fifth day I ate a little.

Then each day I got a little stronger.

I was still very weak. <59(4)>

When it was nearly summer, perhaps two months, my body got strong (again).

Then I stood up.

I sat (up).

I got around a little.

Then, in about two weeks, that particular male doctor took sick. ||123:16|| <59(5)>

That male doctor was a very bad doctor.[12]

Then that doctor stood to his (Tamanawas) dance.

He watched for his Tamanawas-power.

He stood to his dance for five nights.

Lots of Indians came to that doctor's dance of his. <59(6)>

All these Indians here went to it.

My mother, she went to that doctor's dance of his.

Then the doctor stopped his dancing.

He couldn't dance anymore.

He was sick a long time.

Maybe a month (more), then he died. <59(7)>

ᴅɛna·'na ɢutʙʊ'n-aḱwe'ɪnafɪn

pɛ·''ma ɢɪ'n·ʊk ɢuᴅɪnɪḱwe'ɪnafu. ||123:14|| <59(2)>

  tcɪ''ɪ p̓ʊ'fan ɢutwe'ɪᴅɪt.

ɢuᴅɪtha'lʙam-a'a'm·pyan ye·'ᴅj ɢuᴅɪ·'nfyaf-aᴅɪ'nᴅɪn tcɪ''ɪ ᴅɛmhu·'p̓ɪn ɢuᴅʙu'ɢlaɪ.

pɛ·''ma ᴅɛna·na ɢutḱu''ul ᴅɛkwa'l·ak na'u-ᴅɪ'la'qʷ

  ɢuᴅ·i'ᴅ·at pu't'cnaq ɢʊ'ca-a'ntmat ᴅɪkwɪ'tfan na'u ɢu'sa-a'ntmat ᴅɪḱa'ʙya.

  tcɪ''ɪ ɢuᴅḱwi·'han pu't'snaq ɢu'sa-a'ntmat ᴅɪmu·'kʷ. <59(3)>

pɛ·''ma tcɪ''ɪ ɢuᴅɪ'twi·

  ɢuᴅɪtwa·'nfʊ a'mpyan tcɪ''ɪ ɢut_sɪ'y·u.

  ɢu'sa-wa'nfu-a'mpyan tcɪ''ɪ-ɢʊtḱwe'ɪnafʊ pu't'snaq.

pɛ·''ma ʙʊ'ɢulfan-a'mpyan tcɪ''ɪ ɢuᴅ·a'lⱥyu pu't'snaq.

  p̓ʊ'fan tcɪ''ɪ ɢumhe'ɪʙɪnᴅju. <59(4)>

ɢuᴅɪᴅyɛ'ᴅj ɢuᴅɪᴅmɛ·'ɢʷ e'ɪkɪn ɢɛ·'m-aᴅω'ʙ tcɪ''ɪ ᴅɪḱa'pya ɢuᴅ·a'lⱥyu.

pɛ·''ma ɢuᴅ·ɛ'sᴅap

  ɢut_sɪ'y·u

  p̓ʊ't'snaq ɢut'ɪ'ᴅ.

pɛ·''ma e'ɪkɪn ɢɛ·'m-asa'nᴅɪ ɢʊ'sa wa''an a'mu'ɪ apa·'laq ɢutɪ'lfɪt. ||123:16|| <59(5)>

  ɢu'sa a'mu'ɪ apa·'laq mɛ·'nfan ɢutqa'sq apa·'laq.

pɛ·''ma ɢu'ca-pa·'laq ɢutya't·un-ᴅɪyɛ'l'w.

  ɢut'ʊ'ᴅnɪɢwan ᴅɪyu'lmɪ.

    ɢutya't·un ᴅɪyɛ'l'w hu'w·an-awɪ'fyu.

  ʙʊ'ɢulfan-a'w·ɛw amɛ·'nmɪ-ɢʊ'ca ɢuᴅɪnɪᴅɪ't tcɛɢʊ'sa-apa·'laq ᴅɪyɛ'l'w. <59(6)>

    ʙʊ'ɢulfan hɛ'sa a'mɛ·'nmɪ'yak ɢuᴅɪnɪᴅɪ·'f.

    ᴅɛna·'na qɛ'ᴅ·ak ɢuᴅɪ't ᴅjɛɢu'sa-wapa·'laq ᴅɪyɛ'l'w.

pɛ·''ma ɢu'sa-apa·'laq. ɢutʼu'ɢɪ-ᴅɪyɛ'l'w

  wa'ŋq-la'f ɢω·'k ɢumnɪᴅyɛ'l'wi .

  ɢut'ɪ'lfʊt mu'ɪnu.

e'ɪkɪn wa''an-aᴅω'ʙ pɛ·''ma ɢutfu''u. <59(7)>

Another Off-Reservation Work Trip[1]

[previously untranslated]

<60> Preparing to Leave
My father worked on summer days.
 He plowed the ground.
He worked for a month and a half.
Having finished plowing the ground, then he sowed wheat.
 He harrowed the wheat field. ||123:16a|| <60(2)>
Then he sowed oats.
Having finished all that work, then he fixed all the fences on the place.
Having finished with everything, he took the cows and horses.
 He let them go in the mountains.
 Only two horses remained.
Then he said to my mother,   <60(3)>
 "In two weeks we will go to Chemeketa (Salem).
 There I will look for work."
Then my mother prepared everything.
 She placed everything in a trunk.
Then my father took that big trunk to the house of one of our uncles (?).[2] <60(4)>

He said to the uncle (?),
 "You watch over this trunk and my place!
 I am going to go across the Willamette to Chemeketa.   <60(5)>
  There I will be working for two months.
 Then in two months I will come back." ||123:18||

<61> Introduction to Ed Goss
Then a week later we crossed the Willamette River.
 We arrived at Chemeketa.
There my mother's brothers were staying.
My father asked,
 "Do you know where I can find work?"
My mother's older brother said,   <61(2)>
 "Yes, there is a White man who needs lots of fence (rails).

Another Off-Reservation Work Trip

<60> Preparing to Leave

ᴅɛmaʹma ɢѡ·ʹk ɢᴜt_luʹʹnᴜf tcɛmɛ·ʹɢʷ-aʹmpyan.

   ɢѡ·ʹk ɢᴜᴅplaʹɋ̇lu·t haʹŋk̇lu·p.

ɢᴜt_luʹʹnᴜf waʹʹan-aᴅѡ·ʹʙ naʹᴜᴅik̇ʊʹʙfan.

ɢᴜt·ʊʹɢɪ-ᴅᴜmɪnɪplaʹɋ̇lu·t haʹŋk̇lu·p pɛ·ʹʹma ɢѡ·ʹk ɢᴜtɢᴜʹ asaʹʙlɪl tcɛhaʹŋk̇lu·p.

   ɢѡ·ʹk ɢᴜtkuʹm·u·t ɢʊʹsa-asaʹʙlɪl ᴅɪhaʹŋk̇lu·p.   ‖123:16a‖   <60(2)>

pɛ·ʹʹma ɢᴜtɢᴜʹ alawɛ·ʹn tcɛhaʹŋk̇lu·p.

ʙʊʹɢᴜlfan ɢᴜt·ʊʹɢɪ ɢʊʹsa ᴅɪluʹʹnafᴜnak pɛ·ʹʹma ɢᴜtɛ·ʹn·a·n ʙʊʹɢᴜlfan ɋ̇aʹl·ax̣ tcɛɢʊʹca aʹn·u.

ɢᴜt·ʊʹɢɪ ʙᴜʹɢᴜlfan ɢᴜᴅɪʹtɢwɪn ᴅɪmuʹcmᴜc naʹu-ᴅɪkɪʹuᴅɪn,

   ɢᴜᴅɪʹtk̇u tcɛmɛʹf·u,

   yɛʹlfan ɢɛʹm akɪʹuᴅɪn ɢᴜᴅṗiʹn.

pɛ·ʹʹma ɢᴜᴅnaʹɢɪt tcɛᴅɛnaʹna,   <60(3)>

   waʹʹan ɢamɪcaʹnᴅɪ ᴅiʹc ᴅɪᴅɪᴅ·ѡʹʹѡ tcɛtcɛmɪʹɢɪᴅɪ.

   ɢʊʹcaʙɛ·ᴅ tcɪʹʹɪ ᴅɪt'uʹᴅ aʹluʹʹnafᴜnak.

pɛ·ʹʹma ᴅɛnaʹna ɢᴜtɛ·ʹn·atcwu·n ʙᴜʹɢᴜlfan-aʹɢfan,

   ɢᴜt_luʹʹun ʙᴜʹɢᴜlfan aʹɢfan tcɛwaʹʹan alaʹk̇asɛ·t.

pɛ·ʹʹma ᴅɛmaʹma ɢᴜᴅɪʹtk̇u ɢʊʹca waʹʹan waʙaʹl alaʹk̇asɛʹt tcɛwaʹʹan ɢʊʹca   <60(4)>

   ᴅɪᴅɪᴅ_sᴅuʹm'wɪ tcɛᴅʊʹm·aɪ.

ɢᴜᴅnɪʹcɪn tcɛᴅɪᴅ_cᴅʊʹm'wɪ,

   maʹha ᴅɪᴅyuʹᴅnɪgwan hɛʹca laɢasɛ·ʹt nau-tcɪʹʹɪ ᴅɛʹaʹn·u.

   tcɪʹʹɪ ᴅɪᴅɪʹt ᴅjuʹhu· tcɛWillamette tcɛtcɛmɪʹɢɪᴅɪ.   <60(5)>

      tcɪʹʹɪ ɢʊʹsaʙɛ·ᴅ ᴅᴜmᴅɪt_luʹʹnᴜf ɢɛʹm-aᴅѡ·ʹʙ.

pɛ·ʹʹma ɢᴜmᴅɪtɢɛ·ʹm-aᴅѡ·ʹʙ tcɪʹʹɪ ᴅɪtmeʹy·u.   ‖123:18‖

<61> Introduction to Ed Goss

pɛ·ʹʹma ɢᴜᴅɪᴅwaʹʹan-asaʹnᴅɪ ɢᴜᴅɪᴅ·ѡʹʹѡ yɛʹlqfan tcɛWillamette maʹmpɢa,

   ɢᴜᴅwaʹl tcɛtcɛmɪʹɢɪᴅɪ.

ɢʊʹsaʙɛᴅ ᴅɛnaʹna ᴅɪk̇ʊʹn·ayaʙ ɢᴜᴅɪnɪʙiʹʹnᴅ.

ᴅɛmaʹma ɢᴜᴅnaʹɢɪt,

   mɪʹᴅɪ ʙɪcyʊʹɢ·ʊn hɛʹl·a tcɪʹʹɪ ɢᴜᴅɛ·ʹsᴅɛs aluʹʹnafᴜn?

ᴅɛnaʹna ᴅɪʙɪʹgwaɢyak ɢᴜᴅnaʹɢɪt,   <61(2)>

   hɛⁿ·ʹʹa, waʹʹan awuʹm·u· aʹmuʹɪ ṫaʹmᴅju haʹl·u· aɋ̇aʹl·ax̣.

I will bring you to that White man.
  His name is Ed Goss.
  He is a very good man."
They got to the White man's house.   <61(3)>
My father's brother (that is, brother-in-law[3]) spoke to the White man,
  "This is my older brother.
  He wants to work."
The man said,
  "Okay, I want two thousand fence-rails to be made.   <61(4)>
  I will give you a dollar and a half per one hundred fence-rails."
My father said,
  "Okay, I will take that work.
  Tomorrow I will come."
Then they returned to Chemeketa to where they were staying. ||123:20|| <61(5)>
He told my mother,
  "Tomorrow we will go to a place where I will work."

<62> Splitting Fence-Rails
My father took one young man to help make that fence.
Then, when they got ready, they went to the White man's place.
  They got to that man.
Then he took my father to the place where he wanted to make his fence.   <62(2)>
  There he prepared their tent.
Then, when it was morning, they worked.
  My father felled those fir trees, very good fir trees.
  He cut up (sectioned) those fir trees.   <62(3)>
Then the young man split the fence-rails.
  I myself, Bahawadas, was hard at work.[4]
The next day I helped my father.
  I cut (off) the limbs of those fir trees.
  We worked all day long.   <62(4)>
It took us almost four weeks to finish that work.
Then he said to that White man,
  "I have now finished your fence."
Then the man paid my father the money.
Then the White man said,   <62(5)>
  "I want fifty cords of fir wood.

tcɪ′′ɪ ᴅɪᴅɪ′tku tcɛma′ha tcɛgʊ′ca wa′m·u· am′u′ɪ.

    ɢɷ·′k ᴅʊ′ŋkwɪt Ed Goss.

    ṗʊ′f·an mɪtɛ′n·a aᴅja′ŋku.

ɢᴜᴅɪnɪᴅwa′l tcɛgʊ′ca wa′m·u· a′mu′ɪ. <61(3)>

ᴅɛma′′ma ᴅɪku′n·ayaʙ ɢᴜᴅna′ɢɪt tcɛgʊ′sa wa′m·u· am′u′ɪ,

    hɛ′sa tcɪ′′ɪ ᴅɪʙa′n·ak

    ɢɷ·′k ʊmt·a′mᴅju ᴅumlu·′′nʊf.

ɢu′sa-a′mu′ɪ ɢᴜᴅna′ɢɪt,

    ɢu′cwɪ, tcɪ′′ɪ tcɪt·a′mᴅju two thousand aq̇a′l·aẋ ᴅumᴅɪtʙu′n. <61(4)>

    tcɪ′′ɪ ᴅɪᴅɛ′sᴅap wa′′an na′u-ᴅɪku′ʙfan asq̇ɪ′nwaɪmaẋ tcɛwa′′an ᴅʊ′m̌ṗɪ aq̇a′laẋ.

ᴅɛma′′ma ɢᴜᴅna′ɢɪt,

    ɢu′cwɪ. tcɪ′′ɪ ᴅɪᴅɪ′tɢwɪn ɢu′sa lu·′′nafʊnak.

    ɢamɪme′ɪᴅj tcɪ′′ɪ ᴅɪᴅɪtma′′a.

pɛ·′′ma ɢɪ′n·ʊk ɢᴜᴅɪnɪcme′y·ɪ tcɛtcɛmɪ′ɢɪᴅɪ ha′l·a ɢʊ′sa ɢɪnɪᴅa′fʊtc. ||123:20|| <61(5)>

ɢʊᴅnɪ′cɪn ᴅɛna′′na,

    me′ɪᴅj ᴅɪᴅɪᴅ_sᴅɷ·′′ꙍ ᴅjɛha′l·a ɢʊ′sa tcɪ′′ɪ ɢᴜᴅɪᴅ_lu·′′un.

<62> Splitting Fence-Rails

ᴅɛma′′ma ɢᴜᴅɪ′tɢwɪn wa′′an asɪ′nfaf ɢumᴅɪᴅɢɛ′m′yat ɢʊ′sa ᴅumnɪʙʊ′n ɢʊ′sa aq̇a′l·aẋ.

pɛ·′′ma ɢᴜᴅɪnɪtɛ′n·atcwu·n, ɢᴜᴅ·ɪᴅsᴅɷ·′′ꙍ tcɛgʊ′sa-wa·m·u· a′mu′ɪ tcɛᴅʊ′n·u,

    ɢᴜᴅɪᴅwa′l tcɛgʊ′c·a a′mu′ɪ.

pɛ·′′ma ɢᴜᴅɪ′tku ᴅɛma′′ma tcɛhɛ′l·a ɢʊ·′ca ɢᴜᴅɪt·a′mᴅju ᴅʊmbu′n ᴅɪq̇a′l·aẋ. <62(2)>

    ɢu′caʙɛ·ᴅ ɢut·ɛ′n·a·n ᴅɪn·ɪsɪ′lhaus.

pɛ·′′ma ɢᴜᴅɪᴅme′ɪᴅj ɢᴜᴅɪnɪlu·′′nuf.

    ᴅɛma′′ma ɢᴜᴅ_lu′m·ɪ ɢu′sa aha′ṅtwał. ṗʊ′f·an tɛ′n·a ha′ṅtwał.

    ɢɷ·′k ɢutku′ʙk·a·t ɢu′ca ha′ṅtwał. <62(3)>

pɛ·′′ma ɢu′ca asɪ′nfaf ɢɷ·′k ɢᴜᴅṗla′qṗla·t ɢu′ca-aq̇a′l·aẋ.

    tcɪ′′ɪ ʙaxawa′ᴅas ṗʊ′f·an ɢᴜᴅ·ɛ′lq̇yu.

ɢᴜᴅɪᴅme′ɪᴅj tcɪ′′ɪ ɢᴜᴅɢɛ′m′ya·t ᴅɛma′′ma.

    tcɪ′′ɪ ɢutku′ṗk·a·t ɢu′sa ha′ṅtwał ᴅɪnɪᴅʊ′ntkʷ.

    ʙu′ɢʊlfan a′mpyan ɢᴜᴅɪt_lu·′′nʊf. <62(4)>

e′ɪkɪn ta′ʙ-asa′nᴅɪ ɢᴜᴅɪtʊ′ɢɪ ɢu′sa alu·′′nafʊn.

pɛ·′′ma ɢᴜᴅnɪ′s·ɪn tcɛgʊ′sa-wa·m·u·-a′mu′ɪ,

    pɛ·′′ma tcɪᴅɪtʊ′ɢɪ ma′ha-ʙuq̇a′l·aẋ.

pɛ·′′ma ɢu′sa-a′mu′ɪ ɢut·a′ʙna·t ᴅɛma′′ma acq̇ɪ′nwaɪmaẋ.

pɛ·′′ma ɢu′sa-wa·m·u·-a′mu′ɪ ɢᴜᴅna′ɢɪt <62(5)>

    tcɪ′′ɪ-tcɪt·a′mᴅju hu′w·an-aᴅɪ′nfya acord ɢu′c·a-ha′ṅtwal ᴅɪ′wa′ᴅɪk.

I will pay you two and a half dollars per cord.” ‖123:22‖
My father said,
  “Okay.”
Then he and the young man worked.

<63> Mother's Berry Business
Then the White man told my mother,
  “There are lots of berries over here, blackberries.”
Then my mother said to my father,
  “Tomorrow our boy and I will go after those blackberries.
  We will pick those berries <63(2)>
  We'll bring those berries to Chemeketa.
  There we will sell them.”
Then, the next day, she made much food.
Then she said,
  “Bahawadas, go get the horses!” <63(3)>
  I went to get the horses.
  I put on the harnesses.
  I hitched (them) to the wagon.
Then my mother and I picked where there were lots of berries.
  We picked berries there all day long. <63(4)>
  We filled all our buckets.[5]
Then we went back to our camp.
It was nearly dark when we got back to our camp.
  My mother made our food. ‖123:24‖
  I took our horses to the corral. <63(5)>
Then my father and the young man came back to camp.
  They got ready.
Then my mother finished all the food.
Then we ate.
Having finished our meal, my mother cleaned up everything.
Having finished, then she spoke to my father, she said, <63(6)>
  “There are very many berries at that place.”
Then my mother said to me,
  “You go to sleep!
  Tomorrow early you will go get our horses!
  We'll take these berries to Chemeketa.” <63(7)>

tcɪ''ɪ tcɪDɛ'cDʊp ɢɛ'm-nau-DɪKu'ʙfan DɪSǫ́ɪ'nwaɪmax wa''an-Dɪcord. ||123:22||
DEma''ma ɢʊDna'ɢɪt,
   ɢu'cwɪ.
pɛ''ma ɢⱷ'k nau-ɢu'ca-asɪ'nfaf ɢuDɪnɪt_lu''nuf.

<63> Mother's Berry Business

pɛ''ma ɢu'sa-wa'm·u-a'mu'ɪ ɢuDnɪ'cɪn DEna'na,
   hɛ'sa-yʊ'fan ma·ha'l·u· aɢa'y·a'ṇ. a'ntɢwɪl DɪGa'y·a'ṇ.
pɛ''ma DE'na'na ɢuDna'ɢɪt tcɛDEma''ma,
   tcɪ''ɪ nauDa''ʊp me'ɪDj DɪDɪt'u'Dɢwɪn ɢu'sa-a'ntɢwɪl-aɢa'y·a'ṇ.
   sʊ'D·u DɪDɪt_sḱwɪ'tskwa·t ɢu'sa-aɢa'y·a'ṇ   <63(2)>
   DɪDɪDɪ'tku ɢu'ca-aɢa'y·a'ṇ tcatcamɪ'ɢɪDɪ.
   ɢʊ'saBE·D su'D·u DɪDɪt_lu''w·u·t.
pɛ''ma DEna'na ɢuDɪDme'ɪDj ɢuDBu'n ha'l·u· akwe'ɪnafʊn.
pɛ''ma ɢuDna'ɢɪt,
   ʙaxawa'Das, ma'ha DjakDjɪ'wu akɪ'uDɪn!   <63(3)>
   tcɪ''ɪ ɢuD·ɪ'twu akɪ'uDɪn,
   ɢuDBʊ'n Dɪharness,
   ɢuD_lu''un tcɛtcɪ'ɢtcɪk.
pɛ''ma tcɪ''ɪ nau-DEna'na ɢuD_lu'ʙɢu·t tcɛha'l·a ɢʊ'sa ha'l·u· ça'y·a·n.
   ɢu'saBE·D ɢuDḱwɪ'Dḱwu·D aɢa'y·a'ṇ ʙu'ɢulfan-wi·yaha'mpyan.   <63(4)>
   su'D·u ɢuDBu'y·ɪ ʙu'ɢulfan Dɪtɪ'w·at.
pɛ''ma ɢɪD·u'y·ɪ tcɛDɪsɪ'lhaus.
yɛ'Dj ɢuDɪDhu'wɪ pɛ''ma ɢuDɪtwu''ɢ tcɛDɪsɪ'lhaus
   DEna'na ɢuDBu'n Dɪḱwe'ɪnafʊnak. ||123:24||
   tcɪ''ɪ ɢuDɪ'tku Dɪkɪ'uDɪn tcɛǫa'l·ax.   <63(5)>
pɛ''ma DEma''ma nau-ɢu'ca-acɪ'nfaf ɢuDɪnɪt_cmu''ɢ tcɛsɪ'lhaus.
   ɢuD·ɪnɪtɛ'n·atcwu·n
pɛ''ma DEna'na ɢut·ʊ'ɢɪ ʙu'ɢʊlfan-aḱwe'ɪnafʊnak.
pɛ''ma sʊ'D·ʊ ɢuDɪDḱwe'ɪnafʊ.
t·ʊ'ɢɪ-Dɪḱwe'ɪnafʊn DEna'na tɛ'n·a·n ʙu'ɢʊlfan a'ɢfan.
ɢut·ʊ'ɢɪ pɛ''ma ɢuDhɛ'laftcɪn tcɛDEma''ma, ɢuDna'ɢɪt,   <63(6)>
   ṕʊ'fan ha'l·u· aɢa'y·a'n ɢu'saBE·D.
pɛ''ma DEna'na ɢuDna'ɢɪt tcɛtcɪ''ɪ,
   ma'ha cɪ'w·eɪcDa!
   me'ɪDj ɢamɪha'l'wan ma'ha DEDɪ'twu Dɪkɪ'uDɪn.
   DɪDsDu'ku hɛ'ca ça'y·a'n tca'tcamɪ'ɢɪDɪ.   <63(7)>

There my mother sold all of those berries.

  She got maybe eight dollars.

Then my mother bought all kinds of food.

  We went back to our camp.

  She made food.   <63(8)>

  I took the horse to the corral.

When it was evening, my father and the young man came back to camp.

When my mother had finished making food, they prepared for supper.

My mother said,

  "You all eat!"   <63(9)>

Having finished my meal, I went to bed. ||123:26||

  They stayed up talking about everything.

Then it got dark.[6]

Then they went to bed.

When it was early morning, my mother called to me,   <63(10)>

  "Bahawadas, get up!

  Go bring the horses!

  Come back right away, I will have finished the food."

  I came back.

    I got the horses.

    I tied them to a tree.

Then she said,

  "Go call to your father!   <63(11)>

  They are working at the place where they cut wood."

I called to my father,

  "Come, come back for our meal!"

My father said,

  "Okay."   <63(12)>

Then I washed my face and my hands.

Then my father and the young man got there.

  They washed their faces and their hands.

Then we ate.

Finished with their meal, they went back to their work.   <63(13)>

Then I put the harness on the horses.

  I hitched the horses to the wagon.

Then my mother put all the buckets in the wagon.

ɢʊ'saBɛ·ᴅ ᴅɛna'·na ɢʊᴅ_lu'w·u·t ʙʊ'ɢʊlfan ɢʊ'ca-aɢa'ya·n.

ɢʊᴅɪ'tɢwin e'ɪkɪn ɢɪ'm'wei asq̇ɪ'nweɪmax.

pɛ·''ma ᴅɛna'·na ɢʊtya'nᴅ ʙʊ'ɢʊlfan a'w·ɛw akwe'ɪnafʊnak.

ɢʊᴅ_sᴅɪ'ᴅyɪ tcɛᴅusɪ'lhaus.

qɛ'ᴅ·ak ɢʊᴅʙʊ'n-akwe'ɪnafʊn.   <63(8)>

tcɪ''ɪ ɢʊᴅɪ'tk̇u ᴅɪkɪ'uᴅɪn ᴅɪɛq̇a'l·ax.

ɢʊᴅ_ɪᴅɪɛ'ɢ·u-a'mpyan ᴅɛma'·ma nau-ɢʊ'sa-asɪ'nfaf ɢʊᴅnɪtcmu'·ɢ tcɛsɪ'lhaus.

ʙʊ'ɢʊlfan-kwe'ɪnafʊn ᴅɛna'·na ɢʊṫʊ'ɢɪ pɛ·''ma ɢʊnɪtɛ'n·atcwu·n ᴅɪnɪkwe'ɪnafu.

ᴅɛna'·na ɢʊᴅna'ɢɪt,

mɪ'ᴅ·ɪ ʙck̇we'ɪnafu.   <63(9)>

ɢʊṫʊ'ɢɪ ᴅɪck̇we'ɪnafʊn tcɪ''ɪ ɢʊᴅɪt'wei. ||123:26||

ɢɪ''nʊk ɢɪnɪᴅa'f·ʊtc ʙʊ'ɢʊlfan a'ɢ·a ɢɪnɪyu''wn.

pɛ·''ma ɢʊᴅɪt'cɛ·'xᴅɪyu.

pɛ·''ma ɢɪ''n·ʊ'k ɢʊᴅɪnɪᴅɪ'twi·.

ɢʊᴅɪtme'ɪᴅɪ he·'l'wan ᴅɛna'·na ɢʊᴅ_la'l'wi· tcɛtcɪ''ɪ,   <63(10)>

ʙaxawa'ᴅas, sʙʊ'klaɪsᴅa

ᴅɪa'kᴅɪɪ'wu-akɪ'uᴅɪn.

ᴅɪ·'s ᴅumɪmu'·ɢ tcɪ''ɪ ᴅɪṫʊ'ɢɪ akwe'ɪnafʊnak.

tcɪ''ɪ-ɢʊᴅmu'·ɢ

ɢʊᴅk̇wɛ'n-ᴅɪkɪ'uᴅɪn,

ɢʊᴅ'ɛ'm·a·t tcɛ'wa'ᴅik.

pɛ·''ma ɢʊᴅna'ɢɪt,

cla'l'wai tcɛᴅma'·ma.   <63(11)>

ɢɪ''n·ʊk nɪlu'nfun ᴅɪɛhɛ'l·a ɢʊ'sa ᴅɪnɪk̇ʊ'ʙk̇a·ᴅ a'wa'ᴅik.

tcɪ''ɪ ɢʊᴅ_la'l'wɪ tcɛᴅɛma'·ma,

ʙɪsma·'k, cme'y·ɪ tcɛᴅ·ukwa'ɪnafʊn!

ᴅɛma'·ma ɢʊᴅna'ɢɪt,

ɢʊ'cwɪ.   <63(12)>

pɛ·''ma tcɪ''ɪ ɢʊᴅk̇u''uł ᴅɛkwa'l·ak nau-ᴅɛ'la'qʷ.

pɛ·''ma ᴅɛma'·ma nau-ɢʊ'ca-acɪ'nfaf ɢʊn·ɪmu'·ɢ.

ɢɪ''n·ʊk ɢɪn·ɪtk̇u·'ł ᴅɪn·ɪɢwa'l·ak ᴅɪn·ɪ'la'qʷ.

ʙɛ·''ma sʊ'ᴅ·u ɢʊᴅɪtkwe'ɪnafɪn.

ṫʊ'ɢɪ ᴅɪnɪkwe'ɪnafɪn ɢɪ''n·ʊk ɢɪn·ɪᴅɪ't ᴅɪnɪlu'nafʊn.   <63(13)>

pɛ·''ma tcɪ''ɪ ɢʊtɢu·' harness tcɛᴅɪkɪ'uᴅɪn,

tcɪ''ɪ ɢʊṫ·a'xᴅa·t ɢʊ'sa-akɪ'uᴅɪn tcɛtcɪ'k̇tcɪk.

pɛ·''ma ᴅɛna'·na ɢʊᴅṗɪ'n ʙʊ'ɢʊlfan ṫɪ'w·at ᴅɪᴅɪɪɢᴅɪɪɢ.

Then we went to the berry patch.

    We picked berries all day long. ||123:28|| <63(14)>

    We filled all the buckets.

Then we put the berries in the wagon.

Then we went back to our camp.

When we got back to camp near sunset, my mother cooked supper.

    I took the horses to the corral. <63(15)>

Then I came back to the camp.

    My father was at the camp.

    They were waiting for me.

    I washed my face and my hands.

Then we ate. <63(16)>

Finished with our meal, I said,

    "I want to go to bed."

My mother prepared the bed,

    "Come on to bed!" <63(17)>

    I went to sleep.

When it was early morning, my father and the young man went off to their work.

    I got up, went to get the horses, and came back to camp.

    My mother finished all of our food.

    I washed up. <63(18)>

Then I called to my father, for them to come to their meal.

    I hitched the horses to the wagon.

Then my mother and I went to Chemeketa.

    We sold all the berries.

    We sold them all. ||123:30|| <63(19)>

Then we came back to our camp.

This is what we did every day for about five weeks.

<64> Return to the Reservation

Then my father finished their work.

Then the White man paid my father.

Then we went to the place where my mother's brothers were working.

    They were cutting big oaks.

    They were stacking the wood.

    There my father helped his brothers-in-law.

For one week he helped his brothers-in-law here. <64(2)>

pɛ·''ma sʊ'ᴅ·ʊ ɢuᴅ_ıᴅı't ᴅJɛɢʊ'ca ça'y·a'n̦ a'n·u.

  ɢuᴅk̓wı'ᴅkwa·ᴅ aça'y·a'n ʙʊ'ɢʊlfan-ɢʊca-wi'ı'pyan. ||123:28|| <63(14)>

  ɢuᴅ_lu'fu·t ʙʊ'ɢʊlfan atı'w·a·t.

pɛ·''ma ɢuᴅıt_lu''un ɢu'ca-aça'y·a'n̦ tcɛtcı'ɢtcıɢ.

pɛ·''ma sʊ'ᴅ·u ɢuᴅıᴅ_sᴅu'y·ı tcɛᴅ·usı'lhaus.

ɢuᴅıᴅmu''ɢ yɛ'ᴅJ ɢuᴅıᴅJɛ'ɢ·u-a'mpyan ᴅɛna''na ɢuᴅʙʊ'n-ak̓wɛ'ınafʊn.

  tcı''ı ɢuᴅ·ı'tku akı'uᴅın tcɛq̓a'l·ax̣.   <63(15)>

pɛ·''ma tcı''ı ɢuᴅmu''ɢ tcɛsı'lhaus.

  ᴅɛma''ma ɢuᴅʙi·'nᴅ ᴅJɛsı'lhaus.

  ɢuᴅınıyu'w·u·t ᴅJɛtcı''ı.

  tcı''ı-ɢutk̓u''uł ᴅɛkwa'l·ak ᴅɛ'la'qʷ.

pɛ·''ma su'ᴅ·u ɢuᴅıᴅ_c̓kwɛ'ınafʊ.   <63(16)>

tʊ'ɢ·ı-ᴅıskwɛ'ınafʊn tcı''ı tcı'na'ɢıt,

  tcı''ı-tcıta'mᴅJu ᴅumɢu'mwaı.

ᴅɛna''na ɢut·ɛ'n·a·n açwa''an.

  tcı'ᴅ·a si'w·eısᴅa.   <63(17)>

  tcı''ı ɢuᴅ·ıtweı.

me'ıᴅJ-ɢuᴅıtha'l'wan ᴅɛma''ma nau-ɢu'ca-acı'nfaf ɢuᴅınıᴅı't ᴅın·ılu''nafʊn.

  tcı''ı ɢuᴅʙu'ɢlaı, ᴅı'twʊ akı'uᴅın, ɢuᴅıᴅmu''ɢ ᴅJɛsı'lhaus.

  ᴅɛna''na ɢut·ʊ'ɢ·ı ʙu'ɢʊlfan ᴅık̓wɛ'ınafʊnak.

  tcı''ı-ɢutk̓u''uł.   <63(18)>

pɛ·''ma ɢuᴅ_la'l'waı tcɛᴅɛma''ma ɢamnıcme'y·ı ᴅınık̓wɛ'ınafʊn.

  tcı''ı ɢutɢu' akı'uᴅın tcɛtcı'ɢtcıɢ.

pɛ·''ma tcı''ı nau-ᴅɛna''na ɢwᴅı't tcatcamı'ɢıᴅı.

  ɢuᴅ_lu''ut ʙuɢulfan ɢu'ca ça'y·a·n

  ɢuᴅ_lu''ut ʙuɢulfan ɢu' ||123:30|| <63(19)>

ʙɛ·''ma ɢwᴅıᴅ_cme'y·ı tcɛᴅ·ısı'lhaus.

pa'c·a sʊ'ᴅ·ʊ ɢuᴅıᴅmı'ut ʙʊ'ɢʊlfan a'mpyan e'ıkın hu'w·an asa'nᴅı.

<64> Return to the Reservation

pɛ·''ma ᴅɛma''ma ɢuᴅ·ınıt̓ʊ'ɢ·ı ᴅın·ılu''nafʊn.

pɛ·''ma ɢʊ'ca wa'm·u·-a'mu'ı ɢuᴅ·a'ʙnat ᴅɛma''ma.

pɛ·''ma sʊ'ᴅ·ʊ ɢwᴅıᴅ_sᴅı't ᴅJɛha'l·a ɢu'c·a ᴅɛna''na ᴅıʙı'ɢwak ɢun·ılu''nafʊn.

  ɢı'n·ʊk ɢunıkʊ'ʙk̓a·t waʙa'l-amɛ·'f,

  ɢʊnıʙʊ'nhin a'wa'ᴅık.

  ɢu'saʙɛ·ᴅ ᴅɛma''ma ɢuᴅɢɛ'm'ya·ᴅ ᴅınıʙa'naɢyaʙ.

wa''an-asa'nᴅı hɛ'saʙɛ·ᴅ ɢⱷ'k ɢuᴅınıᴅɢɛ'm'ya·ᴅ ᴅıʙa'n·aɢyaʙ.   <64(2)>

My mother worked in the houses of White women.

    She washed clothes for those White women.

After one week, my father said,

    "Tomorrow we will be returning to our place."

Then, early the next morning, my father went to get our horses.   <64(3)>

    My mother packed everything up.

    She put it in the wagon.

Then we left her brothers' camp.

Then we crossed the Big River (the Willamette).

    We travelled all day long.   <64(4)>

We got home around sunset.

Then my father unhitched the horse from the wagon. ||123:32||

    My mother and I brought everything into the house.

Then I played outside.

    I ran all over the place looking at everything.   <64(5)>

Then my mother called to me,

    "Come back for supper!"

Then, when we finished our food, it was dark.

    My mother prepared my bed.

ᴅena′na qe′ᴅ·ak ɢuᴅlu″nuf ᴅJɛ·wa′m·u-ʙu′m·ik ᴅɪnɪᴅʊ′m·aɪ.

  ɢutk̓u′lu·ł a′ɢfan ᴅJɛɢu′ca-wa′m·u-aʙu′m·ik.

ɢuᴅɪtwa″an-asa′nᴅɪ ᴅɛma′′ma ɢuᴅna′ɢɪt,

  me′ɪᴅJ ᴅɪᴅɪᴅ_sᴅu′y·ɪ ᴅJɛᴅu′n·u.

pɛ·″ma ɢwᴅɪᴅme′ɪᴅJ ɢuᴅɪhɛ′l′wan ᴅɛma′′ma ɢuᴅ·ɪ′twu su′ᴅ·u ᴅɪkɪ′uᴅɪn.   <64(3)>

  ᴅena′na ɢut·ɛ′n·a·n ʙu′ɢulfan-a′ɢfan

  ɢuᴅ_lu″un ᴅJɛᴅJɪ′ɢᴅJɪɢ.

pɛ·″ma sʊ′ᴅ·ʊ ɢwᴅɪᴅha′ɢu·t ᴅɪʙɪ′ɢwaɢyaʙ ɢu′ca ᴅJɛᴅɪnɪsɪ′lhaus.

pɛ·″ma ɢwᴅ·ɪᴅɪ′t yɛ′lqfan ᴅJɛɢu′s·a-ʙa′l· ama′mpɢa.

  ɢwᴅɪᴅ′i·′ᴅ ʙʊ′ɢulfan-a′mpyan.   <64(4)>

ɢuᴅɪᴅmu′ɢ ᴅJɛᴅɪᴅʊ′n·u yɛ′ᴅJ ɢwaᴅɪᴅJɛ′ɢ·u-a′mpyan.

pɛ·″ma ᴅɛma′′ma ɢuᴅ_sk̓wi′lsk̓wa·t akɪ′uᴅɪn ᴅJɛɢu′ca-aᴅJɪ′ɢᴅJɪɢ. ||123:32||

  tcɪ″ɪ-nauᴅena′na ɢuᴅ_la′m·ɪ ʙʊ′ɢulfan-a′ɢfan tcɛha′m·ɪ.

ʙɛ·″ma tcɪ″ɪ ɢuᴅ_la′ɢwɪt hɛ·″lʊm.

  ʙʊ′ɢulfan-ha′l·a ɢuᴅɪᴅmɪ′nᴅJɪs t′cɪ′ʙlu·t ʙʊ′ɢulfan-a′ɢfan.   <64(5)>

pɛ·″ma ᴅena′na ɢuᴅ_la′l′wi′fan,

  sma′kcᴅɛ-cme′y·ɪ tcɛᴅɪᴅk̓we′ɪnafʊ.

pɛ·″ma ɢuᴅɪt·ʊ′ɢɪ ᴅɪk̓we′ɪnafʊn ɢuᴅɪᴅhu′wi.

  ᴅena′na ɢut·ɛ′n·a·n ᴅɪqwa″an.

CHAPTER THIRTEEN
Fourth of July Festivities[1]

[previously untranslated]

<65> Agent Demands Support

In the morning my father went to the Agent's house here.

[---] (The agent speaks:)

"You have come back, Kinai.

> *It's so good that you have come back.*

All the Indians want to put on a celebration (a big time)[2] for the Fourth of July.

> *Everyone has given money to buy food for the big day.*

<65(2)>

How much money will you give?"

My father said,

"I can't give any money."

The agent said,   <65(3)>

"Don't you be talking like that!

> *You are chief of the Tualatin people."*

My father said,

"I have a lot of work.

> *I have to cut a lot of wheat, oats, and hay.*   <65(4)>

I need to keep all my money." ||123:34||

Then the agent said,

"You help these Indians!

Every Indian gave three dollars, two dollars,

> *They gave a little bit of money."*   <65(5)>

Then my father said,

"I'm giving one big cow to feed these people.

Whoever is the Indian leader (organizer) of this [_?_][3] of foods, I'll speak to that Indian.

<65(6)>

Four young men will come to my house.

I will take them to the mountains to go find that cow of mine.

They will drive it to where they will be preparing food.

> *There they will slaughter this cow."[4]*

The agent said,

"Alright."

Fourth of July Festivities

<65> Agent Demands Support

ɢᴜᴅɪᴅme'ɪᴅj ᴅɛma·'ma ɢᴜᴅ·ɪ't tcɛhɛ'sa Agent ᴅᴜ'm·aɪ.

[---] (The agent speaks:)

  ma'ha tcumu·'ɢ q̇ɪ'n·aɪ.

    ṗᴜ'f·an tɛ'n·a ma'ha ɢᴜᴅɪᴅ_cmu·'ɢ.

  ʙᴜ'ɢulfan amɛ·'nmɪ nɪṫa'mᴅju ᴅᴜmnɪʙᴜ'n ala·'ɢwaɢ ᴅjɛhɛ'ca ta'ʙ a'mpyan ᴅjɛJuly.

    ʙᴜ'ɢulfan-a'm·ɪm ɢᴜᴅɪnɪɢᴜ' sq̇ɪ'nweɪmax ᴅᴜmnɪᴅya'nᴅ akwe'ɪnafᴜnak ᴅjɛɢᴜ'sa

      waʙa'l a'mpyan.   <65(2)>

  a'hɷ·'lu cq̇ɪ'nwaɪmax ma'ha ᴅɪᴅɢᴜ'?

ᴅɛma·'ma ɢᴜᴅna'ɢɪt,

  wa'ŋq-la'f tcɪ'ɪ ɢᴜᴅɪᴅɢᴜ' asq̇ɪ'nweɪmax.

ɢᴜ'ca-Agent ɢᴜᴅna'ɢɪt,   <65(3)>

  wa'ŋq ma'ha pa'c-numna'ɢɪt!

    ma'ha tcɪt·ca'mʙ·ak tcɛᴅfa'laṫɪ-a'm·ɪm

ᴅɛma·'ma ɢᴜᴅna'ɢɪt,

  tcɪ'ɪ tcɪʙɪ'nᴅ ha'l·u· alu·''nafᴜnak

    ha'l·u· asa'ʙlil nau-la'wɛ·n ᴅamᴅɪᴅkᴜ'ʙᴜn nau-lᴜ'q̇ᵘ.   <65(4)>

  tcɪ'ɪ tcɪṫa'mᴅju ᴅumṗɪ'n ʙᴜ'ɢulfan ᴅɪcq̇ɪ'nwaɪmax. ||123:34||

pɛ·''ma ɢᴜ'sa a'Agent ɢᴜᴅna'ɢɪt:

  ma'ha sɢɪ'm'ya·t hɛ'ca-amɛ·'nmɪ.

  ʙᴜ'ɢulfan mɛ·'nmɪ ɢᴜn·ɪɢᴜ'· hu'w·an-aᴅa·'la ɢɛ·'m-aᴅa·'la,

    pu't'snaq ɢɪn·ɪɢᴜ' sq̇ɪ'nwaɪmax.   <65(5)>

pɛ·''ma ᴅɛma·'ma ɢᴜᴅna'ɢɪt,

  tcɪ'ɪ tcɪɢᴜ' wa''an waʙa'l amu'cmuc ɢᴜmᴅɪᴅ'u'ɢ hɛ'ca a'm·ɪm.

  e'y·a-mɛ·'nmɪ-məᴅja'mʙak ᴅja_ha'sa ṗᴜ'yaɢnak akwe'ɪnafᴜn ᴅɛᴅna'ɢɪt ᴅjɛɢᴜ'sa

    amɛ·'nmɪ   <65(6)>

  ɢᴜᴅɪnɪᴅ_cma'a ta'ʙ acɪ'nfaf ᴅjɛᴅɛᴅu'm·aɪ

  tcɪ'ɪ ᴅɪnɪᴅɪ'ṫku tcɛmɛ'fu u'ᴅnɪɢwaɪ ɢᴜ'ca tcɪ'ɪ ᴅɛmu'cmuc.

  ɢɪ'n·ᴜk ɢɪnɪɢɪ'cɢa·t ᴅjɛha'l·a ɢᴜ'ca ᴅɪnɪʙᴜ'n akwe'ɪnafᴜnak.

    ɢᴜ'caʙɛ·ᴅ ɢᴜᴅɪnɪᴅa'haɪ hɛ'sa-amu'smus.

ɢᴜ'sa-Agent ɢᴜᴅna'ɢɪt,

  ɢᴜ'cwɪ.

<66> Donating a Bull for the Feast

Then, the next day, four young men arrived at my father's house.

One of the young men said,

  "That leader (organizer) is preparing food."

  [He told us,]

    'You go to Kinai's house!'"

My father said,   <66(2)>

  "Alright, I have been waiting for you."

Then my father got his horse.

  He rode a very good horse.

Then he took those young men. ||123:36||

  He went in front.   <66(3)>

  The young men went behind.

[---]

  "You young men watch out here to spot the cows!"

Then one of the young men said,

  "Across over there are many cows."   <66(4)>

My father said,

  "Let's go over there."

  My father rounded up all those cows.

  He found one three-year-old bull.

Then he said to them, those young men,   <66(5)>

  "You go back with this three-year-old bull!

  You drive it to where it is they will be preparing food!

  There you will slaughter this cow."

Then those young men drove the cow.

<67> Pie and Cake

Then my father went to his house.

When he got home, he said nothing to my mother.

When it was dark my father got back.

Then my mother said,

  "Where have you been these last two days?"   <67(2)>

Then my father explained[5] to my mother, ||123:38||

  "All the Indians in my tribe here want to put on a celebration for everyone, White people
    and Indian people.

  That Indian agent, he wanted me to donate money.

<66> Donating a Bull for the Feast

pɛ·"ma ɢwɒɪɒmeʹɪɒj taʹʙ-acɪʹnfaf ɢuɒɪtcmuʹ·ɢ ɒjɛɒɛmaʹ·ma ɒɪhaʹmʹ·ɪ.

waʹ"an-ɢus-asɪʹnfaf ɢuɒnaʹɢɪt,

  ɢuʹsa-aɒjaʹmʙak ɢuɒʙʊʹnhɪn aꞌkweʹɪnafʊnak

    mɪʹɒ·ɪ ʙcɒjaʹ·k tcɛɋɪʹnʹ·aɪ ɒʊʹmʹ·aɪ

ɒɛmaʹ·ma ɢuɒnaʹɢɪt   <66(2)>

  ɢuʹcwɪ_ tcɪʹʹɪ tcɪɒɪɒyuʹwʹ·anfʊʙ

pɛ·"ma ɒɛmaʹ·ma ɢuɒɪʹtɢwɪn ɒɪkɪʹuɒɪn

  ɢuɒyuʹwafɢwuʹ·t ꝑʊʹfan atɛʹnʹ·a akɪʹuɒɪn.

pɛ·"ma ɢuɒɪnɒɪʹtku ɢuʹsa-asɪʹnfaf. ||123:36||

  ɢꞷʹk ɢuɒʹɪʹɒ ɒjɪʹmʹ·.   <66(3)>

  ɢɪʹnʊk sɪʹnfaf ɢumnɪɒʹɪʹɒ haʹntʹc.

[---]

  mɪʹɒ·ɪ sɪʹnfaf ɒɪʙyuʹɒnɪɢwan haʹlʹ·a ɒumnɪɒhꞷʹɒ amuʹcmuc.

pɛ·"ma waʹ"an asɪʹnfaf ɢuɒnaʹɢɪt

  ɢuʹsʹ·a yɛʹlqfan haʹlʹ·u-amuʹsmus.   <66(4)>

ɒɛmaʹ·ma ɢuɒnaʹɢɪt,

  tcɪʹɒʹ·a tcɪɒɪsɒꞷʹ ɢʊʹsaʙɛʹɒ.

  ɒɛmaʹ·ma ɢuɒwɪʹyɪt ʙuʹɢulfan ɢuʹsa-amuʹsmus.

  ɢuɒɛʹsɒɛs waʹ"an huʹpsɪn ɒɪmɪʹtʹsu. ɒjaʹŋku amuʹsmus.

pɛ·"ma ɢuɒnɪʹsʹ·ɪn ɒjɛɢɪʹnʹ·ʊk ɢuʹsa sɪʹnfaf,   <66(5)>

  mɪʹɒ·ɪ ʙɪsmaʹ·k hɛʹca-waɒaʹʙɪt huʹpcɪn ɒɪmɪʹtʹcu waɒjaʹŋku amuʹsmus

  mɪʹɒ·ɪ ʙɪcɢɪʹcɢaʹ·t ɒjɛhaʹlʹ·a ɢʊʹsa ɒɪnɪʙʊʹnhɪn ɒɪnɪꞌkweʹɪnafʊnak.

  ɢʊʹsaʙɛʹɒ mɪʹɒ·ɪ ɢuɒɪpɒaʹhaɪ hɛʹca-amuʹsmus.

pɛ·"ma ɢɪʹnʹ·ʊʹk sɪʹnfaf ɢuɒɪnɪtɢɪʹcɢaʹ·t ɢuʹca-amuʹsmus.

<67> Pie and Cake

pɛ·"ma ɒɛmaʹ·ma ɢuɒɪʹtyɪ ɒjɛɒɪɒʊʹmʹ·aɪ.

ɢuɒɪʹtwuk ɒjɛhaʹmʹ·ɪ waʹŋq-aʹɢʹ·a ɢuɒɪɒnaʹɢɪt ɒjɛɒɛnaʹ·na.

ɢuɒɪɒhuʹ·wɪ ɒɛmaʹ·ma ɢuɒɪɒmuʹ·ɢ.

pɛ·"ma ɒɛnʹ·aʹ·na ɢuɒnaʹɢɪt,

  haʹlʹ·a maʹha ɢuɒɪɒʹɪʹɒ hɛʹca ɢɛʹm aʹaʹmpyan.   <67(2)>

pɛ·"ma ɒɛmaʹ·ma ɢuɒhɛʹ·lafnɪɒʹju tcɛɒɛnaʹ·na. ||123:38||

  hɛʹsʹ·a ʙuʹɢulfan amɛʹnmɪ ɒɛɢaʹwakɪl. ɢɪʹnʹ·ʊk nɪʹtʹaʹmɒju ɒumnɪʙaʹl alaʹɢwak

    ɒjɛʙʊʹɢulfan-aʹmʹ·ɪm. waʹmʹ·uʹ·-aʹmʹ·ɪm. nau-aʹmɛʹ·nmɪyak-aʹmʹ·ɪm.

  ɢʊʹsʹ·a amɛʹnmɪ ɒɪʹAgent ɢꞷʹk ɢuꞌtaʹmɒju tcɪʹʹɪ ɒumcɢuʹ cɋɪʹnweɪmax̣.

I said,   <67(3)>
    'No.'
Then he said to me,
      'You are the head chief of your tribe.'
   I gave that organizer a three-year-old cow to slaughter for feeding all of those people."
                                                             <67(4)>

Then my father told my mother,
   "You must once again make nice food.
      On that day, on the big day, we will take it.
   We will feast."
My mother said,   <67(5)>
   "Alright. What kinds of food am I to make (for) you?"
[---]
   "Oh,"
My father said,
   "Oh, you know all these Indians like those things called 'pie' and 'cake.'"
                                          ||124:2|| <67(6)>
Then my mother said,
   "Alright, I will get to work this very day.
   And tomorrow I will have done all that you have asked."

<68> Grand Ronde Leading Men Assemble
Then my father went to the place where they were preparing the feast.
   He wanted to see all the Indian leaders.
   They were conferring there.
Then Shilikwa and Yachkawa were standing there.
They ran to my father.   <68(2)>
   "When did you get back?"
My father said,
   "I got back two days ago."
Then my father said,
   "Who are all the Indian organizers of this feast?"   <68(3)>
Shilikwa said,
   "Yachkawa and I of the Tualatin people, ||124:4||
   Of the Santiam people, Joe Hudson,
   Of the Umpquas, Bogus,
   Of the Ahantchuyuks, Sambo,   <68(4)>

tcɪ″ɪ ɢᴜᴅna′ɢɪt   <67(3)>

    wa′ŋq.

pɛ″ma ɢɷ′k ɢᴜᴅna′ɢɪt tcɛtcɪ″ɪ,

    ma′ha tcɛha′lʙam ᴅja′mʙak tcɛʙu′ɢᴜlfan ma′ha ʙɪɢa′wakɪl.

tcɪ″ɪ ɢᴜᴅɪ′s tcɛɢu′sa aᴅja′mʙ·ak wa″an hu′psɪn ᴅɪmɪ′t′cu amu′smᴜs. ɢᴜmnɪᴅa′haɪ

    ɢᴜmnɪᴅ′ᴜ′ɢ ɢᴜ′sa ʙu′ɢᴜlfan a′m·ɪm.   <67(4)>

pɛ″ma ᴅɛma·′ma ɢᴜᴅnɪ′sɪn ᴅɛna·′na,

  ma′ha sʙu′n kwa′l·u· watɛ′n·ɪyak k̓we′ɪnafᴜnak.

    ɢᴜ′sa wi·″ɪ′pyan ɢᴜ′sa-waʙa′l-ɪ′pyan ᴅɪᴅɪᴅ_sᴅᴜ′q̓u ɢᴜsa

  sᴜ′ᴅ·ᴜ ᴅɪᴅɪᴅ_sk̓we′ɪnafᴜnak.

ᴅɛna·′na ɢᴜᴅna′ɢɪt   <67(5)>

  ɢᴜ′cwɪ. a′w·ɛu ak̓we′ɪnafunak ma′ha tcɪ″ɪ-ᴅᴜmnɪᴅʙu′n.

[---]

  ᴜ′

ᴅɛma·′ma ɢᴜᴅna′ɢɪt

  ù·′, ma′ha-tcɪ′yᴜ′ɢᴜn ʙu′ɢᴜlfan hɛ′sa-amɛ·′nmɪ nɪt̓a′mᴅju a′ɢ·a ɢᴜ′sa ᴅaŋkwɪt pie nau-

    cake ||124:2|| <67(6)>

pɛ″ma ᴅɛna·′na ɢᴜᴅna′ɢɪt,

  ɢᴜ′cwɪ, tcɪ″ɪ-ᴅɪᴅɪlu″nuf hɛ′sa-wɪ-ɪ′pyan.

  nau-me′ɪᴅj ᴅɪᴅʙu′n ʙu′ɢᴜlfan ɢᴜ′sa a′ɢ·a ma′ha ɢᴜᴅna′ɢɪt.

<68> Grand Ronde Leading Men Assemble

pɛ″ma ᴅɛma·′ma ɢᴜᴅ·ɪ′t tcɛɢᴜ′sa ha′l·a ɢᴜᴅnɪᴅʙu′n ak̓we′ɪnafᴜnak.

  ɢᴜt̓a′mᴅju ᴅᴜmt′cɪ′ʙlu·ᴅ ʙu′ɢᴜlfan ɢᴜ′ca amɛ·′nmɪyak ᴅɪnɪᴅja′mʙ·ak.

  ɢᴜ′saʙɛ·ᴅ ɢᴜᴅɪnɪᴅyu′wᴜn.

ʙɛ″ma ɢᴜ′saʙɛ·ᴅ sɪ′lɪk̓wa nau-yɛ′tcɢawa ɢᴜᴅɪnɪᴅa′·ʙɪt

ɢᴜᴅɪnɪmɪ′nᴅjɪs tcɛᴅɛma·′ma.   <68(2)>

  la′f·ᴜ ma′ha ᴅᴜmɪɢu′m·ᴜɢ.

ᴅɛma·′ma ɢᴜᴅnaɢɪt,

  tcɪ″ɪ ɢᴜᴅɢᴜ′m·ᴜɢ ɢɛ′f·u-a′mpyan.

ʙɛ″ma ᴅɛma·′ma ɢᴜᴅna′ɢɪt

  e′y·a ʙᴜ′ɢᴜlfan amɛ·′nmɪ ɢᴜᴅɪnɪᴅja′mʙaɢ ᴅjɛhɛ′ca k̓we′ɪnafᴜnak.   <68(3)>

sɪ′lɪk̓wa ɢᴜᴅna′ɢɪt,

  tcɪ″ɪ nau-yɛ′tcɢawa ᴅjɛ′atfa′latɪ a′m·ɪm ||124:4||

  ᴅjɛsa′nᴅɪya·m-a′m·ɪm Joe Hudson,

  ᴅja′a′mpɢwa ʙᴜ′ɢᴜs,

  ᴅjaha′nt′cɪyuk sa′mʙu,   <68(4)>

Of the Yamhills, Ilkin,
  Of the Clackamas, Wacheno."
[That's as many as I (Bahawadas) remember.
  I don't remember anything about those Shastas and those Rogue Rivers.
    I don't remember their names.][6]   <68(5)>
  "Alright,"
    my father said.
Then my father said to Shilikwa,
  "How many days do you want to celebrate?"
Shilikwa said,   <68(6)>
  "Three days."
[---]
  "Alright."
Then my father went back to his house.

<69> Meeting with Uncle
When he returned, he went to his uncle.[7]
He got to his house,
  "How are you doing, uncle?"
[---]
  "Oh, I am quite healthy (lit., strong).   <69(2)>
  When did you get back?"
My father said, ||124:6||
  "Two days (ago)."
Then my father explained to his uncle,
  "These Indians are going to put themselves out celebrating for three days.   <69(3)>
  The Indians will prepare all kinds of foods.
  When the Fourth comes, the big day, all the people will gather.
  Many White people will come from all of these little whatevers, what the White people call
    'towns.'
    Our White friends (lit., brothers) will come. ||125:2|| <69(4)>
      The White people from Hillsboro, from Dayton, from McMinnville, all of them will come
        for the big day."
That uncle of his said,
  "Alright, I am very old.
  I can't go to where you all are gathering."   <69(5)>
My father said,

ᴅJɛyɛ'mhɪl ɪ'lkɪn,

ᴅJɛła'kamas wat'cɪ'nu.

pa'sa-ha·''lu tcɪ''ɪ-tcɪ'yʊ'ɢʊn.

wa'ŋq-tcɪ''ɪ ɢuᴅ·ɪtyʊ'ɢʊn ᴅJɛɢɪ'nʊk ɢʊ'sa-aᴅJɛ'stɪ na'u-ᴅJɛɢʊ'sa Rogue River.

wa'ŋq-tcɪ''ɪ ɢɪ'yʊ'ɢʊn ᴅɪn·ɪᴅa'ŋkwɪt.   <68(5)>

ɢʊ'cwɪ,

ᴅɛma·''ma ɢuᴅnaɢit.

pɛ·''ma ᴅɛma·''ma ɢuᴅna'ɢɪt tcɛsɪ'lɪkwa

a'hœ·'lʊ a'mpyan mɪ'ᴅɪ ʙɪsťa'mᴅJu ᴅumᴅɪpla'ɢwɪt?

cɪ'lɪkwa ɢuᴅna'ɢɪt,   <68(6)>

hu'psɪn-a'a'mpyan.

[---]

ɢu'cwɪ.

pɛ·''ma ᴅɛma·''ma ɢuᴅɪ'tyɪ tcɛᴅɪᴅu'm·aɪ.

<69> Meeting with Uncle

ɢuᴅɪᴅɪ'twuk ɢœ'k ɢuᴅɪ't ᴅJɛᴅɪsɪ·''muɪ.

ɢuᴅɪ'twuk ᴅJɛᴅɪᴅʊ'm·aɪ.

a''ma tcɛmɪ'ut ᴅɪsi·''muɪ

[---]

u', tcɪ''ɪ-tcumᴅa'lqᴅʊɢu.   <69(2)>

la'fu ma'ha ɢumɪmu·'ɢ

ᴅɛma·''ma ɢuᴅna'ɢɪt ||124:6||

ɢɛ'm-a'mpyan.

pɛ·''ma ᴅɛma·''ma ɢuᴅhɛ·'lafyʊʙʊn ᴅJɛᴅɪsɪ''muɪ.

ṗʊ'fan hɛ'sa-amɛ·'nmɪyak a'm·ɪm ɢuṅɪla'ɢwak hu'psɪn a'mpyan. <69(3)>

ɢɪ'nʊk ɢusa-amɛ·'nmɪ ᴅɪn·ɪʙʊ'n ʙu'ɢulfan a'w·ɛw akwe'ɪnafʊnak.

ɢamɪta'ʙ-a'mpyan ɢu'sa-waʙa'l a'mpyan ʙu'ɢulfan a'm·ɪm ɢuᴅɪnɪɢɛ'w·u.

ha'l·u· wa'm·u· a'm·ɪm ɢuᴅɪncma''a. ᴅJɛʙu'ɢulfan hɛ'ca waᴅɪ'nt'cit a'ɢ·a ɢʊ'sa wa'm·u· a'm·ɪm ᴅɪnɪkwu'n utown.

ɢu'ca sʊ'ᴅʊ (~sa'ᴅʊ) ᴅɪᴅɪkʊ'n·yaʙ ᴅJɛwa'm·u·-a'm·ɪm ɢʊnɪsma''a ||125:2|| <69(4)>

ɢu'sa-awa'm·u·-a'm·ɪm tcɛHillsboro tcɛDayton tcɛMcMinnville ʙu'ɢʊlfan ɢɪ'nʊk ɢuᴅɪncma''a ɢʊ'ca-wɪ-aʙa'l-a'mpyan.

ɢu'ca-ᴅɪsɪ·''muɪ ɢuᴅna'ɢɪt,

ɢu'cwɪ, tcɪ''ɪ ṗʊ'fan tcɪmyu·'huyu.

wa'ŋq-la'f tcɪ''ɪ ɢuᴅɪᴅɪ't tccɛhɛ'l·a ɢu'ca mɪ'ᴅɪ ɢuᴅɪpɢɛ'w·u.   <69(5)>

ᴅɛma·''ma ɢuᴅna'ɢɪt,

"Alright, you stay home!"
Then my father went back to his home.
　　It was dark when he got back to my mother.

<70> Mother Finishes Food
Then, when it was morning, my mother finished all the fine food.
　　She organized all that food.
　　　　She put it in five tubs.
　　She gave it to my father.
My mother said,   <70(2)>
　　"You take all of this food!
　　You will give it to Shilikwa. ||125:3||
　　He will take care of that food."

<71> Fourth of July
Then it was that fourth day (Fourth of July).
In the morning they banged[8] away.
　　They threw up smoke from two of those things called "anvils."[9]
Then at ten o'clock all sorts of Indians stood in two lines.
Then they went (paraded) around the field.
My father went in front in a wagon.   <71(2)>
　　He carried that which is called the "flag."
Then his tribe went behind him.
Then those Wachenos (Wacheno and his Clackamas people) went behind my
　　father's tribe.
Then these Molala people, they went behind.
Then those Ahantchuyuk people, they went behind.   <71(3)>
Then those Santiam people, they went behind.
Then those Luckiamute people, they went behind.
　　All the Indians' tribes went behind.
　　The Whites stood there to the side (?).[10]
When they finished parading around the field, then they went to where it was
　　that they spoke.   <71(4)>
　　That White agent stood on that which is called the "platform."
　　　　He spoke to his other White people (?).[11]
Then one White man named "Old Doc Sutton" spoke.
When he finished speaking,   <71(5)>

gu′cwɪ. ma′ha sʙi′ɴᴅ ᴅjɛha′m·ɪ.

pɛ·″ma ᴅɛma′ma ɢuᴅɪ′tyɪ ᴅjɛɢɷ′k ᴅɪᴅʋ′m·ai.

ɢʋᴅɪthu′wɪ ɢutmu·′ɢ tcɛᴅɛna′na.

<70> Mother Finishes Food

ʙɛ·″ma ɢuᴅɪtme′ɪᴅj ᴅɛna′na ɢut·ʋ′ɢɪ ʙʋ′ɢʋlfan ɢʋ′ca tɛ′n·a ᴅɪnɪk̇wɛ′ɪnafyak.

ᴅɛna′na ɢut·ɛ′n·an ʙʋ′ɢʋlfan ɢu′sa k̇wɛ′nafyak.

ɢuᴅṗi′n tcɛhu′w·an aṫa′m·ʋltc.

ɢuᴅ·ɪ′ct ᴅɛma′ma

ᴅɛna′na ɢuᴅna′ɢɪt, <70(2)>

ma′ha cᴅɪ′ᴅ̇ku ʙu′ɢulfan hɛ′sa k̇wɛ′ɪnafyak.

ᴅɛᴅɪ′st cɪ′lik̇wa. ‖125:3‖

ɢɷ′k ɢuᴅyu′ᴅnɪɢwan ɢu′sa k̇wɛ′ɪnafyak.

<71> Fourth of July

pɛ·″ma ɢu′sa ɢuᴅɪta′ʙ-a′mpyan.

ha′l′wan ɢunɪṗu′q̇ʙa·t

ɢuᴅɪnɪɢu′ ama′ŋqt ᴅjɛɢʋ′sa a′ɢ·a ᴅa′ŋkwɪt ᴅjɛɢɛ′m anvil.

pɛ·″ma ɢuᴅɪdɪ′nfyaf-a·ᴅɪ′ɴᴅɪn ʙʋ′ɢʋlfan a′w·ɛw amɛ′nmɪ ɢuᴅɪnɪᴅɛ′sᴅap ᴅjɛɢɛ′m aɢu′n.

pɛ·″ma ɢuᴅɪnɪwɪ′y·u ᴅjɛɢʋ′ca amɛ′w·a.

tcɪ″ɪ-ᴅɛma′ma ɢwᴅ·ɪ′·ᴅ ᴅjɪ′m·ɪ ᴅjɛᴅjɪ′ɢᴅjɪɢ. <71(2)>

ɢwᴅɪᴅk̇wɛ′n a′ɢ·a ɢʋ′ca ᴅa′ŋkwɪt aflag.

pɛ·″ma ɢɷ′k ᴅɪɢa′wkɪl ɢuᴅɪnɪᴅ′i′·ᴅ ha′nt′c.

pɛ·″ma ɢʋ′sa wat′ci′nu ɢuᴅɪnɪᴅ′i′·ᴅ ᴅjɛᴅɛma′ma ᴅɪɢa′wkɪl ha′nt′c.

pɛ·″ma hɛ′ca amʋ′lɛ·lɪs a′m·ɪm ɢuᴅɪnɪᴅ′i′·f ha′nt′c.

ʙɛ·″ma ɢu′sȧ ha′nt′cɪyuk-a′m·ɪm ɢuᴅɪnɪᴅ′i′·f ha′nt′c. <71(3)>

ʙɛ·″ma ɢʋ′sa sɛ′ɴᴅɪyɛ′m-a′m·ɪm ɢuᴅɪnɪᴅ′i′·f ha′nt′c.

ʙɛ·″ma ɢʋ′sa la′q̇mayut-a′m·ɪm ɢuᴅɪnɪᴅ′i′·ᴅ ha′nt′c.

ʙu′ɢulfan ɢu′sa amɛ′nmɪyak ᴅɪnɪɢa′wakɪl ɢuᴅɪnɪᴅ′i′·ᴅ ha′nt′c.

ɢɪ′n·ʋk ɢu′ca-wa′m·u·-a′m·ɪm ɢuᴅɪnɪᴅa′f tcɛla′q̇wayu.

ɢuᴅɪnɪt·ʋ′ɢɪ ɢuᴅɪnɪwɪ′y·u ᴅjɛɢʋ′ca amɛ′w·a. pɛ·″ma ɢuᴅɪnᴅɪ′t ᴅjɛha′l·a ɢu′sa

ɢuᴅɪnɪᴅyu′wun. <71(4)>

ɢu′sa-awa′m·u·-a′Agent ɢɷ′k ɢuᴅɛ′sᴅap ᴅjɛ′a′ɢ·a ɢu′sa ᴅʋ′ŋkwɪt aplatform.

ɢuᴅyu′wun ᴅjɛɢɷ′k ᴅɪᴅɪᴅwa′m·u·-a′m·ɪm.

ʙɛ·″ma wa″an wa′m·u·-a′mu′ɪ ᴅa′ŋkwɪt ᴅjɛyu′hu′yu· Doc Sutton ɢɷ′k ɢuᴅyu′wɪn.

ɢuᴅɪt·ʋ′ɢɪ ᴅɪyu′wɪn <71(5)>

"Which of you Indians will stand up and speak to these White people?"
My father said,
   "You, Yachkawa, go on and stand up!
   You go speak to these Whites!"
Yachkawa said,   ‖125:5‖   <71(6)>
   "I don't really know the White people's language."[12]
Then Shilikwa said to my father,
   "You go stand there!
   You speak to those White people."
Then my father went.
   He stood up.
   He spoke to those White people.   <71(7)>
Having finished his speech, then he said,
   "All you White people, come to our feast at one of those tables.
   Indian people will be at a different table."
He having finished his talk, then all the White people came to my father. <71(8)>
They shook his hand,[13]
   "We are very pleased with what you have said."
Then the White people went to the one table.
   They ate.   <71(9)>
   Lots of girls waited on those White people.   ‖125:6‖
   It was like this also at the Indian peoples' meal-table.
When it was two o'clock everyone went to the racetrack.
[---]
   "All of you will race horses, White people and Indian."   <71(10)>
   Part of the Indians went to where they played shinny.
      Tualatin boys played against the Luckiamute people.
When it got dark, all came to where the feast was.
Then part of those young men and girls knew those White people's dance.
                                                                           <71(11)>
Then the White girls and young men, they too stood dancing with the Indians.

   There they stood to their dance.   ‖125:7‖
When it was midnight, everyone went home.

<72> Fifth of July
Then, on the next day, all the Indians gathered at ten o'clock.

e'yʌ mɪ'ᴅɪ mɛ·'nmɪ ɢuᴅɪʙsᴅɛ'cᴅʌp ɢuᴅyu''wɪn ᴅjɛhʌ'cʌ wʌ'm·u-ʌ'mɪm.
ᴅɛmʌ'mʌ ɢuᴅnʌ'ɢɪt,

    mʌ'hʌ yɛ'tcɢʌwʌ sᴅɛ'sᴅʌp

    ᴅɪtyu'w·ʋn tcɛhɛ'sʌ-wʌ'm·u-ʌ'm·ɪm.

yɛ'tcɢʌwʌ ɢuᴅnʌ'ɢɪt, ||125:5|| <71(6)>

    wʌ'ŋq tcɪ''ɪ p̓ʋ'fʌn ɢutyʋ'ɢʋn wʌ'm·u-ʌ'm·ɪm ᴅʋ'mhʌ.

pɛ·''mʌ cɪ'lɪkwʌ ɢuᴅnʌ'ɢɪᴅ tcɛᴅɛmʌ'mʌ,

    mʌhʌ tcʌ·'k cᴅɛ'cᴅʌp ɢʋ'cʌʙɛ·ᴅ

    ʙɪcyu''wʋn tcɛɢʋ'cʌ-wʌ'm·u-ʌ'm·ɪm.

pɛ·''mʌ ᴅɛmʌ'mʌ ɢuᴅ·ɪ't

    ɢuᴅ·ɛ'cᴅʌp

    ɢuᴅyu''wun ᴅjɛɢʋ'cʌ-wʌ'm·u-ʌ'm·ɪm.   <71(7)>

ɢut̓ʋ'ɢ·ɪ ᴅɪyu''wʋn pɛ·''mʌ ɢuᴅnʌ'ɢɪt,

    mɪ'ᴅɪ wʌ'm·u-ʌ'm·ɪm ʙɪcᴅjʌ·'k ᴅɪk̓wɛ'ɪnʌfʋn tcɛwʌ''ʌn ɢʋ'sʌ ʌlʌᴅʌ'm.

    mɛ·'nmɪyʌk ʌ'm·ɪm ɢɪ'n·ʋk ɢɪnɪp̓i'n wʌᴅʌ'ɪ'wʌn ʌlʌᴅʌ'm.

ɢut̓ʋ'ɢ·ɪ ᴅʋ'mhʌ pɛ·''mʌ ʙʋ'ɢulfʌn wʌ'm·u-ʌ'm·ɪm ɢuᴅɪnɪsmʌ·'k ᴅjɛᴅɛmʌ'mʌ.   <71(8)>

ɢuᴅɪnɪᴅɪ'tɢwɪn ᴅɪ'lʌ'qʷ

    p̓ʋ'fʌn sʋ'ᴅ·u ɢuᴅ·ɛ'lʋfɪᴅ ʌ'ɢ·ʌ mʌ'hʌ ɢuᴅɪᴅyu''wɪn.

ʙɛ·''mʌ ɢɪ'n·ʋk wʌ'm·u· ʌ'm·ɪm ɢuᴅɪnɪᴅɪ't ᴅjɛwʌ''ʌn ɢʋ'sʌ ʌlʌᴅʌ'm.

    ɢuᴅɪnɪᴅk̓wɛ'ɪnʌfʋ.   <71(9)>

    ʙʋ'ɢulfʌn ʌ'w·ɛw ʙɪ'nʌ·tst ɢuᴅɪnɪᴅyu'ᴅnɪɢwʌn ᴅjɛɢʋ'sʌ-wʌ'm·u-ʌ'm·ɪm. ||125:6||

    pʌ'sʌ-yu·-wɛ'w ᴅjɛɢu'sʌ mɛ·'nmɪyʌk ᴅɪlʌᴅʌ'm ᴅɪnɪk̓wɛ'ɪnʌfʋn.

ɢʌmɪᴅɢɛ·'m-ʌᴅɪ'nᴅɪn ʙu'ɢulfʌn-e'y·ʌ ɢuᴅɪnɪ''ɪ ᴅjɛɢʋ'sʌ mʌ'nfɪyʌk-ʌɢʋ'n.

[---]

    mɪ'ᴅɪ ɢu'sʌ ɢuᴅmʌ'nfɪyʌn ᴅɪk̓ɪ'uᴅɪn. wʌ'm·u-ʌ'm·ɪm nʌu-ʌmɛ·'nmɪ.   <71(10)>

    k̓u'ʙfʌn ʌmɛ·'nmɪ ɢuᴅɪnɪ''ɪ ᴅjʌhʌ'l·ʌ ɢu'cʌ ɢuᴅɪnɪlʌ'ɢwʌk ʌsk̓ʌ'lkʌl.

       tfʌ'lʌt̓ɪ wʌt̓u'ɪᴅfʌf ɢunɪlʌ'ɢ·wʌɢ ᴅjɛɢʋ'sʌ lʌ'q̓mʌyut ʌmɛ·'nmɪ.

ɢuᴅɪᴅhu''wɪ ʙu'ɢulfʌn ɢuᴅɪnɪᴅ_cmʌ''ʌ ᴅjʌhʌ'l·ʌ ɢʋ'cʌ k̓wɛ'ɪnʌfʋnʌk.

pɛ·''mʌ k̓u'ʙfʌn ɢu'sʌ-ʌsɪn'fʌf nʌu-ʌʙɪ'nʌ·tst ɢuᴅɪnɪᴅyʋ'ɢʋn ɢu'sʌ-wʌ'm·u-ʌ'm·ɪm

    ᴅɪn·ɪyɛ'l'wʌ.   <71(11)>

pɛ·''mʌ ɢɪ'n·ʋk ɢu'sʌ wʌ'm·u· ʙɪnʌ'ᴅjɪt nʌu-ʌsɪ'nfʌf ɢɪ'n·ʋk-yu· ɢuᴅɪnɪyʌ't·ʋn-ᴅɪyɛ'l'wʌ

    tcɛmɛ·'nmɪ.

    ɢu'cʌʙɛ·ᴅ ɢuᴅɪnɪyʌ't·ʋn-ᴅɪnɪyɛ'l'wʌ ||125:7||

ɢwᴅɪᴅk̓u'ʙfʌn-ʌwɪ'fyu_ ʙu'ɢulfʌn-ʌ'm·ɪm ɢuᴅɪnɪᴅɪ'tyɪ.

<72> Fifth of July

ʙɛ·''mʌ ɢuᴅɪᴅmɛ'ɪᴅj ʙu'ɢulfʌn ʌmɛ·'nmɪ ɢuᴅɪnɪᴅɢɛ·'w·u ᴅjɛᴅɪ'nfyʌf-ʌᴅɪ'nᴅɪn.

There the Indians ran on the dirt (track?).

There they raced until noon.

Then the Indians got ready to eat at midday.

Not many White people came that day. <72(2)>

Then the Indians went to the race-track.

The young men went to where it was that they play shinny.

Then Molalas played against the Umpqua Indians.

When it was dark, they came to where the meal place (was).

Then, when it was dark, all the Indians gathered at the place where they stood to their dances. ||125:8|| <72(3)>

Those Umpqua Indians, they stood to their dance.

These other Indians just sat.

They watched the Umpquas as they stood to their dance.

The other Indians gave the Umpqua Indians everything.

Kerchiefs and shawls to those women Umpquas. <72(4)>

To those Umpqua men they gave pants and coats and shirts.

When it was midnight, they finished their dances.

All the Indians returned to their tents.

<73> Sixth of July

Then on the third day, the early ones staying in the tents ate at the place where they prepared food.[14]

Then at ten o'clock all the Indians came to the place at where they gathered.

||125:9||

Then Shilikwa stood up.

He said, <73(2)>

"Today we will wrestle at Indian wrestling."

Then he said,

"We have one boy, he will want to wrestle with any of the Indians."

That Indian was named Antoine (*at'wé·n*[15]). <73(3)>

Shilikwa took Antoine's hand.

He led him to the middle of the grounds.

He was not a very big man.

Then they, the other Indians, took a young man, a Shasta.

They said,

"We have a young man, he will wrestle against your young man." <73(4)>

ɢʊ′ᴄᴀʙɛ·ᴅ ɢɪ′n·ʊk mɛ′′nmɪ ɢʊᴅnɪᴅmᴀ′nfɪf tcɛhᴀ′ŋ̓klu·p.

ɢʊ′ᴄᴀʙɛ·ᴅ ɢɪ′n·ʊk ɢʊᴅɪnɪᴅmᴀ′nfɪf tcɛwɪ′lfu-ᴀ′mpyan.

pɛ·′′ma ɢɪ′n·ʊk amɛ′′nmɪ· ɢʊᴅɪnɪtɛ′n·atcwu·n ᴅumɪnɪk̓wɛ′ɪnafu tcɛwɪ′lfu-ᴀ′mpyan.

wa′ŋq hⱳ·′′lʊ wa′m·u-ᴀ′m·ɪm ɢʊᴅɪnɪᴅᴄmᴀ′′a ɢʊ′ca-wɪ-ɪ′pyan.　　　　<72(2)>

pɛ·′′ma ɢɪ′n·ʊk amɛ′′nmɪ ɢʊᴅɪnɪᴅɪ′t tcɛmᴀ′nfɪyak-aɢu′n.

ɢɪ′n·ʊk sɪ′nfaf ɢʊᴅɪnɪᴅɪ′t ᴅjɛhᴀ′l·a ɢʊ′sa ᴅɪnɪlᴀ′ɢwak askᴀ′l̓kal.

pɛ·′′ma ɢɪ′n·ʊk amulɛ·′lis ɢʊᴅɪnɪlᴀ′ɢwak tcɛ′ᴀ′mpɢwa amɛ′′nmɪ.

ɢʊᴅɪᴅhu′′wɪ ɢɪnɪsmᴀ′′a ᴅjɛɢʊ′ca hᴀ′l·a kwɛ′ɪnfɪyak.

pɛ·′′ma ɢwᴅɪᴅhu′′wɪ ʙu′ɢulfan amɛ′′nmɪ ɢʊᴅɪnɪᴅɢɛ′w·u ᴅjɛhᴀ′l·a ɢu′ca ɢʊᴅɪnɪᴅya′t·ʊn-
　　ᴅɪyɛ′l̓wa.　　　　　　　　　　　　　　||125:8||　　<72(3)>

ɢɪ′n·ʊk ɢʊ′sa a′mpkwa amɛ′′nmɪ ɢʊᴅɪnɪya′t·ʊn-ᴅɪyɛ′l̓wa.

hɛ′sa waᴅa′ɪ′wan-amɛ′′nmɪ k̓ʊ′nfʊ ɢʊᴅɪnɪᴅ_sɪ′y·u

　　ɢʊᴅɪnɪt·′ᴄɪ′ʙlu·ᴅ ᴅjɛɢu′sa a′ŋ̓kwa amɛ′′nmɪ ɢʊᴅɪnɪᴅya′t·ʊn-ᴅɪnɪyɛ′l̓wa.

ɢu′sa waᴅɪ′ᴅᴀɪ amɛ′′nmɪ ɢʊᴅɪnɪᴅɪ′ᴄᴅ ɢu′ca a′ŋ̓kwa amɛ′′nmɪ ʙu′ɢulfan ᴀ′ɢfan.

　　ahɪ′k̓tcʊm alɪ′ᴄⱳ·l tcɛɢɪ′n·ʊk ɢu′ca-waʙu′m·ik aŋk̓wa.　　　　<72(4)>

　　ɢɪ′n·ʊk ᴅjɛɢʊ′ca a′mu′ɪ a′ŋ̓kwa ɢʊᴅɪnɪᴅɪ′ct alu′m·ulu·n na′u-aɢa′ʙu· na′u-aca′·ᴅ.

ɢʊᴅwɪ′lf-awɪ′fyu ɢʊᴅɪnɪt̓·ʊ′ɢɪ ᴅɪnɪyɛ′l̓wa.

　　ʙu′ɢulfan amɛ′′nmɪ ɢʊᴅɪnɪᴅɪ′tyɪ ᴅjɛᴅɪnɪsɪ′lhaus.

<73> Sixth of July

ɢwᴅɪᴅhu′psɪn-a′a′mpyan ɢu′sa hᴀ′l̓wan ɢɪ′n·ʊk ɢu′sa ɢunɪᴅa′fᴅju tcɛɢʊ′sa sɪ′lhaus

　　ɢɪ′n·ʊk ɢʊᴅɪnɪᴅk̓wɛ′ɪnafʊ ᴅjɛhᴀ′l·a ɢu′ca ɢunɪʙʊ′n-akwɛ′ɪnafʊnak.

ʙɛ·′′ma ɢwᴅɪᴅɪ′nfyaf-aᴅɪ′nᴅɪn ʙu′ɢulfan mɛ′′nmɪ ɢʊᴅɪnɪᴅᴄmᴀ′′a ᴅjɛhᴀ′l·a ɢu′ca

　　ɢʊᴅɪnɪɢɛ′wʊfʊn.　　　　　　　　　　　||125:9||

ʙɛ·′′ma ᴄɪ′lɪk̓wa ɢʊᴅɛ′·ᴄᴅap

ɢʊᴅna′ɢɪt,　　　　　　　　　　　　　　<73(2)>

　　hɛca-wɪ-ɪ′pyan ɢʊᴅmᴀ′ntfɪt amɛ′′nmɪyak amᴀ′ntfu.

pɛ·′′ma ɢʊᴅna′ɢɪt,

　　su′ᴅu tcɪᴅṗi′′n wa′′an at·u′ɪᴅfaf ɢutᴀ′mᴅju ᴅumnɪᴅmᴀ′nfɪf ᴅjɛʙu′ɢulfan e′y·a

　　　　amɛ′′nmɪ.

　　ɢu′s·a amɛ′′nmɪ ᴅa′ŋkwɪt atwɛ′·n.　　　　<73(3)>

　　ᴄɪ′lɪk̓wa ɢʊᴅɪ′tɢwɪn atwɛ′·n ᴅɪ′la′qʷ

　　　　ɢʊᴅwu′ᴅwa·t wɪ′lf ᴅjɛhᴀ′ŋ̓klu·p.

　　　　wa′ŋq-p̓ʊ′fan ɢwᴅɪᴅʙa′l aᴅja′ŋku.

ʙɛ·′′ma ɢɪ′n·ʊk ɢu′sa waᴅa′ɪ′wan amɛ′′nmɪ ɢunɪᴅɪ′tɢwɪn wa′′an asɪ′nfaf aᴅjɛ′·stɪ.

ɢɪ′n·ʊk ɢʊᴅɪnɪᴅna′ɢɪt,

　　su′ᴅu tcɪᴅʊṗi′′n wa′′an asɪ′nfaf ɢʊᴅmᴀ′nfɪt tcɛmɪ′ᴅɪ ᴅɪsɪ′nfaf.　　<73(4)>

[---]
   "Alright,"
said Shilikwa,
   "Bring him out!"
Then all the Indians put together their money.
   Perhaps one-hundred dollars they gathered. <73(5)>
Then a Shasta man said, ||125:10||
   "Only one fall, and then he will win one-hundred dollars."
Shilikwa said,
   "Alright."
Then they got ready (?)[16] to wrestle. <73(6)>
   They took off all of their clothes.
Then they took two men to watch over that wrestling (match).
Silikwa said,
   "I will pick Ishilshil as our man."
   The Shastas picked one man, I don't remember his name. <73(7)>
Then they took hold of each other's bodies.[17]
When they had wrestled for nearly an hour, then the Shasta got tired.
Then Antoine threw him to the ground.
Then all the Tualatins were glad. <73(8)>
   They hollered, they jumped around, they threw their hats high into the air.
||125:11||
Then they finished their match.
Shilikwa said,
   "All you Indians get ready and eat!"
When they had finished their meal, those who had racing horses went to the
   racetrack.
   The young men, they went to where they played shinny. <73(9)>
Then at sunset part of the old men and the women went back to their houses.

   My father and mother (and) I went back to our house.
Then I don't know what they did that night.
   Shilikwa was head man at the meal table.
This is as much as I remember. <73(10)>

[---]
   ɢu'cwɪ,
cɪ'lĭkwa ɢuᴅna'ɢɪt:
   cmu'ku hɛ''lʊm.
pɛ·''ma ʙu'ɢulfan amɛ·'nmɪ ɢuᴅɪnɪɢɛ'w·a ᴅɪnɪsɋɪ'nwaɪmax.
   e'ɪkɪn wa''an-ᴅʊ'mp̌ɪ cɋɪ'nwaɪmax ɢuᴅɪnɪɢɛ'w·u.   <73(5)>
pɛ·''ma wa''an ᴅjɛ'cᴅɪ a'mu'ı· ɢuᴅna'ɢɪt, ||125:10||
   yɛ'lfan wa''an ɢwᴅjɛ'ɢ·u. pɛ·''ma ɢuᴅ·u'l·ı ɢu'ca wa''an-ᴅu'mp̌ɪ sɋɪ'nwaɪmax.
cɪ'lĭkwa ɢuᴅna'ɢɪt:
   ɢu'cwɪ.
pɛ·''ma ɢuᴅɪnɪᴅhu'l·ıtcwu·n ᴅumᴅɪᴅma'nᴅfɪᴅ.   <73(6)>
   ɢuᴅɪnɪᴅɢu' ʙu'ɢulfan ᴅɪnı'a'ɢfan.
pɛ·''ma ɢɪnɪᴅɪ'ᴅɢwɪn ɢɛ·'m-a''mu'ı ɢumɪnɪyu'ᴅnɪɢwan ɢu'ca-ama'nᴅfɪᴅ.
cɪ'lĭkwa ɢuᴅna'ɢɪt,
   tcɪ''ı ᴅɪᴅ·ı'tɢwin ı's·ılsil tcɛsu'ᴅ·ʊ tʊ'm·ım.
   ɢɪ'n·ʊk a'aᴅjɛ'stı ɢɪnɪᴅɪ'tɢwɪn wa''an a''mu·ı wa'ŋq ɢuᴅyʊ'ɢ·ʊn ᴅa'ŋkwɪt. <73(7)>
ʙɛ·''ma ɢuᴅɪnɪᴅɪ'tɢwɪn ᴅɪnıǩa'ʙya.
ɢuᴅɪnɪᴅma'nᴅfɪt e'ɪkɪn wa''an hour. pɛ·''ma ɢu'sa-aᴅjɛ'stı ɢuᴅ_lu'ɋyu <60(34)>
pɛ·''ma a̓twɛ·'n ɢutɢu·' ᴅjɛha'ŋklu·p.
pɛ·''ma ʙu'ɢulfan atfa'latı a'm·ım ɢuᴅɪn'ɛ'l·u.   <73(8)>
   ɢuᴅɪnɪᴅ_la'l'wi ɢuᴅɪnɪᴅ'ı'ᴅ·up ɢuᴅɪnɪᴅɢu·' ᴅɪnɪmu'yus ha'lʙam tca'myaŋk .
                              ||125:11||
ʙɛ·''ma ɢuᴅɪnɪt·ʊ'ɢı ᴅɪn·ıla'ɢ·uk,
cɪ'lĭkwa ɢuᴅna'ɢɪt,
   ʙu'ɢulfan mı'ᴅ·ı amɛ·'nmɪ tɛ·'n·atcwu·n ᴅɪᴅʊp̌kwe'ınafʊ.
ɢuᴅɪnɪt·ʊ'ɢı-ᴅɪǩwe'ınafʊn e'ya ɢu's·a wap̌i·'n ama'nfɪyak akı'uᴅɪn ɢuᴅɪnɪᴅɪ't tcɛma'n-
   fɪyak aɢu·'n.
   ɢɪ'n·ʊk ɢu'sa ası'nfaf ɢuᴅɪnɪᴅni''ı tcɛha'l·a ɢu'ca ɢuᴅɪnɪᴅla'ɢ·uᴅ askǎ'lkal.<73(9)>
pɛ·''ma ɢuᴅɪᴅjɛ'ɢ·u-a'mpyan ǩu'ʙfan ɢu'ca-wayu'huyu a'mu·ı na'u-aʙu'm·ik ɢɪ'n·ʊk
   ɢuᴅɪnɪᴅɪ'tyı tcɛᴅɪnɪᴅu'm·aı.
   ᴅɛma·'ma nau-ᴅɛna·'na su'ᴅ·u ɢwᴅ·ı'tyı tcɛᴅuᴅu'm·aı.
ʙɛ·''ma wa'ŋq tcɪ''ı ɢuᴅyu'ɢ·un a'ɢ·a ɢuᴅɪnɪᴅ'mı'u'nan ɢu'cawi-wı'fyu.
   cɪ'lĭkwa ɢʊ·'k waᴅja'mʙak ᴅjɛɢu'ca ǩwe'ınafyak alaᴅa·'m.
ʙa'sa-hʊ·'lu tcɪ''ı-tcɪ'yʊ'ɢ·un.   <73(10)>

<74> Post-Festivities

When we got back to our home, my mother made food.

Finished, then we ate. ||125:12||

Our meal being over, I went out.

   I came back.

   I went in the house.

I said to my mother, <74(2)>

   "I'm going to sleep."

[---]

   "Alright."

Then they went to bed.

It wasn't so very early in the morning (that) they got up. <74(3)>

   My father chopped wood.

   My mother cooked food.

When nearly done with her food, she called out,

   "Bahawadas! get up! come on!

   Wash your face! <74(4)>

   Now we are eating."

Then we sat down to our meal.

When we finished, then my father said,

   "Today I'm going to the mountains (to) round up our horses. <74(5)>

   I'll bring them back to the corral."

   He found all his horses.

Then he drove them to the corral.

   He got home near sunset.

   My mother was finishing up the cooking. ||125:13||

   My father staked his horse outside at a place where there was much grass. <74(6)>

Then he came into our house.

   He got ready.

   He washed up.

Then we ate.

   (We) finished eating.

The next day he went to the mountains to look for his cows.

   Perhaps some of the big cows had had baby calves.

MY LIFE, BY LOUIS KENOYER

<74> Post-Festivities

ɢᴜᴅɪᴅɢᴜ′mwu·ɢ tcɛᴅɪᴅu′m·ɑɪ, ᴅɛnɑ′nɑ ɢᴜᴅʙu′n ak̓we′ɪnɑfʊn.
t̓ʊ′ɢɪ, ʙɛ·′′mɑ su′ᴅ·u ɢᴜᴅɪᴅkwe′ɪnɑfʊ. ||125:12||
t̓ʊ′ɢɪ-ᴅɪkwe′ɪnɑfʊn, tcɪ′′ɪ-ɢʊᴅɪ′t-hɛ·′′lʊm.
  ɢᴜᴅɪ′tyɪ,
  ɢᴜᴅ_lɑ′m·u ᴅɟɛhɑ′m·ɪ.
ɢᴜᴅnɑ′ɢɪt ᴅɟɛᴅɛnɑ′nɑ,   <74(2)>
  tcɪ′′ɪ-tcumsᴅɪ′twɑɪ.
[---]
  ɢᴜ′cwɪ.
pɛ·′′mɑ ɢɪ′n·ʊk ɢᴜᴅɪnɪᴅɪ′twɪ.
wɑ′ŋq p̓ʊ′fɑn hɑ′l′wɑn ɢwᴅɪᴅme′ɪᴅɟ, ɢɪ′n·ʊk ɢᴜnɪcʙʊ′ɢlɑɪ.   <74(3)>
  ᴅɛmɑ′mɑ ɢᴜᴅk̓u′ʙk̓ɑ·ᴅ-ɑ′wɑ′ᴅɪk,
  ᴅɛnɑ′nɑ ɢᴜᴅʙu′n-ak̓we′ɪnɑfʊn.
yɛ′ᴅɟ ɢᴜᴅɪt̓ʊ′ɢɪ ᴅɪkwe′ɪnɑfʊn, qɛ′ᴅ·ɑk ɢᴜᴅ_lɑ′l′wɑɪ
  ʙɑ̓χɑwɑᴅɑs, cʙu′ɢlɑɪ tcɪ′ᴅ·ɑ.
  ck̓u′′uɬ ʙuɢwɑ′l·ɑk!.   <74(4)>
  pɛ·′′mɑ ᴅɪ′sᴅɪᴅkwe′ɪnɑfʊ.
pɛ·′′mɑ ɢᴜᴅ_sɪ′y·u ᴅɪkwe′ɪnɑfʊn.
ɢᴜᴅɪt̓ʊ′ɢɪ-ᴅɪkwe′ɪnɑfʊn pɛ·′′mɑ ᴅɛmɑ′mɑ ɢᴜᴅnɑ′ɢɪt
  hɛ′cɑ-wɪ-ɪ′pyɑn, ᴅɪᴅɪᴅɪ·t tcɛmɛfʊ ɢɪ′sɢɑ·t sʊ′ᴅ·ʊ ᴅɪkɪ′uᴅɪn.   <74(5)>
  ɢᴜᴅɪᴅ_cwɪ′′ɪl ᴅɟɛq̓ɑ′l·ɑχ.
  ɢᴜᴅ·ɛ′sᴅɛs ʙu′ɢulfɑn ᴅɪkɪ′uᴅɪn,
pɛ·′′mɑ ɢɪ′cɢɑ·t ᴅɟɛq̓ɑ′l·ɑχ.
  ɢɪnᴅwɑ′l yɛ′ᴅɟ ɢwᴅɪᴅɟɛ′ɢ·u-ɑ′mpyɑn,
  ᴅɛnɑ′nɑ ɢᴜt̓ʊ′ɢɪ ʙu′ɢulfɑn ᴅɪkwe′ɪnɑfɪyɑk. ||125:13||
  ᴅɛmɑ′mɑ ɢᴜᴅ·ɛ′m·ɑt ɑkɪ′uᴅɪn hɛ·′′lʊm tcɛɢu′cɑ hɑ′l·ɑ hu′l·u ɑlu′q̓u. <74(6)>
pɛ·′′mɑ ɢʊ·′k ɢᴜᴅ_clɑ′m·u ᴅɟɛᴅu′m·ɑɪ
  ɢᴜt·ɛ′n·ɛtcwu·n
  ɢᴜᴅk̓u′′uɬ.
pɛ·′′mɑ su′ᴅ·u ɢᴜᴅɪᴅkwe′ɪnɑfʊ.
  t̓ʊ′ɢɪ-ᴅɪkwe′ɪnɑfʊn.
me′ɪᴅɟ ᴅɪᴅɪᴅɪ′t ᴅɟɛmɛ′fu u′ᴅnɪɢwɑn ᴅɪmu′cmuc.
  e′ɪkɪn wɑʙɑ′l-ɑmu′cmuc ᴅɪnɪp̓ɪ′n ᴅɪnɪwɑ′p̓ɪ ᴅɪ·′t′sɑq ɑmu′cmuc.

Notes and Commentary

CHAPTER ONE

1   This section is from a group of several short texts that Kenoyer dictated to Angulo and Freeland (1929), independently of the autobiography proper. Brackets and curly brackets appearing in the transcript restore Angulo and Freeland's original transcriptions, in cases where their different perceptions have possible morphological implications: see Text Presentation and Translation: The Tualatin Text.

The names of all three chiefs mentioned in this text appear also in texts transcribed by Gatschet (1877:108–114, 298-300; in Jacobs 1945:160–73) from Kenoyer's father, Peter Kenoyer. The three chiefs were Peter Kenoyer's father, Kammach (*k'ám·ač*); his father's brother, Kayakach (*k'áyak'ač*); and the Multnomah-Wakanasisi Chinookan chief Kiesno (Gatschet: <Giáshnu, Kiáshnu>, for Chinookan *k'iásnu;* often encountered as "Casino" in historical reference, misconstrued in Jacobs 1945:161 as "ɢyɛ'cnu," a "Clackamas headman").

Kiesno's home village was Cathlahcumups (*gaɬáq'map*), near modern St. Helens, Oregon. Following the malaria epidemics of the early 1830s, he and other survivors of the epidemics moved across the Columbia River (Kenoyer: "the Big River") to Wakanasisi village (*wak'ánasisi*) near Fort Vancouver. Well known to Euro-Americans of the fur-trade era (Boyd 2011:44–57, 115), Kiesno was also a principal player in the region's early nineteenth-century indigenous slave trade. Slaves originated as captives or descendants of captives. On the lower Columbia, their hereditary status was revealed by the fact that, unlike freeborn people, their heads did not bear the effects of frontal-occipital flattening during infancy—a custom general among Tualatins, although not among Kalapuyans farther south. Indigenous slaves lived in their masters' households, where they were treated much as poor relations (indeed, they were addressed using kinship terms); nevertheless, they were considered the property of their masters.

Tualatins seem to have acted as a client group to lower Columbia Chinookans, obtaining slaves from the south to supply Chinookan chiefly patrons like Kiesno. As in Kenoyer's account in this chapter, they often (perhaps usually) obtained slaves through trade with interior Willamette Valley Kalapuyans, among whom the selling of orphaned or otherwise marginal children into slavery was customary. But it cannot escape notice that the very first unambiguous historical mention of Tualatins (under the historical synonym "Faladin") includes reference to a slave raid in the southern Willamette Valley. John Work, with a Hudson's Bay Company party visiting Indians near Marys River in 1834, has the following entry in his journal:

> They [the Indians] inform us that 4 men of Lautaude Indians [perhaps a miscopied synonym of a name for Long Tom River Kalapuyans; the same source has "Lamitambuff" for Long Tom River] have been killed & 3 children taken slaves a short time since, as they suppose by a party of Faladin or Yamhill Indians. (Work 1923:264)

As in Western classical antiquity, indigenous Oregon slave raiders usually tried to kill or rout the men of a victim group, the preferred prizes being children and young women. A passage in Peter Kenoyer's 1877-dictated text on Kammach may have originally been meant to describe some such practice, although its interpretation is ambiguous in the original—and further complicated in Jacobs's (1945:162–163) published version by the restoration of a text-segment that appears crossed out in the original. The passage appears to have been meant originally as follows (reproducing Gatschet's field translation with bracketed extensions; the part in <_> brackets appears crossed out in the original):

If somebody wanted [to] take away [a] slave Kamm[otch] took him, not he was afraid when he is angry [aroused? ready to fight?] [then] he entered a house he takes hold of the <man and cut him>" (Gatschet 1877:113)

The crossed-out section is replaced by the word for 'slave' ('he entered a house he takes hold of the slave'; the rest of the <_>-marked passage is left crossed out). While an apparently clear explanation is given in a later section of the manuscript devoted to review of the text—"If a slave is ordered for a man, Kamm[otch] is not afraid to enter houses & get slaves" (Gatschet 1877:300)—both the original and the explanation are complicated by demurrers. In the original, "Kamm[otch] never did this"; in the review, "(not true) K[ammotch] never was anywhere else but among the Lákmiuk [Luckiamute Kalapuyans, from whom he obtained slaves by trade] for slaves." The source of these discrepancies is unclear (review by another informant? Peter Kenoyer's second thoughts about the image he was projecting of his father's "greatness"?). The published version was confused by Frachtenberg (whose typescripts of the texts Jacobs worked from), compounded by Jacobs's own parenthesized textual interpretation:

When anyone wanted to obtain a slave, then he [Kammach] would take him. He was not afraid. Should he become angry (presumably at some slave) he would go inside, take the slave, and cut (slash) him up (at least to produce permanent scars if not to cut off a nose or ears). (Jacobs 1945:162–163)

This very troubling portrayal of master-to-slave abuse is not supported by Gatschet's original version of the text. Rather, it appears to be Jacobs's own original interpretation.

2 Angulo and Freeland's free translation of lines 7–9 reads: "Whenever they have anything to say they gather all the people, (to find out) what kinds of games the people want to play."

3 *tókdeluk* (tɑ́'qʊɛlʊq) 'brave': Gatschet glosses 'brave fighter, big warrior', observing that the term implies not only fearlessness in battle, but invulnerability to wounds as well ("shot, but always recovering"). Gatschet reviewed his texts from Peter Kenoyer with his other principal Tualatin informant, Dave Yachkawa, whose reaction to Peter Kenoyer's characterization of Kammach as *tókdeluk,* a great or 'mighty man' (Jacobs 1945:160), is recorded in a marginal note to the original manuscript (Gatschet 1877:109): "he was not, (Dave), but a great eater."

4 The Angulo and Freeland transcript glosses haʼloʼ (Jacobs: haʼlʊ) 'only', yielding the free translation: "He only bought those slaves." Ordinarily, haʼlʊ bears first-syllable stress, and translates 'many, lots of, so many'. Possibly, the shift of stress to the second syllable in the original dictation was expressively motivated, as we have conjectured in our translation. In any case, the apparent implication is that Kammach was not a slave raider—he only bought slaves from tribes that customarily sold off orphans and like persons lacking connections in the community. The historical truth may have been more complicated: see note 1 above.

5   That is, the Columbia River: see note 1 above.

6   Jacobs re-elicited *diditwál* 'we will arrive' for Angulo and Freeland's tɑm.tɪt-wɑ'l (*damditwál*) 'when we arrive'. We translate following Angulo and Freeland's transcript, which shows this clause subordinate to the preceding clause.

7   Jacobs re-elicited *debíkʷakyup* 'my brothers' for Angulo and Freeland's *dabíkʷ·ak* 'my brother('s)'. Context favors the originally given meaning.

8   The placement of this passage in the Angulo and Freeland typescript suggests that Kammach's return from his trading expedition provided the occasion for the celebratory activities envisaged. This plausible interpretation only lacks explicit confirmation in the manuscript.

CHAPTER TWO

1   The Tualatin text of <1-12> is Jacobs's re-elicitation, as it appears written into Angulo and Freeland's typescript (Angulo and Freeland 1929). Jacobs did not independently translate this portion of the narrative, although he did insert many field annotations into the pages of Angulo and Freeland's original translation. The last segment of this chapter (<13>) is wholly from Jacobs, included here because it completes the narrative segment begun in <8>.

   According to Jacobs's field annotations, Kenoyer was about seven or eight when he started school (<2-3>), and his family home was at Old Grand Ronde. Old Grand Ronde was the part of the reservation surrounding Grand Ronde Agency, near where St. Michael's Catholic Church now stands, versus New Grand Ronde, where modern Highway 18 intersects Grand Ronde Road (see map 2).

2   See Introduction, note 1, regarding the tribe name. The usual form is *tfálat'i*, which becomes *atfálat'i* with the addition of the Tualatin nominal prefix. While some historical synonyms do show a terminal *–n* as in Kenoyer's form, Gatschet's voluminous Tualatin field notes do not show it, leaving it uncertain whether Kenoyer's form is entirely genuine or was perhaps influenced by the English local name "Tualatin."

3   The *hánč'iyuk* (or Ahantchuyuk) people were a Central Kalapuya-speaking "tribe" or cluster of villages indigenous to Pudding River and French Prairie—roughly, the part of the Willamette Valley bounded by the modern towns of Canby, St. Paul, and Keizer. They signed the 1855 Willamette Valley Treaty as the "Calapooia band of Calapooias" (Belden 1855). On the reservation, they were counted as part of the Santiam tribe.

4   Although the only census we have for this period (Grand Ronde ca. 1872) shows Peter and Ann (?) Kennoyer [*sic*] with three children: Charles (six years old), Louis (four years old), and Margaret (fourteen months). Apparently, Kenoyer either misspoke when he referred to his *bú·cat* 'elder sister' or there was an unrecorded other sister (or possibly, another relative referred to as an elder sister).

5   Jacobs's annotations add: the boys were seven to eleven years old, divided into two sides fifty to one hundred feet apart; the balls were stuck on the ends of serviceberry switches and were made to "fly with the help of the sticks."

6   For ᴅɛha'mha-ha'mɪ (*de-hámha-hám·i*) 'my language-house', literally. Elsewhere in the narrative, 'language-house' appears consistently with the meaning 'school'. In this line only, the Angulo and Freeland transcript identifies it as the agency office. The only linguistic clue to this changed reference is the presence of the first-person singular possessive prefix *de-* (Angulo-Freeland <ta->), implying that this is the agent's own 'language-house'.

7   Where contemporary postcolonial criticism emphasizes the cultural destruction inherent in the nineteenth-century boarding school experience, what we get from Kenoyer here, as well as in chapters 8, 9, and 10, is a simple, straightforward account of daily living routines, children's play, and classroom lessons at Grand Ronde's on-reservation "Sisters' School." A stint at the Sisters' School constituted a rite of passage for almost all Indians born on the reservation, from the construction in 1876 of the first substantial school building to the generation of elders interviewed by Zenk in the early 1980s. Kenoyer's experience with the reservation's education system goes back further than that, since his first attendance was at one of the day schools preceding the establishment of the Sisters' School: 2<2-3> above. Even after the Sisters' School was established, a portion of the student population attended as day students, not boarders; and we can see from Kenoyer's narrative that special circumstances (a death in the family, as in 2<6>; family economic exigency, as perhaps in 2<7>) could trump the government mandate put forth in 2<4>. Nonetheless, children boarded there normally spent the entire school year in the school, their contacts with their own families (Kenoyer's family home was only a mile away from the school) restricted to monthly visits, as explained by the agent in 2<4(5)>. For an overview of the rather complex history of Grand Ronde Reservation schools, see Cawley (1996:55–62).

8   In Angulo and Freeland's original translation, <5> shows the English present indefinite throughout: suggestive of a typical day (as opposed to a particular day) in the life of the Sisters' School. In Jacobs's Printer's Manuscript translation, the entire section is given in the past tense. See discussion in Text Presentation and Translation: The Tualatin Text, note 1.

9   "The man" referred to is subsequently described as conducting the Catholic daily Mass. According to Fr. Martinus Cawley (personal communication 2014), this could only have been the priest—that is, Fr. Croquet. Fr Croquet is also featured in <6> later in this chapter, as well as in chapters 7 and 9: see chapter 9, note 1.

10 Jacobs notes: "about twelve years old." No name given but quite possibly Charley Kenoyer, whose death Fr. Croquet recorded on August 24, 1874 (Munnick and Beckham 1987, I P. 88).

11 Jacobs: "our relatives from diff[erent] tribes."

12 Jacobs: "my father's niece, a Tualatin."

13 The Tualatin Tamanawas doctor Shumkhi (šúmxi; also: šúmxin, šə́mxən), called Nancy Jack or Jack Nance in English, was a well known and frequently patronized traditional healer in the late nineteenth-century reservation community. John Hudson (Jacobs 1945:48–49) described him as a man who dressed as and assumed the lifestyle of a woman—in anthropologists' terminology, a *berdache*, or in more recent indigenous-inspired terminology, a Two-Spirit. This is how he (she) was remembered also by elders interviewed by Zenk in 1978. Victoria Howard (Jacobs 1958-59:517–519) consistently referred to Shumkhi as a woman, indeed, as her own father's father's sister (Mrs. Howard's father, William Wishikin, was Tualatin; he died when she was a small child, and she was raised by a Clackamas Chinookan-speaking grandmother). Some sources refer to Shumkhi as a "hermaphrodite." Judging by Hudson's and John Warren's descriptions to Berreman (1935:23, 44), "she" was clearly biologically male: in Warren's rather uncomplimentary depiction, "a big fat, coarse featured man" who dressed and rode side-saddle like a woman. Hudson and Howard both identify Shumkhi's Tamanawas power as Coyote, while Jacobs's field annotation from Kenoyer identifies it as "dead-people-power." Both attributions are possible, as Tamanawas doctors typically had an

array of different Tamanawas spirits at their disposal.

14 Note that Kenoyer refers to Shumkhi as *go·k* (ɢɷ·ʹk) 'he' in this line, whereas in the first line of <6(16)> he had used *géd·ak* (ɢɛʹᴅɑk) 'she'.

15 While the Tualatin word t'ɪʹw·ɑt properly refers to an indigenous twined berry basket, Jacobs's annotation notes that "tin buckets [were] already [in use] at that time."

16 For *kúʔus* (quʹʹʋs), the usual Kalapuyan name for Siletz Reservation people. The Angulo-Freeland typescript glosses 'Coos'. While the term could be taken broadly, to include Coosans and other Oregon coastal people to the south of Siletz Reservation, Kenoyer himself uses it elsewhere with explicit reference to people of Siletz Reservation (compare 6<32>).

17 Jacobs starts <12> at this line, which we feel properly belongs to the last line-set of <11>.

18 The White man on whose property Kenoyer and his mother went to pick these berries had deliberately planted them there: see <12(11)>. Probably a kind of blue huckleberry (*Vaccinium* sp.), as it seems unlikely that the locally common red huckleberry (*Vaccinium parvifolium*) would be prized enough to justify such special treatment.

19 Source translation: "he had one of my aunts" (not explained). It seems worth noting that the verb (*p'i·n* 'keep, have, lie, be, remain, put, leave, make' [Berman 1988b]) bears the present/progressive prefix *u-*.

20 Jacobs: "the old man used Santiam(-)hantcyuk [Ahantchuyuk] words: kaʹʙɑɪ; kaʹʙ·ɑɪ is Tualatin." Evidently, he spoke some Kalapuyan, very unusual for local Whites of this period. More usually, Whites used Chinuk Wawa (or increasingly, with the passage of time, English) to communicate with tribal people.

21 The Angulo and Freeland transcript of the autobiography ends with the last line of <12> (as numbered in Jacobs's Printer's Manuscript). The extension of the narrative transcribed by Jacobs at Wapato, Washington, in the summer of 1936 commences with <13>. It was originally recorded in Jacobs's field notebook 122:11, 13, 15.

CHAPTER THREE

1 A field annotation by Jacobs states that Kenoyer was "about twelve at this part of his narrative," which would date it to about 1880.

While the reservation's lands were not officially allotted until 1891, the government agents parceled out the Grand Ronde Valley into individual family farms long before that. Gatschet (1877:18, 188–189) has some contemporary observations on Indian farming on the reservation: a young man of age received twenty acres of land, two single people or a married man forty, a family with two children sixty, a family of four children eighty, a family of six children one hundred; the land was "mostly poor," fit only for raising wheat, with an average yield of only twenty-five bushels ("often only 5–6 in bad ground"); sowing and plowing was in November, the harvest in September–October; pumpkins and melons don't do well at Grand Ronde, beans are "not very sure," while peas, cabbage, and turnips do well.

Kenoyer's use of narrative repetition conveys a good sense of the sheer hard work and daily drudgery (albeit relieved by occasional playful interludes and Sunday rest days) that was the lot of any nineteenth-century small farmer, Indian or White. The old reservation life of hard work on the farm, as described by Kenoyer, was more than just a distant memory for the Grand Ronde elder (and respected community leader) Wilson Bobb Sr., interviewed at length by Zenk in 1982 and 1983. It was a living legacy that guided him throughout his long life. Indeed, it would be no exaggeration to say that that legacy was his salvation, since it was primarily through sheer hard work—including a fifty-year career in the woods ("I high climbed, tended hook, pulled rigging, set chokers, chased, whistle punked, done all of those things"), with added time spent working his own inherited and acquired lands at Old Grand Ronde—that he was able to surmount the disadvantages of a dysfunctional childhood family, made so largely as a result of the reservation drinking culture alluded to in the Introduction: Louis Kenoyer in Later Life. In an interview conducted by Mike Markee (1973), excerpted below, he shares some of his thoughts about farming, both in general and on the reservation, pointing especially to the strong work ethic of the old reservation, too often ignored by local Whites who, to his extreme annoyance, were fond of characterizing Indians as "lazy." Probably, not many contemporary community members would go so far as to concur with him that interest in one's ancestral heritage should be discouraged as "a waste of time"—a potentially harmful distraction from the overriding necessity to "make a living." Yet, that necessity must loom very large indeed, viewed against the backdrop of the old reservation as portrayed in Kenoyer's autobiography, and actually experienced by Mr. Bobb in his earlier years.

> Mike Markee: What was the farming like around here [at Grand Ronde]? Do you think it was pretty good?
> Wilson Bobb Sr.: Farming's no good anyplace.
> MM: What kind of crops? Wheat? Oats?
> WB: Wheat and oats, that's all.
> MM: Now I know over at Siletz they planted a lot of potatoes there and that sort of thing when they originally formed the reservation.
> WB: I think that's the better ground over at Siletz there. But farming is a joke you know. You take all these farms with nice big homes, why, the banks own most of it! Go to MackMinnville [McMinnville, Oregon, twenty miles from Grand Ronde] over here a little ways, why gol', great big machines why, you know very well that a farmer can't make it, with all the machine[s] and the amount of money they have to pay for machinery. I tried it, I know. . . .
> MM: . . . Now, you grew up right here on the reservation now, right?
> WB: Yeah, right here.
> MM: Don't you think it's important that your children and grandchildren know something about their past heritage though?
> WB: I don't.
> MM: You don't think it's important.
> WB: No, that's a waste of time. . . . Because you gotta make a living nowadays, you can't fool around with all that stuff! . . . Was a lot of 'em farmed here, this whole country in here was farmed by Indians at one time. There's no Indians worked as hard as these, these fellers that come from, that was driven from other places to be here. They ALL worked, they either farmed or worked out, cut cordwood or cut wood or something they did. But you, you hear the White man say "the lazy Indian," but that's just the way that the White man is, talks about the Indian.

2   In preparing for their off-reservation trip, Kenoyer and his father had turned their livestock loose in the mountains near their home: <7(3)>. That this was a common practice on the reservation is suggested by local tradition, according to which there used to be feral cattle roaming the mountains west of Grand Ronde—no doubt an unintended consequence of this practice.

3   The Tualatin text actually shows the word for 'elder brothers' (*bíkʷakyap*), not brothers-in-law; Jacobs notes: "bros-in law was meant." Gatschet has *míuf* 'brother-in-law'.

4   Jacobs: "down to Yamhill river right there." Presumably the South Yamhill River, which meanders its way through the middle of the old reservation.

5   Jacobs: "to this (Catholic) church (near Old Grand Ronde Agency)." That is, St. Michael the Archangel Church, here probably the first of three church buildings occupying the same church property. In Kenoyer's time, the Sisters' School and the buildings of Grand Ronde Agency stood in close proximity to the church. The modern St. Michael's Church, located at the junction of Grand Ronde Road and State Highway 47, stands somewhat to the south and west of the original church and agency.

6   Gatschet has *mámiš* specifically for 'cooked camas', as opposed to *mándip* 'raw camas'. Angulo and Freeland (1929) show only the former word from Kenoyer, glossed 'camas'.

7   These are all indigenous Kalapuyan foods, which by this late date (and with the notable exception of blackberries) contributed very little to the overall subsistence economy of the reservation. They would seem here to be ceremonial foods.

8   Jacobs (Printer's Manuscript): "various linguistic groups or 'tribes.'" Presumably, the different Grand Ronde Reservation tribes.

9   Jacobs: "at the ends, corners (of the wheat field)."

CHAPTER FOUR

1   The only proper name appearing anywhere in this extended narrative of a hunting and berrying excursion into the Coast Range to the northwest of Grand Ronde is that of Kenoyer (that is, Bahawadas) himself. Other participants, as well as the mountain peak dominating this part of the Coast Range, are identified only in Jacobs's field annotations. The contents of these, with some additional background information, are summarized in the following key to people and places referred to in this chapter:
That man. Yamhill Joe Jeffries (*túkšin*), a Yamhill hunter.
His (that man's) wife. Mary (*hayash-tutúsh* 'big breasts', a Chinuk Wawa name). Originally Modoc, she had been brought up as a slave among the Clackamas. She spoke Clackamas Upper Chinook and Chinuk Wawa.
One woman, that woman <21(2)> and her husband <21(3)>. Susan Hollingsworth (*xímštani*), a Klickitat (Sahaptin) speaking woman—earlier married to Joe Hollingsworth, here to Molala Sampson, a Molala hunter.
The Big Mountain. Mt. Hebo, in the Coast Range northwest of Grand Ronde. During the ca. 1880 period of this narrative, it was reachable from Grand Ronde via some twenty to thirty miles of primitive trail, much of it over difficult mountain terrain. Jacobs records *hívu* from Kenoyer as the name of Mt. Hebo. It is "Hevo" on the 1899 township sketch accompanying the first land survey of this part of the Oregon Coast Range. Mt. Hebo proper, which stands at 3,154 feet some twenty miles from the ocean coast, is part of a complex of rugged mountain ridges. The region has been a favorite hunting ground for generations of Grand Ronde Indians. The 1899 township sketch also shows a trail, labeled "Grande [*sic*] Ronde and Nestucca trail," going right over the top of the mountain. Darrel Mercier (personal communication 2013), who as a youngster in the 1930s often went on family hunting trips to the mountain, has it from family tradition that Indian trails usually followed ridgelines, and also that Fr. Croquet (who happened to be Mr. Mercier's grandfather's uncle) went by trail over Mt. Hebo to conduct his pastoral visits to the Oregon coast. Very likely, Yamhill

Joe and his party traveled this same trail. The top of Mt. Hebo is broad and flat, and in Mr. Mercier's memory largely bare (this was before a manned radar station, since demolished, was constructed there). Also, much of the country nearby was burned over. Burned-over land makes for the best berrying and hunting habitat, and Mr. Mercier understands (again, from family tradition) that Indians deliberately set fires to keep their berrying grounds from reverting to brush and timber. Today most of the area is clothed in dense second-growth Douglas-fir timber.

2   Jacobs: "this was done for the sake of improving the general luck at hunting."

3   The Tualatin form for 'his rifle' (ᴅɪsɑ' g̱walal) appears in the field text as a correction of the incorrect form: *ᴅɪpa'g̱walal.

4   This may be a restart following a hiatus in the dictation.

5   Jacobs: "in order to discourage wolves black bears or panthers [usually called cougars in contemporary local English], who, smelling the human's coat, will stay away."

6   This and the following lines down to the beginning of <22(8)> appear to recapitulate the preceding three lines.

7   Jacobs: "following another route to get to where the deer lay."

8   Jacobs: "leaves with brush, etc., over the pile of meat, to keep the flies off."

9   In Jacobs's field notebook, the "place" that was "fixed up" is explained with reference to a sketch labeled "Yamhill dry frame": four corner posts set in a rectangular configuration joined by stringers on the long sides, with eight cross stringers joining the two long stringers. The sketch bears the legend: "5–6 ft. high, 3–4 ft. across, 6–8 ft. long (enough for 2 big deer)." Such a structure could have been built by any local hunter, so its identification as "Yamhill" seems a bit odd.

10 Jacobs: "with small fires under the frame for perhaps two days."

11 Jacobs: "berries are laid on the pieces of fir bark, which are placed to the side of the fire."

12 Jacobs: "men stayed to help too."

13 Jacobs: "they were getting red huckleberries, blackberries, a kind of brown huckleberry / mid-August."

14 Jacobs: "they were Yamhill Joe's relations."

15 Jacobs: "removed the dried ones, put fresh ones on the fir bark."
    This annotation is expanded upon on the facing page of the field notebook:
    The berries are dried for about half the night, then the fires are allowed to go out and the people sleep; then next morning the fires are lit again to dry the berries all thru the day. That evening the cured berries are removed and a fresh bunch started.

16 Jacobs: "to dry a fresh batch."

17 Jacobs: "a yearling buck."

18 Jacobs: "it was to be eaten at camp."

CHAPTER FIVE

1   See chapter 3, note 1, for background on the reservation's farm economy and historical work ethic. The off-reservation work trips described in this chapter, as well as in 2<8–13> and chapter 12, also remind us that the Grand Ronde Valley was not ideally suited to intensive agriculture; Grand Ronde Indians had to find piecework and

seasonal employment elsewhere in order to get by.

2   Jacobs: "Ind[ian] girls from the community."

3   Jacobs: "Five miles southwest of Salem on the west bank of the Willamette (at Ed Davis' hopyard)."

4   Jacobs: "to your people (for food when here)."

5   Jacobs: "to a grist mill—west of New Grand Ronde [see chapter 2, note 1]."

CHAPTER SIX

1   Organized competitions on the reservation—such as horse races—generally entailed betting. Judging by this text, the stakes could be significant—five hundred dollars (as in <33>) in the late nineteenth-century American West was no small sum of money. An especially interesting aspect of this text is the insight it affords into the dynamics of individual self-identification on the reservation. In relation to the world outside the reservation, Grand Ronde Indians competed against Whites (<29–31>) or, in <32>, against Indians of another reservation (here, the neighboring Siletz Reservation). Within the community itself, individuals usually aligned themselves first with other individuals of their own tribe. In <33> we see also the influence of the reservation's local tribal clusters (see Introduction: The Grand Ronde Tribes), as the Tualatin leading man Shilikwa assembles a stake from Molalas, Clackamas, and Yamhills, as well as from his own Tualatin people, to bet against the Luckiamutes, a Central-Kalapuya speaking tribe backed here by the Umpquas, Rogue Rivers, and Shastas—all southern Oregon tribes residing in New Grand Ronde (across the South Yamhill River from Old Grand Ronde). In <34> Kenoyer's father lends his racehorse to the Clackamas leading man John Wacheno, to whom he was related by marriage. Backed by "our people" (presumably, Tualatin and Clackamas people, at least) Wacheno proceeds to organize a win against the Umpquas.

2   Jacobs: "east of O[ld] Grand Ronde [see chapter 2, note 1]."

3   Jacobs: "ci'likwa [šílik'ʷa]—a Tual[atin] shaman [also known as] Lame Jim."

4   Jacobs: "to back him up—help him make up the bet—he had not the money himself."

5   Jacobs: "Frank Bond—a Yamhill."

6   Jacobs: "to start at 'ready' rather than at 'go.'"

7   Jacobs: "he didn't want to give the White boy an advantage at the starting jump."

8   Jacobs: "really, they 'used their whips' / they pretty near killed them whipping them."

9   Literally, 'your own heart/mind'.

10 Jacobs: "the Ind[ian]s made outside bets on this race between the two White men's horses."

11 Jacobs: "a judge who had bet on the side [of] the losing horse."

12 Jacobs: "it was Pinky Logan's horse—bro[ther] to Abe Logan." The Logans are a Siletz Reservation family.

13 Jacobs: "who had been picking hops in the valley [Willamette Valley] near Independence—they had come over to Grand Ronde for the sports."

14 We gloss gáwakil (ɢa'wakıl) 'community' where, as here, it refers to the collectivity of Grand Ronde Indians. Where it refers to one or another tribe, we gloss 'tribe'. While Jacobs too appears to understand that the term refers here to the collectivity of Grand Ronde Indians, he usually takes it to refer to the Tualatin tribe, even where context

makes it obvious that it cannot: see discussion in our Introduction: The Story of *My Life, by Louis Kenoyer.*

15 Kenoyer's usual word for measuring distance is *do·f*, which Gatschet glosses 'foot'. Field glosses in this text have the word both as 'pace(s)' and 'yards'; for consistency, we gloss 'pace(s)'. Only in this line does Kenoyer use *lúʔun* 'leg' as a measure word; while this may be a slip, for clarity we gloss as 'yards'.

16 Jacobs: "it was one of cilikwa's [Shilikwa's] horses / named Silvertail."

17 Jacobs: "two white, two black sticks with a cover—a guessing game."

18 Jacobs: "to John Watcheeno [Wacheno] / who had married my father's niece." John Wacheno was one of the three sons of the Clackamas treaty chief *wač'ínu*, the other two being Dan Wacheno, Victoria Howard's first husband, and Foster Wacheno.

19 Field translation. Kenoyer may actually have said: *go·k gut-ténaʔan gusa mánf-yak a-kíu-din* 'he fixed up that race-horse'; but then misheard the verb *-ténaʔan* 'fix up' as a related nominal form (*tén·an* 'good') when Jacobs read the text back for translation. Alternatively, he may originally have misspoken the former for the latter, then corrected his meaning during translation.

20 According to Jacobs's field annotations, the individual referred to in this passage was Umpqua Joe (very likely, the individual also known as Winchester Jo—brother of the Umpqua treaty Chief known as Bogus, and stepfather of John Warren, a contemporary of Kenoyer quoted in our Introduction).

21 Schrock adds: field transcript and translation have plural 'jockeys' here, though from context—father giving advice to "his" jockey—it is clear that the jockey should be singular.

22 Jacobs: "Frank Bond was our jockey in most of our races at that time."

23 Jacobs: "from Eng[lish] hoof—meaning foot, yard."

CHAPTER SEVEN

1 The Church at the center of this chapter as well as of chapter 9 was St. Michael the Archangel Catholic Church, founded by Grand Ronde's first and longest-serving missionary priest, Fr. Adrien-Joseph Croquet (locally, "Father Crockett"). Fr. Croquet's first appearances in the narrative come in 2<5-6>, originally dictated to Angulo and Freeland (1929). The present chapter has the narrative's only explicit identification of this important player in the life of the nineteenth-century reservation; this comes in a field annotation to <36>: "[he was] a Belgian, Father Crockett / he spoke in Jargon [Chinuk Wawa] and English both during services." See chapter 9, note 1, for additional detail on Fr. Croquet.

2 Glossing *gáwakil* as 'community': see chapter 6, note 14.

3 Text and gloss of the first clause, as they appear in Jacobs's field notebook:

   p[ɛ·ʼma] ɢʊt̓ʊʹɢı maʼʼa
   'then you quit [for:] when you die'

   Translated literally, *péʔma* 'then'; *gut-t'úgi* 'you stop, quit'; *máʔa* 'come' (verb-stem -*a* 'come', *ma-* directive prefix). Possibly, the key to this line is to be found in the documented fact (mentioned by Kenoyer himself) that Fr. Croquet preached in Chinuk Wawa. Fr. Croquet used Fr. Demers's "Chinook Catechism" (Chinuk Wawa Dictionary Project 2012:370–72, 378–79, 467–71), which includes the idiomatic compound <kopet chako> '[stop-come:] cease coming to pass, end for all time', as in the following passage from the catechism (transliterated following Chinuk Wawa Dictionary Project 2012:271):

pus kʰəpit-chaku <kopet chako> *kʰanawi-ikta, pi kʰanawi tilixam miməlust pi wəχt kitəp, chxi yaka k'ilapay kʰupa ili?i sesukʰli*
'When all things cease coming to pass, and all people die and rise up again, only then will Jesus Christ return to earth.'

Jacobs's Printer's Manuscript interpretation of this line is very forced:

pɛ·"ma ɢʊt·ʊ'ɢ-ı ma·"a pɛ·"ma
'And when you have finished (have died) you are to come then,'
ɢʊdna'ɢıt dʊm·a·"a ᴅʲaɢʊ'ca-ha'lʙam-aᴅʲa'mʙɑk.
'he [the priest] said, "you will come to the headman above (God).'

We find no other examples in the narrative of *pé·?ma* placed and glossed as a clause-final adverb ('. . . then'). Our reading also varies from Jacobs's in that we understand the grammatical subject of *-nagit* 'say' to be the Lord Above (God), not the priest.

4   Jacobs: "behind me while I walk in front sowing grain."

5   Jacobs: "[you will] lap the harrow the second time."

CHAPTER EIGHT

1   According to a field annotation by Jacobs to <42(3)>, Kenoyer was a second-grader at this point of his narrative. Compare 2<4-5>, in which Kenoyer remembers the opening of the Sisters' School and provides his first account of life there. In this chapter, as well as in chapter 10 below, he provides considerable additional detail on what daily life was like for students boarded there.

2   Jacobs: "a mile from my home." Very likely, the Kenoyer family farm was the same place later awarded to Louis Kenoyer himself, as part of the final allotment of reservation lands in 1891. This allotment was located a mile east of the agency and boarding school (see map 2). The "brothers" in Kenoyer's account were most likely other boys from the tribal cluster occupying the northeast quadrant of the Grand Ronde Valley, where Tualatins, Yamhills, Clackamas, and Molalas co-resided.

3   Jacobs: "it was a two-room school."

4   Puzzling verb form: *-?uknifai*, apparently showing the first-person singular objective suffix *-fai*. Unfortunately, this particular verb form hardly ever appears in the narrative, and Kenoyer's field translation of this sentence (reproduced in full here) appears not to be literal.

5   Presumably, the same "whipping stick" described in Jacobs's field annotation to <42(12)> (next note): a ruler applied to the palm of the hand.

6   Jacobs: "they used a ruler on the palm of the hand."

7   Jacobs: "they had 1 h[ou]r lunch—class from 9–12, 1–4."

8   Jacobs: "there was a diff[erent] washroom for girls." Context elsewhere in the narrative makes it clear that the boys' "washroom" was located outside the school and dormitory buildings. (Kenoyer's narrative takes place long before indoor plumbing was introduced to Grand Ronde.)

9   The anonymously written Catholic *History of Grand Ronde* cited in our Introduction quotes one of the Benedictine Sisters, Sister Mary Augustine (at the school from 1895), regarding a case of two runaway girls:

One Sunday afternoon two of the girls ran away and were not missed until

Benediction. When found, for punishment they were put in the Block House for one day and their meals consisted of bread and water only. (Anonymous 1960:21)

The blockhouse was originally built as part of the Fort Yamhill military garrison that oversaw the reservation during its first ten years. After the garrison was disbanded, the blockhouse was moved from the old site of Fort Yamhill to Grand Ronde Agency, where for some years it served as a community jail. In 1911 it was moved again, to Dayton, Oregon, where it remains on public display.

CHAPTER NINE

1   Although this part of the narrative could be considered simply another episode in the daily life of the Sisters' School, because it so prominently features Grand Ronde's Catholic missionary priest, Fr. Croquet, we present it as a free-standing chapter. Fr. Croquet was known both within and without the Indian community for his humility and self-sacrificing deference to the needs of others, often at the expense of his own personal comfort and welfare. We are indebted to Fr. Martinus Cawley of Our Lady of Guadalupe Trappist Abbey, Lafayette, Oregon, author of an authoritative biography of the good father (Cawley 1996), for reviewing this chapter and providing selected annotations.

Fr. Martinus's biography of Fr. Croquet includes an appendix titled "The Gospel according to Croquet," from which we excerpt the following observations on Fr. Croquet's missionary modus operandi:

Listing of vices, and headlong attacks on them, were not part of Fr. Croquet's strategy. Visiting priests might speak that way, and he would interpret their sermons into Jargon [Chinuk Wawa], but he would tell them afterwards that such a style was not a fruitful one at Grand Ronde, that one did not make people Christian in one day or one month. Instead, one tempered the demands to the capacity of the flock. He told this to his Archbishop in regard to Lenten arrangements, and to Rev. [R. W.] Summers [Episcopal priest at McMinnville, Oregon] in regard to funeral rites. Gradually he would win the adults, but his hope lay in the next generation.

This gradualism built upon the warm welcome that so consoled him in every new beginning. He saw his Gospel as first of all a Gospel of "Help" and "Consolation." He was himself consoled by the welcome, but his aim was rather to console and help the needy among those he met, most especially the abandoned and the dying. There was also the over-all view, in which he saw his work as a propagating of the Faith, of true religion, of the Light of the Gospel, and so on, but most of all he called it the simple "doing of good" or "saving of souls." (Cawley 1996:34)

Fr. Martinus happens to have in his possession a letter from one of the aforementioned "visiting priests," of interest both for the author's firsthand impressions of Fr. Croquet's character; and for the firsthand glimpse it offers of communication within the polyglot Grand Ronde and St. Michael's communities. The letter is dated July 30, 1903, and is written on stationery of the Benedictine Priory, Mount Angel, Oregon. While the flawed Xerox in Fr. Martinus's possession lacks a signature line, peculiarities of style, content, and handwriting have enabled a member of the current Mount Angel Benedictine community, Fr. Augustine DeNoble (personal communication 2016), to positively identify the author as the Priory's founder, Fr. Adelhelm Odermatt, a native of Switzerland. Fr. Adelhelm is credited with arranging for Benedictine Sisters to be sent to Grand Ronde to staff Fr. Croquet's school (Van der Heyden 1906:221–222). Neither Fr. Adelhelm nor Fr. Croquet were native speakers of English. Since Fr. Adelhelm spoke both German and French, the two could well have used French when speaking to one another. But their language of public communication at St. Michael's was of necessity English first, followed by Fr. Croquet's Chinuk Wawa construal of their English.

> When his Grace Archbishop Seghers blessed a new way of the Cross in the new church [the second St. Michael's church, dedicated 1883], . . . I had to preach the English Sermon & Rev. Father Croquet had to translate my English into Chinook language for the old Indians. When the Ceremony was over & we had returned into the sacristy, the Archbishop well pleased remarked: What a change would soon come over that entire reservation, if such a Sermon was preached every Sunday to those Indians. But good Father Croquet was afraid, some Indians might not like some of the strong language I used against certain vices, especially against the holy virtue. . . . Some years after His Grace Archbishop Gross once preached a powerful sermon to the Indians against mixed marriages, & when the sermon was over, & His Grace returned to the sacristy the old Missionary, Father Croquet complimented the Archbishop, by saying: "<u>This would have been a splendid sermon for the white people.</u>" —of course it did not mean or concern his darling Indians.

Although the last comment may betray a hint of sarcasm, Fr. Adelhelm nonetheless affirmed the good father's "saintliness," an appellation frequently encountered in accounts of Fr. Croquet's life and mission: "I was often at Grand Ronde & I thought a great deal of the old Saint & his mortified [*sic*] way of living." And,

> Rev. Father Croquet looked & acted as humble & unpretending as a child. To judge from his appearance, his shabby clothes, & his poor English, with a strong French brogue or accent, one would be tempted to think that he hardly knew the most necessary Latin to be a priest—& yet it is an admitted fact, that he was one of the best scholars, & one of the most profound & learned Theologians among the Catholic Clergy.

The foregoing characterization of Fr. Croquet's English, it must be noted, is from someone who had himself learned English as an adult. According to Fr. Augustine, while Fr. Croquet may have spoken English with a distinct French accent, he did speak it fluently. Fr. Croquet was indeed an accomplished Catholic scholar, holding the degree of bachelor of philosophy from Louvain University in his native Belgium.

2   Jacobs: "boys only here"; "boys had a dining room separate from the girls."

3   Jacobs: "[Daniel] yɛ́'tcɢawa [*yáčgawa, yéčgawa*] / a Tualatin also / died of TB after leaving Chemawa."

4   Jacobs: "back end of the church." Fr. Martinus: The technical term is "the sacristy."

5   Jacobs: "[a] coat-dress/garment—long skirt-like, a white garment; [and] a red (short) coat." Fr. Martinus: The technical terms are "cassock" and "surplice." The cassock was the everyday gown worn by all clerics, and for altar boys in the USA its usual color was red. The surplice was a waist-length smock, always white. Louis seems to remember the colors in reverse.

6   Jacobs: "as altar boys." Fr. Martinus: Normally in liturgical processions—even with only three participants—the juniors go first, but perhaps Fr C[roquet] found the boys too shy to do that, and thought best to have them follow, esp[ecially] if going down the aisle.

7   It is hard to know when to take Kenoyer's circumlocutions (such as, here, "the good man," with reference to Fr. Croquet) at face value (to be translated literally), as opposed to when it may be more appropriate to replace them with familiar English translation equivalents (as, in this case, "priest"). The field translations show both options. Jacobs consistently opts for literal translation, adding English equivalents in parentheses. We usually introduce the first instance of a circumlocution in a given segment of text by providing both a literal gloss and an English equivalent; thereafter, we usually favor the equivalent.

8   Fr. Martinus: ... sprinkling with what is called an "asperory."

9   Fr. Martinus: ... the "choir loft"—an indoor balcony at the rear of the church, above the front door.

10   Fr. Martinus: We call these two little vessels "cruets." ... The servers brought up the cruets twice. First, in preparation for the rite of Consecration they brought them up to the altar for the priest to pour wine into the chalice, adding the traditional few drops of water from the other cruet. Then, after the Communion, [they brought] the cruets up a second time, for the priest to rinse the chalice and wipe it dry.

11   Fr. Martinus: [I poured the wine into his cup. ... [he] washed his hands]: Louis is here describing the second bringing up of the cruets. Out of reverence for any remnants of the consecrated bread and wine, the priest held his fingers over the mouth of the chalice as the boys poured in the wine and water, in order so as to catch any crumbs on his fingers. Then, rather than tossing the mixture down the drain, he respectfully drank it.

CHAPTER TEN

1   With Sunday worship concluded, it is back to the routines of daily school life, as previously detailed in chapters 2<5> and 8. The present chapter adds a good deal of detail on children's games and play. Recall that according to Angulo and Freeland's information from Kenoyer, "at school he and his comrades (from various tribes) spoke the 'Chinook Jargon' [Chinuk Wawa]" (Angulo and Freeland 1929:2). Very likely, Chinuk Wawa was restricted to informal contexts like those described in <46>, <48>, <49>, and <53>, since we can assume that the language of classroom instruction and school authority was invariably English.

One of the charges leveled by contemporary postcolonialist criticism against the boarding school system is that authorities used corporal punishment to enforce the exclusive use of English, thereby actively contributing to the decline and demise of indigenous languages. In this regard, it is of interest that Chinuk Wawa is the only language besides English receiving mention in historical records of the Grand Ronde school system. Reflecting its role as the reservation's original common language, Chinuk Wawa came into general use also within the reservation's multi-tribal cohorts of children and young people, and it survived for some generations as an expression of social solidarity within those cohorts, even as younger people became fluent and literate in English.

Two schoolteachers' reports from the day-school era provide instructive early glimpses of this development. In one of the earliest published school reports, the teachers, encountering children who had had no previous exposure to English whatsoever, had to resort to Chinuk Wawa themselves.

They were all ignorant of the English language at first, and it was found necessary, on the part of teachers, to resort to Chinook, a jargon spoken here by all the tribes, as a means of communicating ideas. We have now almost wholly dispensed with Chinook, as the children understand English very well. (Sawtelle 1863:84)

Only a few years later, however, there comes the following indication that Chinuk Wawa had become embedded in the children's classroom (or more likely, playground) culture, to the extent that the teacher considered it an impediment to their learning.

The boys seem eager to learn. . . . I find no difficulty in making them understand the English language, and I endeavor to make them communicate their ideas in the same language, but they will use that barbarous jargon, the Chenook [sic]. (Clark 1866:82).

The only mention of corporal punishment being used at the Sisters' School to enforce the exclusive use of English, to our knowledge, comes in the following elder reminiscence recorded by Berreman in 1934. It concerns none other than John B. McClane, by unanimous consensus of the elders interviewed by Berreman the best agent ever assigned to Grand Ronde.

He has the usual respect for McLane [sic], and hatred for Kershaw, though is very temperate in expressing it. He describes McLane as a blunt, gruff old fellow. Recalls that he threatened the school boys with severe whipping for speaking Chinook jargon on the playground in playing ball. Made all speak English. (John B. Voutrin interview; Berreman 1935:64)

Chinuk Wawa was still being encountered by teachers in the Sisters' School in 1891, according to the following report.

The progress especially of the elder ones who already understand English, has been very encouraging. Several of the pupils, however, were new from their homes, in which case the lack of civilization and want of knowledge of the language rendered them doubly a charge, but these obstacles gradually succumbed to the patient endeavors of teacher and matron. It is gratifying to notice how even eager our Indian children are to give up their native dialect, the pleasing result being that at the close of school every child could converse in English without any need of taking refuge to "jargon" [sic]. (Butch 1891:371-372)

2   Jacobs: "[I'll be the black man] in this game of black man—who represents bear or panther or some black animal."

3   Jacobs: "aged 15–16."

4   Jacobs: "little chapel (upstairs in the school building)." This little building within a building is also referred to in chapter 2<5>.

5   Jacobs: "Just big boys and girls do this at 5 [a.m.] while the younger children may sleep on."

6   Jacobs: "about 50-60 were in this room composed of beginners / 1st graders / 2nd graders."

7   Field translation: 'hand gong'. The Tualatin word (*díndin*) is a borrowing from Chinuk Wawa, in which the word shows the same range of meanings appearing in Kenoyer's narrative: 'bell; o'clock; music; musical instrument'. We are uncertain what kind of bell is being referred to in this passage; other passages in which *díndin* also refers to a handbell gloss it variously as 'bell', 'handbell', 'gong'. Fr. Martinus (personal communication 2015) remembers that in one of the Australian Catholic schools he attended, the bell was a large bell-shaped piece of metal sounded using an external stick (as opposed to a clapper). Perhaps, the bell referred to here was a handheld version of that kind of bell.

8   Schrock adds: I have translated this text with mostly non-baseball terminology to add flavor. I think there is a lot of information conveyed about Tualatin language in the way that Louis Kenoyer coins his way through the explanation of baseball. I am leaving this literal terminology intact to give the reader a taste of what the language feels like.

9   Jacobs: "This was a sort of pre-modern baseball game."

10   Jacobs: "it was a rubber ball."

11   In the Tualatin field text of this line, *wáʔan* (wa''an) 'one, a particular' appears as an insertion, wedged in between *pé·ʔma* 'then' and *gín·uk gúsa-ginidítgʷin* 'they that had taken (the bat)'. We suspect that it was inserted there in error.

12   Jacobs: "in a circle, quadrille fashion."

13   The boy's "correct" answer appears in Jacobs's field-annotation. Kenoyer cannot be said to lack a sense of humor, however understated.

14   Jacobs: "Indian wrestling is a matter of no foot used at all, just two boys or men in a sort of body embrace, around the trunk, and the winner throws the other one down. No leg or arm holds of any sort. It's a matter of lifting and throwing."

15   Jacobs: "one hand to rear . . . 'sideholds' is wrestling one hand to the rear."

16   Jacobs: "waʹm·u-asi·'l, 'white sail'—i.e., a bed sheet—the children at this Catholic boarding school were given sheets as well as blankets." This note from Jacobs appears to have been meant to expand on "blanket," appearing in the text here. *-sil* is a borrowing from Chinuk Wawa, where it usually translates 'cloth'.

17   The base translation of this section was created by Zenk, then reviewed by Schrock and Zenk. Base translations of subsequent posthumously translated sections were created by Schrock, then reviewed by Zenk and Schrock.

CHAPTER ELEVEN

1   This chapter, with chapters 12 and 13, are from the part of Kenoyer's narrative lacking a field translation. The translations appearing here are from transcripts created by Schrock and reviewed by Zenk and Schrock. See the Introduction: Life on the Nineteenth-Century Reservation for a discussion of traditional healing ceremonialism incorporating content from this chapter.

2   "I was very *yáčfiq*": the verb yaʹtcfiq (*yáčfiq*) lacks a field gloss. Howard Berman (1988b) guesses 'suffer'.

3   Gatschet (1877) recorded some indigenous Tualatin doctoring terminology, including examples evidently showing the same verb stem used by Kenoyer in this sentence: for example, <tchi tchûmaínai tăláků> 'I heat, warm my hands to work the sickness out' (Gatschet 1877:66).

4   See the description of Tamanawas ceremonialism in the Introduction: Life on the Nineteenth-Century Reservation. During a curing ceremony (the full-form expression of which involved a five-night winter Tamanawas dance), the people gathered in support of the doctor took up his or her songs, marking rhythm by pounding sticks (usually canes in a Tamanawas dance proper) against the wooden floorboards of the house hosting the ceremony.

5   We were unable to identify the verb -ᴅuʹtyu (*-dút'yu*).

6   aʹntmat 'chicken' originally designated the ruffed grouse (*Bonasa umbellus*), a native bird locally termed "pheasant." That chickens were meant is confirmed by the use of

the English word at 57(13). Chickens were much more common than grouse on the nineteenth-century reservation.

7   The verb -'uʹkna·t, 'uʹɢ'na·t (-ʔúkna·t, -ʔúk'na·t) (also <57(9)> and <58(6)>) lacks a field gloss from Kenoyer. We restored it with reference to Santiam <o·k'ni> 'warm, warm up' (vb tr) (Berman 1988d).

8   We were unable to identify the verb -lɛ·ʹвnɪtcfuɪ (-lé·bničfui).

9   Had we an identification of the doctoress and her tribal language, we might have more to go on for conjecturing a source of agé·mšandi (aɢɛ·ʹmcɑnDɪ'), given as the name of the doctoress's Tamanawas-power. The Tualatin form given looks like gé·m 'two' conjoined to šándi, a borrowing from Chinuk Wawa translating both 'week' and 'Sunday'. A form gé·mšandi (the same Tualatin form minus the nominal prefix a-) appears in the draft version of Jacobs's (ca. 1937a, mf 000306) Tualatin culture-element list (see Introduction: Life on the Nineteenth-Century Reservation) as the "second strongest" of Tamanawas-powers, described as "boss of the serpents (in m[oun]t[ain]s)." This name, found nowhere else in the Kalapuyan corpus, provides positive confirmation that Kenoyer was indeed the source of Jacobs's list of Tualatin culture elements.

10 The noun in question, waʹmpɢɪ (wámpgi), does not find an exact match elsewhere in the Kenoyer corpus, although there are a number of near matches: ámkʷ 'thunder, lightning', mámpga 'water, river', ámpqʷi 'hazel' (Gatschet: mámpgʷi). The nearest dead ringer is a Central Kalapuya form for 'water': ampgíʔ. While Kenoyer's Tualatin elsewhere shows the influence of his mother's Central Kalapuya dialect, it is unclear why he would use a Central Kalapuya form to refer to water (or some sort of body of water) here, while using Tualatin for 'water' (etc.) everywhere else. wa- is the usual form of the Tualatin adjectival prefix; but Kenoyer shows it also as an occasional variant of the nominal prefix a- (an-, am-).

11 Verb identified by comparison with Santiam -pú·fi 'to blow'.

12 Jacobs: "named Santiago." This is the only Jacobs field annotation to be found in the untranslated portion of the narrative. Gatschet (1877:374) has "Santiago, or San Diego" as a Klickitat living at Grand Ronde in 1877. Olson (2011:384–385) has an entry for a "Henry Santiago," whose last appearance on a Grand Ronde Indian census is on that for 1886.

CHAPTER TWELVE

1   <60–64> are from the part of Kenoyer's narrative lacking a field translation. This translation was created by Schrock and reviewed by Zenk and Schrock.

    The berry-picking excursions described here and in 2<12> illustrate another means by which reservation Indians supplemented their meager incomes from their reservation farms. The berries harvested were mostly sold to Euro-Americans, thus illustrating an adaptation of a traditional economic pursuit to the realities of the new Euro-American cash economy. A like adaptation is illustrated by traditional basketry on the reservation, where indigenous materials and techniques were applied to the manufacture of new basketry forms geared to the Euro-American market.

2   DɪDɪD_SDuʹm'wɪ (apparently, di-didsdúmʔwi) appears to consist of the possessive marker di-, (either '3 singular' or '1 plural', Kenoyer's forms for these two persons being identical) prefixed to a kinship term. Kenoyer elsewhere gives Duʹm'wɪ (dúmʔwi) 'nephew', while Gatschet records <stūmui> 'mother's elder brother'. The source may be a self-

reciprocal term: 'mother's brother : sister's son'. Possibly, Kenoyer was identifying an "other" (*díd·ai* 'different'?) maternal uncle, in contrast to the uncles met at Salem further on in this chapter. The intended denotation is not clear to us.

3 The root or narrow meaning of -ku'n·ayaʙ (*-k'ún·iyap*) is 'younger brothers'; Kenoyer also used the term in extended senses, such as here when referring to his father's brothers-in-law. In chapter 1 it denotes fellow tribesmen; in chapter 8 it refers to Kenoyer's childhood age-mates; and in chapter 13 it is used with reference to Euro-American guests at a major community celebration. His father's brother-in-law calls Peter Kenoyer his -*bán·ak* 'older brother'.

4 Schrock adds: here it is hard to gloss ɢuᴅ·ε'lq̇yu: 'get stronger'?, 'tough it out'? Searching the rest of the autobiography returns meanings of the root √ᴅε'lq related to "strong" or "tough": to show someone's level of strength or level of recovery from illness; to show difficulty, toughness; and to describe a bitter, hard wind, or a tough wrestler. I cannot quite tell what he means here, whether he is bragging that he is a big boy and strong enough to work like the young man, or whether he was admitting that the work was very hard for him. At any rate, I think we can take from this passage that Bahawadas did help his father perform this work.

5 Compare 2<10(4)>: t̓ı'w·at is originally the Tualatin term for an indigenous berry basket, but by this time, tin buckets were usually used for berry picking.

6 Schrock adds: this sentence is completely opaque to me. Howard Berman suggests 'getting dark' so I'm using that.

CHAPTER THIRTEEN

1 In common with their Euro-American neighbors living in and around the small towns of the Willamette Valley, Grand Ronde Indians honored the Fourth of July, making it the occasion of their major annual community celebration. Of note here is the extension of invitations to Euro-Americans from such disparate small towns as Hillsboro (located some fifty miles north of Grand Ronde, in the Tualatins' old ancestral homeland), McMinnville (some twenty miles from Grand Ronde), and Dayton (on the main Yamhill River, some six miles downstream from McMinnville). Note that in <69(4)>, Kenoyer uses the Tualatin term for 'brothers' (*-k'ún·iyap*) with reference to these visiting Whites, reminding us that notwithstanding the inequality inherent in Indian-White relations of the time, person-to-person relationships could be quite cordial. As well illustrated in Kenoyer's narrative, Grand Ronde people often worked for and alongside neighboring Euro-Americans. Note also, though, that during the festivities described here, Euro-Americans and Indians occupied separate meal tables; also, there seems to have been a clear separation between celebratory activities organized for both audiences and those involving Indians only. Only in <71(11–12)> is there anything like open mixing between the races, with the co-participation of young people of both races in a "White people's dance" (square-dance?: cf. 10<49>).

2 For Tualatin ala'ɢwaɢ (*a-lágwak*), elsewhere glossed 'playing, game(s)' by Kenoyer. Berman (1988d) glosses the Santiam cognate word *lága* 'game, playing; having a big time'; the latter gloss seems to best fit the context here.

3 For Tualatin ṗu'yaɢnak, unidentified.

4 Translation of the foregoing quotation is in some doubt. The prefixation of the verbs may convey nuances that escape us. We translate freely, with an eye to the subsequent unfolding of the narrative in <66>.

5   The verb hɛ·ʹlafnɪɒʹju (-hé·lafnič·u) lacks a field gloss from Kenoyer. We suspect it is related to Santiam hé·lenč 'to tell, relate, explain'.

6   Nor, apparently, did Kenoyer correctly remember the names of all of the leading men of the tribes just listed: "Chief Bogus," one of the Umpqua leading men signing the 1854 Calapooia Creek Treaty, died before Kenoyer was born. The identity of the Wacheno mentioned is uncertain: it could be John Wacheno, featured in 6<34>, or wačʹínu (Old Wacheno), John Wacheno's father. The other names are all identifiable from other ethnographic sources, as well as from government records.

7   si·ʹ'muɪ (sí·ʔmui) appears to be related to the unglossed kinship term appearing in 12<60(4)> (see chapter 12, note 2): -(did)sdúmʔwi. Elsewhere, Kenoyer gives dúmʔwi 'nephew'; while Gatschet records <stūmui> 'mother's elder brother'. Gatschet has a clearly distinct term for father's brother: šíšak. Since we have only the gloss 'uncle' for Kenoyer's sí·ʔmui, the exact relationship remains obscure. Possibly, this particular uncle was the same as the -(did)sdúmʔwi featured in 12<60>.

8   Tualatin -ṗuʹq̇ʙa·t (reduplication of p'uq'): no gloss by Kenoyer, but compare Santiam p'úkp'uk (sound of chopping).

9   Schrock adds: Meaning uncertain. I translate literally, having no real idea what is being referenced. Shoeing horses for the forthcoming races? Canons?

10 Tualatin laʹq̇wɑyu, no gloss available. Kenoyer elsewhere shows lakʷ 'hand, arm'; lákfan 'on one side'. Perhaps lákʹʷayu is a related form; hence, our conjectured translation.

11 Conjectured translation of Tualatin ᴅɪᴅɪᴅʙwaʹm·u·-aʹm·ɪm as 'his White people'. The first di- certainly looks to be the third person singular possessive prefix, but we can only guess what did- is: possibly for díd·ai 'different, other'?

12 It seems rather odd that Yachkawa would beg off for the reason given. "Wapato Dave" Yachkawa (yáčgawa, yéčgawa; often encountered as "Yats-kow," etc., in contemporary reference) was one of three leading Tualatin men involved in negotiations leading up to the Willamette Valley Treaty of 1855. According to one of Peter Kenoyer's 1877 text dictations to Gatschet (published in Jacobs 1945:168-169), his main contribution was as interpreter of the government representatives' English. Through the narrative device of quoted speech, Peter Kenoyer had Yachkawa begging off from taking a more active negotiating role: "I (only) translate your words." Note also that Yachkawa too served Gatschet as an informant, and that Gatschet conducted his fieldwork entirely through the medium of English. There seems to have been some degree of rivalry between Yachkawa and Peter Kenoyer, perhaps influencing the latter's son's dictation here.

    Rather odd also is the fact that R. W. Summers' "Indian Journal" describes an utterly disastrous Fourth of July appearance by Yachkawa, during approximately the same period covered by Kenoyer's narrative. Yachkawa did not speak at this occasion either, but evidently not out of innate reticence. Summers' note of Yachkawa's alcoholism and blindness brings to mind his subsequent tragic end, as mentioned in the Introduction: Louis Kenoyer in Later Life.

    Wapato Dave, or Yatz-ka-wah, just here called on the agent, who sat on the porch talking to him for some time. Yatz-ka-wah has been a drinking Indian and is a large, strong man, of bad disposition. Of late he has become perfectly blind. On the Fourth of July he went to a neighboring town "celebration" and when put up on a box to make a speech, fell to the ground, so drunk that several men working together could not make him stand up any more. Somebody had furnished him with whisky—seven bottles of it, the agent said—and officers are now endeavoring to find out who it was. There is a heavy penalty for furnishing Reservation Indians with strong drink. (Cawley 1994:37)

13 In Jacobs's untranslated field text there is, written directly below the Tualatin for 'his hand', the cryptic notation: "(sobs)." Evidently, Kenoyer was overcome by emotion at this point of the dictation. One of the few direct suggestions of deep emotion anywhere in his narrative.

14 Difficult sentence. We are not sure of the syntax.

15 Antoine Metzgar (*at'wé·n*), maternal grandfather of Zenk's consultant Wilson Bobb Sr.

16 For Tualatin -hu'lɪtcwu·n, no gloss recorded.

17 See the description of Indian wrestling in chapter 10, note 14.

References

Angulo, Gui de (Gui Mayo). 2004. *The Old Coyote of Big Sur: The Life of Jaime de Angulo.* Big Sur, California: Henry Miller Memorial Library.

Angulo, Jaime de, and L. S. Freeland. 1929. "The Tfalati Dialect of Kalapuya." Typescript by Angulo and Freeland with 1936 field annotations by Melville Jacobs, ms 96/15 (formerly 91/5) in University of Washington Libraries, Special Collections, Melville Jacobs Papers, Acc# 1693-001, Seattle, Washington.

Anonymous. 1960. "History of Grand Ronde." Manuscript in archives of the Benedictine Sisters of Mount Angel, Oregon.

Anonymous. ca. 1949. "Some Excerpts from the *Annals* of the Benedictine Sisters of Mt. Angel, Oregon." Manuscript in archives of the Benedictine Sisters of Mount Angel, Oregon.

Applegate, Oliver C. 1905. Claims testimony taken at Grand Ronde Reservation, 1901. Manuscript in archives of the Confederated Tribes of Grand Ronde Cultural Resources Department, Grand Ronde, Oregon.

Banks, Jonathan. 2007. "The Verbal Morphology of Santiam Kalapuya." *Northwest Journal of Linguistics* 1(2):1–98.

Barnett, Homer. 1939. "Culture Element Distributions, IX: Gulf of Georgia Salish." *Anthropological Records* 1(5):221–295.

Belden, G. 1855. "Sketch Map of Oregon Territory Exhibiting the Locations of the Various Indian Tribes, the Districts of Country Ceded by Them, with the Dates of Purchases and Treaties, . . ." Map 234, Cartographic Records Division, National Archives, Washington.

Berman, Howard. 1988a. "Santiam Verbal Prefixes." Manuscript in Howard Berman papers, University of Washington Libraries, Special Collections, Seattle, Washington.

Berman, Howard. 1988b. Linguistic slip-files based on Melville Jacobs's Tualatin Northern Kalapuya field texts from Louis Kenoyer. Manuscript in Howard Berman papers, University of Washington Libraries, Special Collections, Seattle, Washington.

Berman, Howard. 1988c. Linguistic slip-files based on Melville Jacobs's Santiam Central Kalapuya field texts from John B. Hudson. Manuscript in Howard Berman papers, University of Washington Libraries, Special Collections, Seattle, Washington.

Berman, Howard. 1988d. Linguistic slip-files based on Melville Jacobs's Santiam Central Kalapuya field texts from Eustace Howard. Manuscript in Howard Berman papers, University of Washington Libraries, Special Collections, Seattle, Washington.

Berman, Howard. 1990. "An Outline of Kalapuya Historical Phonology." *International Journal of American Linguistics* 56(1):27–59.

Berreman, Joel V. 1935. "Field Notes and Various Documents, Research Concerning Cultural Adjustments of the Grand Ronde Indian Tribes, Obtained During the Summer of 1934." Manuscript in archives of the Confederated Tribes of Grand Ronde Cultural Resources Department, Grand Ronde, Oregon.

Boas, Franz. 1890. "Mōlális / Obtained from Tom Gilbert (Grand Ronde Res.) at Portland,

July 1890." Manuscript No. 999 in National Anthropological Archives, Smithsonian Institution, Washington, DC.

Boyd, Robert. 2011. *Cathlapotle and Its Inhabitants*. Cultural Resources Series #15. U.S. Fish and Wildlife Service Region 1, Portland, Oregon.

Brentano, F. T. B. 1894. Indian agent's annual report. In *Annual Report of the Commissioner of Indian Affairs for the Year 1894*, 259–261. Washington, DC.

Brentano, F. T. B. 1895. Indian Agent's annual report. In *Annual Report of the Commissioner of Indian Affairs for the Year 1895*, 266–268. Washington, DC.

Butch, Rosa. 1891. Superintendent's annual report, Grand Ronde School. In *Annual Report of the Commissioner of Indian Affairs for the Year 1891*, 371–372. Washington, DC.

Cawley, Fr. Martinus. 1994. *Indian Journal of R. W. Summers: First Episcopal Priest of Seattle (1871-73) and of McMinnville (1873-81)*. The Trappist Abbey of Our Lady of Guadalupe, Lafayette, Oregon: Guadalupe Translations.

Cawley, Fr. Martinus. 1996. *Father Crockett of Grand Ronde: Adrien-Joseph Croquet, 1818-1902; Oregon Missionary, 1860-1898*. The Trappist Abbey of Our Lady of Guadalupe, Lafayette, Oregon: Guadalupe Translations.

Chinuk Wawa Dictionary Project. 2012. *Chinuk Wawa kakwa nsayka ulman-tilixam łaska munk-kəmtəks nsayka / Chinuk Wawa as Our Elders Teach Us to Speak It*. Grand Ronde, Oregon: Confederated Tribes of the Grand Ronde Community of Oregon.

Clark, J. B. 1866. Teacher's annual report, Grand Ronde Manual Labor School. In *Annual Report of the Commissioner of Indian Affairs for the Year 1866*, 81–82. Washington, DC.

Drucker, Philip. 1934. Clackamas, Umpqua, and Takelma ethnographic field-notes recorded at Grand Ronde, Oregon. Manuscript 4516 (78, 82), Philip Drucker papers, National Anthropological Archives, Smithsonian Institution, Washington, DC.

Du Bois, Cora A. 1939. "The 1870 Ghost Dance." *University of California Anthropological Records* 3(1).

Frachtenberg, Leo J. 1913-14. Yamhill Northern Kalapuya texts and data from Louisa Selky. Manuscript 1923-e, National Anthropological Archives, Smithsonian Institution, Washington, DC.

Frachtenberg, Leo J. 1915. Field re-elicitations from Louis Kenoyer, written in red ink into the pages of Gatschet (1877). Manuscript 472-a, National Anthropological Archives, Smithsonian Institution, Washington, DC.

Frachtenberg, Leo J. ca. 1915. Typed Kalapuyan text transcripts. Manuscript 96/8 (formerly 90/9) in University of Washington Libraries, Special Collections, Melville Jacobs Papers, Acc# 1693-001, Seattle, Washington.

Frachtenberg, Leo J. 1922a. "Coos." *Handbook of American Indian Languages*, ed. Franz Boas. *Bureau of American Ethnology Bulletin* 40(2):297–429.

Frachtenberg, Leo J. 1922b. "Siuslawan (Lower Umpqua)." *Handbook of American Indian Languages*, ed. Franz Boas. *Bureau of American Ethnology Bulletin* 40(2):431–629.

Gatschet, Albert S. 1877. "Texts, Sentences, and Vocables of the Atfálati Dialect of the Kalapuya Language of Willámet Valley, Northwestern Oregon." Bound field note-books with 1915 red-ink field annotations by Leo J. Frachtenberg, Ms 472-a, National Anthropological Archives, Smithsonian Institution, Washington, DC.

Grand Ronde. 1856. "Census List 'A,' Grand Ronde Agency, O. T., Nov. 25, 1856." Oregon Superintendency Records microfilm series, Letter 244, Microcopy 2, Roll 14.

Grand Ronde. ca. 1872. Register of family households on Grand Ronde Reservation. Manuscript in archives of the Confederated Tribes of Grand Ronde Cultural Resources Department, Grand Ronde, Oregon.

Grand Ronde. 1876–82. Laws passed during the annual meetings of the Grand Ronde Indian Legislature. Manuscripts, Grand Ronde-Siletz Tribal Program Records, Box 162, RG 75, Federal Records and Archives Center, Seattle, Washington.

Hajda, Yvonne. 1978. "Marys River Kalapuya Pronominal Subject Prefixes." Manuscript in author's possession.

Hymes, Dell. 1981. *"In Vain I Tried to Tell You": Essays in Native American Ethnopoetics.* Philadelphia: University of Pennsylvania Press.

Jacobs, Melville. 1928–36. Santiam Central Kalapuya texts and data from John B. Hudson and Eustace Howard. Field notebooks nos. 33-37, 46-47, 76-90, University of Washington Libraries, Special Collections, Melville Jacobs Papers, Acc# 1693-001, Seattle, Washington.

Jacobs, Melville. 1929-30. Clackamas Upper Chinook texts and data from Victoria (Wishikin) Wacheno Howard. Field notebooks nos. 52-69, University of Washington Libraries, Special Collections, Melville Jacobs Papers, Acc# 1693-001, Seattle, Washington.

Jacobs, Melville. ca. 1930. "Music and Ethnology / Klikitat and N. W. Oregon." Field notebook no. 51 in University of Washington Libraries, Special Collections, Melville Jacobs Papers, Acc# 1693-001, Seattle, Washington.

Jacobs, Melville. 1931. "A Sketch of Northern Sahaptin Grammar." *University of Washington Publications in Anthropology* 4(2):85-292.

Jacobs, Melville. 1936a. Tualatin Kalapuya texts and data from Louis Kenoyer. Field notebooks nos. 122-125 in University of Washington Libraries, Special Collections, Melville Jacobs Papers, Acc# 1693-001, Seattle, Washington.

Jacobs, Melville. 1936b. "Tualatin File Recorded with Louis Kenoyer at Yakima Reservation 1936." Slip-file. Box 59 (formerly box 41) in University of Washington Libraries, Special Collections, Melville Jacobs Papers, Acc# 1693-001, Seattle, Washington.

Jacobs, Melville. ca. 1936a. "A Tualatin Kalapuya Autobiographical Fragment with Some Other Tualatin Texts." Manuscript 96/11-12 (formerly 91/1-2) in University of Washington Libraries, Special Collections, Melville Jacobs Papers, Acc# 1693-001, Seattle, Washington.

Jacobs, Melville. ca. 1936b. "My Life, by Louis Kenoyer." Manuscript 96/13 (formerly 91/3) in University of Washington Libraries, Special Collections, Melville Jacobs Papers, Acc# 1693-001, Seattle, Washington.

Jacobs, Melville. ca. 1937a. "Northwest Coast Culture Element List: Kalapuya, Santiam and Tualatin." BANC FILM 2216, Reel 78(1), ethnological documents of the Department and Museum of Anthropology, University of California, Berkeley.

Jacobs, Melville. ca. 1937b. "Kalapuya Element List." Manuscript 96/2 (formerly 90/5) in University of Washington Libraries, Special Collections, Melville Jacobs Papers, Acc# 1693-001, Seattle, Washington.

Jacobs, Melville. 1945. *Kalapuya Texts.* Seattle: University of Washington.

Jacobs, Melville. 1958–59. *Clackamas Chinook Texts.* Bloomington: Indiana University Research Center in Anthropology, Folklore, and Linguistics.

Jacobs, Melville. n.d. "Northwest Indian Informants." Scattered notes. Manuscript 115/2-3 (formerly 120/15-16) in University of Washington Libraries, Special Collections, Melville Jacobs Papers, Acc# 1693-001, Seattle, Washington.

Kappler, Charles. 1904. *Indian Affairs: Laws and Treaties*. Washington, DC: Government Printing Office.

Leavelle, Tracy Neal. 1998. "'We Will Make It Our Own Place': Agriculture and Adaptation at the Grand Ronde Reservation, 1856–1887." *American Indian Quarterly* 22(4): 433–456.

Leeds-Hurwitz, Wendy. 1982. "A Biographical Sketch of L. S. Freeland." In *Freeland's Central Sierra Miwok Myths*, ed. Howard Berman, 11–26. Report #3, Survey of California and Other Indian Languages.

Leeds-Hurwitz, Wendy. 2004. *Rolling in Ditches with Shamans: Jaime de Angulo and the Professionalization of American Anthropology*. Lincoln: University of Nebraska Press.

Lewis, J. William. 2003. "Central Kalapuya Phonology: the Segmental Inventory of John Hudson's Santiam." MA thesis in Linguistics, University of Victoria, British Columbia.

Markee, Mike. 1973. Oral history interviews. Audio recordings in archives of the Confederated Tribes of Grand Ronde Cultural Resources Department, Grand Ronde, Oregon.

McCartney, Paul. 2014. "Kalapuyan-English Dictionary" and "English-Kalapuyan Dictionary." Manuscripts in archives of the Confederated Tribes of Grand Ronde Cultural Resources Department, Grand Ronde, Oregon.

McClane, John B. 1886. Indian agent's annual report. *Annual Report of the Commissioner of Indian Affairs for the Year 1886*, 209–211. Washington, DC.

Munnick, Harriet, and Stephen D. Beckham, eds. 1987. *Catholic Church Records of the Pacific Northwest—Grand Ronde*. Portland, Oregon: Binford & Mort.

Olson, June. 2011. *Living in the Great Circle: The Grand Ronde Indian Reservation, 1855–1905*. Clackamas, Oregon: A. Menard Publications (www.grandrondebooks.com).

Olson, June. 2013. Biographical fact-sheet for Louis Kenoyer. Manuscript in possession of author.

Rude, Noel. 1986. "Noun Stripping in Central Kalapuya." *Proceedings of the [Second] Annual Meeting of the Pacific Linguistics Conference*, 423–433. Department of Linguistics, University of Oregon, Eugene.

Sawtelle, C. M. 1863. Teacher's annual report, Grand Ronde Manual Labor School. In *Annual Report of the Commissioner of Indian Affairs for the Year 1863*, 84–86. Washington, DC.

Seaburg, William, and Pamela Amoss. 2000. *Badger and Coyote Were Neighbors: Melville Jacobs on Northwest Indian Myths and Tales*. Corvallis: Oregon State University Press.

Takeuchi, Lone. 1969. "Santiam Kalapuya Vocabulary with Notes on Phonology and Morphology." Manuscript in possession of Scott DeLancey, Department of Linguistics, University of Oregon, Eugene; and Manuscript 45/4 (formerly 23) in University of Washington Libraries, Special Collections, Melville Jacobs Papers, Acc# 1693-001, Seattle, Washington.

Van der Heyden, Rev. J., ed. 1906. "Msgr. Adrien J. Croquet, Indian Missionary (1818–1902) & Some of his Letters." Copied by Fr. Martinus Cawley. Original: *Records of the American Catholic Historical Society* 16 (1905); 17 (1906).

Work, John. 1923. "John Work's Journey from Fort Vancouver to Umpqua River, and Return, in 1834." Leslie M. Scott, ed. *The Quarterly of the Oregon Historical Society* 24(3):238–268.

Youst, Lionel, and William R. Seaburg. 2002. *Coquelle Thompson, Athapaskan Witness: A Cultural Biography*. Norman: University of Oklahoma Press.

Zenk, Henry. 1978–93. Linguistic and ethnographic data from members of the Grand

Ronde community, Oregon. Field notes, sound files, and transcripts in archives of the Confederated Tribes of Grand Ronde Cultural Resources Department, Grand Ronde, Oregon; and in the Henry B. Zenk Papers, University of Washington Libraries, Special Collections, Seattle, Washington.

Zenk, Henry. 1988. "Chinook Jargon in the Speech Economy of Grand Ronde Reservation, Oregon: An Ethnography-of-Speaking Approach to an Historical Case of Creolization in Process." In *International Journal of the Sociology of Language 71: Sociolinguistics and Pidgin-Creole Studies*, John R. Rickford, ed., 107–124.

Zenk, Henry. 1994. "Tualatin Kalapuyan Villages: The Ethnographic Record." In *Contributions to the Archaeology of Oregon, 1989-1994*, ed. Paul W. Baxter, 147–66. *Association of Oregon Archaeologists Occasional Papers No. 5.* Eugene: University of Oregon.

Zenk, Henry, and Jedd Schrock. 2013a. "Learning to Read Tualatin." *University of British Columbia Working Papers in Linguistics* 35. http://lingserver.arts.ubc.ca/linguistics/icsnl/2013.

Zenk, Henry, and Jedd Schrock. 2013b. "Addendum to Learning to Read Tualatin." *University of British Columbia Working Papers in Linguistics* 35. http://lingserver.arts.ubc.ca/linguistics/icsnl/2013.

Zenk, Henry, and Jedd Schrock. 2015. "Chinook Jargon (Chinuk Wawa) and Obsolescent Kalapuya." Paper read at Linguistic Society of America 89th Annual Meeting, Portland, Oregon, January 2015.

Index

Note: Page numbers in italic refer to illustrations. Page numbers with an "n" refer to notes.

Shasta (tribe), 9, 11, *11*, 33n7, 280, 286–288. *See also* Grand Ronde Reservation

Shastan (language), 9

Shilikwa (Tualatin leading man), 10, 144, 162, 278, 286–88, 301n1

shinny. *See* games (competitive)

Shirley, Mrs. Josephine, 34n10

Shoefan (Kalapuyan), 32n2

Shumkhi (Jack Nance, Nancy Jack, a Tualatin Tamanawas doctor), 18, 84, 296–297n13

Silas, Nellie. *See* Frank, Nellie

Siletz Reservation, 8, 9, 35n10, 90, 297n16, 298n1, 301n12: visitors from, 152, 301n13

šílik'ʷa (Shilikwa) 301n3. *See also* Shilikwa

Silvertail (horse), 154

Simmons, Suzette (Kalapuyan speaker), 36n16

Simmons, William (Takelma speaker), 18

Sinnott, Perry B. (Indian agent), 15, 22

sisters (Catholic), 7, *17*, *42*, 76–80, 198, 200, 206: as teachers, 172–78, 182–184, 200–204, 214–222, 230–238; head sister, 170, 246. *See also* Benedictine Sisters; Holy Names of Jesus and Mary; Lord Above

Sisters' School (Grand Ronde government boarding school), 3, 15, 31, 74–80, 170, 296n7, 299n5: alphabet lessons, 182, 214; arithmetic lessons, 202, 214–216, 222, 232–236; children's play in, 172, 178, 184, 194, 197–198, 204–210, 212, 224–226, 240; classrooms in, 182, 200, 214, 230, 307n1; cooking at, 184, 200, 222; daily round, 76–80, 176–184; dining room in, 78, 186, 188, 192, 200, 206, 220, 222; geography lessons, 214, 218–220; illness in, 21; laundry as children's chore, 78, 184; lining up in, 78, 194; whipping-stick (ruler) as discipline, 180, 303; meals, 78, 172, 178, 184–188, 192–194, 303nn5–6; playroom in, 78, 186, 188, 190, 198, 200, 204, 210, 212, 222, 228; prayer (prayers/ words to/of the Lord Above) in, 78, 80, 172, 178, 184, 186, 188, 192, 194, 198–230, 240; preparing firewood as children's chore, 78, 184, 200, 222, 230; readers (school books), 174–178, 182–184, 202–204, 214–220, 230–234; recitation exercises, 182–184; roll-call, 200; running away from, 186, 303–304n9; sleeping quarters in, 74–76, 180, 184, 198, 210, 226–228; spelling lessons, 230, 236–238; washing, bathing, combing

hair in, 76, 78, 178, 180, 184–186, 188, 194, 198, 200, 206, 210, 212, 218, 222, 228, 230, 238, 242; wash-house (laundry) in, 78; washrooms at, 172, 303n8

slavery (indigenous), 66, 68, 293–294n1, 294n4

Smith, Captain John, 35n10

Smith, Doctor (Doc) (Tualatin Tamanawas doctor), 20, 23, 34–35n10

Smith, John (Shasta tribe), 35n10

Smith, Mr. *See* Smith, Doctor

South Yamhill River, 8, *10*, *11*, 299n4, 301n1

Southern Kalapuya (language), 9

Spirit Mountain (Grand Ronde), *24*, *25*

square-dancing. *See* dancing

St. Michael's (Catholic Church and Parish, Grand Ronde), 1, *27*, 36n16, 110, 299n5, 302n1, 304–305n1

strawberries, 88–90

style (narrative), 3, 5, 49, 53, 56, 59, 60: of lower Columbia region, 49–50. *See also* quoted speech

subordination. *See* morphology

subsistence: berry picking (for subsistence), 120, 124, 126, 134; hunting of deer, 68, 120–134; hunting, fishing, gathering (as supplement), 13. *See also* employment (off-reservation); farming; foods

Summers, Rev. R. W., 32n2, 35n10, 304n1, 311n12

surplice, 305n5

Sutton, Doc, 282

sweating, 68, 84

Takelma (language), 9

Takeuchi, Lone, 61–62n

Tamanawas (spirits), 16, 31: *agé·mšandi* as, 254–256, 309n9; and Tamanawas doctors, 16; Coyote as, 296n13; dead people as, 84, 296n13; individuals' relationship with, 21, 31; power from, 16, 19; quests to acquire, 25, 31, 35n10, 36n14; require periodic expression in Tamanawas dances, 21; source of malevolent power, 20, 35–36n12

Tamanawas dance (doctor's dance), 19, 20–24, 30, 35n11, 260, 308n4: jumping dance-step in, 35n11; presence of children at, 35n11; suppression of, *22*

Tamanawas doctors (shamans, Indian doctors), 16, 19, 24, 31, 34–35n10, 35n12, 80, 84, 248–260, 296–297n13: training period, 25